Miguel Herrero de Jáuregui
Orphism and Christianity in Late Antiquity

Sozomena

Studies in the Recovery of Ancient Texts

Edited
on behalf of the Herculaneum Society

by
Alessandro Barchiesi, Robert Fowler,
Dirk Obbink and Nigel Wilson

Vol. 7

De Gruyter

Miguel Herrero de Jáuregui

Orphism and Christianity in Late Antiquity

De Gruyter

ISBN 978-3-11-048235-5
e-ISBN 978-3-11-021660-8
ISSN 1869-6368

Library of Congress Cataloging-in-Publication Data

Herrero de Jáuregui, Miguel.
 [Tradición órfica y cristianismo antiguo. English]
 Orphism and Christianity in late antiquity / Miguel Herrero
de Jáuregui.
   p. cm. − (Sozomena ; v. 7)
 Includes bibliographical references and index.
 ISBN 978-3-11-020633-3 (hardcover : alk. paper)
 1. Orpheus (Greek mythology) 2. Church history − Primitive and early church, ca. 30−600. I. Title.
 BL820.O7H4713 2010
 261.2'2−dc22
                                                      2010004423

Bibliographic information published by the Deutsche Nationalbibliothek

The Deutsche Nationalbibliothek lists this publication in the Deutsche Nationalbibliografie; detailed bibliographic data are available in the Internet at http://dnb.d-nb.de.

© 2010 Walter de Gruyter GmbH & Co. KG, Berlin/New York
Original title: Tradición órfica y cristianismo antiguo
© EDITORIAL TROTTA, S.A., 2007
Translated by AGESTRAD (Granada, Spain)
Translators: Jennifer Ottman and Daniel Rodríguez
Printing: Hubert & Co. GmbH & Co. KG, Göttingen
∞ Printed on acid-free paper
Printed in Germany
www.degruyter.com

Ἑλικῶνα μὲν καὶ Κιθαιρῶνα καταλειπόντων, οἰκούντων δὲ Σιών
Let them abandon Helicon and Cithæron, and take up their abode in Sion!

(Clement of Alexandria, *Protrepticus* 1.2.3)

Preface

Greece and Rome matter because they are related to us. Classics should not be a self-contained realm for the enjoyment of a few, but a source of intellectual, moral and aesthetic inspiration for our own times. And research should not only pursue old questions and open new ones for fellow experts, but should also be able to transmit a deeper and more subtle – even enthusiastic – knowledge of Antiquity, to those approaching classical studies from other disciplines or out of general interest. Thus, this book, stemming from a PhD dissertation, is intended to be accessible not only to classicists and specialists in other areas, but to anyone interested in ancient religion. In order to make it so, I have restricted the use of Greek to a necessary minimum and I have tried to avoid excessive quotation, instead providing the most relevant texts in the Appendices. The introductory chapter seeks to embark upon this sailing ship of Orphism and its related controversies all who have no fear of the voyage. The five chapters that follow are intended to maintain the balance necessary to prevent anyone – either the expert or the general reader – from being tempted to jump ship.

This book deals with issues that have received increasing attention in recent scholarship. General interest in the first centuries of Christianity has spread beyond the confines of academia for a number of reasons – and this has been accompanied by a concomitant curiosity regarding the religions of Antiquity, especially those considered similar to the incipient Christian cult. Ever since its initial scholarly reconstructions in the nineteenth century, Orphism has been prominent among them. Several spectacular finds in the last decades have furthermore brought Orphism to the forefront of studies of ancient religion of the Classical, Hellenistic and Imperial periods.

The present study returns, from a new perspective, to the old question of the relationship between Orphism and Christianity, starting with a study of its form and spheres of influence in Imperial times (Chapters II and III). For the first time, the potential and implications of using the works of the Christian apologists as our primary source for ancient Orphism are fully explored, and the contents (Chapter IV), strategies (V) and perspectives (VI) of their Orphic references assessed. The two main fields of study, always murky, upon which the present work is intended to cast light, are the nature of Orphism within the Greek religious, literary and philosophic context and the relationship between second- to fifth-century Christian literature and Greek culture and religion. My interest here is focused upon an already-developing Christianity, as it attempts to deepen its interaction with the Greek world that surrounds it without compromising its Jewish roots. This Hellenization of Christianity is not only a crucial development for much of Western history, but also one whose exploration has the potential to cast a certain amount of light backwards and to explain some aspects of the Classical world.

The research methodology is purely philological, inasmuch as it stems from the examination of written evidence. Its results do not depend upon any prior theoretical orientation. The fact that linguistic, sociological or anthropological theoretical models are used at times to clarify various aspects of the study does not mean that the research as a whole is structured by these approaches. This is also the case concerning comparisons with other historical eras, including modern ones: their function – to help with the explication of the texts – is simply instrumental to particular points, and is not aimed at developing some general theory.

The same desire for investigative independence applies also to the analysis of theology and religious experience, both Greek and Christian. Any attempt at absolute objectivity is vain in approaching religion, even more so given the fact that Christianity is a living religion which continues to pervade our culture. Doubtless, my attempts to liberate the analysis of Orphism from the Christian categories through which it has often been approached, careful though they may be, will betray the influence of my own culturally determined schemas. At the very least, however, I have tried to avoid an apologetic approach, which has been and still is the main reason for arbitrary and ungrounded extrapolations with regard to one side or the other. Christianity's similarity to or difference from the other religions of its milieu is not a proof of its truth or falsehood. The days when the study of Christian texts was the exclusive province of those seeking to demonstrate Christianity's truth or the contrary seem, fortunately, to have been left behind. Returning to them, in a more or less concealed way, only implies burdening our research with ideological prejudices. Religious experience and the theological constructs it has generated within both the Greek and Christian contexts – as well as in others – are a psychological and historical reality that, as such, deserves scholarly study. Deciding whether this experience corresponds to an objective reality or not is a question that does not depend on empirical research, but on personal choice.

Neither general nor specific conclusions are intended to be absolutely definitive or beyond doubt. In a murky area such as this, subject to the changes introduced every few years by new discoveries and approaches, research must aspire to offer a tool well adapted to the scientific community's pursuit of an always-partial truth. This study explores areas in which passionate debates have arisen in the last two centuries. My approach to previous works stems from an indisputable axiom that should be welcomed, in principle, by those who dedicate themselves to classics: fools do not abound in our scholarly field. Some results of the present work confirm and develop earlier theories; some explore new perspectives; others refute ideas still widely held. However, as wrong as any hypothesis might seem, we will have to investigate the motivations for mistakes made by researchers whose competence is generally beyond doubt, in order to extract from such hypotheses the truth that mistaken overarching visions might contain. The distortions introduced by modern authors, just like those of ancient ones, also contribute to an understanding of the reality which they are distorting. I hope that possible mistakes in my own work will receive an equally benevolent explanation from future critics.

This book is a revised translation of the original Spanish version, finished in 2006. I have introduced some minor changes in addition to those required by the appearance of new studies in the last three years. I am grateful to the readers and reviewers of the Spanish version, specially Olegario González de Cardedal, Alan Farahani and Thomas Figueira, who pointed out some elements that needed revision and / or updating, and also to the translators for their patient and efficacious work.

The Spanish Ministry of Education and Science has funded my research at the Universidad Complutense de Madrid. I am very grateful for its trust. I also owe special gratitude to the Real Colegio de España at Bologna, where I was able to finish this work. I am grateful to Alberto Bernabé, my supervisor in my graduate years, for his constant support, generous work of critical correction, and unfailing openness to different approaches, and to Antonio Piñero, who introduced me to the study of early Christian literature. Discussion with other Spanish researchers on Orphism, associated with the same school of research often from very different perspectives, has been extremely positive on more than one level. I thank, therefore, Antonio Bravo, Francesc Casadesús, Rosa García-Gasco, Ana Isabel Jiménez, Mercedes López-Salvá, Sara Macías, Raquel Martín, Carlos Megino, Francisco Molina, and Marco Antonio Santamaría. I would like to thank Christoph Riedweg for his kind welcome and generous academic supervision in Zurich, just as I would Albert Henrichs and the Real Colegio Complutense at Harvard and Dirk Obbink and Christ Church in Oxford. I would like to thank as well Walter Burkert, Sarah Burges Watson, Giovanni Casadio, Bruno Currie, Renaud Gagné, Carmen Grande, Annewies van der Hoek, Marianne Govers

Hopman, Barbara Kowalzig, Gregory Nagy, Simon Price, and Jean-Michel Roessli for all their suggestions, advice and comments that have contributed to shaping this research and for having freed it from not a few of the errors it originally contained. For those that remain I am solely responsible. To share with all these friends and colleagues the merits of this book is a great honor for me.

Madrid, September 2009

Table of Contents

Preface	VII
I. Introduction	1
1. Orphism and Christianity	1
2. –isms and their subjects Christians, Pagans, "Orphics"	12
II. Orphic religious presence in the Imperial Age	31
1. Orphic literature	32
2. Orphic ritual traces in Imperial times	41
2.1. Direct evidence	41
2.2. General references	73
3. The Orphic tradition in the second to fifth centuries	78
III. Fields of intersection	87
1. Philosophical traditions	89
2. Theological texts	94
3. Gnosticism	104
4. Hellenistic Judaism	108
5. Assimilation and syncretism	116
IV. Orphic Tradition in Christian Apologetic Literature	127
1. Apologetics in the second to fifth century AD	127
2. The figure of Orpheus	139
3. The mysteries of Orpheus	144
3.1. *Protrepticus* 2.12–22 and related Greek texts	147
3.2. Latin texts related to *Protrepticus* 2.12–22: Arnobius and Firmicus	153
3.3. Hippolytus	160
3.4. Justin	164
4. Orphic Theogonies	167
4.1. Athenagoras	167
4.2. Tatian	170
4.3. Pseudoclementina	171
4.4. Origen	172
4.5. Gregory of Nazianzus	173
4.6. Lactantius	177

5. Orphic "monotheistic" poems 179
5.1. The *Testament* of Orpheus 179
5.2. Hymn to Zeus 187
5.3. Other Orphic hymns in *Stromata V* 190
5.4. Other poems in the *Cohortatio ad Graecos* 195
5.5. Didymus the Blind 199
6. Apologetic philology 199
6.1. Orpheus and Homer in the *Cohortatio*. 199
6.2. A treatise *On Plagiarism* in *Stromata VI*. 201
6.3. Fragments on symbolism in *Stromata 5.8* 205
6.4. Christian versions of Orphic-Pythagorean texts 210
7. References to the soul 213
8. The reliability of the Apologists 217

V. Christian Strategies 219
1. General principles 219
2. Continuity with Greek interpretative traditions 224
2.1. Adaptation 224
2.2. Criticism 231
3. Christian attitudes 238
3.1. Rejection 238
3.2. Appropriation 243
3.3. Omission 246
4. Orphism as axis of the Christian/Pagan opposition 251
4.1. The construction of Paganism 251
4.2. Conceptual metaphors 255
4.3. Literary metaphors 259
4.4. Toward the Christian re-creation of Orphism 265
4.5. The New vs. the Old 272
5. Orphism as a bridge between Christianity and Paganism ... 275
5.1. Explanation of the parallels 278
5.2. Presentation of Christianity in Orphic molds 286
6. The triumph of Christian strategies 293

VI. Orphism in the light of Christian apologetics 295
1. The gods and the cosmos 296
1.1. Theogony and cosmogony 297
1.2. The creative voice 304
1.3. Cosmology 306
1.4. Transcendence and immanence 309
1.5. Monism 316
1.6. Personality and abstraction 323

2.	Gods and man		328
	2.1.	The savior gods	329
	2.2.	Nature and destiny of man	335
3.	The ritual experience		344
	3.1.	Pagan and Christian *teletai*	344
	3.2.	Ritual and belief	351
	3.3.	Eating the god?	354
4.	Causes of the parallels		358
	4.1.	Typological resemblances	358
	4.2.	Eastern waves	361
	4.3.	General Platonism	365
	4.4.	Mutual influence	367
Appendices			375
Bibliography			393
Index locorum			421

I. Introduction

1. Orphism and Christianity

Modern interest in the Orphic tradition arose from the perception of its similarities with Christianity, and this is still one of the main reasons for the curiosity that Orphism arouses among scholars of ancient religion. Both are deeply asymmetrical entities that, however, share some apparently common elements, particularly appealing for the contrast these offer with the conventional image of Greek religion. The survival of the soul after death and its reward or punishment in the next world; the devaluation of this *lacrimarum vallis*, as opposed to a transcendent Afterlife; an original state of moral impurity from which only believers are purified; an individual and intimate relation with divinity; the possibility of passing beyond the border between the human and the divine: these notions and others associated with them seem completely inconsistent with the image of the Olympian religion transmitted in the *Iliad*, in Pindar's odes or in Aeschylus' tragedies. There death is an insurmountable boundary, which marks an insuperable distance from the gods. Mortals communicate with the Olympian immortals by means of a public cult, with the declared aim of securing their favour for a life characterised entirely by social and secular aspirations. Two Orphic tablets found in a tomb (*OF* 485–486) say to the deceased, "Now you have died, and now you have been born, thrice blessed one, on this very day." On the other hand, Pindar makes his choir sing in honor of a victor in the Olympic Games, "since death is unavoidable, why spend in vain an anonymous old age sitting in the shade, alien to any kind of glory? No, victory has to be mine!" (*Ol.* 1.82–84). Death is always central in the Greek *Weltanschauung*, always the moment that defines and sets its seal upon the life it terminates. In Orphism, however, death is the beginning of life, and not its end.

The poetic image of Greece, celebrated from Homer to Winkelmann and Nietzsche, is one deeply emblazoned in Western consciousness. In reality, however, this heroic – not to say idealized and biased – image of Greek religion has been constructed partly by a more-or-less conscious opposition to Christianity. Thus the shadow of Orphism, which does not readily conform to the marmoreal patterns of Olympian religion, has inevitably been traced on this template as a kind of Christianity *avant la lettre*, which introduced for the first time in Greece the dualistic and eschatological notions that were to be developed further in the Hellenistic age, and came finally to dominate the Late Antique religious landscape. This apparent similarity may prompt a heavily distorted view of Orphism, onto which the scholarly tradition has attempted, and sometimes still attempts, to project an under-nuanced interpretation of Christian theology, or, even more dangerously, of Christianity's social structure. In turn, it is just this similarity itself that has often motivated the interest or the scorn of modern scholars – themselves seldom free of prejudice. Some saw in Orphism a process whereby the Greek spirit was being prepared for the reception of the greater Christian truth to come. Alternatively, others saw it as the seed of a Hellenistic spiritual decadence, which would lead eventually to the final disappearance of the Classical spirit. Yet others envisioned it as a kind of Protestant reform of traditional Dionysiac worship. All of these interpretations are informed by the underlying idea that Orphism is a forerunner of Christianity in the Greek world – an idea that, as we shall see, had already been formulated by some ancient writers, and that took root again strongly when nineteenth-century philology focused on Orphism as a subject of study.

It is only a small step, and one very easy to take, from postulating spiritual precedence to supposing historical dependence. Here the study of Orphism is framed within a broader intellectual fashion, the comparison of Christianity with ancient mystery cults. The overwhelming presence of Greek philosophy in the formation of Christian dogma made it appear logical to posit similar processes with regard to ritual and religious experience. The *Religionswissenschaft* of the nineteenth century explored the roots of Christianity with great enthusiasm, and many scholars found them in the mystery religions. But many others contested any direct dependence of the dogmas and central rites of Christianity upon the Greek or Eastern mysteries. Of course ideological *parti pris* on the "uniqueness" of Christianity was more or less explicitly present in these quarrels. The debate was long, complex and brilliant, and outstanding figures like the German scholars Albrecht Dieterich (1913), Richard Reitzenstein (1927[3]), Wilhelm Bousset (1913), the British anthropologist Sir James Frazer (1913), or the Belgian Franz Cumont (1929), on the first side, and Carl Clemen (1915) or Arthur Darby Nock (1928), on the other, left many contributions which retain a great significance today. While the comparatists showed the manifold coincidences between Christian texts, rites and ideas and those of the mystery cults, the other side developed various methodological lines which sought to underline the differences. Comparativism discovered many analogies and often deduced a more or less direct genealogy: baptism, for instance, would come from initiation rituals, salvation from mystic soteriology, etc. The compara-

1. Orphism and Christianity

tivists' critics, on the other hand, refuted such genetic dependence, arguing from the differences of language and meaning that underlay the superficial resemblances. For example, Clemen established a rigid threefold filter to establish the dependence of a Christian narrative or ritual element upon a pagan one: 1) The Christian element should be inexplicable as an inheritance from Judaism or from Christian practice prior to its appearance. 2) Its similarity with the pagan element from which it is allegedly derived should not be merely superficial, but also concern its import and meaning. 3) The pagan element should exist before Christianity and in geographical proximity to it.[1] Along similar lines but from a refined linguistic approach, Nock denied that the mysteries played any significant role in the New Testament, since the common vocabulary (*myein, kyrios*) had a very different meaning in the Pauline Epistles than in pagan Greek sources.[2] However, even more than the weight of these arguments, it was the discredit of comparativism after its boldest exaggerations had been refuted that caused its exhaustion until its revindication in our own day along renewed lines[3].

The question of "Christianity and mysteries" gradually disappeared from the forefront of scholarship in the second half of the century. The American historian of religions Jonathan Z. Smith published in 1991 a most influential book, *Drudgery Divine: On the Comparison of Early Christianities and the Religions of Late Antiquity*, which showed with great precision what had long constituted a general impression[4]. The old debates on Greek or Eastern influence on Christianity were largely a more or less conscious reflection of traditional Protestant vs. Catholic polemics over whether primitive Christianity had or had not been corrupted by Hellenism. Apologetic concerns about an unscholarly category like "uniqueness" distorted reality in their zeal to show

---

1   Clemen, though not mentioned by Smith 1991 in his overview of scholarship, is one of the most conspicuous defenders of this restrictive approach, consecrated by Metzger 1955 in a classic, apparently impartial article, where he states that "if any conclusions can be drawn from the preceding considerations of methodology, they must doubtless be, first, that the evidence requires that the investigator maintain a high degree of caution in evaluating the relation between the Mysteries and early Christianity; and, second, that the central doctrines and rites of the primitive Church appear to lack genetic continuity with those of antecedent and contemporary pagan cults."
2   On Nock's arguments, cf. Smith 1991, 66–84. A study of Nock's figure in Casadio 2009.
3   Cf. Patton/Ray 2000, drawing on the seminal study of Smith 1982.
4   On the impact of Smith 1991, cf. the collection of essays in *Numen* 1992. As Elsner 2003 shows, the same old ideological quarrels underlie some categories of the study of art, like the strict divisions among pagan, Jewish and Chistian art.

that the influence was either overwhelming or insignificant, and as a result both Christianity and the mysteries were falsified in falsely symmetrical constructions. Their internal complexity and evolution were ignored, and later elements were projected into earlier times, since all that mattered was the (in) adequacy of the mysteries (taken as a single entity) and the diverse Christianities (also taken as a whole) when measured against the same template.

Fortunately, for some decades the study of the ancient mysteries, though still heavily burdened by concepts inherited from these old religious debates, has been in general free of apologetic concerns.[5] Obviously Christianizing prisms and arbitrary genealogies are avoided, as also is the case with ideological presumptions. Current scholarship generally attributes the majority of the observed parallelisms between the mysteries and Christian practice to their common origin in the spiritual *koinē* that began to emerge in the Mediterranean in the second century BC, rather than to a sole and direct dependence of the latter upon the former or viceversa. Parallel religious situations produce analogous processes that do not imply borrowing, but shared concerns. For example, Hellenistic religions were deeply permeated by popularized Platonism. The aspiration to salvation through union with a divine entity and to moral and ritual purity found in both the Hellenistic mysteries and Christianity arises contemporaneously from the post-Classical individualistic, universalizing, and syncretistic climate portrayed so vividly in Apuleius' *Metamorphoses*. Even the Hellenistic Judaism from which Christianity was eventually to emerge is permeated by this new spirituality, in which all religions of the time participated to some extent – but most especially those that arose from its ferment.[6]

The particular case of Orphism can only be understood within this general framework, for in its case the comparison with Christianity has been the backbone of its study for in its case. It is a clear instance of the enormous weight that ancient religious quarrels and national scholarly traditions have in shaping the terms of the question. Christian August Lobeck is generally – and dubiously – acclaimed as the first modern scholar of Orphism[7]. His monu-

---

5 Among modern studies on the mystery cults, I will refer foremost to Burkert 1979 and 1987, Versnel 1990, Price 1999, and Bremmer 2002.
6 On this spiritual *koine*, cf. Versnel 1990, Trombley 1993. Cf. Hengel 1975 on Hellenistic Judaism. Projecting this environment onto the mysteries of Classical times, such as Eleusis, must be avoided. Burkert 1987 and Price 1999, 108–125 advise against viewing traditional mysteries as entirely oriented towards eschatology, an understanding derived from wrongly projecting onto them a combination of Christian soteriology, the practices of later mystery cults and even the Orphic model.
7 Not only did he follow G. Hermann's edition of *Orphica* (1805) and earlier Ger-

mental *Aglaophamus sive de theologiae mysticae graecorum causis libri tres* (1829) is in fact heir to a long previous Protestant tradition of opposing Greek mysteries as irrational cults similar to Roman Catholic practice. It is in such terms that he portrays the *Orphica*. Orphic priests are explicitely compared to the Jesuits as apostles of a superstition that he condemns as pure phantasy devoid of any true mysticism[8]. Half a century later, Friedrich Nietzsche in his *Birth of Tragedy* and other works envisaged Orphism as a reformation of the true Dionysiac spirit, a forerunner of Christianity like Socrates, responsible for the decadence of the primitive tragic Greece[9]. Others held the same view from the opposite perspective, whereby Orphism was an imperfect precedent of the more advanced religion that was to come. Such was the opinion of the famous French writer Ernest Renan[10]. Eduard Zeller also, the great historian of Greek philosophy, saw in Orphism, as well as in the Essenes, "the prehistory of Christianity." At the turn of the century, German scholars like Erwin Rohde, Ernst Maass, Albert Dieterich, Otto Gruppe and Robert Eisler[11]; the Cambridge ritualist school led by Jane Harrison – who called Orpheus "a reformer, a protestant" and said that the "blood of some real martyr may have been the seed of the new Orphic Church";[12] and also, with less depth and

    man scholarship (cf. following note), but he also must have known N. Fréret's learned commentaries on the Orphics in his study of 1740, "Histoire du culte de Bacchus" (*Histoire de l'Académie royale des inscriptions*, 23, 1756, a reference for which I am indebted to Renaud Gagné). On French eighteenth-century scholarship on Orphism, cf. Juden 1971, 66–98. Nineteenth-century German classical philology created its own *protoi heuretai*, and these fixed images still survive (cf. the introduction of Grafton and Most 1989 to the *Prolegomena* of F. A. Wolf).

8 Lobeck 1829, 964. Cf. Gagné 2008, 112f, who shows that Lobeck echoes earlier Protestant scholarship like J. H. Feustking's *Gynaeceum haeretico-fanaticum* (1704) and J. Lomeier's *De Lustrationibus* (1681). Lobeck's rationalistic approach attacks symbolist and romantic visions of "Orphic wisdom" like those of A. C. Eschenbach in his *Epigenes* (1702, reedited and augmented by M. Gesner in 1764) and G. F. Creuzer in his *Symbolik* (1810).

9 On Nietzsche and Orphism, cf. Biebuyk, Pratel, Van den Poel 2004; McGahey 1994, 51–74; Aulich 1998.

10 Renan 1866, 338: "l'orphisme, les mystères, avaient tenté la même chose dans le monde grec, sans réussir d'une manière durable". Arguing against Renan's downplaying of Greek ancient religion, the French professor Jules Girard dedicated an influential book (1879) to proving that the most spiritual traits of Christianity could already be found in Orphism (pp. 6–9).

11 Zeller 1889; Maass 1895; Rohde 1907[4]; Gruppe 1906; Dieterich 1913; Eisler 1921 and 1925.

12 Harrison 1922[3], 461, 468. The influence of Frazer's *Goulden Bough* and Robertson Smith's *Lectures* on her vision of Orphic "sacramentalism," was also large (cf. p. 270f). Many less scholarly but equally famous books of that time share

rigor but even greater imagination and popularity, the French universal comparatist Salomon Reinach:[13] they all saw in Orphism the proximate source of several ideological, moral and ritual elements later absorbed by the Christians. Though the majority of their hypotheses have been disproved, or at least modified, by subsequent scholarship, the works of these path-breaking scholars are not devoid of interest to the modern reader. They created the classical image of Orphism. Projecting the Christian model onto it, they posited a network of Orphic communities who read the Orphic poems as sacred texts, who celebrated rituals commemorating the sacrifice of Dionysus, and who held uniform practices and religious beliefs. The influence of such portrayals is still largely perceptible.

Other scholars went even further, and purported to find in Orphism the source of the central dogmas of Christian theology. The Italian Professor Vittorio Macchioro expressed this theory in its most radical form in several works, which attained great popularity in the twenties thanks to their clarity and audacity, and which remain as the most extreme statements of the theory of "Panorphism." In Macchioro's view, St. Paul was the actual creator of the Christian theology whereby the Son of God dies for the sins of mortals and through His resurrection gains for them the promise of eternal life. This conception would be a straightforward transplantation of the Orphic myth according to which Dionysus, son of Zeus, died and was resurrected, to become the guarantor of the salvation of mortals – descendants of the Titans who sacrificed him. Christ's theological character is, according to Macchioro, the direct result of the transposition of the Orphic Dionysus into Biblical categories, and the system of Christian salvation stems directly from the Orphic one. Other scholars, like the French liberal priest Alfred Loisy, were heavily influenced by this portrait.[14]

---

such conceptions e. g. the much-reprinted English work by Legge (1915) on the *Forerunners and Rivals of Christianity* dedicates a whole chapter to the *Orphici*.

13 Reinach was particularly fascinated by the pretended parallelism of Christianity and Orphism. He entitled his general history of religions *Orphée* (1909), and he published an article, "La mort d'Orphée" (1902), where he derived the Christian Eucharist from Orphic sacrifice, which had enormous influence on Freud's *Totem and Taboo* (cf. p. 270) Cf. Duchêne's introduction to a reedition of his selected articles (1996). In an article understandably not included in that selection, "Morale orphique et morale chrétienne", Reinach argues for their symmetry from the idea that both would forbid masturbation, and goes on to draw the following conclusion: "ce tabou n'existe pas chez les singes et existe fort peu chez les nègres; c'est peut-être pourquoi les singes sont restés des singes et la plupart des nègres leurs cousins germains" (1923 III, 279).

14 Macchioro 1922 and 1930; Loisy 1919 (on whom Reinach's influence is also clear). Macchioro's works and influence are analysed by Graf-Johnston 2007, 58–61.

To Macchioro's claims, the most conclusive – and, being devoid of apologetic interest, the most objective – response was that provided in 1925 by André Boulanger, one of the most sensible and qualified experts in Greek religion of his time. The French professor demonstrated, with arguments that remain valid today, that Macchioro's theory, besides presenting a much-distorted image of Orphism, did not meet any of the aforementioned conditions enunciated by Clemen. Dionysus's sacrifice is not voluntary and does not bring redemption, but is precisely the crime that condemns mankind. In addition, Boulanger demonstrates the very low probability of any direct Orphic influence upon Paul, given the very slight evidence we have of Orphism's presence in the first century and the lack of any trace in the New Testament.[15] Boulanger's work succeeded in refuting Macchioro over the long term, and though the Italian scholar still published a well-known English version of his writings in 1930 under the programmatic title *From Orpheus to Paul: A History of Orphism*, this path was abandoned.[16] The question of Christianity and Orphism has not been directly posed again, though its shadow is always present in the scholarly discussion. Once the question of direct influence seemed out of place, attention turned elsewhere.

Boulanger's work preceded by only a few years, and to some extent heralded, the sceptical reaction that would shortly place in doubt the very existence of Orphism – and that would cause its disappearance from academic literature for almost forty years. The main cause of "Orpheo-scepticism" then and now, in fact, is a thorough rejection of these early attempts to extrapolate Christian elements into a reconstructed "Orphism." The champions of the reaction – Ulrich von Wilamowitz-Möllendorff, André-Jean Festugière, Ivan Linforth, and Eric Robertson Dodds – protested justifiably against arbitrary visions of an "Orphic Church," complete with communities, dogmas and common rites for which there were no literary witnesses, and which was accordingly best explained as a result of the semi-conscious projection of a template derived from primitive Christianity onto a subject area in which little hard evidence existed.[17] But the sceptics themselves were not

---

15   Boulanger 1925. The only proof adduced by Macchioro that Boulanger does not discuss, and that leaves open the possibility that Paul knew the myth directly, is a speech to the people of Tarsus in which Dio Chrysostom (*Or.* 33. 2–4) mentions a cult to the Titans that might (or not) be linked to the myth. Cf. pp. 329ff regarding parallels and differences between the Orphic Dionysus and Christ.

16   Guthrie 1935, for instance, makes little use of Macchioro and confines the question of Christianity to a few cautious pages at the end of his book. Boulanger's arguments were revived, against Loisy, by Father M.-J. Lagrange 1937, 191–222.

17   Wilamowitz 1931, Festugière 1935, Linforth 1941, Dodds 1951, for whom the

entirely objective: if they were ready to criticize "the unconscious projections upon the screen of Antiquity of certain unsatisfied religious longings characteristic of the late 19th and early 20th centuries" (Dodds 1951, 148) in the classical reconstruction of Orphism, they were not themselves free of their own religious agendas. Repugnance for elements that might stain a pure and idealized, Winkelmannian view of Classical Greece is clearly detectable in Wilamowitz or Linforth. On the other hand, Father Festugière, the pride of Jesuit scholarship, was all too ready to reject the idea of pagan precedents for Christian beliefs and rituals. Finally, a certain Protestant vision of a "Puritan" reform of ritual religion can still be traced in the work of Dodds, who also accepted some other key postulates of previous scholarship, like Dionysiac sacramentalism and Orphic original sin.[18]

Since the 1960s, new discoveries have returned Orphism to a central place in studies of Greek religion and philosophy, and the topic has since been freed of its crudest deformations. I will shortly be returning to the question of what precisely is to be understood by the term "Orphism." For the present it is sufficient to point out that recent studies do not take its historical relationship to Christianity as their central concern. Rather, they are concerned with a phenomenological comparison between religions of salvation intended to illuminate aspects of both, and refrain as far as possible from excessive extrapolation. Mutual borrowing and syncretism are plausible in some contexts of direct contact, but these sporadic assimilations are better explained as a result (rather than as the cause) of the typological affinities between them, as we shall see at the end of the present study. The prevailing principle healthily tries to focus more on analogies among diverse elements than upon establishing a dubious genealogy between them.[19]

It is now necessary to take up again the question of the relationship between Orphism and Christianity, which has been at a standstill since the 1930s. Several studies dealing with related matters have referred tangentially to the

---

Orphic Church was a "historic mirage emerging from our own unconscious projection of our own worries into the remote past" (170, n.88). An epigone of these four great scholars was the French scholar L. Moulinier (1955).

18 Cf. Parker 1995, 505, n. 20 on Linforth; Bremmer 2002, 18, on Dodds; Dodds himself sometimes falls into the same mistaken Christianization he denounces: he speaks of "Orphic apocalypses" to refer to the *katabasis* (1951, 170); for his Eucharistic conception of Dionysian omophagy, cf. p. 270.
19 Cf. for example Bianchi 1966. The debate among several scholars following the exposition of Burkert 1977 includes very accurate observations in this respect.

subject, with brilliant results[20]. The question, however, has not been directly tackled again, as if the lack of any new approach had made researchers afraid of simply repeating well-known topics, or of falling into the same mistakes as their predecessors. A part of the resistance to dealing with the question arises, furthermore, from the vagueness of the terms concerned. This work attempts to avoid both problems by fixing clearly the limits of the questions it poses and the testimonies it uses to discuss them. Its central concern is to study the Orphic tradition that Christians knew, assumed, or rejected in the first five centuries of our era. This raises some new questions and provides some heretofore neglected sources for understanding what Orphism was in Antiquity. The problem of influence has been left to the end, as a validation of what the new approaches can contribute to old questions.

The scope and definition of the various terms involved in such an investigation will be discussed in this chapter. First, however, it is necessary to observe that neither "Christianity" nor "Orphism" are immutable and self-contained realities – despite the tendency of the apologists and their many modern scholarly descendants to present them in this light. Both possess considerable fluidity within their temporal, spatial, and ideological limits. The Orphism contemporary with Christianity is different from that of the Classical period, though of course, lines of continuity between the two can be traced. Moreover, Orphism overlaps with several philosophical, literary, and religious traditions, through which it coincides with Christianity in the Hellenistic spiritual *koinē* as a whole, far removed from any uniform orthodoxy. Chapters II and III will accordingly describe, on the basis of the available literary, epigraphic, papyrological and iconographic material, the character of the Orphic tradition in the Imperial age and the nature of its direct and indirect encounters with Christianity. These chapters, therefore, will depict a very fluid panorama, in which sections are instrumental for presenting the evidence but by no means closed compartments.

Such is the context within which several Christian authors of the second to fifth centuries AD make their multiple references to Orphism. Chapters IV, V and VI, on the other hand, will depart from the strict distinctions introduced by apologetic texts. The description of Orphism detailed in the

---

The methodological cautions of Smith 1991 are also applicable to the particular case of Orphism (cf. Edmonds 2004, 37–46).
20 Riedweg 1993 on Orphic-Jewish literature, transmitted almost entirely by Christian sources; Bremmer 2002 studies the lines of continuity between Christian and Orphic eschatology, and Burkert 1987 refers on several occasions to the similarities and differences in religious experience; the Jewish and Christian iconographic appropriation of Orpheus has fuelled academic debate for more than a century (cf. III).

first part of the book serves as a counterpoint and yardstick for the Christian texts that are studied in the second. In previous works, the near-exclusive attention paid to the question of Orphic influence on the central tenets of Christianity naturally demanded an overwhelming focus on the New Testament – and in particular upon the Pauline texts, in which any passing reference to Orphism is undetectable[21]. The attention paid to subsequent Christian authors, however – whose contact with Greek culture and religion is much more intense than that of the previous generation, and who confront a movement toward which they show ambiguous and mixed reactions – has been much less. Yet these texts are fundamental to understanding not only the Orphism of the Imperial age, but also that of the Classical period, on three levels.

First, much of the material that we have for the reconstruction of Orphism – very considerable in its quantity, and of great importance for its quality – comes from Christian sources: it is enough to look at the *index fontium* of the editions of Orphica. However, this material must not be used without first analysing the sources, intentions, and manipulations of the author who transmits it, since the apologetic literature is anything other than innocent and neutral. Crucial testimonies (such as Dionysus's sacrifice as reported by Clement of Alexandria) have been excerpted from Christian sources without adequate account being taken of their origin, or of the alterations the text may have suffered in the hands of these authors. Sometimes related apologetic passages are treated as independent testimonies, when in fact they have been derived directly from each other in such a way that these apparently numerous witnesses in reality can be seen to resolve ultimately into a single source. Other times, Christian texts have failed to receive the attention they deserve, and evidence that might help us add to or piece together the Orphic puzzle has been overlooked. Chapter IV will deal with these tasks.

Secondly, the analysis of the sources and contents of the Christian texts offers the materials to undertake an indispensable task: a systematic exposition of their strategies. This aspect of the study has, besides its direct usefulness for the analysis of the Orphic evidence, its own inherent value: Orphism is an excellent mirror within which the diverse Christian attitudes toward traditional Greek religion and culture are reflected. Chapter V thus amounts almost to a study in miniature of the Christian strategy in confrontation with the pagan world: it will show how different apologists act when confronted with

---

21 Cf. n. 15. The attempt by Ehrhardt 1951 to find an Orphic source in Paul on the basis of his mention of victory crowns (a very extended Greek notion) is clearly wrong and has had no success: Pfitzner 1967, 86f; Brändl 2006, 6, 231.

the same phenomenon – sometimes in unison and at other times with total divergence, spanning a range of attitudes that runs from total assimilation of Orphism to its most absolute rejection. It is not exceptional that both attitudes and diverse intermediate possibilities coexist in one single author. If Orphism is a flexible and often ungraspable category within the extremely fluid field of Greek religion, apologetics likes neat distinctions and firm boundaries: their mutual encounter provokes extremely interesting results. In modern bibliography, one frequently finds more or less accurate generalizations about a subject as ambiguous and diverse as the Christian reception of Greek culture.[22] Orphism presents itself as a simplified testing-ground for research in this area, while remaining at the same time a topic broad enough to bring together and mobilize an array of characteristic Christian strategies that have to a large extent determined its transmission and reception up to our days.

Thirdly, the apologists[23] are an extremely authoritative source – if obviously a subjective and partial one – regarding the contested question of the similarities and differences between Orphism and Christianity. The perceptions of Christians themselves regarding which aspects of a living tradition in direct competition with their own were similar to or different from their practice – or which elements could be considered compatible with Christian teaching, and which were to be rejected out of hand – should be a guide of great value, if not of absolute accuracy, in reconsidering the question. Scant attention has been paid to the opinions of the Christians concerning whether, and to what extent, Orphism might be considered a proto-Christianity. Of course, the apologists will be the first to project Christian categories onto an Orphism defined by quite different parameters – and it is from these original projections that many of the modern ones are derived. Once conscious of this danger, however, and of the necessity of "de-Christianizing" the information they provide, direct interrogation of these authors' works throws new light on the theological content and religious experience of Orphism. If an external assessment of a phenomenon necessarily distorts it to some extent, it may also be valuable for the new perspectives it is capable of opening up – perspectives which must be taken into account, and which have the potential to reveal points of detail and differentiation imperceptible from a purely internal viewpoint. This task will be attempted in chapter VI.

---

22 Among reference works on the topic, cf. particularly Jäger 1961, Daniélou 1961, Chadwick 1966, Wolfson 1970, Lane Fox 1986, Momigliano 1987, Stead 1995, Burkert 1996, Fitzgerald *et al.* 2003.

23 For the scope of this term I refer the reader to the beginning of Chapter IV.

2. –isms and their subjects: Christians, Pagans, "Orphics"

From its title through to its final chapter, this book uses a number of terms whose interpretation is not uncontroversial, and it should, therefore, be clarified from the beginning in which sense they are to be understood. The use of abstractions in order to understand better the phenomena under discussion is an entirely valid scholarly strategy. An extreme deconstructionism that leads us not to nuance our understanding of general terms, but rather to entirely deny their validity, sometimes simply paralyzes. It is also true, however, that abstract concepts, even as they organize the realities they denote, throw light upon some areas and leave others in darkness. There is also a degree of risk in the mutability of labels, which have the potential to shift in meaning depending upon who is using them, and when. If, however, some consensus can be forged concerning the basic meaning of terms in scholarly discourse, these dangers are minimized, and the advantage of such terms' use becomes obvious. This need is especially urgent in relation to our topic: to the question "What is Orphism?" some scholars have answered "everything," and others have decided it is "nothing." Echoing Sieyès, it would perhaps be better to find "something" in it that turns it into a useful concept.

A second danger is that of being carried away by the linguistic mechanism of supplying every identified '-ism' with a group of followers usefully denoted by the suffix '-ist' or its equivalent. One must avoid the comfortable symmetry of assuming for the sake of apparent consistency that there is a regular relationship between any abstract ideology and its followers and adherents. It is clear that to be a communist and to be a classicist are not existential choices of the same order. A similar disproportion can be found in relation to ancient Mithraism, Orphism, or Hermeticism – which, as we shall see, do not all define their followers in the same manner. It will accordingly be necessary to address also the problem of the so-called "Orphics."

It is, however, desirable to extend the debate on the various -isms of antiquity no further than necessary. Some of these can be easily dismissed in favour of an obviously preferable alternative: for example, I will not use "Dionysism" because the expression "cult of Dionysus" expresses the reality in a much more concrete manner. Other terms, such as "Judaism" or "Gnosticism," are taken in a general sense long sanctioned by academic tradition, and there is no cause to question them here, where they are not the core of the study. It will be sufficient to specify in what sense I use the three terms most fundamental to this inquiry: Christianity, paganism and, in particular, Orphism.

The mere contraposition of "Christianity" and "paganism" should arouse a certain fear in the breast of the experienced reader. The religious situation of the Roman Empire was of such fluidity that any classification in terms of narrowly defined compartments betrays a bookish artificiality that hardly corresponds to the reality. The boundaries among orthodox Christianity, heretical and heterodox movements, the various branches of Judaism, the Gnostic movements, and the diverse array of Greek and Eastern cults were highly permeable. To say "Christianity" without further ado simplifies this complexity excessively. When theological ideas of Christian derivation are discussed, it is always necessary to indicate who it is that asserts or defends them, and when. Nevertheless, precisely because I am concerned not with the theological propositions made in Christian literature, but with its apologetic content and with the strategies this entails, the classification of the authors I will be discussing as "Christians" without further ado is here well warranted. For the purposes of this study, inquiry is focused not upon questions concerning orthodoxy or the Church as a whole, but on those thinkers whose writings on Orphism remain extant. A fundamental aim of the apologetic literature is to delimit clearly what Christianity is and what it is not. If we were to judge these authors by their theological ideas, the conception of Christianity would change according to each one. Some of the authors we are interested in were considered heretics by their contemporaries (for instance Tatian, Tertullian, and Hippolytus), while others supported ideas rejected by later orthodox belief (Origen). All of them, however, share the intention of establishing, in a free-flowing reality, a fixed and clear boundary between Christian truth (according to the more or less orthodox conception of each author) and "pagan" error.

The use of the latter term is the lesser evil. It is true that "paganism" is a construction of apologetics, whereby the term is employed to designate anything that is neither Christian nor Jewish, nor even heretical – in general terms, then, the traditional Greek and Roman religions and the new cults that had arisen in the Hellenistic age. "Paganism," in other words, denotes a variety of cults and trends that seem too heterogeneous to be adequately comprehended under a common term. We will see in Chapter V the central role that the Orphic tradition played in the creation of this concept by the apologists. Attention will also be paid to the role of Orphism in the syncretic and unifying tendencies seen in the traditional Greek and Roman religions themselves – tendencies which accelerate in the Imperial age, in part because of gathering resistance to Christianity. In any case, the term "pagan" is inherently biased, as it is an entirely Christian formulation. But its use, if the negative undertones it may have had in the past are set aside, remains much simpler than the lengthy periphrases that would be necessary were it banished – e. g. "an adherent of any non-Jewish, non-Christian sect in the

Greco-Roman world." Other terms used by the Christians themselves, such as "Gentile" or "Greek," are if anything even more biased. Once note has been taken that the notion of "paganism" is a late artifact of apologetic rhetoric, there is no excessive risk in using the terms "paganism" and "pagans," and qualifying these more precisely where necessary.

Nevertheless, such reductive terminology is far less appropriate with regard to the problem of Orphism, concerning which, for over a century now, there has raged one of the most impassioned debates in the history of Classical Studies, almost comparable to the Homeric Question in its intensity and duration. As was explained in the previous section, only its relation to Christianity brought forth a long and intense debate between scholars of many different countries and orientations. Before explaining in what sense I think the term may be used appropriately, it will be necessary to dedicate a few paragraphs to the succinct exploration of the traditional understanding of the term "Orphism," and some of the issues that surround it.

In its nineteenth-century reconstruction, Orphism[24] emerged as a religious movement born in the sixth century BC under the authority of the mythical singer Orpheus. It is supposed to have arisen as a reform of the traditional cult of Dionysus, whose orgiastic and ecstatic aspects would have been redefined by a minority group in mystical and eschatological terms. This trend is held to introduce for the first time in Greece the idea that the soul is enclosed in the body as punishment for a primordial fault – specifically, the crime committed by the Titans, the ancestors of mortals, when they tore to pieces and devoured Dionysus, son of the supreme god Zeus and Persephone. As a result, the soul is condemned to suffer a cycle of reincarnations from body into body, as well as torments in the Afterlife, until it expiates its ancient fault and can thereby enjoy the happy everlasting life to which its immortal nature aspires. Salvation is achieved by obtaining Persephone's forgiveness through participation in the Bacchic rites (*teletai*) and the observance of conduct that assures purification: an Orphic life (*orphikos bios*) demands – in addition to some imprecise references to justice – observance of a series of dietetic and clothing taboos, including, most importantly, a strict vegetarianism derived from the belief in reincarnation. The followers of this doctrine, transmitted in poems attributed to Orpheus, who practise the rites supposedly founded by him, and who observe an Orphic lifestyle, might thus be termed "Orphics."

---

24 The term "Orphism", only sporadically attested in the first half of the nineteenth century (e. g. E. G. Faber, *Horae Mosaicae*, 1818, 203), becomes very popular in the second half, when scholarship progressively abandons the cautious Latin *Orphica*.

Leaving aside the excesses of pan-Orphism, which have been previously discussed, such a reconstruction remains the classic image of Orphism that, with a number of variations, remains current today. It is based on extant fragments of Orphic poetry and on the information about Orpheus and his rites transmitted by diverse authors in Antiquity. There is also some papyrological and epigraphic evidence associated with these references – in particular, the gold tablets found in tombs that instruct the soul in how to reach salvation in the Afterlife. All these pieces of evidence have been collected in the last two centuries in various philological editions of *Orphica*, which, very different though they are, have all departed from the picture of Orphism described above, and they have contributed to fixing it in place by transmitting the remains of an Orphic corpus that, it is implied, would have been much broader.[25] The most careful and balanced portrait of the classical reconstruction of Orphism is owed to W. K. C. Guthrie, whose Orpheus and Greek Religion continues to be widely read, translated and influential today[26].

Against this reconstruction, the aforementioned "Orpheosceptical" reaction arose – and still retains its credibility in Anglo-Saxon and German circles. Apart from denouncing the projection of Christian categories, as we have seen, its main arguments were two.[27] First, there is no proof of the existence of any religious group known as the "Orphics" in the Classical period. The only witnesses who use the term *orphikoi* to refer not to Orphic poets, but to believers who describe their religious affiliation in these terms, are the Neoplatonists, who suppose these beliefs to have inspired Plato; and this is clearly no proof of their existence one thousand years earlier.[28] Second, it is maintained that under the label of "Orphism" scholars have gathered into a single artificial *constructum* a series of late testimonies of Orphic

---

25 *Orphica* have been edited by Hermann (1805); Lobeck (1829); Abel (1885); Kern (1922) and now Bernabé (2004–2006), whose Teubner edition includes all the new testimonies and reorders Kern's fragments. Cf. Edmonds 2008 for a critique of the way in which editors of fragments impose their interpretation as a system
26 Guthrie 1935 (=1952²). Cf. the preface of L. J. Alderink to the English re-edition (1993). Guthrie's moderation compared to his predecessors may have come from the influence of A. D. Nock, which is repeatedly acknowledged (1952, 271ff.: Nock is very cautious about Orphism in all his works. The long article by Nilsson 1935 also offers a balanced approach.
27 Cf. n. 17 for the early sceptics. More recently, see also West 1983, Brisson 1992, and now Edmonds 1999 and 2004, pp. 37–46.
28 Representative of this sceptical view is the dismissive observation of Wilamowitz (1931 II, 197): "Die Moderne reden so entsetzlich viel über die Orphiker. Wer macht das in Altertum?". The Olbia inscription (*OF* 463) was discovered only thirty years ago.

poems; theological and anthropological ideas, whether of general circulation or derived from Plato, arising in Hellenistic times, or even in Christian and Neoplatonic writings; and a number of ritual rules associated with the name of Orpheus, but with nothing to indicate that they are intended to form a coherent system. In the sceptical view, there is in fact no Orphic reality separable from such well-known and documented phenomena as Pythagoreanism, the cult of Dionysus, or the Eleusinian mysteries, with which the figure of Orpheus has sometimes been linked. A vague and inconsistent relationship with some particular mythical character is not sufficient to give unity to all the material claimed for it. Taken at face value, as the most penetrating of the sceptics observed, the contemporary reconstruction of Orphism would appear to subsume "the entire religion of teletae and mysteries."[29] The label, it was felt, was so general that it had become empty of meaning, and ought to be abolished.

This abolition was in fact achieved for almost four decades, until new discoveries in the second half of the century disproved some of the sceptical theses. The *Derveni Papyrus* – a document serendipitously preserved when it fell off a funeral pyre and was dried rather than consumed by the flames – demonstrates the existence in the Classical period of Orphic theogonies evidently taken as authoritative in connection with mystery rituals. Newly discovered gold tablets reveal a perceived connection between hopes for the happiness of the soul in the Afterlife and the Bacchic mysteries. A bone tablet found in Olbia (Crimea) with the inscription ΟΡΦΙΚΟΙ seems to testify to the existence of a Dionysian thiasus of Orphics in the fifth century BC. All this new evidence shifted scholarly trends. The endorsement of Walter Burkert and his followers, along with the Italian school of historians of religion and lately the Spanish school formed around Alberto Bernabé's edition, has restored "Orphism" as a respectable and academically accepted term.[30]

Apart from the new evidence, new approaches replaced dogma and Christianity as the main focus of scholarly interest in religion. Social questions were asked where the influence of Marxism, of 1968, or of post-colonial anthropology was evident. Orphism was now interesting not as a forerunner of Christianity, but as a protest movement of deviation, repressed by a monolithic polis. The Parisian school has been particularly incisive in this approach[31]. Neither has the long tradition of oralist approaches to early

---

29 See the whole citation in n. 37 below.
30 Cf. Burkert 1977, 1982, 1999; Riedweg 1987, 1993; Graf 1974, Graf-Johnston 2007; Sabbatucci 1965; Bianchi 1974; Casadio 1997; Bernabé-Casadesús 2008.
31 Detienne 1975 and 1977.

Greek poetry in the United States left the Orphic material untouched: notions like "competing traditions" and "performance" have made a startling appearance in the old discussions.[32] However, if such perspectives have found new interest in Orphism, there have also been forceful reactions against its coming back onto the stage. On the one hand, traditional philology proudly maintains a purist distrust of any construction that does not spring directly from the text, preferably a written one.[33] On the opposite side of the picture, the post-modern taste for deconstruction recovered the sceptical arguments in order to fight against an "-ism" instinctively seen as a distorting modern construct.[34] To be sure, the debate is not focused on just one matter, whether Orphism existed or not. There are many different interpretations of each set of evidence (the gold leaves, the myth of the Titans, the reconstruction of the theogonies, etc.). Yet each position on any of these subjects relies heavily on a particular approach to the broader Orphic question.[35]

The use of the term "Orphism" has, therefore, become popular again, if with widely varying interpretations and with much greater nuance than before. Terminology has been refined, and comparisons are made with extreme care. The overlap of Orphism with Dionysiac cult, the Eleusinian mysteries, and Pythagoreanism is insistently underlined, as is the lack of any central governing authority that defined doctrine or ritual practice. Emphasis is placed on the open, uncanonical character of Orphic literature, the itinerant diffusion of Orphic cults, and their evolution under the influence of individual and local circumstances and interests.

Too often, however, this praiseworthy insistence on methodological rigour is confined to prologues and introductions, and is shortly abandoned in favour of again discussing Orphism as though it were a coherent system into which all our scattered pieces of evidence may neatly be fitted, as if a central authority, whose existence is emphatically denied, had disposed them somehow – the very image of Orphics living an Orphic life and performing a few standardized rituals in accordance with doctrines transmitted by the Orphic poems seems to exert an irresistible fascination on the scholarly imagination, not least due to the preexistent Christianizing pattern according to which the Orphic evidence is semiconsciously classified. I cannot pretend to be entirely free from this fault, so congenital to the scholars of Orphism, and it is possi-

---

32 Nagy 2001, Martin 2001.
33 West 1983.
34 Edmonds has raised the loudest protests against the recovery of Orphism as a valid category (1999, 2004, 37–46, 2008). Cf. also the objections of Calame 2001.
35 Parker 1995 presents a good state of the question on "Early Orphism". Cf. Bernabé-Casadesús 2008 for a complete bibliography.

ble that an attentive reading of this book will detect several stumbles into the old traps. Nonetheless, I hope at least to delineate clearly herein the distinction between my ideas of Orphism and either its traditional reconstruction or pure scepticism.[36] I will, in other words, attempt to outline as simply as possible what I consider to be the most plausible path between an *ars nesciendi* that refuses to elaborate the data in order to render them comprehensible and a comfortable adherence to a long-falsified construction.

Three previous warnings, however, are relevant here. First, the following reflections do not attempt to collect and analyze the entire corpus of evidence, but only to justify the use of terms foundational to this study – although they do provide a preliminary sketch of the portrait that will be developed in the following chapters. Second, I will be dealing now only with the Orphism of the Classical period, reserving discussion of its evolution as a tradition in the Hellenistic and Imperial age for later in the book. Third, it will be necessary for the sake of clarity to discuss first the nature of Orphic myths and ideas, deferring for the moment consideration of the existence of the Orphics, more tied to the problem of the rites.

I begin by accepting the minimal definition at which Linforth arrived after an exhaustive examination of the material known in 1941: Orphism is the theology of the mysteries.[37] However, this broadness of reference, which for the American philologist was proof of the term's uselessness, is instead taken here as indicating its centrality as a spiritual and intellectual phenomenon in Classical Greece – and hence in Western culture. To borrow Ugo Bianchi's expression (1978), Orphism represents the earliest stage of Greek mysteriosophy. It is the theological elaboration of the mythical and ritual elements, as well as of the experience, of the traditional Greek mysteries: an intellectual process, which finds its expression in poems, rites and beliefs governed by this speculation. It is a mediate theorizing of immediate experience, which does not fall like a meteor upon traditional Greek religion, but arises from it as a strange but natural fruit. That the mystery cults of the Classical period were focused primarily not on doctrinal content, nor even upon eschatological hope, but on the experience that the special relation-

---

36 The following reflections are heavily indebted to long debates with Alberto Bernabé and Renaud Gagné.
37 Linforth 1941, 173: "If we must call something Orphism, it must be the entire religion of teletae and mysteries with their magical ritual, the poems of Orpheus and others in which their sacred myths are told, and the ideas concerning god and man which were inherent in poems and ritual. The ancients did not call this religion Orphism, but they said what is in effect the same thing, in the Greek manner, when they said that Orpheus was the inventor and founder of it".

ship to the worshipped god prompted *hic et nunc*, is well established in the secondary literature (e. g. Burkert 1987). It is evident, however, that some of the initiators, and perhaps also those to be initiated, turned their minds not only to consideration of the ritual acts themselves, but to theological and anthropological questions perceived to be implicit in them. It is important to bear in mind the spatial and temporal coincidence of Orphism with Presocratic philosophy – with which it exhibits multiple correspondences and links, though differing from it in its preservation of traditional moulds and its reluctance to create new forms of literary and ritual expression[38]. This restriction both marks its cultural limits and, at the same time, confers upon it a cultural authority derived from the prestige of its supposed antiquity. The maintenance of traditional cultural forms is to be expected of speculation arising from the mysteries themselves, as is the attribution of these to Orpheus, poet and cult-patron. The existence of a written transmission, another of the distinctive features of Orphism, however, allows this speculation to innovate, sometimes with considerable audacity, on the basis of this traditional anchorage.

Thus, the most characteristic and famous ideas of Orphism – the "drops of foreign blood" whose origin has often been sought in some source other than "the veins of the Greeks"[39] – are actually a theologizing reading of notions inherent to the mysteries, rather than the result of different Eastern influences. That the soul must be purified of an original fault inherited from the cosmic ancestors, the Titans, is an elaboration of a central concern with the faults of human ancestors whose punishment the descendants inherit, unless they are purified of them.[40] The ascetic prescriptions believed to constitute the *orphikos bios* – that is to say, to refrain from shedding blood, eating certain foods, wearing certain clothes, and perhaps from sexual intercourse, along with a commitment to just behaviour – are precisely the same ritual requirements inscribed upon temples for cultic practitioners before their approach to the deity. Orphism simply extends to the practitioner's entire life the ritual and/or moral purity that were

---

38 Bernabé 2004, Finkelberg 1986.
39 Rohde 1907, 338 coined the oft-quoted expression. Cf. Parker 1995 on the diverse foreign roots proposed.
40 Cf. Dodds 1951, 135–179, and Gagné's forthcoming monograph on ancestral fault in ancient Greece. The evolutionary transference of guilt from human ancestors to cosmic ancestors (Titans) is seen vividly in the Orphic *telete* of *P. Gurob* (*OF* 578), the first preserved line of which reads (with supplements) "receive my gift as compensation for the injustices of my forefathers" (δῶρον δέξ]ατ' ἐμὸν ποινὰς πατ[έρων ἀθεμίστων): it is impossible to clarify whether the faults in question are of the human or the cosmic ancestors, since the formulae would be the same in both cases. Cf. Edmonds 2008 on this line.

only temporarily and momentarily necessary in cultic worship.⁴¹ The hope of religious fulfilment in the Afterlife, with the revaluation of the soul over the body and the future life over the present, looks like the result of theorizing about, and an attempt to explain, the experience of momentary ecstasy attained in ritual – in particular, in the cult of Dionysus – with the aim of rendering permanent its breaking of spatial and temporal limits.⁴² In the Afterlife as described by the gold tablets (and by Plato *more orphico*), Memory guarantees immortality, and Oblivion means death, and the sources of memory and of oblivion appear in the oracle of Trophonius, with multiple echoes in the mysteries. But even beyond the religious sphere, both concepts played a central role in the immortality attained in epic glory, from which Orphism seems so removed at first sight: in epic, the hero must be remembered in order to survive, while in Orphism he must remember to be saved.⁴³ The notions are opposed (from being the object to being the subject of memory), but the formulae to express them are similar, because this speculation develops Greek traditional ideas not only compatible with the cults of the mysteries, but in fact latent within them. The theory of reincarnation, according to which particular bodies are irrelevant to the identity of a soul that bears the imprint of its divine lineage (*genos*), revives and reinterprets the conventional Greek understanding whereby the life or death of individual generations do not matter, and stable identity is found instead in the continuity of the family *genos*.⁴⁴ From the traditional pessimism that finds its archetypal expression in Theognis' *gnomai* that the best possible fate is never to have been born, there is only a short step – if one of enormous importance – to the Orphic slogan *soma-sema* (the body is the prison of the soul), and this is its elaboration in speculative terms. In effecting this transfer from traditional wisdom to innovative cosmo-theology, the Orphic theologian-

---

41 Parker 1983 is the standard work on contamination (*miasma*) and purification.
42 Cf. Eur. *Ba.* 402 (ἱκοίμαν ποτὶ Κύπρον): in their ecstasy, the Bacchants wish to reach the ideal and unattainable land of Cyprus; this impossible spatial transfer is deferred to the temporal transfer in the next life, which thus becomes feasible (e. g. *OF* 493a: "send me to the thiasoi of the initiates", cf. Bernabé-Jiménez 2008, 158). Turcan 1986 on the sense of permanence conveyed by the perfect tense *bebakkheumenos* in the funerary inscription of Cumas (*OF* 652).
43 Cf. Vernant 1969 on the role of memory, and Bonnechère 2004 on the oracle of Trophonius.
44 For example, Glaucos' famous claim (*Il.* 6.145ff), saying that human generations do not matter in comparison with the deeds of one's family. Questioned about his identity, he does not give his name, but his lineage (cf. also *Il.* 20.213–241 and 21.153–160), as the initiate does in the *lamellae* (*OF* 474.10: "I am the son of Earth and starry Sky"). Glaucos uses the same image of the botanical cycle that will be later used to describe reincarnation (*OF* 438).

poets cultivate traditional genres, such as the theogony, the hymn, and the *katabasis*, albeit freighting them with new theological messages.

The list of traditional religious conceptions elaborated and theologized by Orphism could be greatly extended, but these examples will be sufficient. Orphism attains a general language higher than concrete particularities, overcoming the local and ethnic divisions so deeply rooted in all Greek cults, be they mystic or not. In the same way that personal identity is established in terms of a celestial lineage (*genos ouranion*) beyond the barriers of family *genos* or of the polis, the main divinities of Orphism do not have local character either: Dionysus, Persephone, Zeus, and their myths and theologies are not centred, unlike in other cults, upon a local sanctuary. On the contrary, such pan-Hellenic deities tend to be united within overarching theogonies that serve to elide local variations and specificities. The explicit or implicit identification of superficially distinct gods with each other in the Orphic hymns and theogonies reinforces this henotheistic tendency, which purports to find within diverse cults indications of a sole and unique divinity who dominates the cosmos as a whole.[45] Orphic theological speculation, then, not only is pan-Hellenic, but also stretches beyond the boundaries of Greece and Greek culture, to attain an all-embracing perspective that facilitates the evident Egyptian, Mesopotamian, and Persian influences on Orphic thought.[46]

Who could be a better patron of this trend than Orpheus? Himself not Greek, but a Thracian of divine lineage whose figure no local cult could appropriate as its sole right, his mythical experiences as poet, traveller to distant lands, voyager into Hades and founder of religious cults gave him special authority to stamp his imprimatur on poems and rites. The common ascription of these to his figure is, for the sceptics, the only factor that unites them all, whereas supporters of the existence of a unified Orphism believe that such attributions occur because of their common ideological background. The absolute lack of a closed canon or of a central authority could not help but lead to an open tradition spreading out in multiple directions. But leaving aside works in minor genres, such as astrology or botany, that were attributed to Orpheus in later times, the main points of focus in Orphic speculation are three: theo-cosmogony, eschatology, and anthropology. Let

---

45 This tendency is clearly seen in the Derveni Papyrus (Betegh 2004). Six hundred years later we find it quite unchanged in the *Orphic Hymns* (Morand 2001, Ricciardelli 2000). Cf. Herrero 2009a.
46 On Middle Eastern connections of Orphism, cf. West 1983; Casadio 1986 (sceptical, as is Bremmer 2002); Burkert 1992, pp. 9–41, 125–127, and 1999; Bernabé 1997 and 2006a, Herrero 2009b

us examine briefly each of these fields, postponing for later consideration the crucial question of their mutual relationship.

The first quotations of Orphic poetry come from theogonies in the same tradition as Hesiod's, but with significant variations. The Orphic poets maintain the same general outline with regard to the primordial gods and to the myth of Olympian divine succession, but the traditional theogonic images (sexual generation, gulping up as means of engendering) are here used to express new conceptions, which seem to be the theogonic parallel to the monism expressed in prose by Presocratic philosophers such as the Ionians or Anaxagoras, who are free from the bounds of poetic forms and images. The theogony of the *Derveni Papyrus* – dated approximately in the 5th century BC – depicts Zeus as the god who "became the only one" (μοῦνος ἔγεντο), becoming pregnant with the entire cosmos and the gods after devouring everything into himself, and then subsequently "conceiving it" again, so that Zeus becomes "the first, the last and the middle one."[47] The author's fidelity to the theogonic images, which are polytheistic by nature, tortuously complicates the expression of a monistic vision. Orphic theogonies, nevertheless, enjoyed surprising success, giving rise, as we shall see, to variants, imitations, and applications in a wide array of contexts.

At the other end of the spectrum of Orphic speculation lies eschatology. One recurrent element in Orphic sources is to locate in death the key to true life – an inversion more extreme than that found in the traditional mysteries, which are less marked by the hope of an Afterlife. As a consequence, depiction of the blessings and punishments of the next world seems to have been a favorite topic of Orphic poets. A poetic tradition about the descent to Hades (*katabasis*) was attributed to Orpheus, which in itself is hardly surprising, since according to the myth Orpheus went down to the kingdom of the dead in search of his wife Eurydice. Though very little of these poems has been preserved, we have a certain idea of their contents. Plato's eschatological myths are very probably inspired by Orphic eschatology. The most valuable testimonies, however, are the gold tablets, the hexametric lines of which are probably derived from a poem narrating the descent of the soul to the other world, followed by an ascent to the realm of the blessed. Probably the voice in which these verses are sung is that of Orpheus (which other poet had experience of Hades?); but this is not necessary to establish a relationship with Or-

---

47 *OF* 12–14. Cf. Betegh 2004, 112–122 for a discussion of the *aidoion* that Zeus swallows in order to gulp up the entire cosmos, and pp. 278–306 for the comparison of the poet and of the commentator with Anaxagoras.

phism, since their correspondences to other Orphic witnesses are very clear.[48] These poems represent a theological version of the traditional genre of the hero's descent into the underworld (that of Heracles, for instance), in order to rescue another from death by avoiding the dangers posed by the infernal realms and persuading Hades and Persephone to relinquish their captive. Now, however, the soul is the hero that, in a similar way – if under very different circumstances – must find his own salvation.

At a midpoint between the distant domains of theogony and eschatology stands the famous myth of Dionysus' sacrifice by the Titans. Dionysus, as offspring of the incestuous union of Zeus and his daughter Persephone, is directly linked to the contents of the Orphic theogonic traditions; on the other hand, at least in some versions, mortals sprang from the ashes of the Titans when they were thunderstruck by Zeus, which has fundamental anthropological implications intimately connected with eschatology. If the life of the soul in the body is expiation for the primordial fault of the cosmic ancestors of mankind, only after death can this atonement come to an end. There may, of course, have been divergent versions and interpretations of the myth of the Titans. However, in spite of sceptical doubts, it seems clear that the anthropological implications derived from it date back to the Classical period.[49] It is tempting to see in the myth of the Titans the cornerstone that gives unity to the whole Orphic building. Such temptation not only exists for us. It is very probable that the *Rhapsodies* – a collection of the Orphic theogonies compiled in the first century BC – outlined a path from the theogonic origins of the cosmos up to the eschatological destination of the soul, the two being linked by means of the myth of the Titans[50]. Nevertheless, it is necessary to

---

48 See Bernabé/Jiménez 2008 and Graf/Johnston 2007 on the *lamellae*. Riedweg 2002 reconstructs the structure of the *katabasis* of the soul that inspires them. See also Kingsley 1995 on the presence of Orphic eschatology in Platonic eschatological accounts. In Herrero 2007c I synthesize the nature and evidence of Orphic eschatology.
49 Brisson 1992 maintains that the double (i.e., both Titanic and Dionysiac) nature of humans, as progeny of the Titans who ate Dionysus, is an idea of Neo-Platonist origin and does not derive from ancient Orphism. Edmonds 1999 makes it an invention of nineteenth-century scholarship. However, cf. Bernabé 2002a for a recent and convincing demonstration of the existence of the myth and its anthropological implications in Classical times (in spite of Edmonds' response in 2008).
50 Edmonds 2008 objects that the systematicity of the *Rhapsodies* is an invention of modern editors (and of West 1983) and that they could have been a messy compilation of disparate materials. But many references to the *Rhapsodies* call it a theogony, and there are allusions to particular episodes in specific places (cf. Bernabé 2004, 97–101). In this case over-scepticism constructs from a preconceived idea an image of messy disorder without proofs and against the evidence.

exercise caution in supposing that all Orphic poetry followed the apparently tidy structure of this late compilation.

The connection between cosmogony and eschatology is a *desideratum* of modern scholarship, reluctant to conceive of a religious doctrine that is not systematic. Yet such connection is far from assured. A wide array of theogonies and eschatological claims circulated under the name of Orpheus, and not all were compelled to follow the same arrangement. Undoubtedly, there exist some lines of continuity between theogonic interests and Orphic eschatological concerns: theogonies were sung in rituals, the focus of which can be supposed to be the salvation of the soul, and some cosmogonic Orphic accounts may have had eschatological import. But not all Orphic poetry had to deal with anthropogony and eschatology, and not even all Orphic anthropogony had to originate in the myth of the Titans.[51] There are no indications – though the possibility cannot be completely ruled out – that the Derveni theogony continued up to the destruction of Dionysus, since the extant papyrus ends with Zeus's recreation of the universe. Nor should it necessarily be taken for granted that works of theo-cosmogony, anthropology, and eschatology were invariably ascribed to Orpheus. The *katabasis* of the soul that underlies the texts of the tablets may be Orphic, but its attribution to Orpheus is no more than a supposition, and nothing connects it, in any case, with the theogonic poems. In addition, there is no explicit link between Orpheus and the myth of the Titans before the Hellenistic Age.[52] The testimonies adduced to prove that by the Classical period Orpheus was already the obvious poet of the myth are not wholly conclusive, while Plato's attitude, which seems to accept the myth and many other elements of Orphism while deriding and mocking the figure of Orpheus himself, seems to indicate that the two were readily dissociable.[53]

---

51 Cf. Hdt. 1.132 on theogonies sung in rites, as seemingly suggested by the first columns of the Derveni Papyrus, which describe rites before interpreting a theogony. As Seaford 1986 notes for Empedocles, the four cosmic elements may have an eschatological role in Orphic contexts, like fire (Betegh 2004, 325–348) and wind: cf. Gagné 2006, who notes that the Orphic *Physika*, a poem of Classical times, proposed the Tritopatores, and not the Titans, as forefathers of humans.

52 The earliest pieces of evidence are the sources of Diodorus (cf. Bernabé 2000 and 2000b) and Clement (cf. Herrero 2007a), which can be traced back to the third century BC. Fragmentary quotations of Callimachus (fr. 43.117 Pfeiffer) and Euphorion (fr. 92 Van Groningen) allude to the myth but without mention of Orpheus.

53 Plat. *Euthyphr.* 5e, Isocr. *Busir.* 10.38, grouped under *OF* 26. In both cases, the reference to untellable, terrible and extraordinary things does not have to be necessarily to the myth of Dionysus. In the first passage, moreover, Orpheus is not mentioned, and in the second, his death as a Dionysiac punishment (told by Aeschylus

The same lack of systematization can be found in other areas of Orphic theological speculation. Vegetarianism, belief in reincarnation, and the assertion that the soul's fundamental flaw arose with the rebellion of the Titans, for example, were independent elements that on occasion might be presented in a coherent and interrelated fashion – but they did not always have to be so presented. The gold tablets, for example, appear to allude to the myth of the Titans, but contain little indication of an interest in reincarnation, the only exception being an ambiguous reference to a cycle in one of them[54], and it would certainly be arbitrary to conclude that the users of the tablets were vegetarians. The appearance of a new tablet containing the name of Orpheus would in fact add very little to what we know of the theological constructions they reflect. Any construction – as for instance Empedocles' poems – will necessarily privilege certain elements from within this broad range of speculation and reject others, or at least pass over them in silence

The attempt to define a coherent Orphic ideology "from creation to salvation,"[55] then, is doomed to failure not only for lack of proof, but because it fails to take into account the dispersed and always isolated contexts in which our information appears. We are dealing with an array of speculations containing many common elements, but which remains unorganized except for the particular systematizations imposed by particular individuals, as in the case of Empedocles and certain Pythagoreans. Why, then, does so loosely defined a process of speculation deserve to be called Orphism?

The question is whether a phenomenon including elements as diverse as the theogony of the Derveni Papyrus and the gold tablets, lacking any obvious relationship between them, deserves a unitary and unifying label. And the response is in the affirmative, because both, like the rest of Orphic speculation, are attempts to create an abstract and non-local language departing from traditional cultural forms such as the *katabasis* and theogony, in order to express speculative insights arising from the religious experiences of the traditional Greek mysteries. The directions taken by these theological speculations are diverse, and their conclusions cannot necessarily be deduced from one another; but their concerns are not incompatible, tending as they do to converge in line with their common inspiration and method of inquiry.

---

in the *Bassarides*) does not have to be necessarily linked to the content of the myths told by him. Cf. Bernabé 1998 on Platonic treatment of Orphism.

54 A tablet from Thurii mentions (*OF* 488) "liberation from the cycle of deep grief". Cf. Bernabé / Jiménez 2008, 117–120, for the various interpretations of this line.

55 As Alderink 1981 does in his analysis of Orphism as a general systematic doctrine. This endeavour leads him to (wrongly) exclude texts that mention reincarnation because he finds them incompatible with others not mentioning it.

One of the points of convergence (the clearest and latest being the compilation of the *Rhapsodies*) is the name of Orpheus, to whom is attributed much of the theology of the mysteries.

"Orphism," then, is a conventional label that ought to be kept because of the lack of any feasible alternative and because it has been consecrated by academic tradition. Though it will be necessary to qualify the term in many cases – to refer specifically, say, to Orphic eschatology or anthropology – it is possible to claim without valid objection that all these areas are related to Orphism and to investigate such general features as are common to the whole field of study and the diverse particular elements that it comprehends, some of them key to Western spiritual history. It is true that the term has behind it an entire history of misunderstandings, but the word remains useful, when employed with caution, to describe a cultural phenomenon that demands some sort of denomination. Dodds' purposefully anachronistic "Puritanism" is more vague, and Bianchi's "mysteriosophy" is broader in scope, since it includes later stages like Hermeticism and Gnosticism, while reductionist terms such as "Bacchic mysteries" or "Pythagoreanism" can exclude indispensable testimonies. On the other hand, the restriction of sources to testimonies authorized by the name of Orpheus, along with other, clearly connected phenomena such as the tablets, may ignore some evidence that could be intimately related to them, and perhaps it may include some other pieces that are only superficially linked to the general phenomenon. But the portrait of the process of theorization and intellectual unification of the mysteries will be trustworthy in its general lines.

As a process of speculation arising from the experience of the mysteries, Orphism is at the same time something more and something less than this experience: Aristotle said (fr. 15 Rose) that one became initiated in order not to learn (*mathein*) but to experience (*pathein*). From the evidence we have, it appears that Orphism placed more emphasis on the former than on the latter: it is sufficient to observe that in such clearly ritual-related evidence as the tablets, the knowledge that the initiated should possess is much more important than any ritual action undertaken. The consequences are clear: a group brought together by intellectual speculation – even supposing that several people take part in it – is far less stable and characterized by less tight bonds of belonging than a group defined by the celebration of a ritual and the shared experience this produces.[56] Such considerations raise in turn the question of the "Orphics."

---

56 Cf. for example Rudhardt 1958 and Burkert 1983, who from very different perspectives on ritual, and particularly on sacrifice, agree on the power that ritual has to make the group cohesive.

A purely intellectual and literary tradition may broaden the domain of thought and speculation, but it does not create stable groups around this domain. The case of ritual traditions, however, may be different. From Herodotus up to the end of Antiquity references to Orphic rites occur, and possibly many of the later ones allude to rituals that exist only in the imagination of those who mention them (Chapter II). However, authentic proofs of the celebration of rituals under the auspices of Orpheus in the Classical period do exist, as it would be only logical to expect: if Orphic speculation arises from the experience of the rites, it also, in turn, has the potential to generate other rituals – as attested by the presence of Orphic verses in the tablets or in the Gurob Papyrus (*OF* 578), which documents a *teletē*. *Legomena* and *dromena* go hand in hand in these cases. The question is whether these rituals possessed a certain degree of uniformity, referred to the same myths and ideas, and implied similar prescriptions and ritual actions – that is to say, whether groups of people with more or less common beliefs gathered around them, in order to fulfil similar rites. In this case they could appropriately be called "Orphics," whether or not this was the name they gave to themselves.[57] A relative ideological and ritual uniformity allows one to speak with confidence about the beliefs and rites of "the initiates of Isis or Mithra" despite the absence of any term such as "Isiacs" or "Mithraics." On the other hand, the rites associated with Hermetic literature are so vaporous and changeable that one cannot speak of "Hermeticists."[58] There are Orphic rites, but is it possible to talk about "Orphic mysteries"?

The fact is that proofs of the existence of such ritual and ideological uniformity are nearly non-existent, and many indications point entirely in the other direction. The only clear reference to doctrinal or ritual uniformity, the mention of an *orphikos bios*, the "Orphic life," by Plato, occurs in the plural, and is used to denote some imprecise lifestyle that existed in a remote period, the precepts of which do not differ from those of the well-known Pythagorean life.[59] Plato's statement, then, hardly demonstrates the existence

---

57 Denomination of religious movements may vary depending on the adoption of an external or an internal perspective (Mormons= Church of Jesus Christ of Latter-Day Saints). Cf. Casadio 1997, 22.
58 Burkert 1987 on mysteries of Isis and Mitra; Fowden 1987, 187–192 on Hermeticism and its followers.
59 Plat. *Leg.* 782c: "those of yore lead certain so-called Orphic lives (Ὀρφικοί τινες λεγόμενοι βίοι), since they took from all not animated beings and kept away from all the animated instead". The only feature of this *orphikos bios*, the principle of vegetarianism, is the most famous of the *pythagorikos bios*. The plural, "certain" and "so-called" denote a certain indetermination. Note, moreover, that its practice is placed in a distant past, in the same tone as *Leg.* 713e: "the so-called

of a uniform doctrinal formulation of Orphic rules. Instead, the sources do depict the social reflection of Orphic rites, involving two types of agents. On the one hand, there existed itinerant priests who conducted initiations in their *teletai* with varying degrees of sincerity and commitment – morally exemplary specimens of this group being in rather short supply, according to the critics who caricature them.[60] Burkert's classic 1982 study demonstrated that these initiators were very far from attaining the organisational level of, say, a *collegium*, approximating more closely to the model of a loose guild or craft than to that of a sect – in contradistinction to, for instance, the Pythagoreans.

The other aspect of involvement relates to the recipients of these initiations, who might be individuals or even "entire cities," according to Plato's account. In the latter case, the city is not a community formed around that specific rite, but rather already exists as a group when it decides to accept joint initiation, as did Athens when it decided to undergo Epimenides' collective purification after the murder of Kylon by the Alkmaionids.[61] As for the individuals who underwent these purification rites, they do not seem to have formed stable groups, self-conscious *thiasoi*, among themselves. In fact, the only group initiated as such and that retained a stable existence afterwards was the family – which as a unit exists obviously prior to and independently of Orphic initiation. Funeral rites tended to be administered within the family environment, and in addition there exist numerous references to the initiation of close relatives. That leads one to conclude that the family is the area of social shaping and of transmission of Orphic rites.[62] But

---

life under Cronus". The Golden Age (celebrated maybe in some Orphic poem of Pythagorean inspiration) was not a real fact contemporary to Plato. The choir in Euripides' *Cretans* (fr. 472 Kannicht: *OF* 567) speaks about a holy life (ἁγνὸς βιότης) with elements related to Orphism, but its practice is also situated in a remote place and time (Minos' Crete), and its principles seem to stem rather from a poet's imagination, hence mixing hardly compatible ritual elements, such as omophagy and vegetarianism.

60 Plato, *Resp.* 364e and *Leg.* 909a, 933a. Mocking references to the celebrants of Orphic *teletai* made by Theophrastus, Plutarch and Philodemus (*OF* 653–655) seem to derive from an archetypical character like those of the New Comedy. The insult of Theseus to Hippolytus (Eur. *Hip.* 952ff) seems aimed at comparing him with this type of priest (Burkert 1982, 11).

61 *Resp.* 364e; cf. *P. Derv.* XX.1, with similar wording; Aristot. *Ath.* I on the purification of Athens by Epimenides. The city also could adapt mystic initiation to its own institutions, as shown by the Eleusinian mysteries in Athens, which integrated Orpheus and his eschatological poetry (Graf 1974).

62 A shield from Olbia (*OF* 564) bears an inscription referring to a mother and a daughter, both initiated. Plato (*Resp.* 363c) portrays parents threatening their children (Platonic critique of the educator) with the punishments of the Afterlife

the family, just like the city, does not become aware that it is a group by the fact of burying its dead or initiating its members in Orphic rites; on the contrary, it buries and initiates as a group precisely because it already exists as a social unit. Orphism is like a dye extending over an already-existing social fabric; it creates neither a new social environment nor a self-conscious sense of belonging to a defined and distinctive group.

It is true that both the itinerant character of the initiation rites and the universalizing theology of Orphism in themselves tend to elide the structures imposed by family and polis to focus attention upon the community of all men. The well-known Orphic saying that "many carry the *thyrsos*, but only a few are *bacchoi*" (*OF* 576) seems to transcend familial, *polis*-based, and even ethnic distinctions. But union with other *mystai kai bacchoi*, as promised by the Hipponion tablet (*OF* 474.15–16), individuals other than those already known by an initiate through his own political or family community, appears to have been reserved for the other world. The similarity among tablets from very far-flung locations does not prove anything but the expansion of the poetic and ritual tradition into widely separated areas, and any concern for uniformity, and with it a sense of community, is absolutely absent from the tablets and from our other evidence. The *bacchoi* look more like an imaginary spiritual community[63] than a social grouping, unless this might have arisen within a family context. There is no proof of the existence of any Orphic *thiasos* which would have blurred the boundaries of the family, and even less of the polis, in sharp contrast with Pythagorean or primitive Christian communities.

Only one, very exceptional, testimony raises the possibility that Orphic rites produced at a given time a stable thiasos conscious of its own differentiated identity: in Olbia appears the word – of doubtful reading in its last part – ΟΡΦΙΚΟΙ[64]. However, even accepting in good faith that the bone

---

described by "Musaeus and his son", who promise happiness for the initiated and their descendants as well; Demosthenes (*De Cor.* 18–19) describes Aeschines and his mother taking part together in rites with clearly Orphic elements; Theophrastus (*Charact.* 16.11) presents a gullible character taking all his family, with the nanny if the mother is not available, to visit the celebrant of Orphic *teletai*; Plutarch (*Cons. ad. uxor.* 10) reminds his wife about the Bacchic initiation they attended together. It could be inferred from the decree by Ptolemy Philopator (*OF* 44) that the craft of itinerant priest was also passed down from parents to children (Burkert 1982). Paus. 9.27.2; 9.30.12 presents the Lykomids preserving and transmitting Orphic poems at the sanctuary of Phlya.

63   As the συνετοί or οἷς θέμις ἐστ from *OF* 1 (cf. Henrichs 2003).
64   *OF* 463. Herodotus' tale (4.79) of the Scythian Scylas, who took part in the Dionysiac thiasos in Olbia, seems to imply that some groups of initiates on the borders

tablet proves the existence of some self-styled "Orphic" in fifth-century-BC Crimea (that is to say, on the very margins of Hellenic civilisation), this does not allow us to generalize concerning the rest of Greece. There, the pressure of official, public cult as the focus of religious identity did not encourage the creation of alternatives. It is possible – even probable – that the circulation of itinerant rites gave rise to stable groups of initiates in certain contexts. Instances of the spontaneous formation of a thiasos – crystallizations of the process of ritual diffusion – whose similarity to other groups would be at best haphazard, are, however, adventitious developments, an accidental side effect rather than the driving force of the process. If "Orphics" of this kind existed, they are far less important than the Orphic poets and theologians who led the intellectual process just described. Their disappearance without a trace is the best proof of their scarce relevance.

Thus, to turn these self-conscious "Orphics" (or in the most extreme formulation, the archetypal "Orphic") into the protagonists of the intellectual process described above heavily distorts its reality, and tends to turn Orphism once more into an organized ideological system, according to the false social portrait drawn of it. Burkert's 1977 outline of Orphism, wherein it is visualized as a circle superimposed over three different fields, better reflects the situation: there were Pythagoreans, there were initiates of the Eleusinian mysteries, and there were practitioners of Dionysiac cult. Orphics did not exist – or at least, were of marginal importance – as anything distinct from these three spheres. Instead, within these areas, Orphism spread to a greater or lesser degree. To focus the debate on whether the commentators of the *Derveni Papyrus*, the users of the tablets, various Pythagoreans, or even Empedocles, were or were not – or worse, did or did not call themselves or others – "Orphics" prevents us from attending to a question of much greater interest: which elements of Orphism were integrated into each of these systems. This study, therefore, will discuss Orphism, the Orphic tradition, Orphic cosmogony, anthropology and eschatology, Orphic poets and theologians, and Orphic rites, but it will never speak of "Orphics".

---

of the Greek world may have crossed traditional ethnic and political boundaries, though not without resistance (cf. Hartog 1984).

II. Orphic religious presence in the Imperial Age

One of the many paradoxes of the study of Orphism is that, although most of our preserved Orphic testimonies and fragments date from the Imperial period, research has been focused primarily upon its early existence in Classical times, when its originality as a distinctive movement is greater. From the Hellenistic period onwards, the novelties that Orphism had once introduced in the world of the classical polis, like the concern for the soul, were spread all over by new philosophical and religious movements – Stoicism, Platonism, Neo-Pythagoreanism, new mystery cults. The images and ideas once propagated by Orphism for a few select individuals became common currency, and their increasing public visibility was due not so much to Orphic poems or rites as to the much more powerful and prestigious philosophical schools and organized religions. At the same time that the Orphic literary tradition is establishing itself as an achieved fact, however, ancient Orphic rites – for example, the use of the gold tablets – start to disappear, and by the end of the Hellenistic period Orphism seems to be no more than a literary memory.

Yet from the second century AD, there are signs of Orphism emerging afresh within different religious cults, and the Orphic literary tradition increases its prestige as a source of divine revelation. The resurgence of Orphism is surprising, and can only be explained by a re-evaluation of its religious contents within certain contexts. In addition, since Classical Orphism has been reconstructed in great part from late testimonies, the identification of the common threads linking one period to the other remains an important task. This question, however, must be approached with extreme caution: if early Orphism was never a cohesive, doctrinal movement, systematically defined by a series of intellectual oppositions and complementarities, it was even less so in the Imperial period, when the dispersion of materials is geographically even wider. Literary testimonies that may reflect a simply bookish or antiquarian tradition should be separated from those indicative of actual ritual practice. Following the usual procedure, I will first examine the forms of Orphic literary tradition and then its traces in ritual practice. While late Orphic literature has received no little attention, evidence regarding its ritual practice – from inscriptions, papyri, and external references – has not been studied systematically before. Here, however, the latter will be the main object of our interest, in order to to ascertain the religious value of Orphism during the Imperial period.

1. Orphic literature

From the Hellenistic period onwards, the number of poetic works attributed to Orpheus increases drastically – some being directly related to the Orphic poems of earlier periods, with others retaining only certain characteristics of style and the name of Orpheus to connect them to the rest of the Orphic tradition. Despite this diversity, the most important genres to invest Orpheus with significant authority since Classical times remain theogonies, hymns and tales of descent to Hades (*katabasis*).[1] Before effective analysis of these genres can proceed, however, let us say a word about the authorship of the Orphic poems. It was by no means uncontested, and many were aware that at least some of the poems attributed to the mythical Thracian bard had actually been written by another – and much later – hand.[2] This uncertainty, however, did nothing to diminish their perceived religious value. Rather, what we call Orphism nowadays was sanctioned by the name of "Orpheus"; that is, by accepting a conventional attribution of a work, it was assumed that such work possessed particular poetic and religious characteristics. Pausanias, for example, believed the *Rhapsodies* to be the work not of Orpheus, but of Onomacritus. Nevertheless, he invests them with the same authority as he does those *hieroi logoi* whose authenticity is unquestionable. Jewish and Christian apologists would adopt a similar attitude in claiming the authority of Orphic poems that at least some of them suspected were not composed by the mythic singer. It is not as much a question of cynicism or propaganda as a question of the value placed on a poetic tradition, which surpassed by far individual authorship.

The most significant part of the Orphic corpus, both in quantity and in quality, is constituted by the THEOGONIES[3]. The poem commented on in

---

1 Other Orphic literary works in Late Antiquity are the *Orphic Argonautica* and poems on astrology, botany, and the magical use of stones (*Lithica*). Cf. West 1983 and Bernabé/Casadesús 2008.
2 Epigenes (*apud* Clem. Alex. *Strom.* 1.21.131) attributes Orphic works to various Pythagoreans; Cicero (*ND* 1.107) endorses this opinion and supports Aristotle's idea that Orpheus never existed; Pausanias (9.30.12, 8.37.5) follows the biased opinion of the Lycomidai according to which only the poems sung by them in Phlya were authentic.
3 Detailed studies of theogonic Orphic poems are to be found in West 1983, Brisson 1995 and Bernabé 2003a.

the *Derveni Papyrus*, together with Plato's references, clearly indicates that theogonies associated with the name of Orpheus were widespread in the Classical period, even if only some of these seem to have survived into the Imperial period. The Neo-Platonist writer Damascius (fifth-sixth century AD) speaks of three Orphic theogonies – one quoted by the Peripatetic philosophr Eudemus, another composed by Hieronymus and Hellanicus, and the *Hieroi Logoi in 24 Rhapsodies*. The first one is not mentioned by any other author, so it is likely that Damascius was familiar only with a prose summary whose origin was noted in his philosophical sources. The *Theogony of Hieronymus and Hellanicus* coincides with that quoted by the Christian writer Athenagoras: it seems to be a Stoic reinterpretation of traditional theogonic materials, is witnessed by only a few literary testimonies, and presumably enjoyed a limited circulation amongst certain philosophical communities. The *Rhapsodies*, a major collection of all previous Orphic literature, compiled probably in the first century BC, is the most widespread theogony of the Imperial period. It told the origin of all the gods and of the cosmos, probably culminating in the myth of Dionysus and the Titans. It also seems to have included some sections that described the ultimate destiny of the human soul, condemned to be reincarnated until its final liberation from the cycle as expiation for its foundational crime. Also in the *Rhapsodies* there appear hymnic, cosmological, and katabatic fragments from non-theogonic literature, assembled and ordered by the compiler with a greater or lesser degree of coherence.

Damascius' enumeration does not mean that these three theogonies are the only poems to which we might ascribe theological or mythological Orphic quotations. The *Rhapsodies* are a compilation of previously existing poems, and the subsequent immediate disappearance of all other theogonies in circulation cannot be assumed. In fact, some quotations plausibly traced to pre-Rhapsodic sources can be found in the works of Clement of Alexandria, as we shall see. The continued existence of theogonic and mythic poems aside from those of the *Rhapsodies* becomes even more plausible when considering Demeter's myth, since the proliferation of different Eleusinian-inspired cults and the frequent use of the figure of Orpheus to endow them with prestige – as will be discussed below on the basis of the evidence of Pausanias – must have stimulated the production of Orphic versions of the myth.

Whatever their original or derivative links with cult may have been, there is no doubt that theogonies were the most appropriate vehicle for the transmission and dissemination of Orphic myths, from their origins to the end of Classical antiquity. Not only philosophers considered them highly. Still in the fifth century AD Nonnus, Claudian, and other poets betray the influence of

Orphic theogonies[4]. Apart from their role in transmitting and continuing the mythological tradition, however, what was the ideological value of these poems? The best answer comes from the mouth of Apion, the anti-Jewish Greek author, who appears as a literary character in the *Pseudoclementina*.[5]

> Out of all Greek literature dedicated to the beginning of the universe, and out of all authors, two are most relevant: Hesiod and Orpheus. Their works permit a double interpretation – according to the written word, and according to its allegory *(secundum litteram et secundum allegoriam)*. Those passages interpreted according to the written word attract crowds of sullen people – those following the allegory excite the admiration of philosophers and men of taste alike.

The strength of myth as an ideological structure within which religious categories can be set has been studied in depth throughout the last century. Beyond the traditional debates between (post-)rationalists and (post-)romantics on the value of mythical thought, there is little doubt that myths have the ability to appeal to our feelings for the divine and shape our religious experience.[6] The old evolutionary vision of Greece according to which there was a clear progress from *mythos* to *logos* seems now obsolete: along with the ongoing speculations of philosophers, the myths of the poets (and the cults of the cities) were as powerful in the Imperial age as in classical times, and rather than being replaced by *logos*, they were the material upon which *logos* progressed.[7] In addition, several myths exist as *aitia* (tales of origin) for a particular cult or aspect of cult practice. The narration of an aetiological myth may be the full and explicit aim of a poem, as in the case of the *Homeric Hymn to Demeter*. But it can also serve as an attempt to associate a particular cult with the prestige attached to myth, along with whatever ideas the cult may promote or encode. This attraction of the myth as a narrative in its own right – its appeal, in Apion's phrase, *secundum litteram* – is precisely the factor that causes Orphic theogonies to influence ritual practice.

---

4   Cf. Hernández de la Fuente 2002 (Nonnus); West 1983, 265f (Claudian); Turcan 1961 (Martianus Capella).
5   Rufin. *Recognit.* 10, 30 (346, 17 Rehm) = *OF* 669 VII. On this work, cf. pp. 138f.
6   Following the classic study of Cassirer 1923–1929 on myth as a means of structuring thought, cf. Kirk 1970 as representative of the American school, and Vernant 1969, Detienne 1981 and Veyne 1983 as representatives of the French one. Cf. the overview of theories of myth in Csapo 2005.
7   Cf. Most 2007, who vindicates the validity of Varro's statement (fr. 6 Cardauns) that the theologies of the poets, of the philosophers, and of the cities coexisted throughout all of Antiquity, instead of being successive.

The very moment the import of the myth, however, is theorized – that it becomes subject to interpretation *secundum allegoriam* – then ideas are explicated from its narrative by means of two, often contrasted, hermeneutic strategies: exegesis and allegory. The exegetical approach interprets the narrative by accepting it at, essentially, face value, and takes it as the basic conceptual structure – as when, for instance, the commentator of the Derveni Papyrus develops the idea of the world's creation by a single *nous* from a theogony describing the conception of the world by Zeus.[8] His interpretation is more exegetical than allegorical. Another famous instance of exegesis is the cycle of reincarnation derived from the Titanic myth, as a consequence of an event that actually happened. The ideas resulting from exegesis are so intimately linked to the events narrated in the theogonies that they come close to being explicitly stated within them – and, in the latter case, probably were.

Allegorical interpreters, on the other hand, attempt to draw conclusions whose sense is far from the mythological narratives, positioning themselves as external observers and adaptors of the myth to their own mental and ideological structures. Orphic theogonies also proved themselves a fertile source of often-diverse allegorical readings for the various philosophical schools. This method is also applied by the commentator of the Derveni Papyrus, whose interpretations sometimes appear to stray rather far from anything the original composer of the theogony might have intended. In the following centuries, Stoic, Neo-Pythagorean and Neo-Platonic philosophers, and even Christian authors like Clement, enthusiastically applied allegoresis to Orphic theogonies, and they have transmitted to us significant theogonic fragments that have been incorporated into their own traditions.

Associated with the theogonies, there is another genre of Orphic poetry, already mentioned in the Derveni Papyrus: the HYMNS. The extant invocations to the gods under the name of Orpheus all have a similar style. Unlike the *Homeric Hymns*, they are not narrative in form. Instead, they concatenate epithets, cultic titles and names of a markedly theological tone, which refer in highly compressed form to the events told in the theogonies. In fact, such hymns could appear inserted in the theogonies, as in the case of the *Hymn to Zeus* of the *Rhapsodies*, or exist as independent poems. Christian authors, as we shall see, are fond of such poems and quote them often.[9] However, the most important collection of hymns by Orpheus has been transmitted by a single manuscript containing, along with the *Orphic Argonautica*, the *Ho-*

---

8   Betegh 2004, Bernabé 2007.
9   *P.Derv.* col. XXII.11 mentions the *Hymns* of Orpheus. The commented theogony is, in itself, a hymn to Zeus (Betegh 2004, 137) Cf. pp. 187ff.

meric Hymns, and the *Hymns* of Callimachus and Proclus, the so-called *Orphic Hymns*, composed in Asia Minor by the second century AD.[10] Each of the 87 poems is accompanied by a ritual act of libation. According to Pausanias (9.30.12), the hymns by Orpheus that were sung in Phlya were "short and not many," and probably were similar in style. Attempts to represent Orphism as a doctrinal system are frustrated by the absence of any indication of concern for the Afterlife in them – a point which amply demonstrates that Orphism may be very present in literature and cult without necessarily implying any developed eschatology. The cultural and performative character of the hymns is even more evident than that of the theogonies, as the mere fact of reciting them is in itself a form of worship before the god they celebrate – no matter how intellectual and abstract this form of worship might be.

In addition to these hymns, however – written with at least the possibility of recitation and performance in mind – others appeared for which any ritual context was of secondary importance or non-existent, their focus instead being on exploitation of the genre's literary characteristics for the purposes of philosophical speculation. I am not only refering to the neo-Pythagorean *Hymn to Number* (*OF* 695—704), which could have been somehow ritually performed. Macrobius quotes a certain *Hymn to the Sun* that equates Zeus, Helios, Dionysus, Fanes, and Hades (*OF* 539–543). The method used to create such identification is the concatenation of one name to the next as though they were epithets of one another – that is to say, as though they are different manifestations of the same god. The hymn also uses typically henotheistic formulae such as "one is Zeus, one is Hades, one is Helios, one is Dionysus" (*OF* 543). But apart from these hymnical techniques, the author profits from the ritualistic context in which Orphic poetry is supposed to be performed. In a symbolic manner, the poem describes the dress of the priest when the Bacchic rituals were taking place, with the obvious purpose of proclaiming solar syncretism, as the first lines of the poem indicate:

> All these rites must be celebrated covering with paraphernalia
> the body, imitation of the glorious god Sun:
> first, covering the body with a scarlet robe,
> similar to the splendid sun rays, like fire.
> Then, over this, a wide piece of fawn leather, brightly coloured, will be tightly adjusted,

---

10 Cf. the commentary on the *Orphic Hymns* by Ricciardelli 2000, as well as the general study by Morand 2001. On the theological content of the epithets, cf. Rudhardt 1991 and Govers-Hopman 2001. Cf. also Graf 2009.

a wild animal's spotted skin will rest on the right shoulder,
and this will resemble the shiny stars and the sacred dome…[11]

The *Hymn to the Sun* uses this ritual dress as a poetic resource to give expression to a speculative theory. The same applies to other ritual elements that came to serve as the focus of poems and that survive now only as titles: *Enthronement, Sacrifice, Purification, Tightening* (*OF* 602–624). The form of these poems draws upon the Pythagorean poetic tradition of describing objects in accordance with a cosmological model (*Robe, Net, Bowl*). Generally speaking, the poems describe elements of imagined rituals in highly abstract and speculative terms. Nevertheless, and perhaps under the influence of these very descriptions, such rituals may in fact at times have been enacted. A late Imperial alabaster bowl apparently intended for use in the worship of the Sun is inscribed with lines from the *Hymn to the Sun* in praise of Zeus Sun, Father of the Cosmos, and also a line from Euripides that seems to imitate theogonic poetry ('Sky and Earth were one and the same shape').[12] The bowl indicates the capacity of poetry from both the past and the present to stimulate religious devotion, even if this was not the original motive for its composition.[13] The Neo-Pythagorean *Orphica*, then, stand as both a consequence and the start of a tradition of intellectualized Orphic rites that, if generally enacted only in imagination, served also at times to inspire new *dromena* actually put into practice.

One particularly ambiguous instance of this ritualistic/speculative poetry is presented by the *Oaths*. It is well known that ancient mystery rites incorporated an oath intended to maintain the secrecy surrounding the practice of their celebration. Some of the poems attributed to Orpheus are of this type and name various gods as witnesses to the oath in question. The Neo-Pythagorean Theon of Smyrna contrives to find references to the Ogdoad in

---

11 Macr. *Sat.* 1.18.22 (*OF* 541). West 1983 (28, n.77 and 206, n. 96) tentatively identifies it with the poem *Hierostolika*, but Macrobius seems to have taken it from the very same *Hymn to Dionysus* from which all his Orphic quotes of this section come from. The verses follow the old tradition of the *Robe*, which described cosmologically, in line with Pherecydes, Persephone's *peplos* (*OF* 406–407).
12 *OF* 66 III (Eur. *Melanipp.* fr. 484 Kannicht), 539, 540. Delbrueck-Vollgraf 1934, 133 thinks its origin is probably in Asia Minor; cf. Bottini 1992, 124; Martínez Nieto 2000, 255–257; Mastrocinque 2005, 197–199.
13 For example, the use of Aristophanes' *Frogs* for late eschatological funerary epitaphs (Lada-Richards 1999), or the re-emergence of Maenadism after Euripides' *Bacchae* (Henrichs 1978). Along the same lines, the attacks of Irenaeus (*Adv. Haer.* 2.14.1) on the parodic cosmogony found in Aristophanes' *The Birds* (690ff = *OF* 64) is a likely indication that it was taken seriously.

three of the verses of the *Oaths*, whereas a Christian apologist discovers the Creator-Father God in another three. All these verses are believed to have been written without reference to any actual ritual practice, their ceremonial trappings serving merely as a pretext for intellectual and philosophical speculation. Their style is nevertheless similar to that of poetic oaths extant in papyri assumed to reflect ritual practice closely, and which may in fact have functioned as exorcisms.[14] Any clear-cut distinction between the ritualistic and speculative elements within the Orphic hymns is accordingly impossible to achieve.

Another of these poems, the *Lyre*, seems primarily concerned neither with theogony nor with cosmology, but with eschatology. A scholium on Vergil (*OF* 417 1) clearly indicates its content, referring to it as the *Liber de vocanda anima*, or 'book concerning the summoning of the soul [sc. "through the celestial spheres"],' an obvious reference to ritual practice. It is quite possible that, at least in Neo-Pythagorean circles, this poem was not only read, but also accompanied by the sounds of a lyre in some kind of funerary rite, no matter how elementary this might have been. Burkert states that "when we look beyond the façade of analysis and explanations for the harmony of spheres, [its chief concern] is not empirical science or mathematics, but eschatology," and as an example, he cites the anecdote according to which Pythagoras asked someone to play the monochord for him as he lay dying.[15]

The theme of the soul's ascent through the celestial spheres was shared by Pythagorean, Gnostic, and Christian eschatologies alike, as was the topic of the soul's descent to the Underworld after death. Such descent narratives are referred to as CATABASIS, a genre of poetry crucial to Orphism from the earliest periods – in part because of its focus on the soul's fate in the afterlife, and partly for its relationship to the figure of Orpheus himself, whose own descent into Hades endowed him with a near-unique authority to narrate such events.

Since classical times, a poem about the *Descent into Hades* has been attributed to Orpheus. A catabasis of the soul underlies the lamellae containing specific scenes of the soul's encounter with the guardians or Persephone. In the imperial age, it seems that the *Rhapsodies* included scenes of cata-

---

14 Th. Smyrn. *Exp. Rer. Math.* 104.20 (*OF* 619); Ps-Iust. *Cohort.* 15.2 (*OF* 620, cf. pp. 196ff); *OF* 621–623 are similar formulae preserved in papyri (p. 58); *OF* 614–618 on the oath requested in Orphic *teletai*.
15 Burkert 1972, 367 n. 37 referring to Arist. Quint. *De mus.* 3.2. Cf. now Hardie 2004 on music used in mysteries. In Herrero 2007a, n. 13 I propose the use of the lyre in the *telete* described in *P. Gurob* (24: λ]ύρα).

batic origin in their final part, dedicated to the fate of the soul.[16] Version after version of these scenes appeared in successive works, since in such a popular genre, one with which literature has played incessantly from Homer and Dante to Bulgakov, renewal is constant. Its influence is clear in Christian apocalypticism (pp. 368ff). Vergil was inspired by an Orphic catabasis, stemming from his Neopythagorean environment, and such inspiration is certainly evident when he describes the descent of Aeneas into Hades in book VI of the *Aeneid*.[17] The discovery of the so-called Bologna Papyrus, which contains a catabasis originating in the same source as the Vergilian scene, adds to the traditional arguments.[18]

This poem illustrates Orphic literature's mode of transmission and capacity to influence, as well as the ideological content derived from it. The fragments that were conserved, in hexameters of a style belonging to the second and third centuries AD, appear on the pages of a codex found in Egypt that dates from around the third century, preceding a *Homeromanteion*, a divinatory use of Homer. This type of work reveals the possible practical uses of literature, straddling the religious, the oracular, and the magical. A long and interesting debate has been raised by the first lines of the papyrus, which present several sinners who suffer punishments in Hades, among them a woman who would have "torn off" (ἀπορρίψασα) and "done violence" (βιαζομένην) to her child (the mentions of a bed and of Eileithya, the goddess of childbirth, make this certain). The lines are fragmentary and hard to read. Some scholars have argued that they refer to infanticide or exposure of children: the poetic eschatological tradition usually asigns to abandoned children the first place in the Beyond, and the Bologna poem would innovate by presenting the criminals instead of the victims of the crime.[19] Others, however, prefer to read the text as the first reference to abor-

---

16 Clem. Alex. *Strom.* 1.21.131.2 (quoting Epigenes) and probably Cic. *ND* 1.107 allude to the Pythagorean *Descent to Hades* attributed to Orpheus. Cf. Riedweg 2002 for the catabasis of the soul in the gold leaves. *OF* 337–350 are the catabatic fragments ascribed by Bernabé to the *Rhapsodies*.
17 Servius in the fourth century AD had already proposed Orpheus as precedent in his commentary to *Aeneid VI*. Among modern authors, cf. Carcopino 1927, Norden 1957[4], Luck 1973, Molyviati-Toptsis 1994, Bremmer 2009..
18 *Pap. Bon.* 4. Treu 1954 for the complete treatment of the parallels and Herrero 2008b for the *status quaestionis* of the relationship of the papyrus with Vergil. A common source is the most plausible hypothesis. Neither West 1983 nor Brisson 1990 include this poem in their accounts of later Orphic literature. Bernabé edits it as *OF* 717. Cf. some new readings now in Shanzer 2009.
19 Virg. *Aen.* 6.428; Luc. *Cat.* 5. The Christian tradition of the *limbus puerorum*, for non-baptized dead infants, inherits this tradition. Cf. n. 39 *infra* for the possibility

tion in a pagan catabasis, be it due to Judeo-Christian influence or to some Orphic precedent.[20] The mention of Eilithya makes me think the reference to a punishment for abortion more probable, though by no means certain. However, since there are no other allusions in the rest of the preserved Orphic evidence, I do not think this text can be alleged as proof of an early Orphic condemnation of abortion. It is not even necessary to posit a direct Jewish or Christian influence on late Orphic poetry, for opposition to abortion is not exclusive to Judaism in Late Antiquity, but belongs to the general ethics of the time.[21]

Thus, the three traditional genres of Orphism – theogonies, hymns, and catabasis – remained in perfect health in the Imperial Age, not only carrying on a literary tradition the forms and images of which they preserved, but also providing vehicles for new ideas of a diverse nature. This capacity for innovation made them valuable to the "philosophers and men of good taste," in Apion's words, who handed down these genres by quoting them in literary works. Their religious value, however, which also appealed to the "obscure multitude," is seen primarily in their influence on ritual practice.

---

that Orphic mythology provided an *aition* against the exposure of infants.

20 The Latinist Setaioli and the legal historian Nardi had an interesting debate contraposing literary and juristic methods: Setaioli (1970) interpreted lines 3–4 as a reference to abortion; Nardi (1970) questioned this interpretation, arguing that θρ[όνοισι (with abortive poisons) read by Setaioli had no paleographical grounds (the most recent editors, Lloyd-Jones/Parsons 1978, read δ̣ [) and that neither βι[αζ]ομένην nor ἀπορρίψασα find parallel expressions in legal or ritual references to abortion. Setaioli (1973) answered that a poetic text need not necessarily follow legal vocabulary. Nardi (1972: the journal *Iura* appeared later than its official date suggests) insists that there is no basis for abortion. Most scholars remained undecided (Lloyd-Jones/Parsons 1978, 92: *aut ad infanticidium respicere potest aut ad aborti procurationem*; Bernabé *ad OF* 717). Shanzer 2009, 355–360 has recently vindicated Setaioli's arguments.

21 Freund 1983 discusses the ethics of abortion in Hellenistic Judaism and concludes that Judaism adapted to the increasingly anti-abortion moral tendency, rather than being its motor. However, the parallels with the condemnation of abortion in Jewish apocalyptic literature are pointed out by Setaioli 1970, 207–217 (with partial rectification in 1973, 126).

2. Orphic ritual traces in Imperial times

2.1. Direct evidence

The lack of dream and vision accounts revealing traces of the Orphic mythic tradition indicates its marginal status and erudite character; accounts of this sort are the best foundation for reconstructing general religious experience, as Robin Lane Fox (1986) does in his excellent portrait of paganism in the imperial age. Without them, only in ritual practice is it possible to determine whether Orphic myths and images had any real substance in the religion the apologists sought to combat, or whether, on the contrary, these myths were part of a purely erudite tradition without any counterpart in cultural reality. The problem, as in the case of the cosmological ritual works, is that a great part of the Orphic ritual tradition also has been transmitted in literary references, and it is difficult to know when real practices are being alluded to and when it is a case of rites that existed only in the collective imagination. In addition, even when evidence, principally epigraphic and papyrological, of actual ritual practices colored by Orphism does exist, it is necessary to resist supposing a unitary rite shared by all these cults. On the contrary, the extreme variety of evidence cannot be reduced to any prototypical "Orphic ritual," but rather presents a multiplicity of cults – generally connected to the mysteries of Dionysus and of Demeter-Core – tinged with Orphism in varying forms and degrees, with an even greater level of diversity than that found in the literary works. In order to work around these difficulties, I have thought it preferable to examine separately the direct evidence from each region where that evidence indicates the real existence of Orphic practices: Greece, Asia Minor, Egypt, and Rome. In addition, this division will make it possible at a later stage to conduct a comparison with the zones where the apologists who mention Orphism were active. I will then complete the picture with the general references to Orphic rites made in literary sources.

I begin the examination in GREECE because it is here that, thanks to Pausanias, we have more concrete information about some cults specifically linked with Orpheus.[22] This is in contrast to the absence of direct epigraphic evidence – contrary to Rome, Asia, Asia Minor, or Egypt. A few decades ago, before Pausanias's rehabilitation, this contradiction would have been further proof of his alleged untrustworthiness and of the literary nature of his ac-

---

22 A systematic analysis of Orphic references in Pausanias has not been made, except for the brief overview by Sabbatucci 1991 of his mentions of Orpheus.

count.[23] Today this paradox can be attributed in part to chance, which has not furnished us with inscriptions confirming his references to Orphic cults, and in part to the fact that, as will be demonstrated by the analysis of the relevant passages of Pausanias, the Orphic presence in the region consisted primarily in *legomena* that accompanied or explained *dromena* in sanctuaries of esoteric coloration that prided themselves on the divine origin of their rites, open only to the faithful. This secrecy, essential to religious prestige, did not permit the rites to be made public in inscriptions.

When discussing Eleusis at the beginning of his *Periegesis*, Pausanias offers a key to the Orphic poems' function: "It is impossible to attribute the discovery of beans to Demeter; whoever has seen the initiation at Eleusis or has read the so-called *Orphica* knows what I am talking about."[24] Scepticism about the authorship of "the so-called *Orphica*" is not an obstacle to assigning them a function similar to the *epopteia* of the mysteries, at least when it comes to understanding the celebrated taboo on beans. Ritual activity and the reading of poems are not incompatible – they are rather complementary and concurrent – but the verbs clearly mark out each one's territory: the parallel to *seeing* the Eleusinian rite is *reading* the Orphic poems.

Two other, later passages, referring to the mysteries honoring Gaia at the sanctuary at Phlye, corroborate this impression. Pausanias says, "After Olen, Pamphus and Orpheus made verses, and both made poems to Eros, to be sung by the Lycomids as well in the *dromena*, and I read them after conversing with a man who was a daduchus" (9.27.2). Slightly further on he repeats, "Everyone who has a general knowledge of poetry knows that, among the hymns of Orpheus, each one is very short, and the total number is not great. The Lycomids know them and sing them in the *dromena*" (9.30.12). The Orphic poems were recited in Phlye while certain rites took place. The nature of these poems, as brief hymns to the gods, does not seem suited to having a close relationship with the rite carried out, beyond that of simultaneity. The parallelism with the *Orphic Hymns* is clear and provides a clue to their nature.

---

23 The spectacular rehabilitation of Pausanias began with Habicht 1985, who showed that Wilamowitz's condemnation of his reliability was largely due to personal reasons (pp. 165–175); since Habicht, interest in Pausanias has constantly increased: *cf.* Alcock /Cherry /Elsner 2001; Hutton 2005; Pirenne-Delforgue 2008 is an excellent monograph on his treatment of religion (with an up-to-date *status quaestionis* on pp. 9–14).

24 1.37.4. In 8.15.1 (*OF* 649 II) Pausanias mentions a *hieros logos* explaining the beans taboo. Cf. n. 37 *infra* about the inscription presenting the myth of the Titans as the *aition* of this prohibition.

The Lycomids, who since classical times were responsible for the mysteries in Phyle, gave these hymns much importance as a hallmark and symbol of their cult, which kept up a certain rivalry with the Eleusinian cult. They held that only the hymns that they sang were the authentic works of Orpheus and Musaeus. Pausanias, who seems to have had direct contact with a Lycomid and been persuaded by him, says in several passages that the majority of Orphic poems are forgeries.[25] In any case, the cultural function of the "inauthentic" Orphic poems also seems to have been quite similar, in Pausanias's eyes, to that of the hymns sung in Phyle; that is to say, they accompanied the *dromena*. Thus he says, "Onomacritus, taking from Homer the name of the Titans, instituted (συνέθηκεν) the rites in honor of Dionysus and made (ἐποίησεν) the Titans responsible for the sufferings of Dionysus" (8.37.5). Pausanias, probably following his Lycomid source, attributes to Onomacritus the composition of the poem narrating the myth of the Titans, which in this period doubtlessly refers to the *Rhapsodies*. What is interesting is that for Pausanias, instituting the Dionysian rites is equivalent to composing the poem that narrates Dionysus's death at the hands of the Titans: the τε καί coordinating the two propositions unites them very closely, almost in hendiadys. In this case, Pausanias is not limiting himself any more to Phyle, but is rather talking about *orgia* in general, as if in Pausanias's Greece Orphic rites were inseparable from the reading of this poem. However, it is important to note that, unlike what he does with many other cults, Pausanias does not specify any concrete location for these rites, a fact that, once again, leaves in doubt whether he really knew of these rites' existence or simply imagined it.

For Pausanias, Orpheus is mainly a poet and continues to be so despite forming part of a cult, whether as its founder, practitioner, or exegete. There are several cults of Eleusinian heritage that claim Orpheus as their mythic founder, claims to which the Periegetes reacts with mocking scepticism. Thus with regard to the cult of Hecate in Aegina, modelled after that of Eleusis, he says, "They celebrate the ceremony every year, saying that it was founded by Orpheus the Thracian" (2.30.2). Speaking about the cults of the Lacedaemonians, Pausanias comments, "Some say that the Thracian Orpheus built it [the temple of Core Soteira], others that it was Abaris" (3.13.2); "The Lacedaemonians say that they venerate Demeter Chthonia because Orpheus so handed it down to them, but in my opinion the temple was built on account of the one in Hermione, where they held Demeter Chthonia in high regard" (3.14.5).

---

25 In 1.22.7 he considers forgeries the hymns by Musaeus (who for Pausanias is entirely an *alter ego* of Orpheus, *cf* 10.7.2: "Musaeus, who imitated Orpheus in everything"); in 8.31.11; 8.37.5; 9.35.5 he considers forgeries the *Orphica* themselves.

Note the verbs in these last three passages: to found (καθίστημι), to hand down (παραδίδωμι), even to build (ποιέω) the temple where the cult was celebrated. Orpheus's reputation as an originating figure to ground oneself upon is evident. His prestige as a theologian was inseparable from his fame as a poet, since he was an ideal candidate for the authorship of the *hieroi logoi* that every self-respecting mystery cult needed in order to make itself at once ancient and comprehensible. Even the *Rhapsodies* could occasionally take on this function.[26] Like a saint in medieval and early modern Christian cults, Orpheus's active role as poet and founder of rites could lead to his veneration in his own cult. The sanctuary of the Muses on Mount Helicon had a statue of Orpheus enchanting the animals alongside a statue of Telete (9.30.4): he was venerated there as a poet and cultic founder, and was said to have been struck by a thunderbolt for having revealed the mysteries, appearing as Prometheus and at the same time as one of the violently deceased holy men who became more and more fashionable.[27] Similarly, there is Lucian's mention (*Adv. indoct.* 109) of the preservation of Orpheus's head in the *Baccheion* of Lesbos. This "saintly" position may have extended to a quasi-deification that put Orpheus on practically the same level as the gods whom his own hymns addressed: on Olympus "alongside Strife is the image of Dionysus and Orpheus the Thracian and the statue of Zeus" (5.26.3), and in a Lacedaemonian cult site dedicated to Demeter Eleusina, there is "a *xoanon* of Orpheus that they say is the work of the Pelasgians" (3.20.5).

In all these cults the *dromena* performed are, according to Pausanias, of clearly Eleusinian lineage. This picture is in agreement with the first passage analyzed (1.37.4); Orpheus and his poems serve to explain and to lend prestige, to be read and perhaps heard, while what is practiced and seen are the Eleusinian rites. In fact, Orpheus's expansion and prestige among the cults of Hellas coincides above all with the cults of Demeter and Core. Orpheus and his poetry seem to be the complementary *legomena* needed by the imitators of Eleusis all over Greece to promote and explain their *dromena*, in mythological, aetiological (e.g., the taboo on beans), and eschatological

---

[26] Pausanias says (8.31.11) that the Heracles of Demeter's sanctuary in Megalopolis "is one of the Dactyls of Ida, as Onomacritus says in his verses". On *hieroi logoi*, cf. Baumgarten 1998 and Henrichs 2003.

[27] 9.3.5. Cf. Orig. *CC* 7.53, discussed on p. 124. This climactic tale is precisely the only appearance of the word *mysteria*, which had for Pausanias an archaic resonance (Pirenne-Delforgue 2008, 296–298).

terms.²⁸ They were also needed by Eleusis itself in Athens, which had already integrated Orpheus into its ideological scheme in classical times²⁹.

It is little wonder that, in comparison with the multiple mentions in Pausanias, epigraphic traces of Orphism during the imperial age are extremely scarce in Greece. ³⁰ Secrecy was inherent in the very nature of the *legomena*, even more so when their primordial function was to lend prestige to the cult by means of their ancientness and to explain the *dromena* only to initiates. Mentioning the content of the *hieroi logoi* in public inscriptions would contradict their purpose as such.³¹ Pausanias speaks about the *Orphica* profusely, but never reveals their content, stopping with an air of mystery at the threshold of allusion. There is much in this attitude that smacks of imitation of Herodotus, but there is no reason to deny a real respect for the secret in question.

At the same time, paradoxically, Orpheus's poems and his figure itself were not yet instruments of excessive importance for first-rate Greek intellectuals during this period (e.g., Plotinus), although they would become increasingly significant for their heirs, beginning with Porphyry and Iamblichus. The foundations of this prestige in late paganism are to be found in the search for roots and identity undertaken by the Greek cities of the first and second centuries AD, described by Pausanias: great cities like Athens, middle-sized towns like those of the Peloponnese, and even tiny villages like Mesatis, a district of Patras whose name was etymologized by local scholars in accordance with the myth of the Titans.³² This is the most likely

---

28 Pausanias, following Herodotus' model, never reveals the content of the *hieroi logoi* that he claims to know (Pirenne-Delforgue 2008, 342f). But when he describes (10.30.6) a painting by Polygnotus in which there is an Orpheus with a lyre in Persephone's meadows, he mentions, along with the punishments of Sisyphus and Tantalus (10.31.9–11), some women who try to carry water in broken jars, and his explanation is the same: "they are those who did not pay attention to the rites at Eleusis". This is probably the pictorial transposition of an eschatological *hieros logos* (a *katabasis*).
29 Cf. the classic monograph of Graf 1974, with some new thoughts in Graf 2008.
30 Contrary to Asia Minor or even to Rome, we do not find any influence of the Orphic tradition in religious epigraphy, except perhaps in the inscription of the thiasos of *Iobacchoi* in Athens (Prott-Ziehen 1896 n. 46), whose terminology resembles that of the thiasos of an inscription at Torre Nova (*OF* 585) or the group of the *Orphic Hymns*; in that inscription the Eleusinian colour is again predominant.
31 Burkert 1995, Henrichs 2003.
32 7.18.2. I have proposed the reason for this etymology in Herrero 2006a. While the name of Mesatis clearly comes from being in the middle (*meson*) of other two towns, Antheia and Aroe, the myth of the Titans could be the basis for a popular etymology for two reasons: one possibility is that Dionysus was in the middle of the circle of attackers; another possibility is that the name was derived from the

source for the renewed popularity of Orpheus and his poems: among the various old- and new-style theologians who came into fashion, he was better able than anyone else to satisfy the need for religious profundity and Greek national identity, something which in the second century AD looked to the most archaic past for orientation. His acceptance by the local *intelligentsia* – who in various sanctuaries and cities passed on Orpheus's presence, his myth, and his poems to Pausanias as a symbol of religious prestige – is the necessary foundation for understanding the later neo-platonic constructions of Orpheus and the Christian attacks against him.

The region of ASIA MINOR already had an extensive tradition of Bacchic cults from the classical age, in assorted combinations with the Mother Goddess under her various manifestations (Rhea, Cybele) and with other autochthonous deities like Sabazius or Attis. Euripides had the maenads accompanying Dionysus come from Asia in the *Bacchae*, and it is precisely in Asia Minor that ritual maenadism, in whatever form, is best documented.[33] During the Hellenistic age, the Attalids of Pergamum (like the Ptolemies in Egypt) used Bacchic symbolism for propaganda purposes. During the Imperial Age, the cult of Dionysus continued to have great vigour in both public and private spheres.[34] It is not surprising that in the vicinity of the cult of Dionysus there appear the greatest number of elements of Orphic provenance from the second century AD onward.[35] The Orphic literary tradition, probably beginning with the *Rhapsodies*, left a significant epigraphic and literary mark on

---

verb *mesazo* (to be half-cooked), since the Titans would not have had time enough to completely cook his limbs.

33 Eur. *Ba. 62ff*. A Milesian inscription of 276 BC (Sokolowski 1955, n° 48: *OF* 583) shows in the expression ὠμοφάγιον ἐμβαλεῖν a certain will to reflect in ritual the most characteristic element of mythical maenadism, omophagy, although the exact interpretation of the sentence is much discussed; I find Henrichs' (1978) the most persuasive.

34 Cf. Burkert 1993, 265ff for Minorasiatic Bacchic *teletai* in Hellenistic times; Cumont 1911, 47–72 and Quandt 1913, though old works, are still valid for the Imperial Age. Jaccottet 2003 makes a general epigraphic study of Imperial Dionysiac cult, and Jiménez 2008 collects the inscriptions with Orphic traces.

35 Various Orphic elements have been claimed to be present in some inscriptions of the second to first centuries BC. They are dubious cases, since these inscriptions are called "Orphic" due to their ideological contents, rather than their images or the myths alluded to. At such a late date, the restriction of any ideas to Orphism is very risky: e. g. an inscription from Panticapaeum in the first century BC (*OF* 467), is rightly denied the label "Orphic" by Nock 1935; the Orphic elements in another inscription from Halicarnassus from the second or first century BC (*OF* 581) are very dubious in comparison with the later ones that will be analysed here, although there is an unmistakable mystic tone.

cults that reflected its myths and ritual traditions. The legend that Midas, the Lydian king, received his religious knowledge from Orpheus is the mythic tale that accounts for this Orphic presence in the cults of Asia Minor.[36]

The most important witness to Orphic rites in Asia Minor, and probably for the entire Imperial Age, is without doubt the *Orphic Hymns* already mentioned. Even though these poems are a literary source clearly dependent on the theogonies, they need to be mentioned here because one of the characteristics distinguishing them from other Orphic works is their express linkage to a ritual. The manuscript that has preserved them indicates before each hymn the type of ritual that ought to accompany it. The presence of various deities (Hipta, Mise) only known in Asia Minor led Otto Kern (1910) to suppose that these hymns were used by a religious community in this region, something which has been accepted practically unanimously by later scholarship, although the hymns' more precise attribution to Pergamum is more debatable. The question that needs to be investigated is whether they are an exception or part of the general panorama in Asia Minor at the time.

Besides the *Hymns*, there are five inscriptions that reveal, in keeping with them, the influence of Orphic mythology on Bacchic cults. The most important piece of evidence is a second century AD inscription from Smyrna.[37] In it are laid out the conditions that must be fulfilled by all those entering the sanctuary of Dionysus, and in the second part (lines 10ff), some requirements of purity applying only to the *mystai*: they are not to wear black or sacrifice inappropriate victims, and they are not to eat eggs, hearts, mint, and "the roots of beans, arising from the seed (σπέ[ρματος) of the Titans." All of these taboos have parallels in other evidence expressly related to Orphism and Pythagoreanism.[38] In particular, the mention of the Titans as the source for the taboo on beans, from whose seed they arise if we accept the reconstruction of the incomplete word, combines two different motifs habitually separated in Orphic tradition: the taboo on beans and the impure offspring of the Titans. In much the same way, the poetic language

---

36 Clem. Alex. *Protr.* 2.13; Ov. *Met.* 11.92.
37 *Inscr. Smyrn.* 728 (p. 227) Petzl: (*OF* 582). *Cf.* Sokolowski 1955 n° 84 (p.186) *SEG* 14, 1957, 752.
38 Nock (*apud* Sokolowski 1955. 186) saw just remnants of Pythagoreanism that would have influenced the Smyrnaean cult. Yet when prescriptions have mythical *aitia* like the Titans, the label "Orphic" is more than justified: cf. *OF* 650–651 for the dress, *OF* 645–646 for the egg and *OF* 648–649 for the beans. The inscription forbids a "plant of sweet smell destroyed by Demeter". It is probably mint, whose prohibition is attributed by Hippocrates (*De morb. sacr.* 1.10) to "magi, purificators, mendicants and wanderers"; its connection the sacred rites is documented in Sext. Empir. *Pyrrh. hypot.* 3.224.

of the general prohibition of the exposure of children, which threatens divine wrath, makes it possible for a traditional norm to be reinforced in this cult with the mythic *aition*.[39] In contrast to the moralization of ritual norms found in other contemporary inscriptions, justifications for the Syrmnean cult were sought in Orphic mythology for the same purpose of reinforcing and explaining the purity taboos.[40]

Another inscription presenting unmistakable Orphic traits dates from the second century AD and is of Lydian provenance, perhaps from the city of Hierocaesarea. Dionysus is given the epithet Ericepaeus, unequivocally linked to Orphic mythology.[41] It is tempting to suppose that the donors of the altar perhaps called themselves "members of one family" (συγγενεῖς) not only in relation to one another or to the hierophants mentioned, but also in relation to Dionysus himself, of whom they would be descendants in some sense according to the myth of the Titans, in which human beings, as a result of originating from the Titans' ashes, have part of Dionysus in their nature. In the lamella from Thurii, the soul claims to be of the divine *genos* (*OF* 488.3).

An inscription from Perinthus (Thrace)[42] from the second century AD points in the same direction, making a clear allusion to the same myth when

---

39 Lines 3–4: ἀπ' ἐχθέσεως πεφύλαχθε νηπιάχοιο βρέφους, μὴ δὴ μήνειμα γένηται. The expression is parallel to the depiction of Dionysus as νηπίαχος in Clement (*Protr.* 2.17) and Nonnus (*Dion.* 6.168). In the catabasis the first place in Hades usually corresponded to exposed children (cf. n. 19).
40 An inscription from Lindos (Rhodes) dated in the first century AD (Sokolowski 1962, n° 108) orders "abstinence from the pleasures of sex, from beans, from heart. May you be holy in the temple: not cleansed with water but purified in spirit". Porph. *Abst.* 2.19 and Clem. Alex. *Strom.* 4.22.142.3 quote similar rules from the cults of Asclepius in Epidaurus and Serapis in Egypt. *Cf.* Prott-Ziehen 1896 n° 148, with other similar inscription in Lindos with similar ritual prohibitions (having eaten neither cheese nor goat, having neither aborted nor had sex), and the same demand for interior and external purity "pure and holy in hands and intention". Sokolowski 1962, 177 shows other parallels in late inscriptions of this moralizing view of ritual purity. *Cf.* Nock 1964, 17–23, Parker 1983, 321–325 on this increasing moralization, attributed to the influence of Hellenistic philosophy (*cf.* already Plat. *Leg.* 4.717d-e) and of Eastern religion: an inscription from Philadelphia from the second to first century AD (Sokolowski 1955 n° 20, *cf.* Barton-Horsley 1981) is a clear example of moralization stemming from an Eastern cult (Agdistis is the deity granting justice).
41 *TAM* V 2, 1256 (p. 451 Keil-Herrmann): *OF* 662. Ericepaeus is a name of Dionysus in the *Rhapsodies* (*OF* 134) and *HO* 52.6; also in a ritual context: *P. Gurob* (*OF* 578) 22a, and the large lamella from Pherai (*OF* 493).
42 *Epigr. Gr. Suppl.* 1036a (*OF* 661). Cf. Casadio 1990, 200. Edmonds 2008 argues, along his usual lines, against using the myth of the Titans for the interpretation of this inscription.

it places this oracle in the mouth of the Sibyl: "When Bacchus, celebrating with cries of *euoi*, is struck, then blood, fire, and ashes will be mixed." Whether the blood is that of Dionysus or of the blasted Titans, the reference is clear. The last two Dionysian inscriptions make no more than brief allusions to the Orphic myth, and although W. Quandt already pointed them out in 1913, they have been overlooked and left out of the editions of *Orphica*. In Sardis, an inscription from the imperial period venerates Dionysus Coreus, son of Core, in what is a clear reference to the Orphic theogonies.[43] Finally, the last legible line of a Rhodian inscription from the time of Caracalla (third century AD) refers to Dionysus's two descents (καθόδοι).[44] If one descent into Hades is in search of his mother Semele, the second must be the young Dionysus's descent into Hades after his death at the hands of the Titans. Admittedly, Dionysus-Zagreus's descent into Hades after his death is not documented anywhere else. The pattern "sacrificial death–descent into hell–resurrection" recalls Christ's *descensus ad inferos* before his resurrection and may point to Christian influence on this Bacchic cult.[45]

As an outside observer, Lucian (*De Salt.* 79) confirms that Orphic imagery in Asia Minor frequently saturated Bacchic cults: "The Bacchic dance, practiced mainly in Ionia and the Pontic region, although it is a satyr dance, has taken possession of the people there to such an extent that at the appointed time everyone comes, forgetting everything else, and spends all day sitting watching Titans, Corybantes, satyrs, and herdsmen (*boukoloi*)." Satyrs, Corybantes, and Titans mingle in this Bacchic dance belonging to the Ionian and Pontic cult (there are no obvious reasons why Lucian would invent this location) and fitting the pattern that calls for the combination of specifically Orphic and generally Dionysian elements; thus, the Titans are only associated with Dionysus in Orphic tradition, while the satyrs are companions of Bacchus in any context, but especially as god of wine. The Corybantes and *boukoloi* play a more ambiguous role, at times appearing in Orphic contexts and at times not.[46]

---

43 Quandt 1913, n° 177 = *IW* 5219. The binary alternative posed by Quandt (1913, 178), on whether the cult was public or Orphic, is not pertinent in this period, when Dionysiac private associations were under public protection and participated in the public festivals (Nilsson 1957, Burkert 1993, Jaccottet 2003, 81).
44 Quandt 1913, n° 204 = *Oesterreich. Jahresbuch* VII (1904) 92. Cf. now Jiménez 2008
45 1 *Petr.* 3:19 was traditionally interpreted by Christians along these lines. *Cf* Grillmeier 1949.
46 *Cf.* Clem. Alex. *Protr.* 2.19 (Corybantes) and 1.16.2 (*boukoloi*). On *boukoloi*, cf Morand 2001, Jaccottet 2003.

The combination of Orphic traditions with the traditional Bacchic cult is exemplified once more in an inscription from Hellenistic Magnesia in which the figure of Baubo appears as a maenad.[47] Baubo is a central character in the Orphic versions of the story of Demeter and will be a favorite target of Christian attacks.[48] According to the inscription, an oracle commanded the summoning of three maenads, Kosko, Baubo, and Thettale – all names full of significance.[49] This appearance of Baubo in Asia Minor is complemented by a series of small figurines found in the Hellenistic Thesmophorion of Priene that join the face with the vulva, in the likeness of the character in the Orphic tale transmitted by Clement and Arnobius. The proximity in space and time of the two pieces of evidence, the maenadic inscription and the statuettes linked to Demeter, shows the nearness between the Bacchic traditions and those traditions of Demeter that had Orphic roots, a nearness which could give rise to exchanges of mythic elements like these. This fusion of Orphism's various traditions in Asia Minor has a final witness in the spells found on some small lead scrolls from the fifth century AD, intended to influence races in the hippodrome of, precisely, Magnesia (Hollmann 2003). Among the names given to the horses so that the latter might acquire their intrinsic magical power are Orpheus and Baubo. This is a final example of the fact that Orpheus's name was just a single element among all those carried along by the ever-more-voluminous stream of Orphic tradition.

The examination of all this material makes it possible to affirm that the *Orphic Hymns* are not a literary exception, but rather allow glimpses of a situation fully in accord with the general scene in Asia Minor. We find in Asia Minor an uninterrupted continuity of Bacchic cults from the classical and Hellenistic ages until the end of the imperial period. Now, beginning in the first century AD it is clear that cultural and mythic elements with Orphic roots increasingly entered into these cults. The origin of the Orphic elements is clear: the literary tradition, already unified in the *Rhapsodies*, with which

---

47 *I. Magn.* 215(a), 35. *Cf.* Henrichs 1978, 131.
48 Clem. Alex. *Protr.* 2. 21.1, Arn. *Adv. Nat.* 5.25; Greg. Naz. Or. 4.115. Baubo also appears in *P. Berol.* 44 as a nurse. Her role is variable, from nurse to goddess to maenad, and she is paid cult in Naxos (*SEG* 16.478, fourth century BC), Paros (*IG* XII 5.227) and Dion in Macedonia (*SEG* 27.280, 34.610). This character, symbol of feminine sexuality, and the relationship between the Homeric and Orphic versions of the *Hymn to Demeter* (is the former a more primitive version or a later innovation?) have attracted great scholarly attention: *cf.* Picard 1927, Graf 1974, Richardson 1976, Devereux 1983, Olender 1985 and O'Higgins 2003.
49 Thessale is clearly linked to Thessaly, and Kosko to the sieve (κοσκίνον), which had a ritual use similar to the kernos and is the instrument for the eternal punishment of the Danaids in Hades (Plat. Resp. 363d).

the composers of the *Orphic Hymns* or the author of the Lydian inscription mentioning Ericepaeus were doubtless familiar. This tradition contributed to giving shape to religious experience and, therefore, formed an inseparable part of that experience.

EGYPT was for the ancients, as India has been in modern times, the mysterious land from which the most arcane religious traditions supposedly originate.[50] Therefore, the urge to find a foreign origin for the cults of Dionysus and Demeter – an impulse shared by ancients and moderns, arising from the perception of these cults as alien to the "purely" Greek religion forged in the Homeric tradition – found in Egypt an obvious solution to the problem. In reality, Orphism seems to have integrated Egyptian elements during both the archaic and the Hellenistic ages.[51] Since Herodotus (2.82), it was supposed that the Bacchic rites were really Egyptian. The identification of Osiris with Dionysus and Isis with Demeter, easy due to their similarities, further encouraged the idea of the Egyptian origin of the mysteries of Dionysus and Demeter from Hellenistic times.[52] The figure of Orpheus took on a principal role as intermediary in the construction of this ritual chain of transmission, since as in the case of so many other Greek wise men (Solon, Pythagoras, Plato), it was tempting to attribute Orpheus's religious knowledge to a trip to Egypt. Likewise, the Jewish and Christian apologists enthusiastically promoted this supposed Egyptian origin, via Orpheus, of the most prestigious Greek mysteries (pp. 145, 281ff). Now, if the tradition of cultic transmission between Egypt and Greece habitually identifies Egypt as the place of origin, and leaving aside the influences which may have existed

---

50 *Cf.* Hartog 1980 on the Herodotean image of Egypt, which is greatly influential in later tradition. Pausanias (6.20.18) tells a representative tale about the *daimon* Taraxippus, whose statue scared the horses running at Olympia for some unclear reason. After considering whether it might be the tomb of various heroes, the last possible explanation Pausanias offers is that "Pelops received something from Amphion the Theban and buried it". This more supernatural and mysterious explanation is attributed to "an Egyptian who thought that Amphion and Orpheus the Thracian were skilled magicians". *Cf.* Díez de Velasco-Molinero Polo 1994 on the fantastic character of many of these supposed Greek borrowings from Egypt.

51 The clearest cases are the parallels of the gold leaves with the Egyptian *Book of the Dead* (Merkelbach 1999). Some sceptical scholars have thought that the Titanic myth was a result of Hellenistic Egyptian influence (Wilamowitz 1931, Festugière 1935). But there are clear earlier allusions to the myth (as even Liforth or Dodds admit), and the theme of dismemberment has many Greek parallels: if there is any influence between the myths of Osiris and Dionysus, it is probably in the opposite direction (Casadio 1996).

52 Hecataeus of Abdera is the great herald of this idea. *Cf.* Bernabé 2000 and 2002b for the analysis of the Orphic evidence in Diodorus.

in this direction during the archaic period, the evidence for the Hellenistic and Roman periods appears to point in the other direction as well: the Greek mysteries acquired deep roots in Hellenized Egypt and even themselves influenced the ancient Egyptian cults (Casadio 1996). In this process, Orphic elements appear to have played an important role. If the evidence from Asia Minor comes primarily from inscriptions, in Egypt it is papyri, preserved thanks to the aridity of the climate, that provide information on the presence of Orphism at all levels, from mystery cults and magic to fictional literature set in Egypt and philosophy inspired by Egyptian wisdom.

There are four papyri of enormous importance that testify to the celebration of Orphic rites in honor of Dionysus, as well as a series of magical papyri that include elements of Orphic coloration. It is well known that the cult of Dionysus took immediate root in Egypt following its incorporation into the Greek world. Dionysus's general popularity during the Hellenistic age and his identification with the figure of Alexander – where the myth of Dionysus's conquest of India originates – came together with his adoption by the Lagids as the ancestor to whom they traced the divine origin of their dynasty. The Ptolemies encouraged, for propagandistic purposes, all manifestations of Dionysian cult, furthering its identification with the cult of the sovereign, as can be seen in Ptolemy II Philadelphus's magnificent Dionysian procession (280–275 B.C.).[53] Among the forms of Bacchic cult that appeared in the procession, the mysteries were not lacking: among those who marched were the *telestai*, and Ptolemy IV Philopator played the kettledrum as a *telestes* and received the *teletai* of Neos Dionysus.[54] These linkages were probably intended to present the official mysteries as heirs of *teletai* the independent continuity of which they sought to limit. Such can be deduced from Ptolemy IV Philopator's decree, preserved in a papyrus datable to slightly before 215–214 BC,[55] that attempted to control the activities of "those who celebrate rites in honor of Dionysus in the countryside." They are to "be entered in the official register," "declare from whom they have received the sacred instruments (τὰ ἱερά) going back three generations, and hand over the sacred discourses (ἱερὸς λόγος), sealed, each one writing his name."

---

53 Fraser 1972, 202–206, Dunand 1986; Burkert 1993.
54 Plut. *Cleom.* 33.2; 34.2; 36.7 *Mor.* 60a; Clem. Alex. *Protr.* 4.48; Euphronius, *Priapeia* (176–177 Powell); Callixenus FGrH 627 *apud* Athen. 5.197c–203b describes with great detail this Dionysiac procession.
55 *BGU* VI 1211 (*OF* 44). Although most scholars continue to date this papyrus between 220 and 205 BC, Turner 1983 was able to narrow the date down to earlier than 215–214 BC.

What was the purpose of this decree? Four possible explanations have been offered: 1) To convoke a synod of priests of Dionysus in order to unify the doctrine of the Bacchic mysteries; 2) To establish a more or less official Dionysian mystery cult (this is a refinement of the previous explanation, with its excessively Christianizing overtones characteristic of the beginning of the century); 3) To monitor and restrict the activities of these itinerant priests, considered dangerous centrifugal forces by the centralized Ptolemaic state; 4) To compile a census of the priests in order to impose new fiscal measures on the cults. In general, a mixture of the second and third explanations – that is to say, the simultaneous control and promotion of the Dionysian mystery cult, channelled and encouraged by the state – has been the most widely accepted among scholars.[56] The ambiguity in the relationship between the classical polis and the religion of Dionysus, located in the heart of the city yet nonetheless containing dangerous antisocial tendencies that the official Dionysian cult tried to redirect, continued to exist in the Ptolemaic kingdom; the state sought to make use of the attractive force of Bacchic cult and myth in order to reinforce its own prestige, making the cult official, while at the same time trying to smooth away its more centrifugal tendencies. The radicalism of the Roman *Senatus consultum* of 186 BC would have been unthinkable in any Greek state, in which the story of the *Bacchae* was part of the collective identity. The Ptolemies could not associate themselves with Pentheus; they did not suppress the *teletai*, but rather tried to channel and support them within the official cult at the service of the state.[57]

---

56 The extensive bibliography on the decree is commented on by Lenger 1980 and 1990. The most convincing study is in my opinion that by Zuntz 1963. *Cf.* also the comments by Henrichs 2003, 227–231.

57 The Orphic genealogy of Dionysus, born from the incestuous union of Zeus and his daughter Persephone, was different from the traditional genealogy that made Dionysus the son of Zeus and Semele. Since the Ptolemies legitimized the public Dionysiac cult and the identification of the king with the god in their own descent from Dionysus according to the official genealogy, it is clear that the diffusion of the alternative Orphic genealogy mentioned in *hieroi logoi* was not convenient for the Ptolemies. In the *Rhapsodies* the Orphic genealogy of Dionysus is united with the traditional one, thus making Semele the second mother of Dionysus (*cf.* Bernabé 2002, 74 n. 20, and Rudhardt 2002). Perhaps that mythographic conciliation of the two versions, either by the composer of the *Rhapsodies* or by an earlier poet, aimed to integrate the Orphic genealogy of Dionysus into that which legitimized the Ptolemaic dynasty. The epithets of Dionysus in the *Orphic Hymns*, διφυής, τρίγονος (30.2) and διμάτωρ (50.1; 52.9), reflect this threefold mythographic, religious and political interest. The only evidence of the latter epithet applied to Dionysus in pre-Ptolemaic times is in the comic poet Alexis (fourth century BC:

If there has been a great deal of interest in the causes that led to the promulgation of this decree, there has been much less concern for the consequences that it might have had; as there are no references to it in later literature, it is not possible to know with any certainty to what extent it achieved its objectives. The official cult of Dionysus continued to enjoy enormous prominence during the Ptolemaic period and in the time of the Ptolemies' ephemeral epigone, Mark Antony. As far as *teletai* with Orphic elements are concerned, however, the direct evidence is limited to three papyri: the celebrated *Gurob Papyrus* from the third century BC and two others from the second to third centuries AD.

The *Gurob Papyrus* (*OF* 578) is a unique example of the content of a Dionysiac *telete* at the time of the edict. It has even been suggested that the papyrus itself, slightly preceding the edict (it is dated around 275 BC), may have belonged to Philopator's collection of *hieroi logoi*.[58] It contains invocations to various deities of Orphic milieu (Brimo, Ericepaeus, Curetes, and at the end, the formula honoring the principal god of the *telete*, εἷς Διόνυσος)[59] and ritual indications alluding to sacrifice and raw meat, along with toys belonging to Dionysus that unmistakably recall the myth of the god's dismemberment. The mixture of ritual elements and hexameter verses highlights the interrelationship of poetry and ritual. Clement of Alexandria's account of the Dionysiac mysteries sung by Orpheus has numerous parallels with the papyrus, confirming that the information in Clement's source came from an Orphic poem with content similar to that of *hieroi logoi* like the *Gurob Papyrus*.[60]

We will not find new evidence of Orphic rites in Egypt until precisely Clement's text (App. III), in the second century AD: he mentions the *symbola* and *synthemata* of the Dionysian *telete* and of the Eleusinian mysteries, of which Orpheus is the poet, as well as of other cults (Aphrodite, Cybele,

---

fr. 285 K-A). However, nothing else in this fragment links it to Orphic poems, and Dionysus is born twice in traditional mythology (from Semele and from Zeus' thigh), so it could be that the Orphic poet who combined Persephone and Semele as mothers of Dionysus in the Ptolemaic interest freighted the traditional epithet διμάτωρ with new meaning. On the political use of Alexandrian poetry, cf. Stephens 2003.

58 Wilamowitz 1931 II, 378; Burkert 1987, 70f. Hordern 2000 has reedited and commented on the papyrus.
59 The formula "One Dionysus" is typical of the kind of henotheism that considers the specific god to whom cult is being paid as the only important deity (Versnel 1990). The same invocation appears in the Orphic *Hymn to the Sun* (*OF* 543).
60 *Protr.* 2.17.2. In Herrero 2007a I study in detail the relationship between both texts.

Corybantes), with a clear source in an Orphic theogony (p. 147ff). The context is not explicitly Egyptian and, in addition, Clement's source may come long before the second century, almost contemporary with the *Gurob Papyrus*, which does not guarantee the survival of these rites four centuries later. It is worth asking, however, whether Clement would go to the effort of attacking something that he did not perceive to some extent as a living phenomenon in the Alexandria of his day. His denunciation raises the possibility that Bacchic *teletai* of Orphic tradition had an important role in imperial Egypt. This impression is confirmed by two other papyri from the second to third centuries AD that, despite their fragmentary state, refer unequivocally to the dismemberment of Dionysus.

Papyrus *PSI* 850 (*OF* 310 III) preserves portions of twenty lines containing unmistakable allusions to the myth of the Titans. The appearance of Orpheus's name (lines 2–3, 13) indicates that the text's author was discussing the myth on the basis of an Orphic poem, of which the poetic word γαίης (line 14) is probably a quotation.[61] The text may be simply a mythographic treatise. However, the insistent appearance of the same elements of the myth (fire, mirror, possibly raw meat)[62] that are present in the *Gurob Papyrus* as a justification of the ritual makes it probable that the author's intention was to interpret or transmit a rite linked to this episode.

P. Argent. 1313 (*OF* 593) also alludes to the myth of the Titans. The last two lines of the text ("come, blessed one, for the male and female initiates," 29–30) indicate an invocation to a male god (μάκαρ), of the type found in the *Orphic Hymns*. The surviving portions of the previous lines allude to a story – they do not narrate it, as the tale was already known – in which the myth of Dionysus and the Titans can be discerned. The clearest piece of evidence mentions the deception of the child with toys and uses a vocabulary identical to that in Clement's account;[63] "those who bring game" and "those who prepare [it] on the other side" (lines 14–15) are probably the same Titans who deceived the child. Other elements, such as the golden branch with its Vergilian connotations (χρυσανθές ἔρνος in line 29) or the mention of a virgin (παρθένωι in line 27), have led some to see an allusion to the abduction of

---

61 A possible conjecture, along these lines, could be ὑμ[νει for line 4.
62 If the conjecture ὤμοις ἁρπάζοντες is accepted for line 17. The editors also suggest Θ]ρακίων for line 16, but the μει]ρακίων suggested by Bernabé *ad loc* is more consistent with the context. The mirror is not only alluded to in κάτοπτρον (lines 3–4 and 6) but also probably in δίσκος (line 5).
63 Lines 11–12: διηπάτων νιν ˙]ν ἀνθεων ποικίλτ' ἀθύρματα; *Protr.* 2.17.2: ἀπατήσαντες παιδαριώδεσιν ἀθύρμασιν.

Core.⁶⁴ Leaving aside the Eleusinian myth, however, Core is the mother of the Orphic Dionysus, and reference to her would not be out of place. The god invoked is most likely Dionysus himself (εὐα]στὴν θεόν in line 28).⁶⁵ The papyrus testifies to a community probably similar to that of the *Orphic Hymns*, even though it maintains a more narrative tone. It is not clear what ritual actions may have corresponded to the recitation of this hymn, but the parallel with the *Orphic Hymns* suggests a primarily oral rite, one of invocation.

The papyrological evidence does not by itself demonstrate a reality specific to Egypt, since it is only there that the climate has preserved such documents. However, the coincidence between three papyri and the text of an author precisely from Alexandria (Clement), along with the absence of equally clear parallels in other authors, encourages the idea that the myth of the Titans took root in Egypt in a special way. Here there was clearly an essential continuity in the ritual dimension of the myth between the third century BC and the third century AD. This continuity does not seem to be due to the handing down of Bacchic rites within families, the *paradosis* that Philopator's decree described as existing for three previous generations, or in other words, since the beginnings of Greek domination in Egypt. From this period there are multiple literary testimonies – such as those of Diodorus or Plutarch – to Orphic traditions regarding Dionysus, but no document testifying to their ritual use during these six centuries. The absence of direct documentary evidence between the second century BC and the second century AD suggests that this *paradosis* disappeared as a result of Ptolemaic centralization. Philopator's edict probably achieved its objective of "stateizing" the Dionysian *teletai*, and although the transmission of these cults among individuals was not entirely destroyed by this edict, it was certainly weakened to a great extent. The decree will have had as its consequence the preeminence of a public cult of Dionysus and his Alexandrian equivalent, Serapis, generally a stranger to Orphic traditions.

At the same time, however, if it weakened the private *paradosis* of Orphic *teletai*, the edict may very well have consolidated the literary transmis-

---

64 Snell 1937, 108–109. However, he admits inconsistencies: ἐπιφέροντες is not a singular to refer to Hades, and the plural participles are not feminine, so they cannot refer to Core's companions. Kern 1938 III, 197, n.1, and Körte 1939, 96 defend the reference to the myth of the Titans. In *P. Gurob* Persephone, Brimo and Dionysus are combined in the *telete*. Cf. also Epiph. *Panar.* 51.22.10 (p. 372).

65 This conjecture was suggested by Kern 1938, who alternatively proposed κωμα]στὴν. Perhaps χρυσανθὲς ἔρνος, just after μάκαρ in line 29, also refers to Dionysus.

sion of Orphic myths and rituals; it would be strange, indeed, if the collection of *hieroi logoi* resulting from the decree had not aroused the curiosity of Alexandrian scholars, increasingly interested in strange and little-known variants of Greek myths and cults. It is not difficult to suppose that the Orphic theogonies composed during the late Hellenistic period, especially the *Rhapsodies*, might have obtained material, directly or indirectly, from this collection of *hieroi logoi*. What is certain is that the flourishing of the Dionysian *teletai* in Egypt during the third century BC, documented by the *Gurob Papyrus* and Philopator's decree, coincides with a rise of academic interest, especially in Alexandrian circles, in their mythic and religious content: the historians Hecataeus of Abdera (fourth century BC) and Dionysius of Miletus, called Scytobrachion (third century AD),[66] Hellenistic poets like Callimachus and Euphorion (Santamaría 2008), and Clement's source on the mysteries echo Orphic traditions with a precision and lack of ambiguity unknown before this time. Thus, if the decree appears to have driven the direct practice of Orphic *teletai* into obscurity, it did not weaken academic and literary interest in them, but rather, probably, even reinforced that interest by collecting written material.

This idea is supported by the fact that in the literary sphere, the centuries immediately following saw the unification of Orphic traditions in the theogonies of Hieronymus and Hellanicus and the *Rhapsodies*. In the academic sphere, the following centuries bear witness in a good number of authors – Diodorus, Strabo, Philodemus, Plutarch – to a quite extensive knowledge of Orphic mythology, even though the references to Orphic rites are always indirect, as if they were celebrated in a distant time or place. We may suppose, then, that Philopator's decree was a decisive catalyst for the transformation of Orphism into an intellectual tradition, a tradition in which reference to Egypt continued to be of great importance, given that the comparison between the cults of Dionysus and Osiris had been common since Herodotus. The dependence of one set of myths and rituals on the other (or the simple

---

66 Both authors are the main sources for the abundant information that Diodorus transmits on Orphic traditions (Bernabé 2000, 2002b). Hecataeus has Egyptian sources, mainly temple priests who are keen to demonstrate the dependence of Orphic rites on Egypt. There are no reliable proofs of the presence of Dionysius Scytobrachion in Alexandria except for an isolated reference in Suetonius (*Gramm. Rhet.* 7). However, Samothrace was under Ptolemaic power in his time, and some episodes of the Lybian Stories have clear Ptolemaic references (Rusten 1982, 90 Stephens 2003, 39–44). Perhaps Scytobrachion used Orphic tales as inspiration for his fantastic Lybian Stories, where Zeus fights against the Titans and enthrones the child Dionysus in a tale clearly similar to the Euhemeristic tale transmitted by Firmicus Maternus (*De Err.* 6).

identification of the two) was generally accepted. It must not have been difficult to revive the tradition of Orphic *teletai* at any time in Egypt for religious or even literary purposes, as is demonstrated by the two papyri from the second to third centuries AD that return to the myth of the Titans. Thus, Lollianos (around the second century AD) in his novel *Phoinikika* attributes to a group of bandits, who are in all probability the *boukoloi* who camped in Egypt's most inaccessible regions, the celebration of a ritual with clear Orphic resonances: they murder a child, dismember him, and eat his heart, after which the initiates swear to keep the secret. Where but in Egypt could a novelist situate this ritual fantasy?[67]

At the same time, nevertheless, documents of another type bear witness to some degree of direct transmission of Orphic elements in a different but connected sphere, that of magic. Mystery religion, by its individualist nature and emphasis on a personal relationship between man and deity, can easily slip into magic. In fact, it is difficult to define where the mysteries end and magic begins because, among other things, the distinction between the two springs from ancient and modern external perspectives (philosophers, apologists, scholars), rather than from the ancient evidence itself.[68] The permeability of these boundaries is seen in the presence of the deities of the Greek mysteries, alongside other figures of distinct origin, in the invocations preserved in Egyptian magical texts from the third and fourth centuries AD, which manifest no small number of Orphic elements. I will review the five most significant texts.

A clear example of continuity between the Orphic elements that we find in the mystery cults and magical spells are the oaths supposedly sworn by the initiates before the ritual, promising to keep secret what they are about to do, hear, and witness. The *Oaths* attributed to Orpheus have already been mentioned (pp. 37f); they are poems more literary than ritual in intent but very similar to the formulas conserved in papyri (collected in *OF* 623). It is difficult in these cases to differentiate between an oath ("I swear by you, god") and a spell or exorcism ("I conjure you, god"), as the formula with the verb ὁρκίζω + accusative is the same. On a more poetic level, two papyri from the third century A.D. contain an oath of silence with a cosmogonic elaboration of Gnostic tone that seems to manifest traces of the Orphic cos-

---

67 Dio Cassius 72.4 describes such bandits. Novelists like Achilles Tatius and Heliodorus also refer to them. *Cf.* Henrichs 1972 in his edition of and commentary on the papyrus of the *Phoinikiká*.
68 Kingsley 1995 and Bernabé 2003b have shown the links between the South Italian mysteries (in particular the gold tablets) and the Greek magical papyri from Egypt. On the question of magic and religion, cf. III nn. 2–3.

mogonies.⁶⁹ The fact that the text appears in two papyri that mutually complement one another makes it very probable that it was a semi-literary poem that circulated quite extensively for the purpose of use as a ritual hymn.

Various oaths also appear in a papyrus from the fourth century AD in which a lengthy cosmogony with Gnostic characteristics, apparently originating in Egyptian royal coronation rituals,⁷⁰ is accompanied by a number of magical spells in which ritual words are mixed with other incomprehensible ones (among them Dionysus and Baubo in lines 917, 924). Immediately following, one of these spells is introduced with the phrase "the theologian Orpheus handed down in his *parastichis*" (933).⁷¹ Shortly afterward (946), another spell is attributed to Erotylus "in the *Orphica*."⁷² Other illustrious personages to whom spells are attributed include Zoroaster, Moses, and Pyrrhus; the theologians judged most prestigious by the philosophers are also the supreme magi in spells. Whether or not the preceding cosmogony has traces of Orphic influence, the author of this magical compilation believed that he was bringing together texts of a similar nature, which demonstrates that in practice magic and cosmogony were not clearly differentiated. Burkert (1998) has pointed out that it is typical of the "logic of cosmogony," from Mesopotamian to Greek texts, that in order to act on a particular detail, such as a toothache, it is necessary to work back to first causes.

---

69 *PSI* X 1162 and 1290 (*OF* 621). Schütz 1939 and Martínez Nieto 2000 study the Orphic connexions of this poem, though it has many other elements of Egyptian, Gnostic or Jewish origin.

70 *P.Mag* XIII P-H, edited and commented on by Dieterich 1891 and Merkelbach-Totti 1990–1992 (whose title, *Abrasax*, expressly echoes that of Dieterich, *Abraxas*, both divine names formed from the eight letters). The Ogdoad is the fundamental cosmological entity. Let us remember that Theon of Smyrna justifies the Ogdoad with verses from the Orphic *Oaths* (Merkelbach-Totti 1990 I, 208). This would support Dieterich's idea that the Orphic cosmogonies are a direct precedent of this one, although it is difficult to make more precise connexions at such a late date.

71 Dieterich (1891, 165 n. 2) suggested linking this obscure title with some acrostic poems (*AP* 9, 524–525: two hymns to Dionysus similar in style to the *Orphic Hymns*, whose epithets are in alphabetical order). The alphabet has great importance in magic (cf. Dornseiff 1925), and also in this papyrus. Magic and refined literature are not so distant as scholarly labels would have them.

72 *P. Mag. ap. Suppl. Mag.* II 96, 24 (*OF* 833) ascribes to Erotylus new magic words, some of which seem linked to the cult of Demeter and Persephone (1.31: pomegranate; 1.44: Brimo). Other terms refering to androgyny seem derived from Orphic mythology (Phanes): 1.25, 1.30, 28. *P. Mag.* VII 479 (*OF* 832) begins with an invocation to Eros-Erotylus (cf. Martín 2006, 351–359).

A third papyrus calls the magical formula *aski kataski* a *logos orphikos*.[73] This testimony is of great interest, since what it attributes to Orpheus is the beginning of the famous *ephesia grammata*, powerful incantations very popular in late antiquity. Hesychius (*s. v.*) says that there were six words, although some charlatans added others. Clement of Alexandria (*Strom.* 5.8.45.2) reports that the Pythagorean Androcydes, author of a treatise *On Pythagorean Symbols*, allegorized the words in conformity with a cosmological interpretation according to which each magical word corresponded to an element, such as light, earth, or the year. What we would today consider a ridiculous abracadabra was the object of sophisticated scientific interpretations and debates over what was original and what was forged, exactly like the higher-level Orphic literature (theogonies, hymns). In these documents the frontiers among magic, religion, and science, or between higher and lower levels of Orphism, seem to dissolve, revealing themselves to us as a product more of modern desires than of ancient requirements.

The genre of the catabasis, too, seems to have a place among magical spells of this type. Bernabé (2003b) has demonstrated the ties between the *ephesia grammata* and the golden Orphic lamellae that describe the descent of the soul. A fourth magical papyrus includes a formula related to the *aski kataski* and follows it with a phrase containing a liturgical reminiscence of the mystery cult of the Idaean Dactyls, in which the descent to Hades played an important role.[74]

Finally, a lead lamella of similar context and date shows the same union among mysteries, catabasis, cosmology, and magical spells that is found in these papyri.[75] Various primordial deities of Orphic milieu, such as Erebus, Night, and Phaos (line 70), are cited, but the clear and highly-developed catabasis of the soul that can be deduced from most lamellae is deformed here into a spell that was probably incomprehensible even for its users. Four lines (64–69) will do for an illustration: "*Aski* when through the shadowy mountains, through the region of black radiances, from the garden of Persephone, at the hour of milking, the child brings by necessity the holy quadruped, companion of Demeter, the she-goat, to nurse at the fountain of inexhaustible milk, calling for torches for Hecate at the crossroads, the goddess with a terrible voice guides the stranger to the god."

---

73 *PMG* VII 450 = II 20 P-H (*OF* 830 I). Bernabé 2003b shows how the utterance *aski kataski* derives from ritual formulas.
74 *PMG* LXX, 12 = 202 P-H (*OF* 712). Cf. Betz 1980 and Bernabé 2003b, 12, who convincingly argues in favour of mantaining Δακτύλων in line 13 in spite of metrical irregularities.
75 *OF* 830 II = Jordan *ZPE* 72, 1988, 245.

This mixture of mystery-cult deities, spells originating in ancient ritual formulas, and Orphic cosmogonies or catabasis, with occasional mentions of Orpheus, is the context on the basis of which the apologists, especially the Alexandrians like Clement or Athanasius, will brand Orpheus a sorcerer (*goes*).[76] Fostering a rigid separation between religion and magic (and ascribing all things pagan to the latter), they will try to draw distinctions within what was a fluid reality, stretching from the most spiritual mystic cults to the simplest spells. The strategy of the Neoplatonic and Neopythagorean philosophers, on the other hand, was very different: they tried to give to all this world of mysteries and spells an allegorical sense that would satisfy the highest aspirations.

Thus, the Orphic *hieroi logoi* that were used in the mysteries of Dionysus and Core, in the style of the *Gurob Papyrus*, and that Ptolemy Philopator ordered to be collected, served as the foundation of magical spells and at the same time as an inspiration or exegetical instrument for other groups with more elevated interests that were most deeply rooted in Egypt: the cosmogonic speculations of the Gnostics, the apocrypha of the Jews, the allegories of Neopythagorean and Neoplatonic philosophers. Egyptian Christianity spread on this fluid ground and became intertwined with all these dimensions of Greek paganism. Remarkable evidence is provided by two large funerary cloths from around 450 AD, one of which depicts a Dionysiac scene similar to the paintings of the Villa dei Misteri in Pompeii, and the other one scenes from the life of Jesus and Mary. Both were found in the same Egyptian tomb, so they are yet another proof of the easy syncretism of Christianity and pagan religion in the actual life of many individuals. Moreover, they portray the religious atmosphere of the birthplace of the fifth-century poet Nonnus of Panopolis, who composed a Christian *Paraphrase of St. John's Gospel* and also an immense Dionysian epic with numerous elements of Orphic heritage.[77] As a final piece of evidence, let us recall that in direct competition with the Christian monks, there was in fifth-century Egypt a sort of pagan

---

76 This cluster of religion, magic, science and poetry, full of Orphic elements, is beautifully described by Merkelbach-Totti III 1992, 22: "Wir sind in dem merkwürdigen Zwischengebiet, an welchem Wissenschaft und Aberglaube, Theater, Religion und Mystik ihren Anteil haben; und nicht vergessen wollen wir den Anteil der Poesie, denn auf eben diese Lehre von Daimon und Tyche hat Goethe zurückgegriffen, als er das Gedicht "Urworte: Orphisch" schrieb. Die erste Stanze is uberschrieben "Daimon" und beginnt: Wie an dem Tag, der dich der Welt verliehen / die Sonne stand zum Grusse der Planeten / bist alsobald und fort und fort gediehen, / nach dem Gesetz, wonach du angetreten".

77 Cf. Willers 1992 on the Egyptian funerary cloths. On Nonnus' Orphism, cf. Hernández de la Fuente 2002.

ascetic hermit, Sarapion, whose only reading was the Orphic poems.[78] This should not be surprising, since Orphism seems to have achieved in imperial Egypt its greatest aura of prestige at all levels of pagan religiosity, from the most sublime to the most vulgar.

The Orphic presence in ROME presents some particular issues. It was studied in 1937 by André Boulanger, who held that, while the myth of Orpheus had great importance in Latin literature, Orphism only managed to acquire some degree of rootedness by way of Neopythagoreanism. Though we shall see that such an image is incomplete, it is indeed what the evidence from Roman classical literature transmits. In his dialogue *On the Nature of the Gods*, Cicero makes the Academician Cotta say (*ND* 1.107), "Aristotle says that Orpheus never existed, and it is common opinion that this Orphic poem is by one Cercops, a Pythagorean (*hoc Orphicum carmen Pythagorei ferunt cuiusdam fuisse Cercopis*); but Orpheus, that is, his image as you prefer to say, is frequently present in my spirit." Vergil, Ovid, Seneca, Statius and others frequently mention the myth of the poet and his search for Eurydice. Orpheus' image is also very frequent in Roman mosaics as a decorative motif.[79] But this omnipresence of Orpheus as mythical hero contrasts with the lack of references to his religious function. Not only does Cicero, for one, follow Aristotle in denying the existence of Orpheus, but his interest in the Orphic poems (obviously inauthentic for him) is also very scarce and indirect. The attribution to Cercops surely comes from a Hellenistic source.[80] The same bookishness is betrayed by his enumeration of the five Dionysus (*ND* 3.58), the first and fourth of whom have a clear Orphic link: "the first one is the son of Jupiter and Proserpine ... the fourth of Jupiter and Moon, to whom Orphic rites are believed to be dedicated (*sacra Orphica putantur confici*)." Cicero's translation of the probable error of his Greek source (Selene/Moon for Semele) reveals that he has little interest in and knowledge of the most famous myths of the Orphic theogonies – the same attitude maintained by republican and Augustan poets.

---

78 Suda, *s.v.* Σαραπίων (IV 324 Adler); cf. p. 102 on a similar Hermetic figure, Antoninus.
79 Verg. *B*.6.30, *G*.4.453ff, Ov. *Met*.10.11ff, Sen. *Med*.625ff, Stat. *Theb*.5.1.23ff. On Orpheus' presence in Roman decorative arts, cf. Jesnik 1997, Vieillefon 2003.
80 The Pythagorean Cercops appears as an author of *Orphica* in Clem. Alex. *Strom*.1.21.131, who cites Epigenes as his authority. Whether this Epigenes is a disciple of Socrates or a Hellenistic scholar (cf. pp. 207f), he must be Cicero's direct or indirect source. Aristotle is also the source of Cicero's allusion in the *Hortensius* (fr. 112 Grilli) to some *veteres illi sive vates sive in sacris initiisque tradendis divinae mentis interpretes*. Aristotle (fr. 60 Rose) spoke of οἱ τὰς τελετὰς λέγοντες.

Instead, Cicero's passage betrays a relatively broad knowledge of one Orphic poem, which must have been a *Descent into Hades*.[81] The presence of such a poem in Rome in the first century BC is by no means strange: it is very consistent with the eschatological interests of the revived neo-Pythagorean movement, which had no little influence over some Augustan poets, above all Vergil. Many Vergilian texts – notably the famous *Fourth Eclogue* – have been interpreted in an Orphic light, but there are no real proofs that it is not just a taste for the language of the mysteries that the Mantovan poet inherited from his Hellenistic predecessors.[82] On the other hand, his knowledge of Orphic eschatology seems well established. An Orphic catabasis has been postulated from ancient times as Vergil's source for *Aeneid* 6, and modern research has confirmed this impression. Precisely the only mention of Orpheus in the *Aeneid* links music and eschatology: after finding the *Threicius sacerdos* playing the lyre (6.645), Aeneas asks Musaeus, *optimus vates* (6.667) for instructions to find his way in Hades.[83] Varro's imitation of the Orphic poem *Lyra*, which described the ascent of the soul through the celestial spheres, represented as the chords of a cosmic lyre, points in the same direction.[84]

Apart from these traces of neo-Pythagorean Orphism in Vergil and Varro, there are only two isolated mentions of Orpheus' religious dimension: Ovid says that Midas, king of Lycia, received the *orgia* from Orpheus and Eumolpus (*Met.* 11.92), and Horace says in the *Ars Poetica* (391f), *siluestris homines sacer interpresque deorum / caedibus et uictu foedo deterruit Orpheus*. Both references have their origin, not in the presence of Orpheus as patron

---

81 Epigenes (cf. previous note) attributes to Cercops two poems, called κατάβασις εἰς Ἅιδου and ἱερὸς λόγος. Though West 1983a, 248 thinks that with the expression *hoc carmen Orphicum* Cicero refers to the *Rhapsodies*, the reference to a catabasis is much more probable. Several witnesses testify to the presence of an Orphic catabasis in Rome, while the absence of the theogonies is all but certain.

82 In his comment on *Eclogue* 4.10, Servius quotes *OF* 364, an obscure Orphic fragment about the Saturnian age (West 1983a, 107 n.73). Reinach 1900 pointed out the parallel between *B*.4.14–16 and the Petelia leaf: *divisque videbit / permixtos heroas et ipse videbitur illis / pacatumque reget ...*; *OF* 476.11: καὶ τότ' ἔπειτ' ἄ[λλοισι μεθ'] ἡρώεσσιν ἀνάξει[ς]. However, gods, heroes, and mortals are already associated in *Il.* 4.61. On Vergil's use of the language of the mysteries, cf. Luck 1975.

83 Servius quoted Orpheus frequently in his commentary on *Aeneid* 6. Among modern scholars, Orphic influences were proposed by Norden 1957[4] (through the Stoic Poseidonius); Carcopino 1927 (through neo-Pythagorean circles); Boyancé 1963b (through the middle-Platonic Academy). The Bologna Papyrus (*OF* 717, cf. nn. 18–20) has added new material. Cf. Bremmer 2009, with full bibliography.

84 Varr. *Fr.* 11 Büchner (*OF* 419). Cicero may also echo the ideas of the *Lyre* in *De Rep.* 6.18. This poem is also mentioned by Servius in his commentary on *Aeneid* 6 (*OF* 417 II). Cf. West 1983a, 30–32.

of mysteries in Augustan Rome, but in literary tradition: there are many parallels for Ovid's assertion, and Horace's lines echo Aristophanes' *Frogs*, as might be expected from a work dedicated to poetry.[85] In Republican and Augustan times, therefore, the myth of Orpheus and the neo-Pythagorean poems of eschatological content were known and used, but the theogonic poems and the role of the Thracian poet as founder of mysteries, which are so important in Greek contemporary authors, have almost no presence in Rome. The non-literary evidence is equally lacking any trace of Orphic influence in Roman cult in the first century AD.

Such absence is not what might be most obviously expected. It might have been thought that the geographic and cultural proximity between Rome and Magna Graecia, where Orphism flourished with such vigor during the classical and Hellenistic ages (lamellae, Apulian ceramics), would have made Rome heir to Orphic beliefs and practices in the following centuries. Nevertheless, cultural proximity, while opening the way for influences of every kind, may also lead to the rejection of certain elements, a rejection that in addition becomes a factor in the construction of one's own identity. Such was the fate of Orphism in Rome. It was not due to the fact that the language of the Orphic poems was Greek, since many other Greek authors were read with sympathy from the beginning of the Republic. It was their mythic and ritual content that must have motivated their rejection by the guardians of the essence of Romanness from the time of the earliest contacts with Greece, since the Dionysian cult was perceived as intrinsically Greek and, accordingly, not Roman. Dionysius of Halicarnassus referred to the typical themes of Orphic poetic and ritual tradition when he said:

> And no festival is observed among them (the Romans) as a day of mourning or by the wearing of black garments and the beating of breasts and the lamentations of women because of the disappearance of deities, such as the Greeks perform in commemorating the rape of Persephone and the sufferings of Dionysus and all the other things of like nature. And one will see among them, even though their manners are now corrupted, no ecstatic transports, no Corybantic frenzies, no begging under the colour of religion, no bacchanals or secret mysteries, no all-night vigils(θεοφορήσεις, κορυβαντιασμούς, ἀγυρμούς, βακχείας, τελετὰς ἀπορρήτους, διαπαννυχισμούς) of men and women together in the temples, nor any other phantasy of this kind; but alike in all their words and actions with respect to the gods a reverence is shown such as is seen among neither Greeks nor barbarians.

---

85 Cono *FGH* 26 F 1.1; Clem. Alex. *Protr.* 2.13.3; Iustin. *Hist. Phil. Epit.* 2.7.14. Aristoph. *Ran.*1030–1032: the relation with *Frogs* was suggested by Linforth 1941, 69f and has been generally accepted (cf. *OF* 626 II).

It is highly possible that Dionysius's source was a critique of Greek religion that took Orphism as its example, since his paragraph coincides in both content and form with some of the Christian critiques of paganism that we will see in chapters IV and V, which derive from similar sources.[86] The continuity of the critical tradition and its use to demarcate religious frontiers, whether Roman vs. Greek or Christian vs. pagan, is here clearly exemplified.

Dionysius' text, putting these words in the mouth of the legendary Romulus, probably reflects an ancient Roman resistance to the Dionysian cults. This tension exploded in the prohibition of the Bacchanalia in 186 BC. The scandal that produced the *Senatus consultum de bacchanalibus* marked a point of no return in the condemnation of such activities.[87] Our knowledge of these events still has many obscurities, but two things are reasonably clear: first, the popularity that these Bacchic cults, very probably derived from the South Italian mysticism of previous centuries, had enjoyed in Rome up to this point, and second, their prohibition and immediate classification as a dangerous anti-Roman activity, a label they would never entirely manage to shake off. The Senatorial decree limits their practice within very strict bounds. In the more rhetorical account by Livy, both his narration and the discourse of the consul Postumius repeatedly underline the foreign origin of these scandalous rites, which "from Greece through Etruria" come to contaminate Rome's purity, like a virus that enters in an alien body to corrupt it (*huius* [sc. *Graeculi*] *mali labes ex Etruria Romam velut contagione morbi penetravit*).[88] These foreign rites are forbidden because they threaten family and state order, to the point that they constitute a *coniuratio* against the Republic which must be repressed as a political conspiracy. The political basis of the prohibition, to assert the

---

86 *Ant. Rom.* 2.19.1–2. Apart from the coincidences in the critique of Greek religion, we will find in Christian texts the repetition of specific words: ἐκτέμνω (Orig. *CC* 4.48), ἀφανισμός (Clem. Alex. *Strom.* 6.2.26.1), τεράτευμα (Greg. Naz. *Or.* 4.115). Cf. Arn. *Adv. Nat.* 5.24: "these rites do not belong to our Republic".

87 Cf. Pailler 1988; Beard, North and Price 1998, esp. 73–98 and 211–244; Takács 2000; Caerols 2006.

88 Apart from Livy's mentions of Greece and Etruria (39.8, 39.9), Postumius insists on the external origin of the evil rites in 39.15 (*pravis et externis religionibus*) and 39.16 (*sacra externa fieri vetarent ... omnem disciplinam sacrificandi praeterquam more Romano abolerent ... non patrio sed externo ritu sacrificaretur*). Also in the precedent-setting case in 25.1 6 (during the second Punic war, in 213 BC), Livy insists on the foreign origin of the rites introduced by *sacrificuli et vates* (*tanta religio, et ea magna ex parte externa, ciuitatem incessit ... nec sacrificantium nec precantium deos patrio more ... ex alieno errore ... externo ritu sacrificaret*). The *Senatus Consultum* does not mention this fact, for it does not express the grounds of the decree – and the preserved copy (*CIL* I² 581) is addressed to a federate city, where foreignness would have a different meaning than in Rome.

power of the Senate, does not contradict the religious motivations. Instead, one supports the other: the rites are foreign, they violate law and morals, they create alternative groups alien to the traditional familial structures, and for all these reasons, they are dangerous for the Republic and must be prosecuted. Romanness is not a purely ethnic or linguistic notion, but also ideological: a Roman is a loyal citizen who obeys laws and practices state cults. For doing the opposite, the followers of Bacchic cult are compared to "another people" (*alterum populum*), from whom Rome must be freed.[89] To separate the political and the religious in the *affaire* of the Bacchanalia would introduce a fictitious distinction in a world where religious deviation is not condemned per se, but for its eventual political consequences. For similar reasons, the frequent Roman acceptance of foreign cults (among them, the weak Bacchic cults that the decree allows to subsist under strict conditions) was always carried out under rigid political and religious control.[90]

It is clear that Livy's narration of these events, which is full of historiographic *topoi*, need not be a faithful mirror of what actually happened.[91] The cult of Bacchus could have taken root in Italy long before, and the Villa of the Mysteries in Pompeii proves that it did not simply disappear after the decree.[92] Its foreign character may be more a rhetorical invention of those who instigated the persecution, or of the authors who recorded it, than a reflection of a historical reality. The Greeks too believed that the "foreign" cult of Dionysus came from elsewhere (Asia Minor, Thrace, or Egypt) and feared that it would dissolve institutional boundaries. The difference resides in the fact that the Greeks integrated the cult of Dionysus as the quintessence of Hellenism,[93] and Rome, by contrast, preferred to define herself by excluding the same cult, leaving it just on the other side of the religious *limes*, as

---

89 Cf. Liv.39.13, 39.16 and the precedent-setting case in 25.1.12 (*eis religionibus populum liberaret*).
90 Beard, North and Price 1998, esp. 73–98 and 211–244;
91 Caerols 2006 analyses the continuity of narrative elements in Livy's account of religious prohibitions in 428 BC (4.30.7–11), 213 BC (25.1.6–12), 186 BC (39.8), 181 BC (40.29).
92 A great Dionysiac fresco painted in 60–50 BC is preserved in this villa. Its religious meaning is hard to pin down, but in any case the scenes seem to have a deeper meaning than mere decoration. Cf. Beard, North and Price 1998, 161–163.
93 Hartog (1984, 78ff, 109ff) makes the episode of King Scylas in Hdt. 4.76–80 the paradigm for the idea that comprehension of the Dionysiac is the boundary between Greeks and Scythians. The battle for self-definition is always fought on the margins of community life, in the liminal cases. As Otto (1933) supposed and the Mycenaean leaves confirmed, Dionysus' late arrival from a foreign land to the Greek pantheon is not a historical fact, but a myth that express the Dionysiac experience of otherness.

Parthians and Germanic peoples were on the other side of the geographic one. There are multiple testimonies in connection with the anti-Dionysian mentality of the Roman conscience, a mentality compatible with the *de facto* survival of the cult of Bacchus, and many such testimonies expressly recall the *Senatus consultum de bacchanalibus*: the association made between the enemies of Rome, or those whom imperial propaganda sought to present as such, and Bacchic imagery (e. g. Antonius, or the bacchant-like queen Amata in the *Aeneid*) provides more than sufficient evidence of this.[94] A collection of topics about the "other" is formed, which will reappear again some centuries later in a new religious conflict, both in apologetic literature and in imperial legislation: Romans will also accuse Christians of terrible crimes like infanticide and cannibalism and of conspiring against the state, and Christians will also make similar charges against pagan, Jewish and "heretic" cults. These traditions last through the Middle Ages to our own time.[95]

The real presence of Orphic elements in the Dionysian environment from which the prohibited cults arose may have been greater or lesser,[96] but from the perspective of the anti-Bacchic version that would triumph for posterity, Orphism's typical traits fell under lasting suspicion. It was not in vain that Livy's text recounting the events characterized their inciter with the typical marks of the itinerant Orphic priest and stressed his foreign origin: *Graecus ignobilis, sacrificulus et vates, occultorum et nocturnorum antistes sacrorum*.[97] Given that this was above all a matter of propaganda and rhetoric,

---

94 This anti-Bacchic tendency was doubtlessly reinforced by the triumph of Octavian, the self-proclaimed champion of Romanity against the "Orientalizer" Anthony, who identified himself with Dionysus *more Ptolemaico* (Plut. *Vit.Ant.*24.4, 33.6–34.1, 50.6, 60.5, 75). Cf. the portrait of Amata, a transposition of the furious maenad, in Virg. *Aen.*7.385–405, 580. Other references in Pailler 1988, 749–796. Latin apologists like Firmicus Maternus (*De Err.* 6.9) and Arnobius (*Adv. Nat.* 5.19) still refer to the Bacchanalian *affaire* with praise for Postumius as a new Pentheus (Opelt 1968).
95 Cf. Henrichs 1970, and Roig Lanzillotta 2008 for apologetic *topoi*, Fögen 1994 for the imperial legislation.
96 Pailler 1988 sees many Orphic elements in the Dionysiac cult previous to the decree. This is not impossible, given the geographical proximity of the leaves (though they are two centuries earlier). But there is not enough information to be certain of Orphic presence, and in some cases it is improbable, as when he states without any proof (p. 679ff) that the rumor of Romulus' dismembering (Liv. 1.16.4) comes directly from the myth of Dionysus and the Titans: tales of dismemberment of a child are very frequent in the ancient world, as a result of the projection of sacrificial ritual onto supposed human victims (Burkert 1983, 89–212).
97 Liv. 39.8.3ff; cf. 25.1.8: *sacrificuli et vates;* 4.30.7 (*novos ritos sacrificandi vaticinando*). *Cf.* Caerols 2006 on this topic, and Bernabé 2002d on this passage and Strab. 7. fr. 18 as prototypical portraits of the *orpheotelestes*.

it is evident that the stigma of anti-Romanism had a greater impact on the verbal elaboration of Dionysian matters than on the god's cult itself, which continued to exist within the limits marked out by the state. Orphism's fate, therefore, was sealed, since Orphism consisted precisely in speculation drawn from the mystery cults: in *legomena* more than in *dromena*. Roman anti-Dionysian sentiment was more a question of *verba* than of *facta*, but this was also what Orphism was, at least since the Hellenistic age. For this reason, then, we do not find in Rome the patronage of Orpheus or other Orphic elements in cults that did absorb such elements in Greece, nor do we find any reflection of Orphic theogonies in literature.

It is even logical that if the cults of Greece, beginning with Eleusis, took up the Orphic tradition as a sign of their own identity within the Empire, this tradition would be perceived in Rome as something specifically Greek, alien to Romanness, and depending on the rhetorical or political needs of the hour, potentially dangerous for the latter. Thus, the only piece of evidence that speaks expressly about the celebration of *Orphica* in Rome is a text of Plutarch in his *Life of Caesar* that stresses these rites' foreign character. In the temple of the goddess called *Bona Dea* by the Romans, the mother of Midas by the Phrygians, and the unspeakable mother of Dionysus (Persephone) by the Greeks, it is said that "the women perform many rites corresponding to the *Orphica* in the ritual." The series of assimilations of the cult of the *Bona Dea*, the foreign cult *par excellence*, to cults from abroad culminates precisely with this phrase, because the *Orphica* were perceived as essentially alien to the Roman world.[98]

Thus, the Bacchic, theogonic, or Eleusinian dimensions of Orphism were barred from integration into Roman tradition. There is, however, one thread that survives in some Roman evidence, as Boulanger saw: neo-Pythagorean *Orphica*. Pythagoreanism was not accepted in Rome without difficulties either, since the South Italian heritage that continued to exist in Rome (attributed to its affinity with the Pythagoreanism of Numa, the legendary king) barely escaped suffering the same repression as the Bacchic rites. In 181 B.C. some Pythagorean books supposedly found in Numa's tomb were denounced as dangerous and publicly burned in a clear gesture of opposition to the Pythagorizing circles of the time: again, the kind of textual religion so closely associated with Orphism was banned from the

---

98 Plu. *Vit.Caes.* 9.4 (*OF* 584). Plutarch's sources on Roman history are Roman (Pelling 1988), so his evidence allows us, with the necessary caution, to observe the Roman vision of Orphism. Also, Strabo seems to call *Orphica* precisely those Greek rites that are similar to the foreign ones, like those of Bendis and Cotys in Thrace and Phrygia (Str.10. 3.16 [*OF* 528], 10.3.18 [*OF* 577V]).

city.⁹⁹ No doubt the elements of continuity between this Pythagoreanism and the Bacchic cult prohibited only five years before – a continuity similar to that which we find in the world of the gold tablets – did not escape the inquisitorial eyes of those who wished to free Rome from these tendencies toward imitation of the foreign. Nevertheless, Pythagoreanism managed to save itself from being stigmatized as essentially dangerous, and a century later Nigidius Figulus would form his neo-Pythagorean circle, which would have great influence on the Roman poets and intellectuals of the first century BC. There must probably have been some continuity with ancient South Italian Pythagoreanism and its Orphic elements, although the degree of this continuity is difficult to verify. In any case, Orphism did not cease to be the patrimony of a select minority, a fact that explains the complete absence of Orphic evidence from the western part of the empire (Gaul, Hispania), colonized by Romans, in contrast to its constant presence in the eastern part.

Two centuries later, however, the panorama changes quite radically. The influence of the Orphic poetic and ritual tradition becomes evident in several pieces of evidence from a wide range of cults. A funerary inscription dated in the second century AD from a Sabine village near Tivoli has clear verbal Orphic imagery that perhaps was also manifested in funerary ritual. It is an epitaph of a child of Latin name, Elianus: ¹⁰⁰

> Your father dedicated this tomb (σῆμα) to Elianus, good and prudent / burying the mortal corpse (σῶμα), but the immortal heart ascended to the abode of the blessed, for the soul is eternal, / gives life and descends from a divine origin. Retain, therefore, your tears, father; mother, retain the brothers. / The body is the tunic of the soul (σῶμα χιτὼν ψυχή). Honour the god in me.

The epitaph presents some elements of clear Orphic pedigree, not so much on the ideological level – body /soul dualism was a widespread notion beginning centuries earlier – as in the images that transmit such ideas: the purposeful opposition *soma/sema* (the latter is a likely conjecture); the reunion with the blessed; the heart as the core of life; and above all, the body as tunic of the soul. None of these expressions alone would be sufficient as a reference to the Orphic tradition. But all of them together in a few lines are. That the inscription addresses the family may suggest that there was a group sharing those beliefs, which would be also among the blessed. The only important difference from the gold leaves of Hellenistic times is that in

---

99 Liv. 40.29. Plut. *Vit. Num.* 22. On the connections of this matter with the *Bacchanalia*, cf. Pailler 1988, 623ff, and Caerols 2006.
100 *IG* XIV 2241 (*OF* 459). Cf. Casadio 1990b, 201s.

these the soul goes down into Hades, while this inscription expressly says that the soul ascends after death. This ascent, however, is consistent with the Pythagorean theory of the ascending soul, which was also expressed in the Orphic poem *Lyra*.[101]

All these coincidences, however, could seem purely casual, if only a few miles away there had not appeared inside a Roman tomb of the third century AD a gold tablet with the following text:[102]

> She comes pure from among the pure, queen of those below the earth,
> Eucles and Eubouleus, child of Zeus.
> Accept, then, this gift of Mnemosyne, celebrated by men.
> Come, Caecilia Secundina, having become a goddess according to the law.

This leaf clearly pertains to the same genre as the Orphic lamellae of Hellenistic date from Southern Italy: the first two lines are almost identical to the tablets from Thurii (*OF* 488–190.1–2), where the deceased also becomes divine, and Memory is mentioned as in the lamella from Hipponion. There are, however, important differences. The main one is that this leaf declares the name of the deceased in the third person, while in the earlier ones the identity was more general ("son of the earth and starry Heaven"), and the soul introduced herself in the first person.

These differences, plus the six-century void between the ancient lamellae and the Roman one, have suggested a magical use, like that of an amulet, of the ancient ritual formulas.[103] The frontier between magic and religion is in cases like these even more unsteady than usual. The parallels with the nearby inscription for Elianus, which nobody would call magical, are clear, both in content – the soul is deified – and in form – the alternation in both texts between the third and the second person creates a dialogue with the deceased.[104] The formulaic variations, therefore, can be better explained by

---

101 The most direct precedent of the expression *soma-chiton* is Empedocles (31 B 126 D-K). Cf. Gigante 1973 and Beatrice 1995 on the tradition of that expression.
102 *OF* 491, edited for the first time in 1903. Boulanger, as a pioneer of the "Orpheosceptic" fashion, did not consider it Orphic.
103 Zuntz 1971, 334; Kotansky 1994, 115. A fact that seems to support this interpretation is that the leaf from Petelia was reused in a collar of Imperial date (Olmos in Bernabé/Jiménez 2008, 324f.) This leaf, however, is the strongest parallel to Vergil's *Eclogue* 4 (cf. n. 82), would be an argument against a simple magical transmission of the leaves.
104 If we suppose that the introduction of the soul in the third person comes from the catabasis of the soul reconstructed by Riedweg 2002, the sentence should be uttered by the guardians who inform Persephone of the arrival of the deceased (a moment alluded to in the Hipponion leaf, *OF* 474.13).

a gradual evolution of the lamella tradition than by a simple magical reuse centuries later: if the formulas of this lamella had been recited mechanically without being understood, what need would the user have had to modify them? Initiates' proper names already appear in the very brief, golden lamellae of later Hellenistic date, accompanied by the epithet μύστης.[105] Identifying Eubouleus as the son of Zeus confirms that the reference is to Dionysus. Two other major modifications, "celebrated by men" and "in accordance with the law," have parallels in the *Orphic Hymns*, composed during the same period on the basis of the earlier poetic tradition.[106]

There is still another Roman piece of evidence linked to the gold leaves. In the Christian hypogeum of Viale Manzoni, dated around 250 AD, which is mostly painted with Biblical scenes, there is one chamber decorated with clearly pagan themes: a vanishing fresco painting which seems to depict a scene including Mnemosyne, two fountains and a white cypress. A Latin inscription written by a Remius Celerinus seems to express a hope that a defunct (Aurelius Epaphroditus) reaches a *refrigerium* in Afterlife. The scene with Circe below and some black figures seem to indicate some sort of "Gnostic" exegesis of Greek mythology.[107] Although the whole ensemble is difficult to interpret, the chronological and temporal proximity to the Roman gold leaf makes it very probable that the Orphic-Pythagorean tradition had also made its way into Christian-Gnostic milieus.

These three pieces of evidence seem to testify to some underground continuity of religious beliefs and practices from Hellenistic times, probably through the neo-Pythagorean channel. Elianus and Caecilia Secundina are Latin names, and the inscription in the hypogeum for Epaphroditus is written in Latin by one Remius Celerinus. Other testimonies, however, leave little doubt that the resurgence of Orphic images is due to foreign influence. A second-century inscription found in Torre Nova documents a Greek Dionysian thiasos whose members bear titles with clear reference to traditional Bacchic mysteries: δαιχοῦχος, βουκόλος, λικνοφόροι, πυρφόροι,

---

105 These shorter tablets are included in the commented edition of the gold leaves by Graf/Johnston 2007.
106 The expression ἀοίδιμον ἀνθρώποισιν of line 3 finds a parallel in *OH* 72.5, dedicated to Tyche, and νόμωι in line 4 introduces an abstract concept similar to both Tyche and Mnemosyne that, though absent from the other leaves, is the addressee of the *Orphic Hymn* 64 to *Nomos*: it could perhaps be edited with an initial capital letter, as the personal name of a deity linked to a philosophical religion of Pythagorean colour.
107 Chicoteau 1997 and 1999, whose very plausible reconstruction of the inscription is: *REmMEVS CELERINUs KaI IUNIS REFRIGERUM In hEROVM HONOReM Aurel EPAFROditi*. On the *refrigerium*, cf. Olmos in Bernabé/Jiménez 2008, 319–322.

φαλλοφόροι ἱεροὶ βάκχοι, βάκχαι, ἀρχιβάσσαροι, ἀρχιβασσάραι, σειγηταί.[108] The epithets with the suffix -φόρος probably imply that some ritual activity took place. It is a family thiasos including senators, liberti and slaves, sponsored by some aristocratic families who want to continue (or to reinvent) the cult of their ancestors in Lesbos. Whatever the truth of that continuity, the leader Macrinus has the role of the refounder. The usefulness of the Orphic-like elements (e. g. *hieroi bacchoi*) to recover a ritual, the prestige of which lies in being ancient, is beyond doubt.

More important, however, are two pieces of evidence for syncretism between Mithras and the most unmistakable Orphic primordial deity, Phanes Protogonos, the "First-Born" from the cosmic egg. Here we have a clear example of the influence of literary tradition on cultic practice: unlike Mithras, Phanes did not previously have statues or altars or temples, existing instead in the verses of the *Rhapsodies* and, at most, as the addressee of an occasional hymn. Now, thanks to his syncretistic identification with the solar deity of eastern origin, he suddenly acquired the status of a deity presiding over a cult in some Mithraic contexts. So testify a second-century-AD relief preserved in Modena and possibly of Roman provenance, in which a winged youth appears to unite the symbols of both deities (plate 4 p. 126), and a Roman inscription from the third century AD dedicated to "Zeus Helios Mithras Phanes."[109] The eastern origin of both deities, Phanes and Mithra, characterized by their luminosity, must have influenced perception of them as equivalent, even identical; late antiquity thus saw the reunion in Graeco-Oriental syncretism of elements that some time before had originated in the same milieu and then followed different paths.[110]

A similar kind of syncretism of Orphic and Christian images is testified in Rome by some iconographic evidence: apart from the aforementioned frescoes in the hypogeum of Viale Manzoni, a famous gem presents a crucified Orpheus, and the Thracian singer appears in Christian catacombs and sarcophagi (plates 1 and 3, p. 126). This Orphic/Christian evidence will be

---

108 *OF* 585. The thiasos tries to claim a Lesbian origin for its family cult. Cf. Jaccottet 2003, 30–53. The thiasos of the *Orphic Hymns* suggests itself as a clear model.
109 Vermaseren, *Corp. Inscr. Mon. Rel. Mithr.* 695 and 475 (*OF* 678). Iul. *Or.* 11.136 uses an expression of the same syncretistic/henotheistic tone (cf. Versnel 1990): "One is Zeus, one is Hades, one is Helios, one is Serapis". On the Orphic/Mithraic evidence, cf. West 1983a, 253f and Guthrie 1952, 254f, where there is mention of the possible link with a relief in Borcovicum (now Housesteads, in Northumberland, England) where Mithra is born from an egg. Cf. also n. 129 on Julian.
110 On these cases of Orphic/Mithraic syncretism, cf. Clauss 2001, 70–72, 165–167; and Mastrocinque 2009, 46–50.

discussed in the next chapter, but in any case it testifies that also in Christian circles in Rome the Orphic religious tradition had a certain prestige.

There are, therefore, unmistakable traces of a renewed Orphic presence in the second and third centuries AD. We shall see in the following section that some Latin authors like Apuleius or Macrobius make some general statements about Orphic ritual. However, at the end of Antiquity, while the Greek defenders of a dying paganism would make Orphism their banner, the Roman resistance (Praetextatus, Siculus) would not even mention it. In fact, all the Orphic material that has appeared in Rome always presents a clear "foreign" tone, occurring in inscriptions in Greek and associated with the Pythagorean tradition or with Greek or Eastern deities. It is probable that precisely this stigma of foreignness that anything Orphic had in Rome, while preventing its extension in traditional religion, offered to some people the attractive aroma of the exotic, parfumed with the ancient wisdom of Greece, just as today a certain Oriental tone attracts those who find the customs of Western religion too familiar and incapable of infusing any fervor.[111]

To sum up: though there are traces of Greek Orphism in Rome, there was never a Roman Orphism. There was no place for it in ancient Rome's religious and political identity as a city. But as capital of a great empire, Rome also became a huge ideological market where every kind of religious merchandise could be imported, in the certainty that in the Urbs there would be an abundance of customers. And as such, it became the seat of new cults, in some of which Orphic influence can be seen, consonant with its recuperation in the Eastern Empire from the beginning of the second century AD.

2.2. General references

It would have been difficult during the imperial age to find a moderately cultivated person who had never heard of the Orphic rites, and not only because of the presence of Orphism in isolated rites like those examined so far. Above all, the *loci classici* of modern studies of Orphism – contained in passages of Herodotus, Plato, or Euripides – were also known and repeated in antiquity. At the same time, the uninterrupted transmission of the poetic tradition, especially in its theogonic aspect, in a typical process of copying

---

111 Cf. Beard/North/Price *et al.* 1998, 161–166 on Catullus' poem 63, dedicated to the castration of Attis: Catullus plays with the outrage to Romanness this cult entails. The authors argue that the Dionysiac frescoes of the Villa dei Misteri may come from a similar taste for the exotic.

and expansion of which the ancients themselves were conscious, made it easy to imagine a similar process of transmission for rites and *teletai*. As a result, in contrast to the scarcity of affirmations like those of Pausanias or Lucian, already cited, that an Orphic rite was celebrated in a particular place or at a specific time, there are multiple general allusions to such rites in literature. Some are of a general character, a product of the transformation of the terminology associated with the mystery cults into a habitual category of language; Christoph Riedweg demonstrated in his 1987 monograph that beginning with Plato the terminology of the mysteries served as a metaphor to express the process of acquiring philosophical knowledge. The novel also fully exploited the narrative possibilities offered by these mysterious rites, as metaphor and as episode.[112] General knowledge, real or imagined, about the functioning of the mysteries was extended throughout the generality of the empire's population. Here, however, I will analyze only those testimonies that mention the actual celebration of rites.

In the first century BC Diodorus acted as a catalyst for the earlier tradition about the Orphic rites and gave it new force, as Bernabé has shown in two studies of his Orphic references (2000 and 2002b). The Sicilian historian collected various traditions related to Orpheus and his rites, many of them derived from earlier authors, especially Hecataeus and Dionysius Scytobrachion. The very facts that Diodorus collected this information, which he considered to be of interest to his contemporaries, and that he in turn would be cited profusely by Eusebius four centuries later reveal the way in which the tradition of Orphic rites could be passed down and expanded through erudite channels, without anyone throughout the eight centuries between Hecataeus and Eusebius needing to have seen a single rite in order to mention them. Diodorus usually refers to the foundation of rites by Orpheus, "the greatest of the Greeks in accounts of the gods (*theologiai*) and *teletai*" (4.25.3; 1.23.6). He tells several versions of Orpheus's story, according to which he was supposed to have acquired his knowledge in Egypt, in Samothrace, in Crete, or in Thrace.[113] These bits of information appear to reflect different attempts to lend prestige to local cults by making them the origin of the rest, for which Orpheus as the founder of *teletai* was a perfect intermediary. Those who were taught Orpheus's rites, wherever he may have learned them, are always the Greeks in general: "The Greeks took what was most admirable of theirs

---

112 Henrichs 1972 for the specific case of Lollianos' *Phoinikiká*, in relation to the myth of the Titans; Merkelbach 1988 for the mystic patterns of the Greek novel (opposed by Stephens-Winkler 1995).
113 D. S. 4.43.1, 5.49.6, 5.64.4 (Samothrace), 5.75.4, 5.77.3 (Crete). Cf. Linforth 1941, 27, 204–5.

from Egypt; for example, Orpheus took the majority of his mystical *teletai*" (1.96.3); "He was a disciple of the Idaean Dactyls and first brought to the Greeks the *teletai* and the mysteries" (5.64.4). The one time that Diodorus localizes in a particular place these *teletai* handed down by Orpheus "to all men," he turns out to be talking about the rites of Eleusis (5.77.3). Otherwise, he repeatedly mentions Dionysian rites as the work of Orpheus, but without specifying where and when they are celebrated; as far as their content is concerned, the myth of the Titans is their characteristic hallmark (5.75.4). Such is the ritual panorama that can be deduced from Diodorus's texts at the end of the Hellenistic age: the name of Orpheus is put forward and applied as a guarantee of the prestige and antiquity of local rituals: his poems are known, with special emphasis on the theogony recounting Dionysus's death, said to underlie the celebration of Dionysian rites, the time and place of which, however, are never specified; and when it is necessary to resort to mentioning concrete ritual actions, Eleusis is all that we find.

The only geographic localizations offered by Diodorus are distant lands, full of religious prestige and the sites of legendary tales: Egypt, Thrace, Crete. In this he coincides with Strabo, some decades later, who says that the *Orphica* originated in the rites of Bendis in Phrygia.[114] The foreign origin of the Orphic rites is a possible explanation of their exceptional position in the panorama of Greek religion, but it seems that this unusual status should rather be ascribed to the experience of "otherness" that the cult of Dionysus could produce in his followers. Dionysus was for a long time considered a recent arrival in the Greek pantheon – as if the *Bacchae* had some basis in historical fact – until the god's presence in the Mycenaean tablets confirmed W. F. Otto's brilliant intuition in his *Dionysos* of 1933: from antiquity Dionysus's cult was at the heart of Greek religion, even though he always manifested himself as the god who came from (and who led toward) regions beyond the limits of the Greek world. Something similar may apply to the mysteries. In addition, however, this supposed foreign, non-local origin of the Orphic rites complements their Panhellenic vocation, destined for all the Greeks, and therefore not instantiated in any local rite or, at most, in the most universal of them all, Eleusis.

Two centuries after Diodorus and Strabo, and much more original and critical in his treatment of sources, Plutarch also makes frequent mention of Orphic rites (Bernabé 1996). Not all Plutarch's references come from literary sources, in contrast to Diodorus's case; rather, a celebrated passage

---

114 Strab. 10.3.11 (*OF* 528); cf. 10 3.16 (*OF* 570) on the rituals of the Cretan Zeus, similar to those of Dionysus.

demonstrates that he knew the mysteries of Dionysus from direct experience: "And what you have heard from others, who seek to persuade many, saying that for the one who has died there does not exist any evil or pain anywhere – I know that you are prevented from believing it by the teaching of our fathers and the mystical tokens of the celebrations in honor of Dionysus (ὁ πάτριος λόγος καὶ τὰ μυστικὰ σύμβολα τῶν περὶ τὸν Διόνυσον ὀργιασμῶν), which we know from having both participated in them. Well, then, consider that the soul, being immortal, undergoes the same things as birds in captivity."[115] The eschatological preoccupation, the *symbola* that the initiates preserve as mementos of their experience, the theme of the immortal soul as prisoner of the body, even the image of the bird leaving its cage, fit perfectly with the tradition of the Orphic rites and leave no doubt about their real celebration.

Nevertheless, Plutarch does not classify these traditional Bacchic rites as Orphic. He denies this label even to as Orphic an element as the myth of the Titans, attributing it to the milieu of Empedocles or of the "wise ancients" (*De esu carn.* 1.7, 996b), and locating its celebration in some mysterious *Nyktelia*, a name unrecorded to this point, the very etymology of which, drawn from "night," suggests mystery and darkness (*Is. et Osir.* 75, 364f). On the other hand, he does designate as Orphic the exotic, distant, or foreign Dionysian rites, like those celebrated in Macedonia by Olympias, the mother of Alexander (*Alex.* 2.7), or those in honor of the Bona Dea in Rome (*Caes.* 9.4), as if being Orphic gave them an added charge of mystery and exoticism. Otherwise, the remainder of his references to Orphic rites come from the same erudite tradition as Diodorus and on occasion directly from Plato. Likewise, his mention of the *orpheotelestes* before Leotychides, the Spartan king (*Apophth. Lacon.* 224d), is in the same burlesque tradition as those of Theophrastus and Philodemus, reflecting a stock comic personage more than actual acquaintance (*OF* 653–655). Such diverse allusions in a single author raise questions about the real practice of the rites and the literary tradition concerned with them, as well as what the Orphic label added to them. I will address these questions in the next section.

In order to complete the picture, let us turn our attention to another personage active throughout the entire empire during the second century AD, Apuleius of Madaura. Defending himself against the accusation of magic, he says, "Could anyone who has any idea of religion still find it strange that a

---

115 *Consolatio ad Uxorem* 10 (*OF* 595). Bernabé 2007b links this passage with the bird mentioned in the first columns of the Derveni Papyrus, which in his reading would be liberated from a cage.

man initiated in so many divine mysteries should keep at home some tokens of recognition of the cults (*sacrorum crepundia*) and should wrap them in linen cloth, the purest veil for sacred objects? For wool, the excrescence of an inert body extracted from a sheep, is already a profane garment in the prescriptions of Orpheus and Pythagoras."[116] It seems evident that he had in mind a famous passage of Herodotus on the same subject, and that he did not read the *hieros logos* to which Herodotus refers, but rather read Herodotus himself.[117] At the same time, however, Apuleius connects Herodotus's text to the habitual practice among initiates of taking home tokens of the mysteries in order to remember them. The literary tradition about the rites is joined to their practice most efficaciously.

Beginning in the fourth century, allusions to Orphic rites in Greek and Latin authors increase spectacularly. Those of Servius and Macrobius have received the most attention, since they appear to be the most detailed. Vergil's commentator says that in the cult of Bacchus the initiate is purified by means of the three elements: fire, water, and air.[118] No other source, however, indicates that such a thing was ever done, and the passage appears to be more of a reference to an imaginary ritual used to confirm Neopythagorean cosmological theories, which held that the soul is purified from its corporal components after death, ascending through the three elements for this purpose. These theories possibly influenced the Vergilian lines on which Servius is commenting, in which souls are described as purifying themselves in Hades. The common use in Greek cults of sacrificial fire, of water as a method of purification, and of the winnowing fan (λίκνον) for separating wheat from chaff are the real foundation on which it was possible to construct intellectually a ritual that corresponded to the cosmological theory of purifying the soul by means of the elements, but that never existed outside the Pythagorean imagination.

The same confirmation of cosmological theories by means of supposed ancient rituals explains Macrobius's references to Dionysus's dismemberment – "carried out during the rites of the Orphics" to symbolize the intellect (νοῦς) that is dispersed among men – and also to the egg venerated in

---

116 *Apol.* 56 (*OF* 651). In other passages of the same work (*Apol.* 27.1, 30), he says in his own defense that Orpheus was a magician, like Pythagoras or Epimenides, in order to vindicate magic as a respectable discipline. Cf. Jourdan 2008a.
117 Hdt. 2.81 (*OF* 650). Linforth 1941, 39ff points out that Apuleius seems to have read the brief version of Herodotus, omitting "Bacchic and Egyptian" and leaving only "Orphic and Pythagorean". The haplography would, therefore, be very ancient.
118 Serv. *ad Aen.*6.741, *ad Georg.*1.166. Turcan 1961 analyses this imaginary rite, opposing earlier interpretations which wrongly took it as a description of actual ritual.

the same rites as an image of the *vita mundi*.[119] These references to ritual acts are simply reflections of metaphysical theories, for which they serve as allegorical matter in a merely rhetorical linkage. By this point it was not difficult – and still less for a reader of Neoplatonic authors like Macrobius – to be familiar with both the Orphic tradition concerning the myth of the Titans and the anecdotal details like the egg, even without ever having seen them. The same scant credit should be given to the references to the garments of the priests in Bacchic rites, which are found in the aforementioned ritual poems and hymns (p. 36f).

In reality, Macrobius and Servius did no more than follow the model of the Greek Neoplatonists, who discussed the Orphic rites with no qualms whatsoever, from Damascius to Olympiodorus, by way of Proclus and Syrianus. Their innumerable mentions of "the Orphics" and their rites are not evidence of their real existence, and in general they have not been taken into account since the "Orpheo-sceptics" imposed a healthy rigor in the use of sources. It is likely that in the mystical-philosophical milieu of the last Academy outmoded rites of metaphysical meaning were recreated, but these possible re-creations had no influence beyond these circles and prove no more than the lasting capacity of erudite tradition to take physical form in any milieu inclined to receive it.

3. The Orphic tradition in the second to fifth centuries

Examining the presence of a fundamentally literary tradition in ritual practice leads to the formulation of three questions for evaluating the religious value of Orphism during the Imperial Age: Does the evidence reflect a continuous tradition from the classical age or a late reinvention? Are the rites alluded to in literary sources imaginary or actual? And lastly, what difference did it make when a cult of Bacchus or Demeter, a philosophical doctrine, or a magic spell acquired Orphic coloration?

With variations in detail, the direct evidence from Greece, Rome, Egypt, and Asia Minor coincides with the literary tradition in documenting a clear resurgence of Orphism, after centuries of almost complete absence, beginning in the second century AD. It is clear that in many cases there was un-

---

119 Macr. *Comm*.1.12.12; *Sat*. 7.6.18. The same interpretation of the egg is found in Plutarch (*Quaest. Conv*.2.3.2), perhaps Macrobius' source in this passage. Linforth 1941, 271 rightly says that the neo-Platonist usage of mystery language does not imply the existence of "living mysteries", though elsewhere he seems to suppose (231, 241, 284) that Macrobius is referring to specific rites.

derground continuity, as the Roman lamella or the rites of Phlye kept by the Lycomids may suggest. On top of this continuity, however, there was superimposed a resurgence that clearly did not originate in *paradosis* from generation to generation. Does this mean that this renewed Orphism was entirely different from its ancient counterpart? Reviewing the evidence has made it possible to demonstrate that in the evolution of Orphism the transmission of the literary tradition (the external perspective) was as important as, if not more important than, the direct transmission of rites or poems (the internal perspective). It was recourse to the more or less benevolent or accurate categories coined by outside observers of these phenomena (Herodotus, Aristophanes, Plato, Aristotle) that in large measure made it possible for those who, for one reason or another, were interested in giving new life to ancient rituals and beliefs (Plutarch, Apuleius, Neoplatonists) to renew the Orphic tradition and adapt it to new circumstances, at times similar to those that fostered its initial growth and at times entirely distinct. A clear parallel case might be the present-day esoteric movements that claim to be the heirs of, for example, Hermes Trismegistus, reuse Hermetic texts, and recreate Hermetic rituals. New hermeticism is an heir of ancient Hermeticism and may appear similar to it in many ways, but this is not the result of an uninterrupted internal Hermetic tradition (even if its adepts so assert), but rather of the prestige that ancient witnesses, and especially the hostile ones, have conferred on it. The continuity between early and late Orphism is guaranteed as much, if not more, by the evidence of external observers, even the detractors, as it is by the imagined successive handing down of tradition across generations of "Orphics."

Why this resurgence of ancient Orphism? The rise of Christianity and the need for pagan self-reconsideration, whatever the relation between these two phenomena may have been, had an enormous impact on the increase of these antiquarian tendencies in Greek religion from the second century onward.[120] That Pausanias or Apuleius should have imitated Herodotus in referring to Orphism, far from discounting it as a literary and artificial phenomenon, shows the reason for its growing popularity on the imperial religious scene. Its value was based on its preservation and continuation of an extremely ancient tradition, located at the very origins of Greek civilization. Greek intellectual and religious efforts were directed from the end of the Hellenistic age toward recovering the tradition of classical antiquity, linking up with it, and carrying it on. The religious or philosophical or literary con-

---

120 Dodds 1965, Veyne 1983, Lane Fox 1986, Alcock *et al.* 2001 on the causes and consequences of the vindication of the Greek past in Imperial times.

tent that was to be upheld was more credible the more it was rooted in this tradition, guaranteed by its transmission from generation to generation since the most ancient times. Invocations of tradition (*paradosis*) and of what was handed down (*ta paradedomena*) are constant in ritual inscriptions. Connecting a cult with Orpheus or giving it a certain Orphic tone with allusions to Orphism's myths and rituals meant tying it to this venerable *paradosis*. What we call Orphism today was conceptualized at this time as a tradition, and in fact the ancient definition emphasizes more than the modern '-ism' the open character of a bundle of elements the value of which was not in their systematic order, but rather in their link with the past. Their coherence was not horizontal in the present, but vertical in time, and an understanding of them ought to be not synchronous, but diachronic.[121]

Given that its primordial function during the Imperial age was to give a prestigious label to the usual cults, Orphism did not need internal coherence, but rather vivid colors. That is to say that it would be the more anecdotal details, those which precisely for this reason had greater sensible force and greater iconicity, that would spread most widely and successfully. The name of Orpheus was, of course, the principal element. Unsurprisingly, his figure singing among the animals flourishes in iconography – above all in the mosaics of the great villas – precisely between the second and fourth centuries AD. Though this motif may be purely ornamental and does not need to be linked to the Orphic religious tradition, it is clear that it was popular precisely because it symbolized vague notions of harmony, peace, transcendence, and attachment to Classical culture (Vieillefon 2003). But other elements more related to the Orphic religious tradition also flourish in this period: taboos like the prohibition of beans or eggs, idiosyncratic appellations like Phanes or Ericepeus, myths like the incest of Zeus or the crime of the Titans, eschatological images, or slogans like *soma-sema*, in sum, those elements most recognizable as belonging to the Orphic tradition would also be the elements chosen for incorporation by religious cults and even by magic spells (and as we will see, also by Christian apologetics as targets for attack). In this way, the Orphic tradition is paradoxically quite uniform, however diverse the cults to which it becomes attached may be: all these unconnected elements are repeated by different witnesses in different contexts, even in times and places quite far from one another, since repetition is precisely the one thing asked of them in order to link with the past from which they derive,

---

121 Casadio 1990 studies the verb *paradidomi* and cognates in Orphic contexts. On antiquity as the main value of Orphic tradition, cf. Celsus *apud* Orig. *CC* 1.14–16; Julian, *Ep.* 111 and 46; 136b1. Cf. also p. 227.

without any requirement that they maintain a systematic mutual coherence that would make their adaptation more difficult.

So, then, it did not matter so much whether an Orphic element in a cult truly had been passed down or recuperated, but rather that it appeared to be ancient and grounded in the most pristine tradition. In the same way, whether a rite was really celebrated or not was less important than maintaining the idea that it was celebrated on occasion, or even that it could be celebrated at a given time. If the principal motor of transmission and diffusion was the literary tradition, this does not mean that Orphism never left the pages of books. No doubt there were rites – like those mentioned by the Neoplatonists – that only existed on the level of imagination, although they served as metaphors, as literary and conceptual images for articulating everything from philosophical ideas to the plots of novels. Precisely those rites that most emphatically call themselves "Orphic" or present details supposedly most peculiar to the ideal rite, such as the astral garment of the priest, are the most suspect of being no more than literary figurations. Even if these re-creations may on occasion have given rise to actual practices originating in the same metaphor (like the lyre, the egg, or the ritual garments that the Neopythagoreans or even the Neoplatonists may have used), these *dromena* did not cease to be literary and artificial – mere reflections of the philosophical doctrines that inspired them. Yet, on the other hand, there are a series of convincing pieces of evidence (the initiation of Plutarch and his wife, the inscriptions from Asia Minor, the community of the *Orphic Hymns*) that testify to the real existence of rites that contained elements unequivocally linked to Orphism. Contrary to the imaginary rites, the *dromena* seem to have been very simple (libation and singing in the *Orphic Hymns*), while complexity and depth were reserved for the *legomena*.

In the equilibrium between the two poles of imaginary and real existence, the convergence of Orphism with its two old companions in the Greek religious mind, maenadism and Eleusis, is clear. The Orphic tradition is similar to the maenadic tradition, ever vigorous in spirit among those impressed by the force of its myths and images even today, but rarely put into actual practice – as has been evident since Albert Henrichs's 1978 study – precisely on account of the difficulty of giving reality to those images. It was enough to recall them and allude to them, something in which the *Bacchae* of Euripides played a fundamental role. With their similar vocabulary and imagery, proper to their common origin in the cult of Dionysus, Orphic and maenadic tradition must have perforce become mixed on several occasions. The former lent a more esoteric flavor to the cults it inspired, the latter a more orgiastic one, but both fulfilled similar functions. On the other hand, the tradition of the rites of Demeter and Core, of Eleusinian heritage, was different, because these were stable cults, regularly practiced; when Orphism entered the scene, it seems that the result was a division of roles between Eleusinian *dromena* and Orphic *legomena*. In both cases, the link with Orphism fostered the universally accepted idea that the cult was the guardian of an ancient, revealed wisdom beyond the reach of non-initiates: the ancient theology of the mysteries. The Orphic connection, to put it in such terms, gave an "extra" quality of the mysteries to any cult and facilitated its experience as something transcendent. This link to the mysteries was no less appreciated by philosophy and magic than by the religious cults themselves: in the ill-defined frontiers among the three, Orphism spread with particular vigor.

All these regular cults, which are the ones actually practiced, seem to have the typical characteristics of the institutionalized thiasoi that proliferated from the Hellenistic age forward.[122] The inscriptions give a partial impression, as if their interest was focused solely on the most colorful taboos and on the hierarchy of offices, something which has contributed in great part to fostering a vision of these thiasoi as little more than bourgeois clubs that sought out a religious-literary excuse for pseudo-profound entertainment.[123] It is possible that the rites they practiced had only a slight tinge of Orphism, more nominal than real, grounding them in the Orphic tradition, just as in the maenadic and Eleusinian ones. Nevertheless, in all probability it was in a thiasos of this type that Plutarch and his wife participated in the Dionysian *orgia* that made such a profound impression on them. In reality, the sincerity and depth of feeling of their participants could be judged only by themselves, and what is important here is not so much what they were in reality as what they claimed to be, since it was this official image of serious practitioners of Orphic rites that was transmitted to the general public, including the apologists. It did not much matter that the "Titans" of a thiasos did no more than call themselves by this name, if that was enough to cause others (for example, the readers of Lucian's description of the Bacchic dance) to believe in the possibility that they might at some point play the role of these personages in myth. It was these thiasoi, finally, with their presence and their "decaffeinated" rites, that made it plausible to imagine, in philosophy, novels, or apologetics, more idealized rites, much closer to the raw myth and, for that reason, much more rarely practiced, if ever.

What in particular, then, did containing Orphic elements add to a cult or to a speculative work? It is a question that seems to have already roused the

---

122 Nilsson 1957, Turcan 1992, Burkert 1993.
123 Cf. West 1983, 28 on the community of the *Orphic Hymns*. But see Graf 2009.

curiosity of some ancients who, for example, developed the explanation that Orpheus reformed the *Bacchica*, as a result of which they have since been called *Orphica*.[124] It is an artificial explanation, like many of those proposed more recently, but it testifies to a desire to clarify the use of certain mobile, fluid, but not insignificant labels. The Orphic elements in question could be literary (a myth or a god), ritual (a regulation ascribed to Orpheus), or even pictorial;[125] in any case, it was a matter of concrete imagery (including the name of Orpheus), not of abstract concepts. We should not speak of specifically Orphic theological, anthropological, or moral beliefs during the imperial age. Not even a strong Orphic presence implies that definite ideas regarding the divine or the soul were necessarily shared; for example, the *Orphic Hymns*' lack of interest in the life to come is well known. It is clear that the Orphic poems contain ideas about the gods, the cosmos, and man that on many occasions are in the service of very different streams of thought. Nevertheless, there is not one single idea in the *Rhapsodies* or in the remaining Orphic literature that is not present and more extensively developed in other philosophical and religious movements, free of the bounds imposed by the traditional poetic and mythic form. What there is in Orphism is a series of literary and ritual images permitting the expression of certain religious and philosophical ideas in a given form. If certain thinkers or cults decided to link themselves to the Orphic tradition, this was, in my opinion, because that tradition brought them three very important assets: the prestige of antiquity provided by an ancient tradition; the aura of "the mysteries" imparted by Orphism; and alongside these two elements already discussed, a third of no less importance, the consolidation of Greek religious identity around Orpheus, his poems, and his rites.

Reference to Orphism not only reinforced the identity of an individual as an initiate and of a group as a thiasos, but also became an instrument for reinforcing one's identity as a citizen of a given Greek city, as a subject of a Hellenistic state like that of the Ptolemies, or simply as a Greek, distinguished from the barbarians or the Romans. Despite his condition as a foreigner, or precisely because of it, Orpheus became a Panhellenic symbol. Diodorus called him "the greatest of the Greeks." Pausanias reported the

---

124 D.S. 1.23.2 (*OF* 497): according to Egyptian sources, Orpheus reformed Bacchic rites after returning from Egypt; D.S.3.65.6 (*OF* 502): he reforms the Dionysiac rites inherited from his father Oeagrus, king of Thrace.
125 E. g. the painting by Polygnotus described by Pausanias (10.30.6ff), or that of Phlye mentioned by Hippolytus (*Ref.* 5.20.4). The paintings on Apulian funerary vases seem to have clear religious functions (Bottini 1992).

prestige of his name as the founder of local sanctuaries.[126] His popularity as an ornamental figure becomes enormous. For the same reason that Orphism carried the stigma of foreignness in Rome, in Greece it became transformed into a hallmark of Hellenism, by reference to the ancient tradition revealed to all the Greeks. For this reason Orpheus, the Thracian intermediary between the barbarian and the Greek, became a standard-bearer of Hellenism in the same way that the Trojan Aeneas became a standard-bearer of Romanness.

For the very same reason, finally, the Neoplatonists took up Orpheus as a champion of that paganism that sought to save the Hellenic inheritance, and the apologists, for their part, saw him as a representative of that same Greek paganism that they opposed. The religious polemics of late antiquity exponentially relaunched the recuperation of Orphism as a banner of anti-Christian resistance. Celsus already contrasted the writings of the Greek wise men, Orpheus among them, to the Christian prophets (*CC* 1.16–18), and the death of Orpheus (*CC* 7.53) and his descent into and return from Hades in search of Eurydice (*CC* 2.55) to the violent death and resurrection of Jesus. It must be noted, however, that Orpheus always appears among other figures and, above all, that Celsus's aim was primarily to demonstrate that one set of stories was no less false and unworthy of belief than the other. The pagan *teletai* did not deserve much consideration in his view either, since they also used the cheap trick of appealing to fear of the terrors of Hades (*CC* 3.16, 4.10, 8.48). In reality, the advantage that Orpheus (and not only he, but other figures as well), his writings, and his *teletai* had over Christ, the Bible, and the Christian rites was that the former were ancient and traditional, while the latter were a dangerous novelty. The value that they had in themselves, however, was scant in the eyes of the vaguely Platonist Celsus. Nevertheless, the prestige of Orpheus and of the Orphic tradition would see rapid growth, supported precisely by the increasing authority given them by their antiquity.

In the anti-Christian resistance that sought to revitalize paganism, two tendencies can be distinguished, the Orientalizing, which sought new vitality in foreign wisdom, and the traditional, which defended the ancestral religion. Orphism, thanks to its supposed foreign origin (Thrace, Egypt) and to its ancient roots in Greece, was able to satisfy both tendencies at once.

---

126 Plutarch seems, contrary to the general tendency, to be an heir of Plato in his lack of admiration for Orpheus and for the label "Orphic" (Bernabé 1996 and 1998), which he uses to designate the obscure rituals of Olympias and the Bona Dea, but not for his own initiation. Just as Orpheus served as an icon to hold up for veneration in some Greek local sanctuaries, he could be rejected in others. In Delphi, where Plutarch was priest, there is no evidence at all of his presence, whence, along with Plato's influence, a plausible reason for his lack of enthusiasm for Orphic matters.

3. The Orphic tradition in the second to fifth centuries

Porphyry, Iamblichus, and Julian spoke with much greater reverence than Celsus about Orpheus, his poems, and his *teletai*, and the later Neoplatonists took this process to an extreme. Each one in his own way, all these authors sought in Orphic tradition one important key to the "pagan religion" they were struggling to recreate in a revived form. Porphyry integrated neo-Pythagorean trends within neo-Platonic philosophy, and quoted Orphic fragments to defend his critique of sacrifice and his allegorical readings of ancient poetry along neo-Platonic lines.[127] Iamblichus went further and engaged in a revalorization of theurgy and of a mystical form of religious knowledge attainable through the ancient rituals in clear opposition to the Christian revelation: Orphism assumed a central role in these constructions. Iamblichus is probably the creator of the philosophical myth that traces the tradition of the *telestai* to Orpheus – who handed it down to Aglaophamus, the initiator of Pythagoras, who in turn initiated Plato. It reveals the growing need to find a source of divine inspiration on which to support traditional paganism, a role which Orpheus was better suited than anyone else to take on.[128] Iamblichus' line was enthusiastically followed by Emperor Julian in the fourth century, who passionately tried to give new life to a paganism that was already defending itself from increasing Christian preeminence. A devotee of Mithra and of the Sun, Julian tried to integrate Orphic theology and ritual tradition into syncretistic constructions that mirrored Christianity, on the one hand, and had some roots in previous trends within paganism, on the other.[129] Finally, once Christianity definitively prevailed after Julian's death, the last Neoplatonic philosophers in the fifth and sixth centuries AD – mainly Proclus, Damascius, Syrianus, Olympiodorus – recovered Orphism as one of the most ancient and divine religious traditions of their idealized and lost Greek past: they quoted Orphic poems as inspired poetry that only needed to be rightly interpreted through allegory, and they imagined Orphic rites and communities of Orphics. Only once Orphism was definitely dead

---

127 Porph. *Ad Gaur.* 2.2.9; *De abst.* 2.36; 165.3; *De antro nymph.* 7, 14, 16; *frr.* 351, 354, 359 Smith; *VP* 17, 29, 43. Cf. Speyer 2005 on his religious thought and Berchman 2005 on his anti-Christian apologetics.
128 Iambl. *VP* 146; Procl. *In Plat. Tim.* 3.168.9, *Plat. Theol.* 1.5. Brisson 2000 argues persuasively that Iamblichus invents the myth of Aglaophamus (which gave its name to Lobeck's work).
129 Iul. 7.215bc, 216d, 217bc; *Or.* 4.136; cf. n. 109 for the correspondences. Athanassiadi-Fowden suggests some cases of Orphic-Mithraic syncretism around Dionysus in Julian's religious thought (1977, 37; 1980, 135f, 151, 174; cf. also Bidez-Cumont 1938, I, 97). Smith 1995, 147 is more cautious in some cases where Orphism could be the only reference without need of Mithraism.

did it become, in these Neoplatonic re-creations, the consistent and systematic religion it had never been.[130]

Thus paganism in its last days simply gathered and made flower tendencies that had been ever more perceptible since the second century AD. It was in relation to Orphism's three contributions that provoked its recuperation in the imperial age – namely, the prestige of antiquity, the prestige of the mysteries, and the prestige of Greek religious identity – that the whole complex attitude of the Christians toward it would be established. Before examining that relationship in all its details, however, it will be useful to consider the spheres in which Orphism and Christianity encountered one another.

---

[130] Cf. Brisson 2008 for an overview of Neoplatonic tratment of Orphism, and specific studies on Damascius and Proclus in his 1995 collection of studies.

III. Fields of intersection

Sibylla porro, vel Sibyllae, et Orpheus, et nescio quis Hermes, et si qui alii vates vel theologi, vel sapientes, vel philosophi gentium de Filio Dei, aut de Patre Deo vera praedixisse seu dixisse perhibentur ..
Augustine, *Contra Faustum* 13.2

In the next chapter our Christian sources for Orphism will be examined, just as pagan testimonies were in the last. It should be noted, however, that while the need to limit this study's sources to a well-defined corpus might create the impression of two opposing movements with no relation to each other beyond the confrontation transmitted in apologetic literature, the resulting image of binary opposition would be a false one. In reality, there are many points where the Orphic tradition and Christianity overlap. If the boundaries of any philosophical and religious movement are permeable – and they are particularly so in the Imperial age – it is obvious that to restrict our testimonies to those which unmistakeably bear the imprint of Orphism imposes an artificial limit upon its undeniable continuity with other movements, a continuity not only literary, but intellectual and ritual. Various philosophical and religious trends are concerned with the ideas expressed in the Orphic poems, or with similar ritual and literary motifs, under names of similar effect and authority to that of Orpheus. More often than not, Orphism appears on the Imperial religious landscape not as an isolated, self-contained phenomenon, but as one tradition within a broader commonwealth of similar philosophies and ideologies.

Christianity similarly overlaps and converges with these trends, its contours being likewise less than perfectly defined upon the ideological and religious map of the Empire.[1] In reality, Christian apologists are attempting to set boundaries to, and define, their understanding of Christianity within a very fluid religious environment. From Paul onwards, the influence of Greek philosophy on the nascent religion becomes increasingly evident. Its affinity with various pagan cults – and in particular with the mystery cults – is also clear, as is seen in the painstaking care with which the Christian apologists seek to

---

[1] Bultmann 1949, Nock 1964, Smith 1990 present Christianity within the framework of contemporary religions. On Christian reception of Greek philosophy, cf. Stead 1994.

distinguish their movement from those practices with which they appear to have most in common. The Christianization of the Greek world implies in turn a Hellenization of Christianity in several doctrinal and ritual aspects that sometimes makes the boundary between the new religion and paganism difficult to determine – while the borders between Christianity, Gnosticism, and Judaism were often even fainter and more permeable. It was in a very fluid and unsteady context that the apologists confronted an Orphic tradition that had extended its encroachments over many diverse fields.

This chapter is divided into purposefully asymmetrical sections, which aim to describe the main fields, ideological, literary, and ritual, where Christian and Orphic spheres of influence overlapped: philosophical traditions, theological texts, Gnosticism, Judaism and Orphic-Christian syncretism. None of these categories is firm and closed, which contributes to the permeability of these boundaries. Another division starting from a sociological viewpoint would perhaps classify these crossroads differently.

Magic, above all, is a field where contact between Orphism and other religious movements and traditions is often perceivable, as the Egyptian evidence examined in the previous chapter shows. However, magic is a much-discussed category[2] that, in the Greek case, lumps together vulgarized philosophical ideas, Greek poetic formulas, and Eastern, Gnostic, Jewish, and Christian themes. Magical practices are present in all these fields as a bridge that unites different religious and philosophical movements, on a popular, practical level, just as literary speculation, in prose or poetry, links them on a more intellectual and speculative level. Labelling any piece of evidence as "magic" comes from the scholarly need for clarity rather than from the objective data. The needs of modern scholars to be understandable are matched by those of ancient apologists to be persuasive, and both often require neat polarities: "magic" became, perhaps irreversibly, defined by opposition to religion, whatever that meant in each case.[3] Yet we should avoid

---

2   The discussion on the category of "magic" is enormous (cf. a good overview in Collins 2003). Yet its usefulness as a technical term, though much battered by postmodernism, is impossible to deny (Versnel 1991). Sorensen 2007 has proposed an interesting cognitive approach to defining magic in new terms. For the specific debate regarding the Greek world, cf. Faraone/Obbink 1991, Graf 1997, Dickie 2001. For "Orphism and magic", cf. Martín 2006.
3   On magic vs. religion, cf. Versnel 1991, Fowler 1994. Cf. Bremmer 2008, 235ff on the birth of the term "magic" as a scientific term with Frazer. However, its apologetic use is much earlier: the Christian accusations against Greek cults of "superstition" (δεισιδαιμονία) and "witchcraft" (γοητεία) as opposed to "piety" (θεοσεβεία) are the direct precedent of the opposition magic/religion that taints Protestant/Catholic polemics in the modern age. Christian apologists reshape the

falling in that trap. Magic, therefore, will not be taken here as a specific field where Orphic and Christian elements may have overlapped, but as a level of thought and practice that took (and takes) place in all fields of spiritual life.

1. Philosophical traditions

Though its precise degree of influence on his philosophy is debatable, it is indisputable that Plato integrated into and developed within his philosophical system the most original ideas that Orphism had introduced in Greece – in particular, the dualism whereby each human is held to comprise both a mortal body and an immortal soul.[4] Such notions were extended within Platonism and became prevalent, in more or less popularized versions, throughout the greater part of the Hellenistic Mediterranean. As a result of this widespread dissemination, Plato attained the status of principal authority to whom all these ideas are traced, with the Orphic poems coming to be seen to some degree as an ornamental complement and precedent for his works – in much the same manner, by way of analogy, that a modern-day Marxist might view the relationship obtaining between *Das Kapital* and the writings of the early Utopian socialists.

Christianity must also be included as part of the Greek world that inherits Plato's legacy. From the second century onward Christian theology begins to be formulated in Platonic terms – not only because of the prestige of such a vocabulary as a hallmark of Hellenism, but because this is perceived as the model best adapted to providing Christian revelation with a rational and intellectualizing theology. The importance of the process is difficult to exaggerate. It begins with Justin and, following in the footsteps of the Alexandrian Jew Philo, continues with Clement of Alexandria and Origen before assuming its definitive form with the Cappadocian Fathers (Gregory of Nazianzus, Basil, and Gregory of Nyssa) in the East and Augustine in the West; and it is not a coincidence that for both Justin and Augustine – the first and the last of these thinkers – Platonism is the last of the pagan systems of thought to which they are committed before their conversion to Christianity. Its worldview was the closest of these philosophies to the Christian cosmological vision.[5]

---

previous distinctions made by Greek religious thinkers (Heraclitus, Hippocrates, Plato) and set the categories of the modern distinction. Cf. pp. 236f, 254f.
4 Bernabé 1998 on Orphic references in Plato and his transposition of Orphism to his system.
5 Cf. Chadwick 1966, Jäger 1961 and Wolfson 1970 on the reception of Platonism in Patristic literature, and Lilla 1971 specifically on Clement of Alexandria.

The role of Orphism within this process is rather slight, the Orphic texts serving as a rhetorical and literary prop to this Platonic/Christian *rapprochement* rather than providing its content. To return to the comparison made above – why other than for historical or ornamental purposes would a socialist now cite Saint-Simon?

The Platonism of the second and third century AD – that is to say, the Platonism contemporary with the Christian apologists – continued to find little of philosophical interest in Orpheus or in the Orphic tradition, as the few references made by authors such as Plutarch or Plotinus indicate.[6] A cento composed of quotations on so prototypically Orphic a theme as the fall of the soul – used as much by Platonically-minded Jewish and Christian authors (Philo, Clement) as by pagans (Plutarch, Hierocles, Plotinus) – incorporates texts by Plato, Pythagoras, Heraclitus, and Empedocles.[7] But there are no verses by Orpheus. Undoubtedly there existed passages of Orphic poetry relevant to the topic, but they did not yet interest a Platonism that continued to find greater authority in other figures. Orphism only appears indirectly – when a Platonic passage refers specifically to it using expressions like "as Orpheus's disciples say (οἱ ἀμφὶ Ὀρφέα)." In the subsequent tradition, such expressions serve to mark a belief as distinctively Orphic – as for example occurs with the famous *soma-sema* comparison, the body as jail or tomb of the soul. Clement says, "Plato in the *Cratylus* attributes to Orpheus the doctrine that the soul is punished by being in the body." The image is also attributed by pagan and Christian authors to "ancient initiators" as heirs of Orphic tradition.[8] In the few cases in which he makes explicit references to Orphic teachings, therefore, Plato is treated as their direct transmitter in his writings.

This tendency changed in the third century AD with Porphyry and Iamblichus, as we saw in chapter II. Such thinkers were searching for an ancient tradition with the authority of divine revelation to ground their own philosophical speculations based on Plato's texts – a desire that sometimes led them to make such clearly exaggerated claims as 'Plato imitates Orpheus

---

6   Only three Plotinian passages contain possible allusions to anecdotal details in Orphic literature: *Enn.* 1.6.6: the punishment of mud; 4.3.12: the mirror of Dionysus; 5.8.4: Dike (justice) as *paredros* (advisor) to Zeus. Plutarch knows Orphic tradition indirectly and mainly through Plato (Bernabé 1996).

7   Cf. Burkert 1975 and the corrections and extensions made by Mansfeld 1985 with regard to this cento.

8   Plat. *Crat.* 400c; Clem. Alex. *Strom.* 3.3.16.3–17–1; Thdt. *Affect.* 5.13; Cic. *Hortensius* fr. 112 Grilli, *apud* Aug. *Contra Iul. Pelag.* 4.15.78, 4.16.83. Cf. chapter IV, nn. 151–153.

in everything.'⁹ The confluence with Neo-Pythagoreanism, and the integration of the Orphic tradition into Neo-Platonist philosophy is total. This late Neo-Platonism, however, was already opposing the pagan tradition to Christianity and raised Orphism as the alternative standard to which it rallied its philosophical troops. The Christian writers influenced by late neo-Platonism, like Pseudo-Dionysius the Areopagite in the fifth to sixth century AD, do not take account of Orpheus and his texts, for these had already become a symbol of pagan resistance.

Stoicism – with Platonism, the most important philosophical school of the Hellenistic and Imperial ages – shows rather more open interest in the Orphic tradition. This is particularly true with regard to the origins of the school, to the extent that it may be possible to trace in Orphism certain 'proto-Stoic' ideas. Some Orphic theological expressions were traditionally believed to be the result of Stoic influence. Their presence in the Derveni Papyrus, however, dated to the fourth century BC, raises the possibility that the influence runs in the opposite direction, and the Stoics derived inspiration for some crucial points from Orphic writings.¹⁰ In any case, it is known that Chrysippus and the Stoics of the Pergamene school made frequent allegorical use of Orphic poetry in order to adapt it to their ideological system and that both the *Theogony of Hieronymus and Hellanicus* and the *Rhapsodies* betray Stoic influence.¹¹ In the next chapter we shall see that some apologists, such as Athenagoras, are evidently exploiting sources derived from Stoic circles.

The Christian attitude to Stoic theology, however, is marked by strong rejection. Christian views of the nature of God place the religion much nearer to the transcendent divinity of Platonism than to the immanence and near-pantheism of much Stoic thinking. As a result, Orphism of Stoic origin is typically subject to apologetic assaults – as it is, for example, in the writings of Athenagoras and Eusebius. By contrast, Christianity early on shows itself

---

9   Olympiod. *In Plat. Phaed.* 7.10. Kingsley 1995, 131 argues that, despite its exaggeration, the statement has some truth in it. Cf. pp. 85f for a survey of Neo-Platonic treatments of Orphic tradition.
10 Cf. Bernabé 2002c, Jourdan 2003, XIV, XX–XXV. Brisson 2009 and Casadesús 2008 have taken to the extreme this Stoic approach to the *P. Derveni*, to the point of purporting that the commentator was a Stoic, which is hardly likely since it would contradict archaelogical, papyrological, linguistic and ideological dating criteria, as Betegh 2007 shows. However, the parallels show that the Stoics were, to a large extent, depositaries of Orphic theory.
11 On Stoic uses of Orphism, cf. *OF* 407 I and Cic. *ND* 1.41; Philod. *De piet.* 13 (*F Hercul.* VI 16 ff); Gal. *De plac. Hipp. et Plat.* 3.4.15. Cf. West 1983 and Bernabé 2003 and 2008 on Stoic influence on Orphic theogonies.

amenable to Stoic perspectives in the field of ethics. From the moment the early Christians begin to countenance the possibility that the Parousia might be delayed, they begin to endorse a civic morality that is evident already in the pastoral epistles of the New Testament, and that has its most obvious philosophical precedent in Stoic ethics.[12] The emphasis on ethics is in addition very effective in defining Christianity against other religions of the Empire more focused on cultic practice.

In this aspect of philosophical assimilation too, however, Orphism has little role to play. The concern Orphism had for civic ethics was slight and superficial in comparison with the importance it laid upon ritual and personal purity, evidenced by little more than a few vague references to *dikē* or to the just life of those who are saved. It is possible to perceive in several inscriptions from the Imperial age some moralization of ritual prescriptions compatible with aspects of Orphism. But this moral emphasis is more likely attributable to the influence of Stoicism, Eastern cults, or Judaism: there is no real reason to find in it evidence of Orphism. Such moralization may even have affected the Bacchic *teletai* (*CC* 3.59) or later Orphic literature, as may be seen in the katabasis of the *Bologna Papyrus* (*OF* 717).[13] In all these cases, though, Orphism receives influence from a common environment, without being, like Stoicism or Eastern religions, a motor of such inflence.

If Orphism is of little importance to middle Neo-Platonic metaphysics or to Stoic ethics – the two philosophical trends with which early Christianity was most closely aligned – its role in relation to Neo-Pythagoreanism is somewhat more significant. After the annihilation of the Pythagorean communities of Magna Graecia at the end of the fourth century BC, we have little information concerning the survival and development of the Pythagorean tradition before its reappearance in Rome in the first century BC.[14] Over the next three centuries, the movement enjoyed a certain prestige, with outstanding figures like Numenius or Theon of Smyrna or, on a different level, Apollonius of Tyana, and finally converged with the Neo-Platonic school of thought from the time of Iamblichus and Porphyry. In fact, the label "Neo-Pythagoreanism" is somewhat inaccurate, insofar as the movement is asso-

---

12 Cf. Chadwick 1966, 11ff, 21ff, and Willert 2006. E. g. Iust. *Ap.* 1.43, 2.7. Some cosmological notions could also be adapted, as *ekpyrosis* could be adapted to the Last Judgement (excluding its cyclic repetition): Clem. *Strom.* 5.9.4.
13 Cf. n. 40 on inscriptions and pp. 345ff on the moralization of the *teletai*.
14 Cf. Burkert 1961, Thesleff 1961 (and the discussion held by both at the session of the Fondation Hardt 1972) on the survival of Pythagorean literature in Hellenistic times; Carcopino 1927 on its re-emergence in Rome; Kahn 2001 for a comprehensive account of the Pythagorean tradition.

ciated with neither original philosophical doctrines nor new ethical precepts. Rather, the Imperial "Neo-Pythagoreans" participated in the eclecticism typical of the era and never organized themselves into any formally defined school.[15] Precisely because of this lack of overall doctrinal and ethical coherence, however, the beliefs of the Neo-Pythagoreans that distinguish them as such – i.e., those that establish their alleged continuity with the ancient Pythagoreanism from which they claim direct descent – stand out with a particular vividness. These continuities are obscure and in every instance partial; the Neo-Pythagoreans revived and emphasized ancient Pythagorean rules whose authority is apparently derived from the simple fact of being such. The taboos concerning food, dress, and purity that make up the Pythagorean life – along with a focus on reincarnation, the nature of music and numbers, and Pythagoras' maxims – are all valorized simply by the fact that "he said it" (αὐτὸς ἔφα).

Within such a philosophical ambience, in which the value of asceticism was being reassessed and ancient tradition newly endowed with quasi-mystical authority, a phenomenon as closely tied to ancient Pythagoreanism as Orphism was clearly going to be revived – particularly given the Neo-Pythagorean interest in Orphic imagery. The Pythagorean taboos regarding diet and dress might readily be justified with reference to *hieroi logoi* of Orphic ascription.[16] In addition, just as the ancient Pythagoreans composed Orphic poems, the Neo-Pythagoreans assigned to Orpheus such compositions as the *Lyre* and a *Hymn to Number*. The topics selected for such attribution – music and mathematical mysticism – are revealing because of the desire they evince to establish a connection with the most characteristic features of ancient Pythagoreanism. The music-related aspects of Orpheus and his myth attain a new significance in Neo-Pythagorean speculations about musical metaphysics,[17] and the reputation Orphism enjoyed among the Neo-Platonists is a legacy of its revival by the Neo-Pythagorean tradition.

The relationship of Hellenistic Judaism and primitive Christianity to this Neo-Pythagorean movement is obscure and difficult to describe in any detail. Although Neo-Pythagoreanism had little to contribute to Christian doctrine or ethics, and its ritual taboos were both rivals to and incompatible with Christian practice, its literary and eschatological concerns might

---

15 Kahn 2001, 94–138, and the introduction of J. Dillon and J. Herschbell to their edition of Iamblichus' *On the Pythagorean Way of Life* (1991) are good surveys of neo-Pythagorism. On neo-Pythagorean and neo-Platonic eclecticism Dillon 1998.
16 Kingsley 1995, Lizcano 2003. Cf. II n. 22 on the taboo on broad beans.
17 Cf. II n. 13, and Boyancé 1936 on the religious dimension of Pythagorean musical speculation reflected, among other things, in the cult to the Muses.

readily be adapted to the purposes of the new religion. To give an example: both Christian and Gnostic apocalyptic writings are clearly influenced by ideas surrounding the ascent of the soul through various celestial realms or planes of existence. Philo and Clement of Alexandria appear to have been the most open-minded apologists with regard to this movement.[18] Clement, as will be discussed in more detail below, reveals a profound appreciation for Neo-Pythagorean musical speculation – and its supposed relationship to Orpheus would not be of his own invention, but an element already present in his Neo-Pythagorean sources. In all likelihood, furthermore, it is this musical connection that facilitates the appropriation of a singing Orpheus in Christian iconography.

2. Theological texts

The need for a religious figure or tradition endowed with the authority of divine revelation is sharply felt among pagan communities from the second century AD to the end of Late Antiquity. This is in part the result of opposition to an expanding Christianity, in part a reflection of a larger context, and one of which Christian expansion is merely symptomatic – the increased religious longing of the period Dodds (1965) famously called "an age of anxiety." The Orphic poems possess precisely this character of divine revelation, and as such their importance in pagan cult and philosophy steadily increases with time. If Orphism was the most important and oldest of the pagan revealed literatures, however, it was not the only one.[19] During this period other, new, traditions arose or were revived alongside it – or even surpassed it in popularity.

The works of various other poets, both real and fictitious, serve similarly as sources of philosophical and religious authority. In the Classical period the names of Orpheus-like figures such as Musaeus, Linus and, to a lesser extent, Olen, Pamphos, and Abaris, had attached themselves to poems related to mysteries and oracles subject to philosophical interpretation. A certain degree of specialization (as in the case of Musaeus and oracular poetry) does not conceal the evident similarities among all these mythical poets. Poetry attributed to Orpheus and to these other figures comes from oracular sanc-

---

18 Tardieu 1974, Afonasin 1998 on Clement's Pythagoreanism. On Philo, cf. n. 52 below.
19 Colli 1977 collects and comments on the most important texts of the Greek sapiential tradition.

tuaries and from mystery cults, and the patterns of similarity and difference evident in the *corpora* attributed to them correspond to those that existed among various local mysteries, myths and rituals, all of which were quite similar in content, but concern different characters and events. From the sixth century BC there were attempts to organize this diversity by placing the poets in chronological sequence or relating them to additional mystery cults, according to the particular focus of the narrator. The ancient historiographical taste for genetic continuities, whereby current institutions (e. g., royalty) are portrayed as contemporary manifestations and direct descendants of mythological predecessors, is clearly seen in the prevailing genealogical explanation of the similarities and resemblances among these poets.

The mythical poets' common descent from divine entities such as Apollo, the Muses, or the Moon meant that they were, on some level, brothers. More often, however, it was felt preferable to contrive some hierarchical principle of organization whereby one poet becomes son and inheritor of another – or, alternatively, master and disciple, a relationship which enshrines the same hierarchical structure. The genealogy in widest circulation was from an early date that which made Musaeus the son of Orpheus. Perhaps not coincidentally, the lineage Orpheus-Musaeus-Eumolpus acted as a powerful source of legitimacy for the Eumolpidai, the priestly family of Eleusis,[20] and just as the strength of Eleusinian tradition and propaganda tended to promote the centrality of figures such as Orpheus and Musaeus, so were the poets espoused by less prominent cults (Linus, Olen) gradually marginalized. Over time, these diverse local interests united into a single force when pagan reaction against Christianity raised the banner of ancient theologians as practically equivalent figures. Orpheus remains the greatest and most renowned of the ancient poets. Nevertheless, it is not unusual to find occasional references to other poets in both pagan and Christian authors, when a text attributed to them is convenient for argumentation. Quite frequently, Musaeus and Linus follow Orpheus in the enumeration of ancient theologians.[21]

If Orpheus' authority lies in large part in his divine ancestry, however, his mythological character is also the source of his greatest weakness. Whatever his pre-eminence over the other mythical poets, the historical poets easily exceed him in influence and frequency of citation. The poetry of Homer and,

---

20 Eumolpus is either the son or the father of Musaeus depending on the genealogy (*P. Cornell* 55 gives evidence of the debate among mythographers about the genealogies of the Eleusinian characters). The reorganization of the master's work could be attributed to the disciple (Musaeus in *P. Berol.* 44.4 = *OF* 57).

21 For example, Hippol. *Ref.* 5. 20.4; Clem. Alex. *Strom.* 1.14.59, Orig. *CC* 1.16, Eus *PE* 10.4.10; Greg. Naz. *Carm. quae spect. ad al.* 1570; Aug. *CD* 18.14, 18.37.

to a lesser extent, of Hesiod was subjected to a wide array of philosophical and theological readings, and despite their lesser religious reputation, the literary prestige the pair enjoyed made their writings famous throughout the Greek-speaking world.[22] Orpheus' success was also overtaken at times by Empedocles, the poet-philosopher heir to ancient Orphism, who transmits a number of Orphic images stamped with his imprint (such as e.g, 'the body is the tunic of the soul'), and whose work increases in popularity from the period of Middle Platonism onwards. One verse of Empedocles is in fact attributed to Orpheus, just as Pythagorean verses sometimes were.[23] Epimenides also appears frequently in the mentions of ancient theologians. Finally, some new poems, attributed to ancient authors, or derived from earlier poems, as in the case of the *Pythagorean Golden Verses*, gain new prestige from the third century AD for the same reason that ancient poetry is revived[24].

During this new boom in theological poetry, oracular verses, derived as they were from an authority whose divine origin was beyond doubt, assumed a new importance. Already in the Classical period, the oracles of Musaeus enjoyed a prestige parallel to that of Orpheus with regard to theogonic poetry. By the second century AD, however, the undisputed master of the genre is Apollo, in the oracles emerging from the sanctuaries of Claros and Didyma. His versified oracles not only respond to particular requests by petitioners, but can also be used in the derivation of doctrines of much wider scope, applied to the domains of metaphysics and even of politics: they played, for example, a fundamental role in justifying anti-Christian persecution. As with contemporary divinely revealed theological poetry, they offered a fertile field for philosophical and theological speculation of both pagan and Christian stripe. Several apologists, in particular Lactantius,

---

22   Lamberton 1986. Homer and Hesiod's success as religious thinkers is exemplified by their important presence in the middle-Platonist cento on the fall of the soul (cf. n. 7) from which Orpheus is absent.

23   Tertullian, *De an.*15.4 attributes fr. B 105.3 DK on the nature of blood to "Empedocles or Orpheus"; fr. B 141 DK that forbids broad beans is usually considered Pythagorean; Lebedev 1994 demonstrates that some verses quoted by Hippolytus (*Ref.* 5.8.43) that metaphorically describe a vagina, previously attributed to Orpheus, are actually from Empedocles (Kern *OF* 352; Bernabé rightly excludes them from his edition). Cf. II n. 36 on *soma chiton psyches*.

24   The *Pythagorean Golden Verses* have usually been ascribed to the Imperial Age (the first mention of them is in the third century AD), but Thom 1995, in his comprehensive study of the text, boldly argues for pushing their date back at least as far as the fourth century BC on the basis of the parallels with Chrysippus and Cleanthes. As in the case of Orphic poetry, the most probable solution is that later compositions reutilize earlier material.

make frequent use of the oracles of Apollo, together with Orphic poetry and the *Hermetica*, to show that pagan authorities also sensed the truth of monotheism.[25]

Precisely the second century AD is the probable date of composition of the *Chaldean Oracles*, a collection of oracular verse expressed in extremely obscure and abstract language, and supposedly transmitting Eastern wisdom, but really expressing middle-Platonic and Gnostic notions in hexametres. After Plotinus and his circle adopted theurgy as an epistemological principle, this collection was found to lend itself perfectly to Neo-Platonic philosophical interests and intentions, to the extent that it has often been called "the neo-Platonic Bible."[26] Indeed, these oracles were the religious poetry most esteemed by Proclus who, like the neo-Platonist Syrianus also, made great exegetical efforts to reach a concordance between Orphic poems and the *Chaldean Oracles*, very much in the same way that Christian theologians struggled with the contradictions of the different books of the Bible to integrate them into a single theological system.[27]

It was in precisely this field of religious poems that Jewish and Christian interaction with Greek hexametrical poetry was most active. Jews and Christians did not limit themselves to interpreting pagan oracles in accordance with their own convictions; they also readily composed new ones, to assert the truth of monotheism directly. As the case of the *Testament of Orpheus* (App. IX and X) exemplifies, Christians generally limited themselves to using Jewish compositions, though sometimes they also made up their own. These "forgeries" fluctuate in how they strike the difficult balance necessary between credible imitation of a pagan poem and proclamation of the Biblical revelation. A number of Apollo's oracles may be the result of apologetic intervention. However, the most favoured object of oracular falsification was the Sibyl – who began as a single individual in the Greek tradition, but multiplied over time so that by the Roman period ten Sibyls were regarded as canonical. The Senate's attempts to recompile Rome's collection of Sibylline utterances after the destruction of the original Sibylline Books in 83 BC furnishes ample evidence of the ease with which "ancient" oracles might be created and inserted into the tradition. It is probable that several

---

25 Cf. Lane Fox 1986 and particularly the monograph by Busine 2005.
26 The commentary by Majercik 1989 tackles all the relevant questions about the *Chaldean Oracles* (cf. p.2 n. 8 for the expression "neo-Platonic Bible"). Cf. Dodds 1951, 283–311 on neo-Platonic taste for theurgy.
27 Marinus, *Vita Procli* 26, 38. Affinities between the *Chaldean Oracles* and Orphic poetry are noted by Majercik in several places (1989: 164, 190, 202, 207, 210 213f, 218f, 221)

of the oracular responses recorded in this second compilation (destroyed by Stilicho in 404–408 AD) were of Jewish origin or inspiration. The surprising parallelism between some Biblical images (such as Isaiah's predictions concerning the birth of the Messiah) and Vergil's announcement in his fourth *Eclogue* – long so popular with Christian readers – of the imminent birth of a secular saviour may be due to the latter's reading of the Sibyls, for whom he expresses great veneration.[28]

The twelve books of purported Sibylline responses now known as the *Sibylline Oracles* were widely circulated. These hexameter verses – generally of a marked apocalyptic and millenarian character – appear in most cases to be the product of Alexandrian Judaism, although Christian influence is arguable in many cases and palpable in books VI, VII, and VIII.[29] These three books indicate sufficiently the inadequacy of the view that Christians do not, as a rule, forge pagan poems, but instead re-use Jewish compositions. For the same reason we shall not rule out Christian intervention in some Orphic fragments (e.g. *OF* 853). The prestige of the Sibyls, as pagan prophetesses of the truth, along with the malleability of the tradition they represented, caused their popularity with the apologists and the later Christian tradition to surpass that of all other figures of pagan antiquity. In terms of chronology, the Sibylline tradition was held to belong to the remote past and believed to reflect a source of divine inspiration independent of that of the Bible. The form in which the famous medieval hymn *Dies Irae* invokes its authority – *teste David cum Sibylla* – is paradigmatic enough. Christian authors cite the Sibyls alongside Orpheus as pagan prophets of Christianity. This juxtaposition can lead to contamination between their texts caused by their functional equivalence.[30] Such confluence between Orpheus and the Sibyls, however, is not only restricted to the Christian context. The inscription at Perinthus (*OF* 661), in which the response of a Sibyl is made to appear to allude to the Orphic theme of the creation of mortals from the striking of the Titans by lightning, has been discussed in the previous chapter. Here, our pagan prophetic sources cross-reference not the *topoi* of Biblical revelation, but

---

28   Compare *Verg. Buc.* 4.22–26 with *Is.* 9.1–11. Cf. Nisbet 1978 and Lane Fox 1986, 652. The attempt by Reinach 1900 to see Orphic roots in the fourth *Eclogue* lacked any real ground (chapter II n. 83).
29   Cf. Lightfoot's 2007 introduction to her commentary on the first two books, and Suárez de la Torre 1994 and Roessli 2004 with ample bibliography; Bartelink 1993 and Sfameni Gasparro 2002 for Christian attitudes towards the *Sibylline Oracles*, very similar to the attitude towards "monotheistic" *Orphica*.
30   Ps.-Iust. *Cohort* 16.1, 36.4; August. *Contra Faust.* 23.1.15; Lact. *DI* 1.13.11. Cf. *Protr.* 7.74.6 (*Or. Sib.* 3.624) discussed on pp. 181f.

their own religious and intellectual inheritance. The convergence of traditions found in the Christian literature thus reflects that already taking place elsewhere in Hellenic culture.

Finally, it is necessary to mention the considerable corpus of pagan texts that, despite being written in prose, was believed to have arisen by divine revelation, and was accordingly discussed frequently on the same plane as the writings attributed to Orpheus. Plato should in a sense stand at the head of this tradition, as his writings were often seen as directly inspired by a divine spirit. Most of the time, however, it was considered more acceptable to understand his philosophy as descended from some other revelation buried further in the past – a tendency into the service of which the Orphic tradition was sometimes pressed. Similar is the corpus of writings attributed to Pythagoras or his disciples, which grows incessantly from the Hellenistic period onwards, and upon which Neo-Pythagoreanism constructs an idealized Pythagoreanism in which the marks of divine inspiration are everywhere to be found. Even for Pythagoras, however, predecessors to transmit and mediate the original divine revelation are evidently considered necessary. A chain of telestic transmission that runs from Orpheus, as recipient of the initial divine revelation, to Aglaophamos, and thence to Pythagoras and on to Plato is representative of the way in which the figure of Orpheus and his poems were coordinated with philosophical writings felt to need the authority conferred by a divine pedigree[31].

Among the other writers of the Classical period promoted as recipients of divine inspiration, the figure of Pherecydes stands out prominently, his cosmological writings in prose being compared by Celsus and Origen to Christian Scriptures. The same word, γραφή, is used for both types of sacred texts (*CC* 1.16: App. VI). In the same passage we find, in addition to the well-known triad of Orpheus, Musaeus and Linus, the figure of Zoroaster. The legendary founder of the religion of the Magi, as well as other such religiously formidable figures in the Persian world as Ostanes, enjoyed not only the authority granted by direct and ancient revelation, but also the prestige of a foreign exoticism equal to, or even surpassing, that of the Thracian Orpheus. Writings circulated under the names of Zoroaster and Ostanes in various intellectual and religious circles, invoked in contexts ranging from the philosophical to the magical. The highly cultured Apuleius (*Apol.* 27) quotes Orpheus, Pythagoras, and Ostanes in succession as proof that magical practices are not incompatible with religion and philosophy. Similar fac-

---

31 Cf. II n. 128.

tors served to promote the status of Moses as a sage in some pagan circles not yet unrelentingly hostile to Christianity.[32]

The most important prose literature held to transmit divinely inspired content, however, is the Hermetic corpus, so called because it was believed to have been dictated directly by the god Hermes Trismegistus, who evidently felt no need to work through a mortal intermediary. The origin and development of Hermetic literature has been investigated in depth by Garth Fowden, whose 1986 study describes in detail the process whereby this literary religious tradition grows and develops through antiquity.[33]

The chief questions that surround the Hermetic corpus – its formal unity; its relationship to other, similar movements; the degree of correspondence between ritual description and practice; and the level of cohesion among those practicing the rites and reading the works (i.e., the extent to which "Hermeticists" might be said to exist) – are similar or identical to those associated with Orphism.[34] In fact, in the Imperial age Hermeticism functions in many respects as a religious and ideological twin to Orphism, and a number of parallels can be seen between the two movements.

The central ideas of the Hermetic corpus are similar to those of Gnosticism: the soul seeks to realize the divine principle in which it participates, freeing itself from material ties. The Greek, and especially Platonic, affilia-

---

32 Cf. the classic work of Bidez-Cumont (1938) and the recent monograph of De Jong (1997) on "hellenized Magi" such as Zoroaster. Origen in the quoted pasage (*CC* 1.17) protests against Celsus excluding Moses from the list of ancient eastern sages, which shows that his inclusion in them must have been common. His name is frequent as an authoritative source in magical papyri.

33 Fowden 1986. This work updates and surpasses the monumental work of Festugière 1949–1953 and Reitzenstein's classic *Poimandres* (1904), which compare Orphic, Gnostic and Hermetic texts. The standard edition of the *Corpus Hermeticum* and the fragments (except the Nag Hammadi three treatises = *N.H.C.* VI 6, 7, 8) is still Nock-Festugière's 1945 one. In the absence of the publication of some unedited papyri from Oxyrrinchus (I thank Dirk Obbink for allowing me to edit some of them), the only other Hermetic fragment published is *P. Vindob. Gr.* 29456r° and 29828r° (edited by P. Mahé en *Mémorial Festugière*, Geneva 1984). The *Hermetica* preserved in Arabic translation are discussed by Van Bladel 2009.

34 Fowden 1986, 189ff clearly shows the similarities and partially accepts the position of Max Weber (1922) that places the origin of the hope for salvation in a time when the elites begin to lose political power, an schaema that Bremmer 2002 applies to Orphism. The lack of institutionalization is a shared feature, and Hermeticism, like Orphism, does not seem to have been incompatible with other affiliations (Fowden 1986, 187f). The debate surrounding possible Hermetic societies is reduced to the Egyptian sphere, since it is clear that outside Egypt Hermeticism was only a literary tradition (Fowden 1986, 212f).

2. Theological texts

tions of the concept are clear. What distinguishes Hermeticism from Gnosis is its association with a purely pagan figure, Hermes, and the resulting arm's-length relationship it has with the Jewish and Christian tradition so crucial to Gnostic literature. Despite this, the overlap between the two movements is clear, as the appearance of three Hermetic treatises in the Coptic Gnostic library of Nag Hammadi shows. As in the case of Gnosticism, the similarity of cosmological and anthropological Hermetic concepts with Orphism is due in particular to Platonism's expansion and extension of Orphic ideas, and this ideological similarity facilitates a transfer of images and formulae already well-known from one to the other – the body as jail of the soul (*CH* 13.7: *soma desmoterion*) or as its tunic (*CH* 7. 2: *soma chiton*). Some difference between the two is perceptible, as Hermetic writings, just as they are composed in prose rather than verse and are free of poetic rules, disengage themselves from an immediate ritual context and range freely into speculation with more readiness than do Orphic texts.[35] If salvation in Hermeticism is attained purely through intellectual knowledge, the Orphic tradition, from the *Derveni Papyrus* to Proclus, appears never even to have contemplated renouncing or foregoing ritual – even in its least formal and most abstract form – as a means of salvation inseparable from intellection.

However, the value of the comparison with Orphism lies less in its shared focus on ideas already in wide currency at the time than in its literary genre and form. Both Orpheus and Hermes serve as founts of inspiration for, on the one hand, technical writing (in such areas as alchemy, astrology, medicine, and botany), and on the other, a religious literature transmitted, according to a *topos* it itself enshrines, through an informal yet canonical *paradosis* from master to disciple. Orpheus has the prestige of being a poet of Thracian origin, of having divine ancestry, and of being a founder of mysteries. Hermes, on the other hand, possesses the authority proper to divinity itself, and, despite the essentially Hellenic character of Hermetic thought, that derived from his allegedly Egyptian provenance – Egypt being the land deemed most suitable for revelations of religious knowledge in the ancient world. Indeed, according to one tradition, Egypt was the ultimate source of Orpheus' mystical insights as well,[36] and one of the reasons behind the

---

35 Fowden (1986, 149) aptly rules out the *Lesemysterien* imagined by Reitzenstein 1904 in which reading alone would imply an initiation. What matters in the *Hermetica* is not the initiation but the "post-cult phase of the experience of the soul". In this, they clearly differentiate themselves from the *Orphica*. Quite another matter is the fact that the *Hermetica* used initiation's metaphoric vocabulary, popular since Plato's time (Riedweg 1937).
36 Cf. p. 51. They differ in the means of revelation: Hermes would have revealed

development of the Hermetic corpus was an incipient Egyptian intellectual nationalism opposing Roman occupation. At the time the *Hermetica* played much the same role within the Egyptian intellectual tradition as did the *Orphica* in relation to the Greek mysteries: while they may not have furnished much in the way of original intellectual content, they nevertheless spoke with the force of revealed authority and the appeal of a tradition perceived as both native and primordial, moving freely in their concerns among the domains of religion, magic, and philosophy. Interestingly, Cicero in *On the Nature of the Gods* (3.56) discusses the existence of no fewer than five Hermes, and then moves on to discourse upon (3.58) the five "Dionysoi," including the 'Orphic Dionysus': evidently his source considered Hermes and Dionysus to be similar figures. Orpheus writes poems, and Hermes prose, but this is perhaps the reason why they complement each other and coordinate their spheres of action in later pagan thought so well. Hermes was to attain a greater prestige in Egyptian, Gnostic, and Manichean circles, while Orpheus was favoured by the neo-Platonists, who also cite Hermes when they feel they require Egyptian authority for their assertions. Towards the end of antiquity Hermes becomes in addition a figurehead of pagan anti-Christian resistance, undergoing a late "Christianization by opposition." The hermit Antoninus, whose spiritual lifestyle was inspired by devotion to Hermetic teachings, is the equivalent of the Orphic ascetic Sarapion in his imitation of the Christian monks.[37]

Finally, Orphism and Hermeticism at times converge to such an extent that they are no longer easily separable. Some Orphic fragments, for instance, come to be attributed to Hermes (*OF* 620, 778). This assimilation of the two traditions is found particularly in Jewish and Christian authors. To them, Hellenic and Egyptian patriotic claims are of little interest, and

---

his word in Egyptian, which would give rise to translation problems of the revealed word similar to those of the Septuagint, a problem never arising in Orphism. His favourite means would not have been books directly, but steles, traditional in Egypt, which would give evidence of their overlap with magical papyri and Gnostic literature: fr. 23, 66–67 NF, *N.H.C.* VI.6.61 (Hermetic); *N.H.C.* VII.5 (Gnostic); *PMG* 4.1115, 4.1167, 5.96, 5.422, 13.63, 7.215. Greek authors seeking authoritative sources in Egypt state that they based themselves upon steles (Euhem. fr. 36–37 Winiarczyk; Iambl. *De myst.* 1.2; Theo Smyrn. *Exp. rer. math.* 105.5; Procl. *In Plat. Tim.* 1.76.9). On steles as source of revelation, cf. Winiarczyk 2002, 100–103. Judeo-Christian tradition, with its characteristic eclecticism in adopting traditional Greek terminology, refers to the Bible using either the traditional ἱερὸς λόγος (Lampe *s. v.* 670 and Henrichs 2003) or the philo-Egyptian ἱερὰ στήλη (e. g., Phil. Alex. *De somn.* 1.17, *De spec.* 1.280).

37 Eun. *V. Phil.* VI 6.9.1, 15–17; 10.6–11.1; 11.10–12. Fowden 1986, 182–183.

they thus do not hesitate to cite Hermes and Orpheus in the same breath or to consider them on the same plane as each other.[38] Already Artapanus in the second century BC had identified Moses with Musaeus, the supposed teacher of Orpheus, and also with Hermes-Thoth, turning him into the father of both Greek and Egyptian ancient wisdom.[39] In the twilight of apologetic writings, Lactantius, the most enthusiastic proponent of Hermetic literature as a precursor of Christianity, is the most original transmitter of Orphic fragments, with the same force and intention with which he cites the *Hermetica*. Many other Christians mention the two authorities together,[40] with the result that, in a process similar to that which had already occurred with Sibylline writings, fragments previously associated with the Orphic tradition are attributed to Hermes. The three most important prophets of paganism thus merge, because their function and the content of their messages are similar.

All these trends finally work together to coalesce into a single source of pagan theology. The Neo-Platonists forced them into a unified system capable, in their eyes, of standing as an alternative to Christianity; and so too did the Christians, who find in the resulting assemblage either a monolithic enemy or a precursor to their faith. Augustine in his writing against the Manichean Faustus (*CF* 13.2) makes them serve as unwitting prophets of Christian truth:

> If the Sibyl or Sibyls and Orpheus or some "Hermes" or other, or if some poets or theologians or wise men or philosophers of the gentiles have made prophecies about the Son of God or his Father, this can serve to refute the vanity of paganism, but not to increase its authority.

The bishop of Hippo reacts this way against excessively positive Christian evaluations of pagan theology, for he perceived this as a double-edged sword that might also be raised against his own faith. But the prestige of the tradition remained even after Christian victory. The sixth-century-AD compilation known as the *Theosophy of Tübingen* collects diverse theologi-

---

38 Moreschini 2000 and Festugiere 1949–53 on Christian passages referring to Hermes, almost always in a positive light. From a similar *Aussenperspektive*, Mani referred to Plato, Hermes and Jesus as his predecessors, thus covering the three spheres, Greek, Egyptian and Hebrew.
39 Artap. *FGH* 726F 3 (cf. n. 53). Cyril (*CI* 1.48) also compares Hermes and Moses, but does not seem to follow Artapanus. *PMG* 13, 14–16 suggests that Hermes plagiarised Moses. The comparison of both figures seems to belong already to the general religious and theological environment.
40 Athenag *Leg*. 28.6, Tert. *An* 2.3, 15.5–6, Did. Al. *Trin*. 2.27, Aug. *Faust* 23.1.15 *Ep*. 234.1; Fulg. *Mit*. 3.9. Ioann. Mal. *Cronograph*. 10. 36.

cal pagan traditions that supposedly express revealed Christian truths: it includes various oracles, the works of Hermes and other Greek poets and theologians, and in addition a late version of the Orphic Jewish poem *Testament of Orpheus*, which integrates and subsumes earlier versions of the text. In this form – digested and refashioned into a single coherent *corpus* – pagan theology was recognized and valued from Late Antiquity until the end of the Middle Ages by figures such as Synesius of Cyrene (sixth century), Michael Psellus (eleventh century), and Georgius Gemistus Pletho (fifteenth century). Through them, it will be enthusiastically received by Renaissance Neo-Platonism, which then revives this perceived *prisca philosophia* as a source of knowledge complementary, or even alternative, to Christianity.

3. Gnosticism

In discussing the *Hermetica*, we have begun to approach one of the most spectacular products of the confluence of Greek and Judeo-Christian tradition, the body of thought and writing known as Gnosticism. Gnosticism is the result of the distinctive interplay of philosophical, mythological, and religious elements arising from traditional Greek myths, new mysteries and Eastern religions – including Judaism and Christianity – that emerged in late Hellenistic culture. The term "Gnosticism" is used to denote a variety of movements that sometimes seem to share very little in common, to the point that this diversity casts doubt upon the label's validity, as is the case with many other modern *-isms*.[41] The different Gnostic schools and sects (Sethians, Valentinians, Naasenians, Basilideans, Marcionists, Carpocratians, and various others) that flourished during the second and third centuries AD share a radical matter/spirit dualism that extends the Platonic dualism from which it is distantly descended to extremes never conceived of within Platonic philosophy. The shift in values is palpable: in Gnostic literature, the material world is conceived of as essentially bad or evil, and the good can only be attained through liberation from the shackles imposed by the body. In Platonic (and Orphic) writings, the material world and the body may lie far from the perfection of the divine, and they may even be obstacles for the soul in reaching spiritual perfection, but they are not essentially evil, and

---

41 On terminological problems cf. Holzhausen 2001. Williams 1996 and King 2003 have, from a post-modern deconstructionst approach, questioned the usefulness of the term: the former proposed (p. 265) to replace it with "Biblical-demiurgical", a label which has understandably had little success.

they participate, if at several removes, in the essential goodness from which they are ultimately derived. Gnosticism's fundamental and extreme dualism, however, leads to the development of novel soteriologies, fantastic cosmological hypotheses, and extremely diverse doctrines and precepts. And Christian theology was to be constructed – as was, in a somewhat similar fashion, much of the philosophy of Plotinus – to a large extent in opposition to the Gnostic tendencies of various Christian movements. Against these tendencies Christian "orthodoxy" seeks to demarcate firm boundaries – although in practice these boundaries are often more difficult to define than they are in relation to such obvious religious adversaries as paganism and Judaism. Christianity's relationship with the Old Testament and residual loyalty to its Jewish heritage brought it into frequent opposition to Gnosticism and its belief in a malevolent Demiurge potentially identifiable with the God of the Judeo-Christian Bible. After the decline of Gnosticism in the fourth century, its dualistic postulates reappeared with the rise of Manichaeism, against which the Christians fought bitterly – often not just dialectically. In one form or another this radical dualism will reappear at intervals throughout the later history of Christianity.[42]

As might be expected, Gnosticism is another area of confluence and contact between Orphic and Christian elements – a crossroads directly relevant to the concerns of several apologetic texts. Christian writers evidently became aware of several Orphic texts – and, at times, of Orphic rites – through Gnostic sources; at other times, Christians refer to Orphism in their assaults upon various Gnostic authorities. Employing a line of argument similar to that used by Plotinus when he accuses the Gnostics of debasing Greek ideas, Christians quote Orphic texts in order to prove that the Gnostics were not inspired by Biblical revelation, but had their origins in pagan philosophy and religion – which, they sometimes further add, they tend to misunderstand badly.[43] In assessing such claims, however, it is necessary to clarify the extent to which this persistent accusation reflects the presence of actual Orphic elements within Gnosticism.

---

[42] Gnostic literature was still being copied and refuted long after it ceased to have authors and followers. The Gnostic library of Nag Hammadi is dated around 400 and its most likely context was a Pachomian monastery (cf. Robinson 1996). For Manichaeism, cf. Widengren 1965. Cf. Bremmer 2002, 67–70, on Cathars in the Middle Ages and their revival of Gnostic and Orphic elements like the famous slogan *soma/sema*.

[43] Plot. *Enn.* 2.9.6, 2.9.17, as part of the vehement refutation of the Gnostics throughout the chapter. The Christian passages are quoted in n. 47 *infra* and studied in chapter IV.

Within the *corpus* of extant Gnostic texts there is only one reference – in a Sethian text quoted by Hippolytus (*Ref.* 5. 20. 4) – to Orpheus and the entire ritual and literary tradition associated with his name. Within such writings, however, debts to earlier texts are seldom explicitly acknowledged, and there are not a few ideological and intellectual similarities between the cosmogonic, cosmological, and anthropological notions which were introduced in Greece by early Orphism and the ideas expressed in Gnostic writings. The most obvious of these are a marked body/soul dualism; the posited existence of a divine principle within the soul; a desire for purification from the chains that prevent the return of this divine principle to its origin; and the image of the soul's wandering and ascent towards this goal. Such is the similarity that, just as at the turn of the twentieth century Orphism was conceived of as a forerunner of Christianity, in the last decades it has been thought to be a Gnosticism *ante litteram*. It is necessary, however, to be careful not to project Gnosticism backwards in time in order to further reinforce its similarity to Orphism. The ideological and temporal interval between the two movements is a long one. It is particularly important to recognize that this ideological connection is highly mediated, above all by Plato.[44] In his works, Plato systematizes a complex of ideas earlier linked to Orphism, and it is within this general Platonic structure that these ideas typically find expression in the Hellenistic world: a Platonic fragment in Coptic, for instance, was found in the Gnostic library of Nag Hammadi (*Resp.* 588b–589b). As a result, there does not appear to be a single Gnostic idea of philosophical or anthropological note that should be related directly to Orphism rather than to its subsequent Platonic reinterpretation and expression. One must not forget, either, the mediation of thinkers other than Plato whose influence on Gnostic texts is clear, and who were also in contact with Orphism, like Empedocles.[45] Orphism's influence on Gnosticism accordingly occurs via a circuitous route, and it is much transformed in the process.

---

44 Bianchi 1967, Crahay 1967 underline the similarities between Orphism and Gnosticism. Mansfeld 1981, and especially Turner 2001, 18–23 also remind us of the differences and the Platonic mediation.

45 In Book 3 of the *Stromata* Clement criticises the Gnostics, upon the evidence of a cento on the fall of the soul (cf. n. 7). The section on Marcion in 3.12–1-25.1 begins by saying that his roots are "Plato and the Pythagoreans", and 3.16.4 quotes the saying about the *soma-sema*, referring it to Orpheus, Plato and Philolaus. Clement then quotes several fragments that modern specialists have considered to be related to Orphism: Pindar (3.3.17.2 = fr. 137 S-M = *OF* 444), Empedocles (3.14.1 = fr. 118 D-K = *OF* 452), and Euripides (3.3.15.3 = *Polyidos* fr. 638 Kannicht = *OF* 457). Origen (*CC* 7.50) quotes this last passage approvingly. Hippolytus is also right in transmitting texts related to Orphism from Heraclitus (*OF* 455 = 22 B 62 D-K = *Ref.* 9.10.6; *OF* 456 = fr. 22 B 63 D-K = *Ref.* 9.10.6) and Empedocles

Rather than direct ideological influence, then, what one finds between the Orphic and Gnostic movements is a ready transfer of images – a transfer facilitated by the Gnostic taste for genres highly cultivated in the Orphic tradition, such as theogonies and eschatological writings. Many scholars have noted the numerous correspondences between Orphic and Gnostic theogonic, cosmogonic, and anthropological myths and in the central religious imagery of both movements: the bisexed god, the journey of the soul after death, the body as both jail and grave of the soul, the importance of *pneuma*, and others.[46] Christian attacks on Gnostic sects as rooted in Orphism in fact never cite as proof anything beyond certain literary and iconographic images: Irenaeus quotes as a precedent of Valentinian cosmology the theogony described in Aristophanes's *Birds*, generally considered a parody of Orphic theogonies; Clement refers to the *soma-sema* equivalence as an image of dualism and to the bisexed god as an image of universal generation from a single principle; Hippolytus justifies his claim that the Sethians are simply derivative of (pagan) Greek religion by reference to painted depictions of a myth.[47]

Finally, it also appears that there may in fact have been a certain dependence of Gnosticism on Orphism with regard to some elements of its rituals – in particular a central focus on a phallus or snake[48]. The continuity among mysteries, magic, and philosophy as described in the previous chapter – and particularly evident in Egypt – seems to argue in favour of the persistence of rituals; the aforementioned Orphic /Christian paintings in the Roman hypogeum of Viale Manzoni also have some "typically Gnostic" elements like black daemons moving through the air (p. 71f). It must be remembered that it is rarely possible to distinguish absolutely, in either Orphic or Gnostic writings, between imaginary/literary rituals and enacted ones, and that the ritual symbols of Orphism cited by Hippolytus are common to most of the mystery traditions. Direct Gnostic borrowing from Orphic rites or texts, therefore, must be established with caution, since there is a great risk of labelling as Orphic what already belongs to the broad tradition of vulgarized Platonism and Hellenistic mysteries.

(*OF* 449 = fr. 115 D-K = *Ref.* 7.29.14–23; *OF* 451 = fr. 117 D-K = *Ref.* 1.3.1) as possible roots of Gnosticism.
46 Bianchi 1965; Crahay 1967; Quispel 1967, 67f; 1978; Kingsley 1995; Casadio 1997; Albrile 1995, 2000, 2008; Turner 2001, 18–23; Pouderon 2003; Mastrocinque 2005, 197f; Bernabé 2008.
47 Iren. *Adv. Haer.* 2.14.1; Aristoph. *Av.* 690ff (*OF* 64); Clem. Alex. *Strom.* 3.3.17.1, 5.14.125; Hipp. *Refut.* 5.20.4.
48 The evidence of Hippolytus (*Ref.* 5.20.4) is matched by a bowl (*OF* 66 III) with Orphic verses and Gnostic imagery depicting a snake surrounded by naked people: cf. Mastrocinque 2005, 197f.

4. Hellenistic Judaism

However intense Christian contact with Orphic tradition via Greek philosophical, literary, and religious channels may have been, the principal bridge between the two is Hellenistic Judaism. Christian attitudes towards Greek culture were in large part anticipated and mediated by the work of confrontation and coexistence begun by Jewish communities – particularly that of Alexandria – from the third century BC onwards. The various processes of acculturation involved in accommodating the Jewish tradition to the Hellenistic world have been the subjects of intense and continued academic study.[49] The translation of the Bible into Greek in the Septuagint version is the first result of this process of cultural synthesis of the Classical and Jewish/Christian traditions – a process, often called "Athens and Jerusalem," which reaches a high-water mark with the Patristic writings, and that, perpetually incomplete, will remain a source of both friction and inspiration through the Renaissance and beyond until our own day.

Christianity is a movement born from a Jewish stem, and in contrast to Gnostic movements such as Marcionism, it never renounced its relationship with the revelation of the Old Testament. Although Christianity's relationship with the Jews grew more distant as it expanded further into "gentile" circles, its connection with both earlier and contemporary Judaism is close and intense during the new religion's first three centuries – particularly in Alexandria, where both Jewish and Christian communities flourished. Most of early Christian literary and philosophical production is clearly both heir and debtor to Hellenistic Judaism. Although Christian writers show themselves ready to reformulate earlier approaches, and to innovate freely with regard to their Jewish predecessors, Christianity's initial attitudes in engaging with Greek culture and religion, and in particular with Orphism, are to a large extent derived from principles originally elucidated by Jewish thinkers.

The most important figure of Hellenistic Judaism, and the most influential upon later Christian writing, is undoubtedly Philo of Alexandria in the first century AD. His stamp, by virtue of chronological and geographical proximity, is most clearly seen on Clement of Alexandria – and can thus also be perceived upon most of the Hellenization of subsequent Christian literature.[50] His intense dialogue with Greek culture has a theoretical rather

---

49 The updated edition of Schürer (1973–87) and Hengel 1975 are the classic studies of Hellenistic Judaism. Gruen 1998 offers several new insights on the culture of the Jewish Diaspora in the Roman Empire. Cf. Jakab 2001 for Jews and Christians in Alexandria.
50 Van der Hoek 1988 on his influence on Clement. Riedweg 1987 provides evidence of his role as key link between Plato and Clement.

than propagandistic motivation, and perhaps because of this we find in Philo no direct allusion either to Orpheus or to Orphism – which was, at any rate, in the first century AD at the lowest ebb of its prestige, as we saw at the end of Chapter II. Only in his use of the language of the mysteries can one find allusions to Bacchic frenzy, ecstasy and similar concepts. Such terminology, however, belongs to the Platonic tradition of expressing philosophical knowledge through the metaphor of a mystic initiation and does not presuppose that Philo knew any actual Bacchic mysteries.[51] Also, the Pythagorean influence that some later authors, like Clement of Alexandria, saw in Philo is ultimately equivalent to Platonism and does not necessarily imply connexion with Orphism.[52] In the writings of his near contemporary, the historian Flavius Josephus, we similarly find reference to neither the literary nor the ritual aspects of the Orphic tradition. In fact, Josephus denies (*Contra Ap.* 1.12), following Herodotus and Aristotle, the existence of any literature prior to Homer, which would include Orpheus.

To find Jewish connexions with the Orphic tradition, one must turn not to theologians or historians, but to the fragmentary writings of the so-called Jewish apologists, between the third century BC and the first century AD. The Jewish apologists (Artapanus, Theodotus, Ezechiel, and Aristobulus are the best known) have some clear differences with their Christian continuators. As Erich Gruen (1998) has vividly described, they are reluctant to engage in direct confrontation with Greek culture. Instead, they try to link it to their own tradition, in order to secure for Jewish culture a prestigious place within the Hellenistic world, in which many different peoples are suddenly forced to coexist. Conspicuous examples of the means used to attain this prestige include such cultural phenomena as the *Letter of Aristeas* and the falsification of the Spartan genealogy: the former constructs an idealized legend of the translation of the Septuagint that legitimizes it as inspired Scripture at the same level as the original Hebrew text, while the latter makes the Lacedaemonian kings dependent upon Israel. In search of both internal cohesion and external prestige, the Jews of the *oikumenē*, in common with almost all Hellenistic cities and states, participate in the tendentious manipulation of historical facts and the creation of a variety of

---

51 Cf. Riedweg 1987. Scott 2008 discusses Philo's Bacchic imagery in his description of the *therapeutai* in *De vita contemplativa*, although he assumes with excessive confidence that Philo purposefully makes them analogous to actual practitioners of Dionysiac cults.
52 Runia 1995 convincingly interprets in this way Clement's references to "Philo the Pythagorean" (*Strom.* 1.72.4, 2.100.3), although he does not rule out the possibility that it is grounded on Philo's fondness for mystic numerology.

apocryphal literature. Such propaganda was typically produced largely for internal consumption – for the Jewish community itself, so as to strengthen its unity in the face of a Hellenistic "globalization" that threatened to dissolve weak identities. External audiences would presumably be reluctant to accept such campaigns at face value, as each community fabricated its own history using strategies that were similar and often produced mutually incompatible mythographies. Concern for historical veracity and for successful persuasion of external readers were not so important as an overriding interest in internal consistency. At this point, Orpheus emerges as a central character playing a very significant role.

Chronology, for any culture within the Hellenistic *oikumenē*, was a vital instrument of historical insertion. Although Rome and its legend of Aeneas is the best-known example of this technique, the foundation narratives of many Greek cities and states, such as those of the Ptolemies, are just as important. The need for retroactive legitimization was even more pressing with regard to the Jewish population, whose status as the chosen people, ideologically elaborated through several centuries, made the maintenance of internal cohesion a religious imperative. It is from this need that the famous theory of the dependence of Greek wisdom on Biblical revelation, whereby all the most valuable aspects of pagan Greek culture had ultimately been derived from the prophets of Israel, first arose. This notion that the Greek poets and philosophers took all their knowledge from biblical Revelation secured in the first place the historical and cultural supremacy of the Jewish people, and furthermore justified its participation in the wider Greek culture; after this, it was necessary only to assemble the missing links necessary to make the theory plausible, if only on a purely artificial and rhetorical level. The complexity and often-excessive character of these manipulations demonstrates that veracity and *prima facie* credibility were not the ultimate goals of such narratives. Rather, it was their aptness and 'fit' within a rhetorically coherent discourse that played the more important role.

The tradition claiming that the Greek wise men found the source of their knowledge in the Middle East and Egypt has roots at least as old as the tales of Herodotus. As evidenced by the scarce references collected by Guy Stroumsa (1999), the Jews did not particularly stand out among these ethnic groups prior to the Hellenistic search for Eastern insight. Yet it was not difficult for Jewish apologists to insert Israel to the old tradition. Egypt was an ideal place to establish a historical link between the revelation to Moses and Greek wisdom: Moses' presence in Egypt is the keystone of Jewish history, while the Greek need for a divinely inspired source of knowledge located this in Egypt. Once the geographic framework had been established,

Orpheus conveniently steps in to assist in organizing the chronological structure of transmission. The story that linked him to the land of Egypt was commonly known and easily exploitable, since its vague and flexible chronology allowed considerable latitude for bringing Orpheus into connection with Moses. Artapanus extends this theory to its extremes, playing with the phonetic resemblance between the names of Moses and Musaeus in order to identify them, and then inverting them from the traditional order of Orpheus-Musaeus in order to convert Orpheus into a disciple of Moses.[53]

Once the Scriptures had been translated, the adaptation of Jewish history to patterns offered by Greek literary genres provided another form of Jewish enculturation. Ezechiel (second century BC) structures the history of Exodus as a tragedy. The genre of theological literature is even more fruitful for exploitation. As we have seen, a collection of oracles of Jewish fabrication, which attained enormous success, was attributed to the Sibyl. In the same way, supported by the chronological scheme described above, Orpheus turns into a pagan prophet who brings the Biblical message to the Greeks in their own language and style. Imitating the style of the Orphic poems, a well-known Jewish poem popularly called the *Testament of Orpheus* (*OF* 377, 378) depicts the singer renouncing polytheism and proclaiming only one God. This text and similar ones resonate, as we shall see, throughout Jewish and Christian works; however, there is not a single indication of them having crossed the boundaries of apologetic literature into more general circulation. This leads one to conclude that their purpose was to motivate a pre-existing community and convince its members of their cultural superiority, rather than to convince an outside audience.

These historiographical and literary achievements, whatever their tendentious nature, required a certain skill and preparation. Refined falsifications of works such as the *Testament* demand good direct knowledge of the Orphic poems to be imitated. Alexandria was an ideal location, providing materials and methods for the Jewish apologetic enterprise. The library of Alexandria offered space for intense historiographical activities. Aristarchean philology, furthermore, was developed within its walls. We do not yet know much about the relationship between Alexandrian philology and its Jewish counterpart, the aims of which were very different. Yet Jewish scholars did not hesitate to adopt the materials and imitate the methods of

---

53 Artapanus, *FGH* 726F 3 *apud* Eus. *PE* 9.27. This identification must be considered as playful experimenting with tradition-shaping, since Artapanus also equates Moses with Hermes/Toth. Cf. Gruen 1998, 159: "Artapanus did not anticipate conversion by Greeks or delusion by Jews. He relished the process of inverting and reshaping traditions." Cf. Gruen 1998, 159; Siegert 2005, 142–147.

their Alexandrian counterparts.[54] As we shall see, some Christians enthusiastically followed them in this apologetic usage of philological techniques.

In addition to this "orthodox" literature, however, in which the lines of demarcation among various religious movements are clearly drawn, there exists a significant area of Greek and Jewish religious confluence in which Orphism can sometimes be seen to assume a leading role. Some Orphic poetry quoted by Christians betrays markedly Jewish perspectives or concerns, whether this arises from Jewish interpolation and falsification, from Jewish influence on Orphic material, or from Orphic influence on essentially Jewish texts (*OF* 414, 620, 691). We shall study all this material in the next chapter. However, for the nature of such texts to be understood, the processes of influence, syncretism, and assimilation – processes in many cases foreshadowing Christian developments – facilitating Jewish-Greek convergence in closely related cultural areas must be explored in more detail.

First, the Jewish Diaspora does seem to have increased the degree of Jewish influence observable in pagan cults in the eastern half of the empire. It has been suggested, for instance, that the increasingly moral tenor of pagan cult prescriptions for ritual purity seen from the late Hellenistic period onwards is due to the influence of Eastern cults, Judaism among them. This is possible, though it is not always easy to isolate the effects of Eastern influence from those of philosophy, or from the internal evolution of Greek religious practice itself. The clearest cases are those in which the coincidence of ritual details is so precise that the influence of the local Jewish colony on pagan cult worship is the most economical solution. As noted above, similar doubts surround the possible condemnation of abortion found in the katabasis of the *Bologna Papyrus*. Given the lack of corroborating details and the fragmentary condition of the papyrus itself, the moralizing character of the prescriptions for ritual purity is not, *per se*, enough to postulate Jewish or Christian influence upon this Orphic poem.[55]

Jewish influence, in fact, is more readily perceivable in the sphere of theology than in relation to regulations regarding moral and ritual purity, since its strict monotheism seems to have appealed to various cults and

---

54 Honigman 2003, Niehoff 2007.
55 On the Bologna Papyrus, cf. pp.39f (with Shanzer 2009). Two inscriptions from Asia Minor dated to the Imperial period, *IG* XII 787 (Prott-Ziehen 148) and *IG* III 74 (Prott-Ziehen 49), prescribe the same number of purification days for menstruation and birth as in *Leviticus* (7 and 40 respectively). Wide 1909 refuted the idea of Reinach 1906 that the taboo on abortion in these inscriptions was Orphic (once again a mere projection of Christianity) and posits a plausible Jewish influence for this prescription.

groups similarly committed to the notion of a single supreme deity. Groups of pagans with religious inclinations close to Judaism sometimes associated themselves with local Jewish communities, and this kind of Jewish acolyte – from the ranks of which came many of the earliest converts to Christianity – is likely to have acted as a connection to other Greek cults. A recent study by Stephen Mitchell, for instance, clearly establishes that the pagan cult of Theos Hypsistos – a single and transcendent deity, whose name could not be spoken – was the result of strong Jewish influence on pagan culture in Asia Minor.[56] This is the most spectacular example of Hellenic adoption and appropriation of Jewish beliefs. However, the presence of Biblical ritual and theological elements, particularly the use of the name "Iao" – evidently connected with "Yahweh" – in religious and magical papyri of Imperial Egypt, makes clear that this Judaizing influence spread through many other religious and literary circles in which Orphic elements also appear. The existence of Jewish elements is furthermore well established in Hermetic and Gnostic literature, where the influence of Orphism has already been noted. The existence of an Orphic-Jewish or Jewish-Orphic syncretism is a practically inevitable conclusion given such trends.

Ideological assimilation is of course a bilateral process, though ancient apologetic writings tend to transmit only cases of Jewish influence spreading outward to affect the Hellenic culture around it. This bias creates the impression of a Judaism kept free of syncretistic contamination and exerting its energies in a purely unidirectional fashion. It is true that Jewish orthodoxy grows more and more passionate over time in its exclusion of Greek influences: for example, the translation into Greek of the Bible becomes more literal from the Septuagint until the absolutely literal translation of Aquila. However, the strict boundaries set by orthodoxy and apologetics are artificial, and it is not unlikely that users of many of the Orphic-Jewish syncretistic texts were in fact Jewish themselves, or very close to Jewish communities. The motivation behind the reaction of those Jewish purists who resist Hellenic thought and culture, and the work of those internal apologists who seek to reaffirm the strength of orthodox doctrine to the faithful, appears to lie precisely in fear of Jewish religious identity being lost against this syncretistic background. The entirely reactive character of the movement, however, attests to the great fluidity of actual religious practice. It is the

---

56 Mitchell 1999, who moreover puts forward the suggestive idea that the altar to the Unknown God before which Paul speaks in the Areopagus (*Act.* 17.28) belongs in fact that to this Theos Hypsistos. In opposition to this unifying view of the cult to Theos Hypsistos, Belayche 2005.

same situation the Christian apologists will later confront when they come to polemical attack against a nascent pagan-Christian syncretism – whose strength is revealed not only in the direct references made by the apologists themselves, but also in the vitriol with which they decry it.

It is in Palestine that the dramatic ambiguities in religious cult and belief of the time are revealed in greatest detail, and in particular in the cult of Dionysus. The cult in question is connected specifically with Bacchus' role as god of wine, and while we do not have sufficient evidence to link the cult – universal throughout the Mediterranean – with the mysteries or with the Orphic tradition, the Jewish attitude towards it is precisely the same as is found in relation to cults of a more explicitly Orphic flavour. The presence of the Bacchic cult in Palestine and the assimilation of Bacchus to Yahweh are very well attested,[57] and it is presumably because of the pervasiveness of such syncretism that contemporary denunciations of Bacchic rituals are so harsh. When Antiochus Epiphanes established the worship of Dionysus in his attempts to Hellenize Judea in 167 B.C. (2 *Mac* 5–6), he was doubtless trying to institutionalize an already-existing syncretism for political self-interest. His attempt was nevertheless condemned by the ultimately prevailing orthodoxy of the time as "the abomination of desolation" (*Dn.* 12:11). The *Wisdom of Solomon*, the last canonical book of the Old Testament, was written in Alexandria in the first century BC and harshly criticizes the Bacchic *teletai* (*Wis* 12.3–7). Dionysus becomes, in this account, the heir to the Baal of the Canaanites, an object of worship whose relationship to Yahweh was marked, on the evidence of the Old Testament synthesized in the classic work of Ranier Albertz (1994), by a similarly widespread syncretism existing in the face of constant official condemnation. Pagan authors such as Plutarch, Valerius Maximus, and Tacitus differ on whether the Jewish Yahweh should be identified with the Greek Dionysus.[58] The Orphic tradition does not appear to play any direct role in this process of assimilation and separation, but the tendency to Bacchic assimilations should be borne in mind when attempting to explain the absence of Dionysiac elements from those aspects of Hellenic culture ultimately accepted into Jewish orthodoxy. From its perspective, the most similar is the most dangerous, for it tends most powerfully towards uncontrolled assimilation.

---

57 Corn. Lab. *apud* Lyd. *De mens.* 4.53, Macr. *Sat.* 1.18. Origen *CC* 6.32 strongly condemns this syncretism. There is also evidence in inscriptions (Zeegers 1972, 213, n. 2). Cf. Chadwick 1966, n. 7 and above all, Smith 1975, the most complete study on Dionysus' presence in Palestine. Cf. some additional bibliography cited by Wick 2004.
58 In favor, Plut. *Quaest. Conv.* 4.671c–672b, Val. Max. 1.3.3; against, Tac. *Hist.* 5.5.5. Cf. Nieto Ibáñez 1999.

4. Hellenistic Judaism

One may attempt to differentiate from this kind of clear-cut syncretism some instances of cultural assimilation which attest a much more managed process, guided by an orthodoxy that sought to hellenize Judaism while preserving its inner core. External accommodation to the Hellenistic cultural milieu may be in principle distinguished from actual cultic syncretism. For example, when Philo depicts the community of Jewish *therapeutai* as if they were initiates in the Bacchic mysteries, such assimilation is purely an external metaphor that does not mean that these *therapeutai* adored Bacchus in any way.[59] However, such clear distinction is not always conceptually fixed. The figure of Orpheus, precisely, offers an excellent example. There is one possible textual instance of an external assimilation between David and Orpheus. Psalm 151 in the Septuagint version talks about David – the putative author of the Psalm – praising God with his lyre. The Psalm was only known in its Greek translation until 1965, when the Hebrew version discovered in the manuscripts of Qumram was published. This purported original version has two lines (2b–3) which are absent from the Greek version: *"And [so] have I rendered glory to the Lord, thought I, within my soul / The mountains do not witness to him, nor do the hills proclaim; the trees have cherished my words and the flock my deeds."*[60] These lines that state the power of the singer over nature suggested from the beginning that there was a conscious appropriation of the myth of Orpheus, the singer who enchants nature, to depict David's song. The reading and translation of these lines is, however, very controversial, and this interpretation has been hotly debated.[61] However, the fact that the Greek version of the Psalm lacked precisely those two verses may be a sign of some censorship of unclear lines whose assimilation of a Greek myth may have been excessive for the orthodox Jewish translators.[62]

Whatever the facts of the case of Psalm 151, this presentation of David as Orpheus is clearly found in several images found in synagogues of the eastern Empire – the most famous being the frescoes of Dura-Europos in the third century AD and a mosaic in Gaza of the sixth century AD. King

---

59 Cf. n. 51 *supra*.
60 Translation from the edition princeps of the Psalm by Sanders 1963. For other proposed translations, cf. Roessli 2008b. The lines are also absent from the Latin, Syriac, Coptic, Ethiopic and Arabian versions, which are all derived from the LXX.
61 Rabinowitz 1964 denies the reference to Orpheus. Stern 1974, Smith 1980, among others, support it. For a thorough *status quaestionis*, cf. Vieillefon 2003, 105f, and above all Roessli 2008b, who states the common scholarly opinion with a cautious "perhaps". The reference to Orpheus, however, would not imply any assimilation of Orphic-Pythagorean ideas, which are very far from Qumran.
62 Such is the tentative suggestion of Roessli 2008b.

David is depicted as Orpheus, surrounded by the animals he has attracted to him with his voice. It is clear that the iconography of the singer whose music pacifies those who hear him is perfectly adapted to the representation of David, whose music cured the mad soul of King Saul (1 *Sm.* 16:23).[63] The Orpheus myth furthermore occasions the depiction together of various animals who, in listening to the musician's song, forget their natural enemity and live together in harmony – an image characteristic of the Golden Age that the prophets announced would witness to the restoration of David's kingdom (*Is.* 9:1–11). This kind of appropiation of Greek myths to Jewish contexts can be hard to distinguish from free-flowing mutual syncretistic exchange. In fact, the following discussion of Christian encounters with Orphic tradition expands the problems raised by the Jewish evidence.

5. Assimilation and syncretism

The question of Orphism's direct or indirect influence upon Christianity has been a subject of study and debate since the nineteenth century. The opposite influence is also probable in some cases. These topics will be dealt with at the end of chapter VI. For the moment I will confine myself to discussion not of their forms and degrees of influence upon each other, but only of those issues in which deep or superficial resemblances between the two traditions led to assimilation or syncretism between them – the cultural background against which many of the Christian apologetic texts must be read. As in the case of Judaism, some relevant evidence concerns Dionysus, and some Orpheus. Let us examine it in this order.

The parallels between Dionysus and Christ, from the most superficial to the deepest levels, have been subject to intense and imaginative study by many modern authors. The affinities of the individual experience of both deities fostered a long history of competition and parallelism between them.[64] Some passages in the New Testament show a clear Bacchic flavor, although of course Dionysus is never named as such. The Gospel of John shows Christ in clear competition with the wine-god,[65] and the Acts of the

---

63 Cf. Vieillefon 2003, 94f, Stern 1958, 1970; Roessli 2008. Eisler (1925, 3) mentioned (and drew) a painting of Orpheus in a Jewish catacomb of Vigna Randanini in Rome, of which there are no traces.
64 On the common traits of Hellenistic deities, including Dionysus and Christ, cf. Versnel 1990. Still in 617 AD the Synod of Trullo was still resolving to extirpate the practice of the *teletai* of Dionysus.
65 The most relevant passages are John 15:1: "I am the true vine", and the wedding

Apostles unequivocally echo Euripides' *Bacchae* in some passages.[66] As we shall see in the following chapters, these parallels were also seen by some Christian apologists, with varying attitudes. The Bacchic myth is denounced by Justin as a Satanic plagiarization of Christian theology and ritual. On the other hand, Clement of Alexandria, following Philo's example, depicts the mysteries of the Logos as the true Bacchic mysteries, using Euripides' *Bacchae* as the template on which he builds his spectacular *peroratio* in the last book of the *Protrepticus*. Their respective treatments reflect condemnation of equating Dionysus and Christ and their rites, along with acceptance of assimilating Dionysiac imagery. An even more illustrative instance of controlled assimilation is the cento probably composed by Gregory of Nazianzus known as the *Christus Patiens*, which relates Christ's Passion in a tragedy composed almost completely of Euripidean verses.[67] Though Christ's resurrection, for instance, is announced with lines taken from the *Bacchai* (*Chris*. *Pat*. 2530–2574), this text does not posit a syncretistic fusion of Christ and Dionysus into a new figure such as Serapis; rather, it serves as a presentation of Christ in Bacchic colours. The Christian tale is presented in the Euripidean manner, but its contents remain the same. Probably Gregory saw his perception of Christ's death and resurrection well represented by the intense Euripidean depiction of the Dionysiac experience, but he, like the author of the *Acts of the Apostles*, does not even name Dionysus, who in no way is identified with Christ. The same occurs with Orpheus in the exordium of the *Protrepticus* (cf. App. I): Clement presents Christ as the new Orpheus while he condemns the old one, and he draws the line with extreme care so that no confusion between them is possible.

---

at Cana (Jn. 2:1–11). Cf. the recent analysis, underlining the Jewish precedents, by Wick 2004, with previous bibliography.

66 The most evident echoes from the *Bacchae* are the earthquake which liberates both Dionysus (*Ba.* 585) and Paul and Silas (*Acts* 16:25–26); the sudden fall of the chains (*Ba.* 447s, *Acts* 12:7); the θεόμαχος fighting against the new deity (*Ba* 45, 325, 1255; *Acts* 5:39); and the expression "kicking against the goads" (πρὸς κέντρα λακτίζειν: *Ba.* 795 and *Acts* 26:14) to designate the futility of opposing the new god. Seaford 1997 studies these parallels, though his idea of ritual as the basis of continuity is not convicing. The parallels probably proceed from conscious or unconscious literary influence. Tueller's unpublished thesis (1992) has very interesting literary comparisons between Jesus and Dionysus as "new gods".

67 After four centuries of harsh disputes, scholars (Tuilier 1969, Trisoglio 1996) tend to defend the traditional attribution to Gregory of Nazianzus instead of a later Byzantine author. Perhaps the work was inspired by Clement's drawing on the *Bacchai* at the end of the *Protrepticus*. *Cf.* Kott 1973, 200f, comparing the prayers of the chorus asking for Dionysus' arrival with medieval Christian hymns or Biblical passages (Is. 53:1) of similar tone.

All these neat distinctions of apologetic texts become immediately blurred when we approach the evidence unburdened by polemical purposes, which shows the fluid situation on which apologists try to build their conceptual walls. Though we find no direct iconographic identification between Dionysus and Christ, there is significant evidence for Dionysiac imagery in Christian contexts. In the previous chapter, for example, we mentioned the two Egyptian funerary cloths with Dionysiac and Christian scenes buried in the same tomb and an Orphic/Gnostic scene among Christian ones on the walls of the hypogeum of Viale Manzoni at Rome.[68] Visual art gives in fact the most reliable portrait of the mental situation of viewers of all religions in the Late Roman Empire. However, for many years the consideration of iconography was subordinated to that of texts – and often to the same ideological prejudices that haunted philologists and historians. As a consequence, textual categories were applied to the iconographic evidence: the discussions of the evidence presupposed that iconography was firmly pagan, Jewish, or Christian, and at the very best, syncretistic. Today, however, these axioms have been called into question, and the interpretations of the evidence have become more varied and subtler.[69]

One of the best-known examples of such complexity is the famous "Christian Orpheus." There are indeed a great number of Christian representations of Orpheus (or of Christ as Orpheus) in Christian art. Orpheus playing the lyre surrounded by animals is first found near the beginning of the third century AD, in the frescoes of the Roman catacombs (see e.g. plate 1) and in sarcophagus reliefs. According to the traditional interpretation, these images portray Christ with the iconographic attributes of Orpheus that were so fashionable as decorative motifs in Late Antiquity: a Phrygian bonnet, a lyre, and an audience of animals listening to him spellbound. The image is found later in several grand mosaics, most of them in the eastern part of the Empire, and in some Coptic textiles.[70] In the Byzantine period it also spread

---

68 Cf. pp. 61, 71.
69 The latest works by Jas Elsner fruitfully develop this fluid approach: cf. Elsner 1995 (251–60, 271–9) and 1998 (218–220) for evidence that resists firm classification as pagan or Christian; Elsner 2003 for a revisiting of Jewish and Christian art as separate categories, a division in which many distorting ideological prejudices are implied.
70 The Christian representations of Orpheus have produced an immense bibliography. Among general studies, cf. above all Panyagua 1967, Stern 1974, Skeris 1976, Murray 1981, Pringent 1984, Jesnik 1997. There are many studies on particular images or regional representations (cf. e.g. von Falck 1992 on Orpheus in Coptic art). All of them have been recently studied by Vieillefon 2003 (with full bibliography): shorter but useful recent overviews are Vieillefon 2005 and Roessli

to manuscript miniatures. The lyre-playing Christ of many medieval sculptures is a famous direct descendant of such iconographic identifications.[71] According to many interpreters, their clear precedent and inspiration is the Orpheus-David figure found in Jewish mosaics and frescoes, a theory which seems to find support from sound textual evidence. At the beginning of the *Protrepticus* (1.5.), Clement of Alexandria, possibly inspired by iconography, makes David the link between Orpheus and Christ. The assimilation of these three figures in literature, as in art, will become topical with time[72]. However, such a plain genealogical model may not necessarily be true, since the preserved Jewish representations of David as Orpheus are in fact later than the Christian ones. They may have been independent iconographic developments out of the traditional Roman model, and cross-influence among pagan, Jewish and Christian art, which often came from the same workshops, must be taken not as an exception but as a likely possibility in many cases.[73]

The variety of the evidence makes any unitary explanation insufficient. However, an illuminating perspective has been recently suggested by the French art historian Laurence Vieillefon in her comprehensive analysis of the iconography of Orpheus in pagan and Christian milieus. She argues that in both cases the meaning of Orpheus is similar, a symbol of universal harmony, with vague associations of immortality and salvation, and suggests that even in Christian paintings and mosaics his image is not used to represent Christ, but a divine man (*theios aner*) as in pagan imagery.[74] The famous Orpheus-Christ of the catacombs would be, in fact, just Orpheus. Vieillefon's is a bold departure from earlier scholarship and, although it cannot become the sole interpretative key to all the Christian images of Orpheus throughout the Empire, may be fruitfully applied to many central cases like the paintings in catacombs.

2008a. New evidence is continuously uncovered by archeology: the latest piece is a funerary mosaic in a Christian catacomb of the fourth century in Leptiminus (Tunisia). Cf. Ben Lazreg 2002, Vieillefon 2003, 126; 2005, 993.

71   On the medieval tradition of Orpheus-Christ, Goldammer 1963 (particularly the Ravenna mosaics), Friedman 1970 (with the introduction of J.-M. Roessli to the French edition of 1999), Vicari 1980.

72   Stern 1974. As Roessli 2008a points out, George Pisides in the seventh century calls David "*the Orpheus of the Lord*" (*PG*, 92, col. 1437ff). Euthymios Zigabenus (twelfth century: *PG* 128, col. 41), "*our Orpheus*".

73   Cf. Elsner 2003 on this continuity, which makes artificial both Stern's (1974) assumption that Jewish iconography of Orpheus is the immediate precedent of Christian art and Vieillefon's (2003, 106) assumption that it is not.

74   Vieillefon 2003, 148–154. In her article of 2005 she summarizes the argument, restricting her analysis to house mosaics.

It is in fact indisputable that some Christian images of Orpheus certainly do not depict Christ. A ring (plate 2, p. 126) kept in the British Museum and tentatively dated to the fourth or fifth century AD in Asia Minor shows a schematic image of a singer playing the lyre before a number of animals, the whole scene being circumscribed with the legend ΣΦΡΑΓΙΣ ΤΟΥ ΗΑΓΙΟΥ ΙΟΑΝΝΟΥ ΣΤΕΦΑΝΕΤΟΥ ("The Seal of St. John Stephen").[75] The ring thus presumably served as a seal to mark items as the property either of an individual or, more likely, of a monastery or other similar community. Rather than some special relationship between St. John and the myth of Orpheus – for which we have no other testimony than the ring itself[76] – the seal proves the popularity of the image of the singer in Christian circles. Clement of Alexandria recommended that Christians should use as seal symbols "a dove, or a fish, or a ship scudding before the wind, or a musical lyre, which Polycrates used, or a ship's anchor"[77] – and the British Museum seal shows that the assertion is not the result of mere whim on Clement's part, but reflects actual practice in using the lyre as a Christian symbol.

Among the Christian iconographic uses of the image of Orpheus there is also some evidence that shows that Adam among the animals in Paradise is represented following the pattern of Orpheus surrounded by them.[78] This type of iconographic composition will be much used in the following centuries in order to depict scenes of Paradise-like nature as settings for other holy men like Saint Francis of Assisi.

The singer Orpheus, therefore, may have been identified with David, Christ, Adam or other Biblical characters in many contexts, but even when his image is found in unequivocally Christian evidence, this is by no means

---

75 *OF* 679 II; *LIMC s. v.* Orpheus 166; Stern 1974, 16; Godwin 1981, 98.
76 The only study dealing with the seal at some length (Godwin 1981, 98) states that it is due to the proximity of St. John to pagan theology. Apart from the vagueness of this statement, if St. John is the name of a monastery, it does not imply the existence of any specific Johannine theology in the fourth century.
77 *Paed.* 3.11.59. Both Kern (T 152) and Bernabé (*OF* 1089) include it as an Orphic fragment, although its direct relation to Orphism is unclear. The prohibition of carrying the image of a god on a seal, which Clement quotes approvingly in this passage, in *Paed.* 3.18.84 and in *Strom.* 5.28.4 (in contrast to Mosaic law), was characteristic of Neo-Pythagorism: Iambl. *VP* 35.256, Plut. *Quaest. Conv.* 652 (a question, unfortunately fragmentary, dedicated specifically to this issue), Porph. *VP* 42, D. L. 8.17, Macr. *Sat.* 7.13.11. Cf. Chadwick 1966, 147, n.163. Eizenhofer 1960 has studied the text in detail and concludes that the lyre and the ship do not have clear Christian precedents, which could allow us to suspect a pagan origin.
78 An ivory statuette in Bargello and a mosaic in Huarte, Syria. Cf. Vieillefon 2003, 90f; 2005, 993.

the only, nor even the principal, interpretation of his figure. Probably many viewers thought of Christ when looking at his image in Christian contexts (Clement probably was one of them), but many more must have seen, first and foremost, what the artist had painted: the Thracian singer. A second question, however, arises immediately, and fosters corresponding academic discussions: is this Orpheus to be given a religious meaning, or is his function merely ornamental?[79] This is not a specifically Christian debate, for the same problems arise with pagan iconography, like for instance the frescoes of the Villa dei Misterii at Pompeii, where the Bacchic paintings pose similar questions.[80] The arguments for the purely decorative interpretation are very solid: the representation of the myth made it possible to unite in a single subject a multitude of exotic and savage animals and natural motifs of great decorative effect; poets like Vergil and Ovid had made it into a great literary subject in connection with the bucolic imagery that appears in these representations; and, above all, the myth of Orpheus the singer had never been closely united to his role as theologian and patron of the mysteries, whether in literature or in iconography.[81]

On the other hand, it is naïve to suppose a complete lack of religious significance, as also is the case with Jewish representations of David with Orpheus's traits. The effects of both personages' music had some coincident aspects: King David was a citharist and singer, and he knew how to free Saul from madness with his music (1 Sm 16.23). The posited salutary effects of music upon the soul and as a means of communion with God are undoubtedly one of the points that serve to promote the popularity of the myth of Orpheus and of his instrument. Jewish and Christian adaptations of neo-Pythagorean images in this sense show how widespread such conceptions were

---

79 The debate is more than a century long. Against Heussner 1893, who denied the connection to Orphism, Eisler 1925 was the scholar who most earnestly tried to identify the myth of the singer with the mysteries, in order to postulate a religious sense in the Christian use of the image. His approach was met with scepticism by Boulanger 1925, Stern 1974, Skeris 1976, among others. Cf. Roessli 2008a, Vieillefon 2003 and 2005.
80 Cf. chapter II n. 92.
81 The only text that firmly unites the two facets, making the content of Orpheus's song the mysteries themselves, is precisely that of Clement's *Protrepticus*, but the clear apologetic intention of this strategy is not present in the iconographic representations. Rather than Clement's text, their parallel is Eusebius's *De laudibus Constantini*, which makes rhetorical use of the same motif, but without any apologetic intention, and in which the religious dimension is conspicuous by its absence. Cf. Appendices 1 and 2.

in many cultivated circles regardless of religious affiliations.[82] Music as a means for bringing the soul nearer to God takes on an increasing importance in primitive Christianity, and Orpheus in his aspect as an exceptional musician can hardly be thought of independently of this. Even without linking them to Orpheus, the popularity of the symbols of the plectrum and the lyre among the Christians is long-lasting. In addition, the messianic prophecies of a Golden Age brought by a descendant of David, in which "the wolf and the lamb, the panther and the kid, the calf and the lion" would graze together (*Is.* 11:6), had a clear possibility of iconographic representation in the myth of the singer who attracts the animals. The confluence of these prophecies with the bucolic tradition is obvious beginning with Vergil's *Fourth Eclogue*, which makes use of precisely these images to announce a new Golden Age and which will be the subject of enthusiastic Christian interpretations as a pagan announcement of the Messiah's birth.

Orpheus's function in these representations is doubtless much more than merely ornamental. Catacombs and sarcophagi, as places of burial, invite thoughts about the Beyond; the Golden Age acquires in Christianity a primarily eschatological dimension; music has an evocative power that leads toward mysticism; and the association of Orpheus the singer with other aspects of the same personage, as founder and poet of the mysteries or even as author of "monotheistic" poems, may have occurred not only to Clement, but also to other observers of the images, or to the artists themselves. However, there is no surviving evidence that permits us to go beyond the free association of ideas: if the presence of one element of Orphism does not necessarily entail the presence of all the rest, still less does it do so in the case of Orpheus the singer, whose separation from the religious themes of the Orphic tradition is evident and broken only by Clement's apologetic strategy, which is not a source of inspiration for iconography but rather, on the contrary, is inspired by it. Boulanger said (1925, 163), "The citharode of the catacombs is not the doctor of Orphism, the prophet of immortality and of monotheism." Eighty years later, we still believe he was right.

However, the Apollonian singer who enchants nature with his music, and who can be conveniently assimilated to biblical characters when needed, is not the only dimension of Orpheus. In sharp contrast with these bucolic images, there is another piece of evidence testifying to a Late Antique tendency to fuse the figures of Christ and Orpheus in a very different direction. The famous – if unfortunately lost in the Second World War – Seal of the Museum of Berlin (pl. 3), produced in all likelihood originally at Rome, depicts

---

82 Cf. the discussion in pp. 211ff, and Skeris 1976.

a crucified figure crowned by seven stars and surrounded by the inscription ΟΡΦΕΟΣ ΒΑΚΚΙΚΟΣ; furthermore, this description closely matches that of two other gems catalogued by Italian collectors in the eighteenth century.[83] The fusion of Orpheus and Christ into a single figure is different in kind from the iconography that could vaguely associate each with the other, and likewise from the aforementioned St. John seal and similar representations; rather, it is similar to contemporary iconographic evidence of Orphic-Mithraic syncretism that identifies Phanes with Mithra (plate 4). Three religious elements from three different domains are brought together here: speculation about the stars[84], the figure of Christ, and the figure of Orpheus, here appearing already not as a musician but as a Dionysian character of special power.[85] The adjective *bacchikos* indicates that the one represented on the cross is not a god (*Bacchos*), but a follower of the god – if one nevertheless sufficiently important to be crowned with stars and to stand as the protagonist of a piece of personal jewellery, the function of which was possibly to protect its user. That such an image exists in more than one copy indicates that this was not an isolated case, but that the synthesis of the two divine figures had spread to some extent. The misspelling ΟΡΦΕΟΣ for ΟΡΦΕΥΣ – presumably the result of retranscription from Latin – reveals that the artisan's knowledge of Orpheus and his theology was not very deep.[86] This piece belongs to the world of elemental magic, not of elevated speculation. It serves, however, to confirm that the common elements between both figures were sufficient for

---

83   *OF* 679: despite earlier suspicions of forgery of the seal, Mastrocinque 1993 has given definitive arguments for its authenticity based on the autograph descriptions of F. Buonarroti and F. Ficoroni in the eighteenth century. Cf. also Carotta 2009. Vieillefon 2003, 83 still prefers to take it as a forgery, in accordance with her thesis that Orpheus is not iconographically assimilated to Christ in any case.
84   Markschies 2005 suggests that the seven stars could be referring to the cosmic lyre. On the connexion of stars and music, with some references to Orphic texts, cf. Csapo 2008. An astrological interpretation cannot be discarded either: some astrological poems were attributed to Orpheus.
85   Eisler 1921, 54; 1925, 338 proposed a purely pagan origin for this gem upon the basis of the legend of Lycurgus' crucifixion (D. S. 3.65.5). However, Justin (*Apol* 1.55) states that the only thing that the pagans never dared to imitate was the crucifixion. It is true that the other representations of Christ crucified are later, but this may be due to chance, since the cross has been a central motif of Christianity since its origin.
86   Markschies' suggestion (2005, 244, n.61) that it could be read as a genitive, "The Bacchic one of Orpheus," seems to me very implausible. He relates it accordingly (p. 246) to Justin's accusation that Dionysus' death plagiarized Christ's (*Dial.* 69,2; *Apol.*1.54.6). Doubtless due to a misprint, Markschies speaks of Orpheus death instead of Dionysus'.

them to be perceived as a unity: undoubtedly, the story of Orpheus' violent death at the hands of the Bacchants is crucial for their identification. Celsus (*CC* 7.53) explicitly compares Christ to Orpheus: "If you do not like Heracles and Asclepius and those who have been glorified since antiquity, then you have Orpheus – who, as everyone recognizes, possessed a divine spirit (*hosion pneuma*), and who also died violently."

As Celsus' text shows, the main factor that serves to assimilate Christ and Orpheus is their shared character as mediators between the divine and human realms – i.e., their status as *theioi andres*.[87] Such "divine men" acquired enormous importance in the spiritual world of Late Antiquity. These "pagan saints" could be men from the past like Plato or Pythagoras, or even contemporary men like the miracle-worker Apollonios of Tyana. As we saw in chapter II, the prestige of Orpheus as a divine man was *in crescendo* from the second to the fourth centuries AD. From a pagan viewpoint, Jesus Christ could also be one of these divine men. That is the reason why fusion is more easily achieved in relation to a man, Orpheus, than it is with a god, Dionysus, who, as we saw, tends to be identified rather with Yahweh. Jesus is also compared to other mythical deified men like Heracles, the Dioscuri, and Asclepius, as well as to historical figures like Apollonius of Tyana. The *Historia Augusta* tells that the emperor Alexander Severus worshipped Orpheus, Abraham and Christ at his private altar. This eclectic religious attitude does not identify the three figures, but takes them all as similar and inter-compatible semi-divine men. That a Roman Emperor was known to put on the same level such different *theoi andres* testifies that their superficial veneration was not restricted to low magic[88]. Religious syncretism arises from precisely this kind of superficial awareness, which obviates prolonged or deep enquiry into the differences between the various figures it reveres. It is probably this easy slide towards deification that motivates Augustine's clarification that (*CD* 18.14) "these theologians (Orpheus, Linus, Musaeus) founded the cults of gods; they are not worshipped as gods." On the other hand, at the highest level of abstraction – for the philosophers and apologists – this prestige

---

87 On the holy men of late Antiquity, cf. Anderson 1994, Fowden 1982, and Brown 1982.

88 Hist. Aug. *Alex. Sev.* 29.2–3; cf. 31.4–5 (Vergil, Cicero, Achilles and Alexander the Great were also venerated by Severus). Some other sources elevate Orpheus to the category of god or demi-god, or, at least, recipient of cult, in line with Alexander Severus: Cono (fr. 1.45.6), Plutarch (*Alex.* 14.5), Arrian (*Alan.* 1.11.2), Pseudo-Callisthenes (1.42.6), Pausanias (3.20.5, 5.26.3, 9.30.4), Lucian (*Adv. Indoct.* 109), Philostratus (*VA* 4.14), Tertullian (*De an.* 2), Athenaeus (24.632c). Cf. *OF* 1052.

could serve to turn Orpheus not into an equivalent or complement to Christ, but rather into his pagan alternative or rival.

There seems to be *prima facie* a clear difference between the syncretism between Orpheus and Christ evident in the Seal of Berlin and their eventual iconographic assimilation in some Christian catacombs and mosaics. The representation of Christ in iconography or literature with some or all of Orpheus' attributes does not mean a fusion of both characters into a new unity. It implies only that both share some important features in common that allow the former to borrow some of them, without changing his personal identity. This is especially true of the figure of the singer, a motif of very broad application: Fronto compares Marcus Aurelius' task as Emperor to the singing of Orpheus in much the same manner as Eusebius does with regard to Christ in the *Laudes Constantini*.[89] In sharp contrast with these cases, the Berlin Seal freely mixes so distinctive and apparently unique an element as the Crucifixion of Christ with the distinctive traits of other deities, up to and including the personal names (Orpheus and Bacchus), and the resulting amalgam really does posit their complete fusion into a new and syncretic character, just as occurs with purely pagan composites such as Zeus-Helios-Mithras-Phanes.

Assimilation vs. syncretism; Apollonian Orpheus vs. Bacchic Orpheus; Orpheus vs. Orpheus/Christ. Such distinctions may appear too fine-grained and artificial, but they are not just the product of modern scholarly concerns. As we shall see, they have a central place in the apologetic agendas of many Christian authors. These categories were probably more interesting for intellectuals like Clement than for the average spectator of the frescoes. Clement's firm rejection of any identification of Christ and Orpheus, alongside his explicit endorsement of a depiction of Christ as divine singer, betrays a great deal of effort spent to maintain the subtle line that differentiates both types of approach to the assimilation of Christ and pagan figures. However, in the reality outside of the apologetic texts, these two neat solutions, pure syncretism or purely external assimilation, are the two extremes of a very wide range of possibilities, of which the hitherto discovered evidence only shows the tip of the iceberg. The Christian images of Orpheus also corroborate the idea that fixed labels like "pagan" or "Christian" were not at all clear in day-to-day fluid practice. The efforts of apologetic literature to fix these boundaries are better understood in this light.

---

89 Front. *Ep.* 4.1 (cf. Portalupi 1985); Eus. *Laud.* 15.5.15. The topos of the ruler bringing peace as Orpheus had a great continuity well into Late Antiquity: cf. Stoehr-Monjou 2005 for its presence in Dracontius' *Romulea* (fifth century AD).

126 III. Fields of intersection

Plate 1: Orpheus in the Catacomb of San Pietro e San Marcellino in Rome (third century AD).

Plate 2: fourth- or fifth-century-AD ring from Asia Minor with the inscription "Seal of St. John Stephen" (*British Museum*)

Plate 3: Seal (lost in 1945 in the Berlin Museum) with the inscription "Orpheos Bakkikos" (*OF* 679 I)

Plate 4: Orphic/Mithraic relief, second century AD (Modena, Museo Comunale)

IV. Orphic Tradition in Christian Apologetic Literature

1. Apologetics in the second to fifth century AD

Let us now explore the origin and meaning of the appearance of Orpheus, his poems, and his rites in Christian sources. After the analysis of the testimonies of pagan non-apologetic sources in the last chapters, the reliability of Christian references for our knowledge of Orphic tradition can be solidly checked. Furthermore, these texts will be the basis of the next two chapters on Christian strategies and visions of Orphism.

Before undertaking a thematic analysis of Christian texts, it seems necessary to introduce the main authors with whom this chapter is concerned, beginning with an explanation of the rubric under which they are discussed. In the history of ancient Christian literature the authors subsequent to the New Testament are conventionally divided into three principal generations – the Apostolic Fathers, the Apologists, and the Church Fathers. Here, however, the label 'apologetic' will be used in a fashion that traverses all three categories. For the purposes of this study, "apologetic literature" consists of writings that undertake confrontation with paganism.[1] These works often present Christianity to a non-Christian public, at least in terms of their rhetorical form – for as is discussed below, the declared and intended audiences of apologetic literature are not always identical. Because of this rhetorical focus, apologetics follow certain specific strategies, the analysis of which requires the comparison of works separated from each other by up to three centuries and expressing very diverse theological ideas. Their form is usually highly polemical, typically contrasting Christianity and paganism, with the latter being portrayed as an enemy to be combated. Nevertheless, some texts also search for common ground between the two opposed camps. It is within this general context of presenting Christianity and confronting its rivals that each and every appearance of Orpheus and Orphism in Christian writing of the second to fifth centuries occurs. Only much later – when pa-

---

1   On the lives, works and thought of these authors, cf. von Campenhausen 1967 Among the most recent general studies on Christian apologetic, see especially Friedrowicz 2001, Pouderon 2005, *Entretiens Hardt* 51 (2005), and those edited by Pouderon and Doré (1998) and by Edwards, Goodman, and Price (1999).

ganism was extinct and apologetics no longer necessary – is any reference made to Orpheus or his works that does not ultimately have these two aims in view. Most of the authors considered here are among the so-called Apologists. However, some of them, such as Gregory of Nazianzus or Augustine, clearly belong to the generation commonly referred to as the Church Fathers. Because the principal interest of this investigation lies in their apologetic works rather than their theological ideas, however, I believe that they are appropriately discussed here under the general title given above – though of course their apologetic is typically expressed in terms consistent with their larger theological concerns. The term "apologists" will be thus used for convenience in its broadest sense.

We must also recall that these Christian works are in intimate relationship both with the antecedent tradition of Jewish apologetics and with contemporary pagan anti-Christian authors.[2] Orphism plays a very specific role in both, which illuminates certain tendencies within Christian literature. Continuity with pagan and Jewish works is not only a matter of strategies and approaches – as we shall see in chapter V – but also of shared materials and texts. In addition, Christian apologetic literature is often based on previous works of many different kinds, some of which do not spring from Jewish or anti-Christian authors. When tackling all these sources, it must be remembered that there are many different types of relationship between texts. On the one hand, there is direct dependence, a technique similar to modern "cutting and pasting." On the other hand, as Annewies van der Hoek (1996) points out, a more subtle and nuanced version of the same method occurs when an author takes notes while reading or relies on a more or less precise recollection of the text. Thus, the intellectual transmission of Orphic tradition becomes increasingly complex in the process of the interweaving of different interests and approaches, and *Quellenforschung* seldom arrives at more than excessively broad suppositions. For instance, the circulation in Jewish and Christian circles of pagan texts in anthologies intended to refute paganism makes it difficult to determine in each case whether the apologists directly depend on each other or are using common sources, and whether (or how far) the pagan texts are authentic or apocryphal. Detailed and careful philological analysis will often be unable to go beyond probability.

---

2   Zeegers 1972 shows that most apologetic poetic quotations come from Jewish anthologies. Regarding the continuity of the *Testament* in Christian authors cf. Riedweg 1993, and Friedman 1970, 13–38. Cf. n. 59 *infra* on the common pagan source of Firmicus Maternus and the *Wisdom of Solomon*.

The number of strata accumulated between the composition of Orphic texts and our Christian sources makes it advisable to undertake the analysis of Orphic texts in thematic order, according to their subject-matter: the figure of Orpheus; Orphic cults; Orphic theogonies; Orphic poems about God (or interpreted as such by Christians); Orphic texts subject to diverse interpretations; and Orphic texts about the fate of the soul. Before undertaking such analysis, however, it will be useful to begin with a brief, roughly chronological overview of the twenty Christian authors who are most relevant for this study. Ten important texts too long to be cited in the corresponding sections are offered in the appendices.

JUSTIN (early second century–163?) is the first of the apologists to allude to the Orphic tradition. After having passed through different philosophical schools (Stoic, Peripatetic, Pythagorean, and Platonic), this Samaritan of Roman origin converted to Christianity, where he found complete answers to his intellectual and spiritual demands. He died as a martyr under Marcus Aurelius. As Henry Chadwick (1966) vividly described, Justin's optimistic attempts to reconcile Platonic metaphysics and Stoic ethics with Christian theology contrast with his absolute condemnation of pagan cults. Two of his works are preserved: the *Dialogue with Trypho*, in which he converses with a Jew about the Christian fulfilment of the Scriptures, and the two parts of an *Apology* directed to a pagan audience. In both he mentions the mysteries of Dionysus as an example of pagan borrowing from Christian beliefs. There is no evidence to suggest that his acquaintance with Orphism was anything other than literary.

Justin's prestige made him a popular name to which several anonymous apologetic works could be attributed. In this pseudoepigraphic *corpus* (conventionally known as PSEUDO-JUSTIN), two works contain important Orphic quotations. *De monarchia* is a brief work, probably written by a Jewish author between the first century BC and the first century AD, that accumulates Greek literary quotations, among them the so-called *Testament of Orpheus*, in order to prove the existence of monotheism in Greek culture.[3] The work popularly known as *Cohortatio ad Graecos* has much greater importance for this study. It was produced by a Christian author – if one inspired by Jewish sources including the *On Monarchy* itself – whom Christoph Riedweg has plausibly identified as the fourth century theologian Marcellus of Ancyra.[4] The *Cohor-*

---

3   Riedweg 2001. According to Zeegers 1972, 253, the common source would be an anthology of examples of alleged Greek plagiarism of Biblical revelation. Cf. pp. 180, 186 on the mutual relations of apologetic writings, using the *Testament of Orpheus* as example.
4   Riedweg 1994 provides a commented edition, in which he argues that the true

tatio audaciously seeks to demonstrate the dependence of the Greek poets and philosophers on Biblical revelation, relying on the argument that they became acquainted with it during Egyptian sojourns. Orpheus is one of the author's favorite poets: he quotes at length the *Testament* and another three Orphic fragments of great interest, not transmitted in other sources: the first discusses Orphic henotheism, the second refers to creation by the Word, and the last attempts to show that Homer was dependent on Orpheus. The *Cohortatio* is an important direct source of Cyril's *Contra Iulianum*.

TATIAN (*c.* 120–180), of Syrian origin, is the author of a *Discourse against the Greeks*, one of the most violent Christian attacks on Greek culture, which he considers – unlike Justin, with whose work he is evidently familiar – to lack any value when compared to Gospel truth.[5] His radicalism pushed him to extreme positions, such as Encratism. In the *Discourse* (or *Oratio*), Orpheus' antiquity is used to prove the foreign origin of Greek wisdom, and Orphic theogonic myths are taken as examples of the impiety of Greek religion.

It is commonly believed that ATHENAGORAS (second half of the second century) lived in Athens. He is the author of a *Legatio* or *Plea for the Christians*,[6] rhetorically composed as what would now be termed an "open letter" addressed to the emperors Commodus and Marcus Aurelius, where he tries to convince the emperors that Christians do not in fact practice the crimes of which they were often accused, such as atheism, parricide, and incest. He presses these same charges against the Greek poets and philosophers, because they claim that the gods are of material origin, and therefore cannot live forever, and furthermore commit acts unworthy of divine beings. He draws many examples for his case from the Orphic *Theogony of Hieronymus and Hellanicus*.

---

title of the work is *Ad Graecos de vera religione* and attributes it to Marcellus of Ancyra at the beginning of the fourth century. His arguments are persuasive; for ease of reference, however, the work will be cited here under its traditional title of the *Cohortatio* and ascribed to Ps.-Justin.

5 The *Discourse* is a possible source for Clement, since both (Tat. *Orat.* 41 and Clem. Alex. *Strom.* 1.21.131.1) make the same mistake of placing the Peisistratids in the 50th Olympiad.

6 Pouderon (1998) affirms that the treatise *On Resurrection*, of disputed authorship, is rightly attributed to Athenagoras and suggests that it may have been composed in Alexandria, validating the late tradition that Athenagoras was the founder of the Catechetical School in Alexandria. With regard to quotations from Orphic sources, however, the flimsy continuity of Athenagoras with Clement and Origen fails to support the hypothesis – which has at any rate garnered little support.

THEOPHILUS, a bishop of Antioch living at the end of the second century, left a single work – an *Apologia to Autolycus* in three books. Its main topic is the inferiority of Greek culture with regard to Biblical revelation.[7] Theophilus denies that Orpheus discovered music, and quotes the *Testament*.

CLEMENT OF ALEXANDRIA (mid-second century to early third) is the author most crucial to this study, for he attributes the greatest significance to the Orphic tradition both as a representative of Greek religion and as a pagan forerunner of Christian truths. The only information we have regarding his life is provided by Eusebius (*PE* 2.2.64), writing a century and a half after Clement's death. There is no reason to doubt Eusebius' assertions that Clement was born in Athens to a pagan family and was later converted to Christianity. By contrast, the claim that earlier in his life he had been initiated into mysteries appears groundless, as will be discussed in more detail later. Clement's writings display great training and skill in philosophy and rhetoric. After having learnt from his teacher Pantaenus, by 180 he was living in Alexandria, where he taught and composed many important writings.[8] His three main works are the *Protrepticus*, or *Exhortation to the Heathen*, inviting the pagans to convert to Christianity; the *Paedagogue*, outlining a norm of ethical behavior for the good Christian; and the more extended and varied work entitled *Stromata*, depicting the spiritual life of the "true Gnostic." The apparently interlocking structure of these three texts has led critics to believe that with these works Clement intended to create a trilogy, a project he seems to allude to at the beginning of the *Paedagogue* (1.1–3). It is not clear whether the *Stromata* are in fact the *logos didaskalikos* envisaged here, an attractive enigma that has fuelled an extended and heated debate among critics.[9] In any event, Clement's most important Orphic references are found in the *Protrepticus* and the *Stromata*.

In the *Protrepticus* Clement adapts a traditional philosophical genre following all the rhetorical conventions of a suasory discourse.[10] It is built upon

---

7   On Theophilus' attitude towards Greek culture, cf. Zeegers 1999.
8   Beautiful introductory pages in Chadwick 1966, 31ff. On his philosophical and theological thought, cf. now Osborn 2005 and Feulner 2005. On the Alexandrian Church, cf. Jakab 2001.
9   Cf. Osborn 2005, 2–25 and Feulner 2005, 38–47. Chronologically, Clement could have read Celsus or a similar critic, although this is not specifically mentioned (Chadwick 1966, 49). Apart from the above-mentioned texts, Clement's extant works are the essay *Who Is the Rich Man That Shall Be Saved?* and the surviving fragments of *Eclogae Propheticae* and *Excerpta ex Theodoto*.
10 The reference edition is still Stählin's of 1905. Marcovich's (1995) is too speculative to be reliable. A work of such potential interest to both Classicists and specialists in Ancient Christianity furthermore deserves a detailed commentary – a project

the basic and well-established structure *exordium – refutatio – argumentatio – peroratio*, and within each section Orphic elements play a fundamental role. In the *exordium*, Orpheus's old song is juxtaposed against the new song of Christ (Book 1), who is thus presented as a new Orpheus, bringing true religion instead of false superstition; the *refutatio* opens with sharp criticism of Orphic mysteries (2.12–22); at the end of the *argumentatio* Clement proves by means of the *Testament* the conversion of Orpheus himself (7.74.3–6); and in the *peroratio* he casts light upon the proclamation of the mysteries of Christ using Bacchic and Eleusinian terminology (12.119–122). In exhorting the reader to conversion, Clement clearly delimits two symmetrical and antagonistic fields, with the mysteries of Orpheus representing a unified paganism and those of Christ being depicted as their rival. The *Protrepticus*, therefore, offers a fertile field for the analysis of apologetic strategies, as well as much and varied information on Orphism, revealed here not only in its pagan context, but also in its interactions with Christian self-conceptions.

The *Stromata* – the traditional title being adopted here in preference to the equally valid *Stromateis* – is a much more complex work. It is addressed to both a pagan and a Christian readership, with different sections clarifying the means by which the "true gnostic" gains knowledge of God in a manner that varies with the presumed background of the reader. Orphic references are concentrated in Books I, V, and VI. Book I focuses on chronology, while Book V and the beginning of Book VI focus on closely interrelated matters and are similar in many respects. In both these books Clement quotes a number of pagan writers in order to support symbolic interpretation of Scripture and to stress the dependence of the Greeks on the Biblical prophets. In addition, Book III is to a significant extent dedicated to a refutation of the Basilidian Gnostics, in the course of which some indirect references to Orphism occur.

The Orphic fragments in these two works naturally raise the question of Clement's sources. Salvatore Lilla (1972) recognizes three principal currents of philosophical thought in his work: Middle Platonism, Gnosticism, and the Jewish tradition. All three may be recognized in the use he makes of Orphism, which also shows that Clement had close contacts with Neo-Pythagoreanism.[11] Regarding Clement's written sources, it will be patent from his use of treatises on the mysteries, on symbolism, and on plagiarism that he had strong ties to Alexandrian intellectual and scholarly circles. Or-

---

      in which I am currently engaged. On the protreptic genre, cf. van der Meeren 2002 and Van der Hoek 2005. Steneker 1967 makes interesting stylistic observations.

11   Tardieu 1974 and Afonasin 1998 are the only studies on Clement's Pythagorean connections.

phic fragments transmitted by Clement are usually believed to have their origins in the *Rhapsodies* supposedly written in the first century BC; it will be shown, however, that most of these citations were taken from Orphic poems prior to the *Rhapsodies* i.e. of Hellenistic date.

TERTULLIAN (*c.* 160–220) was born in Carthage to a pagan family and studied there to become a jurist. Around 197 he converted, to become one of the most prolific writers of Latin Christianity. His command of rhetoric brought him fame and success. His extremist ideas led him into Montanism, from which he later separated to found his own small movement. Three works from amongst his voluminous writings are relevant here. In the *Ad nationes* and *Apologeticum* he defends Christians against accusations of infanticide and incest, launching counter-accusations against paganism and attempting to convince the authorities to treat the Christians with respect. In the *De anima* he outlines his concept of the soul and refutes all theories contrary to his beliefs, such as the doctrine of transmigration. Among his sources is Clement of Alexandria, and he himself becomes in turn a source of inspiration for subsequent Latin African writers such as Arnobius, Lactantius and Augustine.

HIPPOLYTUS OF ROME (second half of the second century–236) was a presbyter of great eloquence and energy, whose doctrinal rigidity came into full frontal collision with the nascent Church hierarchy. Like the other great western theologian of the second century, Irenaeus of Lyon[12], he wrote in Greek on many different subjects. His only work transmitted in its entirety is *On Christ and the Anti-Christ*. As an apologist he was largely concerned to refute heretics with Gnostic tendencies, a task which is best exemplified in the extant portion of his *Philosophoumena*, also known as *Refutation of All Heresies*.[13] Hippolytus' principal argument rests on the claim that heretical and Gnostic doctrines are ultimately derived from pagan philosophers and mysteries. As in his arguments against the Naasenes, where he conveys crucial information on Eleusis, in his refutation of the Sethians he accuses them of having their origins in the Orphic mysteries, in a passage that is every bit as interesting as it is textually corrupt.

ORIGEN (185–253) appears as the most significant figure in the Alexandrian school after Clement, although he spent the second half of his life in Asia Minor, and Caesarea in particular. Apart from his many Scriptural and

---

12 Irenaeus is conspicuously absent from this list because he makes no explicit Orphic references (cf. p. 217, and III n. 47 on his criticism of a parodic Aristophanic theogony).
13 The only manuscript was first edited in 1951, the most recent edition being that of Marcovich 1986. The most thorough study of this work as a heresiological source is Mansfeld 1992.

theological works, some of them lost in whole or in part because of subsequent condemnation of his ideas (the *De principiis*, for instance, in which Origen accommodates reincarnation to Christian soteriology, exists only in the fragments translated by Rufinus in the fifth century), his literary legacy includes an apologetic text conceived towards the end of his life, *Contra Celsum*, an extended refutation of the attacks of this early pioneer of anti-Christian writing. This work is crucial not only because in it Origen deploys the strongest and most trenchant arguments of Christian apologetic, but also because he thereby reveals the nature of the criticisms he was concerned to oppose. Although Origen knew Orphic literature only indirectly – through references in philosophical works – the *Contra Celsum* provides some significant passages regarding Orphism which come both from Celsus' search for Greek alternatives to Christianity and from Origen's responses.

ARNOBIUS OF SICCA (second half of the third century) was a distinguished orator from proconsular Africa and a convert to Christianity. An active if not exalted participant in pagan controversies in his early life, his *Adversus Nationes* presents a vigorous attack against paganism in which he deploys all the power of his baroque style; in spite of his rhetoric, the accuracy with which he reflects his sources is highly appreciated by historians of Greek and Roman religion. The refutation of Porphyry permeates the entire work. In Book II he focuses on him, while in Books III and IV Arnobius is chiefly informed by the antiquarian work of Cornelius Labeo. The Orphic passages are concentrated in Book V, dedicated to the Greek mysteries. In the section dedicated to further discussion of Arnobius it will be argued that Clement's *Protrepticus* serves as Arnobius' primary source, although he complements this with details taken from other sources and his own general culture. This question, however, is not uncontroversial, and some scholars think that Arnobius' sources were other than Clement.[14]

EUSEBIUS OF CAESAREA (260/5–341) is one of the most prolific and important Christian writers. His life and works spanning the period before and after the Edict of Milan (313), he marks the shift between the time of perse-

---

14 Jerome (*Chron. s. a.* 325–326) provides a detailed account of his conversion and the composition of his work, which Simmons 1995 has shown to be largely accurate. The bishop of Sicca demanded an attestation of Arnobius' conversion; in response Arnobius, having earlier employed the arguments of Porphyry when he was on the pagan side, attacked them in his work of apology (cf. e.g. in Book VII he uses the arguments of Porphyry's *De abstinentia* against those expressed in the *Philosophia ex oraculis* in order to attack animal sacrifice). His work has been preserved in a single manuscript that presents significant textual problems. Mora 1994 has studied in detail Book V, on mystery cults.

cution and the Constantinian period. He was involved in various theological controversies both before and after the Council of Nicaea (323). Although at one point accused of Arianism, Eusebius signed the Council resolutions and became, in a move that was to define his subsequent career, a protégé of Constantine – upon whom he lavishes unstinting praise with regard to his position as protector of the Church and Emperor on Earth, whose rule resembles that of God over heaven. Out of all his works, three are particularly relevant for us. In *De laudibus Constantini* he presents an unusual perspective as he develops a metaphor of Christ as Orpheus, the inspiration of which he found in the *Protrepticus*, although Eusebius adds significant modifications. In the *Praeparatio Evangelica* he presents a large compilation of theological and apologetic arguments and texts, some of which are his own, and many more of which are borrowed from earlier authors. Eusebius' scholarly bent means that he cites texts written by others with great philological precision. He accordingly transmits all the Orphic passages found in Clement and in many other authors, such as the Jewish apologist Aristobulus and the Neo-Platonist Porphyry. Finally, another treatise addressed to a wider and more popular audience, the *Theophany*, integrates themes taken from the *De laudibus* with arguments from the *Praeparatio Evangelica*, with a newly aggressive rhetorical stance reflecting the Christian triumphalist mood after the Edict of Milan. Although Eusebius does not have direct knowledge of Orphic tradition and does not add new information to previous authors, his works reveal how old apologetic topoi can be given new orientations.[15]

LACTANTIUS (*c.* 250–325) is in some ways Eusebius' counterpart in the Western empire, both thinkers bridging the gap between the pre- and post-Edict periods. Converted to Christianity in his native Africa (where he was a disciple of Arnobius), Lactantius travelled as a professor of rhetoric and Latin with the Imperial Court to Nicomedia in the east and Trier in the west.[16] His *Divinae Institutiones*, conceived before the Edict of Milan (after which they are updated in the *Epitome*), are discourses upon diverse theological and apologetic matters, while the contents of the *De ira Dei* and *De mortibus persecutorum* disclose the level of vindictiveness that could be found in certain sectors of the post-Constantinian Church. His Orphic references, however – concentrated in the *Divinae Institutiones* – display a sound knowledge of

---

15 *Cf.* Kofsky 2002 in general on Eusebius' apologetic work, and in particular 276–311 on the *Theophany*. Almost all of this work is preserved in Syriac translations quite true to the Greek originals, of which some fragments are preserved.

16 Ogilvie 1978 reviews Lactantius' sources. He seems to know directly Orpheus the Sibyls, and Hermes Trismegistus. On the parallels between Lactantius and contemporary Gnostic and Hermetic thought, see Wlosok 1960.

the *Rhapsodies*. Lactantius' use of Orphic material is, furthermore, groundbreakingly open-minded: not only is Lactantius the only author to draw some explicit positive parallels between Orphism and Christianity with regard to their portrayal of God as the uncreated Creator; more importantly, he ascribes such insights to Orpheus' reflection and natural reason alone.

FIRMICUS MATERNUS (mid-fourth century) is unknown to later tradition, and we accordingly know of him only what can be concluded from the two works attributed to him, the *Mathesis* and the *De errore profanarum religionum*, which do indeed appear to have been written by the same author, since they present detailed stylistic similarities otherwise difficult to explain. The former, pagan, work explores astrological matters; the latter, a violent assault upon paganism, was composed after his conversion, and it seems as if it had been written to atone for his earlier beliefs. Firmicus' Orphic intertexts in the *De errore* – although direct quotation of Orpheus is lacking, thematic coincidences are obvious – suggest parallels with Clement and Arnobius, although their precise relationship is far from clear. Firmicus is extremely fond of euhemerist versions of pagan myths, including Orphic ones, that allow him to criticize gods as divinized humans.

ATHANASIUS (296–373), bishop of Alexandria, is one of the great doctors of the post-Nicaean Church. In his only reference to Orpheus, Athanasius opposes a contemporary Egyptian trend, well documented in the papyri, whereby traditional paganism *per se* was dwindling, but magical practices were freely incorporating elements from different religions, including Orphism.

DIDYMUS THE BLIND (310–395) also lived in Egypt during the *floruit* of the Alexandrian Church and was head of its Catechetical School for almost half a century. The greater part of his work is lost, the result of the accusations of heretical Origenism later lodged against him. His only reference to Orpheus appears in a theological treatise entitled *De Trinitate*, in which he purports to find evidence of Biblical elements – in particular, the Holy Spirit – in pagan poetry.

EPIPHANIUS (after 310–403), born in Judaea, was a monk in Egypt and later bishop of Salamis in Cyprus. His principal work is the *Panarion* or *Medicine*, where he launches a vigorous attack against diverse heresies, especially those derived from the ideas of Origen. Epiphanius himself admits that his knowledge of the doctrines and cults he criticizes so vehemently is rarely direct, and that he instead relies upon oral reports and literary sources.[17] Later in this study his most explicit reference to Orphic rites will be shown to be derived entirely from Clement; yet he also offers a unique testimony

---

17 At *Panar.* 71 he acknowledges that his arguments are based on hearsay, the point being confirmed by Sozomen in *Hist. Eccl.* 7.40.

concerning a pagan Alexandrian ritual containing elements of late Christianization of Orphic tradition (p. 372).

GREGORY OF NAZIANZUS (325–389) was son of the bishop of Nazianzus in Cappadocia (Asia Minor). As a young man he studied rhetoric in Caesarea, Alexandria, and Athens, where he made contact with other Christian theologians – most notably Basil of Caesarea – as well as with neo-Platonic philosophers, including the future emperor Julian. After fulfilling a great variety of roles, ranging from hermit all the way to bishop of Constantinople, he returned to his birth-place of Arianzus, where he completed most of his poems. His numerous other works can broadly be divided into epistles and discourses. Throughout his writing in these three genres, crafted with great literary quality and theological precision, Gregory proves himself one of the most accomplished writers of Late Antiquity along with the other Cappadocian Fathers, Gregory of Nyssa and Basil. In his apologetic work, his attacks on Orphic myths and cults appear to be largely based on bookish knowledge; some elements, however, betray knowledge of actual practices deeply rooted in this particular area of Asia Minor.[18]

JEROME (347–420) was born in Pannonia and completed the greater part of his outstanding literary work in Palestine. He refers to Orpheus very briefly in two chronological allusions and once more in connection with vegetarianism. His awareness of Orphism is obviously purely scholarly, the result of some readings rather than direct contact.

AUGUSTINE (354–430) is a figure of fundamental importance to the Western Church of the fifth century, as the Cappadocian Fathers are in the Eastern Church. Having gone through several religions – in particular Manicheanism – in his native Africa, he converted to Christianity in Milan under the influence of Ambrose. His autobiographical work, the *Confessions*, offers a glimpse into his brief but crucial passage through Neo-Platonism as he describes the process of his conversion. After baptism he returned to Africa, where he became bishop of Hippo Regius. Orphic references in his works are naturally concentrated in pieces with apologetic tendencies, most notably *Contra Faustum*, written against the leading Manichean of the time; *Contra Iulianum Pelagianum*, in which he defends himself against accusations of Manicheanism lodged against him by a leader of the Pelagians, a movement later declared to be heretical; and the *City of God*, which presents the history of salvation,

---

18 Cf. Demoen 1996 on Gregory's knowledge and use of Greek literature. On his probable authorship of the cento *Christus Patiens*, cf. III n. 67. In Herrero 2007b I have demonstrated that the critique of the doctrine of reincarnation expressed in his poem *De anima* appears to be aimed at the Orphic *Rhapsodies*, along with Empedocles and Pythagoras.

in a formulation that would have lasting impact, as that of a conflict between the *Civitas Dei* and the *Civitas impiorum*. In these works Augustine presents Orpheus as the principal theologian of pagan belief, and he treats him with considerable mistrust. Augustine does not know, nor is he interested in knowing, Orphic literature directly; but he seems to be conscious of the prestige Orpheus enjoyed among pagans and in some Christian circles.

CYRIL (late fourth century–444) is the last great figure of the Church of Alexandria, before its importance declined after the Council of Chalcedon (451). The patriarch fought with the same vigor against his ecclesiastical and doctrinal rivals as he did against pagans, already clearly in the minority. His Orphic references are restricted to his most clearly apologetic work, *Against Julian*, an extended attack upon the "apostate" emperor's failed attempt to revive paganism.[19] Cyril's principal source is, as his use of the *Testament* reveals, the previous apologetic literature (the *Cohortatio*, for example). It seems likely, however, that, like Athanasius, he was aware of the diffusion of the Orphic tradition within his episcopal domain, on both a philosophical and a popular level.

THEODORET (393–457) chronologically closes the series of authors relevant to this study. Born in Antioch, he rose to become bishop of the neighboring town of Cyrrhus – a region in Asia Minor strongly influenced by the Alexandrian Church – and became an active participant in the Nestorian and Chalcedonian controversies. Among his diverse theological, heresiological, and historical works, the *Therapeutikon* or *Healing of Greek Afflictions*, written before 437, is the last and most comprehensive of Late Antiquity's Christian apologetic works. In twelve books, Theodoret describes and refutes the Greeks cults. As can be expected from a work of this scope at this time, he invariably relies upon bookish sources rather than direct knowledge of pagan cults or literature. His Orphic quotes vary a great deal: his quotations of the *Testament* and other texts are taken from earlier apologetic works, but some fragments originate in explicitly pagan sources such as Diodorus and Plutarch.

There is one last work the dating and origin of which is subject to endless debate, for which reason it has been left to the last place on this list. The PSEUDO-CLEMENTINE HOMILIES attributed to Clement of Rome (second century AD) is the title of a work written in approximately the fourth century AD. It has been partially preserved in its original Greek version, while other parts of it can be found in the so-called *Recognitiones*, preserved in the fifth-century Latin translation by Rufinus. Long fragments of both texts were also transmitted through a Syriac summary written by the Nestorian

---

19 Malley 1978 presents a thorough analysis of the apologetic arguments of Julian and Cyril.

monk Theodore Bar-Choni in the sixth century. Yet the Orphic theogonic material mentioned into this work seems to have its exclusive origin in a Jewish apologetic work probably composed in Egypt around the second century AD. The (Syrian?) author of the *Homilies* combined this Jewish piece with other Christian sources (the *Preaching of Peter*, the *Acts of Peter*) in an original composition following the formal models of Greek novels. It is a final example of the complex web of textual and ideological relations through which Orphic texts are received in Christian literature.[20]

This chapter offers an analysis of the sources and contents of the Orphic fragments and information on Orphism transmitted by these twenty Christian writers. Occasionally, writers of the Byzantine period, such as John Malalas, John Lydus, Michael Psellus, John Tzetzes, and the anonymous scholiasts of Clement, Plato, and Gregory of Nazianzus, will also be mentioned in this study. The Orphic references made by these writers, however, invariably consist of quotations from the texts of the authors discussed above. For the later Byzantine writers, the relevance of Orphism is only indirect, as they address objectives far removed from those of the apologists and speak about an Orphism extinct long before their time.

2. The figure of Orpheus

The reception and survival of Orpheus in the iconography and literature of the Middle Ages is well known: his descent into Hades in search for Eurydice was told many times in more or less Christianized versions. Nevertheless, the first step in this reception, the apologetic literature, has received scant attention.[21] The reason is that Orpheus interested the apologists only for the religious value of his figure. Eurydice's tale, for example, is not mentioned in their writings at all. The great literary possibilities of Orpheus' myth, which many earlier and later authors have not hesitated to exploit, meant nothing to them if they did not have a connection to the one objec-

---

20 Cullmann 1930 and Strecker 1981 on the composition and sources of the *Pseudoclementina*. Brisson 1990, 2902–2912, Bernabé 2008 and Roessli 2008 on the Orphic material. Noldeke 1899 on Homer, Hesiod and Orpheus in the Syriac version of Bar Choni.
21 General surveys in Irwin 1980, Naldini 1993, Markschies 2005, Geerlings 2005. Cf. Halton 1983 and Roessli 2002 for specific analyses of the Orpheus /Christ of Clement's *Protrepticus* and Eusebius' *Laudes Constantini*. On the latter, cf. Jourdan 2008c. The medieval Christianization of Orpheus is different from this apologetic treatment, *pace* Tataglio 1999. In the introduction to his classic work on Orpheus in the Middle Ages, Friedman 1970 rightly stresses the difference.

tive that mattered to them, the defence of Christianity and the attack on that paganism of which they made Orpheus a principal figure. The selection of themes that they made among the multiple facets of his myth proves this.

The aspect of the myth of Orpheus in which Christians had the liveliest interest was his chronology. For this reason they repeatedly mention that Orpheus participated in the expedition of the Argonauts.[22] The episode allowed them to date him before the Trojan War, and this early date, in turn, permitted them to place him before Homer. We will see in chapter V the importance that it had for the apologists to place Orpheus at the head of the Greek poets, attaching themselves to the tradition that situated him as the first of them, and hence as the inspiration for the rest. In addition, dating him in remote antiquity placed him in the age of the biblical prophets and thereby made contact between them possible, so that Orpheus's religious knowledge could be made dependent on biblical revelation. This chronology became fixed in Christian tradition, and even when establishing historical contact was no longer the aim, the chronological coincidence of Moses and the Greek theologians continued to be affirmed. This is the case for Augustine (*CD* 18.14, 18.37), who no longer puts forward a theory of historical dependence: he simply opposes symmetrically the *principes* of the *Civitas Dei* and those of the *Civitas impiorum*.

What underlies the debate about priority was the idea that chronological posteriority was a sign of inferiority and dependence. For this reason, another traditional element of the myth of Orpheus, his invention of music, was accepted by Tatian (*Orat.* 1.2), on the one hand, as a demonstration of the non-Greek origin of Greek wisdom (that is to say, its origin in a Thracian poet), and rejected by Theophilus, on the other, because Orpheus lived after the Flood and therefore after the biblical inventor of music, Jubal:

> But also, concerning music, some have fabled that Apollo was the inventor, and others say that Orpheus discovered the art of music from the sweet voices of the birds (ὀρνέων ἡδυφωνίας). But their story is shown to be empty and vain, for these inventors lived many years after the flood (*Ad Autol.* 2.30).

The wordplay that etymologizes Orpheus's name on the basis of birdsong obviously comes from the pagan chronologies that Theophilus refutes with his own.[23] This systematic chronological enthusiasm is, at least in many cases,

---

22 Tat. *Orat.* 41.1, Clem. Alex. *Strom.* 1.21.131.1, Lact. *DI.* 1.5.4, Thdt. *Affect.* 2.47, 3.29. Cyr. *CI* 1,35 ("the most ancient in time"). Cf. *OF* 875–879.
23 Kleingünther 1933 and Thraede 1962 on the figure of the πρῶτος εὑρετής, whose legitimacy was usually supported through etymology. Cf. Pilhofer 1990 on the

consciously elaborated and manipulated. At least some apologists were well aware that these subjects were hotly debated and that their own positions were not the most rigorous. Cyril reports Orpheus's primacy over Homer with a certain distance of tone ("they say") that reveals his scepticism (*CI* 1.35), and Clement, following Epigenes (*Strom.* 1.21.131), recognizes that many Orphic poems were not by Orpheus, but instead by Pythagorean poets. Clement himself, however, had no qualms about citing Orpheus without raising any questions about his authorship and antiquity. The apologists could attach themselves to a respectable older tradition, as did Tatian (*Orat.* 41.3), who says that Orpheus was a contemporary of Hercules and that the poems attributed to him were reordered (συντετάχθαι) by Onomacritus, thereby reconciling the post-Homeric dating of the *Orphica* and their attribution to Onomacritus with their Argonautic antiquity. Exactitude was a secondary preoccupation, however, and the apologists did not hesitate to change the chronology to make it fit their needs, as when Artapanus, as reported by Eusebius (*PE* 9.27), identified Moses with Musaeus and in contradiction to the entire previous tradition, made Orpheus a son of Musaeus.

Some Christian apologists also paid attention to the celebrated myth of the bard whose melodious voice had the power to enchant men, animals, and all of nature. The theme was, as we have seen, the object of iconographic assimilation in the Christ-Orpheus of the catacombs. Some mentions seem critical with this positive valutation of his music. We have seen Theophilus' disdainful mention. Hieronymus, while praising asceticism, alludes to the effect of Orpheus' lyre to show the pernitious effect of music for maintaining the chastity of the soul. The Syrian Christian writer Ephraim seems to imply that Christ's music triumphed where Orpheus failed (i. e. in Hades).[24] Nevertheless, apart from these brief mentions, this theme had limited popularity among the apologists: only Clement, at the beginning of the *Protrepticus* (App. I), and Eusebius, in a passage clearly inspired by the Alexandrian's work (*Laud. Const.* 14.5 = App. II), extensively treat the myth of the singer.

If Clement grants so much importance to Orpheus's song, it is because for him this song had a material content, the mysteries, that would go on to be the target of his *refutatio*. The *Protrepticus* begins by relating the myths of Amphion, Arion, and Orpheus, who drew animals, trees, and stones to them with their music, and then immediately accuses the three of them (*Protr.* 1.3.1):

> That Thracian Orpheus, that Theban, and that Methymnæan, – men, and yet unworthy of the name, – seem to me to have been impostors, who, under

---

apologetic struggle for priority through the comparison of chronologies.
24 Hieron. *Ep.* 117.6; Ephr. Syr. *Carmina Nisibena*, *Hymn* 36.5, 36.11.

the pretext of poetry have corrupted human life; inspired by some artful sorcery (γοητείᾳ) for purposes of destruction, they celebrated crimes in their orgies, divinized woes, and were the first to entice men to idols; and indeed, they built up the somberness of custom with pieces of wood and stone, – that is, statues and images, – subjecting to the yoke of extremest slavery the truly beautiful freedom of those who lived as free citizens under heaven by their chants and enchantments (ᾠδαῖς καὶ ἐπῳδαῖς).

Clement presents Orpheus as a poet and founder of the mysteries, "at once hierophant and poet."[25] The first chapter of the *Protrepticus* is full of references to the myth of the singer, linked by Clement to the role of the theologian. Just as in the myth Orpheus made use of his music to attract animals, he drew men after him to perdition with his rites; that is to say, Orpheus's song is his mysteries. For this reason Clement associates the mountain of the Muses, Helicon, with the mountain on which Dionysus's most famous epiphany took place, Cithaeron, and contrasts both pagan mountains to Mount Sion (1.2.1). In uniting Orpheus's two most important facets, those of theologian and poet, Clement fuses two elements of Orpheus's myth, his song and his mysteries, that in earlier Greek tradition might appear juxtaposed, but not identified (p. 265f). Thus, in contrast to Linforth's opinion, the mention of Orpheus's song in Clement is not ornamental, but rather has full religious value.[26] The content of Orpheus's song is his mysteries (just as the content of Christ's song is the Gospel). Nor is the juxtaposition of both facets causal in other Christian writers: Tatian begins his discourse by recalling that "Orpheus taught you to practice poetry and song, and he himself, initiation into the mysteries," and Gregory attacks "the *teletai* and mysteries of Orpheus, whom the Greeks admired so much for his wisdom that they gave him a lyre that drew everything to him with its notes."[27]

Only in Eusebius's version can a significant change be appreciated: Jean-Michel Roessli (2002) points out that Clement is very explicit about the allegory in order to avoid any confusion among his readers between

---

25 *Protr.* 7.74.3; cf. 2.17.2 (the poet of the *teleté*) and 2.21.1 (mystagogue).
26 Linforth (1941, 225) says that Clement presents Orpheus in the company of Amphion and Arion, as a mere literary resource without religious significance. It was a topos to associate the singers who could move the natural elements with their song (Hor. *Ars Poet.* 391ff; Menand. Rhet. 2.392.19; Mart. Cap., *De Nuptiis Phil. et Merc.* 9.906–8; Stat. *Silv.* 2.2.60–61.), and the exordium of the *Protrepticus* seeks the literary effect. But Orpheus is *primus inter pares* among the musicians (Orpheus is the subject-matter of "another myth", *Protr.* 1.1.1) and has more relevance throughout the whole work as the prophet of Greek mysteries (2.27, 2.22, 7.2). Cf. Jourdan 2008b on the literary association of these poets.
27 Tat. 1.2; Greg. Naz. *Or.* 4.115, *Or.* 39.5; Lact. *DI* 1.22.12.

2. The figure of Orpheus

Christ and Orpheus. When Eusebius repeats the image a century and a half later, he dispenses with such concerns, probably because his audience has by this point become more accustomed to this metaphor and its iconographic reflection, at a time at which, in addition, the balance of power has been reversed, with Christianity thriving and paganism on the defensive. Eusebius's work is more encomiastic than apologetic, and consequently, he does not need to attack the mysteries as the enemy, but to celebrate God. His brief reference to Orpheus is merely a description of the magical power of his song, stripped of any reference to its content. The end of the apologetic age and the gateway to the Orpheus-Christ of the Middle Ages are already announced here in this first appearance of Orpheus as a decorative figure, shorn of religious significance.

Eusebius's ornamental Orpheus, however, is an exception in the apologetic literature, one that looks ahead to the future in celebration of Constantine and of the advent of a new age. The Orpheus who appears in the apologists' violent religious polemics, on the other hand, is the theologian of the mysteries. What is most usual is to mention him as the founder of all the mysteries in general, with a vagueness of clear apologetic utility, since it permits lumping different cults together in one "paganism."[28] The same generalizing vagueness is what leads the apologists on occasion to replace an attack on the Orphic myths or gods with the affirmation that he sung of as many as 365 gods, an affirmation not repeated outside the apologetic literature. Still far from imagining the transformation of the calendar into a succession of saints' days, the Christians thereby summarized their idea of Orpheus as the theologian par excellence of polytheism, a characterization that gives greater value, in addition, to his later conversion in the *Testament*.[29]

Singer, founder of mysteries, and theologian: the Christians put these characteristics to use in their less flattering version of Orpheus's story, distanced from that of a respectable religion. Clement applied to Orpheus (*Protr.* 1–3) pejorative epithets associated with the magical sphere: sorcerer (γόης), sophist, superstitious (δεισιδαίμων), an impostor whose songs (ᾠδαί) are really magical charms (ἐπῳδαί). The apologists' goal was to identify the mysteries with superstition and magic. In order to do so, they needed to do no more than promote the reputation as a magus that Orpheus had carried with him from ancient times and that the magical papyri show that he still

---

28   Clem. Alex. *Protr.* 1.1–5; Thdt. *Affect.* 1.22, and the texts mentioned in the previous note.
29   Theoph. *Ad Autol.* 3.2, Ps.-Iust. *De Mon.* 2.4 (in contraposition to the *Testament*'s monotheism), Lact. *DI* 1.7.6 (not in direct relation to the *Testament*).

had and had even increased. Athanasius does not hesitate to make him the patron of the typical spell that leads away from the truth: "So an old woman, for 10 obols or a quart of wine, hits you with an enchantment of Orpheus, and you end up amazed as an ass, bearing on your neck the quadrupeds' filth, straying from the sign of the saving cross."[30] The bishop of Alexandria brings to the opposition between Christ's cross and Orpheus's spell the same antagonism that a century and a half earlier Clement had ascribed to the contrast between the song and the mysteries of one and the other.

3. The mysteries of Orpheus

In addition to general mentions, the Christians offer abundant information on the theological and ritual content found in the mysteries of Orpheus. When a particular cult is specified, Orpheus is made out to be the founder of the mysteries of Dionysus or of Demeter. This specification may come from general cultural knowledge, since these two sets of mysteries were the most popular among those influenced by Orphism. On other occasions, however, the details offered make it possible to identify the source of the affirmation: they are found in either the descriptions of the mysteries given by other apologists or in the pagan authors who are the sources of general religious culture in the Greek world. Herodotus is the only source for Athenagoras's references to the sufferings of Osiris, who is expressly identified with Dionysus,[31] but it was Diodorus Siculus and Plutarch above all who attained great popularity among the apologists as sources for Greek history. Several authors depend on Diodorus in affirming that Orpheus was a founder of the mysteries, and all of them have one point in common: they refer to the "Osirisized" version of the myth of Dionysus in which Rhea gathers the remains of her son just as Isis did for Osiris, and they use the comparison of Dionysus to Osiris and of Isis to Demeter in order to support the widespread opinion that Orpheus brought the mysteries of Egypt to Greece.[32] The apologetic

---

30 *PG* 26.1320 (*OF* 822). The manuscript reading is ὄφεως ἐπαοιδή. The snake is common in magic papyri (cf. Mastrocinque 2005), but the connection with an enchantment makes very plausible the correction Ὀρφέως. The charge of superstition against Orpheus is particularly widespread among Alexandrian apologists. Apart from Clement and Athanasius, Cyril calls Orpheus "the most superstitious" (δεισιδαιμονέστατον). This is concordant with his presence in the magical papyri (pp. 58ff).
31 Athenag. *Leg.* 28 expressly quotes Herodotus as his source: 2.144, 2.156, 2.90, 2.41, 2.3, 2.61, 2.170, 2.86 (in this order).
32 Diodorus (1.23.2ff, 3.65.6) is the source of the *Cohortatio* 10.2, 14.2; Epiph. *Pa-*

motive that drove them to favor this Egyptian origin is not difficult to guess: such version permitted them to make Greek religious wisdom dependent on an encounter between Orpheus and Moses.

If Egypt is the preferred land of origin among the apologists, there are no lack of other foreign countries as sources of the Greek mysteries. An extreme case of this is Epiphanius's thesis (*Panar.* 1.182.13), according to which Egyptians, Phrygians, Phoenicians, and Babylonians all had a part in the origin of the Greek mysteries, handed down by Cadmus, Orpheus, and others, whence Greek wisdom arose. Other apologists referred to various of these countries, but the insistence on the foreign origin of the mysteries is common to them all, and Orpheus is the most popular mediator.[33] Even when the place of origin is not mentioned, the idea of foreign roots was firmly lodged in the apologetic mind. Lactantius (*DI* 1.22.15) says, "Orpheus was the first to introduce (*induxit*) the rites of Dionysus and the first to celebrate them." Establishing the rites is synonymous with introducing them into Greece.

It is not only this belief in the foreign origin of the rites that follows the model of the earlier tradition. Except, clearly, in the case of the innovative metaphor that describes the mysteries as a song, in which verbs like ἀείδω dominate, the tenor of Orpheus's patronage of the mysteries is similar to that of the Greek tradition by which the apologists were inspired; they use the usual verbs, like the various derivates of ἵστημι (establish, found),[34] καταδείκνυμι (show),[35] and κομίζω (bring).[36] It is curious that the only innovation with respect to pagan authors takes place with the verbs διδάσκω (teach) and ἐπαιδεύω (educate),[37] perhaps because these verbs included a connotation of doctrinal instruction proper to Christianity and absent from the pagan expressions, which were centered more on ritual than on doctrinal transmission. It is also interesting to note that the Christian texts that mention Orpheus never link him to the verb παραδίδωμι (hand down), which is enormously abundant in pagan references (Casadio 1990) and in the Christian texts themselves in references to other rites. The reason is perhaps to be

---

   nar. 1.182.13; Thdt. *Affect.* 1.21 (cf. Casadio 1996, 201, n. 1), 1.114, 2.95. *Cf.* Bernabé 2000 and 2002b on the Orphic sources of Diodorus and Beatrice 1998 on Diodorus in Christian apologists.
33 Eus. *PE* 10.4.4 (from Egypt and Babylon); Clem. Alex. *Protr.* 2.13.3, Thdt. *Affect* 1.22 (from Phrygia); Tat. 1.2 (from Thrace).
34 Eus. *PE* 10.4.4. The same verb is used by Paus. 2.30.2; Luc. *Salt.* 15; Iul Or.7.217c.
35 Hippol. *Haer.* 5.20.4; cf. Ar. *Ra.* 1030ff; Ps.-D. 25.11; D. S. 5.77.3.
36 Thdt. *Affect.* 1.21. *Cf.* the synonym ἀποφέρω in D. S. 1.96.4.
37 Tat. *Orat.* 1.2; Thdt. *Affect.* 1.22.2.

found in the fact that if it was precisely *paradosis* that was the foundation of Orpheus's authority and that of his rites, the Christians refused to grant him this prestige even lexically, since they opposed their own *paradosis* to that of the Greek tradition; the debate over priority (p. 227) would become a faithful reflection of this conflict of traditions. The one exception is Hippolytus (*Ref.* 5.20.4), who used the term once, although he did so in order to denounce the origin of Gnostic ideas in the ancient pagan tradition of the mysteries, explaining his interest in highlighting this claim by the use of the verb.

Nor do the Christians' general mentions of practices and taboos vary from the habitual ones – beans and vegetarianism. When Jerome says that "Orpheus in his poem utterly condemns the eating of meat," it is impossible to know whether the expression *in carmine suo* is referring to the *Rhapsodies* or to another poem, or whether it is more of a general citation based on the assumption that Orphic prescriptions are formulated poetically.[38] In any case, the reference simply brings in the widespread idea of Orphic vegetarianism. Only Clement says more specifically, comparing the ritual precepts of the Old Testament with those of the Greeks, "I believe that the *teletai* not only ordered the avoidance of contact with certain animals, but also excluded the use of parts of the animals sacrificed for reasons known to the initiates." Clement's mysterious tone, similar to that used by Pausanias, may reveal his ignorance or his attachment to literary models, but if the Alexandrian remembered the mythic aetiologies of the prohibitions of pomegranates or celery that he had revealed in his *Protrepticus*, he surely had an approximate idea of the explanations given for the animal taboos.[39]

The Christians, then, knew and received the broad literary tradition about Orphic rites, and they modified it at times for reasons of unconscious projection or conscious convenience. These mentions, however, while valuable for understanding the apologetic *modus operandi*, add little to what the pagan sources already preserve about Orphic rituals. On the other hand,

---

38 *Adv. Iov.* 2.14 = *PL* 22.317c. Cf. Greg. Naz. *Or.* 27.10: "throw me the silence of Pythagoras, and the Orphic beans, and the novel bragging about "The Master said"". The epithet "Orphic" has a tone of mockery, like the reference to the Pythagorean *symbola*. The iconicity which makes the label "Orphic" valuable for pagans (pp. 80ff) is here the first target of Christian critique.

39 *Stromata* 2.20.106. Clement is probably making reference to mythical aetiologies of ritual prescriptions like those of Smyrna (*OF* 582, cf. p. 47). In *Protr.* 2.19.2–3 he mentions the prohibition of celery, because it sprang from the blood of the dead Corybant, and the pomegranate, which sprang from Dionysus' blood. Cf. Paus. 1.37.4 with a similar tone on the beans taboo.

sometimes they transmit more specific evidence which is very important for our knowledge of such cults. The following pages analyse this evidence.

3.1. *Protrepticus* 2.12–22 and related Greek texts

One of the most important ancient literary witnesses to the Greek mysteries, and to the Orphic cults in particular, is the *Protrepticus* of Clement of Alexandria. After comparing the song of Christ to that of Orpheus in the exordium of the work, Clement dedicates substantial paragraphs (2.12–22: App. III) to the *refutatio* of the pagan mysteries of which Orpheus is poet and founder, especially those of Dionysus and Demeter, as the basis for his exhortation later in the *peroratio* to follow the true mysteries of the Logos. Because of information offered by Eusebius (*PE* 2.2.64) when he transcribed the text 150 years later, the traditional idea has been that Clement knew the mysteries from personal experience prior to his conversion. However, Eusebius alleges this direct knowledge in order to give greater authority to Clement's description. The literary structure of this section, arranged conceptually and alphabetically, and Clement's imprecisions make clear that his description comes from a written source and not from personal knowledge, besides what he might know from general cultural knowledge about maenadism or Eleusis.[40]

I have analysed Clement's text in detail in a long article whose results I summarize here now.[41] Clement's source was an alphabetic treatise on the mysteries from the end of the Hellenistic period that was based, in its turn, on an Orphic poem (or, more improbably, several poems) datable approximately to the third century BC – a dating grounded, among other factors, on the exact concordances with the Gurob Papyrus. A synoptic view of these parallels is given in this table:

	P. Gurob 1	Clem. Alex. *Protr.* 2.12–22
Deities	5–6: Βριμὼ με[γάλη Δημήτηρ τε Ῥέα	15.1: Δηοῦς μυστήρια· Διὸς πρὸς μητέρα Δήμητρα ... καὶ μῆνις ... τῆς Δηοῦς, ἧς δὴ χάριν Βριμὼ προσαγορευθῆναι

---

40 Riedweg 1987, 117–123, and supplementary arguments in Herrero 2007a.
41 Herrero 2007a (with one further precision in Gagné/Herrero 2009). Clement's text is given in Appendix 3. On the papyrus, cf. p. 54. On Dionysus' toys in both texts, cf. Levaniouk 2007.

148   IV. Orphic Tradition in Christian Apologetic Literature

	P. Gurob 1	Clem. Alex. Protr. 2.12–22
Deities	7: Κούρητές τ' {ε} ἔνοπλοι 18:]νον καὶ Εὐβουλῆ[α 22a: Εὐβου]λ̣ε̣ῦ Ἰρικεπαῖγε 23b: Διόνυσος 21: Δ]ήμητρος καὶ Παλλάδος	17.2: ἐνόπλῳ κινήσει περιχορευόντων Κουρήτων (17.1, 20.2: Εὐβουλεύς) 17.2: τὰ Διονύσου μυστήρια 18.1: Ἀθηνᾶ... Παλλὰς... προσηγορεύθη
Ritual formulae	24: θεός διὰ κόλπου 25: ο]ἶν[ο]ν ἔπιον 28: εἰς τὸν κάλαθον ἐμβαλεῖν 29–30: κ]ῶνος ῥόμβος ἀστράγαλοι]η ἔσοπτρος	16.2: ὁ διὰ κόλπου θεός 15.3: ἐκ κυμβάλου ἔπιον 21.2: ἔπιον τὸν κυκεῶνα 21.2: ἐργασάμενος ἀπεθέμην εἰς κάλαθον καὶ ἐκ καλάθου εἰς κίστην 17.2: κῶνος καὶ ῥόμβος καί παίγνια καμπεσίγυια 18.1: ἀστράγαλος, σφαῖρα, στρόβιλος, μῆλα, ῥόμβος, ἐσόπτρον, πόκος
Technical terms	3: διὰ τὴν τελετήν 10: κριός 25: βουκόλος 23b: σύμβολα 26: σύνθεμα	14.2, 17.2, 18.1, 19.4: τελετή 15.2: κριός 16.3, 20.2: βουκόλος 15.3, 14.2, 22.5: σύμβολα 21.2: σύνθεμα

The poem on which the treatise was mainly based seems to have had a theogonic structure, still perceptible in Clement's text, in which the mythic elements follow a genealogical order; Orpheus's verses, which are both quoted by Clement and perceivable under his prose, described the myths that provided the foundation for the cults of Aphrodite, the Mother, Sabazius, Dionysus, and Demeter at Eleusis. It is this Orphic poem that provides the most extended descriptions of the myth of the Titans and of the Orphic version of the Eleusinian myth, in which Iambe is replaced by Baubo.[42] The treatise perhaps added other mysteries, like those of the Cabiri, and paid special attention to ritual elements (*symbola*, *orgia* and *synthemata*) that it linked to the mythical accounts. Although Clement adds certain mythographic elements of euhemerist tone, his description is quite faithful to the content of his sources, making his testimony especially valuable, particularly since there is only one other text derived from the same source – a set of brief scholia on Lucian. A stemma of the sources is offered on figure 1 (p. 159).

The importance of Clement's text is evident in the fact that the great majority of the Christian apologists' mentions of the mysteries are inspired by this section of the *Protrepticus*. The texts that depend directly on this passage add no new information (other than the few details I will point out) to what Clement provides, so that it is unnecessary to suppose either additional literary sources or direct knowledge on the part of these authors of the mysteries or of Orphic literature, and as a result, they should not be used as independent sources on the Greek mysteries. A factor in this popularity is that Eusebius quotes Clement's text in full without adding or suppressing anything, as is characteristic of his historiographical style. By acting as a channel for the transmission of Clement's text, Eusebius multiplied its effect on later audiences, ancient and modern. This is so much the case that Origen, in the generation immediately following Clement, nowhere appears to echo this section of the *Protrepticus*. After Eusebius's citation, on the other hand, there are a whole series of mentions probably originating there.

The following description of the Greek mysteries and *teletai* in Epiphanius is clearly an enumeration of the most scandalous aspects that this apologist could find in Clement's text: "And how many mysteries and rites do the Greeks have? As the women who go to the *megara* and those who celebrate the Thesmophoria are different between themselves, so many other things are different: the mysteries of Deo and Pherephatta at Eleusis, and shameful actions in the sanctuaries there, nakednesses of women, to put it politely,

---

42 The treatise may, of course, have used more than one Orphic poem. However, the theogonic order the treatise seems to follow seems to point to one poem as the main source, since the criterion of the treatise is alphabetical order (cf. Herrero 2007a). Apart from the Orphic lines which are literally quoted (*OF* 306, 395), some sentences show clearly that Clement (or the treatise) paraphrases the Orphic poem: eg "and Apollo did not disobey his father" (*Protr*. 2.18.2) echoes the formula of *Iliad* 16.677 (where Apollo must bury another son of Zeus, Sarpedon). Cf. Herrero 2008a.

drums and cakes, a bull-roarer and a basket, worked wool and cymbals, and *kykeon* prepared in the beaker."[43]

Gregory of Nazianzus also refers on various occasions to the Orphic tradition, even quoting verse, and it is clear that he had other sources for his knowledge of Orphism besides the *Protrepticus*. Nonetheless, roots in Clement's work can be presumed for the Cappadocian's criticisms of the Orphic version of the Eleusinian mysteries when he mocks their mythic and ritual elements with disdainful plurals. In his *Second Discourse against Julian* he exhorts his readers to "cast off your Triptolemuses and your Celeuses and your mystic serpents; be ashamed of what there is in the books of your theologian Orpheus!" and in the *Discourse on Holy Lights* he says, "We do not have a girl ravished from us, nor does Demeter wander, nor bring us Celeuses and Triptolemuses and serpents, nor do this or that, nor suffer other things."[44]

A text by Theodoret of Cyrus (*Affect.* 1.22) should be given equal consideration. Theodoret's principal source for his quotations regarding Orpheus – besides the *Testament* – is Diodorus. He expressly cites Diodorus, Plutarch, and Demosthenes as witnesses to Orpheus's introduction of the mysteries of Deo and Dionysus to Athens, adapting the Egyptian mysteries of Isis and Osiris. Immediately following, however, he gives this information about the Orphic origin of the Phrygian mysteries: "Demosthenes says that Orpheus showed them the most sacred rites. And also those of Rhea, Cybele, Brimo or however you want to call her – for much abundance you have for names, not for the facts that lie behind them. And in the same way, those called as witnesses show clearly that the Greeks received their feasts and initiations in Greece from Phrygia." Demeter's epithets, the Phrygian origin, and the judicial metaphor of calling witnesses coincide with Clement's text. Since these elements do not appear in Diodorus's discussion of Cybele, nor in Demosthenes' text, it is probable that Theodoret is taking them from the *Protrepticus*.[45]

---

43 *Expos. fidei* 10 (*OF* 592). This is the only information that is not explicit in Clement: ἐρέα ἐξειργασμένη seems an interpretation, perhaps by Epiphanius himself, of what is inside the basket of the mysterious Eleusinian *synthema* of 2.21.2: ἐργασάμενος ἀπεθέμην εἰς κάλαθον. The word μεγαρίζω (to go to the crypts) is only attested in Clement's *Protrepticus* (2.17.1) and in this text.
44 *Or.* 5.31, *Or.* 39.4 (*OF* 384). A reference to Baubo (*Or.* 4.115), which will be analysed in the next section (p. 177), perhaps also stems from Gregory's knowledge of Clement's text.
45 *Cf.* D. S. 3.58.59; Ps.-Dem. 25.11. Another, more speculative possibility, is that an unknown text by Plutarch is the source for this passage, since we do not know the Plutarchean work that Diodorus is using (*cf.* Linforth 1941, 195). It is not improbable that Plutarch knew Clement's source or a similar work.

A famous scholion to Plato (*Gorg.* 497c: *OF* 589 II) contains a moral critique of the Greek cult with clear apologetic roots. This commentator, of indeterminate date, made evident use of Clement as the source for his description of the Eleusinian Greater Mysteries: "The Greater Mysteries were celebrated in honor of Deo and Core, for Pluto raped her and Zeus was united with Deo. In these mysteries many shameful acts took place, and the initiates were told, 'I ate from the tympanon, I drank from the cymbal, I carried the sacred jars, I went into the nuptial chamber,' and so on." The scholion presents the *synthema* (strangely addressed to the initiates) of the Mother as that of Eleusis. Rather than a real fusion of the two cults, as suggested by Scarpi (2001,147) and others, this is a confusion characteristic of someone who knows little more of the cults than what he has read in Clement. The error is a result of the similarity of both *synthemata* and of the linkage of the two sets of mysteries under the epiclesis Deo.

Finally, the Byzantine polymath Michael Psellus (eleventh century) offers a description of the Eleusinian mysteries obviously derived from earlier sources; it is evident that these were ninety percent dependent on the *Protrepticus*. Psellus summarized and compressed Clement's text in order to make the various mysteries described in it into a single one, that of Eleusis, in which different episodes would have taken place one after another. The vision of the mysteries as pure representation (*deiknymena*) develops the theatrical metaphor used by Clement when he presented the myths by speaking of their entrance on stage (*Protr.* 2.12.2). The text is eloquent on its own:[46]

> And the mysteries of these daemons, like for example those of Eleusis, represented the mythical union of Zeus with Deo or Demeter and with her daughter Pherephatta (or also Core). As in initiation there were going to be sexual unions, the marine Aphrodite comes out from some testicles thrown over. Then (εἶτα) the nuptial hymenaios is told about Core, and the initiates sing, "I ate from the tympanon, I drank from the cymbal, I carried the sacred jars, I entered under the nuptial chamber." The birth pains of Deo are represented (ὑποκρίνεται). Finally (αὐτίκα), the supplications of Deo and the drinking of the gall and the pains of the heart. After that (ἐφ' οἷς), the imitation of the kid that suffers in its testicles because Zeus paid the compensation for his violation of Demeter by cutting off the testicles of a kid and throwing them onto her bosom as if they were his own. After all that (ἐπὶ πᾶσιν), the rites in honour of Dionysus,

---

46 *Quaenam sunt Graecorum opiniones de daemonibus*, 3 (PG 122, c 878D 3–4 Migne). Despite the interest of this opuscule as an example of the progressive distortion of the image of Greek religion, its value as historical evidence is nil, since it is entirely based on a phantastic reinterpretation of Clement's information. However, Harrison 1922³, 568–9, among other influential authors, uses the text as evidence for the supposed Eleusinian *deiknymena*.

and the baskets and the cakes of many globes and the initates in the cult of Sabazios and of the Mother, and the Clodons and Mimallons[47] and the resounding cauldron of Thesprotis, and the bronze of Dodona and another Corybant and another Couret, imitations of daemons. And after that (ἐφ' οἷς), Baubo who uncovers her thighs and the femenine comb: since thus the ashamed call the sexual organ. And so they celebrate the rite in shame.

Six centuries after the extinction of Eleusis, nine centuries after the *Protrepticus*, the effort to unify the mysteries in a single ritual culminates in the Byzantine texts, the heirs of a tendency perceptible in all the Greek apologists who followed Clement, in a growing process of confusion and mixture of the various cults described in the *Protrepticus*. In reality, however, the later authors did no more than continue along the lines set out by the Alexandrian himself, who already presented all these cults as an ensemble characterized by common traits of sex and violence: "The mysteries are, in a word, murders and tombs" (2.19.2: συνελόντι φάναι, φόνοι καὶ τάφοι). Burkert took this phrase as a motto for his *Homo Necans* in the idea that it reflected the essence of sacrificial religion. Even if Clement might be unintentionally correct in this anthropological judgment, it is clear that he had good apologetic motives for summarizing the mysteries in this way. It should not be forgotten, however, that he himself was following (with new propagandistic goals) the clear tendencies of his Orphic sources – the theogony and the treatise – toward the unification of the mysteries, and not only in placing the essence of the mysteries in violence, as already suggested by the treatise when it identified μύσος (crime) and ὀργή (anger) as the respective etymological roots of μυστήρια and ὄργια (2.13.1). At a much more profound level, the genealogical and narrative continuity that links the myths of some cults with others; the parallel presentation of various rites with very similar *symbola* and *synthemata;* the identifications of different gods like Deo/Cybele (15.1), Sabazius/Zeus (16.2), Dionysus/Attis (19.4), Cabiri/Corybantes (19.4); even the placement of them all under the patronage of Dionysus and Demeter as gods and of Orpheus as poet: all these factors were already clearly present in his sources and perceptible merely by a straightforward reading. As I said in the first chapter, Orphism is a process of unification of the mysteries, and Clement's Orphic sources show this clearly. The history of his later reception does so as well: pan-Orphic enthusiasm has always valued Clement's description of the mysteries highly (and those of the Alex-

---

47 These two names constitute the only piece of information that we do not find in Clement. They appear in some descriptions of Bacchic rites; cf. Plut. *Alex.* 2.7, a possible (in)direct source of Psellus, and *OF* 579.

andrian's followers up through Psellus) and has frequently treated them all as an ensemble. "Orpheo-scepticism," on the other hand, is in the habit of suspiciously critiquing each fragment of the text, as if every common element of the mysteries was entirely the product of Clement's rhetoric.[48]

3.2. Latin texts related to *Protrepticus* 2.12–22: Arnobius and Firmicus

Besides these Greek authors, there are two Latin apologists whose descriptions of the pagan mysteries have too many points in common with Clement's text not to be related: Arnobius of Sicca and Firmicus Maternus. Unlike the writers previously discussed, these authors tend to accentuate the multiplicity of the mysteries and to delight in their details, instead of tending to unify them, as a result of which the parallels with Clement are dispersed in various passages and manipulated by the baroque rhetoric of both writers. Whether they depend on Clement and to what extent are debated questions difficult to resolve.

In book V of his *Adversus nationes*, Arnobius brings all his rhetorical artillery to bear against the pagan mysteries. The extensive section dealing with the mysteries of Dionysus and Demeter (5.19–26) has extraordinarily clear correspondences with the text of the *Protrepticus*. Arnobius transforms and adapts the text in order to make it fit his rhetorical tastes and his polemical needs, but the topics discussed and the verses quoted are the same, although the translation sometimes gives them a different meaning. Themes attested only in Clement are repeated in Arnobius's text, such as the castration of Zeus before Rhea, Dionysus's toys, or the episode of Baubo with the same verses quoted (although their Latin translation is quite different from the Greek). Nevertheless, Arnobius adds certain pieces of information that do not appear in Clement's work, as is revealed simply by reading the two.

The differences have given rise to various speculations about the relationship between the two texts. There are two contrary points of view, which I will now present. The most widely held opinion is that Clement is Arnobius's principal source in this section. The coincidences between the two are thereby explained, while Arnobius's additions are ascribed to other complementary sources or to his own general knowledge of the mysteries. As far as

---

48 Cf. the interpretations by Lobeck, Harrison, Eisler and Macchioro, and the opposite ones by Wilamowitz and Linforth, mentioned in V nn. 75–77. Festugière 1935, 37–47 undertakes a true *diasparagmos* of Clement's text in an artificial attempt to neatly distinguish the different mysteries as separate entities.

the passages in which Arnobius's translation fails to agree with the sense of Clement's text – for example, the verses referring to Baubo – these may be explained by corruption of one or the other's text or, according to an ingenious hypothesis put forward by Miroslav Marcovich, by corruption of the copy of Clement's text that Arnobius was using.[49] Nevertheless, some years ago Fabio Mora rejected the traditional assumption that Arnobius depended on Clement in his account of the mysteries. Emphasizing the many differences between the two, Mora maintains that Arnobius primarily used another source and that he became acquainted with the *Protrepticus* only in the final stage of composition. Scholarly opinion has been divided with regard to this theory:[50] the fundamental objection is that the argument can be easily reversed, making the *Protrepticus* the principal source and the divergences the result of Arnobius's own reworkings or of his use of other sources. As long as Mora is forced to admit that Arnobius did know Clement's text, it is naturally easier to suppose that Clement was his principal source and was used by him prior to a presumed last stage of composition, rather than postulating another, unknown source.

The objection appears to be well founded, and as a result, the traditional hypothesis appears more likely to correspond to reality. However much the differences may be magnified, many can be explained by the disparity in context and intentions, rather than by different sources; and it will always be more economical to postulate a known text as a source rather than a hypothetical one, since Mora never identifies Arnobius's presumed other source. Nevertheless, if Mora is right and Clement was not Arnobius's source, then his source could only be the same treatise used by Clement or its close derivative: this would explain, on the one hand, the agreement between the two, while on the other hand, it would make it easier to justify Arnobius's additions, since Clement could have omitted certain information in the treatise; and finally, it would explain the differences of translation, since it would allow a longer chronological lapse for possible textual corruption. It seems to me more probable that one apologist's source for information on the mysteries would be another apologist, as a general matter. In light of the differences pointed out (and in my judgment exaggerated) by Mora, however, the

---

49 Röhricht 1893, Rapisarda 1939, Graf 1974, 195–199; Marcovich 1986 specifically on the text about Baubo.
50 Mora's (1994) forerunner was Tullius 1934, refuted by Rapisarda 1939. Sfameni Gasparro (*BStudLat* 26.2, 1996, 636–639) and Humphries (*CQ* 46.1, 1996, 53f) supported Mora's view; more sceptical were the reviews by Turcan (*AC* 65, 1996, 352–355), Champeaux (*Latomus* 55.2, 1996, 427–430) and Zeller (*Kernos* 9, 1996, 440–442).

3.2. Latin texts related to Protrepticus 2.12–22: Arnobius and Firmicus 155

possibility that Clement and Arnobius shared a pagan source, the treatise on the mysteries, should not be entirely excluded.

Mora and his predecessors have analyzed in detail Arnobius's text and his differences from and similarities to Clement. I will only point out two significant examples. Some of the divergences that Mora puts forward as evidence of a source distinct from Clement appear to be simply additions to Clement's text – the product of Arnobius's general culture and his taste for rhetorical amplification. In addition, it is necessary to take into account that as a rhetor and former reader of Porphyry, Arnobius must surely have had sufficient knowledge of pagan cults, from his reading and his own experience, to permit him to add details to Clement's description. Thus, when he says (*Adv. Nat.* 5.20) that the serpent that symbolized the mysteries of Sabazius was made of gold, Arnobius gives more information than Clement, who does not mention this detail. Nevertheless, another Christian, Athenagoras (*Leg.* 20.2), says that the staff of Hermes is a *symbolon* of Zeus's incest in the form of a serpent. The association of the caduceus with a chthonic animal like the serpent is easy to make, and in various famous passages of Greek literature the caduceus is said to be of gold (e. g. *Od.* 24.3). Arnobius's baroque taste for details may be sufficient to explain his addition of *aureus* without needing to postulate a specific source other than Clement. In the same way, when he quotes the verses on the "bull father of the serpent" that Clement attributes to an "idolatrous poet" (*Protr.* 2.16.3: ποιητὴς εἰδωλικός), Arnobius translates them with the comment that they are a "well-known Tarentine senarius sung by antiquity" (*Adv. Nat.* 5.20: *Tarentinum notumque senarium quem antiquitas canit*). The tenor of the phrase clearly demonstrates that the verses were familiar to him on the basis of his general cultural knowledge, so it is unnecessary to suppose that he took this supplementary information from another specific source.

The problem posed by Firmicus Maternus's sources is even more difficult. His *De errore profanarum religionum* has much in common with Clement, Arnobius, and other apologists throughout the entire work. Most of these common contents repeat what Clement took rom the treatise he used, generally following the same order: Cinyras the founder of the mysteries of Aphrodite (10.1); the serpent of Sabazius (10.2); the mysteries of the Corybantes (11); Zeus's incests with his mother and daughter (12.4); the *symbolon* of the mysteries of the Mother (18.1); the aforementioned verses on the bull as father of the serpent (26.1). Firmicus makes rapid allusions to these subjects, with more rhetoric than content, and does not add anything to the information in Clement, except for two small details. One is that the *symbolon* of the Mother transmitted by Firmicus (18.1: ἐκ τυμπάνου βέβρωκα, ἐκ κυμβάλου πέπωκα, γέγονα μύστης Ἄττεως) is slightly different from that in Clement (*Protr.* 2.21.2: ἐκ τυμπάνου ἔφαγον· ἐκ κυμβάλου ἔπιον· ἐκερνοφόρησα· ὑπὸ τὸν παστὸν ὑπέδυν). Firmicus's version is more coherent, simpler, and easier to understand, so that it can be supposed to be more recent: a modification of the ancient *symbolon* that perhaps the *mystai* themselves no longer understood, and still less the mysteries' external observers, into which category Firmicus's source would fall. The second detail is that Firmicus (26.1) calls the two lines about the bull and the serpent a *symbolum*, which neither Clement (Protr. 2.16.3) nor Arnobius (5.20) does, and which they probably would not have failed to do had their source considered the verse a *symbolon*, since they always record this sort of information. Once again, Firmicus's information appears to be somewhat modernized and systematized in comparison to that of the other two apologists.

Firmicus's relationship with Clement and Arnobius has been a subject of some controversy, since it is unclear whether he knew both directly, knew only Clement, knew Clement only by way of Arnobius, or simply used anthologies in which the apologists' material appeared, to which he added material from pagan sources.[51] None of these hypotheses can be definitively proved, but at the same time, they are not mutually exclusive and may even all be possible at once: Firmicus would have used all the material he had at his disposal to write his treatise.

His euhemerist version of the myth of the Titans (*De err.* 6 = App. 4), which turns it into a palace conspiracy against Dionysus, the son of Jupiter, the king of Crete, deserves to be considered separately. Euhemerism distorts myths to a great extent, but it may also serve to shed light on aspects that remain obscure in more canonical versions. Thus, some elements occurring in the euhemerist account confirm the importance of these details in other contexts in which they are less clear or in which they might be supposed to have only anecdotal value: Athena's preservation of Dionysus's heart (*cor divisum sibi soror servat*); the strange way in which Dionysus's dismembered parts are cooked in various manners (*decocta variis generibus*); the importance of the toys and the mirror (*crepundiis ac speculo*) in his dethronement. The fact that the euhemerist version, so different in other respects, should have chosen to preserve these elements is a very powerful indication of their importance in the myth and perhaps in the ritual on which the euhemerist version is based, and this is even

---

51 While Rapisarda 1939, 36, and Forbes 1970, 29–31 have no doubt that Clement is a main source for Firmicus, Turcan 1982, 50–52 is more sceptical and points out that the correspondence with Clement may come through Arnobius (similarly Sanzi 2006, 51). Apart from the Orphic parallels commented on here, cf. other correspondences with Clement in *De err.* 12.1, 12.7, 15.1, 16.1.

3.2. Latin texts related to Protrepticus 2.12–22: Arnobius and Firmicus   157

more the case when the latter departs in many other aspects from the usual versions of the myth, like those preserved by Clement and Arnobius. Besides the variations arising from the need to humanize the actors of the story in order to euhemerize it successfully, the following details differ: the Titans' evildoing is instigated by Hera's spite at once again having been deceived by her husband; Athena is complicit in the conspiracy and the crime, although in the end she betrays her co-conspirators; they eat all of Dionysus, instead of tasting him and then having their banquet interrupted by Zeus; Dionysus's heart, the only remaining part of his corpse, is enclosed in a plaster statue, while in other versions either Apollo buries his remains or Demeter gathers them up; the Titans do not receive just one punishment, the blast of Zeus's thunderbolt, but are instead punished in various ways (*vario genere excruciatos necat*).

Some of these details may be supposed to be newly created – the product of the tale's adaptation to a pseudo-historical episode. The euhemerist impulse lends force to novelistic elements like Hera's grudge, which although it is already present in the *Rhapsodies*, seems clearly to be a late mythographic incorporation of Hera's traditional jealousy as a motivation for the Titans' crime, since the Titans have no need of such a banal motive to take on the role of cosmic evildoers assigned to them from ancient times.[52] It also makes a difference that the personages in question are now not gods but men; it is easier for the Titans to eat all of Dionysus because the scruples provoked by theophagy disappear, since he is not a god (pp. 354ff). Other details, however, may derive from an ancient mythic tradition not preserved in other sources: Athena's implication in the crime exceptionally converts her into a malicious character, as in the line of the *Iliad* (I. 400) that implicates her in a conspiracy against Zeus, together with Hera and Poseidon. It may be an ancient detail, since no other version explains how she managed to be present at the scene of the crime in order to save Dionysus's heart if she had nothing to do with events. In the same way, the variety of punishments inflicted on the Titans should probably be connected with *OF* 319, which assigns Atlas the penalty of holding up the heavens, while others suffer other fates; it is possible that some were chained to Tartarus and other directly struck down by Zeus's lightning bolt. The plaster statue into which Dionysus's heart is introduced also deserves consideration. Some have considered this to be an ancient version reflecting ritual performance, while another opinion supposes it to be the result of euhemerist rearrangement of two more ancient elements, the plaster with which the Titans cover themselves and the heart from which Dionysus returns to life. The version with the statue has

---

52   All the allusions to Hera's jealousy (collected in *OF* 303) are late, possibly springing from the *Rhapsodies*. On the evil character of the Titans, *cf.* Bremmer 2008, 73–95.

an unmistakable euhemeristic tone, while the ritual use of such a statue is not attested by any source, so the second option is clearly preferable.[53]

Where Firmicus's text appears least trustworthy, and where it has nevertheless exercised the greatest influence over modern scholarship (pp. 370ff), is his description of the Cretan ritual instituted by the king of Crete in order to commemorate his son's death. Crete's mysterious aura for the purposes of all religious activity allows Firmicus to mix in any and every Bacchic ritual element, whether it has anything to do with the myth or not, without worrying about internal contradictions. Thus, after expressly stating earlier that the child was cooked in various manners (*decocta variis generibus*), he says (6.4), "They imitate point by point everything that the child did and suffered in dying; they devour a living bull with their teeth..." (*omnia per ordinem facientes quae puer moriens aut fecit aut passus est; vivum laniant dentibus taurum...*). Leaving aside the practical difficulty of devouring a live bull with one's teeth (even for the toughest Cretans), what is clear is that this is not an imitation of the fate of Dionysus, who was obviously not devoured alive but rather sacrificed beforehand. Instead, what we have here is a mixture of various elements of Dionysian ritual mythology, derived both from this episode and from the maenadic tradition (sacrifice, omophagy, Bacchic ecstasy). The union of different aspects of Greek religion in a single *constructum* grows ever more audacious as the need for plausibility grows less.

It is clear that the source of this text is not Clement or Arnobius or any other known apologist, since none of them includes this version. Neither is it due to Euhemerus himself.[54] However, there is a curious case of correspondence that permits an approximate localization of the source. The *Wisdom of Solomon*, composed in Jewish circles in Alexandria during the first century BC, contains a passage that seems to come from the same source as Firmicus's text; the passage condemns a king who, grieving over the death of his son, commissions an image of him and converts him into the object of a mystery cult.[55] Thus,

---

53 West 1983, 162f imagines a ritual performance with the statue, but his only evidence for that is Frazer's description of the Niska Indians of British Columbia, which is hardly enough of a basis to suppose an ancient Greek ritual. Bernabé 2003a, 198 defends the alternative option, as a consequence of the fact that Dionysus' rebirth from Semele on the basis of this heart is an early Orphic version integrated into the *Rhapsodies* (Bernabé 2000 and Rudhardt 2002). The survival of the heart would be, therefore, oriented to Semele's version, not to any ritual. There might, however, have been more than one version regarding Dionysus' heart. On the gypsum and its possible implications, *cf.* Bettini 1985 and Ellinger 1993, who take for granted, perhaps too readily, that anthropogony was linked in all contexts to the myth of the Titans and all its details.
54 Forbes 1970, 37, n.116, and Winiarczyck 1991, 55 and 2002, 168–172.
55 *Wis.* 14:15–16. West 1983, 172 n. 101; Burkert 2005, 184.

3.2. Latin texts related to Protrepticus 2.12–22: Arnobius and Firmicus 159

the first century BC becomes the *terminus ante quem* of Firmicus's source, and the third century BC, when euhemerist mythological critiques become widespread, is the *terminus post quem*, although it is clear that the euhemerist author transformed earlier Orphic theogonic accounts like those on which Clement's version was based. The divergences in detail are the result of the euhemerization of the story, yet there are indeed several significant points of agreement with the Orphic myth: the toys and the mirror are mentioned, Pallas preserves the heart, Dionysus is cooked "in various ways." The Alexandrian connection reinforces the link: the poem reworked by Firmicus's euhemerist source may be the same one that underlies Clement's text.

With Firmicus the texts related to the description of the mysteries in the *Protrepticus* come to an end. A diagram of the sources and relationships might take the form of the figure on the next page (with the broken lines representing relationships I consider probable but not certain):

Figure 1

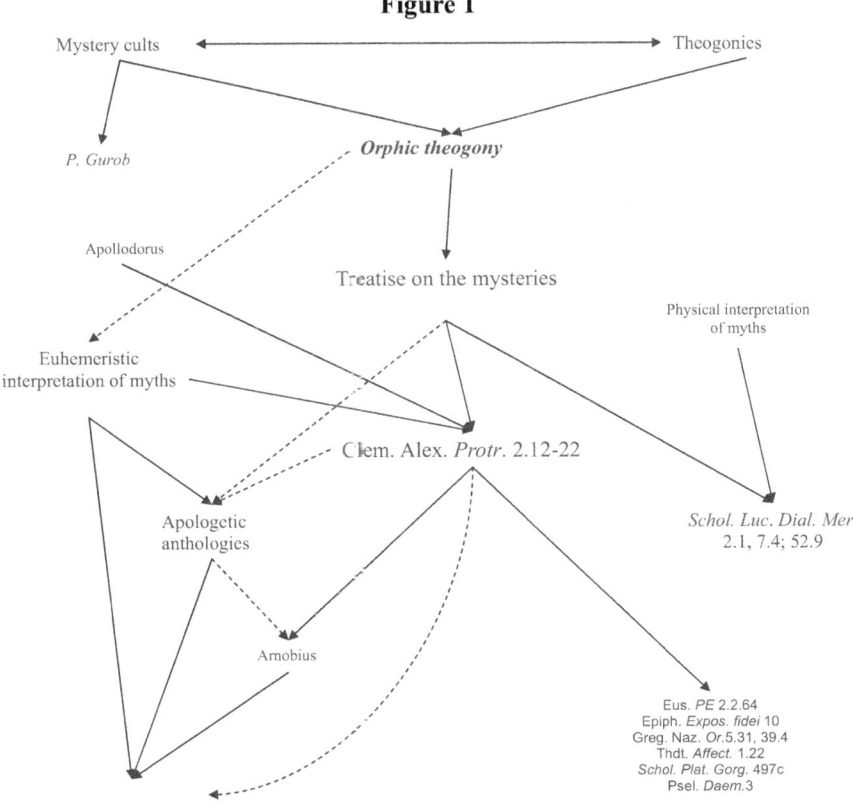

3.3. Hippolytus

A paragraph of Hippolytus's attack on the Gnostic sect of the Sethians, in which he accuses them of taking their doctrines from Orphic rites, heads in a different direction from the texts just discussed.[56] An additional difficulty is the extreme corruption of the only surviving manuscript, which makes it necessary to emend it in various places on which its interpretation depends to a significant extent. In order to facilitate my commentary, I have numbered the lines. The words on which I will comment are given in Greek in the reading I consider best, although some of these readings are conjectures emending the manuscript, for reasons I will explain. I direct the reader to Bernabé's edition (*OF* 572) for the complete bibliography on each variant.

> Their entire doctrine is derived from the ancient theologians, Musaeus, Linus, and Orpheus, who is the main revealer of the initiations and of the mysteries. For their doctrine concerning the womb and the snake and the navel, which is virility, is clearly found in the Bacchic rites of Orpheus (ἐν τοῖς βακχικοῖς τοῦ Ὀρφέως). These orgies have been celebrated and [5]handed down to men in Phlya of Attica (ἐν Φλυῇ τῆς Ἀττικῆς), prior to the observance of the mysteries of Celeus, and Triptolemus, and Demeter, and Core, and Dionysus in Eleusis. For before the Eleusinian mysteries there are enacted in Phlya (ἐν Φλυῇ) the rites of the so-called Great (*Megale*). There is a portico there, and on the portico (ἐπὶ δὲ τῆς παστάδος) is inscribed still today a representation of all the words that are spoken. There are many things [10]inscribed upon that portico, which Plutarch discusses in his ten books *On Empedocles*. And in the front part of the portico (τοῖς κλισίοισι) is also drawn the representation of a certain aged man, grey-haired, winged, having his *pudendum erectum*, pursuing a retreating woman like a dog. And over the aged man is the inscription "Fluent Light" (Φάος ῥυέντης) and over the woman "peree Phicola" (περεη Φικόλα). According to the doctrine of the Sethians, [15]"Fluent Light" appears to be the light, and Phicola the darkish water; while the space in the middle of them seems to be a harmony constituted from the spirit that is placed between. The name "Fluent Light" manifests, as they allege, the flow from above of the light downwards. Wherefore one may reasonably assert that the Sethians almost celebrate among themselves those rites of the Great (Megale) that are observed in Phlya (Φλυῇ). And the discourse of the Sethians tells that they composed their dogma plagiarizing those of the Greek [20]wise men, Musaeus, Linus and Orpheus.

---

[56] *Ref.* 5.20.4 (*OF* 572). Cf. Casadio 1997, Edwards 1991, Mansfeld 1992, and Montserrat 1993 on the Sethians. A similar passage, though without reference to Orpheus, is *Ref.* 5.6–10, accusing the Naassenes of finding inspiration in Eleusis (Sourvinou-Inwood 2003).

3.3. Hippolytus

The passage is a paradigm case of the fascinating complexity presented by the texts of the Church Fathers on Greek religion: the superposition of levels from the original nucleus – the Orphic text, rite, or in this case, painting – to the final source preserving it – the medieval manuscript of Hippolytus – is even greater than in Clement's work. Besides the textual corruption, it is necessary to work through, at the least, the filters imposed by Hippolytus and by his Sethian Gnostic source. In addition, two other sources are mentioned: some debated *Bacchica* by Orpheus and a work of Plutarch on Empedocles that has not survived.

Fortunately, Hippolytus's intervention appears to have been minimal and limited to the first seven lines, devoted to justifying his initial affirmation that the Sethians were dependent on the pagan theologians, as he also repeats in the last phrase of the passage. In order to justify this claim, he cites at the end the Sethians' own treatise (ὁ κατὰ τοὺς Σηθιανοὺς λόγος) as the source handing down the Orphic information; he needs only to summarize it, not to manipulate it. The quotation of this *Sethian Logos* clearly begins in line 7 ("since prior to the Eleusinian mysteries..."), which justifies the earlier affirmation about Phlye and the general reference to Eleusis. If Hippolytus had been able to take advantage of modern editorial techniques and insert footnotes, most likely the whole summary of the Sethian *Logos* from line 7 onward would have been covered with one note.

Let us now concentrate on Hippolytus's contribution (lines 1–7). The information on Eleusis is of the most trivial sort, limited to naming the personages of the Eleusinian myth, for which a certain level of general cultural knowledge that we can presume Hippolytus to have had would suffice.[57] What is interesting is the affirmation that what was instituted before Eleusis were the *bacchica* of Orpheus. What were these *bacchica*? On the one hand, the preceding phrase, "it clearly appears thus" (διαρρήδην οὕτως ἐστὶν), calls to mind a written work. However, it seems to me that we can rule out reference to a concrete work titled *Bacchica*; the phrase "the *bacchica* of Orpheus" had the same meaning as the similarly common "Bacchic and Orphic rites" (Hdt. 2.81, Plut. *Alex.* 2.7), and even if some scholar of a later age may have interpreted the generic title as a specific one, this is not a sufficient basis for thinking that it in fact designated any specific text.[58] If Hippolytus

---

57 The inclusion of Dionysus among the Eleusinian characters may refer to Iacchus (Graf 1974, 52 n. 10); it may be influenced by the previous mention of the *Bacchica*; or it may be yet another instance of the Christian apologetic tendency to amalgamate all the mysteries and their characters.

58 The catalogue of Orpheus' works in the *Suda* is the only specific reference to a work *Bacchica*, attributed to Nicias of Elea. Hippolytus' passage would be the only external support. Unlike Bernabé (*OF* 835), Kern trusted the *Suda* and at-

was referring to a more specific work than the *Orphica* in general, it might have been the *Rhapsodies*. The "womb, the serpent, and the navel that is a virile member" of the Sethians refer back to earlier paragraphs that described the Sethian doctrine according to which a serpent fertilizes the womb of a virgin and also to the way that the heavens and the earth are similar in form to a womb with an *omphalos* in the center (5.19.19–21). If there is anything similar to this related to Orpheus, it is doubtless the theogonic poetry, with the primordial couple of Uranus and Gaia and with Zeus's intercourse with Core in the form of a serpent. The most widespread theogony narrating these events at the time was the *Rhapsodies*, and Hippolytus – or even his Gnostic source, if the relation to Orpheus was established by the latter – might well have designated this theogony with the general title of *Bacchica*. The connection to Phlya may also suggest that this was the title designating the hymns of Orpheus sung by the Lycomids (Paus. 9.27.2, 30.12). On the other hand, however, Hippolytus immediately goes on to say of the *bacchica* that "they have been celebrated and handed down" (τετέλεσται καὶ παραδέδοται), which suggests that the term should rather be understood as "Bacchic rites," comparable to those of Eleusis. It is unjustified (*pace* Edwards 1991) to think that Hippolytus misinterpreted the title of a book; rather, on the contrary, he maintained the ambiguity – and perhaps it was for this reason that he chose an ambiguous term like *bacchica* – because in this way he reflected the tension between the erudite tradition and its real or imagined ritual actualization, a tension that was an inseparable part of both Orphism and Gnosticism.[59]

The unity of the text on the pre-Eleusinian mysteries beginning with line 8 guarantees its origin in a single source, the Sethian *Logos*. The passage describes certain paintings of Orphic inspiration and interprets them in accordance with the Gnostic mythology previously described, in which the triad of Light, Water, and Spirit is the cosmogonic principle. How did the Sethian author come to know these paintings? It is impossible to prove that he had not seen them himself, but what can be said for certain is that if he expressly cites Plutarch as an authority on these paintings, it is most likely that Plutarch's lost work on Empedocles is his principal source.[60]

---

tributed to the *Bacchica* his fragments 236–242; Linforth (1941), Edwards (1991) and Casadio (1997) also believe it refers to the title of a work.

59 Cf. Paus. 8.37.5: "And Onomacritus, taking from Homer the name of the Titans, composed the rites in honor of Dionysus, and made the Titans the authors of the sufferings of Dionysus". Cf. the same ambiguity between rites and writings in Hdt. 2.81, or Macr. *Sat.* 1.18.22. Cf. pp. 73ff.
60 Hippolytus does not read Plutarch's work on Empedocles directly, but a summary made by the Sethian writer. Mansfeld 1992, 295 n. 174.

3.3. Hippolytus

The next question is the location of the paintings. Is the reference to the mysteries of Phlya in Attica or to Phleious in the Peloponnese? Both options require emending the text: in the first case, replacing Φλειοῦντι by Φλυῇ on the three occasions on which it appears, and in the second, suppressing τῆς Ἀττικῆς in lines 7–8. The first option is clearly preferable. To start with, it is more plausible that a scribe (or even Hippolytus himself, if he misread the Sethian Logos) changed the mysteries of Phlya to the better-known mysteries of Phleious than that someone interpolated τῆς Ἀττικῆς for no apparent reason. What is more, however, Pausanias's testimony weights the balance definitively in this direction, since he says that the Lycomids sang Orphic hymns in the sanctuary (9.27.2; 9.30.12), that they had an Orphically-tinged cult to Gaia Megale (1.31.4), and that they alleged that their cult was older than Eleusis (1.5.1). In addition, the sanctuary of Phlya had been decorated with paintings since classical times; Plutarch bears witness to the fact (*Them.* 1), demonstrating that he could have seen the paintings personally and described them in his work on Empedocles.

It is precisely Pausanias who can help us to pin down where in the portico (παστάς) the paintings were: in line 11 the manuscript has τοῖς πλείοσι, which has generally been considered corrupt and for which various emendations have been proposed.[61] I would like to add the following one: Pausanias (4.1.7) says that a statue was dedicated in the κλισίον of the Lycomids in Phlya. This word is a Homeric *hapax* the exact meaning of which was already a subject for discussion among the ancient students of Homer: Porphyry says that the κλισίον is the part of the house that is πρὸς τὰς παστάδας.[62] It would not be difficult for a copyist to make a mistake – especially if κλισίον was an unusual word – by transcribing the dative plural ΚΛΙΣΙΟΙΣΙ (or ΚΛΕΙΣΙΟΙΣΙ with a common iotacism) as ΠΛΕΙΟΣΙ. It fits with Hippolytus's text that the paintings in question should have been in the κλισίον, as something contiguous to (or part of) the παστάς that was painted. A plausible translation is "in the front part of the portico."

These pictures, of explicitly sexual content, are an "image of the words spoken" (τῶν εἰρημένων λόγων ἰδέα); the expression calls to mind the Orphic hymns recited by the Lycomids during the rites. The connection with Orpheus – given that they must have had something Orphic about them in

---

61 Cf. Bernabé's *apparatus ad loc*: τοῖς πλείοσι] τοῖς πλείοσι‹ν ἄλλοις› Marc. ibid., coll. I 639 et Hippol. *Ref.* 5.21.1 : ταῖς παστᾶσι Wendland : τοῖς πυλεῶσι dub. Miller : τοῖς κείοσι dub. Maass. : 'Hippolytus has probably misread his source' Sandbach

62 *Quaest. Hom. ad Od.* 24.208. Cf. Eustathius and the scholia *ad loc.*, as well as the lexical works Harpocration, Hesychius and *Etymologicum Magnum* (*s. v.* κλισίον)

order to serve as evidence of Hippolytus's affirmation – is based on the two figures that must have been the protagonists of an Orphic episode, Resplendence (Φάος) and Phicola.[63] A relationship between Resplendence and Phanes-Eros was proposed long ago, on very convincing grounds: the common root of the name suggesting luminosity, the wings, and the sexual emphasis.[64] More recently, Giovanni Casadio has proposed relating Phicola to Baubo, on account of her canine imagery, her nocturnal associations, and her function as recipient of the virile member. The fact that Plutarch mentions these pictures in relation with Empedocles supports the association: if Empedocles composed explicitly sexual verses on the female *genitalia* and even used the term βαυβώ, as seems to have been the case, it would not be surprising for Plutarch to mention these obscene paintings in commenting on his work.[65] In any case, it must have been one or some of the many sexual unions of cosmic or ritual meaning sung in Orphic poetry that constituted the ground for the Sethian's proud claim of Orpheus' patronage of his doctrine-and also for Hippolytus' accusation.[66]

3.4. Justin

Finally, Justin has two references to the mysteries of Dionysus in which, although he does not allude to Orpheus directly (for which reason these passages have never been included in the editions of *Orphica*), the Orphic myth is clearly intended.

> *Apol.* 1.54: It was thus predicted: "There shall not fail a prince from Judah, nor a lawgiver from his thighs, until He come for whom it is reserved; and

---

[63] Marcovich 1974 proposed a Semitic origin for the name Phicola. Of the possible solutions for περεη in line 14, the most convincing proposals are γεραίη (Marcovich 1974) or ῥέη (Edwards 1991). I suggest also as possible readings ἱερῆ (sacred) or even ἱερέη (priestess, cf. Call. *Epigr.* 41) which would easily fit both paleographically and semantically.

[64] Maass 1895, 303, Harrison 1903, 644. Cf. *OF* 830.8, in which Phaos is invoked among other cosmic deities.

[65] Casadio 1997, 19–66. Hesychius (*s. v.* Βαυβώ) says that Empedocles used the name of Baubo to mean *koilía* (cavity of the body). Cf. Lebedev 1994, which shows that three verses describing a vagina, quoted precisely by Hippolytus (*Ref.* 5.8.43) in a similar attack on the Naassenes, are in fact by Empedocles.

[66] Casadio (followed by Bernabé in *OF* 572) also proposes to associate these paintings with the *symbola* of Ge Themis described in *Protr.* 2.22.2. However, Wilamowitz's emendation Ge has been shown to be wrong, so these symbols of Themis do not belong to Phlya but to Eleusis (Gagné / Herrero 2009).

3.4. Justin

He shall be the desire of the nations, binding His foal to the vine, washing His robe in the blood of the grape" (Gn. 49:8–10). The devils, accordingly, when they heard these prophetic words, said that Dionysus was the son of Jupiter, and gave out that he was the discoverer of the vine, and they number wine [or, "an ass": οἶνον/ὄνον] among his mysteries; and they taught that, having been torn into pieces, he ascended into heaven.

Dial. 69: Be well assured, then, Trypho, that I am established in the knowledge of and faith in the Scriptures by those counterfeits that the so-called Devil made to be said among the Greeks, just as he acted through the Magi in Egypt, and through the false prophets in Elijah's days. For when they say that Dionysus, son of Zeus, was begotten by the intercourse Zeus had with Semele, and that he was the discoverer of the vine; and when they tell that after he had been torn into pieces and died, he rose again, and ascended into heaven; and when they introduce wine [or, "an ass": οἶνον/ὄνον] into his mysteries, ¿do I not perceive that the Devil has imitated the aforementioned[67] prophecy of the patriarch Jacob, recorded by Moses?

The two passages are almost identical and refer to the same subject. Justin continues with the same accusation of plagiarism against Bellerophon, Perseus, Heracles, and Asclepius in the *Apology* and against Heracles, Asclepius, and Mithras in the *Dialogue*. The slight differences between the texts suggest that one is not a copy of the other; instead, Justin must be either summarizing the same source in different ways or, more likely, quoting from memory. The most probable direct or indirect source of the Dionysian references is the *Rhapsodies*, since they include Dionysus's birth from Semele, his identification with the vine, his death, and his resurrection. Nevertheless, the possibility cannot be dismissed that Justin is freely combining in both passages various episodes of Dionysian mythology with which he is familiar from standard handbooks or from his general cultural background.[68]

The texts raise two questions of interest. First, Boulanger (1925, 93) supposed that Dionysus's ascension to heaven was an unconscious projection by Justin of his own Christian narrative onto the Orphic myth: his ardor for

---

67 He is alluding to the same passage quoted in *Apol.* 1.54 (*Gn.* 49:8–12), mentioned in *Dial.* 52 and 54. The reference to Semele must be due to the biblical expression "lawgiver from his thighs" (ἡγούμενος ἐκ τῶν μηρῶν αὐτοῦ). Perhaps Justin mentions Semele because just before he has spoken of birth from a Virgin (*Dial.* 66, quoting *Is.* 7:10–16). In the *Apology*, instead, Semele is not mentioned, but after mentioning Dionysus he speaks of Danae, who is not alluded to in the *Dialogue*. Danae and Semele are evidently closer to the biblical tale than Core's rape by Zeus, even if Justin had known the Orphic myth. Cf. Tert. *Apolog.* 21.7–9, quoted in p. 285.
68 Cf. p. 234: in *Apol.* 1.21 "Dionysus who was torn apart" is mentioned in a typical list of "sons of Zeus", among Hermes, Heracles, the Dioscuri, Perseus and Bellerophon.

levying accusations of plagiarism would have led him to attribute to Dionysus an ascension, in imitation of Christ (*Acts* 1:9), that really never appeared in an Orphic *logos*. Although ingenious, the French scholar's idea does not seem likely for two reasons. First, Origen also says that Dionysus ascended after his resurrection in two passages (*CC* 3.23, 4.17) that do not seem to depend on Justin, since their context is entirely different (p. 214). Although Origen is again a Christian witness, unconscious projection is more difficult to postulate for two distinct cases, whose agreement in this point would be too much of a coincidence. Second, and more importantly, the *Rhapsodies* seem to imply that the Dionysus who returned to life by way of Semele resides in Olympus (*OF* 334–336). Thus, Justin's and Origen's testimony supports the idea that the *Rhapsodies* included the narration of some form of ascent of Dionysus to Olympus, as one line of a hymn by Proclus also suggests (7.11 = *OF* 327 II: "From Semele Dionysus ascended through the cosmos"). It should be remembered, nevertheless, that there was no reason for this ascent to be depicted in the same way as that of Christ.

The second problem is whether what the demons introduced in the mysteries of Dionysus was the ass or wine. The majority of the manuscripts have οἶνος, but an inferior manuscript and a marginal gloss to a principal manuscript read ὄνος.[69] Given the similarity of the two texts, what is decided for one passage applies to the other as well. The problem is that both wine and the ass appear in the prophecy that Justin proposes as the model being plagiarized (*Gn.* 49:8–12), which may have inclined the copyists as much toward one word as toward the other. Now, although it is tempting to read ὄνος on account of the ass's esoteric connotations in the *Frogs* of Aristophanes and in the *Gurob Papyrus*,[70] reading οἶνος is ultimately preferable. Not only is it the case that this reading is better attested in the manuscripts and that wine is much more common than the ass as an element of Dionysian mysteries, but in addition, the passage on Dionysus in the *Apology* is followed by a diatribe against Bellerophon for having copied the prophesied ass with Pegasus and against Perseus for having copied the virgin birth; given that the mention of Perseus complements the *Apology*'s passage on Dionysus with an element not included there, it is to be supposed that the same is true of the mention of Bellerophon as well, and hence that Dionysus's plagiarism involved not the ass, but wine. The later correction to ὄνος may be the result of simple error or of the effort to find all of the elements of the biblical prophecy in the mysteries of Dionysus.

---

69 Cf. the commentaries of Munier's edition of the *Apology* (1995) and Bobichon's edition of the *Dialogue* (2003).
70 Aristoph. *Ran.* 31. *P. Gurob* (*OF* 578) 25: ο]ἶν[ο]ν ἔπιον ὄνος βουκόλος.

4. Orphic Theogonies

We have seen that alongside his role as founder of mysteries, Orpheus most frequently appears in Christian texts as a theologian. *Theo-logia* in its etymological sense – discourse about the gods – exactly defines the Orphic theogonic poems, which additionally provide a basis for allegorical interpretations to which the same name might be applied in a more abstract sense. Although recounted in theogonic poems, episodes about Demeter, Core, and Dionysus have also been mentioned in ritual contexts because of their evident connection to the mysteries. Let us focus now on the references to the primordial gods who culminate in Zeus. In the theogonies, different principles coexist: Orpheus was the singer as much of the henotheistic tendencies that identified the various gods with one another or gave primacy to Zeus as he was of the episodes involving each individual deity. In the following section we will see how the Christians took advantage of the henotheistic tendency, generally making use of the hymnic genre. In the theogonies, on the other hand, their usual practice was to emphasize those episodes that forcefully brought out the contradictions of polytheism, with the interesting exception of Lactantius.

4.1. Athenagoras

The paradigmatic author in this sense is Athenagoras, who introduces an entire section of the *Legatio* on the Greek gods by saying that Orpheus, Homer, and Hesiod were those who established the genealogies and names of the gods (*Leg.* 17.1). Of the three, it is the most ancient, Orpheus, whom he will place at the center of his exposition.[71] Athenagoras's testimony has been much studied, since he describes in some detail an Orphic theogony the characteristics of which correspond to those offered by Damascius for the *Theogony of Hieronymus and Hellanicus*, a re-elaboration of earlier Orphic theogonies originating in a Stoic milieu and preceding the *Rhapsodies*, with which it shares its principal mythic themes, although orienting them more clearly toward a Stoic

---

71 He specifies this in *Leg.* 18.3 "Orpheus, whom Homer follows more than anybody". This contrasts with his previous quotation from Herodotus (2.53) about Homer and Hesiod having invented the genealogies and names of the gods. The second part of the quotation (i. e. that in his opinion they had been the most ancient poets) is omitted by Athenagoras, who used Herodotus as his favourite source for themes of Greek religion (cf. n. 31) but did not want to throw away the apologetic advantages of Orpheus' chronological priority (pp. 227ff).

interpretation.[72] The general opinion is that, in order not to multiply entities without necessity, it is to be supposed that all of the fragments attributed by Athenagoras to Orpheus come from this theogony, since they are perfectly coherent with one another. Given that Athenagoras's texts are provided in Appendix 5, I will limit myself here to discussing their content and purposes.

The first fragments (*Leg.* 18.4) are the ones that coincide with Damascius and permit the localization of the theogonic material. From the waters there arose a monstrous animal, a serpent with the heads of a bull and a lion, Heracles/Cronus by name, which engendered an egg, which was divided into Heaven and Earth and from which arose Phanes. Heaven and Earth, in their turn, had additional descendants (Moirai, Hecatonchires, and Cyclops), whom Heaven cast down into Tartarus in order to avoid being dethroned by them, causing Earth to engender the Titans in revenge. All these details are intended to demonstrate that the gods are corruptible, since they are not eternal, but rather arise from matter and are consequently subject to the laws of generation. For this reason the emphasis on the noun γένεσις (four times in 18.3–6) and the verb γίγνομαι (seven times) is constant. Nevertheless, it need not be thought that Athenagoras was doing excessive violence to his source: an ἐγείνατο appears in what he quotes from the poem (*OF* 83.1) and is also in agreement with the spirit of the theogony.[73]

Shortly afterward (*Leg.* 20), Athenagoras returns to these same episodes, elaborating now not on the corruptibility, but instead on the monstrosity of these primordial creatures: he mentions once again the god-serpent Heracles and the Hecatonchires and adds the daughter of Zeus and Demeter-Rhea, Core, who had four eyes, four horns, and two faces, as a result of which Rhea fled in

---

72 West 1983, 176–226 and Bernabé 2003a, 89f suppose that the *Theogony of Hieronymus and Hellanicus* is previous to the *Rhapsodies*, while Brisson 1990 is the only scholar to maintain that it is a later version. The debate on the *Pseudoclementina* is obviously linked to this question (cf. nn. 76 and 77).

73 It is debatable whether the other quotation in which γένεσις appears is Orphic. The Homeric line (*Il.* 14.246) Ὠκεανός, ὅσπερ γένεσις πάντεσσι τέτυκται is attributed to Orpheus. West 1983, 184 suggests that it could be an inserted gloss, and Bernabé does not include it as Orphic fragment. However, the parallel with *HO* 83.2 and Plut. *De fac. orb. lun.* 938d, which documents a line *Il.* 14.246a of clear Orphic coloration (Nagy 2001, Herrero 2008a) make it probable that Athenagoras' text is reliable and that Ocean was in the original text of the *Theogony of Hieronymus and Hellanicus*, interpreted as water by the Stoics. His partner, interpreted as primordial *ilys*, is Thetys for West 1983, Ge for Jaeger 1947. The first one is a better option, since Ge was the partner of Ouranos in the same theogony. However, Bernabé (*OF* 75) considers that Ocean and Thetys were not in the theogony and that water and mud appeared as ἀρχαί in the poem itself, on the grounds that Damascius does not exchange proper names for common elements anywhere else.

fright without nursing her, leading to her mystic name Athela (from ἀ-θηλύς). This is information found nowhere else and reveals not only a taste for allegory in the Orphic poet, but also a baroque aesthetic that is clearly Hellenistic and, in turn, a certain interest in ritual, as seen in Core's mystical epithet. Further on he mentions the castration of Uranus by Cronus and the dethronement of the latter by Zeus, who after battling the Titans,[74] raped in serpent form both Rhea (herself also turned into a serpent) and the fruit of their union, Core, who became the mother of Dionysus. He ends with the verses describing the terrifying appearance of Echidna, engendered by Phanes (*OF* 81), who is said to have also had the form of a serpent and to have been devoured by Zeus "in order to be infinite." He ends the section by asking, "To what end are we going to turn to those who are born in forms like those of the beasts and have the shapes of wild animals and a horrible appearance?"

The last reference to the theogony is in *Leg.* 32.1, where after refuting the accusations of incest and cannibalism made against the Christians, he counterattacks, "If they want to present free union as a crime, they should start by hating Zeus, who begot children on his mother Rhea and his daughter Core and took his sister (Hera) as his wife, or the poet who tells of all this, Orpheus, who made Zeus more impious and abominable than Thyestes, since the latter united himself to his daughter on account of an oracle, in order to reign and to avenge himself." Nothing new is to be found in this paragraph, which only recalls episodes previously mentioned, this time emphasizing incest.

Various other general references in the work to the parricides, incests, and monstrosities of the Greek pantheon have as their background the events expressly referred to here. It is clear that Athenagoras was interested in highlighting them in their crudest possible form, for which reason he emphasizes (*Leg.* 20) that these poems describe "their deeds exactly, just as they suppose them to be," without admitting any allegorical or symbolic interpretation of these episodes. Precisely this rejection of interpretation provides a clue as to the source through which Athenagoras knew this theogony. In *Leg.* 22 he criticizes those who argue that 'these are all poetic fantasies and that there is a physical explanation for all this." The most logical supposition is that these interpretations rejected by Athenagoras came from the same source as that through which he knew the theogony, referenced immediately before. Probably this was a Stoic commentary, perhaps by the same Hieronymus

---

74 A Titanomachy shows that the Titans did not sacrifice Dionysus in this Orphic theogony (West 1983, 181), unlike in the *Rhapsodies* or in Clement's source.

cited by Damascius, that used the theogony as the basis for naturalistic interpretations, in a format like that of the Alexandrian *Hypomnemata* on the Homeric text or, as a more distant precedent, the *Derveni Papyrus*.[75]

4.2. Tatian

Tatian's diatribe against the immoral actions and passions of the Greek gods also mentions the typical Orphic theogonic episodes:

> Zeus has intercourse with his own daughter, who becomes pregnant by him. I will have as witnesses now Eleusis, and the mystic snake, and Orpheus saying, "Close the gates, you profane!" Aïdoneus carries off Kore, and his deeds have been made into mysteries; Demeter bewails her daughter, and some persons are deceived by the Athenians. In the precincts of the temple of the son of Leto is a spot called Omphalos, but Omphalos is the burial-place of Dionysus (*Orat.* 8.6).

Slightly later (*Orat.* 10.1), criticizing the metamorphoses of the gods, he specifies, "Rhea turns into a tree, and Zeus into a serpent on account of Persephone." The reference to Zeus's transformation into a serpent in order to unite himself with his daughter has suggested that Tatian's source is the same theogony used by Athenagoras, that of Hieronymus and Hellanicus (*OF* 74 and 89 in Bernabé's edition). Nevertheless, Zeus's union with Persephone in the form of a serpent is also a prominent episode in the theogony that is at the basis of Clement's text, in which it is an *aition* of the mysteries of Sabazius. Probably, the episode was also included in the *Rhapsodies*. In fact, "the mystic serpent" that Tatian appears to associate with Zeus's union in his first reference suggests a ritual context more than the baroque aesthetic of Athenagoras's multiple serpents, and if Tatian was inspired by the same source, he probably would not have failed to mention that Zeus also transformed himself in order to unite with Rhea. What can be said for certain is that Tatian (or an apologetic source, if he himself was not the compiler of this list of gods) could recall the episode of Core as sung by Orpheus on the basis of his general knowledge of pagan religion, just as he could the Orphic *sphragis* of "Close the doors, you profane ones" (*OF* 1), without making a concrete reference to any particular theogony. If we prefer to suppose a specific theogony, nevertheless, it should also include the ravishment

---

75 Cf. Casadesús 2001 and Schironi 2001 on the similarity between the methods of Alexandrian philology and those of the Derveni commentator.

of Core by Aidoneus and the burial of Dionysus in Delphi, both alluded to immediately afterward. Moreover, these episodes, as myths of the mysteries of Eleusis and Dionysus, were included both in the theogony underlying Clement's text and in the *Rhapsodies*, making these works the most probable candidates for the direct or indirect basis of Tatian's references.

4.3. Pseudoclementina

The Christian apologetic novel preserved in different Pseudo-Clementine writings also transmits several fragments of an Orphic theogony. The section in which these appear has a clear Jewish stamp, in both literary and ideological dimensions, and it seems clear, as Luc Brisson has convincingly argued, that the author of this Christian novel integrated into it a Jewish apologetic work dated approximately in the second century AD. This section (*Homil.* 6.2–13, Rec. 10.17–19) presents a dialogue between three characters: a Jew, Clement, his brother Nicetas (a convert to Judaism) and Apion, the renowned enemy of the Alexandrian Jewish community, against whom Josephus had written a work *Contra Apionem*. All three discuss an Orphic theogony, among other pieces of Greek poetry, especially Hesiod, within a general discussion about how myths should be interpreted (cf. p. 34). While Clement prefers euhemerism, Apion interprets myths as physical allegories, a method rejected by Nicetas as devoid of any value. It is tempting to think that Apion's approach, and perhaps some of the actual words put in his mouth, are taken from some previous pagan work, perhaps even by the historical Apion, but waters are too deep there to undertake a successful *Quellenforschung* further than this supposition.[76]

The relevant texts are long and complex and have been analysed in detail in other recent works, so a brief summary of the main facts will be sufficient here. The Orphic theogony is particularly difficult to reconstruct due to the fact that the three characters interpret it together with Hesiod. Such harmonizing interpretation of different Greek poets in order to achieve a naturalistic cosmological reading points clearly to Stoic circles, whence the Orphic poem must ultimately come. Both the *Rhapsodies* and the *Theogony of Hieronymus and Hellanicus* are well known to have been subjected to this kind of interpretation by Stoics. The contents are also coincident with what

---

76 Cf. n. 20 for general studies on the *Pseudoclementina*. Brisson 1990 for the *Quellenforschung* of Orphic material. Bernabé in his edition attributes these fragments to "Apio ap. Ps.-Clem. Rom." (vol. III, 330).

we know of both poems from other sources. The emergence of a cosmic egg out of the primordial chaos, due to the combined action of personified Time and the generative *pneuma*, and the subsequent birth of Phanes out of this egg are the main episodes that are narrated and interpreted. Scholars have proposed different theories on whether the original poem is Hieronymus' or the *Rhapsodies*, or even some other theogony that would be close to both but would not coincide exactly with any of them. Alberto Bernabé has recently made a detailed and forceful case for the *Rhapsodies* based on stylistic and formal coincidences, which makes this the preferable option.[77]

4.4. Origen

Among the various references to Orphism made by Origen in *Against Celsus*, there are some that criticize the themes of incest and parricide characteristic of the theogonies (*CC* 1.17 = App. VI; 3.23; 4.17). Lacking direct quotation and full of apologetic topics, these references hold scant interest for the reconstruction of the theogonies. A claim for novelty has been made only with regard to *CC* 4.48. However, the textual variant that I believe to be correct, transmitted by one line of manuscripts (**A** in the edition of M. Marcovich 2001), belies this:

> What can be said to be more truly shameful than the Greek histories taken literally? In these, gods who are sons castrate the gods who are their fathers, and gods who are parents devour their own children, and a goddess-mother gives a stone to swallow instead of his own son, the "father of gods and men" (ἀντιδίδωσιν υἱοῦ τοῦ πατρὸς ἀνδρῶν τε θεῶν τε λίθον), and a father has intercourse with his daughter, and a wife binds her own husband, having as her allies in the work the brother of the fettered god and his own daughter! (cf. *Il.* 1.399)

The text is customarily edited as ἀντιδίδωσιν υἱοῦ τῷ πατρὶ «ἀνδρῶν τε θεῶν τε» λίθον, which when translated as "she gives a stone in place of her son to the 'father of men and gods,'" grants this title to Cronus in Orphic tradition.[78] Nevertheless, Greek poetry (*Il.* 1.544), including Orphic poetry

---

77 Bernabé 2008. On pp. 80f he provides a *status quaestionis*, with Kern 1922 (frr. 55–56) and Brisson 1990 attributing the Orphic fragments to the *Theogony of Hieronymus and Hellanicus*, while West (1983, 266) prefers the *Rhapsodies*. He gives new arguments for the latter position. He disagrees with Roessli 2008c, who postulates an independent theogony, close to the *Rhapsodies* but different in some points.
78 Cf. Bernabé in his edition (*OF* 201). The only other basis for giving Cronus this title is a text by Gregory of Nazianzus, but it will be shown in the following

(*OF* 244, 282), always designates Zeus with this expression, never Cronus. Therefore, in my opinion, it is preferable to adopt the genitive τοῦ πατρός and grant the title to Zeus, as in the translation given above and as Origen himself does when referring to him in *CC* 3.23. The earlier reference to Cronus would permit the omission of the dative, the lack of which must have motivated the scribe to change the case of πατήρ without realizing that this would award to Cronus a title he never enjoyed. Of course, it is possible to argue that the genitive is precisely a later correction intended to normalize the text, but the arguments in favor of the *lectio facilior* seem superior to me.

Did Origen know the Orphic theogonies at first hand? Probably not: he does not quote Orphic verse directly (except for the 'father of men and gods' just mentioned, which could perfectly well be a quotation of Homer from memory), unlike what he does in a similar critique of Hesiod (*CC* 4.35), whose work he did know, for example. This agrees well with the affirmation in *CC* 1.18 (App. VI), "And it does not seem that the books of your wise men and poets still endure, and they would have been preserved if they had been perceived as having any use." If the Orphic theogonies the episodes of which Origen relates were lost for him, it is clear that he must have had a different source, "the philosophers" (mentioned together with wise men and poets immediately before, but omitted in this last phrase) who interpreted and allegorized these myths in the Neoplatonic mode. In fact, the target of Origen's attacks is, as much as the myths themselves, the allegorical interpretations that the philosophers apply to these myths and to which Celsus nevertheless objects when they are applied to the Bible. The text of *CC* 4.48 is followed by criticism of an interpretation made by Chrysippus of the Samian painting of Zeus and Hera in full ἀρρητοποιία. A philosopher-theologian like Origen acquired his knowledge of Orphic poetry from other philosophical and theological works originating in the rival camp.

4.5. Gregory of Nazianzus

Two passages of Gregory of Nazianzus should be viewed in connection with those of Origen. In his *First Discourse against Julian* Gregory says:[79]

---

section that it also probably alludes to Zeus. *OF* 244 and 282 also give Zeus the traditional title that he is always given by all Greek poetry.

79 *Or*. 4. 115, distributed by Bernabé across fragments 134 V, 200 VII, 201 II, 395 III, 676 III, 848 II. The sixth-century commentator of this discourse known as pseudo-Nonnos expands largely on Gregory's allusions to Orphic theogonies, apparently drawing from some informed handbook. Cf. Nimmo Smith 2001.

Let Orpheus come forward with his harp and all-attractive song; let him thunder out in honour of Zeus the great and supernatural words and concepts of his theology: "Zeus, greatest of the gods, rolled up in dung, be it of sheep, or of horses, as well as of mules" (*OF* 848: Ζεῦ κύδιστε, μέγιστε θεῶν, εἰλυμένε κόπρωι, / ὅση τε μηλείη, ὅση τε ἵππων, ὅση τε ἡμιόνων), in order that henceforth may be exhibited the life-giving and life-maintaining (τὸ ζωογόνον καὶ φερέσβιον) power of the god: for in no other way could it be done. Nor should he spare the rest of his magniloquence: "The goddess spoke, and both her thighs exposed" (*OF* 395 III) in order to initiate her lovers, a thing she still does by means of figures (ἃ καὶ νῦν ἔτι τελεῖ τοῖς σχήμασιν); and after all, Phanes, and Ericepaeus, and he that swallows up all the other gods, and throws them up again, so that he may become "father both of gods and men." Let these things be brought on the stage for the benefit of the marvellous audience of this theology, and over and above all this, let there be contrived allegories and exhibitions of miracles: and let the sermon, running wild from these premises, advance into pits and precipices of speculation that has no solid foundation.

In the *Discourse on the Holy Spirit* he says:[80]

Nor do those whom the Greeks worship as gods and *dæmons (as they say themselves)* need us in any respect for their accusers, but are convicted by their own theologians: some as subject to passion, some as given to faction, and full of innumerable evils and changes, and in a state of opposition, not only to one another, but even to their first causes, whom they call Oceans and Tethyses and Phanetes, and I do not know what other names; and last of all a certain god who hated his children through his lust for rule, and swallowed up all the rest through his greediness that he might become the "father of all men and gods" whom he miserably devoured, and then vomited forth again.

Both texts are very similar and have an extremely strong rhetorical charge, using the metaphor of putting paganism on trial. Information is not used as evidence for an argument previously given, in the manner of a footnote, but rather is itself the argument, since "the theologians accuse themselves." This creates an opening for suspecting the manipulation of their testimony, but it also makes their content more interesting, since it comes directly from the Orphic poems or from allegorical interpretations of them. It is appropriate to rule out a previous apologetic source, on account of the original content of Gregory's references, not repeated in other authors, on account of his wide reading, and on account of his references to ideas about the soul contained in the *Rhapsodies* (p. 213). The *Rhapsodies* are probably the source of these references, if they

---

80 *Or.* 31.16, distributed by Bernabé across fragments 191 II, 200 VI, 201 III, 215 I.

are indeed derived from a specific theogony.⁸¹ Gregory's disdainful "Oceans, Thetyses, Phanetes, or whatever they are called" does not encourage the reader to assume a great deal of precision. This tendency to lump things together and provoke confusion leads to a problem in the second text, in which the first causes (πρῶται ἀρχαί) are clearly contrasted to the ultimate god (τελευταῖον θεόν). Who is this? The adjective would seem to indicate Zeus, characterized as ultimate (ὕστατος) already in the *Derveni Papyrus* (*OF* 14.1) and the successive Hymns to Zeus (*OF* 31.1, 243.1), and in whom culminates the dynastic succession that begins with Oceanus-Tethys or Phanes, the first causes. "Who hates his children on account of love of power" (μισότεκνον διὰ φιλαρχίαν), however, points to Cronus, who devoured his children out of fear of being dethroned. I believe that, as part of his strategy of fusing various sources and mythic elements, Gregory amalgamates into a single episode the traditional myth of Cronus and the Orphic myth of Zeus's ingestion of Phanes and all the other cosmic elements, including the gods, and his posterior regeneration of them all (*OF* 240). This amalgamation permits him to denigrate an episode much celebrated among admirers of Orphism (e.g., the Neoplatonists), the re-creation of the world by Zeus, by putting it on the same plane as the myth of Cronus, a favorite target of Christian mockery, since his aim is to attack the most philosophical myths and those most susceptible to allegorization. In addition, this fusion of the two episodes explains why the title of "father of men and gods" (πατὴρ ἀνδρῶν τε θεῶν τε), much more appropriate for Zeus than for Cronus, is displaced in both of Gregory's texts to the latter. Thus, neither Origen's use of the title nor Gregory's uses are a sufficient basis for arguing that the Orphic poets gave to Cronus a title belonging only to Zeus.⁸²

Nevertheless, the error may be enlightening in other respects. Out of malice or confusion, Gregory mixes Zeus's swallowing of Phanes (and with him of the entire universe) with Cronus's devouring of his children in order to retain power. The Orphic theogonies, in their turn, present the ingestion of Phanes as a solution to the problem of the One and the Many, under the auspices of Night. In swallowing Phanes, the primordial generative principle, Zeus,

---

81   West 1983, 186 deduces from the allusion to Ocean and Thetys as first causes that he refers to the *Theogony of Hieronymus and Hellanicus*, which, unlike the *Rhapsodies*, perhaps had them as primordial couple. However, the presence of this couple in that theogony is not certain (cf. n. 73). Besides, the interpretations of both gods as first causes were usually made on the basis of *Il.* 14.201 and 14.302, and perhaps this is the reference that Gregory has in mind, for he is speaking generally and need not necessarily be restricted to Orpheus.
82   *OF* 201, therefore, should be suppressed in my opinion as an independent fragment. Cf. n. 78 *supra*.

causes everything to become once again one within him. This myth has a common foundation with Hesiod's account of the devouring of Metis (a name that Phanes also receives in the *Rhapsodies*), an action taken by Zeus in order to avoid his dethronement by his possible descendants.[83] The ingestion of Phanes for metaphysical reasons seems to be the more ambitiously speculative Orphic version (since the name of Metis, "Counsel," already reveals a certain level of Hesiodic speculation), of the old myth of one god devouring another in order to interrupt the chain of succession, as Cronus does. Thus, in erroneously identifying the two acts of ingestion with one another, Gregory brings to the fore their fundamental connection, as the same mythic image gives rise to different speculative results. The distortion inherent in Christian apologetics at times reveals a certain amount of truth, a path that will be explored in chapter VI.

Besides the theogonic references, Gregory's first text includes two quotations of distinct origin. The verses of *OF* 848 mocking the omnipresence of Zeus, present even in animal excrement, do not seem to come from the theogonies. Their origin may be in parody, or they may have been intended as a serious expression of pantheism taken to its radical extreme, since they are quoted in Philostratus (attributed to Pamphus) in a non-parodic context.[84] The adjective ζωόγονος that follows the quotation also appears in Philostratus's text, so that it is probable that this word, as well as φερέσβιος, which the Cappadocian also mocks, appeared in the poem to which these two lines belong, since both words fit hexameter meter and imply the same pantheistic orientation.

The quotation about the goddess who shows her thighs seems to come from a poem derived from a more ritual context. Clement, whose work we have seen that Gregory knew, quoted a verse in which Baubo makes a similar obscene gesture. Gregory's text is slightly different, since it is a goddess who makes the gesture.[85] Unless the Cappadocian was quoting from memory and made a mistake or changed the text deliberately, it must be supposed that he is reflecting an Orphic tradition parallel to that used by Clement, whether Demeter herself is the protagonist of the action or whether Baubo has divine rank, as seems more probable to me. In any case, this reference should probably be related to Baubo's presence in Asia Minor, as a maenad in Magnesia and as

---

83 Hes. *Theog.* 888–900; *OF* 140–141. Cf. West 1983, 88, 106.
84 Philostr. *Her.* 25.2 (*OF* 848 I). Cf. Lobeck 1829, 745; West 1983, 53. Bernardi *ad loc.* suggests that Gregory purposefully transforms the second line to make it sound more ridiculous: in Philostratrus' text it has adjectives instead of genitives μηλείηι τε καὶ ἱππείηι καὶ ἡμιονηίηι.
85 The line quoted by Clement (*OF* 395 I) says: "ὡς εἰποῦσα πέπλους ἀνεσύρατο, δεῖξε δὲ πάντα", while that in Gregory (*OF* 395 III) says: 'ὡς εἰποῦσα θεὰ δοιοὺς ἀνεσύρατο μηρούς'.

a figure of feminity in the statuettes of the sanctuary to Demeter in Priene. It is most probable that it is this kind of image that Gregory has in mind when he says that "she still initiates by means of figures." Likewise, the mention of Ericepaeus recalls the inscription from Halicarnassus (*OF* 662) that invokes Dionysus under this name.[86] However literary Gregory's references, he knew which elements of the Orphic tradition were present in the cults of the region of Asia Minor, and he chose precisely these as the targets of his criticism.

4.6. Lactantius

In contrast to all these attacks on the theogonic myths, Lactantius is the only apologist who takes the theogonic material in a different and original direction. In a lengthy passage of the *Divinae institutiones* he singles out Orpheus from among all the ancient poets to praise him for having intuited in Protogonos-Phanes the first, uncreated, and creator god (1.5.4). Immediately afterward, he contrasts Orpheus's profundity in this to the lesser depth of the poetry of Homer, which only narrates human adventures, and of Hesiod, whom Lactantius criticizes because he "traces the origin of everything not to a creator god but rather to chaos ... when he should rather have explained that chaos itself" (1.5.8). He praises Vergil and Ovid, on the other hand, for their reflection of the doctrine of a creator god, and he ends the section by recalling (*DI* 1.5.13) that Orpheus and the Latin poets attained this intuition of the truth. The entire text, translated in Appendix 7, is of enormous importance because it proposes an *interpretatio christiana* of the Orphic deity, the scope of which will be analyzed in detail in chapter VI.

The passage is complemented by two other references along the same lines. In *DI* 4.8.4 (*OF* 134 IV) Lactantius discusses the double sexuality of Phanes: "And we will not consider that God is male and female, as Orpheus thought, since he could not conceive of another form of generation that did not have the power of one sex and the other, as if he were to copulate with himself and could not procreate without coitus." In *Epitome* 3 (*OF* 153 II), then, he specifies the elements of the cosmic creation mentioned in the *Divinae institutiones*: "Orpheus says that there is a principal god who established the heavens and the sun with the other stars, the earth, and the sea."[87]

---

86 II. nn. 41, 47–49.
87 The anaphoric enumeration of the elements in the universe is typical of cosmological passages in hexametric poetry: cf. *OF* 237 (from the *Rhapsodies*), probably inspired by *Il*. 18.482–485. Lactantius' Latin shows that he reads Greek Orphic poetry directly. Cf. pp. 298f for his playful translation of *archos* as *princeps*.

The source of the references to the creator god (Phanes) is doubtless the *Rhapsodies*, since the episodes agree exactly, especially regarding the birth of Phanes from the ether.[88] The citations must derive from direct acquaintance with the *Rhapsodies* or, alternatively, with pagan Neoplatonic works that quoted them frequently. They do not appear to come from Christian anthologies;[89] the great interest of Lactantius's quotations arises precisely from the originality of his perspective, which leads him to preserve fragments of which he is the only route of transmission. His approach is quite the opposite of that of the other apologists who refer to theogonies: instead of satanizing Orpheus, he puts him on the same level as the gods, using the voyage of the Argo as evidence; instead of harmonizing him with Homer and Hesiod, he looks for what distinguishes his poetry from that of the other two; instead of attributing the fragments of truth that he finds in him to plagiarism of Moses and the prophets, he attributes them to natural reason that led him to "apprehend the truth"; and when he has to criticize a failure in his theology, the double sexuality of Phanes or his birth from the ether, instead of elaborating on Orpheus's errors, Lactantius excuses them indulgently, appealing to the theogonic categories that pushed Orpheus to conceive of creation in terms of generation (*quia concipere animo non poterat*). While Athenagoras insists on the presence of generation in the Orphic theogonies in order to demonstrate the corruptibility of the gods, Lactantius sees in Orpheus the intuition of postulating an ungenerated creative principle.

Thus, Lactantius works within the same categories as the other apologists, but inverts them. He is much closer to the Neoplatonists who see in Orpheus the inspiration for the demiurge in Plato's *Timaeus*.[90] Instead of highlighting the polytheistic side of Orphism, he emphasizes the henotheistic tendency. This aligns him far less with the authors seen up to now than with those we will look at next.

---

88 Ogilvie 1978, 26 supposes that Lactantius wrote ἠερός instead of Αἰθέρος because he translates it into Latin as *aer*, but the manuscripts can be interpreted in both senses (ιερος **R** : ‹ηε›ρως **B** : θερος **MP**), and translating *aither* as *aer* is not unthinkable. Proclus (*In Plat. Tim.* 1.433.31 = *OF* 124) says περικαλλὴς Αἰθέρος υἱός. Betegh 2004, 156 concludes from this line of reasoning, among other evidence, that Aither is already a god in the Derveni theogony.

89 Such is also the opinion of Ogilvie 1978, 26f. The only exception is perhaps *OF* 363 (*DI* 1.7.11), an obscure fragment of euhemeristic tone (Cronus and Zeus are kings), preceded by the chronological topos that Orpheus is later than the Sibyl. Both elements are typical of apologetic anthologies (cf. pp. 233f, 98).

90 For example Procl. *In Plat. Tim.* 1.306 (*OF* 153 V), 3.227 (*OF* 58 I), 3.68 (*OF* 58 II). This tradition is still alive in some Byzantine authors (Malalas, Suda in *OF* 153) and it is renewed by Renaissance Platonists.

5. Orphic "monotheistic" poems

No direct source in earlier apologetic works can be located for Lactantius's use of the *Rhapsodies*, but it is clear that he participated in a tradition that began with the Jews and that the Christians expanded. According to these authors, Orpheus already proclaimed the revealed truth, at least in part. Some texts, like the so-called *Testament*, were composed for this purpose in imitation of Orphic poems; others were pagan Orphic poems whose orientation (at times a product of Jewish influence) was sufficient to serve as evidence for the thesis of Orphic monotheism.

5.1. The *Testament* of Orpheus

The Orphic poem most cited by the apologists was the one popularly called the *Testament*,[91] a poem in which Orpheus announces to his son Musaeus his abandonment of the polytheism he previously defended and proclaims his belief in a single God. The poem is a Jewish composition imitating the poetic and theological style of earlier Orphic poems. The Christians' predilection for the poem is explicable, since it was composed precisely for apologetic ends and did not need to be taken out of context and reinterpreted, as was the case with other Orphic poems that did not originally carry such meanings. References to it are customarily preceded or followed (*OF* 368–376) by expressions emphasizing Orpheus's previous polytheism in order to highlight his conversion. Its enormous popularity is precisely what gives rise to the principal problem associated with the *Testament*: the great textual variation revealed by the quotations that preserve it, all of them in Christian apologetic works.

Various versions of the poem are preserved, apparently resulting from the expansion of a primitive version in a process tending to make the announcement of the Mosaic revelation clearer and to refine the image of the one God. Two theories have been proposed in this regard, and the debate between them remains unresolved. The one I believe to be more convincing is that of Christoph Riedweg (1993), who proposes a briefer first version (*Urfassung*: *OF* 377), of Jewish origin and Stoic tendencies, not greatly different from the Orphic poems on which it was modelled, and a longer version, perhaps composed by Aristobulus (*Aristobulische Überarbeitung*: *OF*

---

91 Theophilus (*Autol.* 3.2) and Ps.-Justin's *De monarchia* (2.4) call it Διαθῆκαι (*Testament*), a title that I will use for convenience, although probably it did not designate the poem originally. Cf. Riedweg 1993, 44.

378), in which biblical elements are made much more explicit and certain theological ideas change substantially. The respective texts, commented on in great detail by Christoph Riedweg, are presented in Appendices IX and X, and merely reading them clearly brings out their differences; for example, *OF* 377 (ll. 11–12) makes God responsible for good and evil, while *OF* 378 (ll. 13–15) relieves him of responsibility for the evil that men cause for themselves. The two versions were fused in the *Tübingen Theosophy* in the sixth century AD. Clement seems to have known and partly quoted both. The *stemma* of the various authors' relations of dependence has been studied in depth by Riedweg (1993, 24) and offers few secrets. I reproduce it here:

Figure 2

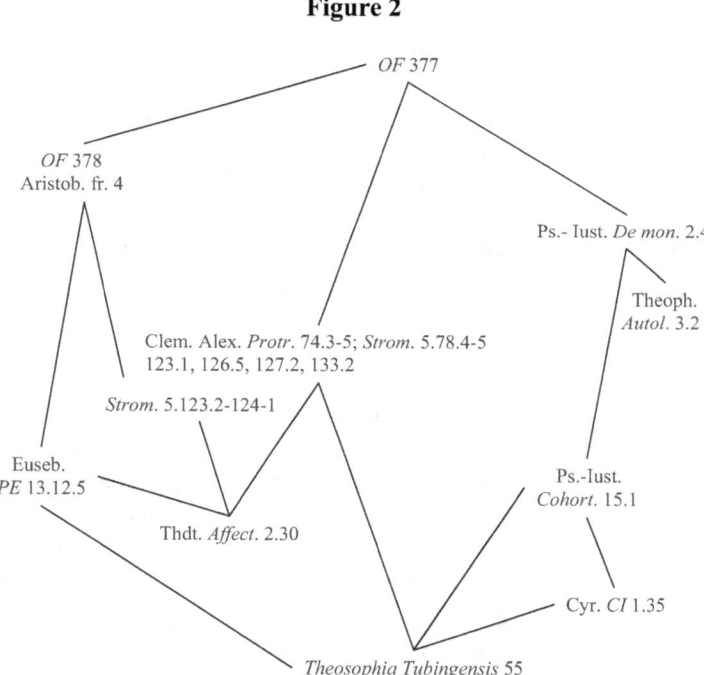

The alternative to Riedweg's proposal, advanced by Carl Holladay (1996) following the indications of Niklaus Walter (1964), postulates four recensions, each successively amplifying its predecessor: A (recension used by the *Cohortatio*), B (recension used by Clement, the presumed source of all his quotations), C (recension used by Eusebius), D (recension used by the *Theosophy*). Given that the question of whether the *Theosophy*'s version expands the one preceding it or compiles all of the earlier ones seems to be more a matter of names than of substance, the principal problem lies in determining whether there is a specific version of the poem quoted by Clement, or whether he simply quotes parts of the two versions in different passages.[92] Riedweg (1993, 15ff) defends the second option and denies the existence of a *redactio clementina* separate from the other two, because he considers it unnecessary to require that Clement quote every line of the two versions; rather, he could omit lines according to his tastes and needs. The detailed analysis of Clement's references to the *Testament* can, in my opinion, contribute to clearing up the question. I will focus on this point, because it is here that this book can add something to the meticulous studies of the text made by the authors mentioned.

Let us begin with the quotation in the *Protrepticus* (7.74.3–6). After citing Aratus, Hesiod, Euripides, and Sophocles, Clement offers several lines from the brief version of the *Testament* (*OF* 377). Unlike the quotations from the other poets, however, the quotation from Orpheus is preceded by a phrase emphasizing the contrast to his singing of the pagan mysteries, denounced in the earlier *refutatio*. Orpheus's own conversion should impel that of Clement's readers.

> But the Thracian Orpheus, the son of Œagrus, hierophant and poet at once, after his exposition of the orgies, and his theology of idols, introduces a palinode of truth by singing, albeit late, the real *hieros logos*: ... (*OF* 377, 1.–7a). Then proceeding, he adds with precision: ... (*OF* 377, 8–10). Thus far Orpheus at last understood that he had been in error: "But linger no longer, O man, endued with varied wisdom; / But turn and retrace your steps, and propitiate God" (*Sib. Orac.* 3.624).

The insistence on Orpheus's palinode and on his singing (ᾄδων) the true *hieros logos*, although belatedly, picks up on the metaphors of Book I surrounding the old song of Orpheus and the new song of the Logos. This intimate connection with the beginning of the work also explains the choice of verses. What is quoted are the first ten lines of the brief version, which emphasize exhortation to conversion and end with three lines describing the object of conversion, the one God. Beginning with line 11 the poem becomes more philosophical as it amplifies this description, and these lines are

---

92 Kern 1922 edits a Clementine version as an independent version (fr. 246); Bernabé does not, since he accepts Riedweg's theory (*OF* 377–378). Radice 1995 arrives independently at the same conclusions as Riedweg 1993. A new monograph on the *Testament* by F. Jourdan is expected to appear soon.

not of so much interest for Clement's hortatory aims; on the other hand, the lines from the Sibyl that follow the quotation are a perfect fit.⁹³

The sole omission in these ten lines is the phrase "about this there is an ancient account" (παλαιὸς δὲ λόγος περὶ τόδε φαείνει) in line 7a, which was undoubtedly in the text that Clement was reading, because before quoting l. 8, he says, "And then, further below, he adds with precision." The probable reason for excluding this phrase is that its traditional reference to the authority of a *palaios logos* (perhaps a remnant of the Jewish imitator's Orphic model) would contradict Clement's efforts throughout the whole work to oppose the "ancient error" of Orpheus to the "new truth" of Christ (παλαιὰ ἡ πλάνη, *Protr.* 1.6.3).

The most probable source for this brief version of the *Testament* is an anthology of pagan texts suited for apologetic use, like those studied by Nicole Zeegers (1972); this is because all of the citations preceding it on the topic of divine omnipotence appear in other apologists and will be repeated by Clement in book V of the *Stromata*. Nevertheless, the *Stromata* were addressed to the instruction of the already-converted Christian, and in this work the aim of conversion is secondary. This is immediately evident in the citations of the *Testament* in book V, from which disappear the initial hortatory lines that were key in the *Protrepticus*. Now what matters to Clement is demonstrating correspondences with the prophets, and this is his sole criterion for selecting verses.

---

93 One might think that Clement mistakenly attributes those two lines to Orpheus (Bernabé edits them as *OF* 844). But Clement knows the *Sibylline Oracles* well, as his many quotations show. Besides, it is not strange that he quotes allusively without mentioning the author (e.g. *Protr.* 1.2.4; 1.5.3; cf. van der Hoek 1996, 131–133). The oracle simply underlines the process of conversion undergone by Orpheus. But the effect pretended by Clement is possibly to lead the reader who knows neither the *Testament* nor the *Oracles* to think they belong to the same poem, while a more attentive or expert reader cannot accuse him of being mistaken. *OF* 845 is another case of confusion of an oracle with an Orphic poem. The proximity between Orphic and oracular poetry (pp. 97f) provokes their convergence in a non-apologetic context in *OF* 661.

The first quotation (of *OF* 377) shows up in *Strom* 5.12.78.3–5. After demonstrating agreement between Plato and Moses on the inaccessibility of God, Clement says:

> And when the Scripture says "Moses entered into the thick darkness where God was" (*Ex.* 20:21), this shows to those capable of understanding, that God is invisible and unspeakable, And "the darkness" – which is, in truth, the unbelief and ignorance of the multitude – obstructs the gleam of truth. And again Orpheus, the theologian, taking it from there, says:
>
> "He is one, perfect in himself, and all things are made (τέτυκται)
> the progeny of one" (8)
> or "are born," for it is also written thus
> (ἢ 'πέφυκεν', γράφεται γὰρ καὶ οὕτως). He adds:
> "Him no one of mortals has seen, but He sees all" (9–10).
>
> And he adds even more clearly:
> "Him see I not, for round about, a cloud has settled;
> for mortals have in their eyes mortal pupils
> and are not able to see the sovereign through everything" (14–16).

There follows a quotation from the New Testament (2 *Cor*. 12:2–4) on the same theme of divine inaccessibility, showing that Clement is not following slavishly a Jewish source, but making some scriptural comparisons of his own. The citation here of the brief version is of great importance for the question of the poem's redactions, because the phrase "πέφυκεν is also written" after τετύκται in line 8 demonstrates that even within a single version there were significant variants, and that Clement was conscious of them.[94] Admittedly, this phrase could perfectly well be a medieval gloss inserted into the text of the manuscripts, but as it is a variant attested nowhere else, it probably belongs to Clement's original text.

In addition, this paragraph once again shows Clement's criteria for quotation: only those lines that support the idea of the inaccessibility of the omnipotent creator God deduced from the preceding biblical passage are selected. The clearest link is that between the cloud (νέφος) of line 15 and the cloud of *Ex* 20:21 (γνόφον). In contrast, the beginning of line 9 ("he

---

94 In line 8 Clement also presents the variant αὐτοτελής instead of αὐτογενής, contrary to his quotation of the same line in the *Protrepticus*. It seems a contamination of the short version by the longer one, perhaps due to Clement's quoting by heart, since he had both versions at hand when composing the *Stromata* (Riedweg 1993, 16, 29).

himself revolves around all") is omitted because this pantheistic principle would contradict the idea of God's inaccessibility.

In *Strom.* 5.14.123.1 the quotations are lengthier, and more importantly, they include the two versions in the same paragraph. After various citations of pagan poets, among others of Orphic texts that we will see later, Clement says:

> And the same Orpheus speaks thus: (*OF* 377.5–7a). And again he says of God that He is invisible, and that He was known to but one, a Chaldean by race – meaning by this either Abraham or his son – with these lines: (*OF* 378, 23–27). Then, as if paraphrasing the expression, "Heaven is my throne, and earth is my footstool" (Is. 66:1), he adds: (*OF* 378, 29–39, with omission of lines 36–37), and so forth. For in this he indicates these prophetic utterances: "If you open the heavens, trembling will seize the mountains in your presence, and they will melt, as wax melts before the fire."

Here the focus is on describing the omnipotent God: the lines from the brief version (*OF* 377) are the same as in the *Protrepticus*, and the same policy of breaking off the quotation in the middle of line 7a is continued, whether on account of the same desire to avoid the reference to the *palaios logos*, or because Clement was copying his earlier quotation. He is aware that there are two different poems, since he separates them with the adversative αὖθις ("in another place").[95] Upon quoting *OF* 378 he skips line 28, a line that, perhaps not coincidentally, is corrupt in the complete version of Aristobulus transmitted by Eusebius.[96] Riedweg thinks that Clement omits ll. 36–37 of *OF* 378 because the direct reference to the laws of Moses was too crude for him; I believe, rather, that these two lines would be a digression from his theme of divine omnipotence.[97] Finally, he ends the quotation just before ll. 40–41 of *OF* 378, which once again address Musaeus (a conscious omission,

---

[95] Instead, when he jumps from line to line within the same poem he uses εἶτα. This is Riedweg's convincing argument (1993, 16) to show that there is no *redactio clementina*, but instead Clement is using both versions at the same time.

[96] *PE* 13.12.4. Riedweg (1993, 17) suggests that perhaps it was not present in Clement's manuscript due to its being corrupted. In any case, confusion around the same line is another proof that this quotation corresponds to the same version quoted by Eusebius (*OF* 378).

[97] Riedweg 1993, 17 n. 56. Another possible reason is that line 36 of *OF* 378 speaks of the "tradition of the ancients" (λόγος ἀρχαίων) as the basis for attributing to Moses the saying that God was "beginning, middle and end" (Plat. *Leg.* 715e). Clement, unlike other Christian authors (cf. V n. 101), does not attribute this quotation from a "*palaios logos*" to Moses, not even in *Stromata* V: if for some reason he does not share this idea, it would be logical that he omitted these verses that imply it.

as the phrase "and what follows" shows). As always in this work, Clement's program is one of confining himself to doctrinal parallels and not insisting on exhortation, the contrary of his approach in the *Protrepticus*.

In the following passages he quotes anew some lines from the brief version (*OF* 377), *à propos* of other comparisons between poets and prophets. As a correlate to the Deuteronomic phrase "I will kill and give life; I will strike and heal" he cites lines 11–12,[98] and afterward ll. 19–20, "clearly taken" from Jeremiah when the latter says, "He who made the earth with his power."[99] Shortly afterward (5.14.133.2) he quotes l. 17, an expression of radical monotheism ("There is no other besides the great king"). The content of all these verses fits the biblical parallels to which they are compared, for which reason their selection is fully justified. The amalgam of pagan and Old Testament citations in this section suggests that the origin of the whole section is an anthological source. The slight variations with respect to the standard text of *OF* 377, discussed in the notes, do not justify postulating an independent version, but are rather the product of different paths of transmission.

These are the texts. Discussion of the recensions of the *Testament* known to Clement should take into consideration the extent to which Clement slavishly copied his apologetic sources, which established the comparison between pagan authors and the Scriptures, and the extent to which he reorganized this information and added texts of his own. To begin with, given that direct knowledge of Aristobulus, to whom he refers frequently, seems clear, his source for the long version, which he quotes only in the section on divine omnipotence (*Strom.* 5.14.123–124), was probably the Jewish apologist.[100] On the other hand, given the frequency with which and the diversity of contexts in which Clement cites the *Testament* alongside scriptural comparisons that seem to be his own,[101] it is highly possible that he had at his disposal a copy of the brief version of the *Testament* (perhaps originating, as Riedweg 2001 notes, in the *De monarchia*, with which he shares an almost identical text, or else in a common source), besides the quotations of the same version that he

---

98 *Strom.* 5.14.126.5, *Deut.* 32:39. In line 11 there are two slight variations from the standard text of *OF* 377: αὐτός for οὗτος and φυτεύει for δίδωσι. Both can be explained (Riedweg 1993, 29) as a result of quoting by heart: the first as contamination from the longer version (*OF* 378.13), the second from Homer (*Il.* 15.134, *Od.* 5.340).
99 *Strom.* 5.14.127.2, *Jer.* 10:12. The second part of l. 20 is contaminated by l. 18, be it due to a copying mistake, due to a memory lapse, or on purpose, since the result is closer to the following biblical text. Cf. Riedweg 1993, 17.
100 Riedweg 1993, 18 n. 60.
101 Cf. the New Testament quotations in *Strom.* 5.12.78.1, and the confusion of Hosea for Amos 4:13 in *Protr.* 8.79, repeated in *Strom.* 5.14.126.3.

doubtless found in the apologetic anthologies. It would be highly surprising if these apologetic sources did not include so well-known and important a testimony as this poem, and it is probable that the text at Clement's disposal did not always coincide with the one in the anthologies; a text transmitted in this way is susceptible to permanent changes in accordance with the taste or the needs of the apologist in question, as the *Testament*'s history demonstrates. The anthologies would be, then, a second source for Clement's citations of the brief version. The *varia lectio* in *Strom.* 5.12.78.1 and the variants that Clement offers in *Strom.* 5.14.126–127 with respect to other patristic witnesses can be easily explained by this dual source. The possibility of quotation from memory should also be taken into account. Finally, it is clear that Clement quotes while choosing and omitting lines according to what interests him, for which reason postulating an independent Clementine recension, on the grounds that he is obligated to quote every line, is without sufficient basis and multiplies entities without necessity. In this way Riedweg's theory that Clement consulted the two recensions is confirmed, although with the additional nuance that the anthologies may have provided him with alternative variants of the brief version by another route. The earlier diagram could be revised as follows, as far as Clement of Alexandria is concerned:

Figure 3

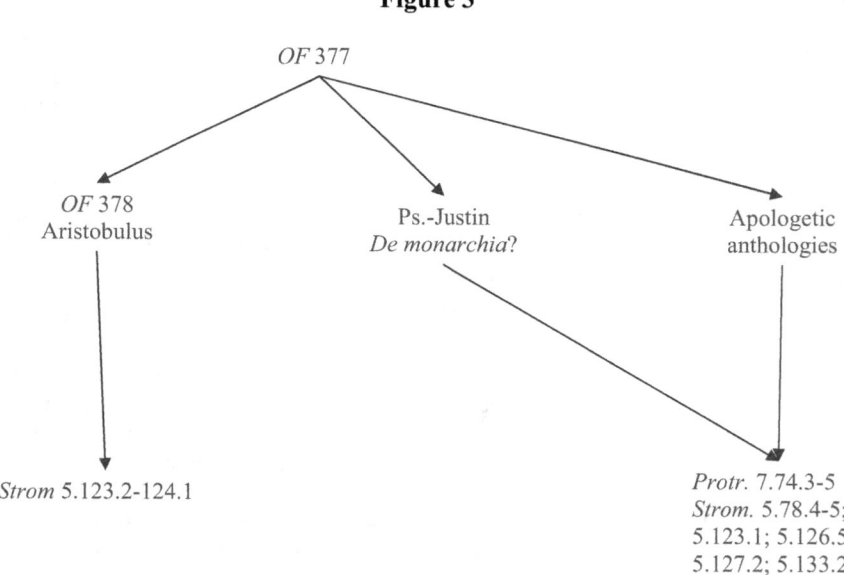

5.2 Hymn to Zeus

One of the most celebrated texts in Orphic literature is the *Hymn to Zeus*, which proclaims him the beginning and end of all things. Already alluded to by Plato (*Leg.* 715e) and inserted into the *Derveni Theogony* in a first, reduced version (*OF* 14), it was expanded, probably under Stoic influence, in a hymn transmitted by the Pseudo-Aristotelian treatise *De mundo* (*OF* 31) and inserted into the *Rhapsodies* in an even longer version (*OF* 243). The hymn in its various forms enjoyed enormous popularity among the Neoplatonic philosophers. Among the Christians, Clement of Alexandria and Eusebius refer to it, although in very different ways. Clement's two references are in the same section of the *Stromata* as his two references to the *Testament*. In 5.14.122.2 he says:

> We shall find expressions similar to these also in the Orphic hymns, written as follows:
>
> "For having hidden all, he brought them again to gladsome light forth from his sacred heart, solicitous" (*OF* 31.8–9).
>
> And if we live throughout holily and righteously, we are happy here, and shall be happier after our departure there, not possessing happiness for a time, but enabled to rest in eternity.

These verses are inserted after various texts of the comic playwright Diphilus, Euripides, and Pseudo-Sophocles (probably a Jewish forgery) and before a fragment of Empedocles on the end of the world, divine wrath, and the immortality of the just. The eschatological interpretation of these verses is in perfect consonance with the previous texts and makes it very probable that they came from the same anthology. The verses quoted are the end of the celebrated *OF* 31, a *Hymn to Zeus*, and it is noteworthy that they are the only two lines of the poem that do not refer to Zeus by name; the seven previous lines are excluded in order to apply them with greater purity to the biblical God. To whom is this filter to be attributed? Given that Clement in other passages has no problem quoting pagan texts that announce the truth using the proper names of pagan gods,[102] while on the other hand the fragments surrounding this one in this passage follow the same policy of abstaining from proper names, maintaining the respectful "God," it can be supposed that Clement's apologetic source already had only these two lines.

---

102 *Strom.* 5.14.125.1: Bromius (although this is a rhetorical reference to autumn); *Strom.* 5.14.127.1: Zeus.

In addition, the Orphic text receives here an eschatological meaning that it did not originally have: "hiding them all" refers to the gods swallowed by Zeus in the Orphic theogony, but Clement takes it as referring to all men whom God will raise to new life. As there is no allusion to the theogonic episode of Zeus's ingestion anywhere in his works, it is highly possible that Clement did not know the story or considered it sufficiently marginal to enable him to change the meaning without disturbing his readers. Lack of knowledge of or interest in theogonic themes (except for the section on the mysteries in the *Protrepticus*) is a constant in his work.

The following citation, slightly further on (*Strom.* 5.14.128.3), is inserted in a section on God's omnipotence. The verses are introduced following references to Phocylides, Philemon, and Sophocles, and preceding references to Pindar and Hesiod, without any comparison to the prophets, and probably come from the same anthology for apologetic use as the earlier verses. Clement says:

And Orpheus:

"One Might, one god exists, the *great, the flaming heaven;*
all things are made one Being, in whom all these revolve,
fire, water, and the earth."

And so forth.

These three lines offer two variants (highlighted here in italics) of great interest when compared to the versions that appear in the hymn inserted in the *Rhapsodies* and recorded by Porphyry and other Neoplatonists:

"One Might, one god exists, the *great, sovereign of everything;*
one is the real body, in whom all these revolve,
fire, water, and the earth, night and day" (*OF* 243.6–8).

The two variants[103] that Clement offers have a common trait: they do not place as much emphasis on the kingly nature of the god they invoke as they do on his pantheistic essence. Clement interrupts his quotation in the middle

---

103 The Greek is as follows: Clement: ἓν κράτος, εἷς δαίμων γένετο, μέγας οὐρανὸν αἴθων, / ἐν δὲ τὰ πάντα τέτυκται, ἐν ᾧ τάδε πάντα κυκλεῖται; *OF* 243.6–7: ἓν κράτος, εἷς δαίμων γένετο, μέγας ἀρχὸς ἁπάντων,/ ἓν δὲ δέμας βασίλειον, ἐν ᾦι τάδε πάντα κυκλεῖται. There are some other variants for the γένετο of *OF* 243.6 (ἔγκρατος, ἐγένετο, γενέτωρ, and Bernabé's conjecture γενέτης, cf. Bernabé *ad loc*). They do not affect, however, the comparison with Clement's variant.

5.2. Hymn to Zeus

of the third line, although he makes clear that more text follows. West's brilliant analysis of *OF* 243 supposes that the compiler of the *Rhapsodies* "after the recital of Zeus' predicates inserted a passage of 25 lines in which the physical world is described and anatomized as the body of Zeus ... the Rhapsodist has evidently interpolated into the theogony a passage of separate provenance, probably from a hymn and presumably current under the name of Orpheus. It assumes an anthropomorphic Zeus with golden locks, horns, and wings: this is not the Zeus of the theogonies, but the Zeus of some Hellenistic syncretism."[104] Given that Clement's verses do not mention the kingly nature of the god, which integrates the hymn into the theogonic narrative, but instead describe the god's function more philosophically as kindler of the heavens and modeler of the universe, and that moreover these verses' relationship with those of the *Rhapsodies* is undeniable, then why not believe that Clement's lines belong to the hymn the compiler inserted, with certain modifications, into the *Rhapsodies*, and that they preserve their form prior to insertion? It is logical to suppose that they were the first two lines of this Hellenistic Orphic hymn to Zeus.[105]

---

104 West 1983, 239–240. In note 25 he offers some Greek and Eastern parallels to this sort of pantheism. We could even suppose that lines 10 and 20, the only ones that invoke this universal god as "Zeus" (called θεός in line 24), resulted from the insertion of this hymn into the *Rhapsodies* and were not in the original version, dedicated to some impersonal god or to some other divinity whose name was changed by the Rhapsodist. However, Zeus is the best candidate to have been invoked in hymns of this sort.

105 West 1983, 239–241 describes the efforts of the Rhapsodist to insert the hymn into the theogonic structure of the great poem, for which he had to introduce slight changes in the initial series of Zeus' predicates (the first seven lines of *OF* 31): he altered the line that in *OF* 31.7 reads Ζεὺς βασιλεύς, Ζεὺς ἀρχὸς ἁπάντων ἀργικέραυνος. In the *Rhapsodies* (*OF* 243.5) it reads Ζεὺς βασιλεύς, Ζεὺς αὐτὸς ἁπάντων ἀρχιγένεθλος. According to West, this change is due to the fact that the first line of the new Hellenistic hymn already had ἀρχὸς ἁπάντων, and the Rhapsodist would have tried to avoid repetition. This idea is incompatible with my supposition that the first line of the Hellenistic hymn is the line transmitted by Clement. But if we concede to the compiler some interest in maintaining a certain theological consistency, it is easily perceivable that αὐτὸς ἁπάντων ἀρχιγένεθλος underlines that Zeus gives birth to all things himself, precisely the theogonic episode into which this hymn is inserted (a strategy identical to that by which West himself (1983, 241) explains the insertion of line 8 and the changes in line 31). According to my proposal, the predicate ἀρχὸς ἁπάντων, which the Rhapsodist is interested in keeping since it expresses the theogonic idea of supreme power, would be transposed to the following line (*OF* 243.6), thus modifying the first line of the inserted hymn. Thus the only lost predicate is the traditional epithet ἀργικέραυνος, which is already in the first line, and also οὐρανὸν αἴθων in the first line of the inserted

Therefore, *OF* 243 is composed from the fusion of the initial series of invocations to Zeus (the six first lines of *OF* 31) and the hymn whose first lines Clement quotes. The fact that an apologetic source cites them separately under the name of Orpheus not only gives us a relative *terminus ante quem* for this source – before the composition of the *Rhapsodies* – but also demonstrates that both hymns circulated together in Alexandrian milieus. The citation also confirms that the pantheistic Hellenistic hymn integrated into the *Rhapsodies* was already circulating independently under the name of Orpheus, and it confirms, once again, that the majority of the Orphic material that Clement is using is pre-Rhapsodic.

The other Christian author who cites the *Hymn to Zeus* is Eusebius. His quotations are not derived directly from the *Rhapsodies*. In the same way that he cites the preceding passage of Clement in *PE* 13.13.55 as evidence of pagan wisdom's dependence on the prophets, in *PE* 3.9 he begins with a lengthy quotation from Porphyry's *On Statues* (fr. 354 F Smith) and a detailed refutation of his theological principles. Porphyry quotes the hymn inserted into the *Rhapsodies* in full (*OF* 243), and it is thanks to Eusebius's quotation that it has been preserved for us. In the following refutation he singles out a handful of lines for commentary. If this refutation, however, is of great interest for the next two chapters as an example of Eusebius's theology and strategy – very different from those of Clement insofar as he will use the verses not as support for monotheism, but rather, *more athenagorico*, in order to criticize the immanence and materiality of the pagan god – from the perspective of the text there is no mystery whatsoever, as his only source for his knowledge of the *Hymn to Zeus* is Porphyry, who himself took the text from the *Rhapsodies*.

5.3. Other Orphic hymns in *Stromata V*

A good part of book V of the *Stromata* (5.14.89 - 5.14.141), the subject of a magisterial commentary by Alain Le Boulluec in 1981, is dedicated to dem-

---

hymn, an expression of lighting up the universe that is not completely coherent with having swallowed it previously. In the second line of the insertion, the replacement of ἓν δὲ τὰ πάντα τέτυκται, an expression of philosophical tone, by ἓν δὲ δέμας βασίλειον, which underlines the ideas of a universal body and Zeus' kingship, would have the same intention of inserting the Hellenistic hymn into the theogonic narration. The Rhapsodist did not achieve perfect consistency, and later lines of the hymn betray its separate origin, but syncretistic amalgams rarely achieve total cohesion, and the compiler would presumably have concentrated his efforts on the first lines.

5.3. Other Orphic hymns in Stromata V

onstrating the coincidences between pagan philosophy and poetry on the one hand and the Christian revelation on the other. Besides the *Testament* and the *Hymn to Zeus*, there are two other quotations in the same section from Orphic hymns of henotheistic orientation. The more extensive reference is to the following hymn (*Strom.* 5.14.125: *OF* 691):

> And he said this through Isaiah, "Who has measured the heaven with a span, and the whole earth with His fist?" (Is. 42:12). Again, Orpheus says:
>
> Ruler of the aither, of Hades, of the sea and the earth,
> who shakes with bolts the strong home of Olympus;
> whom the daemons (δαίμονες) dread, and whom the throng of gods fears;[106]
> even the unsoftening Fates obey you
> immortal, mother-father (μητροπάτωρ), you shake everything in your heart,
> you move the winds, you cover all with clouds,
> you cut the broad aither with storms; in the stars
> is your order, following your inalterable commands,
> around your fiery throne stand the much-labouring
> messengers (ἄγγελοι), who care that everything is fulfilled for mortals;
> your spring flourishes anew with purple flowers,
> your winter comes among chilly clouds,
> Bacchic thunder (βακχευτὴς βρόμιος) reigns in your autumns...
>
> And then he adds, calling God expressly "almighty":[107]
>
> deathless, immortal, speakable only for immortals,
> come, oh greatest of all gods, with powerful necessity,
> fearsome, unconquerable, great, deathless, crowned by the aither.
>
> By the expression "mother-father" he not only intimates creation out of nothing (ἐκ μὴ ὄντων γένεσις), but also gives occasion to those who introduce emissions to imagine a consort of the Deity.

---

106 I have translated δαίμονες as *daemons* since the presence of angels in line 10 suggests the parallel existence of evil beings who would dread the mighty God, a dualistic conception of Persian origin with great success in Judaism. However, the traditional fear of the gods before Zeus (*Il.* 1.580f) is also present in the second half of the verse. It is a clear instance of transition between two different conceptions linked by one word (cf. p. 277).

107 Clement argues that Orpheus calls God παντοκράτωρ by making a word-play with line 15 (μέγιστε θεῶν πάντων, κρατερῇ σὺν ἀνάγκῃ). Clement is very fond of etymology and word plays as an apologetic and hermeneutical method (cf. pp. 276f). The εἶτα may suggest that Clement is dropping some lines (cf. n. 95).

This hymn is cited just after the *Testament* in relation to the quotation from Isaiah. Once again, it is difficult to know whether this fragment formed part of the "anthologies of plagiarism" used by Clement in this section, or whether he knew it from somewhere else and inserted it here *motu proprio*. Nevertheless, there are four indications that support the second option. *a*) The prophetic citations following the poem are repeated identically in the *Protrepticus* (even with the same error of saying Hosea instead of Amos), in a context unconnected to plagiarism,[108] suggesting that the comparison originates with Clement himself, as with his comments on μητροπάτωρ. *b*) The poem is quoted just after the long version of the *Testament*, which comes directly from Aristobulus. *c*) The hymn invokes the god using pagan names, unlike other Orphic fragments – of Jewish manufacture or excerpted like the *Hymn to Zeus* – derived from anthologies. Finally, *d*) the hymn does not appear in any other source, not even in other apologetic works that use anthologies extensively.

Clement knew the hymn, then, from a non-apologetic source, and a hint of the route by which it reached him is offered by the content of the poem itself. It is a hymn composed in Alexandria, an exponent of the pantheistic and syncretistic tendencies of Hellenism, and although the hymn is not a Jewish work, Jewish and perhaps also Gnostic influence is evident.[109] The angelology and demonology surrounding the king of the universe, of Eastern origin, are combined with traditional religious images and terminology very close to those of the *Orphic Hymns* and other hexametrical poetry like the *Sibylline* and *Chaldean Oracles*. Line 4 on the Moirai reveals the internal contradictions of this amalgam between tradition and new ideas (immutable destiny versus omnipotent God) that expanded in Egypt more than anywhere else. What Clement says about the epithet μητροπάτωρ is of great interest.[110]

---

108 *Protr.* 8.79.1–3. *Am.* 4:13, *Jer.* 19:13, *Deut.* 32:9.
109 Cf. West 1983, 36, n. 108, with some *loci paralleli* of late syncretistic texts, and Le Boulluec 1981 *ad loc.*
110 Cf. Le Boulluec 1981 *ad loc.* Its usual sense is "mother's father". Here it expresses the notion of a first uncreated creator, like αὐτογενής in the *Testament* (cf. Firm. Mat. *De err.* 5. *praef: Deus tu omnium pater pariter ac mater*) or the bisexual Phanes in *OF* 149. The notion of a masculine and feminine Zeus was already in line 4 of the *Hymn to Zeus* (*OF* 31), and it was traditionally thought to be Stoic (Festugière 1953, 45–46). But the Derveni theogony, with a hymn to Zeus that is the clear precedent of *OF* 31, already presents Zeus bearing the Universe (*OF* 12 and 16), so it is possible that the Orphic image was inherited by the Stoics rather than vice versa (p 91). This notion is a clear link between the three "monotheistic" hymns quoted by Clement (*OF* 31, his version of *OF* 243 and this one), and also with the earlier hymn of the Derveni theogony. Lactantius was probably right when he thought this a characteristically Orphic image (*DI* 4.8.4): *deum, sicut Orpheus putavit, et marem esse et feminam.*

On the one hand, he gives it as evidence that Orpheus had intuited the biblical idea of creation *ex nihilo*. On the other hand, with his constant ambivalence with regard to Orphism, he deduces a second consequence. For if the text indeed prefigured Christian truth, it also contributed to fomenting error: "It inspired those who introduced the doctrine of emissions and perhaps even thought of a spouse of God." The vocabulary makes clear that, more than to Hera or to a traditional goddess, the allusion is to the doctrine of the Valentinian Gnostics, whom Clement combatted frequently:[111] they postulated a series of "emissions" (προβολαί) and "relations of marriage" (συζυγίαι) starting from the divine *Pleroma* and characterized the Eons as "male and female" (ἀρσενοθέλυες) principles. Perhaps the Valentinians took this notion, like various others, from Orphism. The accusation that the Gnostics inherited their "heretical" conceptions from the pagans was a favorite idea of the apologists (e. g., Hippolytus), and it is not always a credible one. Clement's nearness to Gnostic milieus and to Gnostic thought, demonstrated by Salvatore Lilla (1971), gives a certain degree of trustworthiness to his information, the objectivity of which he himself guarantees with a cautious τάχα, and puts us on the track of the route by which this hymn could have come into his hands, namely, Gnostic literature. The ease with which he links it to hymns derived from Jewish apologetic sources reveals the similarity of the literature circulating in Gnostic, Jewish, and Christian milieus. The proximity of these circles doubtless facilitated the expansion of the corpus of Orphic literature.

Shortly before citing this hymn (*Strom.* 5.14.116.1), Clement quotes another Orphic verse:

Homer also manifestly mentions the Father and the Son by a happy bit of divination in the following words:

"If, alone as you are, no one uses violence on you,
there is no avoiding the sickness sent by *great Zeus* (*Od.* 9.410f),
for the Cyclopes do not concern themselves over *aegis-bearing Zeus*"
(*Od.* 9.275).

And before him Orpheus, speaking of this, had said:

"Son of *great Zeus*, father of *aegis-bearing Zeus*" (*OF* 690).

It is probable that this section, which accumulates citations of different passages of Homer, Orpheus, and Xenocrates in order to attempt to discern, rather forcedly, a pagan intuition of the Father and the Son, originates more

---

111 *Excerpta ex Theodoto* 32.1; 64; *Strom.* 3.1.1.1; 4.13.90.2.

in Clement's powers of invention than in his sources in this part of the work. The great majority of the comparisons between pagan authors and the Bible refer to the Old Testament and are of Jewish origin. The persons of the Trinity, however, are a Christian notion, and we have seen already that Clement makes additions to his Jewish sources.[112] In addition, Homer and the Platonist Xenocrates (perhaps by way of Plutarch) are two authors he could have known directly. The comparison between Orpheus and Homer, in the apologetic tradition that made Homer depend on Orpheus, may be inspired by the treatise on plagiarism that Clement will cite in book VI. Here the two citations are complementary, since the epithets of μέγας and αἰγίοχος are taken, thanks to the Orphic quotation, as if they referred to two different Zeuses in Homer. It must be recognized that the philological quality and apologetic force of the passage are rather slight, which lead Eusebius to omit it when he copied the whole section (Le Boulluec 1981 *ad loc*).

In any case, where did Clement find the Orphic verse? The invocation clearly points to a hymn, generally thought to be addressed to Cronus, the only god in the Greek pantheon to whom the epithets of Father and Son of Zeus can be simultaneously applied, since in the Orphic theogonic tradition Zeus swallows all the gods, including his father, and afterward gives birth to them anew.[113] In Egypt, in addition, the veneration of Aion helped to recuperate the figure of Cronus as a principal god by way of the old equation Cronus-Chronos (Time).[114] However, the possibility should not be ruled out that the reference could be to Zeus himself, who with this act of re-creation becomes his own successor, and whose two epithets in the verse would indicate, in the somewhat ineffable manner appropriate to the genre, his two successive reigns, before and after the re-creation. This hypothesis is strengthened still more if we accept the idea that the verse quoted belongs

---

112 This passage is similar to *Strom.* 5.70.3–6, where Clement quotes a fragment of Euripides (fr. 912 Kannicht) as a pagan intuition of the Father and the Son. Le Boulluec 1981 *ad loc.* suggests that the source could be Gnostic, which could also be the case here. In the Euripidean passage traces of Orphism have been proposed in a possible allusion to Dionysus Zagreus (cf. Bernabé *ad OF* 458).
113 West 1983, 35 n. 107, whose suggestion is accepted as plausible by Bernabé (*OF* 690: *in Saturnum?*). Cf. *OH* 8.13: Χρόνου πάτερ, ἀθάνατε Ζεῦ. Le Boulluec 1981 *ad loc.* thinks the line is a Jewish forgery like the *Testament*, but this does not seem probable, since the only reason for making it up would be to create a pagan precedent for the Christian notion of the Father and the Son.
114 Both Ptolemaic and Roman propaganda in Egypt identifies the Cronus associated with the Golden Age with Aion, symbol of the eternity of the Empire (Zuntz 1988). In addition, Gnostics venerated Aion as a metaphysical concept. Cf. the reference of Epiphanius to Aion's birth (*Panar.* 51.22.10, p. 372). Cf. n. 145 *infra*.

to the hymn that we just finished examining, cited soon after.[115] The reason for uniting them, given that there is nothing in the content of *OF* 691 either to contradict or to support the hypothesis, is one of simple economy: it is more logical to think of one hymn cited in two places than of two hymns, of the first of which only one line is quoted. In addition, Clement acknowledges that he is not quoting the entire hymn (εἶτα after l. 13). The qualities of dominion over Olympus and over the atmospheric elements and the title of "the greatest of the gods" (l. 15) are most suggestive of Zeus, although a transfer of Zeus's qualities to Cronus is not impossible in an Alexandrian context.

5.4. Other poems in the *Cohortatio ad Graecos*

The *Cohortatio ad Graecos* includes another two Orphic texts that should be added to the discussion in this section. Just after the brief version of the *Testament* (*OF* 377), derived from *De monarchia*, the text says:

And again he says somewhere:
One Zeus, one Hades, one Helios, one Dionysus,
one God in them all[116]: why shall I tell you in two ways? (*OF* 543)

The first line belongs to an Orphic *Hymn to the Sun* with syncretistic tendencies, of which most of the surviving fragments have been preserved in the *Saturnales* of Macrobius (1.18), who quotes the same verse.[117] As this fragment is not attested in any other work, it is unlikely that the source is an apologetic anthology, as Zeegers recognizes (1972, 249). Rather, it probably comes from some pagan philosophico-theological work in the style of the *Saturnales*. Nevertheless, there is room to doubt the authenticity of the second line, of which the *Cohortatio* is the sole witness. The expression "one is God" (εἷς θεός) is documented in pagan texts, and as an expression suggestive of monotheism, it may be what has attracted the author. However, the Orphic poems do not customarily invoke an impersonal god, and as Macrobius does not

---

115 *Strom.* 14.125–126. The idea is always suggested with much caution: West (1983, 268: "perhaps"), Bernabé (*OF* 690: "probabiliter").
116 The Greek εἷς θεὸς ἐν πάντεσσι could also be translated as 'one God in everything'. But the line focuses on divine equivalences rather than on immanence.
117 *OF* 538–545; cf. Fauth 1995, and West 1983, 206. Julian (*Or.* 11.136) also quotes this line as belonging to an oracle of Apollo, with the variant of replacing Dionysus by Serapis. Cf. pp. 72, 85.

transmit this line, it must probably be considered a Christian addition to the Orphic original.[118] Perhaps it is the work of the author of the *Cohortatio* himself, who shows quite a bit of originality in daring to put forward the proper names of pagan gods as allusions to the one God, coming dangerously close to syncretism. It may be as a result of this risk that the mysterious fragment does not appear in any other apologetic work, either before or after Pseudo-Justin.

Immediately after citing the *Hymn to the Sun*, the *Cohortatio* continues (15.2):

> And in the *Oaths*:
>
> I swear it upon you, heaven, wise work of the great God.
> I swear it upon you, father's voice, which he first sang
> when he fixed the whole cosmos with his will. (*OF* 620)
>
> What does he mean by "I swear it upon you, father's voice, which he first sang" (αὐδὴν ὀρκίζω σε πατρός, τὴν φθέγξατο πρῶτον)? He calls here "voice" (αὐδή) the Word (Λόγον) of God by which heaven and earth and the whole creation were made, as the divine prophecies of the holy men teach us; and Orpheus himself also paid some attention to them in Egypt, and understood that all creation was made by the Word of God; and therefore, after he says, "I swear it upon you, father's voice, which he first sang," he adds this besides, "when he fixed the whole cosmos with his will." Here he calls the Word (*logos*) voice (*aude*), for the sake of the poetic metre. And that this is so is manifest from the fact that a little earlier (*viz. OF* 377.5), where the metre permitted it, he names Him "Word."

This fragment is also cited by Cyril and by various later Byzantine authors – who, with Ioannes Malalas as their source, attributed it to Hermes Trismegistus – as a prefiguration of the incarnate Logos.[119] As Cyril is dependent on the

---

118 Neither Riedweg 1994 *ad loc.*, nor Zeegers 1972, 249, nor Bernabé *ad loc.* seems to have any doubts that the line stems originally from the Orphic *Hymn to the Sun*. The expression εἷς θεός is current in pagan epigraphy and literature (Peterson 1926), and also in Christian contexts: it appears in 1 *Cor.* 8.6, a direct precedent of its key position in the Credo. It also appears in texts of the Fathers (Peterson 1926, 255f), Christian inscriptions (Peterson 1926, 300f) and Christian oracles (Busine 2005). A parallel case is the "monotheistic" lines by Xenophanes (e. g. fr. 23 DK: εἷς θεὸς ἔν τε θεοῖσι καὶ ἀνθρώποισι μέγιστος) transmitted solely by Christian sources, which also has cast some doubt on their authorship (cf. Herrero 2005b, defending their authenticity against Edwards 1991).

119 Cyr. *CI* 1.46; Malal. *Chronograph.* 2.4 (20 Thurn); Georg. Cedren. *Historia compen.* 1.37 (*PG* 121, 64D); Suda *s. v.* Ἑρμῆς (II 414.7 Adler); *Chron. Pasch.* 47d (*PG* 92, 172). Malalas mistakenly attributes the lines to Hermes, who was quoted immediately afterward by Cyril. This error was transmitted to the later Byzantine authors.

5.4. Other poems in the Cohortatio ad Graecos

Cohortatio, and Malalas in turn expressly acknowledges that he is taking his citation from Cyril, these other witnesses are of interest only as evidence of the success that these verses had among Christian authors, and on account of the significant fact that beginning with Malalas they change αὐδή into φωνή. Pseudo-Justin himself probably took the text from another, earlier apologetic work.

Pseudo-Justin's precision in naming the title of the work containing the quoted verses is noteworthy and indeed unique in the *Cohortatio*, which consistently limits itself to citing the author. Perhaps this precision is because Pseudo-Justin thought that these verses would not be so well known to and hence accepted as genuine by the pagan public he was addressing. Saying that they belonged to a recognized Orphic work like the *Oaths* (pp. 37f) would increase their authority. Another citation of the *Oaths* originating with Theon of Smyrna (*OF* 619) is preserved, and it manifests the same style, one similar to that of the spells found in the magical papyri. As in this case, whether or not the verses belong to the same work as that cited by Theon, it is impossible to determine whether they truly had a ritual use or were a purely literary composition more suited for allegorical interpretation than for ritual oath-taking, even if they made use of the appearance of such oaths in order to increase their effectiveness.

In any case, however, there is a more fundamental issue. There hangs over these verses the suspicion that they may be a Jewish forgery comparable to the *Testament*. The verses' Judaizing tone is conveyed through four elements: *a*) the heavens as a divine work, and *b*) the great and wise Father God who *c*) set the cosmos on its foundations and *d*) spoke the first word. The first three elements could perhaps also be justified on the basis of the theogonic accounts of Zeus's creation of the world, but the fourth element, creation through the word, gives the text an unmistakable biblical stamp.[120] The text following the quotation reveals that this was precisely what most attracted Pseudo-Justin to these lines. He offers Orpheus as a pagan witness to the creative force of the divine word, a biblical notion alien to Greek and Roman religion that the apologists tried to introduce by way of Orphism. Are the verses a forgery with apologetic aims that imitates the Orphic *Oaths*? Or is it rather a case of Jewish influence on a pagan Orphic poem? The debate[121] is centered precisely on the

---

120 Cf. for instance the two biblical parallels offered by Riedweg 1993 and Bernabé *ad loc*: Ps. 32:6: "by the word of the Lord were the heavens made; and all the host of them by the breath of his mouth"; *Wis.* 9:1: "You, who made all things with your word".

121 Brisson (1990, 2923) has no doubt that the text is a Jewish forgery. Also West (1983, 35), although he leaves open the possibility that it is Hermetic (cf. N.H.C. VI, 6.63.16). But the attribution to Hermes is a later mistake of Malalas (n. 119

point that also concerned Pseudo-Justin, whose discomfort proves the exceptional nature of the text: the use of the word αὐδή to designate the creative λόγος of the Bible.[122] Hebrew *dabar* is systematically translated by λόγος in the LXX.[123] The replacement of αὐδή by φωνή beginning with Malalas bears witness to the dissatisfaction produced by the former word. Pseudo-Justin's metrical argument does not appear sufficient, because it would have been easy to construct the line some other way. As a result, a case of influence seems more plausible to me than forgery. Given that the same idea of the creative word, of Jewish (or Egyptian) origin, appears in magical papyri and in the Hermetic treatises, it would not be strange for it to have also influenced the late Orphic poems.[124] In fact, an Orphic cosmological poem, the *Smaller Krater* (*OF* 414.2), identifies Zeus with the ether and praises him as god of all things and as the one who "fused all together, his words whistling as they mixed with the winds" (πνεύμασι συρίζων φωναῖσί τε ἀερομίκτοις). If an Orphic poem, doubtless late, but pagan and in no way apologetic, has undergone Jewish influence in making the word a creative agent, there is no obvious reason why the same could not happen in the case of the *Oaths*. The problem of αὐδή is thus resolved, since it can be explained as a Greek poetic term receiving Jewish influence. It is worth highlighting, in addition, that this influence results in the original metaphor of a poetic word of creation, as is also indicated by the verb φθέγξομαι and for which I know of no parallels, Jewish, Greek, or Egyptian. In addition, the question of which elements of Orphism permitted the reception of this influence (or even could be the object of apologetic forgery) remains open; it will be discussed in chapter VI.

---

supra). Riedweg (1994, 334) is cautiously inclined to take it as a forgery. Zeegers (1972, 215) is probably right in defending a pagan origin.

122 This is Zeegers' objection (1972, 215) to considering it as a Jewish forgery. Another element of dubious orthodoxy that makes this possibility unlikely is that swearing oaths is not recommended in the Jewish and Christian tradition (e. g., Clem. Alex. *Paed.* 3.79, *Strom.* 7.50–51, quoting *Mt.* 5:36–37 and *Prov.* 8:9), above all if one swears by heaven in a pagan ritual context. But Pseudo-Justin does not seem to worry about this issue, so this argument is by no means definitive.

123 The only exception, pointed out by Riedweg 1994, 335, is *Is.* 55:11, where *dabar* is translated by ῥῆμα.

124 Cf. Merkelbach 1967, 57ff, who points out that creation by the Word is also an Egyptian notion (Bickel 1994). Cf. *PGM* I 16, I 126, II 63 PH. However, Jewish influence on another Orphic hymn quoted by Clement, mentioned above (*OF* 691), makes it more likely that this is also tha case here. Nevertheless, labelling these influences as Jewish or Egyptian has relative value in a fluid syncretistic context.

5.5. Didymus the Blind

A fragment cited by this Alexandrian author is of the same genre as the preceding ones. While discussing various passages proving the dogma of the Holy Spirit, he says (*De Trinitate* 2.27: *OF* 853):

> Orpheus, the first theologian among the Greeks, says:
>
> For under the great favor of the immortal god (ἀθανάτοιο θεοῦ), everything is fulfilled by men under the wise impulse of the Spirit (πνεύματος ὁρμῆι).

The poem from which these lines come is impossible to discern, but the apologetic use that Didymus makes of it is what we might expect. The force of the spirit that impels men's realizations seems to be a foretelling of the Holy Spirit, the divine breath. It is possible that this is another forgery, but once again, I am inclined to think that this is an instance of Judeo-Christian influence on a pagan poem. The Christians, who assigned more importance than the Jews to the divine *pneuma*, to the point of making it a person of the Trinity, did not customarily forge poems themselves, but rather took advantage of Jewish forgeries. Christian forgery, as in the case of parts of the *Sibylline Oracles*, cannot be entirely ruled out, but there are precedents in the ancient Orphic tradition in which *pneuma* appears as a physical element and as philosophical concept, and *pneumata* appear as accompaniments to the divine voice in the line of the *Smaller Krater* (*OF* 414.2) just cited as an example of Jewish influence. Provoked by Jewish and/or Christian influence, the leap to the spirit as divine breath was not difficult, given that the Orphic *pneuma* and the biblical one may have the same origin in Near Eastern mythology (pp. 361ff).

6. Apologetic philology

6.1. Orpheus and Homer in the *Cohortatio*

We have seen a comparison between verses of Orpheus and Homer in Clement (pp. 193ff) in order to show their intuition of the Father and the Son. The author of the *Cohortatio* also participates in the same tendency of using more or less rigorous philological techniques to attain apologetic goals. In 15.2 he justified the use of *audé* instead of *logos* by metrical reasons. In 17.2 he tries to prove Homer's dependence on Orpheus. Pseudo-Justin's enumeration of Greek poets who provide evidence for revealed truth is in chronological order, perhaps following the source that provided him with most of the texts. Thus, after Orpheus and the Sibyl comes Homer, supposedly later than Orpheus. Probably because he knew that this was a debatable supposition,[125] he went to the trouble of justifying it in the following way:

> And the poet Homer, abusing the authority of poetry, and jealous of Orpheus' glory for having inaugurated polytheism, mentions several gods in a mythical style, so he does not seem to differ from the poem of Orpheus, which he so distinctly proposed to emulate that even in the first line of his poem he indicated the relation he held to him. For as Orpheus in the beginning of his poem had said
>
> Sing, O goddess, the wrath of Demeter, who brings the goodly fruit (*OF* 386),
> Homer began thus,
>
> Sing, O goddess, the wrath of Achilles, son of Peleus (*Il*. 1.1)
> preferring, as it seems to me, even to violate the poetic metre in his first line, rather than that he should seem to have remembered for the first time the names of the gods.

According to Pseudo-Justin, Homer was really a monotheist, as he will demonstrate with other quotations from the *Iliad* and the *Odyssey*, but the prestige of the polytheist Orpheus led Homer to imitate him in his polytheism. The evidence for this is provided by the verse that begins an Orphic poem on Demeter,[126] supposedly imitated by Homer in the *Iliad*. The quotation gives us definitive evidence that the author knew Orphic literature directly by way of pagan sources, and not only by way of other apologists' citations: Pseudo-Justin is the sole witness to this Orphic verse, and unlike the earlier examples, the content of this verse is of no apologetic use, ruling out the possibility that it could be a Jewish or Christian fabrication.[127] He brings it into the discussion as evidence for an original argument of his own (ὡς ἐμοὶ δοκεῖ) to explain the metrical lack of perfection of the first verse of the *Iliad*. Like Clement, the author of the *Cohortatio* was fond of applying philological methods to bring home apologetic arguments.

---

125 Cf. V n. 8.
126 Demeter's wrath is probably due to her daughter Core's rape by Hades, which would be the subject-matter of the Orphic poem, although it cannot be ruled out that the line refers to the μῆνις provoked by her own rape by Zeus, mentioned by Clement (*Protr.* 2.15.1).
127 The quotation by Tzetzes *Ex. Il.* 26.5 Herm surely depends on the *Cohortatio*.

6.2. A treatise *On Plagiarism* in *Stromata VI*

After demonstrating the similarities between the pagan poets and the biblical prophets at the end of book V of the *Stromata*, Clement begins book VI by reinforcing his earlier arguments: why would the Greek poets not plagiarize the biblical revelation if their mutual copying of one another proves their natural inclination to plagiarism? In order to back up this somewhat tendentious argument, he goes through numerous examples that he takes from a treatise *On Plagiarism* (Περὶ κλοπῆς), which appears to be of pagan origin given that it has no apologetic intention, the date of which may be assigned to the Hellenistic age, not long after Callimachus (end of the third century BC), the latest author cited.[128] Since the treatise generally follows a chronological order, Orpheus leads off the parade of authors, and as a result various Orphic fragments have been preserved. Once again, Homer is made to depend on Orpheus, with the similarity between their verses as evidence. Clement (*Strom.* 5.14.122.2) and Pseudo-Justin (*Cohort.* 17.1) did the same in sections in which most passages are derived from Jewish apologetics. The rudimentary comparisons made by Clement and Pseudo-Justin themselves are inserted within the apologetic tradition that made Homer – and consequently, all the Greek thinkers and poets – depend on Orpheus. In using the pagan treatise *On Plagiarism*, Clement carried on the Jewish tradition.

The treatise is a philological study that fits within the interests of Alexandrian scholarship. Nevertheless, it follows the traditional order Orpheus-Musaeus-Hesiod-Homer, pointing to philological work of the second rank,[129] marginal with respect to the school of Aristarchus; this school maintained the primacy of Homer over all the other Greek poets and sought accordingly to purify the Homeric text from the additions of later *neoteroi*, among whom the Orphic poets were also reckoned.[130] The treatise in question accepts the traditional order, so it cannot be linked to Aristarchus' circle. If it comes

---

128 Stemplinger 1909 studied this section in detail. He proposes as Clement's original source Aretades, an Alexandrian philologist about whom nothing is known apart from his having written a work Περὶ κλοπῆς. Ziegler 1950 postulates two different sources, since the second part about complete works subject to plagiarism is much briefer, but Van der Hoek 1995 shows that the *excerpta* of other works tend to be progressively shorter. Even if he used two different sources on plagiarism, Clement fits them together very easily, which proves that both were of very similar type.
129 Research on plagiarism was not among the most prestigious philological tasks. Only these excerpts from Clement and others by Porphyry have been preserved. Cf. Ziegler 1950, 1991.
130 Cf. Severyns 1928, Nagy 2001, Herrero 2008a.

from outside Alexandria, the Stoic school of Pergamum would be the most plausible provenance, since there Homer was harmonized with his predecessor Orpheus in order to allegorize both of them according to Stoic doctrine (Nagy 2001). Alternatively, the treatise may come from a para-Aristarchian or post-Aristarchian Alexandrian philological school. Yet who in Alexandria could pursue philological research aside from Aristarchus? Given that Aristarchus's was the only philology financially supported by the Ptolemies, there must have been some kind of ideological, and not merely professional, motivation for these studies. The Alexandrian Jews, for example, carried out intensive philological labors. However, there are no traces of apologetics in this treatise, so it is necessary to look for another ideological group. The only one for which there is evidence in Alexandria is the school of the Neopythagoreans, who, during the Hellenistic period in Alexandria, Magna Graecia, and Rome, were reborn from their ashes and produced a series of apocryphal texts in which the desire to forge links to an ancient authority is manifest.[131] Moreover, the Neopythagoreans were among those who placed Orpheus at the head of Greek tradition, so it would not be strange for the author of this treatise to be close to this school. Thus, the possible origins for the treatise are the Stoicism of Pergamum or Alexandrian Neopythagoreanism. Examination of the texts will show that the second alternative is the more probable.

The treatise has three quotations from Homer supposedly copied from Orpheus. One quotation is a misogynist line devoid of any context.[132] The other two fragments belong, according to Clement's source, to two theogonic episodes (the "disappearance of Dionysus" and "Cronus"), which, given the dating of the treatise not long after Callimachus, must belong to poems previous to the *Rhapsodies*.[133] Of course, the real explanation of the similarities between the two is that Orphic poetry imitates Homer. However, the treatise explains them the other way round, a model that, as we have seen, was enthusiastically followed by the apologists.

---

131 Cf. III n. 14.
132 *Strom.* 6.2.5.3: *OF* 846, "There was nothing more deadly or more vile than a woman," as a model of *Od.* 11.427, "There is nothing more vile or more horrible than a woman". Given its topical content, it is possible that the similarity of both formulas comes from common hexametrical tradition rather than direct borrowing (Herrero 2008a). Since the Homeric line comes from the Odyssey's *Nekyia*, the Orphic line could come from a katabasis (West 1983, 276). Cf. n. 145.
133 *Strom.* 6.2.26.1 (*OF* 330 = *Il.* 17.53), 6.2.26.2 (*OF* 223 = *Od.* 9.372). Since the second passage describes Cronus going to sleep, *OF* 223 probably refers to Cronus's sleep before his castration by Zeus. Cf. n. 145.

A similar case occurs with another Orphic fragment, supposedly a source of inspiration for Heraclitus (*Strom.* 6.2.17.1):

And Orpheus having said,

"Water is death for the soul, and earth for the water;
from water is earth, and what comes from earth is again water,
and from that, soul, which is interchanged with the whole ether" (*OF* 437),

Heraclitus, putting together the expressions from these lines, writes thus:

"For souls it is death to become water, for water death to become earth; from earth arises water, and from water soul" (fr. B 36 DK).

It seems clear that these three lines are the basis for the later affirmation, drawn from the same treatise, that Heraclitus took most of his ideas from Orpheus (*Strom.* 6.2.27.1). However, it is evident that exactly the reverse took place, at least as far as these three lines are concerned, since the Orphic lines are clearly inspired by the fragment of Heraclitus.[134] The question is who composed these Orphic-Heraclitean verses. The immediately following passage may shed light on the matter (*Strom.* 6.2.17.2):

And Athamas the Pythagorean having said, "Thus there are four principles and roots of all the non-generated – fire, water, air, earth: for from these are the generations of beings," Empedocles of Agrigentum wrote:

"The four roots of all things first do you hear –
Fire, water, earth, and ether's boundless height:
For of these comes all that was, that shall be, and that is."

The Pythagorean Athamas only appears elsewhere in a list of Pythagoreans given by Iamblichus (*VP* 267). This fragment enunciates a cosmology based on the four elements, which give rise to the succeeding generations of beings. Given that it seems clear that the ancient Pythagoreans did not have a theory

---

134 Stemplinger 1909; West, 1971, 151; Sider 1997, 147; cf. *OF* 454–456 for other Heraclitean fragments which may be really influenced by Orphism. Clement has been censured as a blind copy-and-paste author who does not understand his sources well (Stemplinger 1909, 63, 66, 73), since he should know that at least some Homeric poetry was composed by later authors (*Strom.* 1.21.131ff). But one must take into account that it is part of the apologetic strategy to situate Orpheus at the beginning of Greek thought, and that it better suits Clement's use of Heraclitus (Wiese 1963) to make him depend on Orpheus than vice versa.

of the four elements,¹³⁵ a theory that was first formulated by Empedocles and later expanded by the Stoics, we can be certain that we have here a case of paraphrase and chronological inversion similar to the preceding example. The three lines from Empedocles are artificially strung together in order to facilitate the comparison with Athamas and to encourage the supposition that the former took the verses from the latter.¹³⁶ The objective is obvious: to lend prestige to the Pythagorean school by making one of its members the first discoverer (*protos heuretes*) of any theory finding a place in the eclectic amalgam of Stoicism and Platonism that was beginning to dominate the scene at the end of the Hellenistic age. There is plentiful evidence for this intellectual imperialism of the Neopythagoreans, who were forced to affirm their distinctiveness by way of these formal aspects of chronological priority since they could scarcely do so by way of the originality of their ideas.¹³⁷

The case of Athamas is so closely parallel to that of *OF* 437, cited just before, that common sense requires looking for a single explanation. And this explanation is not difficult to find if we recall Heraclitus's attacks on the man most venerated by the Neopythagoreans, their own school's principal source of a distinctive identity. In fr. 129 D-K Heraclitus accuses Pythagoras of having taken his doctrine from ancient books, alluding probably to Orphic works.¹³⁸ It would be very foolish to accuse Heraclitus of dependence on Pythagoras, since their enmity must have been proverbial. The better solution would be to accuse him of having taken his ideas from Orpheus, as Clement does in *Strom.* 6.2.27.1, drawing on his source. The Neopythagoreans considered themselves the guardians of Orphic wisdom, and an accusation of this kind was an excellent way to elevate themselves above Heraclitus and facilitate the appropriation of whatever Heraclitean ideas they wished through the medium of Orphic verses, naturally interpreted *more pythagorico*. Along the way they responded to Heraclitus's insolence toward their master by turning his own accusation against him.

As far as the content of the fragment is concerned, *OF* 437 appears to show the Pythagoreans' effort to conciliate their traditional doctrine of the cyclical movement of the soul with the Heraclitean cosmic cycle in which the soul participated (probably interpreted from an early date in combination

---

135 Burkert 1972, 297 n. 101.
136 These lines of Empedocles' are not taken as a genuine fragment, since they are composed out of fr. 6.1; 17.18; and 21.9 DK. Let us remember that Clement, inspired to such methods by the treatise he is using, also united in *Strom.* 5.14.116.1 two separate lines from Homer in order to demonstrate his borrowing from Orpheus (*OF* 690).
137 Burkert 1972, 94ff. Dillon 1988, 119–122.
138 Burkert 1972, 130–132.

with the theory of the four elements), and to present the result as their own theory going back to ancient times, by means of the effective instrument of Orphic poetry.[139] The third line (ἐκ τοῦ δὴ ψυχὴ ὅλον αἰθέρα ἀλλάσσουσα: "And from the water, the soul, which mingles with the universal ether") is the Pythagorean forger's addition to Heraclitus's thought, and it is there where we should look for novelty in comparison to the earlier thinker; Aristotle said (*De an.* 410b27) that the Orphic poems contained the idea that souls entered bodies from the air. In order to reconcile this information with the traditional doctrine of metempsychosis, it is usually supposed that the souls destined for rebirth occupied the levels of the air,[140] which is precisely what the third line of this fragment aims to say.

Thus, our study of this section on plagiarism began by situating it within the Christian continuation of the Jewish apologetic tradition and has ended with a source of clearly Neopythagorean roots. The connection between Alexandrian Judaism and Neopythagoreanism has been little studied, but it seems clear that Clement at least drew from the largely common stream of both traditions. Let us now turn to other Orphic fragments of Neopythagorean origin that can be related to the previous ones.

6.3. Fragments on symbolism in *Stromata* 5.8

The beginning of book V of the *Stromata* seeks to justify the allegorical interpretation of the Bible, subject to attack both from the pagan anti-Christian reaction and from other Christians who feared such interpretation was vulnerable to contamination from Greek philosophy. Clement's argument against the pagans, which held that they also interpreted their "scriptures" in a symbolic and allegorical manner, was of great value, and the fact that Clement dedicates this section to presenting examples of symbolism in pagan texts is evidence that he wrote the *Stromata* for an audience made up in part of pagans. Among the authors introduced for the benefit of these readers, Orpheus and his followers could not fail to appear: "The poets who learned the theology of the prophets do a great deal of philosophizing by means of allegory, I mean Orpheus, Linus, Musaeus, Homer, and Hesiod, and the wise in these matters. For the poetic guidance of the soul is the façade they put up before

---

139 Cf. West 1971, 151 for the cosmic cycle of Heraclitus in fr. 36 D-K. From man's participation in the cosmic cycle to the cycle of reincarnation there is only a small step. If this is the case, and *OF* 437 implies reincarnation (*pace* Sider 1997, 147), it must be attributed to neo-Pythagoreans rather than "pre-Stoic Heracliteans" (West 1971, 51).
140 Guthrie 1952, 186.

the common people" (5.4.24.1). Clement transmits three Orphic fragments in this section: *OF* 438, 357, and 407. At first glance they differ greatly among themselves and, stripped of context, are scarcely comprehensible; as a result, scholars have paid them very little attention. When interpreted together, however, they acquire a certain degree of clarity. After giving the interpretation of the *ephesia grammata* by the Pythagorean Androcydes (*Strom.* 5.8.45.3), Clement says:

> Also Dionysius Thrax, the grammarian, in his book *On Signification*, says this about the symbolism of wheels: "some actions are signified not by words only, but also by symbols: by words, as is the case of what are called the Delphic maxims, 'nothing in excess,' 'know yourself,' and the like; and by symbols, like the wheel that is turned in the temples of the gods among the Egyptians, and the branches that are given to the worshippers." For the Thracian Orpheus says:

> "Whatever works of branches are a care to men upon the earth,
> not one has one fate in mind, but all things
> revolve around; and it is not lawful to stand at one point,
> but each one keeps an equal part of the race as when they began" (*OF* 438).

> The branches are either the symbol of the first food or that the multitude may know that fruits that last for a very long time spring and grow universally, but that the duration of life allotted to them is brief. And it is on this account that they will have it that the branches are given; and perhaps also that they may know that as these are burned, so will they speedily leave this life, and will become fuel for fire.

However these obscure Orphic verses are interpreted, the idea of the cyclical movement of the cosmos (including men, who cannot escape this circular destiny) is clear, and is expressed through the metaphor of the branches given to men. Nevertheless, the botanical sense is not lost in the metaphor, because "upon the earth" (ἐπὶ χθονός) may indicate "this world" while simultaneously retaining agrarian connotations, as in Hesiod, whom these verses clearly recall (*Op.* 90, 822).

Shortly afterward, in a section for which the grammarian Didymus seems to be the source, Clement quotes an entirely cryptic line without context (*Strom.* 5.8.46.4):

> And indeed the learning of the alphabet for children implies the interpretation of the four elements; for it is said that the Phrygians call water *bedy*, as also Orpheus says:

> "And the *bedy* of the nymphs is poured down as bright water" (*OF* 357).

6.3. Fragments on symbolism in Stromata 5.8

This line is quoted as an example of Didymus's explanation of the Phyrgian word *bedy* as 'water.' The presence of a foreign word is very rare in hexameter poetry, and it should probably be linked to some magic or ritual utterance. However, Didymus draws a serious hermeneutical connexion between the alphabet (στοιχειωτική) and the four elements (στοιχείων).[141] The "water of the Nymphs" brings fertility to mind, and once again this line that seems to be related to the abundance of the fields is used in a text conceived as an explanation of the four elements that make up the cosmos. As in the previous fragment, there is a cosmic interpretation built on an agrarian foundation. This constant is even clearer in the last Orphic reference in this section (*Strom.* 5.8.49.3):

> So what? Does not Epigenes, in his book *On the Poetry of Orpheus*, in exhibiting the peculiarities found in Orpheus, say that by "the curved rods" (κερκίσι) is meant "ploughs'; and by the warp (στήμοσι), the furrows; and the woof (μίτος) is a figurative expression for the seed; and that "tears of Zeus" signify a storm; and that the "parts" (μοῖραι) are, again, the phases of the moon, the thirtieth day, and the fifteenth, and the new moon, and that Orpheus accordingly calls them "white-robed," as being parts of the light? Again, that the Spring is called "flowery" (ἄνθιον) from its nature; and Night "still" (ἀργίς) on account of rest; and the Moon "Gorgonian," on account of the face in it; and that the time in which it is necessary to sow is called "Aphrodite" by the theologian? In the same way, too, the Pythagoreans spoke figuratively, allegorizing the "dogs of Persephone" as the planets, the "tears of Cronus" as the sea.

The fragments of Orphic poetry referenced in this paragraph are attributed to the poem *Peplos (Robe)*, which described Persephone's mantle as a cosmological image (*OF* 407). Epigenes' agrarian interpretation could well have been suggested by the poem itself, given that the *peplos* already appeared as a symbol of the earth in the *Theogony* of Pherecydes. In addition, the Pythagoreans seem to have gone even beyond the agrarian interpretation to arrive at astronomical and physical readings about the planets and the sea.

The declared sources of these three fragments are, respectively, the grammarian Dionysius Thrax (first century BC), the scholar Didymus, epigone of the Alexandrian school (first century AD), and Epigenes. The first two are mentioned in the immediate context of the quotations, but it is not clear

---

141 This whole section (5.8.46–49, cf. Le Boulluec 1981 *ad loc.*) reinterprets magical texts in allegorical ways. Here the χαλινοί (nonsense words that help to learn the alphabet) are allegorized. Cf. Dornseiff 1925 on the magical uses of the alphabet. The process of loss of meaning and reinterpretation of these formulas and words is similar to those of the *ephesia grammata* (cf. Bernabé 2003b and p. 60).

where their contributions begin and end.[142] On the other hand, Epigenes, the author of a lost monograph on Orphic poetry, is cited in *Strom.* 1.21.131.5 as an authority for ascribing certain Orphic poems to various Pythagoreans – among them, Brontinus is credited with the *Peplos* and the *Physika*.[143] Epigenes's dates are debated. Even though Linforth ingeniously proposes identifying him with a disciple of Socrates, the consistency with the rest of the sources of this section rather suggests that Dodds is right in dating him in Hellenistic times.[144] Clement appears to know Epigenes directly and not by way of the other authors cited. The possibility cannot be ruled out that Epigenes was cited by Dionysius or Didymus and that he is the one who provided Orphic texts to them and only indirectly to Clement, but there is no evidence that any of these authors was a source for another. On the contrary, Clement refers to them all on the same level.

The fragment on which Epigenes commented, then, comes from the *Peplos* that he himself attributed to the Pythagorean Brontinus. With the other two fragments (*OF* 438 and 357), this one shares the Pythagorean tone of cosmic speculation derived from a base of natural and agrarian elements. It is impossible to know from which poem the other fragments are taken, although it is tempting to relate them to the *Physika* that are also attributed to Brontinus for their Pythagorean content. In *OF* 438, the fragment on the branches, the cosmic cycle is explicitly alluded to with the same words (πάντα πέριξ) that appear in the episode of Zeus binding the whole with a golden chain (*OF* 237), convincingly interpreted by West (1983, 237) as a Stoic allegory of *heimarmene* – that is, of an inevitable destiny conceived as circular. It would not be difficult to find in this fragment a reference to the transmigration of souls as well. In fact, the message of the first two lines

---

142 *OF* 438 is introduced after a quotation of the Περὶ ἐμφάσεως (*On Signification*) of Dionysius Thrax (Schmidt 1852, 370 may well have been right in seeing him behind many of the examples on symbolism in this section), but it is not clear whether the fragment comes from him or it is introduced by Clement by association (cf. Bernabé *ad loc.*). Didymus is also mentioned immediately before *OF* 357. Since he is chronologically the latest of these authors, and a great collector of previous works, it could also be possible to presuppose that he is Clement's direct source for both Dionysius and the Orphic quotation.
143 Brontinus is a semi-legendary figure of ancient Pythagoreanism, contemporary to Pythagoras himself (Burkert 1972, 114). In later times some works were attributed to him (Thesleff 1961, 55). The poem *Physika* is dated by Gagné 2007 in classical times, with theogonic, physical and eschatological content. On the *Peplos*, cf. West 1983, 35.
144 Linforth 1941, 114ff, followed by West 1983, 9 and Gagné 2007; cf., however, Dodds 1951, 162 n. 96.

seems to be an affirmation of metempsychosis: "There is not one life alone for each mind, but rather all is cyclical." The next two lines would then recall the impossibility of escaping the circle of reincarnation. The cycle of reincarnation is thus integrated into the cosmic cycle in *OF* 438 by means of the imagery of the natural cycle. This is exactly the same as what happens in the fragment inspired by Heraclitus, *OF* 437, which we have attributed to a Pythagorizing milieu and which spoke of a cycle of the soul in relation to the four elements.[145] Finally, Clement's final comment (perhaps made by his source, Dionysius Thrax) that "the people" (οἱ πολλοί) should know their terrible destiny of fire after death may preserve something of the content found in the Orphic verses' continuation: it would be the most logical of topics in a poem on the fate of the soul.

Besides speculation on the their sources and content, two conclusions can be deduced from these texts. First, by means of a poetic image they manage to combine the cycle of reincarnation, the cosmic cycle, and the four elements, thereby shedding light on the routes by which Orphic literature was extended to new themes. The fragments analyzed here are neither astronomical nor botanical, but rather theological and cosmological poetry of Neopythagorean tone. Nevertheless, the idea of a cosmic cycle expressed by means of natural and astronomical imagery offers an excellent basis for reuse in astrological poetry, in the same way that the Orphic vocabulary of the cycle of reincarnation had been suitable for adapting Stoic doctrines. The same can probably be said about the botanical poetry (*OF* 784–791) also attributed to Orpheus, which may have originated in the vegetable and agrarian images of earlier Orphic poems. Late Orphic poetry came to embrace an enormous mass of poems without any common religious or philosophical bonds, to the point that the name of Orpheus is the only link that unites them. However, this expansion was not carried out in a chaotic and senseless manner, but instead followed an evolutionary path in which existing elements provided the starting point for internal development or for the adaptation of

---

145 Cf. pp. 203ff. Besides, the three Orphic fragments used for comparison with Homer from the treatise *On Plagiarism* have some features that link them to these texts. *OF* 330 mentions natural elements like a tree, water and the winds; *OF* 223 is centred on Cronus, in whose tears Epigenes says that the Pythagoreans see the sea; and the misogynist *OF* 846 may be linked to Pythagorean sexual abstinence. If the treatise was influenced by Pythagorean ideology, as we saw, it is no wonder that the Orphic fragments selected were fit for Pythagorean speculations. One could add to this cluster of Pythagorean themes in Orphic texts quoted by Clement in the fifth and sixth books of the *Stromata OF* 691, where God's omnipotence means above all that he governs the natural seasons, and *OF* 690, perhaps addressed to Cronus.

new elements, in order to preserve a permanent link to the ancient tradition that was a source of authority.

Second, it is clear that Neopythagoreanism made use of and encouraged a kind of philology of lesser scientific category, parallel to the great philology of Aristarchus. This minor philology was a movement probably centered in Alexandria and similar to the Stoic philology of Pergamum, in the sense that it was interested not so much in the texts in themselves as in the consequences that could be deduced from them. Para-scientific topics like symbolism or plagiarism were studied from this perspective. These Neopythagorean philologists commented on Orphic poems and in turn composed new poems that were imitations of the former but susceptible to more convenient interpretations. The Jewish and later the Christian apologists learned from this ideologically influenced philology,[146] dedicating themselves enthusiastically to the imitation of its work, as in the comparisons of Orpheus to Homer made by Clement and Pseudo-Justin. Let us now take a look at two other cases in which an Orphic image used by the Pythagoreans was adapted to Christian ideas.

6.4. Christian versions of Orphic-Pythagorean texts

The texts commented on in the last few pages show that some Christian authors had direct contact with Orphic-Pythagorean texts. This contact produced more than quotations. Some of the speculative and poetic images of these texts may also have inspired some passages where they serve as templates for Christian content. Let us point out two famous cases where images like the divine loom or cosmic harmony, which we have seen developed in Orphic-Pythagorean texts, also appear in Christian contexts. A passage of Hippolytus cited by Kern (*OF* 33) and Bernabé (*OF* 407) as similar to the *Peplos*, makes use of the same textile metaphor (*Antichr.* 4):

> For whereas the Word of God was without flesh, he took upon Himself the holy flesh by the holy Virgin, and prepared a robe which He wove for Himself,

---

146 A parallel case is the Alexandrian cento that accumulates quotations by Plato, Pythagoras, Empedocles, Heraclitus and other poets about the fall of the soul, used by Christians (Clement, Hippolytus), Jews (Philo) and pagans (Plutarch, Plotin, Hierocles). Cf. III n. 7. The quantity of quotations from Empedocles and Heraclitus that appears in the treatise *On Plagiarism* used by Clement is noticeable: this is logical if we think that it was composed in the same ideological atmosphere as the anthology on the fall of the soul.

6.4. Christian versions of Orphic-Pythagorean texts

like a bridegroom, in the sufferings of the cross, in order that by uniting His own power with our mortal body and by mixing the incorruptible with the corruptible, and the strong with the weak, He might save perishing man. The web-beam (ἱστόν), therefore, is the passion of the Lord upon the cross, and the warp (στήμων) on it is the power of the Holy Spirit, and the woof (κρόκη) is the holy flesh woven by the Spirit, and the thread (μίτος) is the grace which by the love of Christ binds and unites the two in one, and the rods (κερκίς) are the Word; and the workers are the patriarchs and prophets who weave the fair, long, perfect tunic (χιτῶν) for Christ; and the Word passing through these, like the rods, completes through them the will of His Father.

The Orphic-Pythagorean *Peplos*, probably incorporated into the *Rhapsodies* (*OF* 286–290), could well have inspired, more or less distantly, this Christian image, the terminology of which coincides with that of the quotation in Epigenes. Orphic poetry is not the only channel of transmission for this image, developed even more decidedly by Pherecydes. Let us remember that Orphic roots are always found in the midst of numerous intermediate stages of transmission and parallel tendencies. However, just as the *Robe* influenced the pagan Claudian, it may well have also inspired Hippolytus.

The clearest case of direct transfer – on account of the explicit reference to Orpheus, among other things – is once again offered by Clement of Alexandria. In book I of his *Protrepticus* Clement opposes Orpheus's song, the mysteries, to his new song, the mysteries of the saving Logos (Appendix 1). Exalting the virtues of this Logos, he expands upon several musical metaphors that are extremely similar in appearance to the Pythagorean theory of musical harmony as a foundation of the cosmos.[147] The Orphic-Neopythagorean poem *Lyra* is based on the image of the cosmic lyre, which we can suppose was not far from that of other Orphic texts of Pythagorean tone like *Orphic Hymn 34 to Apollo*, in which the god's lyre is praised as a foundation of the universe. Faithful to his metaphor, Clement transfers this effect from the divine instrument to song itself, as Thomas Halton (1983) elegantly describes. The agent of cosmic harmony is now the voice, not the lyre, but the idea is the same. The coincidences between both texts, which are italicized in the texts presented immediately below, are too clear to be the result of chance; it is unnecessary to postulate an intertextual relationship, but it is evident that the texts were inspired by the same conceptions.

It also composed the universe into melodious order, and tuned the discord of the elements into harmonious arrangement, so that the entire cosmos

---

147 On Pythagorean cosmic harmony, cf. Burkert 1972, 350–369, West 1983, 30–32 and Molina 1998.

might become harmony. It let loose the fluid sea, and yet has prevented it from encroaching on the land. The earth, again, which had been in a state of commotion, it has established, and fixed the sea as its boundary. And it has softened the violence of fire by the air, *as the Dorian is blended with the Lydian strain*; and it has moderated the harsh cold of the air by the embrace of fire, *harmoniously arranging these most extreme tones of the universe*. And this pure song – *support of the universe and harmony of all – reaching from the centre to the limits, and from the extremities to the centre, has harmonized this universe*, not according to the Thracian music, which is like that invented by Jubal, but according to the paternal will of God, which David admired. (*Protr*. 1.5.1).

It is noticeable that, as in many of the texts we have seen, the four elements are, of course, also present in this cosmic depiction. In the *Orphic Hymn*, harmony acts on the seasons of the year (cf. the hymn in *OF* 691), in a very similar way (*OH* 34,13–23):

Hear me, with benevolent mind, while I pray for mankind:
For you see this boundless æther
and this blessed earth below, and through darkness
in the quietness of night under the obscurity of the astral eyes
you have seen the roots under earth, *and you hold the bounds of the whole*
cosmos: and the beginning and end are in tune with you;
you make everything bloom, *you harmonize all the celestial sphere*
  with your lyre
of many tones; sometimes going to the extreme of the shortest string,
sometimes of the longest; sometimes, according to the Dorian rhythm,
you balance the poles, and you keep the living species distinct,
mixing with harmony a destiny for all men,
uniting equally winter and summer for each one,
distinguishing winter in the longest strings, summer in the shortest ones,
in the Dorian string the exuberant flower of lovely spring.

In the next chapter we will see the use Clement makes of these Pythagorean ideas in order to present the most novel aspects of the biblical Logos in familiar molds. Here it is sufficient to confirm that Clement had the *Lyra* or another, similar Pythagorean text in front of him when composing his work; the relationship between these speculations and the myth of Orpheus may be an idea which we find only in Clement, but he probably took his inspiration, directly or indirectly, from what was already to be found in his Pythagorean sources.[148]

7. References to the soul

In contrast to the abundance of fragments of theogonic and cosmological content preserved by the apologists, references to the nature and destiny of the human soul are surprisingly scarce. There are no doctrines on the soul explicitly attributed to Orpheus in Christian pages, although there are certain allusions that prove that the apologists were familiar with Orphism's eschatological content. Origen, for example, recognizes that the terrors of Hades in the Bacchic *teletai* do not differ in content from those of Christian eschatology (*CC* 3.16, 4.10, 8.48). However, we should recall that in linking Orpheus more to the *arche* than to the *telos*, the apologists did no more than follow the tendency of the pagan witnesses – considered in chapter II – who looked rather to Plato, the preserver and renewer of the Orphic tradition in this sphere (Orig. *CC* 1.32, 7.28; Thdt. *Affect.* 11.33). Even so, there are some isolated references of no little interest.

Elsewhere I have argued in detail that Gregory of Nazianzus's criticism of reincarnation in his poem *De anima* (ll. 22–52: App. VIII) was aimed principally at the *Rhapsodies*.[149] The target here is a theory combining the inspiration of souls from the air, reincarnation in animals and plants, and final punishment. Such a combination is found only in the Orphic poems, and there is nothing strange about Gregory dedicating himself to its refutation precisely in a hexameter poem, intended to surpass and substitute for its rivals in content and in form. Pythagoras and Empedocles are also alluded to, but the coincidences with the *Rhapsodies* are too clear to be the result of chance. In addition, after refuting the rival theories, Gregory offers his own theory of the soul, and in expounding it he uses expressions characteristic of the Orphic poems.

---

148 Clement's passage also offers affinities to Philo's *De plantatione* 11.167 (Halton, 183f). Mystic-musical speculations, though originally typically Pythagorean, soon were extended to other spheres that Christians also knew: Celsus (*CC* 6.22) describes the Mithraic mysteries and the cosmology derived from them, including a *mousikos logos*. Cleanthes (I 502 Arnim) is quoted by Clement (*Strom.* 5.8.48) as identifying the sun with a lyre that maintains the cosmic harmony.
149 Cf. Herrero 2007b. The poem is edited and commented on by Moreschini/Sykes 1997.

Nevertheless, there is no reference in the poem to the cause proposed by the *Rhapsodies* for the soul's wanderings – namely, the myth of Dionysus – nor does there appear in Clement's, Arnobius's, or Firmicus's mentions of this myth the least allusion to any of the ideas that might be derived from it: the original impurity of mankind's Dionysian nature, the cycle of reincarnation, the final liberation and entrance into a happy Beyond. It is doubtful, nevertheless, that this silence is due to lack of knowledge, rather than to a conscious choice to omit these themes (pp. 246ff). The proof of this is given by Origen, whose Orphic sources, as we have seen, were not the theogonies directly, but rather philosophical interpretations of them. Defending the Christian idea of the immortal Logos, he says (*CC* 4.17)

> But will not those narratives, especially when they are understood in their proper sense, appear far more worthy of respect than the story that Dionysus was deceived by the Titans, and fell (ἐκπίπτοντος) from the throne of Zeus, and was torn in pieces by them, and his remains being afterwards put together again, he returned as it were to life, and ascended into heaven?[150] Or are the Greeks at liberty to make a doctrine of the soul out of these things, and to interpret them figuratively, (τοιαῦτα εἰς τὸν περὶ ψυχῆς ἀνάγειν λόγον καὶ τροπολογεῖν) while the door of a consistent explanation is closed against us?

The mention of the myth of Dionysus does not come from Celsus, but from Origen himself, who knew that theories "about the soul" could be extracted from it. He does not say what these theories were, and there is no passage about the soul in all his preserved works – which encompass various eschatological speculations, including reincarnation – that shows signs of inspiration by Orphic literature. Given that Origen did not know the *Rhapsodies* and said in *CC* 1.18 that the poems of Orpheus were lost, this reference must have reached him by way of some philosophical interpretation of the myth, probably very similar to that of the Neoplatonists.[151] There is a detail that makes it possible to confirm this: the passage (like *CC* 3.23: καταβαλλόμενοι) alludes to Dionysus's "fall" from the throne, in another indication that Origen is not reading the theogonies directly, but rather philosophical interpretations. No

---

150 On Dionysus's ascension to heaven, cf. also pp. 156 and 332f.
151 Origen quotes Celsus (*CC* 8.53–54, 8.58) about a theory of the soul of Egyptian origin, according to which the soul is imprisoned in the body and entrusted to daemons as prison-keepers. But Celsus does not relate it to Orpheus nor to Dionysus' myth, since he is not interested in the cause of this state of man (*CC* 8.53): "Since men are born united to a body, whether to suit the order of the universe, or that they may in that way suffer the punishment of sin, or because the soul is oppressed by certain passions until it is purged from these at the appointed period of time".

other testimony to the episode speaks about a fall; instead, Dionysus is lured into abandoning the throne by the Titans. His fall from the throne smacks of an interpretation along the lines of the fall of the soul from its divine origin. Perhaps Origen did not know exactly what the consequences were that were derived from the myth, or rather he had no interest in commenting on them, but only in pointing out that the Christian case was similar.

The only Orphic anthropological image that is frequently repeated while maintaining its "guarantee of origin" is the theme of the soul shut up in the body as in a prison or a tomb (*soma-sema*).[152] In referring to these images, Clement and Augustine preserve the memory of their distant origin in Orphism. Clement dedicates book III of the *Stromata* to demonstrating that the Gnostics (Valentinians, Carpocratians, Marcionites) derived their radical dualism not from the Bible, but rather from a poor interpretation of the Greek poets and philosophers who valued the soul more the body.[153] A central text is the passage of Plato's *Cratylus* in which he explicitly attributes the expression *soma-sema* to "the disciples of Orpheus" (οἱ ἀμφὶ Ὀρφέα). Just before quoting this passage, Clement says that Plato "attributes to Orpheus the doctrine of the punishment of the soul in the body,"[154] and just afterward, he quotes the Pythagorean Philolaus, saying, "it is also worth mentioning the remark of Philolaus (B 14 DK). This Pythagorean speaks as follows: 'The ancient theologians and seers testify that the soul is conjoined to the body to suffer certain punishments, and is, as it were, buried in this tomb.'" (*Strom.* 3.3.17.1). His immediate source is the fragment of Philolaus, but the latter author himself acknowledges that he is drawing on the ancient theologians and seers. It is very tempting to identify these figures with οἱ ἀμφὶ Ὀρφέα as Plato does. The same line of identification between Orphism and Pythagoreanism seen in the quotations from Epigenes is maintained here, but the image preserves the hallmark of its origin not among the Pythagoreans, but rather among the Orphic theologians.

This hallmark is also perceptible in another Christian reference to the *soma-sema* pairing. Augustine in his polemic against the Pelagians, who denied original sin and the devaluation of the body (in reaction against its demonization among Gnostics and Manicheans), cites with approval the pa-

---

152 Courcelle 1965 and 1966 collect many testimonies witnessing to the popularity of these two images among neo-Platonists and Christians.
153 The source for many of these references is the cento mentioned in n. 146.
154 *Strom.* 3.3.16.3, literally repeated by Theodoret (*Affect.* 5.13). The Platonic passage is *Crat.* 400c; Bernabé 1995 demonstrates (against Dodds 1951, 169 n. 87 and his followers Moulinier 1955, 24–26, Courcelle 1966, 102) that the image of the body as a tomb has an Orphic origin.

gans who, "even without knowing the doctrine of original sin," hit the mark in coining this expression:[155]

> It seems significant that some of them approximated the Christian faith when they perceived that this life, which is replete with deception and misery, came into existence only by divine judgment, and they attributed justice to the Creator by whom the world was made and is administered. How much better and nearer the truth than yours (sc. Julian the Pelagian) were the views about the generation of men held by those whom Cicero, as though led and compelled by the very evidence of the facts, commemorates in the last part of the dialogue *Hortensius*. After mentioning the many facts we see and lament with regard to the vanity and the unhappiness of men, he says, "From which errors and cares of human life it results that sometimes those ancients – whether they were prophets or interpreters of the divine mind by the transmission of sacred rites (*veteres illi sive vates sive in sacris initiisque tradendis divinae mentis interpretes*), – who said that we are born to expiate sins committed in a former life, seem to have had a glimpse of the truth, and that that is true that Aristotle says, that we are punished much as those were who once upon a time, when they had fallen into the hands of Etruscan robbers, were killed with studied cruelty; their bodies, the living with the dead, were bound as exactly as possible, one against another: so our souls, bound together with our bodies, are like the living joined with the dead." Did not the philosophers who thought these things perceive more clearly than you the heavy yoke upon the children of Adam, and the power and justice of God, though not aware of the grace given through the Mediator for the purpose of delivering men?

Chapter VI will discuss the ideas on original sin and liberation from original sin that can be deduced from this passage. Here it is only of interest to note that across all the intermediate sources – Augustine takes the reference from the *Hortensius* of Cicero, who took it in his turn from Aristotle – consciousness of the origin of the *soma-sema* in the poet-seers, interpreters of the divine and teachers of rites, is a constant.[156] The Orphic connotations of the expression *vates sive interpretes* are evident: Horace called Orpheus *vates*

---

155 *Contra Iul. Pelag.* 4.15.78 (*PL* 44.778). He insists again on this image (*Contra Iul. Pelag.* 4.16.83), underlining that the philosophers who coined this image "did not know and did not know the sin of the first man".
156 Cic. *Hortensius* fr. 112 Grilli; Arist. fr. 59–61 Rose. The particular image of tying prisoners to corpses is always referred to Aristotle (cf. Bos 2003), and consequently, to οἱ τὰς τελετὰς λέγοντες (Iambl. *Protr.* 8, Macr. *Somn. Scip.* 1.11.3), while the simpler body/tomb pairing has a much broader diffusion. Cf. Courcelle 1966, esp. 110f. A possible point of comparison is the Orphic saying "many bear the thyrsus, but few are *bacchoi*" (*OF* 576), which the Christians often quote, but attributing it always to Plato, *Phaed.* 69c (Clem. Alex. *Strom.* 1.19.92.3, 5.3.17.4, Thdt. *Affect* 12.35).

interpresque deorum (*Ars poet.* 392). This hallmark of Orphic authorship on the *soma-sema* surely comes from its nature as a memorable motto; however, it mainly comes from the express references to its Orphic origin in the *loci classici* of Plato (and through him, of Philolaus as well) and Aristotle, the effect of which has endured until today.

8. The reliability of the Apologists

It has been possible to confirm that the apologists' sources on Orphism were above all literary: these included the Orphic poems directly (on very rare occasions), their philosophical or literary interpretations, the works that gave information on Orphic myths and cults, like Plutarch or the *Treatise on the Mysteries* used by Clement, and the works produced in the course of earlier apologetic efforts, Jewish or Christian. There is very little direct acquaintance with Orphic cults, about which the great majority of the apologists' information is derived from the literary tradition.

It must be noted that Egypt becomes the center for the diffusion of this tradition, as is demonstrated by the success of Clement of Alexandria's Orphic passages, of the *Testament*, and of the "Osirisized" versions of the myth of Dionysus. It is logical that this was so, since in Egypt Orphism spread, as we have seen, both at the most cultured level of society among the philosophers of Neoplatonic tendency and at the more popular levels glimpsed in the magical papyri. In turn, the golden age of apologetic literature coincided with the apogee of the Alexandrian Church, whose literature attained wide diffusion. Nevertheless, various authors also arose in the regions of Asia Minor, Athens, and Rome, with her extension in proconsular Africa, who considered it necessary to concern themselves with Orphism, in order to attack it or use it for support. This geographical distribution of Christian witnesses broadly coincides with that of the pagan evidence reviewed in chapter II. For example, it cannot be a matter of chance that Irenaeus of Lyon makes not the slightest reference to Orphism and that not one piece of Orphic evidence is to be found in Gaul, while the concentration of apologists and pagan evidence in Asia Minor or Egypt is so large.

This geographical coincidence shows that false conclusions should not be drawn from the fact that the majority of the Christian information is of bookish origin. Orphism was a not a dead reality that the Christians resurrected as a phantom enemy; rather, they attacked it – or used it for support – particularly in those places where they knew that the Orphic tradition had prestige. In reality, this is no more than a confirmation of what common sense might suggest: apologetics generally does not go to the trouble of resurrecting dead doctrines in order to combat them. It has been some time since the Church has launched diatribes against Manicheans or Apollinarists, and today's apologists will turn their attacks against atheism, agnosticism, or esoteric syncretism. It is difficult to think that the ideas and myths attacked by Gregory of Nazianzus were entirely absent among his contemporaries, or that the cults that Clement believed were celebrated in the mysteries were not equally considered to exist by his pagan audience. Whether they were really celebrated is a different question, but their scant practice in reality does not at all diminish the religious value of the general belief that they took place. In fact, it was enough for it to be believed that they ever took place at all, since that belief fostered the actualization of the mythic ritual – an actualization merely intellectual but nonetheless effective. This principle, studied in chapter II, explains the use of antiquarian literature by the apologists. It is clear that they highlighted ridiculous and obsolete aspects of paganism, but ancient religion was permanently oriented toward the past, and still more so during the Imperial Age. The apologists did not engage in polemics out of mere erudite enthusiasm, attacking writings of previous centuries that had already lost all currency; rather, these same writings were a source of inspiration for the contrary camp. Making references to Orpheus, Empedocles, or Pythagoras did not mean battling ghosts, since the antiquity of these personages did not diminish their value as religious and philosophical symbols, but instead increased it. Rather, these attacks were something like, *mutatis mutandis*, denying the resurrection of a Jew who died two thousand years ago as the most efficacious means of criticizing contemporary belief in life after death.

The portrait offered by the Christians, then, complements quite well that drawn from the pagan evidence: an Orphic tradition of growing prestige, sufficient on occasion to stand as a representative for paganism as a whole, alongside a surprising absence of specific ideas or practices, since what we are dealing with is an intellectual tradition of myths and rites handed down primarily through poems and their interpretations. Despite constant apologetic manipulation, it is clear that the general picture of Orphism offered by the Christians coincides with the reality presented by the pagan evidence. The trustworthiness of the details, as we have seen, varies depending on the case and the context. Some general rules can be deduced easily enough: the more concrete a piece of information, the more trustworthy it appears, and when a text functions to prove a different idea, almost as a digression in a footnote, it is more to be trusted than when it forms a principal part of the apologetic argument.

V. Christian Strategies

γλυκύ τι καὶ ἀληθινὸν φάρμακον πειθοῦς ἐγκέκραται τῷ ᾄσματι
A sweet and true charm of persuasion is mixed with this song
Clement of Alexandria, *Protrepticus* 1.2.4

1. General principles

The texts discussed in the previous chapter make it possible to carry out now a study in miniature, taking advantage of the particular case of Orphism, of the various strategies toward Greek religion and culture used by second- through fifth-century Christianity. Some shared lines of approach can be traced, but it is useful first of all to point out the variety of orientations that we will find within the framework of shared apologetic objectives. The audience and the contexts of this literature are not questions with a single solution.

There is no reason why the supposed audience of the apologetic works must coincide with the real one; rhetorically, they are addressed to pagans, commonly in the second-person plural, or in the case of an *ad hominem* refutation, like that of Origen against Celsus, in the second-person singular. Nevertheless, it seems clear that this rhetorical artifice does not reflect the real audience, since few pagans not in contact with Christianity would be interested in this type of literature; the audience that would deign to read and believe an apologist must in principle have had some confidence in his authority, something which presupposes at least a certain nearness to Christian circles. On the other hand, however, the content of these works is useful only for confrontation with paganism. The most probable solution is that apologetic literature sought to instruct the Christian in tools for confronting paganism, offensively or defensively, both in relation to others and in his own interior life. It was not only a matter of demolishing the arguments of those pagans with whom the Christian reader might come into contact, but also one of preserving him from the contamination of syncretism with the cults he had practiced before his conversion or might still be practicing after it. That is to say that if the direct audience was primarily Christian, the indirect audience was paganism, whether by way of the oral apologetics that these works' readers would then carry out in pagan circles, or by way of paganism's survival in the customs of Christians who came from such circles.

Even if the principal adversary in the passages that concern us is Greco-Roman paganism, we cannot forget two secondary battlefronts that also appear in these works, sometimes in combination: the Jews and the Gnostics. If when confronting the Jews – brandished at times as allies by anti-Christian polemicists like Celsus[1] – the apologists affirm the validity of the New Testament, when confronting the Gnostics they reverse the process: they insist on an indissoluble linkage with the Old Testament, contrary to the Gnostic constructions that aim to do without the biblical tradition and that the apologists stigmatize as aberrant deviations from pagan philosophy. In addition, we must take into account the existence of various currents within orthodox Christianity that disagreed profoundly on issues central to apologetics, such as the positive or negative valuation of pagan philosophy. For example, in the *Stromata* Clement has these different types of readers very much in mind, which explains the complex composition of the work.

It must be added as well that the evolution of the religious situation between the second and fifth centuries obviously affects apologetic objectives and strategies. There is a great difference between the defensive situation in which Athenagoras or Justin is writing – when Christianity is still a very small, minority religion in search of a façade of intellectual respectability – and the final offensive launched by Cyril or Augustine against a dying paganism. The growing effect of anti-Christian polemic on the apologetic works that respond to it is perceptible as well, with very similar strategies on both sides: Origen responds to Celsus's invective, Eusebius responds to Porphyry, Augustine writes his *Civitas Dei* in response to the accusations made by Rome's last pagan circles that the city's fall to Alaric was due to abandonment of the ancestral religion, and Cyril writes his *Contra Iulianum* half a century after Julian's day in order to convince the few but stubborn pagans of Alexandria.

Another factor of variability is the different tastes and individual objectives of each apologist. Firmicus Maternus's aim in the fiery anti-pagan diatribes of the *De errore profanarum religionum* is probably to make up for the astrological theses advanced in the *Mathesis* prior to his conversion; his con-

---

[1] Celsus defends Judaism as an ancient tradition perverted by Christianity (Chadwick 1966, 23), at the same time that he uses arguments against the God of the Old Testament that are similar to Marcion's (Chadwick 1966, 26): the apologetic arguments from the Christian, pagan, Jewish and Gnostic sides are all very similar.

cern is not so much to construct a well-argued refutation of the rival religion as it is to demonstrate his ardor as a recent convert, with the consequence that he is less careful to maintain rigorous standards in his descriptions of paganism than other authors who strive for greater credibility. In the same way, Eusebius takes from Clement the image of Orpheus the singer in order to describe Christ in his *Laudes Constantini*, but his purpose is encomiastic, not apologetic, and his use of the image does not require the precautions taken by Clement a century and a half before. Eusebius is an example of variation even within one author, since his doubts about the achievements of paganism increase perceptibly as Christianity becomes predominant: in the *Theophany* he accuses Plato of saying in the *Timaeus* that Homer, Hesiod, and Orpheus are the sons of gods and of paying heed to their gods and myths, even though he expelled poets from the ideal commonwealth in the *Republic*. This attack does not appear in the *Praeparatio evangelica*, more inclined to acknowledge Plato's achievements.[2]

Alongside these factors diversifying the apologists' strategies and objectives, there are others that tend to unify them. The principal one is the unity of formats, sources, and objectives inherited from a genre originating in the Alexandrian Judaism of the second century BC. The Christian apologists in their turn read one another and have no hesitation about repeating and paraphrasing the arguments and descriptions they consider valuable (e.g., those of the *Protrepticus*). Their individual variations are produced within the framework of shared patterns of thought.

A good example of how these two principles of variation and continuity were combined is the varying presentation of the *Testament* in the different apologists who discuss Orpheus's monotheism (*OF* 368–373: cf. figure 2 on p. 180): Theophilus of Antioch, Clement of Alexandria, and Pseudo-Justin (second and third centuries) place Orpheus's recognition of the truth and his retraction (palinode) of polytheism at the end of his life, after he had already taught the Greeks the mysteries. Eusebius's reference (fourth century) already has a colder tone and is restricted to reproducing the passage of Aristobulus in which the latter makes various philosophers dependent on Mosaic law. Cyril's text (fifth century) introduces an interesting novelty: "They say that Orpheus was the most superstitious of men and preceded the poetry of Homer, since he was earlier in time, and he composed poems and hymns to false gods and won no small share of glory by doing so; afterward, condemning his own doctrines and understanding (συνέντα) that in abandoning the high road he had departed from the right way (τὴν ἀμαξιτὸν ἀφεὶς ἐν

---

2   Eus. *Theoph.* 2.41. Cf. Kofsky 2002, 282–286.

ἐκβολῆι γέγονε τῆς εὐθείας ὁδοῦ), he turned back to what was better (μεταφοιτῆσαι πρὸς τὰ βελτίω) and chose truth instead of falsehood." Orpheus's polytheism is now an abandonment of true religiosity, to which he later returns repentant. This variation can be explained as a projection onto Orpheus' conversion of Julian's return to paganism, since Cyril is precisely combating Julian's *Against the Galileans*. Theodoret (fifth century) presents yet another new version of Orpheus's monotheism. Here the journey to Egypt during which Orpheus came into contact with Hebrew ideas came *before* his polytheistic poems: "Although he learned (μεμαθηκώς) this from the Egyptians, who had received some knowledge of the truth from the Hebrews, he mixed (παρέμιξε) a certain amount of error into his theology and handed down the impious mysteries of the Dionysia and Thesmophoria, and as it were anointing the edge of the cup with honey, he offered the baleful drink to the deceived." The view of Orpheus's hypothetical successes is now a negative one: they only served as bait, as a disguise with which to attract his unfortunate victims to paganism. Augustine (fifth century) holds the same attitude toward the pagan theologians: "If in the midst of their many vain falsehoods they sang something of the one true God, they did not serve Him in an orderly way in mixing others who are not gods with Him and offering them the service owed only to God, nor could Orpheus, Musaeus, and Linus themselves abstain from putting their own gods to fictitious shame." Later, in the sixth century, the *Tübingen Theosophy* introduces a compiled version of the *Testament* with a positive valuation of Orpheus's conversion: "Orpheus realized the impiety of his action and was converted to the one Good."[3]

The conclusion is clear: Christian authors have no qualms about using their common materials in whatever way is useful to each one of them on each particular occasion, giving the same text different meanings by the simple device of locating Orpheus's conversion before, during, or after the composition of his polytheistic poems. Until the third century, paganism was still vigorous, and in order to attract its devotees, there was no better propaganda than the end-of-life conversion of the pagan prophet par excellence. As the Christians began to predominate, their tone became more aggressive, and the poem was used to prove Orpheus's dependence on the one true revelation and to criticize the pagan gods and mysteries, no longer an error induced by

---

3   Theoph. *Autol.* 2.3; Clem. Alex. *Protr.* 7.74.3, Ps.-Iust. *Cohort.* 15.1; *De mon.* 2.4; Eus. *PE* 13.12. Cyr. *CI* 1.35 (Riedweg 1993, 12 suggests that the metaphor of going astray is inspired by lines 6–7 of the *Testament*: εὖ δ᾽ἐπίβαινε ἀτραπιτοῦ, an explanation compatible with the one I offer here); Thdt. *Affect.* 2.30–32; Aug. *CD* 18.14 (the translation "in an orderly way" does not require the emendation *recte* against the manuscript reading *rite*, cf. Evans 2002, 40f); *Theosoph. Tub.* 55–56.

the demons, but rather a deliberate deception by one who has known the truth and rejects it. Finally, the *Theosophy* sets the stage for the early medieval recuperation of a positive image of Orpheus, when the paganism of which he had been made the patron is already practically extinct.

This variety of attitudes with regard to a single episode raises questions that are tempting to ask in every case of apologetic manipulation. What did the apologists really think? Was their manipulation a conscious distortion of the facts? There are contradictions with respect to Orphism even within the works of a single author: for example, in book I of the *Stromata* (1.21.31), Clement reports Epigenes's opinion that the Orphic poems are really the work of Pythagoreans of the late period, but in books V and VI he has no qualms about citing Orpheus profusely as an authority, or even about affirming that he preceded Homer. Even this incoherence might be explained as the reflection of uncertainty about Orpheus's existence and the authorship of his poems, but such a charitable interpretation cannot be applied to the evidently biased presentation of Orphic myths and rituals. Did the apologists really believe that these myths and rituals were so terrible, or were they conscious of their manipulation? Did they really believe that Orpheus had converted to and preached monotheism, or did they know that the *Testament* was a forgery?

Although they seem quite natural, these questions actually stem from mistaken assumptions, and not only because the concepts of forgery and authorship were different in the ancient world, giving rise to the extensive Christian and pagan pseudepigraphic literature (Speyer 1971). A glance at politics or mass media in our own time is enough to demonstrate that what one side sincerely perceives as an incontestable truth is for the other side, with equal sincerity and fervor, a manipulation and a lie. The same was true for the polemical literature of every philosophical or religious school in Antiquity, including Christianity. Orpheus's chronology and the authority of his works had been subjects of debate at least since Herodotus, and the content of Orphic rites was a traditional matter for taboos and secrecy. When the Christians chose in each case the version most compatible with their own interests, it is probable that, in the majority of cases, they did not do so with a conscious intent to lie, at least as we understand the word. The only truth they recognized was that of Revelation, and the presentations of reality that would safeguard that truth needed to fit perfectly within its categories; thus, an idea like the dependence of Greek wisdom on biblical revelation, ridiculous to modern eyes, must have appeared perfectly coherent to them, and the adaptation of Orpheus's chronology to this scheme must have meant for them not a self-interested falsification of the truth, but rather a purely logical operation, necessary in order to make the pieces fit together within the only possible scheme of reality of which they could conceive. Moreover, the seriousness of the objective was no obstacle to making use of exaggeration and even a certain sense of irony (as in Artapanus's identification of Moses and Musaeus), because these were part of the existing rhetorical conventions.

What was demanded both by the need to persuade readers and by the author's own conviction of the rightness of his theses was the attainment of a balance between manipulation and plausibility. The more scandalous affirmations, like those of Clement and Athenagoras, are accompanied by quotations from the Orphic poems themselves that give evidence of their veracity. The apologists are aware that in order to be credible, they cannot take their manipulation so far as to make it obvious. Of course, they were not all equally interested in achieving credibility: Firmicus had no scruples about presenting a fantastical euhemerist tale without evidence, while two centuries earlier Clement had proved his descriptions of the *symbola* of the mysteries of Dionysus and the episode of Baubo with detailed quotations of the Orphic verses.

This principle of plausibility has an important consequence: when it comes time to analyze the information transmitted by the Christians about Greek religion, it needs to be taken into account that they very rarely invent their material *ex novo*. That is to say, they may select from, manipulate, exaggerate, and deform the earlier tradition, but they start from information provided by their pagan literary sources or rooted in some aspect of cultic reality. They engage in a labor of criticism, interpretation, and manipulation in various senses of the Orphic tradition, but one that is almost always developed on the basis of principles established by earlier and contemporary pagan authors.

2. Continuity with Greek interpretative traditions

2.1. Adaptation

The Orphic myths and rites and a good part of the Orphic poems transmitted by the apologists are not mere products of their invention, since, as the last chapter has proved, they coincide to a large extent with the pagan evidence. It is their presentation that is subtly different. However, the ways in which the apologists break with the previous tradition regarding Orphism are often so slight and so well camouflaged that they may pass unnoticed by a reader not intent on discovering them. At times the Christians' efforts involve not so much the addition of new elements as simply the selection and expansion of one among various earlier traditions. Let us begin with the two most evident cases on the purely mythographic level: Orpheus's journey to Egypt and his priority with respect to Homer.

That Orpheus acquired his religious knowledge in Egypt was an earlier tradition well integrated into the mythography on Orphism since Herodotus and enthusiastically developed by Egyptian historiography (Manetho, Khairemon, Apion). Many sources of Egyptian orientation, like Hecataeus, were collected by Diodorus, who is especially concerned with spreading this tradition, and not only with respect to Orpheus.[4] The same was said of many Greek sages (Solon, Pythagoras, Plato), because Egypt was the land of mystery, admired for its antiquity and grandeur, from which knowledge of magic and religion par excellence was thought to come. The Alexandrian Jews, enthusiastically seconded by the Christians (*Cohortatio*, Clement, Eusebius), modified this tradition slightly in promoting the idea that Orpheus had become acquainted there with the Mosaic revelation, to which they ascribed all of the usable elements of his message; Diodorus was precisely the authoritative source to which they turned most often (although not the only one) in order to justify this claim.[5] By way of a (consciously?) erroneous interpretation of a passage in which Diodorus clearly distinguishes the first Egyptian lawgiver Menas (inspired by Hermes) from the Jewish lawgiver Moses (inspired by Iao), the *Cohortatio* identifies the two figures with one another and cites Diodorus as support in order to make Moses the first Egyptian lawgiver.[6] This is another field in which Orphism and Hermeticism come together as functionally equivalent movements, now as transmitters of revelation in the service of Judeo-Christian apologetic. We have already encountered Artapanus taking advantage of the phonetic similarity to identify Moses with Musaeus and make Orpheus his disciple; it cannot surprise us that in another passage he also identifies Moses with Hermes to the same end.[7]

The debate surrounding priority of doctrines is a key to the polemic between pagans on the one hand and Jews and Christians on the other, and

---

4 Hdt. 2.82. Hecataeus *FGH* 264 F 25; D. S. 1.96.2–4; cf. Plut. *de Iside* 9 p. 354d.
5 Ps.-Iust. *Cohort*.9.3–4, 14.2; cf. Riedweg 1994 *ad loc*. Eusebius (*PE* 10.8.1–16) also quotes Diodorus as evidence for the Egyptian journeys of Greek sages, along with Clement, Porphyry, Plato, Flavius Josephus, Julius Africanus and Tatian (although in *PE* 3.1 and 3.12 he denies that Orpheus traveled). Cf. Beatrice 1998. Athenagoras (*Leg*. 28) quotes Herodotus to prove the equivalence of Egyptian and Greek rites, but does not speak about dependence.
6 D. S. 1.94.1.2, cited by Ps.-Iust. *Cohort*.9.3, and hence by Cyr. *CI* 1.19. On the textually awkward passage of the *Cohortatio*, cf. Riedweg 1994, 191f.
7 Artapanus, *FGH* 726F 3 *apud* Eus. *PE* 9.27. Cf. III n. 53.

the case of Orpheus offered a marvelous argument to the latter group. Egypt was the physical place of encounter between the two traditions, the tangible proof that the Greek religious tradition was dependent on the Hebrew tradition for whatever truth it contained. Jewish and Christian insistence on the historical factuality of the events of salvation history was thereby fully satisfied, since it required no great effort to reconcile the chronology of Orpheus and Moses. Postulating an encounter between the two during Orpheus's journey to Egypt meant only adding a detail that integrated the theory of Greek dependence on the prophets into the earlier tradition almost without effort. The real consequences of this detail for the vision of Greek religion were vast, but the manipulation that enabled its incorporation into the tradition was extremely slight by comparison.

The insistence on Orpheus's chronological priority with respect to all other Greek poets, especially Homer, fits within the same framework. The traditional chronology of the ancient poets was Orpheus-Musaeus-Hesiod-Homer, although certain discordant voices of no small prestige, like Herodotus, Aristotle, and the Alexandrian philologists, made Homer the first of the Greek poets and, as a result, denied Orpheus's existence, attributing his poems to other, later authors like Onomacritus and the Pythagoreans.[8] The Christians who mention Orpheus place themselves enthusiastically on the side of his existence and priority, although they are highly conscious of the division of opinions.[9] Clement and the author of the *Cohortatio* give express "philological" proofs of Homer's dependence on Orpheus, proofs both of their own invention and taken from earlier works. Other passages of Christian authorship affirm Orpheus's priority as an evident fact that needs no demonstration.[10] This curious unanimity in defending their archenemy's ex-

---

8   The traditional order is stated by Aristoph. *Ra.* 1030–1036, Hippias fr. 86 B6 D-K, Plat. *Apol.* 41a, D. S. 1.96.2, Plut. *Sept. sap. conv.* 16; it is questioned by Hdt. 2.53.3, Aristot. *apud* Cic. *ND* 1.107, Sext. Emp. *Adv. Math.* 1.203. Following Aristotle, Alexandrian philologists (like Epigenes) considered Orphic poets as *neoteroi*, i.e. later than Homer. Cf. Nagy 2001, Herrero 2008a.

9   Clement (*Strom.* 1.21.131) refers to Epigenes, who denies that the *Orphica* were written by Orpheus. Tatian (*Orat.* 42.5) prefers to adhere to an intermediate solution: Onomacritus compiled the poems attributed to Orpheus. Yet both speak confidently of Orpheus as author in many other passages, as we have seen. Only Eusebius (*PE* 3.9.14) doubts the authenticity of an Orphic poem when quoting it, with the clearly polemical intention of undermining Porphyry's allegorical interpretation of the *Hymn to Zeus*. Cf. the Herodotean attitude of Flavius Josephus in *Contra Ap.* 1.12.

10 Clement (*Strom.* 5.14.116.1, 6.2.5.3, 6.2.26.1–2), Pseudo-Justin (*Cohort.* 17.2), Athenagoras (*Leg.* 18.3), and Cyril (*CI* 1.35) expressly indicate that Orpheus pre-

istence and primacy, when they were fully aware of the alternative, is due not only to the desire to define a rival on whom to focus their attention, but also to the convenience of situating him at the head of the Greek tradition as πρῶτος θεολόγος or διδάσκαλος, on the basis of the generally accepted notion of the transmission of wisdom from a first founder.[11] The apologists in this case simply took advantage of an already widely extended tradition and so consolidated its validity for the tradition that came after.

Adherence to the claim of Orpheus's priority was coherent with the widely extended scheme of the genealogical transmission of ideas and permitted the apologists to explain the achievements and errors of the Greeks by way of Orpheus. The approximations to the truth of later thinkers – especially Homer – could ultimately be traced back to his figure. As his dependence on Moses was easy to prove, the priority of biblical revelation over all the achievements of Greek thought was guaranteed. The same framework is found in the inverse explanation that makes sense of Greek paganism: in the *Cohortatio*, Orpheus's character as founder of polytheism (ἐν ἀρχῇ τῆς πολυθεότητος, 17.2) gives greater value to his later conversion (36.4) and explains the error of those who, like Homer or Plato, would have imitated him before they came to know the truth in their own journeys to Egypt (14.2); Homer imitated his polytheism, but afterward he gave his true opinion about the one God (17.2). Emphasis on Orpheus's priority was not intended here to explain the continuity of transmission of revelation, but rather that of polytheistic error.

In drawing on Orpheus's chronology and his fame as a traveler and religious founder, and adapting them to their own interests, the apologists behaved exactly like their pagan predecessors and contemporaries. The manipulation of tradition is perceptible above all in the sphere of the origin of rites. Disputes between cities over the location of heroes' tombs had a clear political purpose, as struggles over the location of saints' tombs would have in the Middle Ages. Let us recall the legend of St Mark's body, stolen from Alexandria when the Egyptian city fell into Muslim hands: its transfer to Venice symbolized the transfer of legitimate dominion over the maritime East to its new home. We must take a similar view of the assorted pretensions that, as Diodorus reports, various regions (Samothrace, Crete, Egypt) had to being the cradle of the mysteries, supposedly transmitted by Orpheus

---

cedes (and is the model for) Homer; Eusebius *PE* 10.4.10 (like Clement in *Strom* 1.14.59.1) just calls him "the most ancient" (παλαιότατος).

11 *Cohort.* 15.1, Athenag. *Leg.* 18.3; Eus. *PE* 1.6.4, 10.4.4. Cf. Kleingünther 1933 Thraede 1962 on the πρῶτος εὑρετής. Cf. Pilhofer 1990 on the use of ancientness and priority as arguments for primacy in pagan and Christian circles.

to the rest of Greece.[12] The region of origin thereby acquired evident religious prestige and consequent political advantages: Athens insisted for the same reason on the primacy of the Eleusinian rites over other Greek festivals of Demeter. Orpheus was the ideal transmitter of rites and religious knowledge, and that he should now play the same role in the transmission of the Mosaic revelation to Greece was only another step in the same tradition of seeking prestige on the basis of religious primacy and of using the Thracian poet as a mediating instrument.

This continuity with Greek tradition is less evident on the literary level than on the purely mythographic one, since the myth of Orpheus, a favorite topic in the Orphic tradition among the Greek and Latin poets, generally did not interest the Christians. Only Clement and Eusebius make use of the myth of the singer, as we saw. However, the themes of the mysteries had also become instruments of literary composition, and on this level Christians did follow Greek trends. I am not only referring now to the use of the terminology of the mystery cults and of initiation as a metaphor for describing the acquisition of philosophical or religious knowledge, a common practice since Plato and one adopted by Philo, Clement and others. The myths and rites of the mysteries themselves also had great potential as literary narratives, a potential much taken advantage of in Imperial times. It has been suggested that the Greek novel was regularly composed on the basis of a ritual framework, using the process of initiation as a model for developing the plot.[13] Whether or not this is true of the genre as a whole, the mysteries clearly lie in the background of some novels: the fragments of Lollianus's novel *Phoinikika* preserved on papyrus clearly exploit the themes of the myth of the Titans, with the horror aroused by the cannibalism of a child and with the imagined possibility that rituals of this kind might actually be celebrated; in order to achieve this effect, the culinary details are especially emphasized.[14] It is clear that when the apologists allude in more or less general or detailed terms to this myth, one of their favorite themes, they are exploiting the same sensations of terror and gory suspense. Clement says, "The mysteries of Dionysus are utterly inhuman; he was still a child ..." (*Protr.* 2.17.2), and he recounts the myth highlighting details like the toys, the tripod, and the roasting spits, with a purpose similar to that of the novel: causing his reader to shudder with horror. It is left deliberately ambiguous whether the rite that

---

12 Samothrace: D.S. 4.43.1; 5.49.6; 5.64.4 (cf. Linforth 1941, 27, 204f.). Crete: 5.75.4, 5.77.3. Egypt: 1.96.6.
13 Merkelbach 1962 and 1988; Kerenyi 1962. The thesis is met with scepticism by Stephens/Winkler 1995.
14 Henrichs 1978, Winkler 1980, Herrero 2006

commemorated the episode really celebrated so "inhuman" a ritual. There is no reason to think that Clement was inspired by any specific novel (although the *Phoinikika* is set precisely in an Egyptian milieu), but he certainly appeals to the same sentiments and uses similar narrative techniques in describing the ritual. So do Arnobius or Firmicus in their own accounts.

Besides serving as literary inspiration, Orphic poetry was the object of study and philological criticism. On this level one can also find clear continuity between pagan and Christian approaches. Among Clement's sources are a treatise on the Orphic mysteries, a treatise *On Plagiarism*, and a work with Orphic fragments on symbolic interpretation, in addition to the mention of Epigenes's *On the Poetry of Orpheus*. These works should be ascribed to an Alexandrian context, as products of a lesser philology far from Aristarchus's quality and ideological independence. Clement and the *Cohortatio* not only report some of the results of this ideological philology that made use of Orpheus, but also continue its methods, making comparisons between verses of Homer and Orpheus for apologetic ends. For their part, the Stoics in Pergamum defended, in opposition to Aristarchus, the existence of an Orpheus prior to Homer, in order to harmonize the two poets and allegorize their works according to their own requirements. Christian continuity with this Stoic method is evident in the case of Athenagoras or the Pseudo-Clementine writings, whose sources for the interpretation of Orpheus and Homer come from Stoic circles.[15]

In fact, this sort of literary criticism already comes very close to philosophical interpretation of the Orphic poems. A variety of schools drew on Orphic poetry in order to spread their own ideas by way of a vehicle that was prestigious because of its antiquity and because it was the product of the Muses' revelation to the poet par excellence. A first method for adapting Orpheus to a given philosophical tendency was the composition of new poems, an endeavor facilitated by the open character of the Orphic tradition The first to draw on Orphic poetry in this sense were the Pythagoreans; Epigenes's testimony is eloquent in this regard. The Stoics also appear to have composed Orphic poems, or at least to have colored compilations and versions of the theogonies, like that of Hieronymus and Hellanicus or the *Rhapsodies* themselves, with their ideas.[16] Jews and Christians were conscious of the existence of these Orphic-Pythagorean poems, and nothing must have

---

15   Clem. Alex. *Strom.* 5.14.116.1; Ps.-Iust. *Cohort.* 17.2. Athenag. *Leg.* 17.1. On para-Aristarchean philology in Alexandria, cf. pp. 201f, 210; on Pergamene philology, cf. Nagy 2001.

16   Epigenes in Clem. Alex. *Strom.* 1.21.131. On the Stoic influence on the *Rhapsodies*, cf. West 1983, 176–259.

seemed more natural to them than forging and circulating Orphic-Biblical poems like the *Testament*.

Aside from composing poems, however, Pythagoreans and Stoics had also practiced from ancient times the allegorical interpretation of already-existing Orphic poems, whose quotations served as support for their theories. They were not the only ones who allegorized Orpheus: this method of interpretation was already being practiced by the Derveni commentator, who is in many ways a predecessor of the Stoa, and even earlier, as early as the sixth century BC, Theagenes was using allegory to defend Homer from attacks on his anthropomorphic theology by critics like Xenophanes. However, it was undoubtedly the Neoplatonists who took this approach the furthest; the majority of the surviving fragments of the *Rhapsodies* come from the quotations they made that allegorized the Orphic theogony, adapting it to their philosophical system.[17] Allegory was also used by Christians (Clement and above all Origen) to overcome the difficulties posed by literal interpretation of the Bible, although controversies with Gnostics and heretics finally led to strict limits on its use, since there was no lack of Christian critics who saw allegory as a perversion of the pristine sense of Scripture by the Greek philosophical categories to which it led.[18] In book V of the *Stromata* Clement appeals to Pythagorean interpretations of Orphic poems in order to justify the practice of similar methods with Scripture. In addition, in their own treatments of Orphic poetry, Clement and Lactantius extend to the Christian milieu the Greek philosophical tradition of using that poetry to support the interpreter's own ideas. Clement quotes Orpheus on various occasions in support of Christian doctrines, at times with an interpretation very far from the literal sense: the last two lines of *OF* 31 are read as referring to the resurrection of the dead, and *OF* 691 as pagan testimony to the Father and the Son. Lactantius cites the theogonic passages of the *Rhapsodies* in order to find in them an imperfect expression of the creator God of *Genesis*. However forced these interpretations may appear today, they are of the same type as the ancient interpretations of the Derveni commentator and the contemporary ones of the Stoics and Neoplatonists, rivals in doctrine but colleagues in the methods employed.

An apparent paradox, explicable as a matter of apologetic convenience, is that these same allegorical methods are inadmissible for the Christians

---

17 Cf. Pépin 1976 (without mention of the Orphic poems) and Brisson 2004 on allegory in general; Brisson 1995 and 2008 on neo-Platonic interpretations of Orpheus. Cf. Ramelli 2007 with a very complete anthology of commented allegorical texts. Cf. III n. 11 for Stoic interpretations of Orphic poems.
18 Chadwick 1966, 95–101.

in the exegesis of Greek myths. Focused on criticizing the myths' literal sense, the apologists deny the validity of interpretations that take Demeter and Dionysus as symbols of wheat and wine. Conversely, the pagan critique of Christianity engages in the same literalistic interpretation of the Bible and does not allow its allegorization (Orig. *CC* 4.17, 4.48–51). Just like the euhemerism that we will look at shortly, the allegorical method is a double-edged sword that one accepts for one's own side while denying its use to one's rival, and vice versa.

There is continuity not only in the interpretative method, but also in the content of the interpretation, since shared sources work to produce a certain commonality of ideas. The purpose of the majority of the Orphic poems given a Christian sense is above all the defense of monotheism: the *Testament*, the *Hymn to Zeus*, the *Hymn to the Sun*, a *Hymn to the Mightiest God* (*OF* 691). Many pagan authors had cited the *Hymn to Zeus* in a similar sense, as proof of the Orphic intuition of the unity of the divine.[19] The *palaios logos* cited by Plato in the *Laws* on Zeus as beginning, middle, and end came from Orpheus in the eyes of the Neoplatonists and from Moses in those of the Christians.[20] In another clear case of common sources, Judeo-Christian Platonism (Philo, Clement, Origen, Augustine) drew on a Neopythagorean cento that quoted other figures of growing prestige, such as Empedocles, Heraclitus, Pythagoras, and Plato, the theme of which was the soul's fall from its original divine status, a cento that we also find being used by contemporary Middle Platonists like Plutarch, Plotinus, and Hierocles.[21]

2.2. Criticism

The Christians were in agreement, then, with the philosophical tradition in valuing certain aspects of Orphism positively. However, the continuity is even greater in the sphere of criticism. The attack on the myths as inappropriate representations of the image of the truly divine is a constant of the Greek philosophical tradition going back to Xenophanes in the sixth century B.C. The mythological gods' subjection to human passions is incompatible with the venerable impassivity that philosophy presumed of the divine. Pindar already refused to believe some especially crude myths about

---

19 Plato, Pseudo-Aristotle, Apuleius, Porphyry, cited as sources of *OF* 31. Cf. pp. 187ff.
20 Plat. *Leg.* 715e7. The Derveni Papyrus (cf. *OF* 14) has confirmed that the neo-Platonists were right. Cf. the Christian quotations of the passage in n. 100.
21 Cf. III n. 7.

the gods, like that of Tantalus. Plato proposed the expulsion of the poets in book X of the *Republic* principally on account of the lies they told about the divine. Precisely Orpheus is mentioned by Isocrates as the narrator of especially scandalous tales, a reputation that he still had in Diogenes Laertius's day: doubtless his theogonic myths were especially difficult to accept in their literal sense for those who were seeking a more spiritual image of the divine.[22] The way to "save" these poets was allegorical interpretation, an endeavor in which the Christians, when it suited them, did not hesitate to join. Much more frequently, however, they attached themselves to the tradition that criticized the poets for the scandalousness of their myths. Justin praises Plato for expelling Homer and the poets "because in this way he taught men to abandon the evil demons and the deities who committed the crimes recounted by the poets, and invited them to search, by means of the Logos, for God, whom they did not know."[23] The attacks on Orpheus by Athenagoras, Tatian, Clement, Origen, Gregory, Arnobius, and Firmicus are direct heirs of the Presocratic and Platonic criticism of myth, and their intellectual authority comes from their continuity with so prestigious a tradition.

The Christians also join in the originally Platonic and Peripatetic criticism of the material conception of the gods to which Stoic pantheistic theology led. So close to Stoicism in ethical matters, the Christians are much more inclined to Platonic transcendent theology than to Stoic immanentism. Athenagoras makes use of the Stoic source in which he finds the *Theogony of Hieronymus and Hellanicus* in order to criticize the materiality of gods who, having originated in water and earth, cannot be eternal: "The gods do not exist, if they have been born when they were not yet (εἰ γεγόνασιν οὐκ ὄντες)." However, the most blatant attack is the verses quoted by Gregory of Nazianzus that make Zeus roll about in the "dung of horses, sheep, and mules," in an evident caricature of the Stoic pantheism that locates Zeus in everything. Whether these verses were originally a joke or were intended as the expression of a profound pantheism, Philostratus had already held them up for mockery, attributing them to Pamphus.[24] The continuity between pagan and Christian critiques of Greek theology could have no more expressive example.

---

22 Pind. *Ol.* 1.50ff; Plat. *Resp.* 595–607; Isocr. *Busir.* 10.38; D. L. 1.5. Julian (Cyr. *CI* 2.44a = *OF* 59 VII) makes a critique *more xenophanico* of Orphic theogonic myths that Cyril uses against them, discarding any allegorical solution.
23 Iust. *Apol.* 2.10.4–8. On the pagan side, Celsus criticizes Jesus as the clearest example of the divine anthropomorphism that Christians are so quick to mock when attacking Greek religion (Chadwick 1966, 27).
24 *Leg.* 19.3. Greg. Naz. *Or.* 4.115, Philostr. *Her.* 25.2 = *OF* 848.

2.2. Criticism

A particular type of criticism of myth is the euhemerist theory according to which the gods are really men of the past divinized for their great works, and the myths are an idealized account with divine trappings of what were really historical events that can be reconstructed by way of the mythological version. This, however, is a criticism of religion (it was not in vain that Euhemerus was quickly included in the catalogues of atheists) that at the same time preserves, in a certain way, the content of myth as a channel for the transmission of truth, by attributing to it a historical foundation obscured by the divine costuming.[25] The Christian reception of euhemerism is very extensive and is split between two poles: on the one hand, a negative view of Euhemerus as an atheist, and on the other, a use of euhemerist techniques as apologetic weapons against Greek religion.[26] In this reception, texts having to do with Orpheus and Orphism occupy a prominent place.

The Alexandrian Jews had already drawn on techniques similar to euhemerism in transforming myths into historical events, as Artapanus did when he identified Moses with Musaeus and Hermes-Thoth. More than an apologetic weapon, however, this was for the Jews above all a tool for integrating their own culture into Greek historiographical frameworks.[27] The Christians continued this labor of chronological adaptation, and Tatian and Clement (who probably depends on Tatian here) had no doubts about including Dionysus in their chronologies as a divinized man.[28] In addition, they developed the use of these techniques as apologetic weapons for demonstrating the falsity of pagan cults. Even there, a certain continuity with Jewish practice is evident, as is implied by the probable euhemerist source shared by the *Wisdom of Solomon* and Firmicus Maternus's account of the mysteries of Dionysus. In any case, the Christian enthusiasm for this approach is much greater: in the *Protrepticus*, Clement integrates a euhemerist explanation of the mysteries of Aphrodite, which he says were founded by Cinyras for his

---

25 Cf. Winiarczyk 1991 (edition of the fragments) and 2002.
26 Condemnation as an atheist in Theoph. *Autol.* 3.7, Eus. *PE* 14.16.1, Thdt. *Affect* 2.112, 3.4; vindication in Clem. Alex. *Protr.* 2.24.2. On Euhemerus' Christian reception, cf. Winiarczyk 2002 168–175, Pépin 1986 and above all Zucker 1905, who shows that only Eusebius and Lactantius were familiar with Euhemerus through Diodorus and Ennius respectively. The others knew him through anthologies and summaries. Euhemeristic approaches to myth had enormous success in medieval historiography. Note that the transformation of ancient gods and heroes into saints is exactly the inverse process (cf. Wilson 1983).
27 Artapanus, *FGH* 726F 3 *apud* Eus. *PE* 9.27. Cf. Winiarczyk 2002, 176–181 or other Jewish texts that reveal euhemerist influence: Eupolemus, Theodotus, *Sibylline Oracle* 3.
28 Tat. *Orat.* 39 ≈ Clem. *Strom.* 1.105.1, 1.79.2.

prostitute lover, into the information provided about these mysteries by his Orphic source, and later on he even goes so far as to praise Euhemerus's atheism as recognition of the falsity of pagan cults and myths.[29]

Apart from these passages of Firmicus and Clement, originating in earlier pagan sources that they put to use in an apologetic manner, Dionysus also appears often in lists of divinized men of euhemerist antecedents, in which his death and resurrection are frequently singled out as his most remarkable characteristics, alongside figures like Asclepius and Heracles.[30] In addition, there are indications that the figure of Orpheus was added to these lists.[31] Christian attitudes toward these divinized men are also ambivalent. Justin compares Hermes, Asclepius, Dionysus, Heracles, the Dioscurii, and Bellerophon with Jesus as proof that the Christians "are doing nothing new" in proclaiming a man who is also "Son of God" and is venerated as such after his death and resurrection. However, still far from the most acrimonious moments of the apologetic struggle, Justin fails to see that the argument can be reversed: Celsus compares Jesus to Asclepius, Dionysus, Heracles, and the Dioscurii, and Origen has to refine his Christological arguments in depth in order to do exactly the opposite of Justin and differentiate these others from Jesus.[32] A comparable case is that of Antinoüs, Hadrian's lover who was deified after his death: the Christians put him forward as an example of divinization that demonstrates the falsity of the Greek gods, but Celsus equates his case with that of Jesus. In fact, euhemerist critiques had as firm a basis of support in the historicity of Jesus as in that of Antinoüs.[33]

---

29 Firm. *De err*. 6 and *Wis*. 14:15–16. *Protr*. 2.13.4, 2.14.2 (cf. Herrero 2007a), 2.24.2.
30 Cic. *ND* 2.62, 3.39 and 45; *Leg*. 2.19; D. S. 6.1, Aet. *Plac*. 1.6. This list exemplifies the continuity between the Christians and their pagan sources: Augustine quotes Scaevola (*CD* 4.27), Lactantius quotes Cicero (*DI* 1.15). The list is also in Athenagoras (*Leg*. 29–30), Clement (*Protr*. 2.26, 2.30, *Strom*. 1.21) and Tertullian (*Apol*. 21.7–9).
31 Celsus in *CC* 7.53 replaces Dionysus by Orpheus in the list, along with Asclepius and Heracles, of divinely inspired men who suffered violent death, as Jesus did. On Orpheus as a *theios aner*, cf. III nn. 87–88.
32 Cf. Iust. *Apol*. 1.21, who makes a lexical distinction, calling Jesus γέννημα τοῦ Θεοῦ as opposed to the υἱοὶ τοῦ Διός (just as in *Apol*. 1.55 he remarks that no pagan god has been crucified); Orig. *CC* 3.22–43. On this debate of euhemeristic tone, cf. Gamble 1979.
33 Christian attacks against Antinous in Iust. *Apol*. 1.29, Athenag. *Leg*. 30.2, Theoph. *Autol*. 3.8, Clem. Alex. *Protr*. 4.49, Tert. *Apol*. 13.9, Athanas. *Contra gent*. 9; for his comparison with Jesus, cf. Celsus *apud* Orig. *CC* 3.36. A euhemerist approach to Jesus is also clear in the story (perhaps originating in Jewish circles) about his being born from the soldier Panthera, in what seems a clear deformation from *parthenos*: Celsus echoes the story in *CC* 1.32.

2.2. Criticism

In their mutual polemic, Christians and pagans enthusiastically made use of euhemerist arguments against which they nevertheless had to defend themselves at the same time.

Not only were the Orphic myths a target of the traditional philosophical critique, and consequently of the Christian one, but the ritual and social sides of Orphism were as well. Let us recall that Plato expels itinerant priests from his ideal city, along with poets. He coincides with Heraclitus in harshly criticizing these initiators (*magoi* for the Ephesian, *agyrtai kai manteis* for Plato), who are the best-known actual manifestation of Orphic initiations. The basis of their criticism is the transformation of rituals of purification into a mechanical initiation in exchange for money. The philosophers are not the only ones with such complaints. At the end of the *Second Olympian Ode*, Pindar contrasts his song for those who understand to the croaking of crows, which rather than referring to his rivals in the composition of choral lyrics, as it is usually interpreted, alludes to the fact that the guarantor of the hero's true immortality is still the poet, not the wandering initiators who flutter about like crows. Theophrastus, Plutarch, and Philodemos mention the figure of the "orpheotelestes" in a comic and mocking tone that raises the possibility that this label comes from a stock comedic character. In reality, criticism of these wandering priests had become a literary topos about initiatory cults, especially Bacchic ones. Doubtless the relevant passages of Plato contributed a great deal to keeping the association with Orphic rites alive even after the "orpheotelestai" had disappeared: Livy uses these traits of a dishonest wanderer to characterize the Greek who introduced the *Bacchanalia* in Rome, and Strabo calls Orpheus himself a sorcerer (*goes*) and a beggar (*agyrtes*).[34]

These commonplaces for describing the ritual officiants of mystery cults also became part of the polemic between pagans and Christians. Celsus uses the traits of the *goes* to characterize Jesus and the Christians in various passages. He compares them on repeated occasions to the "initiators and mystagogues" who cheat the people, frightening them with the terrors of Hades (*CC* 3.16, 4.10, 4.23, 5.14, 8.48–49), and to the *goetes* and diviners who utter prophecies, cast spells, and perform various prodigies (2.49, 2.55, 7.9–11). The vagabonds who wander from city to city begging, without a fixed place of cult, are a constant theme, linked to the ancient prototypes of the itinerant charlatan (*CC* 7.9). Origen's defense in these passages tries to

---

34 Plat. *Resp.* 364e; *Leg.* 909a, 933a; Heracl. fr. 14 DK (cf. n. 76); Pind. *Ol.* 2.83–89; Theophr. *Charact.* 16.11; Plut. *Apophth. Lacon.* 224d (*OF* 653–655); Liv. 39.8.3ff; Strab. 7, fr. 18; 10.3.

show the difference between the thaumaturges of every stripe who abounded in the Late Empire and the miracles of Christ and the Christian saints, and between the diviners' oracles and biblical prophecies. He accuses Celsus of drawing on this topos to classify them all as sorcerers and vagabonds (*CC* 4.35). Although in this passage his defense is precisely the same as the one an Orphic initiator would have made – that is to say, he appeals to the authority of written texts – Origen had a point in claiming that this was a topos that could be applied to distinct cases (*CC* 2.34). A similar polemic can already be found in Flavius Josephus with regard to pagan accusations of *goeteia* against Moses.[35] In works in which the Christians are on the offensive, on the other hand, it is paganism that finds itself accused of *goeteia*. Whether Clement with regard to Orpheus and the mysteries (*Protr.* 1.1.3, 2.11.3, 2.12.1), Eusebius with regard to the pagan priest Theognetus (*HE* 9.3 and 9.11), or Augustine with regard to the Neoplatonists' revived theurgy (*CD* 10.9–10), they all reduce the rival religion to pure sorcery, using terminology that had been topical since the classical age: *goeteia, epodai, teletai, katharmoi*.

The terms of the polemic are exactly the same on each side. The pagans classify Christianity as a whole as magical charlatanism, without distinction, just as the Christians do in reverse when referring to traditional religion, especially the mysteries. The vagueness of the boundary in both directions between "magic" and "religion" (both modern terms) provided ready arguments to the attackers. The central role of literacy and bookishness both in Orphism and in the Judeo-Christian milieu paved the way for the assimilation of sacred texts to magical spells, since the very same religious text composed with elevated theological aims could be employed with lower, purely practical, aims and methods. Correspondingly, each side labored to distinguish superstition from religion within its own camp: in the passages cited, Origen differentiates Christian miracles and prophecies from those of wandering wonderworkers and diviners; Porphyry and other Neoplatonists differentiate theurgy, the elevated and mystical use of purification rituals, from *goeteia*, the magical use of the same rites. What the defender tries to distinguish is what the attacker tries to identify and fuse together, and both strategies use methods and a vocabulary of argumentation that had been (and still are) a recurring element in religious debates since Plato.

---

35 Ios. *Contra Ap.* 2.14.145. Echoes of the accusation against Moses in Orig. *CC* 4.33 and 2.34. Eusebius' *Praeparatio* has long passages aiming to differentiate between Jesus' miracles and pagan sorcery (Kofsky 2002, 165–214).

2.2. Criticism

In reality, each side tries to define the limits of its own identity as a communal religion by excluding its adversary, accused of seeking individual profit outside the bonds of community. The process is similar to what happened during the classical age, when the *goes* went from having an ambiguous status between magic and religion to being clearly excluded from communal religious constructions, both in the official city and in Plato's ideal polis.[36] Now, both pagan and Christian literature and pagan and Christian imperial legislation exclude and persecute the new *goetes*, the only difference being that each side includes its rival in this category, as a representative of superstition as opposed to religion, of disorder as opposed to rationality. In the fourth century BC as in the fourth century AD, every age of crisis in the political community is propitious for the appearance of these figures charismatic priests and skillful charlatans, and the reaction of those in power against them is equally predictable.[37] The continuity of vocabulary and topos corresponds to a continuity of intentions.

Among the elements that reveal this intimate bond among the criticisms of the *goes* in different times and places, besides the mentioned vocabulary characteristic of initiations, is the connection with Orpheus. In the same way that Plato, Theophrastus, or the Theseus of Euripides' *Hippolytus* associated his name with the activities of the wandering priests, because many of them called on his name, magical papyri also invoked his authority in the imperial age, just as did magi of a more elevated level, like Apollonius of Tyana and, in a Roman milieu, Apuleius, or the Neoplatonists who assigned new value to the theurgy of the rituals Orpheus founded. On the attacking side, Celsus (Orig. *CC* 2.55) compared the resurrection of Christ to the journeys to Hades by Orpheus and other heroes, from a perspective that considered them all falsehoods meant to deceive the people. On the other side, Clement made Orpheus the patron of all *goeteia*, lumping together magic, oracles, and the mysteries. If the Platonic critique of wandering initiators is an underlying element in Celsus, Clement expressly invokes Heraclitus following his at-

---

36 Burkert 1962, 53f.: "Thus religion is separated from magic; not only the deepening of thought on the idea of the divine is relevant, but even earlier, the discovery of the citizen". Cf. Martin 2004, and Sfameni Gasparro 2002, on the Greek and Christian construction of superstition (and magic) vs. religion, with the *goes* on the first side. Cf. nn. 53–57 and III nn. 2–3.

37 Fögen 1993 on the continuity in forms and intentions of Late Imperial pagan and Christian legislation. Some groups, like the Manicheans, were persecuted by all sides. Plato's heritage is also perceptible here. Following him, and previous Roman tradition (cf. pp. 64ff), Cicero (*Leg.* 2.21.18; 2.37.4) had already suggested prohibiting cults dangerous for the city, and Late Imperial legislation puts this idea into practice.

tack on the mysteries, condemning "night-wanderers, magi, Bacchics, *lenae*, and *mystai*." The quotation makes manifest the continuity of the Christian (and anti-Christian) attitude with the Platonic and Presocratic critique of Orphism.[38] It should be kept well in mind, therefore, that the various Christian strategies that will be examined in the remainder of the chapter continue along the lines of the Greek tradition, like those of the Christians' contemporary rivals.

3. Christian attitudes

3.1. Rejection

The majority of Christian references to Orphism clearly tend to take the offensive. It is a matter of demonstrating that the gods who are protagonists of such myths and recipients of such cults are unworthy of this divine rank. The Christians juxtapose two very different levels of religiosity: rituals and myths are not the object of belief as dogmas are, and myths are not judged on ethical criteria. The Greek poets do not share the biblical prophets' ethical preoccupations when speaking about the divine, but rather have very different interests (e. g., cosmology). Nevertheless, the Christians place their poems in the same category as the prophetic and legal writings of the Bible in order to compare the two sets of texts from their own historical and moralizing perspective. The pagan myths were a fundamental element in the representation of the gods, which did not imply identifying a god entirely within the limits of an image and believing in him only within the parameters of a myth. However, the Christians applied their criteria of the identification of images with idols and of the full historicity they ascribed to biblical accounts. Even in primarily defensive works, like those of Athenagoras and Origen, this critique became an efficacious counterattack as the apologists compared the Greek myths to their own doctrines as the only ones worthy of

---

38 *Protr.* 1.1.3, 2.11.3, 2.12.2, 2.22.2 (= Heraclit. fr. 14b DK, cf. n. 76). The text of 2.22.4 has a lexical coincidence with the Derveni Papyrus, col. VI.1 that also shows the continuity of pagan and Christian critiques: these are the only two appearances of the generalizing expression πόπανα πολυόμφαλα. Other mentions of *omphala* have, instead of the abstract prefix *poly-*, specific numerals like *tetra-*, *penta-* (cf. Henrichs 1984, 261). Generalizing terminology belongs more to the descriptions of a religious phenomenon by external observers, which tend to categorize it in abstract terms, like the Derveni commentator or Clement (and his source).

the divine. Despite this basic homogeneity, it is possible to discern among these attacks two orientations with distinct roots.

On the one hand, a good portion of these critiques do not declare that these "gods" are entirely non-existent, but only that they do not deserve to be considered divine, since their material nature and subjection to the passions make them clearly unworthy of divinity. The existence of these beings is not totally denied, but instead their status is lowered, whether to the role of immanent material principles (Athenagoras), of demons (Justin), or of divinized ancient men (euhemerism). In the same way, moreover, more than denying the veracity of the stories of crime and incest that shape the myths, the apologists admit them as real events that reflect the immorality of these demons or men, an immorality that makes them unfit for divinization. For it must be remembered that the fundamental conception against which the Christians were fighting was the generally accepted idea that the cult of one deity did not exclude that of the rest.

This orientation is fundamentally Greek in its roots: Paul Veyne (1983) demonstrated that even the most rationalist ancient critics of Greek myths tried to find a foundation of truth underlying their mythological verbiage, instead of entirely discarding them. Alongside this approach, however, there are to be found also claims of the total non-existence of the pagan gods, no more than statues of wood and stone, and of the falsity of their myths, no more than inventions of the poets. In sum, their cult is idolatry pure and simple, and there is nothing more than error behind it. This strictly monotheistic orientation is of clearly biblical lineage and coexists with the previous one without apparent contradiction, since the two are easy to reconcile in a rhetorical argument. In Clement's *Protrepticus* we find intermingled criticism of the *daimones* venerated as gods (4.55.4), of the cults of divinized men (4.54–56), and of the idolatry entailed in the rendering of cult to images of stone and wood (4.46–53).

There is a third orientation in the attack on Orphic myths. Hippolytus denounces them not for their content in itself, but as a source of inspiration for the theories of the Sethian Gnostics. This criticism is not exclusive to Hippolytus: a brief allusion by Clement to those who, taking Orpheus as inspiration, "introduced the doctrine of emissions and perhaps even thought of a spouse of God" shows that it was more widely extended. Irenaeus also accuses the Valentinians of drawing inspiration for their cosmogony from Aristophanes's *Birds*, generally considered a parody of Orphic poetry.[39] On

---

39 Cf. III n. 47. Plotinus (*Enn.* 2.9.6, 2.9.17) also accuses the Gnostics of devaluing Greek ideas.

this second battlefront, with a different audience, the Christians' strategies are necessarily different from those used against traditional paganism, although they are connected. What the Christians denounce is that the Gnostics take their doctrines from Greek religion and philosophy and that in doing so they pervert the biblical tradition containing the true revelation; as a result their doctrine is at the same time novel and obsolete, in the most negative sense of both adjectives.[40] The accusation that heterodoxy had its origin in the pagan mysteries was a recurrent one: Montanism was accused of emerging from the mysteries of Cybele (Hieron. *Ep.* 41; Tert. *De ieiun.* 2.4.16.7). Apart from the topos, in this case the idea is supported by geographical continuity and similar rigorist practices; apologetic topoi may hide a *mica veritatis*. The reproach has the same form as that of Celsus when he insists on accusing the Christians themselves of copying Greek and Eastern ideas and, moreover, perverting them with a new construction that diverges from tradition.[41]

If the attacks' intentions correspond to traditional frameworks, their content is also not excessively novel. The favorite mythical themes attacked by the apologists, the stories of sex and violence, were also common topoi of religious accusation. The charges of cannibalism and incest that had been directed against the Roman Bacchanalia and that formed part of the general imaginary about secret rituals were now directed against the Christians,[42] and predictably, the Christians hinted at similar charges against the Greek mysteries, which they presented as a collection of murders and rapes in the myths whose ritual reflection they exploited: in the *Protrepticus* Clement presents the myths and rituals of Aphrodite, the goddess of sex, the castrations of Uranus, Zeus (simulated), and Dionysus, the incests of Zeus with his mother and daughter, Baubo's obscene gesture. The violence of the myths appears to be reflected in the ritual acts, in which (e. g., in those of Dionysus) Clement hints that the repetition of the mythological crime took place, to the point of putting together a pure assemblage of "murders and tombs" (*Protr.* 2.19.2). We have seen the success that Clement's account had in later apologetic. In reality, these accusations are probably as inaccurate as the ac-

---

40 Iren. *Adv. Haer.* 2.14.2. Cf. Mansfeld 1992, 159ff.
41 *CC* 1.4, 1.16, 2.5, 4.11, 4.41. Chadwick 1966, 22–24. Cf. pp. 256ff, on legitimate intellectual descent.
42 Cf. Dölger 1934, Henrichs 1970. They had previously been directed against Jews: Flav. Ios. *Contra Apionem* 2.91–96. Sex and violence inside the community has been a topical accusation against the barbarian "other" since classical times: cf. Eur. *Androm.* 170–177. Cf. pp. 64ff on the Roman use of the same accusation against Greek rites.

cusation that the Eucharist was a cannibalistic rite. However, the force of a set of extremely long-lived *topoi* (one must merely recall the similar accusations levied against the Jews during the medieval and early modern periods) was immense, and it was nourished by the mutual polemic. Cultural wars in our own times also dedicate enormous efforts to demolishing the mythical foundations of the rival camp.[43]

On other occasions, by contrast, it was the Christians who gave a much more aggressive tone to strategies that they took from the earlier Jewish or pagan tradition, but that had not previously been used to such polemical ends. A clear case is the accusation of dependence on the biblical tradition, which in the Jewish context was meant above all to create a place in the sun for Hebrew culture within the Hellenistic world, but which in the hands of the Christian apologists could be turned into an accusation of "stealing" the biblical revelation. Clement, at times among the most philhellenic of the apologists, drew evidence from the pagan treatise *On Plagiarism*, which had originated in a context foreign to this polemical intention. Lurking in the background of this aggressiveness is the desire to respond to accusations, like those of Celsus, that whatever was good in the Christian message had been said before, and better, by the Greek sages, as well as the eagerness to tranquilize those segments of the Christian public that looked askance at any excessive consideration of pagan philosophy.

Whether on their own initiative, as a reaction to criticism received, or as a repetition of traditional polemical *topoi*, the apologists always accompanied their presentation of myths and rituals with a series of rhetorical techniques that increased the aggressiveness and multiplied the effect of the attack. The tendentious use of poetic quotations – truncated, taken out of context, or rejected – is the most evident, and has been carefully studied by Zeegers (1972, 102–105), but there are strategies of much greater subtlety and reach. The attacks are presented rhetorically under the cover of a variety of metaphors characteristic of the apologetic genre: a supposed discourse before the emperor in favor of the Christians (Athenagoras), a trial of Greek religion (Clement, Origen), a competition between the Greek mysteries and the Christian mystery, ending, of course, in the victory of the latter (Clement, Gregory), the presentation of the secrets of the mysteries as if this were a profanation of their secrecy (Tatian, Clement). The effect is not only rhe-

---

43 A clear parallel to the content and tone of the apologetic attacks against Greek myths is the sarcastic summary of the *Nibelungenslied* by Joseph Roth in 1934 (*Das Neue Tage-Buch*, 7/7/1934 = K. Westermann, *Werke*, Köln, 1989–90–91, vol. III, p. 511): the sex and violence scenes of the German epic song are, for the great Jewish author, representative of the Nazi spirit.

torical, but also contributes to constructing, on the basis of this metaphorical foundation, the antagonistic concepts of paganism and Christianity that constitute the pillars of apologetic strategy, as we shall see.

The immediate reaction that the descriptions of pagan myths and cults aim to provoke is indignation or laughter, for which reason the tone of the presentation always emphasizes those elements capable of inducing scandal or mockery, or both at once. In this process what is fundamental is the selection of themes: the episodes of violence and sex, like those described by Clement; the monstrous images, like the image of Phanes described by Athenagoras; the trivial formulations, in comparison to their expected solemnity, of the *symbola* and *synthemata* that, once again, we find in Clement. The fundamental criterion of selection is iconicity: the details and the version that will be chosen are those that entail the greatest motivation for ridicule or scandal, and that are capable of causing the greatest damage to paganism's foundations. This is the reason that Orpheus ends up as the apologists' preferred enemy: he is a figure of recognized prestige, but at the same time highly vulnerable to attack because he is the one who presents the most scandalous myths. Origen singles him out for this reason among all the pagan prophets presented by Celsus ("written by Orpheus above all," *CC* 1.17). Gregory of Nazianzus, too, does not choose a moderate and rational form of the theory of reincarnation, like that postulated by Plotinus, for example, to criticize in the poem *De anima*, but rather an extreme version that includes metempsychosis even in animals and plants, represented by Empedocles, Pythagoras, and the Orphic *Rhapsodies*.

As might be expected, Gregory does not present a philosophical version of transmigration, but rather engages in a crude and literal exposition of the theory that permits him to mock it more easily. The apologists coincide in taking the myths they present literally and rejecting any allegorical interpretation that might make them more acceptable. Eusebius (*PE* 3.9–10) refuses to accept Porphyry's interpretations of the *Hymn to Zeus* contained in the *Rhapsodies* and prefers to attack the hymn's pantheism on the literal level. Athenagoras (*Leg.* 22) rejects the Stoic interpretation of the Orphic myths, and Arnobius (*Adv. nat.* 5.32–45) and Firmicus (*De err.* 1.1–7), after describing Orphic myths, explicitly reject interpretations of Dionysus as wine, whose dismemberment signifies the transformation of grapes into wine, and of Demeter as wheat. Perhaps because they are more inclined to apply allegorical interpretation to the biblical texts themselves, Clement and Origen do not explicitly disavow this method and, what is more, they make use of the example of the symbolic interpretation of Orphic poems to justify their own symbolic interpretations of certain biblical passages (*Strom.* 5.8,

CC 4.17). Even so, when they attack the scandal of the Orphic myths, they naturally do so on the literal level, not in allegorical versions. In this regard, literal quotations from Orphic poems do not have only evidentiary value: the words of the Greek poet himself are also an element that obviously presents the myth in its most purely literal form.

However, the literalness that makes the quotations trustworthy is not incompatible with accompanying (or at times replacing) those quotations by paraphrases that expand and modify them slightly. Singular elements are transformed into generalizing plurals that additionally increase the scornful tone. Origen scorns the theology in which "the son gods castrate the father gods, and the father gods eat the son gods" and "those who are dismembered by the Titans and fall from the heavenly throne." Gregory of Nazianzus cries out against "your Triptolemuses and your Celeuses and your mystic serpents," "Oceans and Tethyses and Phanetes and others, whatever they are called," and Epiphanius follows him: "How many mysteries and *teletai* are there among the Greeks? ... the shameful actions in sacred spaces there, nakednesses of women, to put it politely, and drums and cakes ..." These disdainful plurals serve to emphasize the idea that Greek religion is a chaotic assemblage of cults, but at the same time, paradoxically, they give it a certain unity in the negative sense, by dissolving all such cults into a single rival of Christianity, the common elements of which are the "murders and tombs" with which Clement summarizes the Greek mysteries and the ubiquitous serpents that contribute to associations with the Lucifer of *Genesis*.[44]

3.2. Appropriation

At the opposite pole to these attacks we find the use of Orphic poems as support for Christian ideas. The most widespread case is undoubtedly the *Testament*, used as evidence for monotheism by various apologists. Other hymnic poems are used by Clement in the *Stromata* (*OF* 243, *OF* 691) and by the author of the *Cohortatio* (*OF* 543) as illustrations of the same theme of monotheism. Lactantius uses the *Rhapsodies* to show pagan intuition of the uncreated Creator God. Pseudo-Justin uses the *Oaths* (*OF* 620) to support the biblical notion of the creative force of speech. Didymus quotes two verses (*OF* 853) in support of the Christian doctrine of the force of the Spirit in man. The next

---

44 Orig. *CC* 4.48, 3.23; Greg. Naz. *Or.* 5.31, 39.4; *Or.* 31.16; Epiph. *Expos. fidei* 10; Clem. Alex. *Protr.* 2.19. On these disdainful plurals, whose usage can be traced back to archaic poetry and some Presocratics, cf. Herrero 2005c.

chapter will consider to what extent this strategy took advantage of tendencies really existing in Orphism. Apologetic enthusiasm, however, did not always need a foundation in reality: Clement takes the *interpretatio christiana* to its fantastical limits when he sees an Orphic announcement of the resurrection of the dead in the last lines of the *Hymn to Zeus* (*OF* 31), or when he finds in an isolated line (*OF* 690) an allusion to the Father and the Son.

This Christian appropriation of pagan poetry has its first and most prestigious antecedent in Paul's discourse in the Athenian Areopagus: his quotation from Aratus in order to show the *syngeneia* of God and men is compatible with other passages in which he disdains Greek wisdom as vain and conducive to error.[45] The apologists follow his example and have no difficulty combining simultaneous attacks on and assimilation of Greek culture and religion, as can be seen with special clarity in the case of Orphism. If in their criticism the Christians follow along the lines of Greek philosophy, in the assimilation of Orphism they follow in the footsteps of the Alexandrian Jewish tradition, imitating its methods and using the same texts (except for Lactantius, who seems to be inspired more by the Neoplatonists). The move to take advantage of mythographic traditions surrounding Orpheus (journey to Egypt, pre-Homeric chronology) in order to defend the thesis that Greek wisdom depended on that of the Hebrews is of Jewish inspiration, and the great majority of the texts cited along these lines are Jewish. In only a few cases can there be discerned a specific orientation that develops the Jewish strategy for the defense of specifically Christian ideas: the resurrection and the Father and the Son in *OF* 31 and 690, cited by Clement; the *pneuma* in Didymus's interpretation of *OF* 853. The three citations are brief and forced. In general, the Christians add little to their Jewish predecessors in the art of adapting ancient texts to their own ideas. It was enough for them to take advantage of the existing material and to develop its methods with greater enthusiasm and aggressiveness.

We already know that Jews and Christians followed a Greek tendency in adapting Orphism to their own ideological frameworks. Nevertheless, dis-

---

[45] In *Acts* 17:28 Paul quotes Aratus *Phaen.* 5; in *Tt.* 1:12 Epimenides' invective against the Cretans is cited (whence Athenag. *Leg.* 30.2, Tat. *Orat.* 27.1 and Clem. Alex. *Protr.* 2.37.4 also cite it); in 1 *Cor.* 15:33 a line from Maenander on bad habits (*Thais* fr. 165 K-A) is quoted, though it could be a popular saying. These three quotations by Paul seem to spring from his general culture, and not from written sources (Zeegers 1972, 19f.). Clement (*Strom.* 1.51 and 1.91) alludes to these pasajes to justify the Christian use of pagan culture, against other Pauline expressions of rejection of Greek wisdom that were held up for imitation by important sectors of the Alexandrian Church (Chadwick 1966, 43).

3.2. Appropriation

tinctions must be made. The Pythagoreans and Stoics deduced some of their own ideas from an Orphic starting point, and once elaborated in their own philosophical categories, these ideas in turn had influence on Orphic poetry by way of new interpretations and compositions. This interrelationship between Orphic speculation and philosophy is very different from the Jewish and Christian appropriation of Orphism, which is far more similar to that of late Neoplatonism. The Orphic quotations of the Jews and Christians (and of the Neoplatonists) are not foundations for these writers' ideas, which are drawn from other sources, but rather external supports that merely contribute to the propagandistic presentation of doctrines of independent origin.

Orphism's function is to adorn the Christian theological edifice, not to hold it up. However, it is an adornment with a great external effect and is one that enjoys enormous popularity among the apologists, since it presents paganism's principal theologian as a defender of Christian truths. On the one hand, Orpheus lends prestige to these ideas in the eyes of those for whom the authority of the Bible is not sufficient; on the other, his individual conversion serves as a model for the conversion that the apologists aim to generalize. The harangue in the final part of the *Cohortatio* (36.4) makes this quite clear:

> For the above-mentioned men, presenting their elegant language as a kind of bait, have sought to seduce many from the right religion, in imitation of him who dared to teach the first men polytheism (*scil*. Orpheus). Be not persuaded by these persons. I entreat you, but read the prophecies of the sacred writers. And if any scruple or old ancestral superstition prevents you from reading the prophecies of the holy men through which you can be instructed regarding the one and only God, which is the first article of the true religion, yet believe him who, though at first he taught you polytheism, yet afterwards preferred to sing a useful and necessary palinode – I mean Orpheus, who said what I quoted a little before; and believe the others who wrote the same things concerning one God. For it was the work of Divine Providence on your behalf, that they, though unwillingly, bore testimony that what the prophets said regarding one God was true, in order that the unanimous rejection of polytheism might lead you to the knowledge of the truth.

Now, this use of Orpheus as a proto-Christian may give rise to the placement of his figure at a level as exalted as that of the prophets. This is perhaps the origin of his iconographic association with David and Christ, which independently of whether or not it constitutes evidence of assimilation or syncretism (pp. 116ff), entails a high opinion of Orpheus in some Jewish and Christian circles. For those apologists who seek to create a dualistic antagonism between paganism and Christianity, this prizing of ornamental elements (Orpheus) alongside sustaining ones (the prophets) can occasionally appear excessive, leading them to exert themselves to mark the difference. For this reason Clement makes Orpheus the champion of the enemy side in the *Protrepticus*. For this reason the *Cohortatio* specifies that the true saints are the prophets and that Orpheus and the pagans spoke the truth "though unwillingly" (καὶ ἄκοντας, 36.4) or only "partially" (ἐν μέρει, 15.2). For this reason, finally, we have seen Augustine saying that the achievements of Orpheus and his peers "may serve to refute the vanity of paganism, but not to increase its authority."[46]

3.3. Omission

This phrase of Augustine's may show us the way to resolve a more difficult question when it comes to evaluating the apologists' criteria for selecting themes from the Orphic tradition. It is clear that they picked out the most scandalous themes, as well as those that, with a greater or lesser degree of distortion, could be made to support Christian doctrines. However, it is less clear why certain elements of Orphism prominent in pagan sources are entirely absent from Christian references. Although any argument *ex silentio* must always contain some degree of uncertainty and is subject to chance in the form of the partial transmission of ancient texts, we can suggest some causes for the apologists' omissions.

A first possible reason is lack of knowledge. Orphism did not have the same presence everywhere in the Roman Empire, and some apologists surely did not mention it because they were not familiar with it or it did not appear to them to be an important component of paganism. The Christians who mention Orphism, positively or negatively, come precisely from those regions in which epigraphic and papyrological evidence proves that it had some presence: Rome, Egypt, and Asia Minor. In addition, however, many of them have no more knowledge of Orphism than what they can find in their anthological sources or in earlier apologists. It is logical that they do not report other details than those their sources offer. Personal taste or convenience may induce them to add their own contributions from other sources or from general knowledge, as Arnobius does with Clement. In general, however, the most common tendency is to summarize more briefly the episodes that their sources recount in greater detail. The rhetorical style of Gregory and Origen is more inclined to rapid, disdainful, and generalizing allusions to some laughable myths than to the detailed and expanded transla-

---

46   *Contra Faustum* 13.2; a similar statement in *CD* 18.14.

tion of the *Protrepticus* undertaken by Arnobius; besides, given the practical difficulty of keeping several rolls of papyrus open at once, the most common method of citation in antiquity was to refer to notes taken during a previous reading of the work cited, which was rarely consulted again directly.[47] Referring to notes clearly tends to produce ever-more-summary versions of the original account.

Another possible cause for the apologists' silence is their lack of interest in certain themes that had greater literary than religious value. Apologetic literature has clear objectives, to which everything else is subordinated: drawing a clear line between paganism and Christianity, defending the former and attacking the latter. While rhetorical techniques are highly valued for the purposes of an eminently persuasive genre, literary fancies are not to the apologists' taste when they do not contribute to this central objective. The myth of the singer is only alluded to when it contributes to presenting Orpheus as patron of the mysteries or Christ, in the same mold, as healer of the soul. Orpheus's participation in the expedition of the Argo is mentioned only when it is a matter of locating him chronologically. The complete absence of references to the story of Eurydice, perhaps the best-known episode of the myth of Orpheus, may be due to lack of interest in this literary element, which is without immediate religious value. During the Middle Ages, by contrast, when apologetic is no longer necessary following the complete Christianization of the empire, the literary themes of Orpheus the lover and the singer will once again become writers' favorites, while the theologian and founder of mysteries will be forgotten until the Renaissance.

Nevertheless, besides ignorance and disinterest, there is also a third, less obvious, possible explanation, which may be suggested by tracing the implications of the quotation from Augustine about the undesirability of increasing Orpheus's authority. The Fathers were interested in avoiding the placement of Orpheus on the same level as Christ or the prophets, because the confusion between sustaining and ornamental elements, the extreme case of which is syncretism, goes against the whole apologetic labor of fixing a clear boundary between paganism and Christianity as two antagonistic and incompatible entities. Now, Celsus highlights some aspects of the myth of Orpheus that make him comparable to Christ: his descent into Hades (*CC* 2.55) and his violent death (*CC* 7.53). It is highly revealing that neither of these two episodes makes the slightest appearance in any Christian text. An episode that is as celebrated as Orpheus's death at the hands of the Thracian women is glaringly absent among the apologists. It is precisely a sacrificed

---

47 Van der Hoek 1996, with special reference to Clement of Alexandria.

and martyred Orpheus who is most clearly fused with Christ in the syncretistic image of the Berlin Seal (*OF* 679). Orpheus's descent into Hades, which medieval authors do not hesitate to compare with Christ's descent *ad inferos* after his death,[48] is also never mentioned by the apologists, who were undoubtedly uncomfortable with comparisons like those made by Celsus between the two figures.

Not only does Orpheus's figure contain aspects that the Christians prefer to avoid: certain Orphic myths are also the object of censorship. Besides the omission of Orpheus's descent into Hades, it is also notable that there is not one Christian reference to the entire tradition – still very much alive in the Imperial Age – of Orphic catabasis, which was very similar to Christian eschatological literature. It is clear that the Orphic genre that possibly had the most direct influence on Christian literature, and with which there was possibly the greatest coincidence of imagery, could not be the object of apologetic attacks.[49] On some level, the apologists perceived that manipulating Orphic texts by means of an *interpretatio christiana* in order to defend monotheism or creation did not encourage syncretism as much as did certain aspects of Orphism in which the reader could perceive excessive similarity with aspects of Christianity without prior manipulation.

This self-censorship is even clearer in references to Dionysus, the pagan god simultaneously most similar and most opposed to Christ. Celsus indicated that Dionysus, like Heracles or Asclepius, could also be considered a man divinized *a posteriori* as the son of a god, and he also compared Dionysus's death and resurrection to those of Christ (*CC* 3.22–43). Origen's responses appeal to the ignoble myths of Dionysus, in comparison to which Christ's story shows more seriousness (σεμνότερος, 3.23, 4.17), as well as

---

48 Cf. Friedman 1970. The first Christian allusion is found in Ephraim the Syrian, who writes in Syriac in the fourth century AD: he compares the failed descent into Hades of Orpheus with the success of Christ, who was capable of vanquishing death: *Carmina Nisibena, Hymn* 36.5, 36.11. His insistence on difference makes any identification impossible.

49 The only reference to Orphic eschatology may be a general allusion by Clement, who in 5.14.123 says, "Punishments after death, retribution by fire, were pilfered from the barbarian philosophy both by all the poetic Muses and by Greek philosophy". He then exemplifies this with Plato, who "knew of the rivers of fire and the depths of the earth, and Tartarus, called by the barbarians Gehenna, naming, as he does prophetically, Cocytus, and Acheron, and Pyriphlegethon, and introducing such corrective tortures for discipline". All these eschatological elements in Plato are well known to be inspired by Orphic poetry (Kingsley 1995). The accusation of plagiarism reveals the affinity of Orphic and Christian eschatological images. Cf. p. 368 on these parallels.

denying the reality of Dionysus's resurrection: "as if he had risen again and ascended into heaven" (οἱονεὶ ἀναβιώσκοντος καὶ ἀναβαίνοντος εἰς οὐρανόν, 4.17.) Justin also stresses the parallels between the two and attributes them directly to the demons' plagiarism, intended to confuse (*Dial.* 69, *Apol.* 1.54). Other apologists, by contrast, opt to emphasize the differences and omit the similarities. The strategy employed by Clement and Arnobius along these lines in their accounts of the myth of Dionysus is highly revealing: both authors avoid expressly stating that Dionysus was the son of Zeus; both speed up their narration and jump from the cooking of Dionysus to the arrival of Zeus in order to avoid mentioning the moment at which the Titans eat Dionysus, perhaps because they can criticize other aspects of the myth, but not theophagy, given that the Christians themselves were accused of cannibalism for saying that they ate the body of a god;[50] and the most telling detail, both leave out Dionysus's resurrection entirely and end the story with his burial on Mount Parnassus. It is possible that Arnobius was merely following Clement, but it can scarcely be doubted that Clement deliberately omitted an episode contained in his source, since the preservation of Dionysus's heart by Athena, which Clement himself reports, makes no sense other than as a prelude to Dionysus's return to life on this basis. Firmicus Maternus, who presents a euhemerist version in which Dionysus is the son of a Cretan king, has no difficulty discussing his parentage, the anthropophagy, and the statue that commemorates the dead child, because since Dionysus is not a god in this case, there is no room for a comparison to Christ.

Finally, it may be asked whether the omission of the anthropological consequences of the myth of Dionysus might have the same explanation. It may be the case that Clement's source was silent on the subject, since there is no reason to think that every version of the myth necessarily had attached to it the story of men's birth from the blasted Titans. There is only one Christian allusion to the episode: after summarizing the myth of Dionysus, Origen says, "If it is permitted to the Greeks to derive a theory and allegorize such things about the soul, why should it be closed to us to follow the same method?" (*CC* 4.17). It seems probable that a theory of the soul extracted from the myth would have been its double Titanic and Dionysian nature. The vagueness of the allusion coincides with the complete absence of any reference in other retellings of the myth (Justin, Clement, Arnobius) and in Gregory of Nazianzus's poem *On the Soul*, which engages in a critique of the *Rhapsodies*. Gregory criticizes and describes in detail the cycle of reincarnation, but he never says where the cycle comes from. When Clement (*Strom.*

---

50   *Protr.* 2.17–18, *Adv. Nat.* 5.19. Cf. Henrichs 1970, Herrero 2006.

3.3.17.1) and Augustine (*Contra Iul. Pelag.* 4.15.78) report the doctrine of the *soma-sema* "on account of a primordial crime," it cannot be thought that a theologian as cultivated in Platonism as Gregory was not familiar with this idea. His omission of it in his critique can only be explained by the fact that soon afterward, in expounding his own doctrine of the soul, he will have to explain Adam's sin that imprisons man in his bodily tunic (*Poem. Arc.* 7.115: δερματίνους δὲ χιτῶνας ἐφέσσατο σάρκα βαρεῖαν) and makes him the bearer of his own corpse (7.116: νεκρόφορος). Expressions so similar to the *soma-sema* for designating the situation produced by the primordial fault make it clear that Gregory considered the Christian doctrine of original sin similar to the Orphic idea of an antecedent sin. He could, then, make use of Orphic expressions to express his own idea, but he obviously needed to avoid criticizing the same thing in the rival camp. This attitude of Gregory's can be extended, on a more or less conscious level, to the other Christians who avoid mentioning the subject: the intentional wall of silence around the meaning of what remained the myth of a minority became the best weapon for avoiding competition from it.

The various attitudes we have just analyzed arise in part from a basic consciousness of the similarity and continuity between certain aspects of Orphism and Christianity. This consciousness gives rise to attacks on the competition that must be defeated and, at the same time, to the use of Orphism as support for Christian positions and to silence when faced with certain elements too much in agreement. However, the attacks also arise from consciousness of fundamental differences in some aspects in which Orphism and Christianity went in different directions. Even the manipulation of Orphic texts does not seem to produce fear of syncretism, probably because of the consciousness that these Orphic notions are sufficiently far from the Christian ones, even if manipulation brings them closer together. Chapter VI will consider to what extent the perceptions of Christian authors reflected Orphic reality. What I aim to show in the next two sections is that these two factors, similarity and difference, were at times combined by them to make Orphism the axis around which to construct the opposition that sustains all the apologetic literature, the opposition of Christianity versus paganism, and that various elements of the Orphic tradition also served to articulate the relationships that the apologists needed to establish between these two opposing camps.

4. Orphism as axis of the Christian/Pagan opposition

4.1. The construction of Paganism

The late Neoplatonists took up Orphism as the banner of ritual and theological tradition and turned it into a cornerstone of the Greek religion opposed to the rise of Christianity. Orphism's role is equally significant in the construction of paganism in Christian authors. The image of Greek religion transmitted by their texts would endure for many centuries, during which Greek religion was seen as a unified assemblage of beliefs and cults whose only real linkage is their non-Christianity, of which Orpheus becomes the principal patron. However, this image is an artificial creation, the product of late-ancient religious polemic. Paganism only exists as such in opposition to Christianity and appears for the first time in the works of the apologists; some of the latter, especially Clement of Alexandria, see in the Orphic tradition the most appropriate foundation on which to construct the new concept.

It is in the *Protrepticus*, as part of a genre making a direct invitation to conversion, that the need to construct paganism becomes most pressing.[51] To use the terminology of cognitive semantics, conversion is a conceptual metaphor structured in spatial terms, as movement from one place (ignorance, error, evil) to another, different one (wisdom, truth, virtue). The underlying metaphor is a very common one: "states of mind are places."[52] Conversion is a spiritual journey presented in terms of physical displacement between a point of departure and a point of arrival, both of which are perfectly defined. The Greek terms closest to the modern concept are μετάνοια and ἐπιστροφή, which may be translated by both "conversion" and "repentance." In general, the verbal prefix μετα-, which primarily indicates a change of place, forms similar terms with various verbal roots of primarily spatial meaning, such as βάλλω (throw) or ἵστημι (be in a place). The prepositions used in the texts that exhort to conversion show that the dominant metaphor is that of displacement: ἐξ, ἀπό for the origin, εἰς, πρός for the goal. This spatial

---

51 On the protreptic genre, cf. van der Meeren 2002, van der Hoek 2005; on conversion, cf. Nock 1933; Gnilka 1993; Herrero 2005b, from a cognitive approach Casadio 2009.

52 Lakoff and Johnson (1980, 477ff), in their groundbreaking study that laid the foundations of cognitive semantics, give as a typical example the English "to be in love". On conversion as a spatial metaphor, cf. Herrero 2005b. For example, in the *Testament (OF* 378) after the proem addressed to Musaeus, three verbs in the imperative imply a movement of the soul in exhorting to conversion: "look to" (προσέδρευε), "walk" (ἐπίβαινε), "watch" (ἐσόρα).

valuation is illustrated even better by the root of προ-τρέπω (urge, exhort), which gives its name to the protreptic genre. This brief text shows it with great plasticity:

> Let us therefore repent (μετανοήσωμεν), and pass from (ἐξ) ignorance to (εἰς) knowledge, from foolishness to wisdom, from licentiousness to self-restraint, from unrighteousness to righteousness, from godlessness to God (*Protr.* 10.93.1).

These pairs of opposites are reduced to a single one: paganism versus Christianity. The delimitation of these points of departure and arrival invites the reader to conceive of them as two unitary entities, opposite and to some extent symmetrical. Not only do reasons of rhetorical convenience press in this direction (it is more convenient to focus on a single enemy on a single front than to confront many different rivals), but it is also difficult to escape this dualist construction once the framework of conversion is accepted. In addition, it fits with the biblical tradition, probably of Persian roots, of dualistic expressions introducing Lucifer as a malign agent. Clement says:

> Therefore, since he is one and the same, he who at the beginning seduced Eve and now brings down to death the rest of mankind, our ally and helper is also one and the same – the Lord... (*Protr.* 1.7.6).

Clement makes Orpheus the champion of the enemy warband, a prophet of the pagan mysteries, in the same way that he proclaims himself a prophet of the mysteries of the Logos. Thus, the two camps confronting one another are not only unitary, but also symmetrical. On the one hand, this symmetry affects the presentation of Christianity, which takes on pagan garb in order to show itself as the true equivalent that is to replace the false imitation, for example when Clement speaks of the "mysteries" of the Logos. However, it also affects Orphism, onto which the Christian framework is projected. Origen's response to Celsus (*CC* 1.16–18 = App. VI), who had said that Orpheus, Linus, and Musaeus "had written their dogmas in books," challenges his opponent: "Compare books with books (βίβλους βίβλοις παραβάλλεσθαι); contrast the poems of Linus, Musaeus, Orpheus, and the prose of Pherecydes with the laws of Moses, comparing histories with histories, ethical discourses with laws and commandments." Origen attributes to the legendary figures of Greek religion books comparable to the Bible and doctrines in the style of Christian dogmas, when in paganism books and doctrines had an entirely different function, one far less central and more flexible. The presentation of Christianity in pagan molds entailed, on the other side, the Christianization of Orphism by projection.

However, symmetry and equivalence also brought with them, in the framework of conversion, a radical separation between the two poles: the point of departure A could be symmetrical to the point of arrival B, but it could in no sense be equal to B, since then conversion from A to B would make no sense. The whole biblical tradition of exclusivist monotheism, incompatible with other cults or with syncretism, is present in this aspect of the opposition between paganism and Christianity. The call to conversion is directed to a *homo optans* who must choose between two mutually exclusive entities. The *Protrepticus* (12.123.2) ends with this sentence:

> It is still up to you to choose which conclusion will profit you most – judgment or grace. I, for one, do not think it is worth doubting which of these is the better; nor is it allowable to compare life with destruction.

If the opposition is indeed symmetrical, the hierarchy between the two poles is always absolute. The presentation of the new singer (Christ) and of the old (Orpheus) puts them on the same level with respect to their image, but it leaves no doubt about their moral difference. Clement manages to combine symmetry and subordination by exploiting a series of concepts, the ambivalence of which allows him to distribute them at whim between the two camps. With regard to Orphism, there is much of interest in the manner in which Clement, upon establishing a strict separation between paganism and Christianity, untangles the ambiguity that certain concepts, now polarized between the two extremes, had maintained since ancient times.

The key criterion of separation is that which opposes religion to superstition. The opposition between *theosebeia* and *deisidaimonia* runs through the entire book under the criterion that the former is a luminous truth that saves and the latter a dark lie that destroys: ὡς ἀπολλύει δεισιδαιμονία καὶ σῴζει θεοσέβεια.[53] Clement charges paganism as a whole with superstition in what seems a clear instance of the modern principle that "one man's religion is another man's magic." The rigid distinctions marked out by the apologists divided definitively into two sharply different categories, inherited by later generations until our own day, what had until then been a *continuum* where internal boundaries were far more diffuse.[54] In the orbit of Orphism we have found everything from sophisticated philosophical speculation to vulgar

---

53　*Protr.* 10.90.3. Cf. also 1.2.1–3; 4.58.4; 8.77.1; 10.108.3–4; 12.121.1–2.
54　The continuity of magical and religious practice and theory in Greece has been dealt with in chapter II; for the modern discussion cf. III (nn. 2–3). On Greek precedents for the construction of superstition, cf. pp. 235ff. Fowler 1994 (esp. 21f) explains the "social" opposition of magic and religion in the Greek world.

magic spells, by way of the mysteries. Besides, the criteria of Greek religious thinkers for classifying spiritual reality were different, and Orpheus's ambivalence as a magus and a theologian did not pose a problem for them, because they had no need for as strict a separation between magic and religion as that at which the Christians aimed. Plato and the Derveni commentator also established distinctions in this fluidity, but their central criteria were different, principally that of the commercial mentality with which wandering priests and their clients approached initiation, versus a more spiritual understanding of purity and salvation.[55] In Clement the primary criterion is that of truth versus falsehood, a criterion which doubtless had classical precedents, but which with the Christian triumph came to mark the vision of the spiritual world of antiquity, and hence of Orphism, until our own day.

As Clement tries on the one hand to reject Orphism and on the other to supplant it, appropriating its traits, he assigns to Orpheus all the burden of magic and attributes to Christ all the religious value of Orpheus's figure. Orpheus's ambiguity thus becomes another trait favoring his adoption as an axis of Clement's discourse. The separation is reinforced by drawing rigid lexical boundaries between the two camps, assigning negative or positive values to words that had previously maintained a certain ambivalence: for example, *goes* and *sophistes*, applied exclusively to Orpheus, take on a clearly negative sense.[56] He is never given the traditional title *theologos*. Instead, *poietes* is systematically awarded to him as "poet of the mysteries," while Christ is the singer (ᾠδός). When two synonyms over which to effect the distribution, as in this case, cannot be found, it is well and clearly indicated with an ὄντως ("really") or an ἀληθῶς ("truly") that there is a bad and deceitful side to the concept as well as a good one: for example, Clement says that only upon his conversion did Orpheus sing "a really sacred tale" (ὄντως ἱερὸν λόγον).[57] In sum, Clement is presenting the "true Orpheus" to the Greeks, in contrast to the "false Orpheus" who has deceived them until now, and he distributes Orphism's traits symmetrically between the two opposing camps.

---

55 Plat. *Resp.* 364e; *P. Derv.* col. XX. Clement also uses this dismissive language against religious charlatans, drawing probably on Plato: cf. *Protr.* 11.115.2, Plat. *Charm.* 157a4.

56 Though in classical times the *goes* was already excluded from the *polis* (Burkert 1962), the term still had some ambiguity when applied to Orpheus in Greek contexts, as in Strabo 7 fr. 18: ἄνδρα γόητα ἀπὸ μουσικῆς ἅμα καὶ μαντικῆς καὶ τῶν περὶ τὰς τελετὰς ὀργιασμῶν ἀγυρτεύοντα τὸ πρῶτον. The same was true in the case of *sophistes*: Clement echoes Plato's *Protagoras*, where the term is used negatively.

57 *Protr* 7.71.4. Cf. also 1.3.1; 1.4.4; 10.104.1; 10.110.5; 11.117.1 (ὄντως); 9.87.1; 12.120.1 (ἀληθῶς).

Conceiving of this "paganism" was not an easy task, among other things due to the absence of clear precedents that the apologists could follow in this case. Until then, various strategies for imagining the "other" existed in the Greek world, but the absence of the idea of conversion meant that symmetrical opposition was not a requirement. Likewise, the rejection of Greek myths as an identifying sign of Roman religion did not set up two symmetrical opposing camps, although it shared the contents of the Christian critique.[58] An additional factor was that Christianity's own self-definition was not clear and also needed to be established on definite foundations.[59] The construction and presentation of two unitary, symmetrical, opposing entities in hierarchical relationship to one another was a complicated task that Clement skillfully performed, albeit on the basis of pagan and biblical precedents, by means of an elaborate system of metaphors. In reality, his use of conceptual and literary metaphors is representative of the importance of metaphor as an instrument of Christian self-definition, and hence of the definition of Christianity's adversary. The Orphism that Clement presents is thus very much shaped by being worked into the metaphors to which I now turn.

4.2. Conceptual metaphors

Cognitive semantics applies the name of conceptual metaphors to those metaphors that shape the manner in which we conceive an object that cannot be perceived by direct experience (Lakoff-Johnson 1980). That is to say, the abstract object is conceived and imagined in terms of something else previously experienced. Christian apologists constructed their religion within the conceptual frameworks of the ancient world, through three traditional metaphors of group definition (family, city, philosophical school), which necessarily also affect its opposite, paganism.

---

58 Dion. Hal. *Ant. Rom.* 2.18–20 (cf. pp. 64f). The Persian wars create a Greek identity in confrontation with the "barbarians", transforming a hitherto aggregative identity, where Greeks and barbarians were not defined in mutual opposition, into an oppositional one (J. Hall 1997). This construction of identity does not need the element of symmetry in describing the barbarian: Scythians or Egyptians were not modeled symmetrically to the Greeks in Herodotus (Hartog 1980), nor were the barbarians of tragedy an inverse reflection of the Greeks (E. Hall 1989).
59 Rizzi 1993 on the "other" in apologetic literature; Buell 1999 and 2005 on the construction of Christian identity on ethnic basis, especially in Clement and Justin; Johnson 2006 on the continuity of this strategy in Eusebius.

Genealogical metaphors are those that had the greatest success. The classical city conceived of itself in terms of descent from a founding hero, and it inherited the categories of the family clan that was its historical predecessor as a nucleus of collective identity. Later, the family decayed somewhat as an image on which to model the political community with the *polis*'s loss of independence. However, the biblical tradition also conceived of the people of God as the legitimate descendants of Abraham (and, in contrast, it conceived of other neighboring peoples as the descendants of Ishmael), and the impact of this tradition with the rise of Christianity revitalized the metaphor of the family as a model for group definition in Greece: for example, Justin (*Dial.* 11.5) defines the Christians as the *verus Israel*, the genetic heirs of the condition of chosen people. Denise Buell (2005) has recently studied this type of ethnic reasoning in early Christianity. By way of this image, dualism can be represented in the form of two opposed descent groups, as in the image, so popular among the Gnostics, of "Children of Light" opposed to "Children of Darkness" (*1 Thes.* 5:5). Clement makes use of this genetic framework to designate the founders of the Greek mysteries:

> These I would say are the founders of evil (ἀρχεκάκους), the parents of atheistic myths and of deadly superstition, who sowed (ἐκαταφυτεύσαντας) in human life that seed (σπέρμα) of evil and corruption – the mysteries (*Protr.* 2.13.5).

A similar but subtly distinct image within the same field is the characterization of the two camps as legitimate descendants–*gnesioi*–opposed to illegitimate descendants–*nothoi*.[60] The symmetry and the hierarchy of one over the other are maintained untouched, but in addition, unlike in the radical opposition of the preceding case, this image, given that it presupposes a common ancestor, makes it possible to exploit the ambiguity that the metaphorical adjective *nothos* inherits from the familial and legal situation of the real bastard child, sometimes accepted as part of the family, sometimes excluded from it. To begin with, it makes it possible to admit the existence of certain fragments of truth in paganism, a bastard and obscure inheritance from the revelation of the prophets, the sole source of wisdom. The genealogical metaphor is thus a perfect fit for the argument of Greek dependence on the Bible beginning with a first founder (Orpheus). Thus Pseudo-Justin introduces the *Testament:* "For Orpheus, your first teacher of polytheism (πολυθεότητος πρῶτος διδάσκαλος), to put it in such words, at the last announced the one God to his son (υἱόν) Musaeus and to the rest of his legitimate (γνησίους)

---

60   Cf. Herrero 2005a on the origin and development of this image.

disciples..." (*Cohort.* 15.1). Legitimacy coincides with the announcement of the truth, in the conceptual framework of the genealogical transmission of ideas. Pseudo-Justin must have picked up here an epithet characteristic of the debates between philosophical schools over who interpreted figures like Plato, Pythagoras, and Orpheus correctly, that is to say, legitimately.

At the same time, the more pejorative sense of *nothos* as a false copy, the fruit of adultery and corruption, made it possible to explain and entirely reject the uncomfortable similarities between Greek religion and Christianity. Thus, the ambiguity of the bastard in real life, on the frontier between acceptance and exclusion, made this image one of the apologists' favorite resources for characterizing paganism, especially in those aspects that were similar and hence bothersome and in need of explanation. It is not surprising, then, to find it in passages referring to Orphism. Clement presents devotion to Greek mysteries as a reverse conversion, a spurious deviation from original truth: "The mysteries are really a new custom and a supposition, an imposture of the serpent,[61] which receives cult when men convert with bastard piety (εὐσεβείᾳ νόθῳ προστρεπομένων) to profane mysteries and unholy rites." Eusebius, too, brands the theogonies of the Greek poets "bastard truth" (νόθος ἀλήθεια), and Theodoret condemns "the mixture of bastard dogmas (ἐπιμιξία τῶν νόθων δογμάτων) of Rhadamanthys, Minos, and the Isles of the Blessed, and the solitary souls that are punished upon leaving their bodies."[62]

Going a step beyond the familial metaphor, Augustine appropriates the most consolidated ancient image for defining a closed group, i.e. the city. Its Jewish inheritance already enabled Christianity to define itself as God's people, and its transformation into an official religion with Theodosius facilitated the assimilation of the religious community to the state. Augustine's metaphor would attain a success that would endure for centuries. However,

---

61 This translates the text that I believe is closer to the original (Protr. 2.22.3: Νόμος οὖν καὶ ὑπόληψις καινὴ τὰ μυστήρια καὶ τοῦ δράκοντος ἀπάτη τίς ἐστιν): in my opinion, the scribal correction κενή for the original καινή has been too readily accepted by all editors (cf. Stählin and Marcovich *ad loc.*). The context makes clear that here Clement is contesting the claim that the mysteries are truly old and is arguing that they are a later invention of the Devil to turn mankind astray from truth. It is also possible that both words were in the original text, in one of Clement's typical phonetic plays on words (cf. pp. 276ff). In addition, this collocation of τὰ μυστήρια instead of after τοῦ δράκοντος, as some manuscripts have it, makes much better sense.
62 Clem. Alex. *Protr.* 2.22.3 (following Philo, *Cher.* 94); Eus. *PE* 1.10.40; Thdt. *Affect.* 11.33. Cf. the same accusation against heretics in Thdt. *Epist.* 118.5, translated in n. 85 *infra*. On Eusebius's ethnic reasoning, cf. Johnson 2006.

the *Civitas Dei* needs the *Civitas impiorum* as its symmetrical counterpart, and it cannot be surprising at this point to find in the same passage, after the familiar criticisms of the pagan gods as men, elements, or entities inferior to God and undeserving of divinization, these gods' greatest theologian, Orpheus, as prince of the City of the Impious, singer of the pagan gods and a specialist in "the sacred, or rather sacrilegious, rites of the netherworld" (*Orpheum nescio quo modo infernis sacris vel potius sacrilegiis praeficere soleat civitate impiorum*, CD 18.14). Even at the end of antiquity and in a Western author who knows the Orphic tradition only from secondary references, as he himself seems to admit (*nescio quo modo*), Orpheus continues to be a figure of maximum prestige as head of the theological and mystery-cult side of a paganism that receives in this work its maximum elaboration as a negative concept.

A third way of conceiving Christianity, one which takes shape among the apologists with reasonable success, is as a philosophical school in possession of the truth, in contrast to the falsity of the rest. For example, this image is prominent in Justin, who describes in this way his conversion after having passed through various schools: "I found that this was the only sure and profitable philosophy, so that I am therefore also a philosopher." The New Testament refuses to compare Christianity to pagan philosophy, but the following generations would take as a mark of glory the title of "barbarian philosophy" with which their critics themselves taunted them.[63] In this type of metaphor, however, Orpheus does not appear; for example, he is absent in Justin. On only one occasion (Greg. Naz. *Or*. 27.10) is the mention of "Orphic beans" placed within a context of pretended Greek philosophical achievements (ideas of Plato, Epicurus, Aristotle, Stoics, and Cynics) that cannot bear comparison with Christianity, and this one reference is essentially anecdotal. Orpheus's absence should not seem surprising, since there were more prestigious names than his with which to defend any philosophical idea that might be found in Orphic poetry. Tatian says, "Orpheus taught you the playing of the lyre and the mysteries" (*Orat*. 1.2). Orpheus is not the patron of an ideological system, but of a tradition of poems and mysteries, and as Augustine shows, his place is in the field of religion and poetry, not in that of philosophy. For this reason, on the other hand, he will be very much present in the image of Christianity as a mystery, located on the boundary between conceptual and literary metaphors.

---

63 Iust. *Dial*. 8.1, *Col*. 2.8. Cf. Stroumsa 1999.

4.3. Literary metaphors

In contrast to a conceptual metaphor, a literary metaphor does not shape our conception of its object, but rather fits itself to an already-existing conception. On the other hand, what it can do is exploit its overlap with a conceptual metaphor, extending it, modifying it, even countering it (Lakoff-Turner 1987). In the *Protrepticus* there are some especially effective literary metaphors, because they are perfectly adapted to the basic conceptual metaphor of conversion as a spatial movement and to the contrast of two symmetrical, opposed, and hierarchically related entities.

The most important is the musical metaphor, indissolubly linked to Orpheus. This metaphor has evident literary possibilities and serves to give unity to the *Protrepticus* as a whole,⁶⁴ but its role goes beyond the merely literary. By means of this metaphor, paganism is unified through its presentation as Orpheus's song, but Clement's Logos also takes on the traits of this miraculous music and is given the name of "celestial song" (ᾆσμα, ᾠδή οὐράνιος: 1.4.3–4). In this way the desired symmetry between the point of departure and the point of arrival in the process of conversion is achieved, and the replacement of the first by the second is facilitated. In addition, it makes it possible to amalgamate the fields of religion, magic, and poetry into a *continuum* that corresponds to the continuity that the three have in Orphism and that enables Clement to lump them together as the general *deisidaimonia* of paganism. Let us recall the passage in which Clement makes the mysteries Orpheus's song (1.3.1). It is easy to observe how the poetic-musical lexicon (μουσικῆς, ἐντέχνῳ, ᾠδαῖς) is joined to that of magic (γοητεία, ἐπῳδαῖς) and to that of religion and the mysteries (δαιμονῶντες, ὀργιάζοντες, πένθη, ἐκθειάζοντες). Thus, all aspects of Orphism are lumped together as idolatry and corruption. By contrast, the Logos's song (1.5.1) has the same beneficial effects on men that Orpheus's song has on nature in the myth, and that Pythagorean music has on souls. In identifying Orpheus's music with the mysteries, Clement not only gives cohesion to his figure, synthesizing his Dionysian facet (founder of the Dionysian rites) with his Apollonian one (music and the lyre), but also, precisely, creates a linkage between these two sides of Greek religion that he aims to unify

---

64 The musical metaphor allows intertextual references (e.g. the cicadas of the *Phaedrus*) and wordplays using terms like *nomos*, *logos* or *pneuma* (cf. pp. 290ff). It dominates the exordium and is recalled several times later on (*Protr.* 8.81.1; 12.120.4). It is not always fully consistent: sometimes the Logos is the song (1.4.3; 1.5.2; 1.7.3), sometimes the singer (1.2.4; 1.3.2), even the musical instrument (1.6.1). As a good rhetorician, Clement prefers greater expressiveness to full consistency.

For Christ is presented in this work as the substitute for Dionysus and Apollo simultaneously.[65] What better to give them unity than the figure of Orpheus, already presented in ancient times (e. g., by Aeschylus in the *Bassaridae*) as caught between the two antagonistic deities? Thus, characterized in accordance with Orpheus's miraculous song that He aims to supplant, the Christian Logos can replace both, previously unified in the Thracian singer, at a single stroke. In addition, the metaphor suggests an association with the song of David in the biblical tradition (1.5.2–4), is evidently parallel to the iconography of Christ-David-Orpheus, and will serve to introduce biblical notions to a Greek public little accustomed to them. At the end of the chapter we will come back to these themes.

Even before the musical image, there appears in the *Protrepticus* another image that simultaneously combines and opposes biblical and Greek tradition: nothing better expresses the spatial nature of conversion than its representation as a journey from pagan mountains – Helicon, the mountain of the Muses, Cithaeron, the mountain of the Bacchic mysteries – to the Christian mountain, Jerusalem. The italics indicate the phrases that set out the metaphors:

> But the *dramas and the Laenean poets*, now completely drunk, crowned with ivy, completely senseless in their Bacchic rite, with the satyrs, and the frenzied thiasos and the rest of the chorus of demons, *let us confine to Helicon and Cithæron, now antiquated*, and let us bring from above, out of heaven, Truth, with Wisdom in all its brightness, and the sacred chorus of the prophets, down *to the holy mount of God*; and let Truth, darting her light to the most distant points, *cast her rays all around on those who are wrapped in darkness*, and deliver men from delusion, stretching out her very strong right hand, which is intelligence, for their salvation. And raising their eyes, and looking above, *let them abandon Helicon and Cithæron, and take up their abode in Sion*. "For out of Sion shall go forth the law, and the Word of the Lord from Jerusalem" (Is. 2:3) – the celestial Word, the true athlete *crowned in the theatre of the whole universe* (*Protr.* 1.2.2–4).

Following the canons of ring composition, the *peroratio* will take up this image again at the end of the work: "This is the mountain truly chosen by God, not material for tragedies like Cithaeron, but rather consecrated to the dramas of truth, a pure mountain shaded by holy groves" (12.119.1). Conversion as displacement and the union of poetry and religion acquire highly concrete

---

65 Christ is Dionysus' substitute in the metaphor of the Christian *Bacchai* (*Protr.* 12.118–120, cf. Jourdan 2006), Apollo's substitute in the musical images and the defeat of the serpent (*Protr.* 11.111.1, cf. Halton 1983, 181 n.10).

imagery in the mountain metaphor. However, the passage also permits us to observe the other two images that it is of interest to examine, due to their importance in the presentation of the mysteries (2.12.1) theater and light.

It is well known that the theater was a Dionysian phenomenon. The opposition of the Christians, Clement included, to theatrical performances is likewise well known and was generally based on moral objections. If Clement chooses this element as a component of his pagan-Dionysian construction, by contrast, it is due to the value that it has for extending another metaphor throughout the text. Christ triumphs on the stage, confronting the "dramas and poets of the Lenaia" in an imaginary theatrical competition: "the celestial Logos, the legitimate victor crowned in the theater of the whole world." As if it was a matter of a theatrical agon, Clement will make the Greek myths, gods, poets, and philosophers parade across the stage, and afterward he will present the prophecies that announce the Logos (8.77.1) in order to finally proclaim him the victor (9.82.1). It is easy for Clement to exploit theatrical terminology because a good portion of the myths he condemns and the texts he cites are presented by dramatic authors: "You have made heaven a stage setting, and the divine is for you a drama, and you have made the holy a comedy, and your superstition has turned true religion into satire' (5.58.4). In addition, taking advantage of the similarity between the theatrical stage and the platform of a tribunal, Clement presents his diatribe against the Greek gods as a legal case: the pagan authors give depositions and are refuted and condemned.[66] Moreover, it is in this way that he announces his presentation of the mysteries:

> And what if I go over the mysteries? I will not dance them in mockery, as they say Alcibiades did, but I will expose right well by the word of truth the sorcery hidden in them; and those so-called gods of yours and their mystic rites, I shall display, as it were, on the stage of life, to the spectators of truth (τοῖς τῆς ἀληθείας ἐγκυκλήσω θεαταῖς).

This metaphor has exerted a capital influence on perceptions of the mysteries, since it gives the impression that they were a matter of *deiknymena*, of representations of the myths recounted. In 2.12.2 Clement says that "Deo and Core have already been turned into a mystical drama," and in 2.17.1, upon recounting Core's ravishment, he affirms that in the Thesmophoria,

---

66 E. g. *Protr.* 7.73.1: μαρτυρεῖν; 7.75.1: ἐλεγχεῖν. The metaphor of a legal case has great success in apologetic literature, partly due to Clement's influence. Cf. Greg. Naz. *Or.* 4.115, 31.16; Thdt. *Affect.* 1.22. On Christian treatment of pagan theater, both on metaphorical and real levels, cf. now Lugaresi 2008.

Scirophoria, and Arre(to)phoria women "celebrate this mythology in many ways" and "represent (ἐκτραγῳδοῦσαι) in many ways Pherephatta's ravishment." The omnipresence of the theatrical metaphor that we have described partially invalidates Clement's text – and the texts of those authors who, like Gregory and Psellus, depend on him and even extend the theatrical imagery – as solid support for the much-debated idea that Core's ravishment was represented in the Eleusinian mysteries. However, the metaphor's influence is also not sufficient to entirely rule out a certain level of veracity and simply say "goodbye to these fantasies," in Wilamowitz's characteristic expression, since a representation of this episode is witnessed to by other sources independent of Clement.[67]

The section specifically on the mysteries in the *Protrepticus*, structured as a retelling of the myth plus a description of the *symbola*, *hagia*, and/or *synthemata* that recall it in the ritual, tends to give the impression of a certain commemoration of the myth, however abstract it may have been. In Eleusis there must have been at least a symbolic remembrance of Core's return, with a ritual search outside the *telesterion* and the display afterward inside of an ear of wheat.[68] The theatrical metaphor perhaps simply exaggerates this commemoration by imagining a dramatic representation, but the distance between the two is not very great, and there could be many intermediate possibilities, since, as Clement says, the episode was represented in various ways (πολυτρόπως) and in various places and festivals besides Eleusis. The same consequent lability between more or less faithful representation on the one hand and symbolic commemoration on the other can be deduced for whatever ritual commemoration-representation of the myth of the Titans may have occasionally taken place.

Finally, in quoting *Protr.* 1.2.3 I have italicized the phrase "that projecting its light to that which is most distant, the truth may illuminate those who are wrapped in darkness." The opposition between light and darkness is a

---

[67] Wilamowitz 1931 II, 374. The most explicit references to a dramatic performance are Christian (Tert. *Ad Nat.* 2.7, Lact. *Ep.* 23), but there are also pagan allusions (Arist. *Eleus.* 19 p. 422 Dindorf, Luc. *Cat.* 22). The debate is a classic one in studies of Greek religion, since archeological and literary data are hard to reconcile in a consistent picture veiled anyhow by secrecy. Sourvinou-Inwood 2003 makes an elaborate proposal about what kind of performance may have taken place, which in my opinion is quite plausible, although she uses as trustworthy independent sources (p. 29) both Clement and a passage of Gregory of Nazianzus (*Or.* 39.4) that draws on him. Harrison 1922³, 568–9 goes much further when she uses Psellus' account (*Quaenam* 3, cf. p. 151).

[68] The key testimony is Hippolytus *Ref.* 5.8.39–40. Cf. Sourvinou-Inwood 2003.

4.3. Literary metaphors

universal method of expressing dualistic confrontation and would not even be worth pointing out if it were not for the fact that light, of great importance in the biblical tradition as a fundamental element of the divine presence,[69] helps Clement to incorporate Eleusinian imagery. Thanks to the reference to the lights of Eleusis, he presents Christianity to the Greeks as the true mysteries of the Logos, replacing the falsity of the Greek mysteries.

Here we enter the realm of an intermediate type of image, halfway between conceptual and literary metaphor. If indeed this image began as a literary metaphor for presenting a Christianity that in the New Testament did not yet use mystery cult as its main conceptual template, it ultimately established itself with extraordinary success as a basic category for understanding Christian experience.[70] Once again, Clement is the pioneer of this image, which will also reappear, contrasted to the Greek *teletai* of Orphic coloration, in passages of Origen and Gregory of Nazianzus that demonstrate its success.

One mystery confronts the other: Clement proposes Christ as hierophant of the mysteries of the Logos, replacing Orpheus, mystagogue of the Eleusinian mysteries (2.21.1). Just as at the end of the section attacking the pagan mysteries, they are all reunited under the aegis of Eleusis, in the final *peroratio* Clement presents the Christian mysteries using the Eleusinian image. Both texts are easy to compare:

> O manifest shamelessness! Once night was silent, a veil for the pleasure of temperate men; but now for the initiated, the holy night is the tell-tale of the rites of incontinence; and the glare of torches reveals the passions. Quench the flame, O Hierophant; revere, O Torch-bearer, the torches. That light exposes your Iacchus (*Protr.* 2.22.6–7).

> O truly sacred mysteries! O stainless light! Like a Torch-bearer I illuminate the heavens and God; I become holy while I am initiated. The Lord is the hierophant, and seals while illuminating him who is initiated, and presents the believer to the Father, to be kept safe for ever. Such are the Bacchic festivals of my mysteries (*Protr.* 12.120.1).

---

69 Bultmann 1951, Bremmer 2002, 60.
70 The appropriation of mystery terminology in Christianity, following Jewish precedents (cf. Riedweg 1987 on Philo and Clement) is immense from the second century AD: its use in the New Testament is limited to some key words (cf. Nock (1933b, 1964), with the observations of Smith 1991, 64–86). The New Testament uses the general term *mysterion*, while a ritual, more technical term like *telete* is incorporated into Christian literature by Clement (cf. Lampe 1982⁶, *s. v.*). Cf. pp 2–4 for the relationship between Christianity and the Greek mysteries.

It is logical that it would be the Eleusinian mysteries that stood for all the others in the irresistible simplification that aimed to oppose one pagan mystery to one Christian one: not in vain were they the best known, to the point that a certain idea of how they functioned was part of the general culture of every educated Greek, initiated or not.

The identification of Christianity with the mysteries arises not only out of Clement's metaphor, but also out of the general perception of Christianity by both sides. Origen accepts Celsus's image of Christianity as a *telete* and defends it as such, as it is the only one that accepts sinners and fosters their repentance and conversion (*CC* 3.59–61). He transforms the verb μύω and its derivates (μύστης, μυστήριον) – which in the Pauline Epistles referred to the incomprehensible and secret, without ritual connotations – into the ritual equivalent, parallel to that of the other rites (τὰς ἄλλας τελετάς) mentioned by Celsus. The reapplication of the mysteries' lexicon to ritual is a constant among Christian authors, bringing it down from the level of abstraction at which it had been used since Plato as a metaphor for initiation into religious and philosophical knowledge. With the Christians the vocabulary of initiation reacquires a specific ritual sense.[71]

Gregory of Nazianzus also proposes the true mysteries of Christ instead of the Orphic mysteries that, following Clement, he subjects to his sarcasm (pp. 150). In his *Second Discourse Against Julian*, just before his outcry against the Eleusinian episodes described by Orpheus, Gregory says (*Or.* 5.31):

> Let *your* herald hush his disgraces, let *mine* cry aloud the divine things (φθεγγέσθω κῆρυξ ἐμὸς τὰ ἔνθεα); close your books of sorcery and divination (γοητικὰς καὶ μαντικὰς βίβλους), let only those of the prophets and Apostles be opened; put a stop to your infamous nights, so full of darkness: I will raise up against them our sacred vigils of the Light (τὰς ἱερὰς καὶ λαμπρὰς παννυχίδας); close your sanctuaries (ἄδυτα) and the roads (ὁδούς) leading unto Hades; I will show the brilliant road that leads to heaven!

The use of Eleusinian terminology to define Christianity is clear, in perfect correspondence with the Eleusinian elements that Gregory has chosen as representatives of the pagan mystery. Likewise, in the *Discourse on Holy Lights*, before criticizing the same Eleusinian characters (*Or.* 39.4) and Orpheus's initiations and mysteries (39.5), he described Christianity as "again a mystery; not deceitful nor disorderly, nor belonging to Greek error or drunkenness (for so I call their solemnities, and so I think will every man of sound sense); but a mystery lofty and divine, and allied to the Glory

---

71 Riedweg 1987, 158–161, and 1988 on the two texts of the *Protrepticus*.

above" (39.1). The image of light, of clear biblical roots, is combined with Eleusinian imagery, but in addition, the references to "books of sorcery and divination" and to Bacchic wine subsume all the Greek mysteries under the heading of Orphism. The fact that these are precisely the passages in which the Orphic references are clearly drawn from Clement suggests that the latter's metaphors about the mysteries may have also influenced Gregory, who renovates them with his own rhetoric. This very continuity of the image of the "true mysteries" proves its success as a suitable approach to presenting Christianity as paganism's symmetrical opposite.

4.4. Toward the Christian re-creation of Orphism

It is clear, then, that all the Orphic references we find in the Christian attacks are fitted within a dualistic framework that locates them in the opposing camp. In cases like that of Clement, these references are even the foundation on which the concept of "paganism" is constructed. The consequences of this insertion of elements of the Orphic tradition into a newly constructed entity are extremely important: scattered or accumulated elements become part of a system, whether that system is conceived of as paganism, Hellenism, superstition, or *civitas impiorum*. The elements of the Orphic tradition acquire in Christian descriptions a function in the contrary camp that they did not previously have: they represent paganism, above all its mystic and theological side – and to a lesser extent, behind Homer and Plato, its philosophical one. We should keep in mind, however, that a very similar phenomenon occurs with the other side's Orphic references, now recuperated as a central component of anti-Christian resistance.

The practical consequence of this systematization – which obviously never becomes absolute, but which shows itself to be an increasing tendency – is that it resulted in an amalgamation of religious traditions that appear more separate in previous non-Christian evidence; or to put it another way the Christians foster the tendency toward the unification of various cults and traditions that already existed within Greek religion and in an especially marked way within Orphism. For this reason Orphism is very useful to them in order to achieve this unification of paganism. At the beginning of the *Protrepticus*, Clement unites Orpheus's aspects as theologian and as musician and makes the pagan mysteries the material content of his song. The association of the myth of Orpheus's song with his mysteries is taken further in Clement than in any previous ancient author. Music and religious instruction frequently go together in the Greek imaginary, and if Orpheus had not been the singer par excellence, the Greeks probably would not have attributed so many rites and religious poems to him. However, the two facets coexist separately within his figure, at most overlapping or juxtaposed, as connected but distinct aspects.[72] Clement now makes the legend of the singer entirely coterminous with the religious tradition associated with his name, the myth of Orpheus with Orphism.

In addition, however, the content of this song – the superstition of the Greek mysteries – is also the result of a synthesis of various aspects of Greek religion that, despite their contacts and overlappings, were never joined so closely together as in these passages of Clement. Clement takes advantage of the strong tendency toward the unification of the mysteries present in his Orphic source (p. 152), but in his own narrative he increases the connection between the various mysteries to the point of presenting them as a single assemblage of "murders and tombs." In this unification Eleusis is the key. It is from these passages that there comes the recuperation of Orphic Eleusinian traditions in Christian writings, where they appear only after Clement. Thus, the connection between Orphism and Eleusis appears much stronger in Christian works than in other evidence that suggests a more labile connection.[73] The tendency to integrate all the mysteries under the Orphic-Eleusinian standard is the evident cause.

Not only Eleusis suffers this insertion into Clement's assemblage, however: the above-mentioned text of the *Protrepticus*, after accumulating Eleusinian elements, ends by saying, "These are the Bacchic festivals (βακχεύματα) of my mysteries" (12.120.1). Eleusinian and Bacchic imagery are also amalgamated. Orphic "glue" also serves to unite more closely, on the basis of a previous labile overlap, the tradition of Dionysian mysteries and that of Bacchic maenadism, with its highest expression in Euripides's *Bacchae*. Granted, Arnobius distinguishes between maenadic Bacchic festivals and the mysteries of Dionysus with the clarity of a modern academic: "the cruel bacchanals called omophagies in Greek ... and these other bacchanals in which an arcane secret is revealed and manifested to the initiates."[74]

---

72 Cf. D. S. 1.23.6: "Orpheus, who obtained great glory among the Greeks for his melody and his rites and his theology"; 4.25.3: "the greatest of the Greeks in theologies, rites, poems and melodies"; Strab. 7 fr. 18. Cf. Burkert 1962 and Versnel 1999 for the connexion of music, magic and religion.

73 Cf. Mylonas 1961 and Graf 1974, who reject a close connexion with Orphism and therefore minimize the importance of these Christian accounts as evidence for Eleusis.

74 *Adv. nat.* 5.19: *Bacchanalia inmania quae nomen Omophagiis graecum est... sed et illa desistimus Bacchanalia altera praedicare, in quibus arcana et tacenda res*

4.4. Toward the Christian re-creation of Orphism

However, the African jurist's taste for clarity was the exception and not the rule in the world of apologetics, in which confusion in the pagan camp was encouraged, and it would not be his enthusiasm for distinction, but rather Clement's tendency to unification that would triumph in the subsequent tradition. In the final *peroratio*, just before the Eleusinian metaphor, Clement directly associates the imagery of the *Bacchae* with that of the mysteries in order to describe paganism and present his equivalent reply. The text combines religious, mystery-cult, maenadic, and biblical references with such skill that it deserves to be read in full:

> Then shall you contemplate (κατοπτεύεις) my God, and be initiated into the sacred mysteries (ἁγίοις τελεσθήσῃ μυστηρίοις), and come to the fruition of the hidden secrets (ἀποκεκρυμμένων) of heaven that I protect (τετηρημένων), which "ear has not heard, nor have they entered into the heart" of any (1 *Cor.* 2:9). "I seem to see two suns, and a double Thebes' (*Ba.* 918f), said one in Bacchic frenzy (βακχεύων) in the worship of idols intoxicated with pure ignorance (ἀγνοίᾳ μεθύων ἀκράτῳ). I would pity him in his intoxication (παροινοῦντα), and thus frantic I would invite him to the sobriety of salvation; for the Lord welcomes a sinner's repentance, and not his death (*Ez.* 18.23). Come, you madman, not leaning on the *thyrsus*, not *crowned* with *ivy*; throw away the *mitre*, throw away the fawn-skin (νεβρίδα); come to your senses. I will show you the Logos, and the *mysteries* of the Logos, expounding them after your own image. This is the mountain beloved of God, not the subject of tragedies like Cithæron, but consecrated to dramas of the truth – a mount of sobriety, shaded with forests of purity; and there revel (βακχεύουσι) on it not the *mænads*, the sisters of Semele, who was struck by the thunderbolt, practicing in their initiatory rites unholy division of flesh (αἱ δύσαγνον κρεανομίαν μυούμεναι), but the daughters of God, the fair lambs, who celebrate the holy rites (σεμνὰ ὄργια) of the Logos, raising a sober choral dance ... Come also, you aged man, leaving Thebes, and casting away from you both divination and Bacchic frenzy (τὴν μαντικὴν καὶ τὴν βακχικήν) allow yourself to be led to the truth. I give you the staff (ξύλον) on which to lean. Haste, Tiresias; believe, and you will see. Christ, by whom the eyes of the blind recover sight, will shed on you a light brighter than the sun; night will flee from you, fire will fear, death will be gone; you, old man, who saw not Thebes, shall see the heavens.

This mixture of images of wine, maenadism, and the mysteries in a general "Dionysism" is also reflected in the section of greatest interest for the study of Orphism, the description of the mysteries in the *refutatio* of 2.12–22. Clement uses verbs characteristic of maenadism to describe Dionysus's dis-

---

proditur insinuaturque sacratis. This neat distinction between maenadism and mysteries corresponds to that made by modern scholars (e. g. Henrichs 1996).

memberment by the Titans, as if instead of a ritual dismemberment characteristic of sacrifice, prior to cooking the flesh, it were a *diasparagmos* in which the flesh is devoured raw. In reality, in mixing images of sacrifice and of *diasparagmos* Clement continues the earlier tradition that already presented the two together in the Titanic myth,[75] but he takes their amalgamation further. In the introduction to the section on the mysteries, he says:

Διόνυσον μαινόλην ὀργιάζουσι Βάκχοι ὠμοφαγίᾳ τὴν ἱερομανίαν ἄγοντες καὶ τελίσκουσι τὰς κρεονομίας τῶν φόνων ἀνεστεμμένοι τοῖς ὄφεσιν, ἐπολολύζοντες Εὐάν...

The Bacchic initiates hold their orgies in honor of the frenzied Dionysus, celebrating their sacred frenzy by the eating of raw flesh, and go through the distribution of the parts of butchered victims, crowned with snakes, shrieking out "euai" (*Protr.* 2.12.1).

The masculine *bacchoi* enunciates the intention to fuse something as intrinsically feminine as the maenads (*bacchai*) with the participants in the mysteries, men and women, designated collectively with the masculine gender. Immediately afterward (2.13.1) comes the mention of the outrage (μύσος) done to Dionysus, in reference to the etymology of μυστήριον, and the myth of the Titans will follow shortly. In addition, in 2.16.3 Clement offers a Bacchic interpretation of the βουκολικὸν κέντρον as a thyrsus, facilitating its replacement by the κέντρον of the true shepherd, Christ, in the "true mysteries." All these details work together to lead the reader to simply identify the *bacchoi* of the mysteries with the *bacchai* of maenadism in a single image. This subtle fusion of traditions is then crowned (2.22.1) by a quotation from Heraclitus, who condemns "night-wanderers, magi, *bacchoi, lenae,* and *mystai*" (14a DK) on the same level, "since they are impiously initiated into what men consider mysteries" (14b DK).[76]

---

75 D. S. 3.62.6; Philod. *De Piet.* 44. 16.1 Gomperz; Plut. *Alex.* 2.7–9; Luc. *Salt.* 79 show the overlapping between Orphic and maenadic tradition. Robertson 2003 tries in vain to distinguish an originary tale of maenadic *diasparagmos* from another, later tale of sacrificial ritual in the Titanic myth. Both, however, seem to be linked in the earliest sources, a combination which is deeply embedded in the core of the myth: Herrero 2006.
76 The authenticity of fr. 14a DK has been contested, but the μάγοι and μύσται of the Derveni Papyrus (col. VI) suggest that, though Clement might have introduced changes in the syntax, the substance of the sentence belongs to Heraclitus (bibliography in Bremmer 2008, 236). Cf. Herrero 2005c with other arguments in favor of the authenticity of the fragment, and Wiese 1963 and Osborn 2005 on Clement's reception of Heraclitus.

4.4. Toward the Christian re-creation of Orphism 269

The success of Clement's work of fusion is evident in the understanding of the *Protrepticus*'s medieval scholiast, who explains the expression "impious division of flesh" of 12.119.1 in this way:

δύσαγνον κρεανομίαν· ὠμὰ γὰρ ἤσθιον κρέα οἱ μυούμενοι Διονύσῳ, δεῖγμα τοῦτο τελούμενοι τοῦ σπαραγμοῦ, ὃν ὑπέστη Διόνυσος ὑπὸ τῶν Μαινάδων.

For the initiates of the mysteries of Dionysus ate raw flesh, doing this rite in commemoration of the dismemberment that Dionysus suffered at the hands of the maenads.

The scholiast attributes Dionysus' death to the maenads. The reference to actual cult ensures that it is not a simple confusion between Orpheus and Dionysus. Clement had accentuated the elements that encouraged identification of the myth of the Titans with maenadism, but he did not make this identification entirely explicit, doubtless because he was conscious of a degree of difference, as Arnobius was even after him. Free now from the apologists' subjection to the reality of paganism, the scholiast has fused the maenads with the Titans and has transformed the mysteries of Dionysus into a full scene of *diasparagmos* and *omophagia* corresponding to an idealization of Dionysiac cult, with a vaguely Eucharistic perfume, which never took place in reality. The scholiast is not the only one to complete Clement's associative labors with total fusion of the different dimensions of Dionysiac cult. Firmicus Maternus (*De err.* 6.5) and, now in the ninth century, the lexicon of the Byzantine patriarch Photius (*s. v.* νεβρίζειν) also present an image similar to the scholiast's. The former also makes the sacrificial victim a commemoration of Dionysus: "They do in order everything that the child did and suffered in dying; they tear apart a live bull with their teeth, renewing their cruel festivities in annual commemorations" (*crudeles epulas annuis commemorationibus excitantes*). It is not necessary to insist on the imaginary character of such a fantastic rite. The latter, for his part, explains the word "to act like a fawn" in this way: "To wear the skin of a fawn or to dismember fawns, in imitation of the suffering related to Dionysus (κατὰ μίμησιν τοῦ περὶ τὸν Διόνυσον πάθους)."

The three texts say expressly what no pagan text ever reaches the point of affirming, that Dionysian rituals involved the dismemberment (and eating) of an animal in "commemoration" (δεῖγμα, *commemoratio*, μίμησις) of the dismemberment of Dionysus. Commemoration does not demand the immediate identification of the animal with the god, but the term is too close to the Eucharistic words of institution not to suggest slippage in these Christians' minds in the direction of a quasi-Eucharistic formulation.[77] These three texts are the only real basis for the Eucharistic interpretation of maenadism, according to which the maenads in trance ate Dionysus in an omophagic ritual in order to enter into communion with him, an idea still very popular today in works of popularization and in superficial references to maenadism, although more serious scholars are justly sceptical in this respect, without need for apologetic motivations, since the idea's foundations are very fragile.[78] Nevertheless, the error serves to shed light on the taboo nature of theophagy for the Greeks (pp. 354ff).

Clement adds other elements of the Dionysian universe, such as the theater and wine, to this maenadic-mystic cement. We have already seen their presence in his final exhortation: μεθύων, παροινοῦντα, τραγῳδίαις (12.118.5–119.3). In accordance with the rules of rhetoric, the final images take up again in *Ringkomposition* those offered in the initial exordium, in which Clement condemned tragic dramas, actors, and poets, "drunk, crowned with ivy, maddened by the Bacchic *telete*," who deserved to be imprisoned "with the satyrs and the maenadic thiasus, and with the rest of the chorus of demons, in the aged mountains of Helicon and Cithaeron" (1.2.1.1). The mixture of mysteries, maenadism, wine, poetry, and theater in a single *constructum*, paganism, which Clement has created in order to oppose it to his own side, could scarcely be more explicit. Clement does not deny his amalgamation's evident aims when he says that he "mixes in his song a sweet and true balsam of persuasion" (1.2.4).

---

77 Cf. 1 *Cor.* 11:23–26, the first testimony to the Christian Eucharist, which explictly identifies bread and wine with flesh and blood, but also incluyes a commemorative element: "Do this in memory (ἀνάμνησιν) of me". Many Christians also maintained an ambiguous attitude regarding the meat of pagan sacrifices, which they refused to eat, supposing that the daemons-idols were present in it (literally, seated on it: cf. Lane Fox 1986, 444), although they did not explicitely identify them with the sacrificial victim.

78 The point of departure of the sacramental interpretation is the totemic theory of sacrifice by Robertson Smith 1894; Freud reelaborated it in *Totem and Taboo* (1912), while Frazer 1912³ and Harrison 1922³, 478–491 applied it to maenadic Greek sacrifice, followed by scholars like Cumont 1922, Loisy 1919, Dodds 1951, 270–282 (and n. 52) and Kott 1973, 186–230. Against Dionysiac sacramentalism were already Wilamowitz 1931–1932, II, 68; Otto, 1933, 99 and 121; Festugière, 1935, 366–396, who considered omophagy a consequence of Dionysiac exaltation and not the way to attain it. Today scepticism predominates: Henrichs 1982, 159–160; Burkert 1987, 110–112; Obbink 1994. The decline of the idea is perceptible in retractations by scholars who accepted it at first: Nock, Nilsson, Henrichs (references in Henrichs 1982, 235, n. 217). I have studied the question in detail in Herrero 2006.

4.4. Toward the Christian re-creation of Orphism

Not a few ancient and modern readers of Clement and other Christian sources have drunk this persuasive cocktail, in effect, and suffered the consequences. Like the scholiast, Photius, or Michael Psellus during the Byzantine period, many modern students of ancient religion have succumbed to Clement's persuasion and elaborated constructions in which the *Protrepticus* and the texts inspired by it play a fundamental role: they present a unified image of the different traditions of the mystery cults, which were only relatively in contact with one another (e. g. Orphism and Eleusis),[79] of the mysteries and maenadism,[80] and of the myth of Orpheus and the Orphic tradition.[81] The symmetric opposition of Bacchic mysteries to Christian ones has also led to the extrapolation of elements from one side to the other.[82] Despite the reaction to which their exaggerations gave rise, these works remain classics in the field (e. g., Jane Harrison's *Prolegomena*) that even today exercise a great deal of influence on our image of Greek religion, and it is useful to be alert

---

79 Harrison 1922³, 568 follows the tendency of Clement (and of his Orphic source), carried to the extreme by Psellus, of taking for granted an internal linkage among all the mysteries described in *Protr.* 2.12–22, with Orphism as the common principle inspiring all: she interprets the different mysteries as successive phases of the same ritual. Maass 1985, 89–92 attributes all Clement's information to Apollodorus, and constructs on this basis his whole idea of locating Dionysus' ritual dismemberment in the Thesmophoria, thus fusing what Clement only intuitively associates. Cf. Mylonas 1961 and Graf 1974, with a much more prudent position regarding the presence of Orphism at Eleusis and the value of Clement's information.
80 Lobeck 1829, 587 and especially Harrison 1922³, 483, 490, did not hesitate in interpreting together the texts of Firmicus Maternus (*De err.* 6.5), *Protr.* 2.17.2 (mysteries of Dionysus), *Protr.* 2.12 (maenadic orgies of Dionysus Mainoles), fr 472 Kannicht of Euripides' *Cretans* and the scholion to *Protr.* 12.119.8–9. For the Eucharistic interpretation of omophagy defended among others by Harrison (cf. n 78), this amalgam was extremely convenient, since it allowed fusing maenadism and Bacchic mysteries at all levels (e. g. when she interprets as Dionysus the kid fallen into the milk of the Thurii leaf, p. 594).
81 Harrison 1922³, Eisler 1925, Macchioro 1930. The scholarly identification of Orpheus and Orphism had as a consequence an excessive separation of both in the subsequent sceptical reaction: cf. Wilamowitz 1932 II, 374: "Dionysiac mysteries have nothing to do with Orpheus: that anonymous poetry, supposedly or really ancient, is attributed to him in later times does not prove any internal link"; Linforth 1941, 225, refuted in IV n. 26), maintained that Orpheus in the *Protrepticus* had no religious meaning at all.
82 Macchioro 1930, 76, besides deriving the Christian Eucharist from a sacramentally interpreted "Orphic omophagy", uses the image of the *Bacchai* in *Protr* 12.119.1 as evidence for a contraposition of Christian sacred dances against the maenadic dance. Also, Eisler 1925, 61–86, bases on Book I of the *Protrepticus* his claims of influence of Orphic-Bacchic mysteries on Christian iconographic and literary symbolism.

for the distortions in their portrait of it. Clement makes use of pre-existing overlaps and tendencies toward unification, but he gives them a definitive impetus that alters them substantially. Analyzing and admiring his rhetorical techniques should also mean knowing how to discern the underlying reality beneath them, less unified in a single system than his text would suggest.

4.5. The New vs. the Old

The strategy of contrast between two symmetrical camps aims at the replacement of error by truth, of superstition by religion, of the spurious by the legitimate. There is also a very interesting conceptual implication. We have heard Clement say that his melody, his song, and his instrument are new (καινός *Protr.* 1.2.4). We have also heard him proclaim that Helicon and Cithaeron have grown old (γεγηρακόσιν, 1.2.2) and that the poets of the Lenaia have *already* reached a state of complete drunkenness (τέλεον ἤδη παροινοῦντας, 1.2.2). Shortly afterward he says, "Error seems ancient, and the truth something new (παλαιὰ δὲ ἡ πλάνη, καινὸν δὲ ἡ ἀλήθεια φαίνεται)" (1.6.4). Let us recall that the *Cohortatio* encouraged its readers to leave behind the "ancient superstition of your fathers" (παλαιὰ τῶν προγόνων ὑμῶν δεισιδαιμονία, 2.36.4). The emphasis on Christianity's newness in contrast to paganism's decadent old age is difficult to exaggerate.

Newness is an unrenounceable aspiration of the Christian message.[83] The Incarnation happened in recent historical time, in contrast to the Mosaic revelation or the Greek myths that took place long ago. Christianity makes this novelty a source of pride and breaks away from Judaism in ever-growing opposition to the ancestral tradition, with the desire to complete – if not replace – the Old Law with the New (*2 Cor.* 5:17; *Gal.* 6:15). The presentation of a new truth in contrast to ancient error is even more marked with regard to paganism. In addition, this aspiration to novelty fits perfectly with the temporal dimension implied by the conceptual metaphor of conversion as a journey from A to B. Arrival necessarily comes after departure: the subject was first at the point of departure (Helicon and Cithaeron, to follow Clement's image) and, if he converts, will later be at the destination of arrival (Sion). Conversion unavoidably entails movement from the old location to the new one, and as a result, an exhortation to conversion is an exhortation to prefer the new to the old, a new religion to the old one, a new life to the previous one.

---

83 *Lc.* 22:20; *Eph.* 4:22–24. The expression "new song" also has biblical roots: *Ps.* 33:3; 40:3; 96:1; 98:1; *Is.* 42:10; *Ap.* 5:9; 14:10.

4.5. The New vs. the Old

Precisely this aspect of novelty in Christianity earned the disdain of both Jews and Greeks, whose defense of religion was based on tradition above all. The entire message of Celsus, Iamblichus, Porphyry, Julian, and other Neoplatonists was centered on the preservation of the old, and the old (*palaios*) continued to be a mark of authority while the new (*kainos*) was rejected. This tendency even increased during the Imperial Age, when danger imposed the necessity of finding a category for traditional religion the venerable antiquity of the Orphic tradition was the virtue that made the greatest contribution to its revaluation in late paganism. The difference in the treatment dispensed by the authorities to Jews and Christians (e. g., both groups refused to sacrifice to the emperor, but only Christians were persecuted) arose precisely from the fact that the Jews did no more than follow a very ancient ancestral tradition, and the Christians, by contrast, were a recent sect preaching a dangerously novel message.[84]

The Christians' defense against the principal line of attack they suffer falls into three categories. On the one hand, they try to maintain a link with the Old Testament tradition, unlike various Gnostic currents, and to present themselves as heirs of the ancient biblical revelation, as the *verus Israel*, the true descendants of Abraham in whom the ancient promises are fulfilled.[85] This also permits them to appropriate the Hellenistic Jewish argument that claimed chronological priority with respect to the Greeks, a claim that can only be understood in this context in which authority arises from the sheer fact of antiquity.

On the other hand, the Christians transpose the terms of antiquity and novelty to a cosmic dimension that makes it possible to reconcile the two. The *Easter Hymn* by Melito of Sardis characterizes the Logos through pairs of metaphysical opposites that define Him as eternal and momentary, mortal and immortal, *arche* and *telos*, *palaios* and *kainos* at the same time. Clement specifies that the novelty of his song is compatible with the greatest possible antiquity, since it has always existed: "Do not consider my saving song as new in the way that a piece of furniture or a house is new; it existed before

---

[84] Cf. Lane Fox 1986, 487ff. Cf. Iambl. *Myst.* 7.5 against Christian καινοτομία; Iul. *Ep.* 46, 111, 136.

[85] Iust. *Dial.* 11.5. Turn and turn about, orthodox Christians accuse heretics and Gnostics precisely of proclaiming a new doctrine that breaks the link with apostolic tradition: e.g. Thdt. *Epist.* 118.5: "They have abandoned the doctrine that has triumphed in the Churches of the Saviour God until today, introducing a new and spurious (καινὴν καὶ νόθον) one, radically opposed to the tradition of the Apostles, and they fight openly against those who maintain the ancient messages (τὰ παλαιὰ κρατοῦσι κηρύγματα)". Cf. Herrero 2005a and 2005b.

the morning star, and in the beginning was the Logos, and the Logos was with God, and the Logos was God." Augustine, too, confesses along the same lines, "Late have I loved you, O Beauty ever ancient, ever new, late have I loved you!"[86]

Third, and this is the aspect of greatest interest here, the apologists pursued a campaign of radical delegitimization of antiquity as a source of authority for Greek religion and especially for the Orphic tradition. Being ancient (*palaios*) was an indisputable motive for the prestige of Orpheus's "deceitful songs": Plato cites with veneration the Orphic *palaios logos* (*Leg.* 715e, *Epist.* 7.335a). In Clement, by contrast, this adjective designates error (1.6.4). We will not find it used in a positive sense in the entire *Protrepticus*. Correspondingly, Clement omits (7.74) line 7a of the *Testament*, which says that "about this (monotheism) there is a *palaios logos*," in order to avoid turning to the old as a source of authority in a positive context. His attacks on the two related concepts of *ethos* and *synetheia*, so positive in the Greek realm of ideas, should be interpreted in the same spirit (e. g. in 10.90.2):[87]

> Why do they flee to this fatal brand, with which they shall be burned, when it is within their power to live nobly according to God (θεόν), and not according to custom (ἔθος)? For God bestows life freely; but evil custom, after our departure from this world, brings on the sinner unavailing remorse with punishment. By sad experience, even a child knows how superstition (δεισιδαιμονία) destroys and piety (θεοσέβεια) saves.

It is worth observing the opposition between *ethos* and *theos*, highlighted by means of the play on words that takes advantage of the phonetic similarity and made comparable to the radical general opposition between *deisidaimonia* and *theosebeia*. With this attack on the old, Clement undermines the

---

86 Mel. Sard. *Hymn. Pasch.* (ed. Perler 1963); Clem. Alex. *Protr.* 1.6.3 (quoting *Ps.* 109:3 and *Jn.* 1:1); Aug, *Conf.* 10.27. These formulas solve the tension between "new" and "ancient" patent in texts like 1 *Jn* 2:7–8: "I write no new commandment to you, but an old commandment that you had from the beginning. The old commandment is the word that you heard from the beginning. Again, I write a new commandment to you…".

87 *Nomos* almost always has a positive sense in both pagan and Christian contexts (though there are also some critiques of *nomos* as an empty convention, cf. *Protr.* 2.22.3 with n. 61). *Ethos* and *synetheia* are usually taken positively in Greek literature when speaking of religion or politics (Plat. *Leg.* 808c), fields dominated by respect for tradition, while in ethics they might be the cause of deeply rooted vices (Aristot. *EN* 1154a.33). Christians apply the latter use to the former, as if the cult of ancient gods was a vice (e. g. Clem. *Protr.* 10.89–90). Cf. Gnilka 1993, 104–113 and Lugaresi 2003 on Christian attacks on *synetheia* and *mores*.

foundations of the authority of pagan religion and of Orphism in particular. The play of metaphors contributes to facilitating this inversion of values, whose importance for the vision of time and history can scarcely be exaggerated. The new song replaces the old; the new mysteries replace the old ones; the *palaios logos* is supplanted by the *kainos Logos*. In Clement's work we are present at a changing of the guard in which the new is dressed in the garments of the old, a changing of the guard between the "swan song of classical antiquity and the morning song of the new creation," in Halton's eloquent expression (1983, 193). In the following pages we shall see how this change of guard was accomplished.

5. Orphism as a bridge between Christianity and Paganism

The construction of two opposing sides aims to break all possible fluidity between one side and the other. On the other hand, it forces the apologists to establish some bridges between both sides that make it possible to insert Christianity into the Greek cultural system by taking advantage of all possible linkages with paganism. Orphism was a fundamental axis of opposition, and for this very reason it also became a bridge that made it possible to overcome the cultural and religious distance between Greek religion and Christianity. In the same way that in the theological sphere assimilation would take place with Platonism in metaphysics and with Stoicism in ethics, in the literary sphere it was necessary to present the biblical images on which Christianity is based to the Greeks in such a way as to make them comprehensible, associating them, whether by opposition or by identification, with traditional Greek images.

This effort directed at integration into Greek paradigms is perceptible in the constant juxtaposition of biblical and classical citations that we find in all apologetic works, situating Greek and biblical literature on the same level of argumentation, although, clearly, assigning them very different statuses. Even such apparently insignificant details as innocent plays on words, however, fulfill an assimilative function, not only an ornamental one. Such humble methods also contribute to bridging the valley that separates the mountains opposed by Clement, and for this reason it is useful to examine them, taking the *Protrepticus* as our point of reference and mine of examples, since it contains the Orphic citations of most interest here.[88]

---

88 Cf. Steneker 1967 on the rhetorical and stylistic techniques of the *Protrepticus* and Riedweg 1987, 148f on Book XII in particular.

At the beginning of his attack on the mysteries (2.12.2), Clement associates the maenads' cry "Euoi" (εὐάν), deforming it slightly, with Eve (Εὔαν), the name of the first woman, the cause of sin, and with the name of the serpent in Aramaic (Ἔυιαν). It must be noted that the inexactitude of the correspondence is its least important aspect.[89] Clement himself is conscious of it, since he notes that the Aramaic word has an initial aspiration. What matters to him is that the pagans mentally associate the cry and the symbol of the Bacchic mysteries, the impiety of which will be criticized in what follows, with the woman and the serpent who are the causes of perdition. In this way Clement familiarizes his pagan audience with the story of *Genesis*, a story less well known to them, and by this simple mechanism he incorporates the Bacchic cry into the Christian lexicon, in this case with a negative connotation. It must be pointed out that the etymology of *euoi* was already the object of pagan speculation and that in keeping with his habitual practice of drawing inspiration from pagan precedents and Christianizing them, Clement adds the etymological link with Eve and the snake to this tradition.[90] The omnipresence of serpents in Christian descriptions of Orphic myths and rituals is not only due to the real linkage of snakes with chthonic cults, but also to the association with Satan that Clement here makes explicit with a highly forced etymology.[91] Likewise, in *Protr.* 1.7.5, 2.16.2, and 2.22.3 the serpent of the mysteries is identified with Lucifer himself. The notion that women are to blame for the original misfortune, common to the Greek (Pandora) and biblical (Eve) traditions, is also brought together with their reputation as devotees of maenadism, on the one hand, and of the superstition of the mysteries, on the other.[92]

---

89 "The exact Hebrew pronunciation" (i. e. Aramaic written with Hebrew characters) does not support, in any case, the correspondence of *hawwá* (Eve) and *hiwyá* (snake). Cf. Van der Hoek 2004 on Clement's (and Origen's) apologetic use of etymology.

90 Arignote, a possible candidate for the authorship of Clement's source in this section (cf. Herrero 2007a) etymologized it as derived from the celebration (εὖ) of the discovery of the mirror (Harp. *s. v.* εὗοι σάβοι cf. Tresp 1903, 173). Pausanias (4.31.4) etymologized the Messenian mountain Eve (Εὔα) as derived from the Bacchic cry, since there Dionysus and his followers would have uttered the ἐπίφθεγμα βακχικόν for the first time. This constitutes another instance of Christianization of pagan etymologies, studied by Opelt 1959 and 1966.

91 Athenag. *Leg.* 20 (the *Theogony of Hieronymus and Hellanicus* placed a "curious emphasis on snakishness", cf. West 1983, 182); Tat. *Orat.* 8.6, 10.1, Greg. Naz. *Or.* 5.31, 39.4 and above all Clement, who in the *Protrepticus* takes great advantage of the serpentine presence in Orphic mysteries and theogonies (2.12.2, 2.16.1, 22.4) and Apollinean oracles (1.1.2; 2.34.1) in order to represent paganism as a whole (1.4.1–3).

92 Not only are all maenads female, but women were also considered prone to be

The importance Clement concedes to this apparently ingenuous etymological-associative method is shown by the fact that the presence of the fourth singer, Eunomos, in the beginning of the *Protrepticus* (1.1.2–3) is justified only by a play on words: this play on the singer's name will serve to introduce the idea of the biblical Law (*nomos*) while assimilating it to the meaning of *nomos* as "melody" in the musical metaphor originating in the myth of Orpheus. Even simpler than these etymologies, however, is the mere play on words that takes advantage of phonetic similarity in order to associate two words on the level of discourse, without positing an etymological relationship between them, as in 11.119.1: "the maenads (μαινάδες) do not celebrate the feasts of Bacchus ... but rather the little lambs (ἄμναδες) who form a chorus of wisdom." The phonetic similarity facilitates Clement's opposition of the two words, so that the "maenads" end up Christianized in reverse, as an impious mob contrasted to the flock of God's sheep, in an image very frequent in biblical tradition but not in Greek tradition. In this case, the new Christian image is made comprehensible to the pagan by contrasting it to an image with which he is familiar.[93]

Of greater penetration than these etymological games is the effort to profit from the "cultural polysemy" made possible by certain terms that have one meaning in the Greek context and another in the biblical one. Thus, for example, δαίμων means "god" in traditional epic usage, but the evolution of the concept meant that the LXX already chose the word to designate a demon. It is obvious that the many poetic passages in which the word designated the Olympian gods were highly useful to the apologists in classifying these deities as demons.[94] Celsus still considers the "daemonic forces" (διαμονίοι δυνάμεις) positive divine energies, while Origen in his response interprets them as evil powers (*CC* 8.48). The same semantic ambiguity is taken advantage of by Clement when he identifies the beam (ξύλον) to which Odysseus is tied to keep him from succumbing to the Sirens with the Cross of Christ that saves from temptations; in addition, in the following paragraph the same word designates the staff offered to Tiresias as a Christian replacement for the Bacchic thyrsus.[95]

---

    seduced by superstition and guilty of its expansion, in both pagan and Christian circles. Cf. Polyb. 12.24.5: τῆς δεισιδαιμονίας ἀρχηγοὺς οἴονται τὰς γυναῖκας On Pandora and Eve, cf. Bremmer 2008, 19–34.
93 Steneker 1967, 18f.
94 Iust. *Apol.* 1.5, Clem. Alex. *Protr.* 2.40.4, 4.55.4. Pagan gods are called "daemons" in 1 *Cor.* 10:20, which alludes to *Ps.* 95:5.
95 *Protr.* 12.118.4, 12.119.3. The word ξύλον is used to refer to the Cross several times in the New Testament: *Acts* 5:30; 13:29; 1 *Pe* 2:24. The Church Fathers will

Besides their rhetorical efficacy, such plays on words carried no small ideological charge, since they familiarized the Greeks with notions initially strange to them. Here an interesting fact must be noted: in the classical age, Orphism made use of very similar methods to introduce new ideas (possibly of Eastern origin) foreign to the Greek world until then, inserting them into the Greek imaginary by means of associative phonetic-etymological games (*soma-sema, telete-teleute*) and the exploitation of polysemy (*arche* as "power" and as "beginning" to designate Zeus in *OF* 14). Plato caricaturized these methods in the *Cratylus*, a depiction which, paradoxically, may have served to inspire later imitators like the Christians. The similarity of the problematic of inculturating new ideas prompts similar responses.

On a small scale, these plays on words demonstrate the subtle superposition of images by which two distinct traditions, the biblical and the Greek, began to be amalgamated into a single one, maintaining the distinction between two opposing sides, paganism and Christianity. At a more profound level, dialogue with the rival camp had two facets: the various ways of explaining parallels and the exploitation of Orphic images to present Christian ideas foreign to paganism in familiar molds.

5.1. Explanation of the parallels

The apologists used and even exaggerated religious parallels with their rival to support their own position, but these parallels were also a cause of discomfort, since they endangered the unique nature of the biblical revelation and could foment syncretism. We have seen that violent attacks emphasizing those aspects of paganism most different from Christianity, omission of the most similar aspects, and the euhemerist explanation of myths were recurrent techniques to solve the problem by denying (or avoiding mentioning) the parallels. However, this type of solution was not always possible, because its very use to support Christian ideas with arguments from pagan literature demanded an explanation of these resemblances. Acknowledgment and explanation of the parallels served at times to bring the two sides together and at times to highlight their differences.[96]

---

develop this theme, interpreting as allegorical prophecy the text of *Ex.* 15:25. The term can also designate pagan idols (*Protr.* 1.7.5).

96 The only specific study of this subject known to me is Pépin 1986, although many authors refer to it tangentially (cf. bibliography in Pépin's study). Fear 1999 studies the Christian reaction to the perceived similarities with Cybele's mysteries; from pagan intuition of truth (Aug. *In Ioh. Evang tract.* 7.6: *et ipse pileatus chris-*

5.1. Explanation of the parallels

The attitude that might be considered most open-minded today supposed that God inspires everyone and that although the truth is only revealed in its purity and plenitude in the Bible, certain fragments of truth may have been grasped by the pagans, whether because the Spirit saw fit to inspire them or through their own gifts of religious intuition. The principal beneficiary of this explanation was the Sibyl, whose oracles (composed *ex eventu* by the Jews and Christians themselves, of course) were so astonishingly accurate that she was frequently placed on a level with the biblical prophets. This explanation is occasionally applied to the achievements of the Orphic poems with different nuances in each author: Clement, Lactantius, and Augustine.

Clement maintains an ambiguous attitude. His belief in the theory of Greek dependence on the biblical prophets is well attested: book I of the *Stromata* gives chronologies demonstrating the priority of the prophets in time, and book V gathers Christian and pagan parallels, with a central place for Orpheus while constantly affirming dependence. Nevertheless, Clement also includes expressions that seem to point toward the idea of an independent enlightenment ("as if he had a happy intuition," 5.14.116.1), and the text that follows the citation of the *Testament* in the *Protrepticus* (7.74.7) leaves no room for doubt: "Orpheus understood with the passage of time that he had been mistaken ... for if the Greeks have gathered some sparks of the divine Logos and have sung a few truths, they demonstrate that the force of the truth was not hidden, but they accuse themselves of weakness for not having persevered to the end." This affirmation supposes knowledge of the truth not originating with the prophets. In Clement, then, the two theories appear to coexist, and when he decides to give an explanation for them, he reduces them to a single outline:

> And we showed in the first *Stromateus* that the philosophers of the Greeks are called thieves, inasmuch as they have taken without acknowledgment their principal dogmas from Moses and the prophets. To which also we shall add, that the angels who had obtained the superior rank, having sunk into pleasures, told to the women the secrets which had come to their knowledge; while the rest of the angels concealed them, or rather, kept them for the coming of the Lord. Thence emanated the doctrine of providence, and the revelation of high things; and prophecy having already been imparted to the philosophers of the Greeks, the treatment of dogma arose among the philosophers, sometimes true when they hit the mark, and sometimes erroneous, when they comprehended not the secret of the prophetic allegory (*Strom.* 5.1.9.10).

---

tianus est) to the topical plagiarism of demons (Firm. *De err.* 22.3: *Habet ergo diabolus Christos suos*), Christian explanations are similar to those prompted by parallels with Orphism.

By means of the two myths of plagiarism and of the union of the fallen angels with human women, Clement "rationalizes" the two theories he maintains.[97] His admiration for Greek culture leads him to admit that it may contain "sparks of the divine Logos," but when it comes time to explain how this Logos reached the Greeks, the urge to safeguard the unity of revelation imposes a solution intermediate between the theft of wisdom and the plagiarism of the demons, that is, the fallen angels. Nevertheless, even though at times he condemns "plagiarism," Clement's presentation sometimes has a positive tone of *felix culpa* that does not appear in other authors.

Fewer scruples are evident in Lactantius, who unqualifiedly attributes the Orphic intuition of a creator God to pure natural capacity: *Natura igitur et ratione ducente intellexit... ratio perduxit* (*DI* 1.5.4). Orpheus's defects of conception arise precisely from his attainment of the truth on his own and not in revealed form like the prophets: *quia concipere animo non poterat*. In other Christian authors these defects would be the fruit of the corruption of the truth originally revealed. The general evaluation of pagan wisdom is hence more positive in Lactantius than in any other Christian author: "They defended what they perceived of eternity under the guidance of nature (*natura ducente senserunt*), and if the truth be grasped (*comprehensa veritate*), they maintained the same doctrine that we follow" (*DI* 1.5.13). Possibly, his nearness to the Neoplatonic interpretation of Orpheus led him to this original position, at the antipodes of any kind of theory of plagiarism.

At the extreme opposite pole we find Augustine, who acknowledges (*CD* 18.37 and *Contra Faustum* 13.2) that Orpheus and the pagan theologians were able to foretell (*predixerunt*) part of the truth, but in whose eyes their having fallen into the error of honoring the pagan gods takes away all value from these intuitions. Augustine is forced to admit this explanation of natural enlightenment because he recognizes that the theory of dependence is highly unlikely.[98] Unlike Lactantius or Clement, however, he is not prepared to admit the existence of virtue among the theologians of the enemy camp. It will not be the first or the last time that greater historical or scientific knowledge and greater intellectual rigor are accompanied by greater narrowness of mind.

---

97 Cf. Le Boulluec 1981 *ad loc* for a detailed commentary on the origin of this myth in the interpretation of *Gn.* 6:2 and its appearance in other Christian authors like Tertullian (*De an.* 2.3) or Athenagoras (*Leg.* 24). Cf. n. 92 on women as cause of universal evil.
98 Aug. *CD* 8.11–12 retracts his earlier acceptance of the theory of dependence, which he had accepted on the authority of Ambrose.

5.1. Explanation of the parallels

In these three authors it can clearly be seen that the same train of argument about the same set of facts can be used in very different ways. However, insofar as this explanation admits that God may reveal Himself in some way other than through Scripture, it is less popular than other explanations that, although less rigorous from the historical perspective, preserve the uniqueness of Scripture as the only path to knowledge of the divine and so reinforce Christianity's pretensions to a monopoly on truth. Without doubt, the most celebrated of these is the idea expressed in Clement's aforementioned text that the Greeks were acquainted with the revelation of the prophets and that their successes and approaches to the Truth arose from this acquaintance.[99] The chronologies presented by Tatian, Theophilus, and Clement are intended to show the prophets' priority with respect to the Greeks (including Orpheus) in time, and hence the chronological plausibility of dependence. They are merely an *a posteriori* support for a theory that originated independently of any chronological considerations. Theophilus already said as much: "What does it matter whether they are the last or the first!" (*Autol.* 2.38).

This argument of dependence is inherited from Jewish apologetic, which in its search for a respectable position and a reinforcement of Jewish identity in the Hellenistic world had developed it with great enthusiasm. Orphism offered various elements that were easily manipulated along these lines: Orpheus's journey to Egypt made it possible to explain his contact with Moses, and his chronological priority placed him at the head of all the Greek poets and philosophers. In addition, Orphic poetry offered various themes, especially the tendency to sing about a supreme god, that were readily susceptible to an *interpretatio biblica* and gave rise to forgeries like the *Testament*. Of course, Orpheus was not the only possible link through which to establish a connection between the prophets and the Greeks, since other sages were also said to have gone to Egypt. Above all, Plato was the principal object of this construction, since he was the one with whom the Christians could most easily establish points of agreement, and the (true?) tradition of his journey to Egypt was firm. For example, when citing as inspired the passage of Plato in which he mentions a *palaios logos* that makes Zeus the beginning, middle, and end of all things (an expression that stems from an Orphic poem, as the *Derveni Papyrus* has shown), the *Cohortatio* does not hesitate to make Moses the author of this *palaios logos*, rather than Orpheus.[100] In addition,

---

99 Droge 1989, Ridings 1995 are the latest studies of this idea; cf. also the bibliography in n. 11 on the on the closely related arguments of chronological priority and descent from a primordial founder as grounds of authority and legitimacy.
100 *Cohort.* 25.4 (with Riedweg 1994 *ad loc* for other quotations of Plat. *Leg.* 715e). Ps.-Justin, whose taste for philological-ideological deductions is patent in *Cohort.*

it is worth noting that certain pagan admirers of Hebrew wisdom accepted this argument, like the Pythagorean Numenius of Apamea who called Plato "the Moses who speaks in Attic" (Μῶσης Ἀττικίζων) and thereby earned the Christians' permanent gratitude.[101]

In general this pagan dependence is presented as a knowledge that is insufficient to contemplate the truth, as it is mixed with erroneous doctrines, but that nevertheless makes it possible to glimpse the truth on occasion. A less amiable version of the argument of dependence is that the Greeks "stole" or "plagiarized" this knowledge from the prophets, with a negative tone originating in the specification that they neither acknowledged nor showed gratitude for the debt (οὐκ εὐχαρίστως εἰληφότας, *Strom.* 5.1.10.1). After offering a large number of pagan parallels in support of Christian doctrines, and perhaps wishing to prevent any impression of excessive Hellenism, Clement develops this argument of theft with sudden aggressiveness in 5.1.14.140 and at the beginning of book VI, taking from a treatise *On Plagiarism* his evidence that, given that the Greeks were capable of plagiarizing one another, they could very well have copied the prophets also. This insistence on Clement's part cannot be separated from the immediate polemical context, on the one hand with the Gnostic movements, which he himself had accused in book III of drawing inspiration from a misinterpretation of the Greek philosophers and poets, no doubt seeking to avoid being the target of a similar reproach, and on the other hand with pagans like Celsus (perhaps known to Clement), who accused Christianity precisely of having copied the doctrines of the Greeks and presenting a corrupt caricature as something new.[102]

In fact, the argument of priority and dependence may appear ridiculous to contemporary eyes and has provoked both modern disdain for the apologists who used it and the minimization of its importance among those seeking to defend their good name. Neither of these extremes, however, is justified. This argument occupies an important place in the thought of highly cultured and talented authors, like Justin, Clement, Origen, Eusebius, and Theodoret.[103]

17.1, is the first to identify the author of the *palaios logos* with Moses. He is the most likely source of Eusebius' statement in that sense (*PE* 11.13.5, the source of Thdt. *Affect.* 6.26 and Suda *s. v.* Πλάτων). Cf. *OF* 14 with the fragment of the Derveni theogony and Chadwick 1966, 11–16, 129 n.27 on Plato's journey to Egypt.

101 Numenius fr. 8 Des Places; cf. Clem. Alex. *Strom.* 1.22.150.1–4, and Origen's praises in *CC* 1.15, 4.51, 5.38, 5.57. Cf. Edwards 1990.

102 Cf. nn. 39–41. Amelius, a disciple of Plotinus, supposed that Saint John had taken inspiration from Heraclitus for his doctrine of the Logos (Eus. *PE* 11.19.1).

103 Ridings 1995 shows the central place of the argument in Clement, Eusebius and Theodoret. Chadwick 1966 for Justin and Origen. Both offer ample bibliography.

Only at the end of antiquity does Augustine mildly recognize its implausibility. In his day, however, polemics on this subject were already largely out of place, while in previous centuries this argument had been current coin in various spheres of debate. Pagans used it against Christians and vice versa, but both groups started from a lengthy earlier tradition in which priority in a discovery or an institution entailed prestige and religious and political primacy. Orpheus in particular had not only been used as a propaganda tool by the Jews; Egypt, Samothrace, and Crete had made him the transmitter of their indigenous rites to Greece, and the themes of his journey to Egypt and his chronological priority with respect to Homer, necessary for the defense of this scheme, were fully part of the earlier tradition, as we saw at the beginning of this chapter.

In addition, the arguments of priority and dependence fit perfectly with the genealogical metaphor that is the basis for Christianity's self-definition as a family. If Christianity is understood as the family of the legitimate descendants of the prophetic revelation, and pagan wisdom as that of the illegitimate descendants, tracing the channels of genealogical transmission from a common ancestor is entirely coherent with this manner of conceiving reality. The framework of legitimate and illegitimate descent explains both the coincidences that the apologists use for support and those that they brand as bastard thefts that corrupt the truth and transform it into a road to perdition (e. g. the mysteries). It was very difficult to escape a type of reasoning so clear, so widely extended, so convenient for argumentation, and so well fitted to the general intellectual framework.

Finally, it must be added that this formulation of dependence on the prophets simply makes an apologetic weapon out of earlier ideas of Greek dependence on various Eastern peoples, ideas that, although for the most part forming "cultural myths," hide a *mica veritatis* that should be taken into account when it comes time to evaluate the argument. In the same way that many ideas of the netherworld were influenced by Egyptian conceptions (e. g. gold lamellae and Book of the Dead), even if Orpheus's journey to Egypt was a myth, it is also possible to find a certain common Eastern origin for some of the parallels that the Christians spotted between the biblical and Orphic traditions (and transformed into the formula of dependence on the prophets). For example, biblical monotheism may have been influenced by Persian Zoroastrianism, which may also have influenced the monistic formulations with respect to the divine that we find in the Orphic poets and Xenophanes.[104] Centuries later, the Christians observe the similarities and suppose that the two notions had a common origin: if their idea is detached from the apologetic

---

104 Albertz 1994; Burkert 2004 and 2008.

formulation that makes it almost ridiculous, it contains a certain accurate intuition. Chapter VI will return to this subject when examining the possible shared Eastern roots of belief in the unity of the divine, of certain theogonic formulations, and of the presence of a creating and vivifying *pneuma*.

An even more negative way of interpreting the parallels that made the Christians uncomfortable was to explain them as plagiarism by the demons for men's confusion. Justin explains in this way the similarity of the mysteries of Dionysus, which use wine and proclaim the death, resurrection, and ascension of the god, as an imitation, according to him, of the prophecies that announced these events with regard to Christ.[105] It is clear that such an idea is intimately linked to the equation between pagan gods and demons. The argument is similar to that of Greek plagiarism, but more negative, since it avoids locating the origin of the parallels in revelation and hence impedes the recognition of a degree of truth in them. It is rather a case of anti-revelation, of a caricature that confuses. It takes to the extreme the theory of the transmission of secrets by fallen angels to human women that Clement laid out in *Strom.* 5.1.9.10, an account from which the idea of demonic plagiarism may have been derived (as pointed out by Le Boulluec in his commentary to the passage). However, in Clement this knowledge, although illegally transmitted, was originally good, the contrary of the case here. The framework into which this argument fits is not that of legitimate and illegitimate genealogy, but rather the strict dualism of two opposed camps, one of which is the truth and the other pure falsehood. Justin radically separates Greek philosophy, in which he finds much that is positive, from pagan religion and cult, which he considers abominable. As a consequence, he applies the explanation of dependence to the former and that of demonic plagiarism to the latter.

Note, in addition, that the similarity of the Christian sacraments to pagan ritual and of the death and resurrection of Christ to that of Dionysus are precisely the themes that other apologists choose to pass over in silence. It is clear that the argument of demonic plagiarism has its dangers, since, like that of dependence, it can be reversed, as Celsus shows, and Justin's optimism in finding no difficulty in explaining these parallels was not universally shared.[106]

Finally, the simplest and most drastic solution to certain discomfiting parallels was to insist on the superficiality of the similarity in contrast to the

---

105 *Dial.* 69, *Apol.* 1.54. Other Greek myths are equally accused of evil plagiarism, like the story of Danae (Chadwick 1966, 13). Cf. n. 97 for this argument in other authors like Athenagoras or Tertullian.

106 Cf. Chadwick 1966, 18f on Justin's characteristic innocence that makes him incapable of hiding any subject, contrary to other authors, and 22f and 132f with n. 59 on the solid basis for believing that Celsus is directly answering Justin.

vast ethical and aesthetic difference between Christian dogmas and pagan myths. This explanation makes equals out of two modes of belief that had little to do with one another, that of the Greeks in their myths and that of the Christians in their dogmas.[107] In the area of interest here we find it applied above all to Christ's divine sonship in comparison to other Greek sons of gods, Dionysus among them. Tertullian says:

> God's own Son was announced among us, born – but not so born as to make him ashamed of the name of Son or of His paternal origin. It was not his lot to have as his father, by incest with a sister, or by violation of a daughter (*scil.* Persephone) or another's wife, a god covered with scales, or horns or feathers, or transmuting himself for love into the gold of Danae. They are Jupiter's, all these human evils! But the Son of God has no mother from impurity; she, whom men suppose to be His mother in the ordinary way, had never entered into the marriage bond (*Apol.* 21.7–9).

I have chosen Tertullian's text for its clarity, even though it is not mentioned in the editions of *Orphica*. However, Origen makes exactly the same claims in order to differentiate Jesus from Dionysus, with whom Celsus had compared him along with other sons of gods like Asclepius and Hercules. Far from the sophisticated theological elaborations on the subject of the Trinity that fill his theological works, Origen in *Against Celsus* limits himself to highlighting the more scandalous myths of these "sons" as sufficient proof that they are irrelevant, scarcely troubling to justify Jesus's sonship. A century before, Justin had chosen precisely these examples to demonstrate, using the opposite method, that the Christian idea of a son of God was not an unusual belief.[108] The contrast is a good demonstration that apologetic does not choose the arguments of greatest philosophical weight, whether in this case or in others, but rather those believed to be strongest from a rhetorical perspective. In this enterprise, efficacy is a principal measure of truth.

---

107 Veyne 1983, cf. pp. 351ff.
108 Texts quoted *supra*, nn. 31–32.

5.2. Presentation of Christianity in Orphic molds

These explanations lay the foundations for a relationship between the two opposing camps that aims at their strict differentiation in order to be able to substitute one for the other, in such a way that alongside the principle of differentiation, there is one of assimilation. Perhaps the most celebrated aspect of the relationship between Orphism and Christianity, as we saw, is the literary and iconographic identification of Orpheus and Christ. The reasons are precisely the same as those that led to the use of Orpheus as a pagan counterpart to Christ: above and beyond the coincidence in certain episodes of their lives (violent death, descent into the netherworld), and independent of the subtleties of Trinitarian theology and the debates on Christ's nature, of interest neither to pagans nor to adepts of a superficial syncretism, the similarity between the two figures was above all their status as divine men, θεῖοι ἄνδρες. Their intermediate and mediating position between the divine and the human entailed a functional similarity that gave rise to Celsus's comparison of the two as "men possessed by a divine spirit" (*CC* 4.17) and even to syncretistic identifications like the Berlin Seal (*OF* 679).

It is in the context of this type of identification that we need to understand Clement's decision to use Orpheus's molds to present Christ to the Greeks at the beginning of his *Protrepticus*. Clement makes Orpheus's song the cause of the seduction that leads to magic and the error of the mysteries, yet the myth of the singer also offers him the possibility of presenting Christ in the same mold, although with opposite effects. After describing Orpheus's false and enslaving song, he says:

> But not such is my song, which has come to loose, and that speedily, the bitter bondage of tyrannizing demons … It alone has tamed men, the most savage of animals; the frivolous among them answering to the birds, deceivers to snakes, the irascible to lions, the voluptuous to swine, the rapacious to wolves. The fools are stocks and stones: still more senseless than stones is a man steeped in ignorance! (*Protr.* 1.3.2–4.1)

Immediately following and throughout book I, which describes the effects of Christ's song on man and the cosmos, Clement justifies the image with a variety of biblical passages that praise God's power over nature and over the human soul. Among these biblical references, there stands out the appeal to the figure of David, whose song to the sound of the cithara cured Saul of his madness (*1 Sam.* 16:23, alluded to in *Protr.* 1.5.2–4). Roessli (2002) has pointed out that this search for biblical support to justify the presentation of Christ as Orpheus aims to take the precautions necessary to avoid giving rise

5.2. Presentation of Christianity in Orphic molds

to a possible identification of the two, along the lines of their presentation as equals or of the syncretism documented by other evidence (a concern for which Eusebius would no longer see the need). The negative characterization of Orpheus, prior to the attribution of his traits to Christ, runs in the same direction. However, all these precautions prepare the presentation of Christ as Orpheus's replacement in Orpheus's own shape. It is a matter of making notions strange to the mentality of the Greeks more comprehensible to them by way of their presentation in the dress of pagan images. Let us review the biblical ideas, strange to the Greek world, that Clement wraps in the framework of the Orphic tradition: the concepts of Logos and Nomos and the novelty of Christianity as compared to traditional religion.

Clement's protagonist is the Logos. The Alexandrian uses the names of Christ and Jesus very little in comparison with this omnipresent name, naturally much more attractive to the Greek mind, not only of the audience, but probably also of Clement himself.[109] The Christian Logos unites the abstract philosophical concept and the incarnated divine person.[110] The Christian theology of the Logos as the Second Person of the Trinity, identified with Christ, is developed on the basis of the *dabar* of the Old Testament, the Word of God, invariably translated by the LXX as *Logos*. Now, *dabar* has a meaning of "word" and "thing" that is much more immediate than the Greek Logos, whose philosophical development since the Presocratics had taken it far afield from its primary meaning associated with the verb λέγω (to say). Even stranger yet to the Greek idea of the Logos was its essential trait in the Old Testament, the healing (*Mt.* 8:8), vivifying (*Ps.* 10:20), and creating (*Gn.* 1:3) power of the Word of God, which in the Fourth Gospel comes to be conceived of as a personal being identified with Christ (*Jn.* 1:1–14).

How could the pagans be made to understand a Logos with traits so different from the habitual ones of the Greek concept? Clement chooses the myth of Orpheus as the mold in which to introduce this novelty. The ambiguity of the presentation of the Logos as singer (ᾠδός, 1.3.2), as song (ᾆσμα, 1.4.4), and as instrument (ὄργανον, 1.5.4) is fruit of the ambivalence of the Christian Logos as a living person, an abstract entity, and an agent of the di-

---

109 Celsus' bitterest criticisms (which Origen is most at pains to refute) focus on the recent historicity of the Christian God, who became man and rose from the dead. In the presentation of Christianity to the pagans this aspect is left in the shade, while its roots in ancient biblical tradition and its wrapping in Greek molds are underlined. Cf. Zeegers 1972, 317–324.
110 Clement juxtaposes (*Protr.* 1.6.5) an expression of abstract impersonality (ἀρχὴ θεία τῶν πάντων ἦν τε καὶ ἔστιν) with an affirmation of the personal Logos (ὄνομα ἔλαβεν τὸ πάλαι καθωσιωμένον, δυνάμεως ἄξιον, ὁ Χριστός).

vine. Making this Logos equivalent to Orpheus helped to personify the term, which for the pagans was an impersonal entity. In the Orphic milieu the *logos* also had undeniable value as the vehicle of oral and written tradition (*hieros logos*, *palaios logos*, *orphikos logos*), fitting it to serve simultaneously as a pendant to and mold for the Christian Logos intended to replace it. Moreover, the identification of the Logos with song brought it near to its primordial meaning of "word," closer to the biblical meaning, and the myth of the singer served as a letter of introduction to the Greeks for the healing and vivifying power of the biblical Logos.

In myth, Orpheus's song has the power to draw the trees and the wild beasts with its sounds. Clement identifies the animals with the vices of the soul (1.4.1) and makes use of this image to announce the purifying power of the Logos, which heals physically and internally. The equivalence between animals and vices was not new,[111] and the cathartic power of music on the soul was a widespread Pythagorean notion, which must have made use of Orpheus's song as a mythic expression of this philosophical concept.[112] Thus, the idea of an interior cure produced by the Logos is introduced without problems in the mold of the pagan singer.

A more difficult step than curing is giving life to the lifeless: Clement's song is capable of raising the dead (1.4.4; 1.6.1). Together with the myth of giving life to trees and stones, Clement makes use of two images of biblical heritage to attribute such a power to this song: making fertile the desert and the womb of a sterile woman (1.9.3). We are no longer in the realm of restoring life to what once had it, but rather in that of infusing it where it has never been. Now, the power of Orpheus's song also served on occasion to bring the dead back to the world of the living (Eurydice). Between invoking Orpheus for cures, as some magical papyri do, and invoking him to restore the spirit of life to the dead, there is a distance easily bridged.[113] On a philosophical level the connection is parallel: if music is cathartic for the soul, it is possible that it continues to exercise power over the soul after death. The only surviving fragment of the Pythagorean poem *Lyra*, attributed to Orpheus, speaks of the ascent of the soul through the planetary spheres thanks to the power of the cithara (*OF* 417–420). Assisted by the myth, which includes stones and trees as well as animals, Clement presents this vivifying power of music in his text as the continuation of its purifying power.

---

111 It is a popular theme, present already in fables and in compositions like Semonides fr. 7 West. Plato applies it in *Tim.* 91 to the reincarnation of wicked people in animals.
112 Iambl. *VP* 64; Aristox. *apud* Mart. Cap. 9.923. Cf. Laín Entralgo 1970.
113 *PMG* 7.450 and 13.933 P-H; Eur. *Alc.* 357ff, 967ff.

5.2. Presentation of Christianity in Orphic molds

A third function of the Logos is to appear as the sustainer of the cosmos (*Protr.* 1.5.1). Clement is clearly inspired by Pythagorizing speculations on universal harmony, expressed for example in *Orphic Hymn* 34 (p. 212). In this case it must be noted that the biblical Logos is entirely adapted to the Pythagorean image (even if the agent of harmony is the voice instead of the lyre) and thereby loses something of its own character. The Word of God in the Bible is the agent of the cosmos's creation and not merely the sustainer of its harmony, but this aspect of the Logos is absent from the opening chapter of the *Protrepticus*. This choice to omit the creative aspect is all the more remarkable in light of the fact that in order to introduce this notion the author of the *Cohortatio* (15.2) takes advantage of precisely those verses of the Orphic *Oaths* (*OF* 620) that say that God created the heavens upon singing (φθέγξατο) a poetic utterance (αὐδήν): the Greek notion of *poiesis* has been influenced in these verses by the Judeo-Christian idea of creation. However, Clement does not go so far as to take this relatively easy step and avoids slipping the concept into the text; perhaps his ill-defined position with regard to the problem of creation *ex nihilo* (Runia 2002) leads him to omit this aspect of the Logos and adapt it merely to the Pythagorean idea of a sustainer and orderer (not creator) of the cosmos. All the connections traced at the beginning of the *Protrepticus* between the myth of Orpheus, the Pythagorean notion of music, and the power of the Christian Logos can be represented in this way:

Myth of Orpheus	*Pythagoreanism*	*Clement*
Song	instrument (lyre)	singer, song, instrument
Orpheus	Apollo	Logos
attract animals	Cathartic power of music	healing power
attract trees, stones	cause souls to ascend	vivifying power
influence the cosmos	give order to the cosmos	give order to the cosmos

Note that these are proximate notions, but not coincident ones, and hence that the connection is not perfect, but is nonetheless sufficient to introduce the biblical notions in a non-jarring manner, by way of the closest pagan images and ideas. It is probable that Clement had a Pythagorean text similar to the *Lyra* or to *OH* 34 as a model when composing his work. In any case, he certainly had in mind at least the speculative outline of works of this kind, on which his own text may shed some light. Not only is the probability confirmed that the Pythagorean theories that inspired him already made use of the figure of Orpheus, but in addition, in choosing the figure of Orpheus and the Pythagorean speculations associated with his music to present his Logos, Clement has intuited with marked perceptiveness one of the key elements of the Orphism of his day: the power of the voice. This idea is what makes it possible to find a common element in the sophisticated Pythagorean who trusts in the power of Orpheus's song to cause souls to ascend by way of the cosmic lyre and the user of magic spells who believes that he will obtain his desire by repeating some incomprehensible words. It is unsurprising that both – just like the individual who entrusts his salvation to the *legomena* of the mysteries – should link themselves to the poet par excellence, in whom the principle of the power of the word is found elevated to its highest expression. Clement appreciates that this principle is shared by magic, religion, and Pythagoreanism. Therefore, if his singer saves with his music, he does not fail to attribute to his rival the same power of attraction toward evil with his ᾠδαῖς καὶ ἐπῳδαῖς (1.3.1), in an expression that makes it quite clear that he perceives the intimate conceptual and etymological relationship (surviving in English in the connection between "chants" and "enchantments") forged between poetry and magic through the notion of the power of the voice.[114]

Also worth highlighting is the important role that the word *nomos* plays in this metaphor. In 1.2.3–4 Clement plays on the technical-musical sense of the word: measure (law) that governs a given melody.[115]

> "For out of Sion shall go forth the Law (*Nomos*), and the Logos of the Lord from Jerusalem" (Is. 2:3) – the celestial Logos, the true athlete crowned in the theatre of the whole universe. What my Eunomos sings is not the melody (*nomos*) of Terpander, nor that of Cepion, nor the Phrygian, nor Lydian, nor Dorian, but the immortal melody of the new harmony (τῆς καινῆς ἁρμονίας τὸν ἀίδιον νόμον) that bears God's name.

---

114 The *goes* is linked to magic, poetry and music (Burkert 1962, 45). Poetry and magic share the principle of creation of a new mental world (Versnel 1999), which has some links to the biblical creation *ex nihilo* (pp. 304ff).
115 Cf. West 1992, 215–217 for this technical sense of the term: since it is opposed to dithyramb in some authors, *nomos* can contribute to the Christian opposition to Bacchic mysteries in the exordium of the *Protrepticus*. Cf. a similar wordplay with Pindar's famous sentence Nomos basileus (fr. 169 S-M), quoted by Clement (*Strom*. 1.29.181) to refer to biblical law.

5.2. Presentation of Christianity in Orphic molds

Clement opposes the *nomos* of the pagan singers to the new *nomos* of Christ. Furthermore, he makes use of the figure of another mythical singer, Eunomos (good *nomos*), compared to Christ and to the cicada that sings an *autonomous* song to the true God, to round out the play on words.[116] However, it is evident that besides its technical sense, which contributes to the opposition of the new song to the old, the word has a more general sense that Clement's reader, ancient or modern, cannot escape. *Nomos* means "law" in various senses: originally the law of the city, conceived of as custom of divine origin, it was also defined by the sophists as human positive law, in contrast to *physis*; in Hellenistic and Imperial legislation, it was the will of the divinized *basileus*; and in Stoic and Pythagorean philosophy, it was the cosmological order governing the world. Nevertheless, in no case in the political, philosophical, and religious spheres of paganism did it have the sense of the *Torah* of the Old Testament, a Law given by the one God to his people, completed and surpassed in the "New Law" of Christ. The biblical sense of the word is expressly presented in the quotation from Isaiah: "From Sion will go forth the Law, from Jerusalem the Logos."

It is precisely the adjectives αἰδίος and καινός, which accompany Christ's *nomos* in the text, that mark a great difference between the pagan and Christian ideas of *nomos*. "Eternal" (αἰδίος) is not an attribute of *nomos* in the political sense, and in the Stoic and Pythagorean philosophical sense it is more the cosmological order that holds sway over the world than the moral law given by God. To be "new" (καινός) is something even more alien to a *nomos* conceived of above all as tradition and custom, the ancientness of which is a guarantee of its authority.[117] Only the metaphor of song makes it possible to slip the Christian notion of *nomos* into the text without too much of an alienating effect. Now, the constant exercise of substitution that Clement carries out with regard to Orphism in this work allows us to suppose that this text may add valuable material to certain pieces of evidence that suggest that, at least in late Orphic speculation, Nomos fulfilled a not inconsiderable function: seated next to Zeus (πάρεδρος) and father of Justice (*Dike* or *Dikaiosyne*) in the *Rhapsodies* (*OF* 247–248), this abstract divinity is the sole subject of *Orphic Hymn* 64, and it is possible to interpret the νόμῳ of the

---

116 The adjective, with the sense of inner independence (Soph. *Ant.* 821), implies that the hints of truth found in the Greek poets come not from their own wisdom but from divine revelation: cf. *Protr.* 1.1.3: "It is not Eunomos's song that moves the cicada ... it moves and sings of its own will, but the Greeks think that it is the singer".
117 Cf. n. 61 on the consideration of mysteries as a *nomos* (kené) and *hypolepsis kainé*. According to my reading, if the mysteries are a "new supposition," they lose weight against the really ancient truth.

second-century Roman lamella (*OF* 491) in a personal sense. This theorization of Nomos as companion of the supreme God, sustainer of all and savior of the deceased's soul, bears witness to the coincidence of interests between late paganism and Christianity.

Another Christian metaphysical concept introduced by Clement through the musical metaphor is that of *pneuma*. The divine Spirit, which was already a participant in creation (*Gn.* 1:2) and which Christianity elevates to the Third Person of the Trinity, enters the scene here disguised as the breath of life necessary for playing the divine instrument (*organon*), man. After describing how the music of the Logos harmonizes the cosmos, Clement describes its effect on man (*Protr.* 1.5.3–4):

> The Logos of God, despising the lyre and harp, which are but lifeless instruments, harmonized by the Holy Spirit (ἁγίῳ πνεύματι) the cosmos and also, even more, the microcosmos, man, composed of body and soul, and makes melody to God on this instrument (ὄργανον) of many tones; and sings accordingly to this instrument – I mean man – : "For you are my harp, and pipe, and temple."[118] A harp for harmony; a pipe for breath (πνεῦμα); a temple by reason of the word (λόγον); so that the first may sound, the second breathe, the third contain the Lord. ... A beautiful-breathing (ἔμπνουν) instrument of music the Lord made man, after His own image.

By means of the musical metaphor, the Holy Spirit is easily introduced as the breath that makes the instrument (man) sound.[119] It must be remembered, in addition, that the key word that links all these layers of meaning, *pneuma*, was a key concept in traditional Greek (and especially Orphic) cosmological and anthropological speculation: blown air (πνοή) is already a vivifying element in the *Derveni Theogony*, where the commentator translates it into prose as *pneuma* (col. XVIII.3). Judeo-Christian apologists did not fail to take advantage of the importance of *pneuma* in the Orphic tradition in order to introduce it into their own Orphic poems (*OF* 378, 853). We will return to this subject in the next chapter, since this convergence of the Orphic and biblical traditions possibly arises from a common Eastern origin for the image of a divine breath in both. What needs to be pointed out here is that

---

118 On this *adespoton* and similar biblical and pagan texts, cf. Skeris 1976, 211ff.
119 The traditional Greek idea of the poet inspired by the Muse, whose paradigm is Orpheus, fits well within the metaphor of the *organon* (Plat. *Ion* 534c; Plut. *De Pythiae Orac.* 404b, *Sept. sap. conv.* 163e). The image of man as instrument of the divinity has Biblical and Greek precedents, mainly Platonic and Pythagorean: cf. Skeris 1976 (178–9, 193–196) on these and the Christian reception of the theme: e.g. Ps.-Iust. *Cohort.* 8.2, and Riedweg 1994 *ad loc.* Cf. also the late fragment *OF* 414 with a similar image.

Clement's text suggests the possibility that the image of a divine breath that animates man like an instrument was to be found – like that of the cosmos sustained in musical harmony – in Orphic-Pythagorean speculations that inspired Clement in his introduction of the biblical concept.

6. The triumph of Christian strategies

The strategies of selection, manipulation, and presentation of the Orphic tradition practiced by the Christian apologists determined the perception of Orphism that prevailed until the nineteenth century and that endures in part even today. Though the apologetic motives that gave rise to them have been left behind, their results still flourish under very different circumstances. The Christ-Orpheus inaugurated by Clement was tremendously popular both in Byzantium and in Western Europe. Once the apologetic battle against paganism was over and the threat of syncretism had become a distant one, the last barriers to the identification of both figures, enriched with the recovered theme of Eurydice, fell away: on the threshold of the Middle Ages, Fulgentius and Boethius allegorize and draw moral consequences from the story, celebrating the fact that Christ, *Noster Orpheus*, was able to save man's soul from hell.[120]

However, it was not only the Orpheus-Christ presented by Clement and Eusebius that survived from the apologetic literature. Orpheus the prophet and founder of the pagan religion that the Christians proclaimed with such insistence, like their Neoplatonic rivals, also was celebrated as such throughout the Middle Ages. To mention only two famous examples, Thomas Aquinas and Dante placed him at the head of the great civilizing sages of paganism. Orpheus the theologian was definitively recovered in the Renaissance. The great difference was that, far from the atmosphere of apologetic polemics in which Orpheus arose as paganism's representative, his figure was now considered very positively, as the symbol of a pagan mysticism believed reconcilable with Christian truth. The *Testament* entered a new period of popularity, this time not in confrontation with Orpheus's earlier doctrines, as in the apologetic age, but as the logical culmination of his pagan theology, seen through a Neoplatonic prism in the works of Pico della Mirandola or Marsilio Ficino. The key element of this representation of Orphism at the head of paganism, his priority with respect to Homer, was inherited from Neoplatonics and Christians across the Middle Ages. Commenting on the golden chain

---

120 Pòrtulas 2000 on Orpheus' presence in Byzantium, Friedman 1970 and Vicari 1982 on his figure in the Middle Ages. Cf. also III nn. 70, 71, 89.

mentioned by Homer, the Byzantine Michael Psellus said that he introduced it into the *Iliad* "after having frequently attended the Orphic mysteries." Renaissance Neoplatonism took up this chronology and developed the idea of Orpheus as head of the *prisca philosophia* that served as a complement (or even at times an alternative) to Christianity.[121] The editors of and commentators on *Orphica* in the following centuries pursued the same idea: it was the principle that inspired A. C. Eschenbach in his work of 1702 (naturally titled *Epigenes*), re-edited and expanded by M. Gesner in 1764. In 1810 G. F. Creuzer proclaimed this mystic vision of Orphism in an enormously successful book, *Symbolik und Mythologie der alten Völker*. Only when the rational spirit of the Enlightment triumphed and imposed the critical treatment of Classical Antiquity were these daydreams definitely abandoned. After the pioneering work of N. Fréret in the previous century, Lobeck's *Aglaophamus* officially inaugurated the scientific study of Orphism in 1829.[122]

Yet even modern scientific study of Orphism falls into the nets of the Christian apologists on many occasions, whether because of overconfident reliance on their texts, or because of excessive reaction against them, without realizing that their Christianization of the Orphic tradition stemmed from previously existing elements. The idea of Orphism has always oscillated between perception of it as a proto-Christianity and refusal to accept the presence of any element similar to Christianity in ancient Greece. Both attitudes have such clear precedents in the apologetic presentations of Orphism that it is easy to see the inheritance in modern minds, most often unconscious, of the Christian categories for perceiving Greek religion.

---

121 Cf. Thomas Aquinas, *Commentarium de anima*, 1, 1, lect. 12 and 190; Dante *Convivio* 2.1.3; Psel. *Aur. Cat.* 164–167 Duffy (in reality the gold chain of the *Rhapsodies* is one of the clearest Homeric elements in the poem, cf. West 1983, 237f.). On Renaissance reception of Orpheus, cf. Walker 1953 for Italian Neoplatonism, Edsman 1946 for German Protestant humanism.
122 Cf. chapter I nn. 7–8 for the beginnings of the modern study of Orphism.

VI. Orphism in the light of Christian apologetics

> *Quid ergo Athenis et Hierosolymis?*
> *Quid Academiae et Ecclesiae? Quid haereticis et christianis?*
> What does Athens have to do with Jerusalem,
> the Academy with the Church, heretics with Christians?
> (Tertullian, *On the Prohibition of Heretics*, 7.9)

The apologists' strategies distort the real image of Orphism, but they maintain a certain basis in reality in order to appear plausible. This last chapter investigates the question of whether this external and often distorting perspective, which approaches Orphism from the standpoint of Christian interests, can at times shed some light on it, precisely because such a perspective views it from a unique position. When the apologists find Orphic parallels to Christianity, they are projecting their own categories onto an alien phenomenon, but perhaps they also perceive some real point of connection that suggests an *interpretatio christiana* to them. Modern scholars who have reconstructed an Orphism that is too similar to a Christian model have not erred due to a lack of expertise or rigor. Orphism offered certain aspects similar to Christianity, although not identical with it, which led to perception of it as a proto-Christianity. However, the effort to avoid projecting Christian categories onto Orphism should not go too far in the other direction and prevent recognition of these similarities.

Given that a certain amount of comparison between Orphism and Christianity must be made in order to shed light on Orphism from this perspective, it is helpful to recall a few points. First, Christianity and Orphism are not symmetrical phenomena in their mode of existence: in the first chapter I presented a vision of Orphism as a theology of the mysteries in which actual ritual practice was secondary to theological speculation. The network of Christian communities, the hierarchical organization they developed, and the localization of identity in a self-defined group of "Christians" are phenomena foreign to Orphism. The lack of an opposition between orthodoxy and heterodoxy and of an effort at doctrinal systematization of the assemblage of theological ideas that gradually accumulated within the Orphic tradition are direct results of this basic social difference. In addition, this comparison is not between two stable and uniform realities, as if it were between philosophical systems: in both camps, ideas evolved over time and were not even understood in the same way by all their interpreters at any given time. It is more appropriate to establish two ideal extreme poles (e. g., polytheism vs. monotheism, transcendence vs. immanence) and then determine on the basis of the texts where along the imaginary continuum between them Orphic and Christian positions tend to be located. The immense complexity of primitive Christianity, which here serves primarily to shed light on the Orphic tradition, necessarily has to be presented in a simplified manner, restricted to the authors who have been used up to this point.

Even so, a comparison limited to that strand offered by the apologists' texts is possible and desirable. In Orphism theological ideas coexist with a religious experience close to that of the mysteries. In Christianity, the same is true, and the apologists establish relationships of identity, similarity, and opposition between the theology and the experience of each. I will leave the question of the origin of these similarities for last. Right now, the analogy of ideas matters more than their possible genealogy, which could lead to projecting later concepts onto their supposed precedents.

1. The gods and the cosmos

The great majority of Orphic fragments preserved by both pagans and Christians are of theogonic and cosmogonic content. In the purest Greek tradition, the Orphic poets were concerned about the origin of the gods and the world and their mutual relationship, as much as or even more than they were concerned about the destiny of the human soul. Man's nature and destiny appear only at the end of the Orphic theogonies (and in some of them do not appear at all), or else are the subject of other, less prominent genres like catabasis. Let us recall that even the *Orphic Hymns* are dedicated entirely to the praise of the gods and practically ignore the destiny of the faithful.

The Christian authors also refer most often to these subjects, both to attack the polytheism of the theogonic myths and to draw support from Orpheus's supposed monotheism. Despite all their exaggerations, their assertions have a basis in reality: the Orphic poems join a polytheistic framework to a clear monistic tendency. Forgeries like the *Testament* originated in earlier poems that celebrated the unity of the divine, a trait that already appears in the *Derveni Papyrus* as a great intellectual achievement of Orphism. The task at hand is twofold: first, to untangle whatever truth there may be behind the Christians' exaggerations in both directions, the polytheistic and the monotheistic; and second, to describe how these two apparently opposite extremes could fit together and coexist.

1.1. Theogony and cosmogony

The fundamental difference between the unique and uncreated biblical God and the succession of theogonic gods is evident at first sight. Athenagoras places special emphasis on the verb *genesthai* that indicates the generation and hence the corruptible materiality of the gods of the theogonies. The genealogical logic of the theogonies is nothing more than an absurd scandal, without the least shred of theological or cosmic profundity, for Christians like Origen or Gregory of Nazianzus, who mock the "father of gods and men" for the mere fact of this paternity and for being himself the son of another god.

Lactantius is the sole exception. He considers (*DI* 1.5.4: App. VII) the Protogonos of the *Rhapsodies* to be an imperfect expression of the uncreated god. According to him, Orpheus intuited in Protogonos the *deus verus et magnus*, the *praestantissima potestas* who created Heaven and Earth, to whom he gave this name because nothing was begotten before him (*quod ante ipsum nihil sit genitum*); Orpheus also called him Phanes because before anything existed, this god was the first to "appear" (φαίνω) and come into existence from the infinite (*quod cum adhuc nihil esset, primus ex infinito apparuerit et extiterit*); and for lack of a better expression, he said that he had been born from the boundless air (*ex aere inmenso natum esse dixit aliud enim amplius quod diceret non habebat*); everything was generated from Phanes. There are three aspects of Protogonos that Lactantius highlights as shared with the biblical God: being the first, being the only principle of generation, and being the creator of the cosmos. These three aspects are intimately intertwined, but we will consider them in this logical order.

Unlike other apologists, Lactantius does not take the references to birth and generation literally, but rather as metaphors enfolding ideas that the biblical tradition expresses using other images. Whether taken by Lactantius himself or by the philosophical circles that inspired him, this intellectual step is of great importance: Lactantius himself recognizes that there is no room for the eternal and uncreated God in the theogonic framework, since He would necessarily have to be born (as the etymology of "theogony" itself indicates), but he tries to look for content beyond the metaphor. The point he fastens onto in order to drag the god of the *Rhapsodies* toward a biblical interpretation is the trait of "first born" proclaimed by his name, Protogonos.[1]

---

[1] Lactantius is original in this point also with regard to neo-Platonic interpretations of the *Rhapsodies*: both Proclus and Damascius take Time to be the representation of the One (Brisson 1995 I, 70. II, 171). His interpretation of the name Phanes as the "appearing" god does not coincide with the Neoplatonic one, which refers it to his luminosity.

This proper name that puts so much emphasis on temporal priority must have previously been an epithet that designated another primordial god (surely Uranus) and that an Orphic poet had the brilliant idea of nominalizing in a deity of this name. A god whose essence is to be the first-born implies that the previous divine generations cannot be considered to have been born, but rather only to have arisen from the initial chaos.² The theogonic framework does not permit an uncreated god, but it can postulate a god who *marks the transition from primordial chaos to cosmic order*: Protogonos's nominalization establishes an inaugural principle that was lacking in the traditional myth of generational succession. It has been endlessly debated whether Protogonos-Phanes is already present in the *Derveni Theogony* or whether the πρωτόγονος of the papyrus is still an adjective describing Uranus, and what Zeus swallows is Uranus's phallus, and not Phanes as in the rest of the theogonies.³ If the latter scenario is accepted, the epithet reflects an Orphic poet-theologian's intuition of a divine being (Uranus) whose fundamental trait is to be the first, like a presentation in mythological terms of the *arche* sought by the Milesian philosophers. The subsequent nominalization of this "first god" in later Orphic theogonies further develops this theological discovery. If the first scenario is chosen, and Phanes-Protogonos is already present in the papyrus, this emphasis on priority can even be moved up several centuries. In both cases, in devouring the phallus or the first god born, Zeus aims to acquire that condition of being first for himself. The play on words set up by the Orphic poet when he characterizes Zeus as *arche* ("primacy" in its double meaning of "temporal priority" and "command") is maintained in Lactantius's Latin translation with the root of *primus*: "Thus, under the guidance of nature and reason, he understood that a power of principal greatness (*praestantissimam potestatem*) founded heaven and earth. And he could not say that Jupiter was the principle of all things (*principem rerum*), since he was born from Saturn; nor could he say that Saturn himself was their principle, since it was reported that he was produced from Heaven; but he did not venture to

---

2   The previous generations would be Chronos and Ananke in the *Rhapsodies* and the *Theogony of Hieronymus and Hellanicus*. Their abstract essence (Time, Necessity) makes it easier to consider them unborn, for the same reason that another Orphic line quoted by Plato (*Crat.* 402b = *OF* 22) says that Ocean and Thetys were the first to marry, implying that the previous union of Uranus and Gaia was not worthy of that name. These forced interpretations may result from the accumulation of different divine genealogies (West 1983, 119f).
3   West 1983, 85f, Brisson 2003, Kouremenos 2006, 26–28, support the presence of Protogonos-Phanes in the Derveni Theogony. Burkert 1992, 90–92, Bernabé 2002c and Betegh 2004, 120–122 support phallophagy (with stronger arguments, in my opinion – and Richard Janko's, cf. *BMCR* 2005.01.27).

set Heaven as the primeval god (*deum primum*), because he saw that it was an element of the universe, and must itself have had an author. This reason led Orpheus to this first-born (*primogenitum*) god, to whom he assigns and attributes the primacy (*principatum*, from *princeps* = *primus caput*)."

Orpheus's second intuition, according to Lactantius, is Phanes's double-sexed nature, the only form in which Orpheus could express that Protogonos is the sole principle of generation, since "he did not conceive of another form of generation, if he did not have the power of both sexes, as if he were to copulate with himself and could not procreate without coitus" (*DI* 4.8.4). Thanks to this, Phanes does not need a *partenaire* for his acts of creation, unlike other generations of gods. The epithet of Eros also indicates that the power of creation (conceived of as sexual in nature) is rooted in him alone. Several mythological generations later, the fact that Zeus unites himself with his mother (Demeter) and daughter (Core) to beget Dionysus entails another form of expressing the idea that the new king, Dionysus, has a unitary origin, not a dual one, since his ancestry is reduced to a single line, the paternal one. The egg from which Phanes is born (*OF* 78–79, 114–116) is another clear image of the monism of the universe's origin. With these images taken from the theogonic tradition, the Orphic poet seems to insist on the unity of creation: his work is the mythological counterpart of the search for a single *arche* in Milesian philosophy.[4]

Finally, even more relevant than Protogonos's temporal priority and monistic self-sufficiency is his creative and demiurgic activity. This creative activity is already a fundamental part of the *Derveni Theogony* (whether Protogonos appears in it or not), since Zeus is presented, following his act of devouring, as the one who gives rise to the gods and the universe. Lactantius does not waste the opportunity to propose that this Orphic creation can be assimilated to the biblical one, to which end he even passes over the images of sexual generation, which for him are purely secondary, and speaks about the "foundation" (*conditrix, condiderit*) of Heaven and Earth, a Latin translation of the κτίσις that designates the biblical creation, assimilating the Orphic god to Ovid's *fabricator mundi* and *opifex rerum*. Lactantius is not the only one to see in Orphism a parallel to the Judeo-Christian creation: Clement interprets the epithet father-mother (μητροπάτωρ) in an Orphic hymn

---

4   Bisexuality, an egg and incestuous procreation are common in mythological tales of different cultures. Another image for a single principle of generation is the masturbation of the Egyptian god Re (Bickel 1994, 72). Eastern cosmogonic myths images of this kind have been collected by Eliade 1964. Cf. Brisson 1997 on the image of the double-sexed god. On the coincidences between Orphic and Milesian thought, cf. Finkelberg 1986 and Bernabé 2004.

as carrying the idea of an "origin from what is not" (γένεσις ἐκ μὴ ὄντων), an idea near to the Christian *creatio ex nihilo*.[5] Along these lines, W. K. C. Guthrie proposed that the one original idea of the Orphic theogonies was precisely their introduction of a creator god, closer to the Jewish and Christian God than to Greek ideas about the cosmological reordering of matter.[6] It is worth pausing to consider a question of such relevance and examining in detail to what extent the Orphic and Jewish/Christian conceptions resemble one another.

First of all, we should not speak blithely of the Jewish/Christian idea of creation as if it were a monolithic block. Speculation about the origins of the universe undergoes an evolution within the Bible itself, as well as, of course, in the very diverse later interpretations of the beginning of the account of Creation: "In the beginning God made the heaven and the earth. And the earth was without form, and void, and darkness covered the abyss, and the spirit of God moved upon the waters. And God said, 'Let there be light,' and there was light ..." (*Gn.* 1:1).

A lively debate surrounds these verses in both Jewish and Christian circles from the Hellenistic age well into the fifth century.[7] The problem was adapting the biblical idea of God's absolute primacy and transcendence with respect to the material universe He created, an idea made explicit both in these verses and in many other passages in both Testaments, to the categories of Greek philosophy. The principal problem rested in the matter with which God creates the heaven, the earth, and the other elements of the cosmos. If it is preexistent, there is a risk of creating an entity independent of God and shattering the monism that is fundamental to Jewish-Christian theology. If it is conceived of as proceeding (or emanating) from God Himself, however, God's transcendence and the creator's independence with re-

---

5   Lact. *DI* 1.5.4–13, *Epit.* 3; Clem. Alex. *Strom.* 5.14.125 (*OF* 691). Clement's stand on creation is not wholly consistent, even though it falls within the "monarchic dualism" described by Runia (2002): the lack of "being" in matter is compatible with its preexistence. To talk about creation "from what is not," as Clement does (already in 2 *Mac* 7:28), does not automatically imply creation *ex nihilo*, for it can refer either to "not being" or to "not being truly," i.e., to what has no real substance and, nevertheless, exists in a certain way (Lloyd 1966, 114).
6   Guthrie 1952, 106; Parker 1995, 492 notices the difference from biblical creation.
7   Cf. Runia 2002 on this debate and the crucial role of Plato's *Timaeus* in it; on the development of the idea of creation *ex nihilo*, cf. May 1994. As pointed out in n. 5, it is not so much a question of terms (apart from the *locus classicus* of 2 Macc 7:28, Scholem 1970, 61 points out that in Jer. 4:23 the LXX translate as οὐθέν the Hebrew *tohuwabohu*, which means "chaos") as of the establishment of mere "nothing" as *causa materialis* of creation.

spect to His creation come into question, and the field opens for the infinite problems of theodicy.

Plato's *Timaeus* is the principal model appealed to in order to make the biblical creation fit within philosophical molds, beginning with Alexandrian Hellenistic Judaism. Following the *Timaeus*'s model, matter is conceived of by Philo and various Christians, such as Justin and Clement, as existing prior to the Creation, that is, as not created by God, but without granting it the status of an active *arche*, since the only creative principle is God. The "monarchic dualism," in David Runia's expression (2002, 139), contained in this position is not free of internal contradictions, since however inert and lacking in active status matter may be, if it is not created by God, there exists a cosmological principle independent of Him. With Gregory of Nyssa and Augustine comes the perfection of the theory of creation *ex nihilo*, developed beginning in the second century AD by the Christians (and Basilidians), especially Irenaeus, in response to the dualism of Gnostics like Hermogenes, who, since they considered creation essentially evil, made preexisting matter an evil principle independent of God and opposed to Him. Creation *ex nihilo* develops the principle of matter's insubstantiality that was already taking form in the statement in *2 Mac.* 7:28 that God created the world "not from being" (οὐκ ἐξ ὄντων) and postulates that matter appears by an act of the divine will, without this entailing that it is a part of God Himself, who remains entirely independent and transcendent with respect to it.

It is clear that the idea of creation *ex nihilo* conflicts with the fundamental principle of Greek philosophy according to which *being* cannot come from *non-being*.[8] Neoplatonic philosophy responded to the difficulty of matter's existence by means of emanations from the One. On the other hand, Jewish-Christian creationism, due to its relegation of the *causa materialis* and its subordination of everything to an omnipotent will (the Aristotelian efficient cause), was, for the same reasons as the belief in the resurrection of the body, the target of Greek mockery and attack as contrary to all philosophical logic.[9]

---

8   This principle, fully formulated by Parmenides (frr. 292–299 DK), became a basic axiom of all Greek philosophical tradition. For example, Aristot. *Phys.* 1.4.187a27. Plutarch (*Quaest. Conv.* 8.9.2) says that to come into being out of non-being would be uncaused (*anaitios*) and contrary to custom (*paranomos*); also "what there is before the genesis of the cosmos is *acosmia*" (*De an. procr. e Tim.* 5).

9   Gal. *De usu part.* 11.14; Celsus *apud* Orig. *CC* 5.14. The polemics against biblical creationism repeat arguments used against the Stoics, who were also theorizers of divine omnipotence. For example, Alexander of Aphrodisias (*De fato* 200. 22 Bruns) says that God cannot make two times two be five or undo a past event.

The Orphic theogonies follow the principle of matter's eternal existence and include nothing resembling its creation *ex nihilo*. The image of sexual generation implies that matter proceeds directly from the divine being. However, unlike the Hesiodic theogony (as Lactantius himself notes), they present this generation as a conscious process of ordering that inaugurates the cosmos.[10] The figure of a creator god was clearer in Pherecydes: the god Zas gives form to the cosmos by drawing it on the peplos he gives to his wife Ge. That is to say, creation takes place on the basis of preexisting matter, to which it gives form and order, although not existence.[11] However, instead of this new image, resembling that of an artisan making the objects of his craft, the Orphic poets develop the theogonic metaphors of sexual generation: in the Derveni theogony Zeus becomes pregnant with the cosmos in order to beget the gods and the elements of creation anew. In the *Rhapsodies*, the first creation of Phanes-Protogonos-Eros is also the result of sexual generation, since he has that creative capacity that is conceived of as a generating power in the theogonic mold. The Orphic poets take the images imposed on them by their poetic genre (gulping up and generating) to the limit of their possibilities in order to present a god who creates consciously, as if he were an artisan. The verb μήσατο that defines Zeus's creative generation has, like its English translation, "conceive," the double sense of biological and intellectual conception.[12] That is to say, sexual generation is at the same time a conscious act of cosmic design. Polysemy is exploited to the maximum in order to introduce new ideas into the traditional poetic mold: thus, the creative "conception" of the Orphic gods is the equivalent of the cosmological craftsmanship of the Zas of Pherecydes, who as a prose writer had more freedom to innovate. The figure of the Demiurge in Plato's *Timaeus* seems to have been distantly inspired by these creator gods of the Orphic cosmogonies and of Pherecydes,[13] even as it goes beyond them: in calling the Demiurge

---

Cf. Walzer 1949 (esp. 23–39) on these critics. Numenius (*apud* Porph. *De antr. nymph.* 10, Orig. *CC* 4.51) and Ps.-Longinus (*De subl.* 9.9) valued the first verses of Genesis positively, due to the role of *pneuma* and the divine power, but there is nothing to indicate that they accepted any sort of creationism *ex nihilo*.

10 *DI* 1.5.8. Lloyd 1966, 298 points out that the difference between the philosophical cosmogonies and Hesiod's is that the former are not a product of randomness, but have a concrete direction: he does not take into account the Orphic material, which is more akin to the philosophical model in that sense.

11 Schibli 1990, 54–57.

12 *OF* 16–18. Bernabé 2003a, Betegh 2004. Cf. Parmenides fr. 13 DK μητίσατο for giving birth to Eros and Aphrodite. On the coincidences between Parmenides and Orphic poetry, cf. West 1983, 109 and Bernabé 2004b.

13 As suggested by Classen 1962, 19. The Demiurge of the *Timaeus* has precedents

the "maker and father" (ποιητὴς καὶ πατήρ) of the cosmos, Plato unites the images of the artisan and sexual generation in a single figure.[14] The Platonic formulation would have much greater resonance than the preceding ones, becoming for both Christians and Neoplatonists the principal point of reference for a creator god in Greek literature.[15]

It is the case, then, that in Orphism we find for the first time in Greece the idea of a creator god, that is, of a god who does not shape preexistent matter, but rather produces it. Nevertheless, there is a great distance from the Jewish/Christian effort to separate God from created matter, leading ultimately to creation *ex nihilo*. There are other Eastern parallels, especially in the Egyptian milieu, to which the Orphic creator god can be much more easily compared.[16] For there is a great difference between "begetting" the created world and "making" it, and the consequences are significant: even if Lactantius perceives a certain separation between creator and creation in Protogonos, who unlike Heaven-Uranus is not part of the cosmos (*DI* 1.5.4), what can be said for certain is that since the created world is born from him, the cosmos proceeds directly from the deity. The same is true of the creation ἐκ μὴ ὄντων that Clement wants to see in μητροπάτωρ: since they are begotten by him, the products of this begetting do not come from nothing, but from the god himself, even if they are different entities. The continuity between creator and creation indicated by the images used has as a consequence the immanence of the divine, an issue to which we will return shortly.

---

in other dialogues, where he is also described with other images: in the *Politicus*, for instance, he is not only artisan (270a5, 273b1) and father (273b2), but also guide (269e6) and dominator (ἄρχος: 271d3). Cf. Lloyd 1966, 220, 276.

14　*Tim.* 28c, although the name of Demiurge itself, from the same root as ῥέζω, gives preference to the image of the artisan, like Pherecydes, perhaps because prose gave both writers more freedom than poetry to use this image. Lloyd 1966, 208f explains that the image of the artisan is not used in archaic poetry because of its lack of prestige in Homeric society. The first appearance of the creator-artisan is probably Alcman's cosmogony with Tethys as primordial modeler, possibly due to Eastern influence (West 1997, 525). Orphic poetry incorporated the image of the artisan into some hymns: (μέρμερα ῥεζων, *OF* 31; κεραστής, *OF* 414).

15　Most quotations of the *Rhapsodies* and of Pherecydes come from Neoplatonic commentaries on the *Timaeus*. The Christian references to a supreme God sung by Orpheus are always accompanied by much lengthier allusions to the *Timaeus* as in Lactantius, Clement or Pseudo-Justin.

16　Cf. Bickel 1994 for a detailed study of the diverse images of creation in Egyptian cosmogonies, be it through sexual generation or otherwise (spitting, sweating, weeping, speaking).

1.2. The creative voice

The metaphor of generation explains the origin of matter from the deity himself, while that of the artisan, popular primarily from the *Timaeus* onward, implies its preexistence, with a more or less devalued status as cause, depending on whether it is inserted into a framework tending more toward monism or toward dualism. In addition, however, another image can be observed in the opening of *Genesis* that is more suited than either of these to the creation *ex nihilo* in which the interpretation of the biblical account culminates: creation by speech. From light onward (1:3), the elements of the universe come into being as a result of mere divine will expressed through the word. The Word of God (*dabar*, *Logos*) is in this and other biblical passages the divine will's agent, which the Christians will identify with the Son, a co-participant in Creation (*Jn.* 1:3). What can be said for certain is that this metaphor of creation by the word is much better suited to expressing the idea of matter's creation *ex nihilo*, emanating not from the divine being himself, but from his will, since unlike the case of the image of generation, the voice is not perceived as transmitting matter. Although it is not stated that the initial creation of heaven and earth in the first two verses of *Genesis* is a product of divine speech, it was easy to apply the creative acts of the following verses by analogy. Undoubtedly, we must distinguish (with May 1994, 21 ff) between creation *ex nihilo* and creation through the word: the former is a philosophical idea, and the latter an image of creation like so many others. It should be kept in mind, however, that the image allows the development of the idea, not only by facilitating the interpretation of the biblical text in this sense, but also by shaping the mental image of the abstract idea, albeit in anthropomorphic terms.[17]

The same metaphor can be found in some of the Orphic texts examined in chapter IV. The verses from the *Oaths* (*OF* 620) cited by the *Cohortatio* (15.2, p. 196) invoke the "utterance (αὐδήν) that God first sang (φθέγξατο πρῶτον) when he affirmed the entire cosmos with his designs (βουλαῖς)." As was said before, this seems to be a matter of Jewish influence on an

---

[17] Augustine (*Conf.* 12.27) speaks patronizingly of those who imagine the act of creation in anthropomorphic terms: "They imagine God as an omnipotent man ... who by a new and sudden decision, would have produced out of himself, far from him, so to speak, the heaven and the earth ... they imagine words that begin and end, which cease to be when what they have ordered to exist comes to existence." Augustine does not share such ingenuousness, but thinks that it is a simple version of the metaphysical truth, acknowledging in this way that the image of the word that creates from a distance is the most adequate image for *creatio ex nihilo*.

1.2. The creative voice

Orphic poem, although a forgery in the style of the *Testament* cannot be ruled out. In any case, the question now is whether there was any element in ancient Orphism that might give a creative role to the voice and hence facilitate the later entrance of this biblical idea into an Orphic poem, whether by influence or by forgery.

What can be said for certain is that no element even distantly recalling this creation by the word appears in the Orphic theogonies (or in any other Greek theogony). In order to find this image, it is necessary to turn to Egypt.[18] We can only tug on the thread offered by the expression "his designs" to find a certain linkage to the Judeo-Christian idea. God's βουλαί, apart from echoing the venerable Homeric "will of Zeus", has as Orphic precedents the verb μήσατο and the μοῖρα that already appear in the theogony of the Derveni Papyrus, entailing an unquestionable emphasis on Zeus's consciousness and will in his creation.[19] This importance of divine volition in the creative act, which we do not find in Hesiod, may have provided the occasion for introducing the biblical creative word, the maximal expression of this will, in the (probably late) Orphic poem known as the *Oaths*.

The expression αὐδὴν φθέγξατο may also shed light on an element that might have been perceived as a possible connection to creation by the word. Both αὐδή and φθέγξομαι are words that are clearly linked more to the sphere of poetic song than to that of the spoken word. The former signifies the poet's utterance, and the latter his action of producing it. Plato chooses the term ποιητής to characterize his Demiurge, and Jews and Christians have no difficulty enthusiastically following him in using the same term to characterize God.[20] The ποιητής, "maker," designates in Greek both the artisan and the poet, who is conceived of in the same terms: he does not create his poetry out of nothing, but rather gives form to already-existing material provided to him by the Muses. We must not Christianize the concept by attributing creation to the poet.[21] Orpheus himself, the poet par excellence, gave things their

---

18　Bickel 1994, 100–113.
19　Cf. *OF* 14.3, *OF* 16.1–2. The *Hymn to the Sun* quoted by Macrobius says (*Sat.* 1.17.42: *OF* 544), "It has the *noos* and the *boule* of the father" (πατρὸς ἔχοντα νόον καὶ ἐπίφρονα βουλήν). Cf. Hom. *Il.* 1.5: Διὸς δ'ἐτελείετο βουλή (never in a cosmogonic context).
20　Phil. *Aet.* 15; Athenag. *Leg.* 8; Eus. *PE* 3.10.4. Chadwick (1966, 128, n. 21) suggests that the LXX translator of the adjectives for the earth in *Gn* 1:2 (ἀόρατος καὶ ἀκατασκεύαστος) echoes *Timaeus* 51a (ἀνόρατον καὶ ἄμορφον), which designates a primordial chaos denied by Plato, who probably alludes to current theogonic ideas.
21　Curtius 1953, 146: "To translate ποίησις as 'creation' is to inject into the Greek view of things a foreign idea – the Hebrew-Christian cosmogony. When we call

names (ὠνόμασε), but he did not bring them into existence.²² Nevertheless, it need not be denied that once the Demiurge came to be represented as a poet, it was easy for there to be slippage in the direction of the biblical idea of the creative word. However, conceiving of the Creator God as a poet (and not as an artisan) by specifying the sense of the word ποιητής and making His song the act of creation are both slippages of meaning due to Jewish influence (or forgery) in Orphic poetry and should not be projected back onto ancient Orphism. Neither αὐδή nor φθέγξομαι are attributed to a god before *OF* 620, and even if they were, no reasonable Greek would ever have accepted that poetic song entailed creation. Let us recall that even Clement, when he identifies the Logos with a poetic song (ᾆσμα) at the beginning of the *Protrepticus*, does not go so far as to attribute to Him the power to create.

1.3. Cosmology

What Clement does do without hesitation in this same text is adopt a cosmological theory of Neopythagorean origin to describe the functioning of this cosmos about the creation of which Christians and pagans held such different views. The only other Orphic fragments focused on cosmological themes and cited by Christians are of Pythagorean and Stoic coloration and are alluded to by Clement in his discussions of symbolism applied to pagan texts and of plagiarism among Greek authors. Athenagoras also refers approvingly to the cosmological ideas, clearly Stoic in orientation, that could be extracted from the *Theogony of Hieronymus and Hellanicus*, in order to show the material nature of Orphic gods. The texts are few and are cited in discussions of subjects generally unconnected to cosmology, but they clearly illuminate the shared Orphic and Christian attitude in this regard: all the ambiguity and discrepancies surrounding the creation of the cosmos become easy parallelism upon turning to its functioning, an attitude that can be summarized in three principles, cosmological optimism, theoretical flexibility, and subordination to theology.

---

the poet a creator we are using a theological metaphor. The Greek words for poetry and poet have a technological, not a metaphysical, still less a religious, significance." Some examples in Lieberg 1982, esp. 159–173. Cornford 1937, 34f and Lloyd 1966, 279 warn against a too-biblical image of the Platonic Demiurge.

22 *P. Der.* col. XVIII.6; Malal. *Cronograph.* 4.7 (*OF* 97, 139). Versnel 1999 explains how poetry and magic respond to the same principle of creation of another world, even though this creation is not comparable to the biblical *creatio ex nihilo*, since it starts from previous material.

That the Christians consider the world good in itself is an inevitable consequence of their idea of creation itself, as God's work: the first chapter of *Genesis* notes explicitly that following the creation, "God saw all that He had made, and it was very good" (*Gn.* 1:31≈1:8, 10, 12, 19, 21, 26). Of course, the influence of vulgarized Platonism and the spread of ascetic practices gave high standing to the idea that the material world impedes perfect connection with God and therefore is to be renounced as much as possible, but orthodox Christianity never came to consider it evil in itself, among other things due to the weight of biblical tradition. It is not a coincidence that those who took this idea to the extreme of considering the world essentially evil, a prison from the chains of which the soul must free itself in order to re-encounter the divine, were a variety of important Gnostic currents (Marcionites, Hermogenians) who took the indispensable prior step of renouncing all of the Old Testament, and even considered the biblical God as a secondary deity, a malignant Demiurge who created an evil world.[23]

The question of whether Orphism's anthropological dualism could lead to considering the body as essentially evil will be discussed later, but even if such were the case, there is no reason to think that the Orphic poems included the idea that the cosmos is also evil. In the theogonies, the universe is the work of Zeus, and even in the *Rhapsodies*, pantheism of Stoic roots makes the elements of the cosmos the parts of the divine body (*OF* 243). Similarly, no sign of cosmological pessimism can be glimpsed in the Pythagorean construction of the world as harmony that makes use of Orphic poetic images (*OH* 34, *Lyre*). The logical consequence of theological monism is that the cosmos, as something derived from the divine, may be less than the divine, but does not cease to participate in its essential goodness.

The parallelism between Orphism and Christianity in the idea of a good cosmos – given that it is not only the work of an intrinsically good god, but also governed by him – takes on form in the shared image of the King of the Universe: the *Derveni Papyrus* (*OF* 14.4) already calls Zeus βασιλεύς and ἀρχὸς ἁπάντων. The Bible also frequently repeats the idea (e.g., *Ps.* 47:3, 95:3, 148:2). It is not a matter of any kind of influence, but rather of the common idea of a god who holds dominion over the cosmos. It is no surprise that the *Testament*, in which the two traditions are joined, speaks of the βασιλεύς (*OF* 377.8 and 13). The image of the charioteer, of Greek

---

23 Mansfeld 1981, 312–314 explains that this theory exhausted the logical possibilities and was, therefore, expectable: for Plato and the Stoics the world is good and the Demiurge is good; for Aristotle, the world is good but there is no Demiurge; for Epicureans, the world is not good, and there is no Demiurge; for (some) Gnostics, the world is not good, and there is an evil Demiurge.

roots (Plat. *Phaedr.* 264e), is accepted by both the *Testament* (*OF* 378.27) and Philo (*Som.* 1.25) because it expresses the same idea.

This optimism shared by Orphism and Christianity is complemented by great flexibility when it comes time to adapt different cosmological theories. The primitive Judeo-Christian tradition was little concerned with cosmological problems, and as a result, in contrast to the difficulty of reconciling the cosmogonic theories of the biblical and Greek traditions, it had no great difficulty in adapting a number of alien theories on the configuration of the world, which would also serve to make its scorned barbarian philosophy more presentable. The Bible's simple cosmology (Jacobs 1975) could not be compared to the elaborate Greek cosmological models. For this reason Galen, habitually a critic of the Christians, could say, "One can teach new things more easily to the followers of Moses and Christ than to the physicists and philosophers who cling firmly to their schools."[24]

Christianity did not even have difficulty integrating the multitude of gods that populated the pagan cosmos. It needed to do no more than identify them with the Bible's omnipresent demons. The apologists' efforts were directed toward demonstrating the unworthiness of the pagan gods more than toward denying their existence. The elaborate demonology that the Middle Platonists, for example Plutarch, had constructed to populate the intermediate space between men and the higher sphere of the divine was integrated into Christian demonology: the meaning of δαίμων simply took on its more negative coloration as an evil spirit impeding relations with the divine.

The Orphic poetic tradition also served to take in both Platonic-Pythagorean visions and Stoic ones without the least difficulty. If even the unity of Orphic theology is more a matter of form and principles than of content, still less is there such a thing as an "Orphic cosmology"; instead, the cosmological conception depends in each case on the philosophical orientation of the Orphic poet in question. We know that the Pythagoreans made extensive use of Orphic poetry to develop their cosmological ideas, but the cosmological system is the Pythagorean one, not the Orphic one, which is a mere container: for example, the world beyond the grave can be described in Orphic verses as a subterranean Hades (gold lamellae) or as what is beyond the heavenly spheres (*Lyre*).

It is clear that neither Christian nor Orphic theological frameworks are compatible with every possible cosmological position. For example, atomism is adapted by neither one, for obvious reasons, since it is incompatible with

---

24 *De pulsuum differentiis* 3.3. Cf. Walzer 1949 on Galen's references to Jews and Christians.

their respective cosmogonic visions. Precisely due to its much greater dogmatic unity around a theological and cosmogonic orthodoxy, Christianity has a greater range of incompatibility than Orphism: on the one hand, various apologists strive to separate themselves from the complicated cosmologies of the Gnostics, in order to avoid being confused with them (Orig. *CC* 6.25), while at least the latter was integrated a variety of visions more than to exclude, as is evident in works of compilation like the *Rhapsodies* and the *Orphic Hymns*;[25] on the other, fatalist ideas like eternal recurrence and astrological determinism are rejected as incompatible with Christianity, while at least the latter was integrated into Orphic poetry. In general, however, among the cosmological models expressed in poems attributed to Orpheus, elements incompatible with Christianity cannot be singled out. For this reason, Clement in *Protrepticus* 1.5 is happy to also accept a cosmological model of musical harmony that we find in Orphic sources. The biblical ideas that, as we have seen, he takes this opportunity to introduce are not cosmological but theological (*Nomos, Logos*). For this reason, too, Athenagoras (*Leg*. 17) will not contradict Stoic cosmology, but on the contrary, will make use of it as evidence for the materiality and hence corruptibility of the Orphic gods.

It is easy to observe that this convergence in attitudes toward cosmology comes from a common primordial interest in theology, to which cosmological interests are entirely subordinated: any theory that does not contradict theological principles is acceptable. Unlike other philosophical and religious movements that united cosmology and theology much more firmly,[26] the first Christians and the Orphic poets were not so much concerned with how the cosmos functioned as with how it was related to its Creator.

1.4. Transcendence and immanence

In addressing the question of creation, there arose the question of the immanence or transcendence of the creating deity: whether the creation is one

---

25 This is more difficult to prove for the most ancient Orphic poetry, where some opposition to Homeric cosmological notions is perhaps detectable: for instance, Achelous seems to be the origin of seas and rivers in *OF* 16, quoted by the Derveni Papyrus, in clear opposition to *Il.* 21.194–7, where such a role is attributed to Ocean (cf. Herrero 2008a). However, the later *Orphic Hymn to Ocean* (83.4) accepts traditional Homeric cosmology.
26 Stoic pantheism, for instance, meant that cosmology had a religious significance (e. g. the *ekpyrosis*). Cosmology may also have held great importance in some mysteries (cf. Celsus *apud* Orig. *CC* 6.22 on Mithraic cosmology).

with its creator or the two are distinct entities. There was a very lively debate between Platonists and Stoics on this subject, and the Christians sided decidedly with the former (Verbeke 1945). As far as Orphic theology is concerned, Eusebius and Lactantius sought a debating partner in it in this regard.

Between the two poles of the opposition between immanence and transcendence, there is a broad space for intermediate, nuanced, and ambiguous positions. The opposition is more clearly sketched, nevertheless, by contrasting the extremes on each side. Total immanence is expressed in the pantheism that considers God to be in every element of the cosmos, elements that are part of His very being: the creator is not separated from his creation, but instead his creation is merely an extension or form of his all-encompassing being. In the Greek milieu, the Stoics were the ones who most decidedly defended this immanent pantheistic vision. Total transcendence entails an absolute separation between God and his creation, which is his work but not part of his being, even granting that he creates it, has dominion over it, and encompasses it from beginning to end. Platonism was the philosophical school with the greatest tendency to differentiate the divine being from the cosmos, which ultimately emanates from the One but is not confused with him. The extreme position of an even purer transcendence would be marked out by those Gnostic visions that located above the creator God a superior deity whose total separation from the cosmos thereby became even more marked.

Nevertheless, complete consistency is difficult to attain in any dichotomy of this kind. The apologists' Christianity is clearly located on the side of transcendence, in consonance with the previous biblical tradition. All the same, the questions of the appearance of matter and of God's action in the cosmos posed certain problems for an entirely coherent acceptance of absolute transcendence, problems to which it would take Christian theology some time to find a definitive solution. Let us recall that creation *ex nihilo*, which simultaneously solved the problem of matter's creation as an entity separate from God and that of a single primordial cause, only attained its definitive formulation with Gregory of Nyssa and Augustine. Trinitarian theology and its Eucharistic sacramental correlate, constantly undergoing redefinition until the fifth century, are also in large part responses to the problem of a transcendent God who is nevertheless capable of participating in his creation without becoming confused with it.

Orphism, although we will see that it leans more toward immanence, also fluctuates between the two extremes – even more so insofar as it has no drive toward dogmatic coherence – since it presents elements of both. The philosophical schools that used Orphic poems – Stoics, Neoplatonists – exploited this ambiguity in order to adapt it to their own very different frameworks. Orphic poetry provided interpretative material for both tendencies, since it combined images and expressions compatible with both, although those pointing toward an immanent deity predominated.

Thus, the *Hymn to Zeus* (*OF* 31) cited in the Pseudo-Aristotelian treatise *De mundo* (401a25) is used to illustrate Platonizing ideas tending more toward transcendence, because it illustrates the thesis that Zeus is the cause (αἴτιος) of the cosmos, not identical to it: "By Zeus is everything perfectly disposed, foundation (πυθμήν) of earth and heaven" (*OF* 31.2–3). However, this same hymn is cited (and imitated) in their turn by Stoics who take advantage of other expressions of pantheistic value: Zeus is identified with "the breath of everything," "the impulse of fire," "the root of the sea," "the sun and the moon" (*OF* 31.5–6). These Orphic pantheistic ideas are customarily attributed to Stoic influence, when in reality their presence already in the *Derveni Papyrus* should suggest that the influence went in the other direction and that Stoic pantheism found inspiration in Orphic expressions rather than the reverse.[27]

The flexibility of the Orphic expressions and their utility in the debates among Stoics, Platonists, Jews and Christians is even more evident in their later fortune. On the one hand, the *Hymn to Zeus* (*OF* 31) was transformed in the *Rhapsodies* (*OF* 243) into a far longer poem that, amalgamated with another Hellenistic hymn (p. 188ff), presents an absolutely pantheistic Zeus, whose body is formed by the various elements of the cosmos (his head is the heaven, his eyes the sun and the moon, etc.). On the other hand, it was poems in the style of *OF* 14 and *OF* 31 that inspired the Jewish author of the *Testament* for his imitation. The first version (*OF* 377: App. 9), close to Stoic ideas, does not present a transcendent god: he circulates among his offshoots (l. 9), his throne is in heaven, he walks on earth, his hands reach to the limits of the ocean, and the mountains, the rivers, and the sea tremble around him (ll. 17–21). In contrast, the re-elaboration (*OF* 378: App. 10) reworks aspects of the earlier poem by adapting it more to biblical theology and, in addition to mentioning Abraham and Moses, introduces images that better reveal the deity's transcendence, possibly due to influence from the treatise *De mundo*:[28] the king (ἄναξ, l. 7) of the world is transformed into its shaper (τυπωτής), who guides (ἡνιοχεῖ) with his spirit (πνεῦμα) the coming

---

27 Cf. III n. 10 on this matter.
28 Riedweg 1993, 90–95 on the question of immanence and trascendence in both versions; 93f for the possible influence of the treatise *De mundo* (or of a common source); 61 for the Stoic influence in the first version (*OF* 377).

into being of his work (l. 27), from which he appears more separate with these images.²⁹ Nevertheless, expressions of immanence like his circulation among his offshoots (l. 11) are preserved, and he is even called "entirely celestial" (ἐπουράνιος, l. 24). The author of the re-elaboration, like the author of the *De mundo*, seems to accept an intermediate solution, postulating a transcendent god separate from his creation, who nonetheless guides it by way of his *pneuma* and who in passing through it is united to it.³⁰ This intermediate, semi-transcendent idea is acceptable for the *Testament*'s author and for all the Christians who cite him later.

In effect, some apologists appear to be comfortable with Orphic expressions that seem closer to immanence: besides the *Testament*, Clement cites the hymn, later inserted into the *Rhapsodies*, that proclaimed that "one power alone, one god alone exists, great, embracing heaven; one being alone gives form to the universe, in whom everything turns, fire and water and earth."³¹ Granted, the context is apologetic, and Clement is only interested in highlighting one aspect of the verses he quotes, the proclamation of a single god, but the reference does not show excessive discomfort with expressions of immanence, possibly because Clement himself had trouble conceiving of expressions of pure transcendence, as we saw in the case of creation *ex nihilo*.

A century later, the apologetic urgency is less, and the refinement of Christian theology is greater. For this reason, we find in Eusebius, Gregory, and Lactantius protests against the expressions of immanence that they find in Orphic poems. Eusebius – who on the other hand has no qualms about offering quotations from the *Testament* – subjects the *Hymn to Zeus* from the *Rhapsodies* (*OF* 243), the same one that Clement cited with approval, to a ferocious attack. His argumentation allows us to see that Christian consciousness of divine transcendence is now much firmer and that it finds in this hymn's immanent pantheism a useful opponent against which to cement its own position. Eusebius perceives the Stoic foundation that impregnates the *Rhapsodies* and says that this hymn "is in agreement with the Stoics who

---

29 The *hapax* τυπωτής expresses the separation of creation and creator even better than the images of king or charioteer, which underline power rather than separation: a king or charioteer may be seen as different from the cosmos, but they can also be seen as the head with respect to the body. Cf. Lloyd 1966, 272.
30 The *pneuma* is, for the author of the treatise *De mundo* (5.396b28, 6.398b8) the *dynamis* that goes through the whole cosmos. The image of the charioteer stems from Plato (*Phaed.* 246e) and will be accepted by Philo also (*Somn.* 1.157, *Aet.* 83); cf. Verbeke 1945 and Riedweg 1993.
31 *Strom.* 5.14.128.3 (*OF* 243); cf. p. 188; *OF* 543.2, quoted by *Cohort.* 15.2, does not express pantheism, but henotheism (cf. IV n. 116).

claim that ... God is a body, and the Demiurge himself is nothing other than the power of fire" (*PE* 3.9.9), and shortly afterward (*PE* 3.10.3–5), he rejects immanence in all its forms, from the hymn's basic pantheism to the more elaborate formulations that make God the *nous* of the cosmos. It is worth reading the text to see how the attack on immanentist positions (that is, on Stoic pantheism) facilitated the affirmation of transcendence, nuanced by recognition of divine intervention and relying on the experience of revelation when faced with the difficulty of offering philosophical arguments:

> The greatest impiety is to say that the parts of the cosmos are parts of God, and even more, to declare that the cosmos and God are the same, and furthermore, that the Intellect that guides the cosmos is Demiurge of the Universe. In effect, it is pious to declare that the one Maker and Father of the world (cf. Plat. *Tim.* 28c) is other than his work, but it would not be holy to say that an Intellect of the cosmos, like the soul of a living being, is totally united to it, and has all as its dress. Instead, that He is present for all, and cares about the cosmos, is taught by our Sacred Scriptures (τὰ καθ' ἡμᾶς ἱερὰ λόγια).[32]

Gregory of Nazianzus also ridicules pantheism in the verses that make Zeus present in the dung of sheep, horses, and mules (*OF* 848).[33] From the perspective of his appreciation for the Orphic poems, Lactantius (*DI* 1.5.4), with divine transcendence in mind, considered Protogonos to have come into being as creator in the face of the impossibility that the creator could be Uranus, who is identified with heaven and cannot be simultaneously the work and the work's author (let us recall that Cronus and Zeus were ruled out by their condition of being born of others). The extent to which Lactantius was correct to project his own concerns onto the Orphic poet is a question that should be approached with prudence. It is possible that it was an intuition of separation between the creator and his work that impelled the Orphic poet to introduce Protogonos as creator in place of Uranus, or that impelled Pherecydes to prefer the image of the artisan, but we cannot prove it. Nevertheless, Lactantius's observation can shed light on the expressive mechanisms that reflect theological ideas like immanence and transcendence.

We have seen that despite the difficulty of maintaining an absolutely coherent position, the biblical tradition – like the Platonic one – tends toward

---

32 This is an explicit confrontation of Scripture with the *Rhapsodies* (entitled ἱεροὶ λόγοι), according to the symmetrical confrontation explained in chapter V (e. g. Orig. *CC* 1.18).

33 Greg. Naz. *Or.* 4.115. These lines may be a parody by some opposed philosophical school or a serious formulation of extreme pantheism. In any case, Gregory follows an earlier polemical tradition (already in Philostr. *Her.* 25.2).

a transcendent conception of the deity, the theological formulation of which is gradually refined over time. On the other hand, Orphism, although capable of manipulation in both directions, tends to formulations more inclined to immanence, a propensity that culminates in the pantheism of the Zeus of the *Rhapsodies*. Thus, despite the multiple variations on each side and the convergences produced by apologetic needs, like the *Testament* and the apologists' quotations from Orphic poems, the two contrary tendencies can be established as the more stable positions that oppose Orphism (in agreement with the Stoa, due to reciprocal influence) and Christianity (agreeing here with Platonism) in this regard.

This divergence has multiple causes. In the biblical tradition, for example, it is easy to associate the presence of God in the elements of the cosmos with their idolatrous adoration. However, I want to focus solely on an aspect that the texts studied make it possible to highlight: the role of metaphor in the formation of concepts. The Greek theogonies' ideas about the divine and creation are essentially incompatible with the Jewish/Christian ones, because ideas are not adapted to different images and metaphors while preserving the same essence; rather, the metaphor itself gives them being. Such abstract concepts are not conceived outside of metaphor, and if the metaphors are different, so are the ideas. The literalness with which Athenagoras takes the verb *genesthai* is more accurate, even though it paradoxically requires much less intellectual complexity, than the doubling of metaphor and content asserted by Lactantius.[34]

Thus, the images of physical generation that are characteristic of theogony (gulping up and procreation) tend in essence to unite the procreator with the procreated in a single nature. For the same reason that the gods of various generations can be identified with one another (Zeus with Phanes and with Cronus), one god can be identified with other gods and elements generated by him.[35] The image of ingestion is even clearer: as everything is

---

34 Athenag. *Leg.* 17.1–18.6, Lact. *DI* 1.5.4. Cf. Lakoff/Johnson (1981) for metaphor as a conceptual template. Lloyd 1966, esp. 205–209 anticipates several cognitive approaches in his consideration of Greek cosmogonies.

35 It is probably the desire to be free from the generative image in order to better express transcendence that led to designating God with the epithet προπάτωρ (pre-father), very popular in Hermetic circles (fr. 23 NF), which is also found in Iamblichus (*Myst.* 8.4) and also in magical papyri (*PGM* IV 949, 1988, XII 236), in another example of the continuity of philosophy, religion and magic. The same intention may underlie the term πάππος (grandfather), coined by the Neopythagorean Numenius to describe the principle above the Demiurge (*apud* Procl. *In Plat. Tim.* 1.303.27). Cf. Athanassiadi/Frede 1999, 18. However, none of these alternatives is able to completely eliminate the generative conceptual frame.

1.4. Transcendence and immanence

within Zeus and forms part of him, it continues being part of him when he gives birth to it. It should not be surprising that in Orphism, whose principal poetic genre is theogony, an immanent conception is prevalent, which can even easily end up in pantheism. Let us recall (p. 188) that the pantheistic hymn to Zeus (*OF* 243) not only appears in the *Rhapsodies*, but also was already circulating independently under Orpheus's name before being integrated into them, demonstrating the immanentist tendency imposed on the Orphic tradition by the theogonic images.

In contrast, the metaphor of the artisan (and that of creation by the will expressed through the word) is better suited to conveying the separation between the creator and his work[36] (so much so that it entails, as we have seen, a problem for monism as a result of matter's independence). This image of the artisan is the one that prevails in Platonism with the Demiurge of the *Timaeus* and in the biblical tradition as well, in which God makes and shapes the Creation and does not beget it. The images and vocabulary of generation are reserved in Platonism for the emanations from the One, and in Christianity for the emanations that explain the Trinity (God the Son is "begotten, not made"). It is not surprising, then, that Platonism and Christianity converge in the transcendent conception of God.

The process should not be imagined in terms of an *a priori* abstract concept – immanence or transcendence – in search of the most suitable metaphors for its expression. On the contrary, it is from the metaphors imposed by the poetic or mythological tradition in each case that there arises the immanent or transcendent conception toward which each philosophical or religious movement will tend and to which it will ultimately give abstract formulations, now independent of metaphor but formed on the basis of it. The mythological image is not a literary adornment, but rather is what gives forms to and determines the theological idea extracted from it. Thus, theogony is not only a poetic genre that makes use of mythological material, but also a form of conceiving of and speculating about the origin of the cosmos, a true conceptual metaphor of enormous power in the Greek world until the end of antiquity: Proclus himself acknowledges that sexual generation (*genesis*) is even in his day the conceptual mold in which the abstract philosophical concept of "cause" can be most vividly imagined.[37] It is the

---

36 Cf. Aug. *Conf.* 12.27 (n. 17). Lloyd 1966, 291 says about Plato's Demiurge that the image of the artisan is at the origin of the notion of a *causa efficiens* separated from its object, and also of the idea that this object results from a rational and predetermined design (a notion that Orphic poetry is able to introduce in the theogonic image with the verb μήσατο, *OF* 16).
37 Procl. *Theol. Plat.* 1.28.5. Plato distinguished between rational demonstration and

continuity of metaphors that gives a certain cohesion and unity to the Orphic tradition through all of its ideological fluctuations.

1.5. Monism

The differences between Orphism and Christianity on the subject of creation can be passed over in the face of their great common element, the monistic tendency that postulated the unity of the divine. This tendency is already present in the most ancient Orphic evidence and not only continues, but becomes stronger with the evolution of the Orphic tradition until late antiquity, becoming one of the most effective moving forces behind so-called Greek "monotheism."[38] With this term the discussion descends from pure theological abstraction and begins to venture into the difficult terrain of cult.

The term "monotheism" is too simple to reflect the ambiguous complexity of belief in a single deity. What can be said for certain is that the simple contrast between Jewish/Christian monotheism and pagan polytheism, a clear product of Christian apologetic insistence, is absolutely unsustainable. Especially in philosophical religion, belief in a god no longer merely supreme, but unique, was common coin during the Imperial Age, with clear precedents already during the classical period. Explicit manifestations of adoration of a single deity in the cultic sphere were also not lacking, above all in the solar cults.[39] In wide sectors of paganism, the unity of the divine was felt in practice and theorized in philosophy beginning long before the appearance of Christianity on the scene, and this tendency gained strength with the anti-Christian opposition. Julian was at least as much of a monist as his rivals. This tendency also made it easier for the Christians to construct their theology on the basis of categories drawn from monistic philosophy, making use of the dominant theological *koine*.

However, "monotheism" is not a neutral term. If the philosophical formulation of Greek and Judeo-Christian monism could be similar, the religious reality was very different. In formulations like the biblical and Islamic

---

mythical image, and sometimes explicitly renounced the former because only the latter was capable of expressing the indemonstrable (Lloyd 1966, 300).
38 On the validity of this term for a clear pagan religious trend in Late Antiquity, cf. Athanassiadi/Frede 1999. Against, Edwards 2004. In the recent volume on the subject edited by Mitchell/Van Nuffelen (2009), alternative designations like megatheism and monolatry are discussed.
39 Cf. West 1999 and Frede 1999 on philosophical religion; Fauth 1995 and Liebeschuetz 1999 on solar cult.

1.5. Monism

ones, monotheism not only expresses the belief in a single god, but also implies the idea – which is not a philosophical idea, but a purely religious one – that the One God is a particular personal god, revealed in a specific manner and adored in a concrete way, to the exclusion of any other. This conception was practically unknown in the Greek world, in which the cult of one particular god was never considered the only proper cult of the true deity.[40] For the Greeks, the cult of one god did not demand the renunciation of the rest. For this reason, the term "monotheism," without specifying adjectives such as "exclusivist," is loaded with theological connotations and can be a dangerous way to designate the vast majority of Greek beliefs in a single god, even if the philosophical formulation of those beliefs might be as monistic as the Christian one: the religious expression of those beliefs lacked in Greece the Christians' biblical exclusivism.

If it is necessary to assign a label to the Greek religious tendency toward theological monism, a more suitable one appears to be the term "henotheism," coined on the basis of the acclamation "one is god" (εἷς (ὁ) θεός), much repeated in hymns, inscriptions, and papyri.[41] The phrase does not mean "there is no other god than this one" so much as it does "there is no other god like this one."[42] Such an expression can easily be pushed in the direction of exclusivist monotheism (in the Christian Creed *heis* designates each Person of the Trinity), but it does not necessarily deny the existence of other gods. It simply gives primacy to the god acclaimed, a primacy that may be more or less absolute. This attitude maintains the ambiguity that permitted Greek religion to fluctuate without glaring inconsistency between a monistic conception of the divine and a polytheistic traditional language. Such is also the ambiguity that we find in Orphism.

In general terms, the polytheistic framework is transformed into a monistic one in two ways: the first is the hierarchization of the gods, that is to say, their subordination to one supreme god whose designs they are limited to carrying out and who ends up being more divine than the rest; the second is syncretism, the identification of some gods with others to the point that they

---

40 The best-known exception is the cult – very popular in Imperial times – of *Theos Hypsistos* (the Highest God), which has an exclusivist orientation, resulting precisely from probable Jewish influence (Mitchell 1999; against his thesis, Belayche 2005).
41 Petersen 1926 collected all the available testimonies of this expression and analyzed its meaning. The first instance is in Xenophanes fr. 23 DK. Cf. West 1999, 32.
42 Versnel 1990 is the best study of the henotheistic attitude and its ramifications. It could also be called (Versnel 1990, 194 n. 332) "affective monotheism," in the sense that for the individual there is no other god in the moment of cultic worship.

all become equivalent and as a result, really only one, invoked under the name preferred by the believer.[43] For example, the epithets "father" or "king" customarily accompany the first path toward unity; the adjective *polyonymos* (of many names) reflects the second path.[44] Both processes take place over a long span of time, are never entirely linear, and share a common trait: they tend toward henotheism while maintaining polytheistic language.

Orphic poets cultivate both methods with particular success, due to their skillful handling of two traditional poetic genres, the theogony and the hymn. In effect, theogony, as an account of the succession of the gods, is a genre more inclined to reflect the subordination of younger generations to their elders or, once the struggles for succession begin, at least to whoever holds power. That is to say, in the theogonic framework the henotheistic orientation is achieved through the hierarchization of the gods. In hymns, in contrast, the typical series of strung-together epithets make it possible to also juxtapose the names of gods, who are thus very tangibly identified with one another, without need for explanation, more by mystical intuition than by logical reasoning.[45] The Orphic tradition not only cultivates both genres separately, but also combines them from the beginning: the *Derveni Theogony* reaches its climax in a four-line hymn to Zeus, and the *Rhapsodies* end up expanding this hymn to thirty lines. Both hymns celebrate that Zeus has gulped up the entire universe, the gods included, and hence made them part of himself. This episode of gulping up, originating in a traditional mythological image,[46] is transformed in the hands of the Orphic poet into the justification for the absolute centrality of a single god, Zeus, to whom the theogony at this point dedicates a hymn.

The Orphic poets also cultivated the composition of independent hymns, besides those included in the theogonies, and in these independent hymns the possibilities of syncretism by juxtaposition were systematically exploited. We find a line of this type already in the *Derveni Papyrus*: "Demeter Rhea Ge Meter and Hestia Deo" (*OF* 398). The *Orphic Hymns* are evidence

---

43 Cf. Athanassiadi / Frede 1999, 8f on these two categories. I have treated the Orphic use of theogony and hymn to achieve hierarchization and syncretism, respectively, in Herrero 2009.
44 The epithets πατήρ or βασιλεύς are traditional; πολυώνυμος appears for first time in the *Homeric Hymn to Demeter* (18), for Zeus. Arguments for the *polyonymia* of the divinity in [Arist.] *De mund.* 401a 12, Apul. *Met.* 11.5, Celsus *apud* Orig. *CC* 8.12, Max. Tyr. 39.5.
45 Sometimes the name given is justified through conjunctions like οὕνεκα (*OF* 60).
46 If Zeus swallows Uranus's phallus, the precedent would be the Hurrite myth of Kumarbi; if it is the god Protogonos whom Zeus gulps up, the image is obviously the same as Zeus swallowing Metis in Hesiod (*Theog.* 886ff). Cf. n. 3.

1.5. Monism

that this style of theological composition remained in vogue. It must be pointed out that the Sun appears to have played a central role in this syncretistic path, as can be demonstrated in the hymn cited by the *Cohortatio:* "One is Zeus, one is Hades, one is Helios, one is Dionysus" (*OF* 543). It is no surprise that the Sun, as an evident image for the one who holds dominion over the universe, should become the point of integration for a variety of deities who could easily be identified with a solar god. In the imperial age this syncretistic role was crucial.[47] It was also key within Orphism: not only are a variety of Orphic deities united in the Sun (*OF* 538–545, *Orphic Hymn* 8), but the Sun also becomes the connection that facilitates syncretism between the luminous Phanes and another solar deity, Mithras (*OF* 678). However, the logical identification of Helios with Phanes, and his consequent integrative role, certainly goes back to the Hellenistic period, in which the evidence shows Phanes-Helios accumulating a variety of divine names, especially that of Dionysus.[48] Moreover, there are sufficient indications to affirm that the Sun (traditionally associated with Apollo) already had a central role in at least some Orphic theological speculations during the classical age,[49] a prominence that would facilitate the identification of a variety of deities with the Sun and their consideration as a single deity. Even in the *Derveni Theogony* Helios's presence cannot be entirely ruled out, although this possibility is not customarily considered, since the sun's appearance in the papyrus is taken to be a result of the commentator's allegory more than of a mention in the Orphic theogony.[50]

---

47 Cf. Fauth 1995. This kind of syncretism also includes the biblical God (e.g. Iao identified as Helios in *PGM* 50.6, or in Apollo's oracle in Claros quoted by Macrobius *Sat.* 1.18.20). The solar elements integrated into Christianity are evident (e.g. the date for the birth of Christ). Julian made the Sun the core of his neo-traditional theology (Liebeschuetz 1999, 187–192).

48 D. S. 1.11.2 quotes a *Hymn to the Sun* (*OF* 60 I) that is a direct precedent for Macrobius' (West 1983, 206 n. 95). Cf. also Helios' presence in one Thurii leaf (*OF* 492.3, fourth- to third-century BC), and in an inscription from Olbia in Crimea (*OF* 537), similar to the bone tablets of the fifth century BC in the same city: Βίος-Βίος, Ἀπόλλων -Ἀπόλλων, Ἥλιο[ς]- Ἥλιος, Κόσμος-Κ[όσ]μος, Φῶς-Φῶς .

49 Aeschylus in the *Bassarai* presented Orpheus adoring Apollo-Sun as the supreme god (*OF* 536); cf. West 1983, 13 n. 34 for some traces of intellectual solar cult in Sophocles.

50 In the Derveni Papyrus there are two mentions of the Sun that the commentator seems to put it in Orpheus' mouth: col. XIII 9: αἰδοίωι εἰκάσας τὸν ἥλιον; col XIV.3: γενέσθαι φησίν ἐκ τοῦ ἡλίου τῆι γῆι. If in the poem Zeus swallows Uranus' phallus (n. 3), it is probable that the commentator takes it as allegory of the Sun for its vivifying power (so Betegh 2004, 123); if Zeus instead swallows Protogonos-Phanes, a double allegory is more complex (from "venerable" to

In any case, the combination of hierarchization and syncretism makes the Orphic tradition a very important vector of the general tendency toward henotheism that culminates in the Imperial age. Stoics and Neoplatonists exhibited no more hesitation in taking advantage of this potential for their monistic constructs than the Jewish and Christian apologists, as we have already learned. Now, in order to characterize this Orphic henotheism, and above all, in order to make clear what it is *not*, the comparison with its Jewish and Christian parallels, which we have seen the apologists rely on for support, turns out to be of great interest.

Biblical monotheism developed out of a context as polytheistic as the Greek one, with the intermediate step of henotheism.[51] Multiple biblical passages speak about other gods inferior to the God of Israel. In a slow process, there was a shift from the prohibition of adoring those gods to the denial that they were eligible to be adored, that is to say, to postulating not Yahweh's supremacy, but his status as the sole true God. However, the biblical passages that speak about "gods" led to some flexibility, in both Jewish and Christian circles, when it came time to speak about the intermediate beings that inhabit the space between God and men, like angels and demons. A variety of passages in the apologists' works admit the existence of the pagan gods, just as the existence of the foreign gods was admitted in various passages in the biblical prophets, pointing out their inferiority and unworthiness. In Christianity, in addition, the introduction of the incarnate Son and of the Holy Spirit led to multiple debates that forced constant theological refinement in order to avoid their subordination to the Father, while maintaining divine unity. A useful distinction can be drawn (Dillon 1999, 69) between an extreme monotheism, like that which dominates Jewish and Islamic theology, and a moderate monotheism that admits the existence of less-divine beings, who are nonetheless still granted the title of gods, under the supreme deity, as Platonism did. Christian orthodoxy (not to mention its multiple heterodox variants) occupies an intermediate position and one that during the first few centuries fluctuated between both poles.

"phallus" to "sun"), so there would be a greater possibility that the poem identified Phanes and Helios. The case for Helios' presence in the poem was defended by Rusten 1985, 135–137.

51 Albertz 1993 provides a grand synthesis of the evolution toward monotheism in ancient Israel. West 1999 describes such processes in several Middle Eastern religions and in Greece.

Thanks to the philosophico-theological *koine* coined fundamentally by Neoplatonism, the Fathers of the Church succeeded in solidifying a great intellectual construct that managed to combine into a coherent system the not-easily-reconcilable principles provided to Christian theology in less philosophical terms by historical revelation. In the opposing camp, the Neoplatonists fitted Orphism and other pagan traditions into a similar and equally monistic enterprise that sought to explain multiplicity. This shared tendency toward monism enabled both Orphism and the Bible to fit into constructs of similar design. The apologetic use of the monotheistic Orpheus was based on this concordance. However, this basic agreement should not hide a crucial difference, which gave rise to the simplistic ancient and modern opposition of (pagan and especially Orphic) polytheism to monotheism: the language used to express this monism.

On the one hand, Christianity's basic language for referring to its God, despite all its ambiguities, is inherited from Judaism and consequently tends to reflect not only the unity of the divine (as would be indicated by *heis*), but also the exclusivity of the Bible's jealous God (marked by the prefix *mono-*). This language arose in a polytheistic context out of the specific historical circumstances of the Jewish people, who took their God as the basis of their identity as a people. The simple solution of adoring this one God under a variety of manifestations was not accepted by Hebrew theology as a result of the constant struggle with neighboring peoples. For the biblical tradition, Yahweh is not the equivalent of Baal: the history of pre-Exilic Israel revolves in large part around the struggle to prevent the syncretism that identified Yahweh with the Canaanite Baals and that became the most abominable sin, idolatry. Precisely the frequency with which the Israelites fell into such sin helped them to develop a purer conceptualization of Yahweh's exclusivity and of the idolatry that violates it, above all during the Babylonian Exile. Post-Exilic Israel maintained this exclusivity as a mark of identity, and despite the multiple witnesses to the participation of Iao-Yahweh in Hellenistic syncretistic conglomerates, such identifications were never accepted at the level of orthodoxy (pp. 113f).

This exclusivist radicalism was inherited by the Christians, who would also make it their mark of identity. The God incarnated in Christ is the God of Abraham, Isaac, and Jacob, and the Christians considered themselves the *verus Israel* that has understood the revelation. Considering other gods as existing or equivalent continued to be idolatry. The persecutions that imposed sacrifice to the traditional gods undoubtedly reinforced this perception of exclusivity. The *Acts of the Christian Martyrs* are full of examples of perplexed Romans who try to convince them to adore their god under whatever invocation they wish, only to be confronted with a refusal to identify God with any other name.[52] Despite the fact that syncretistic practices were widespread, the dogmatic formulation would ultimately carry the hallmark of the exclusivist current. Christianity doubtless inherited much from pagan religion, but that inheritance was never accepted as such: pagan practices were Christianized after first removing the pagan label, not accepting them as equivalents.

In the other camp, in Orphism (and in paganism in general), we find the complete reverse: although there is a clear tendency toward monism, polytheistic language is maintained, emphasizing the unity of the various gods without denying their personality (on the contrary, exalting each one of them). So great a divergence on the basis of similar principles is due to the fact that the historical circumstances that fostered the leap to total monotheism in Israel never applied in Greece and Rome. On the contrary, the traditional gods were maintained as objects of cult despite all social and ideological changes, and any innovation in this terrain ran the risk of being considered laughable or dangerous. No Greek ethnic or political group took the adoration of its god as its principal mark of identity in contrast to another. In the Orphic context, only once do we find a note of exclusivity: the *Derveni Theogony* says (*OF* 12) that when Zeus swallowed the Universe and the gods, "he came to be the only one" (μοῦνος ἔγεντο). However, what this *monos* emphasizes is that there is nothing outside of Zeus, implying the unity of everything within him, and for this reason, it is generally translated as "solitary" (Burkert 2008). That it is not incompatible with the other deities is obvious, since they are born again of him.

Two lines from the brief version of the *Testament* (*OF* 377) illustrate the difference of language and emphasis, coexisting in a single poem in which the combination of conceptions is of great interest. We read in l. 8, εἷς ἔστ', αὐτογενής, ἑνός ἔκγονα πάντα τέτυκται. The line is very similar to others in the *Hymn to Zeus* that emphasize this unity, and it is clearly inspired by this Orphic model. However, shortly afterward in l. 13, the poem says, οὐδέ τις ἔσθ' ἕτερος χωρὶς μεγάλου βασιλῆος. The explicit denial of "another god" is of undeniably Jewish/Christian coloring. The first line emphasizes unity; the second, exclusivity. The difference can occasionally be lost sight of due to apologetic convenience, when it is unity that is to be highlighted, but it never ceases to be present. The fact is that the apologists, on the alert for a syncretism they judge dangerous and impious,

---

52 E. g. *Mart. Pion.* 19.163. Cf. Lane Fox 1986, 419–492. A century later, this exclusivity will turn into intolerance against pagan cults, an intolerance which pagans like Praetextatus or Symmachus eloquently deplore (Liebeschuetz 1999, Gnilka 1993).

never lose sight of the fact that Zeus is not simply the *interpretatio Graeca* of the biblical God: they have the issue of the personality of the gods very much in view.

1.6. Personality and abstraction

The two formulations of theological monism, the henotheistic and the monotheistic, coexist in the *Testament*. However, this is an exceptional case, made possible only by the omission of the gods' personal names under the impersonal *ho theos*. Were this not the case, compatibility would be very difficult. Even when Judeo-Christian apologetic appropriates Orphic frameworks in order to adapt them to its own god, it depersonalizes them entirely, removing all the mythological baggage they carry with them and leaving them stripped down to their monistic essence. In this regard, it is clear that hymns in the Orphic style, in which the deeds of the gods are not recounted in narrative form, but instead epithets are strung together, are much better suited to this impersonal god whom the Christians can identify with their own than the theogonies, whose narrative passages include tales that personalize the god. The *Testament of Orpheus* is inspired by the Orphic hymns to the supreme god, surely Zeus, but names him only as *theos*. In the same way, the three passages with which Clement accompanies his citations of the *Testament* in *Stromata* V come from other Orphic hymns surely addressed to Zeus, but in none of them is he named as such, but rather as the sole Lord of the universe and the universal Father (*OF* 243, 690, 691).

There are only two exceptions to this general rule. First, the *Hymn to the Sun* (*OF* 543) cited by the *Cohortatio* (15.2), which calls the single god (εἷς θεὸς ἐν πάντεσσι) by the names of Helios, Zeus, Hades, and Dionysus in the previous line. The emphasis is on the unity of the divine, not on the names, but it must be recognized that Pseudo-Justin goes against the common tendency here. Perhaps he does so in order to give plausibility to a second line, a possible Jewish or Christian forgery (pp. 195f), which if it were not accompanied by the first would be too neutral to be credible as Orphic. The other exception is Lactantius (*DI* 1.5.4), who takes Phanes and his creation (of which he omits the details) as an example of the creation of the world by God. He is more open-minded than other apologists, but he does not fail to note that Orpheus uses these names because he cannot attain the truth (although he does have an intuition of it). Let us recall, in addition, that neither Pseudo-Justin nor Lactantius criticizes these gods in the same work (unlike Clement, for example): they have not spoken of Zeus's incests or Phanes's monstrosity, and this permits them, after having depersonalized them as much as possible, at least this timid identification of them with God. The silencing of the theogonic acts, absent from all these assimilations, is even clearer. When Clement cites the last two lines of the *Hymn to Zeus*, which allude (without naming Zeus) to the re-creation of the gods he had devoured in his belly, he calmly interprets them as an allusion to the future resurrection of the dead (*Strom.* 5.14.122.2).

The names of the Greek gods, and even more their theogonic acts, are loaded with the heavy weight of personality. They cannot be assimilated to the biblical God, whose revelation is entirely personal, with deeds that his faithful cannot forget. The Marcionites did indeed take the step of renouncing the entire Old Testament revelation. Unlike the apologists, the Gnostics were not in the habit of attacking the Greek myths, but rather adapted them frequently to their own frameworks, which were far more flexible insofar as they did not depend on a concrete and historical tradition of revelation. The fact is that calling Yahweh Zeus or Dionysus entailed forgetting his previous history, turning it into a mere symbol at most.[53] Moreover, the historicity of revelation was for Jews and Christians an irrenunciable argument in support of their position. For them, the gods' "past" made up part of their essence and made them concrete deities not easily interchangeable.

If we measure the distance between the extremes of the gods' impersonality and absolute personality, the biblical God is very close to the latter end of the spectrum, far more so than the Orphic gods. The biblical God cannot be *polyonymos*, however much the pagan camp insists on equating Him with other supreme gods,[54] while the Orphic gods can be, even more easily than those of other Greek traditions.[55] However, the Orphic gods, despite their

---

53 That these identifications take place in syncretistic practice or erudite discussions (cf. III n. 58) only increases their rejection by Christian apologists and theologians: e.g. the argument by Origen (*CC* 5.45–46) against Celsus' suggestion that Zeus can be invoked as Hypsistos, Amon or Adonai Sabaoth. Origen refers as a parallel case to a magical incantation that would not work if one single word were changed.

54 Cf. notes 44 and 53. A clear example of this incompatibility is that the epithet πολυώνυμος is eliminated from an oracle of Apollo quoted by Christians (Lact. *DI* 1.7, *Theos. Tub.* 169 Erbse) as a monotheist poem, while a pagan inscription preserves it (cf. n. 60).

55 The epithet *polyonymos* is frequently used in the *Orphic Hymns* (2.1, 10.3, 11.10, 16.9, 27.4, 36.1, 40.1, 42.2, 45.2, 50.2, 52.1, 56.1, 59.2.) In most cases it is at the beginning of the hymn, which shows its importance. The same principle is perceptible in other hymns like those to the Sun (*OF* 544) or to Demeter-Ge-Rhea-Hestia in the Derveni papyrus (col. 22.7: *OF* 398). Cf. Theodoret's criticism

1.6. Personality and abstraction

polyonymia, are also closer to the personal end: they do not reach the point of becoming an abstract *theos* (although they do offer opportunities for extracting such a god from their texts through interpretation and manipulation), but rather preserve their names, their personality, and their "past."[56] The epithets of the *Orphic Hymns*, which allude to theogonic episodes, demonstrate this.[57] The theogonies never speak of an impersonal *theos*, but instead always name the gods, even if they do so in order to say that Zeus is the one god.[58] This personality of the Orphic gods, the result of their origin and permanent survival in a poetic tradition, which always preserved the mythological form, however many speculative ambitions it packed within it, had advantages and disadvantages from the perspective of acquiring and maintaining prominence in the religious panorama.

We already know that the traditional theogonic form maintains the prestige of the antiquity and authority of poetic revelation. In addition, the gods' personality in these poems has the effect of encouraging the experience of their presence. Save for exceptional spirits like Plotinus, abstract concepts like "the One" or "the divine" are less able to induce an experience of presence, which in the ancient world was generally epiphanic and sensorial, than the traditional gods with their anthropomorphic forms and their myths. The latter were consequently better able to receive cult and the adhesion of the devotees. Chapter II discussed the ambivalence of the Orphic gods in this regard, between speculation and experience, literature and cult. However, it can scarcely be doubted that their undeniable degree of cultic influence and of intervention in religious experience was due more to their figures' personal traits than to their metaphysical potential. The *Orphic Hymns*, which allude far more to the personal traits arising from each god's mythology than to those traits' philosophical interpretation, are evidence of this.

Nevertheless, the gods' personality also has disadvantages for maintaining an important place in the religious framework. The first disadvantage is that any "past" makes its owner vulnerable, however much he tries to hide or

---

(*Affect.* 3.58): "Rhea or Cybele or Brimo or however you want to call her, for you have plenty of names, not of deeds."

56 A specific case is the omission of the name of a god in mystic contexts (e. g. Core-Persephone), which is due to the fondness of mystery cults for secrecy and taboos (Burkert 1995, Henrichs 2003). This secrecy, however, does not mean that the deity loses his or her personal name. On the contrary, it gains more importance.
57 Cf. Govers-Hopman 2001 and Ricciardelli 2000.
58 The designation of the god as *theos* or *daimon* is more frequent in later Orphic hymns (e. g. *OF* 543.2, *OF* 243.6), which are, in consequence, easier for Christians to use. However, they never have the article, which implies a more complete depersonalization (*ho theos*).

sublimate it, and the gods are no exception. Christian attacks on the Orphic myths always choose the most scandalous passages, continuing thereby a philosophical tradition that opposed the myths' naked literality. The second disadvantage is that the mere name of the god, even if it facilitates his cult, turns him into a concrete entity too close at hand to reflect divine grandeur in the eyes of more restless spirits.[59] Still more is this the case, logically, for his necessarily anthropomorphic mythology, already denounced by Xenophanes. The third disadvantage, finally, is that the gods' mythological past and their concrete nature make their adaptation to an abstract philosophical system more difficult. The philosophers carried out this adaptation due to the mentioned advantages of the myths, especially the prestige of antiquity and poetic authority, but at the price of sometimes rather awkward allegorical interpretations, the forcedness of which was also an easy target for the attacks of the Christians or of other rivals. The Neoplatonists, despite all their enthusiasm for the Orphic poems, were conscious of this limitation. To begin with, they subordinated all mythology to commentary on Plato, whose abstract language was better suited for philosophy. And besides, Orphic poetry found itself at a clear disadvantage with respect to the *Chaldean Oracles*, later poems with a far more theologized and abstract language: Proclus chose to compose a commentary on the *Oracles* instead of the *Rhapsodies*, and he used to say that, if he could, he would only leave in circulation the *Timaeus* and the *Chaldean Oracles*, because the rest was dangerous.[60] For all his admiration for the *Orphica*, he recognized that they could be misinterpreted, since only abstract language guarantees conceptual exactitude. For the same reason, the more abstract and depersonalized passages of the Or-

---

59 A celebrated passage of Aeschylus (*Ag.* 160ff) admits that Zeus' divinity is far higher than his name; Plato (*Crat.* 400e) openly admits that names are pure human convention for prayer. Cf. Norden 1913, 144ff, commenting on these passages and other similar ones. This tendency will increase in later periods, when even in prayer a personal name is avoided: the Apollinean oracle quoted by Lactantius (*DI* 1.7: also found in a pagan inscription, cf. Lane Fox 1986, 168–200 and Mitchell 1999, 80–92) refers to a god who is at the same time πολυώνυμος and nameless (οὔνομα μὴ χωρῶν). The cult to Theos Hypsistos doubtless tried to avoid a more specific name, perhaps due to the influence of Jewish taboos about the name of Yahweh. Mitchell 1999, 122 suggests that the "unknown god" before whose altar Paul preaches in the Areopagus (*Acts* 17:16–34) is precisely Theos Hypsistos. For some Gnostic groups even the title of "god" is not adequate for the supreme Monad (*NHC* II, 1–32; cf. Dillon 1999, 72).
60 Marinus, *Vita Procli* 26 and 38. On the *Chaldean Oracles*, cf. pp. 196f. Apollo's oracles, which depend on the question they are asked, and not on previous mythology, are also more susceptible to speaking in conveniently abstract terms.

phic poems were preferred for Neoplatonic commentary, just as they were for apologetic appropriation, in contrast to other more narrative and *évenémentiel* passages that required a more bothersome allegoresis.[61]

The same advantages and disadvantages posed by a sharply defined personality, far from abstraction, for success in the ancient religious marketplace can be identified in the case of the Christian God, but to an even higher degree, since His personality was even more marked and gave far more occasion for religious experience, cult, and a community of the faithful. The Christian dogmas, too, were the object of the scorn produced in refined minds by scandalous and absurd myths, and the attempts at theologization and allegorization of the biblical accounts were likewise attacked by the anti-Christian camp (and by literalist Christians) at every stage: Celsus, Porphyry, and Julian repeatedly insisted on these arguments, very similar to those of their antagonists.

Thus, we once again discover the abyss separating Orphism and Christianity in their degree of cultic implantation. The Christian God's personality is highly marked, as is His cult, and in logical conformity, His faithful center their identity as a group on Him. This is so much the case that Christianity did not integrate itself into a philosophical system, but rather used this system as scaffolding for upholding its own mythological and historical revelation. The Orphic gods' personality is more diffuse, as are their cult and their followers. Orphism did not adapt any philosophical system to its mythology, but instead adapted itself to philosophical systems. I do not mean to debate here whether cult leads to the strengthening of the god's personality or the god's strong personality leads to cult, which would be a variant of the old debate on whether rite precedes myth or vice versa. I simply want to note that both go together and reinforce one another: the scarceness and vanishing character of the phantasmal "Orphics" and the rootedness and cohesion of the Christians are, once again, at the root of many differences between their respective gods.

---

61 The *Hymn to Zeus* in its two versions (*OF* 31 and 243) is much more often cited by different authors of various philosophical orientations than theogonic passages, which are often transmitted by just one single quotation by an author fond of allegoresis like Proclus or Damascius (see the sources in Bernabé *ad loc.*). This continues the tendency of the commentator of the Derveni papyrus, who quotes together in column XVI the four lines addressed to Zeus (*OF* 12) and comments on them easily, in contrast to other episodes that need to be alluded to in scattered and fragmented quotations in order to achieve a much more complex allegorical interpretation.

2. Gods and man

After theo-cosmogonic themes, the nature and destiny of man also occupied the attention of some Orphic poets, and to an even greater degree, have occupied that of modern scholars, whose interest in these aspects has been encouraged in good measure by their parallels with Christian theology. The religious polemic that came with the academic debate about these similarities at the beginning of the twentieth century was only a pale reflection of the tension that framed the apologists' citations, but it poses an additional difficulty for approaching the subject. Facile criticism of polytheism and confident praise of Orphic monotheism as derived from the biblical version give way to ambiguous references and mysterious silences when the focus shifts to this side of Orphism, due to its awkward parallels with Christianity that make both criticism and praise more difficult for the apologists. However, the ambiguity and obscurity of the Christian information corresponds to the scarcity of pagan references, due in part to the secrecy that surrounded the *legomena* of the mysteries, but also to the fact that, contrary to what is generally thought, but according to the preserved evidence, the most relevant dimension of Orphism appears to have been its theo-cosmogonic side, rather than its myths and anthropological ideas. This does not mean that man's relationship with the gods and the cosmos was not an important issue, but rather that making it the cornerstone of Orphism may be the result of unconscious Christianization. This projection of Christian categories may also lead to forgetting that the Orphic ideas of salvation did not form part of a system, but rather of a tradition. That is to say, even though we can already find the Zagreus myth and its anthropological interpretation in the classical age and handed down until the sixth century AD, not every mention of Orphism implies acceptance, or even knowledge, of this scheme, still less of its details. The *Derveni Theogony* could end without even alluding to Dionysus. There could also be in this whole conglomerate of ideas many references to the Zagreus myth without there being any anthropological consequences derived from it (*OF* 34, 35, 36, 39, 58, 59), or visions of expiation that did not include reincarnation and others that did, or that explained the punishment as due for one's own sins and not for those of the Titans. I will therefore consider each element (the primordial sin, anthropological dualism, reincarnation, and eschatology) separately, without assuming that one necessarily leads automatically to another.

2.1. The savior gods

Several Neoplatonists speak about "the happy life, after having wandered lost, desired by those who are initiated through Orpheus in the rites of Dionysus and of Core, to whom Zeus 'commended the granting of release from the cycle and a respite in misfortune'" (*OF* 348). Dionysus and Core are the principal deities of the cults tinged by Orphism, in which Zeus, the protagonist of the cosmogonies, delegates, as it were, the tasks of salvation. As is logical, it is against these two deities that the Christians direct their harshest attacks and accusations of scandal and plagiarism. Are these criticisms the reflection of any points in common with the protagonists of Christian salvation? I will leave for later the similarities or differences in the experience of the respective deities. The comparison to be made now is from a narrative and theological perspective, that is to say, the history and personality of these savior gods and their interpretation in Orphism.

Femaleness marks the divine personality of the figure of Core, even her very name ("maiden"). Exactly the same is true of her inseparable mother Demeter. This femaleness makes any narrative approximation to the distinctly masculine Christian deity very difficult. When Clement presents the Logos in the *Protrepticus* as the protagonist of the Christian mysteries, in the mold of the pagan ones, he does not hesitate to dress Him in Dionysian garb when imitating the *Bacchae* (12.119), but when he makes use of the metaphor of Eleusis, he does not identify Him with Persephone or Demeter, for the obvious reason of gender difference, but rather with the hierophant (12.120.1). On the other hand, this same trait makes it easy to approximate the Eleusinian goddesses to the highest-ranking female figure in the Christian pantheon, the Virgin Mary, who as Mother of God is represented from very early on with the attributes of other mother goddesses characteristic of Mediterranean religiosity (Core with Dionysus, Isis with Osiris). The influence of the female figures of paganism on the idea and the image of the Theotokos is obvious and well known. This clear resemblance should not make us forget the profound theological differences between them. In the apologists' orthodoxy, the Virgin Mary does not attain Persephone's divine status, and her eschatological role is that of intercessor, not that of judge. Unlike what they do with Danae, the apologists do not approximate the two figures, either as an example of convergence or as one of demonic imitation, probably because they perceived the differences as too great. They limit themselves to attacking Zeus's incestuous union with Core as a scandalous myth, in contrast to the purity of the Virgin Birth.[62]

---

62 Tert. *Apol.* 21.7–9. Immediately after Dionysus, Justin mentions Danae as an imi-

The case of the Orphic Dionysus is far more complex, since several elements of his myth approximate him to the figure of Christ. Justin (*Apol.* 1.54, *Dial.* 69) mentions the more obvious ones, in his opinion the result of imitation by the demons: "They said that Dionysus was the son of Zeus ... and gave out that after having been dismembered, he ascended into heaven." The text makes manifest the three elements we should analyze: sonship, sacrifice, and resurrection.

Divine sonship is the trait most clearly shared by the two, too clearly, even, for the taste of the apologists, who for the most part avoid mentioning it explicitly: Clement and Arnobius, in their lengthy accounts of the myth of Dionysus, neglect to say explicitly that he is the son of Zeus, although this can be deduced by way of the Orphic theogony that underlies their texts. There are only two exceptions: Firmicus Maternus insists that Liber (i. e. Dionysus) is the son of Jupiter, but since in his euhemerist account these are now not gods but men, the problem of divine sonship disappears; and earlier, Justin includes Dionysus in a list of Zeus's sons meant to justify the legitimacy of the title of Son of God given by the Christians to Jesus. However, Justin is still in the early days of apologetic, trying to make Christianity believable to the Greeks by insisting on similarities, and the weak argument of demonic plagiarism is enough for him with which to defend himself, without perceiving that this resemblance will become a powerful anti-Christian argument. For this reason, other, later apologists like Tertullian or Origen strive to separate Christ's divine sonship from the sons of Zeus in Greek mythology and from other "divine men" who received this title, for which Jesus's historicity, the Trinitarian theology that makes Him the preexistent Logos, and the Virgin Birth are their great supports.[63] However, this emphasis on marking out the enormous differences only confirms a certain parallelism.

---

tation of Mary (*Dial.* 70), for virginal birth is closer to the image of golden rain than to the crude rapes of the Orphic Zeus. Proof of this is the iconographic adaptation of Danae's image to represent the Annunciation (Lissarrague 1996).

63 Clem. Alex. *Protr.* 17.2; Arn. *Adv. Nat.* 5.19; Iust. *Apol.* 1.21 (cf. p. 294). Tert. *Apol.* 21.7–9. Celsus apud Orig. *CC* 7.9 compares Jesus with other thaumaturges who proclaim themselves "God, Son of God, or Divine Spirit" (ἐγὼ ὁ θεός εἰμι ἢ θεοῦ παῖς ἢ πνεῦμα θεῖον). Like a modern Origen, Nock 1964, 44–46 underlines Jesus' differences from the miracle-mongers who received these titles: Christ's sonship was not an honorific title, but a central matter of belief and cult; besides, Zeus' sons were not invoked as υἱοὶ θεοῦ. Jesus' historicity distances Him from the gods of Greek mythology: for pagans it makes his proclaimed sonship ridiculous (Celsus apud Orig. *CC* 7.53), while for the Christians it makes it unique.

2.1. The savior gods

The sons of gods in Greek tragedy, like Prometheus, Hercules, and Dionysus, are "personifications and instruments of mediation in a universe split between the superior and the inferior."[64] The same can be said of the Son of God in Christianity: the theological construction of Jesus's sonship manages to combine the transcendence of the biblical Father, who cannot be confused with His creatures, with the immanence implied by the Incarnation, at the same time that Trinitarian doctrine preserves divine unity. The degree of theologization in Orphism is far less, but we can suspect that the scant role played by Zeus in human salvation, which he "delegates" to Persephone and Dionysus, to some extent expresses the same functional separation: the idea was a traditional one, since Zeus reigned over the living and did not interfere in Hades's reign over the dead. It is the perception of this similarity that leads Clement to attribute the intuition of the Trinity to Euripides when he quotes the playwright's verses on Dionysus (without naming him, according to the principle mentioned previously), "who shares the scepter with Zeus and power over the dead with Hades" (*Strom.* 5.70 = fr. 912 Kannicht = *OF* 458), as if they were alluding to the Son.

As far as the god's sacrifice, leaving aside the obvious resemblance of the deaths of Christ and Dionysus, the profound differences were already pointed out by Boulanger (1925) in response to the distorted identification between the two outlined by Macchioro (1922). First, Christ's sacrifice is voluntary, and that of Dionysus is not: the very fact that he is a child seems to emphasize the impossibility of any idea of a voluntary sacrifice. Second, Christ's sacrifice entails the moment that makes salvation possible, while that of Dionysus, when it is put into relationship with humans, is always the primordial crime that leads to the soul's punishment. Zeus would have liked to prevent the Titans' crime, which he can only punish too late, while God the Father not only permits His Son's sacrifice, but even sends Him into the world for that purpose. This divine plan of salvation that gives the figure of Christ its meaning is entirely absent from the Orphic myth: only the rhetor Himerius (*Or.* 45.4), in the fifth century AD, gives a clearly Christianized version of the myth in which Zeus sees everything and intervenes at the last moment to save his son (p. 372). If the sacrifice of a god was already in conflict with the Greek conception of the divine as immortal (which made Dionysus's case already an exception, an *arreton* spoken of rarely and obscurely), the voluntary sacrifice of a god was an inconceivable and senseless "scandal" (*1 Cor.* 1:23). It is useful to keep this difference very much in mind if we suppose that certain rituals might have commemorated Dionysus's

---

64 Kott 1973, xiv–xv.

sacrifice: they do not commemorate the event that brings salvation, like the Eucharist, but rather the crime that should be expiated. For this reason, neither Clement nor Arnobius has any qualms about describing Dionysus's death, which they do not perceive as close to that of Christ.

However, the very different theologization of the deaths of Dionysus and Christ – which, in Boulanger's accurate judgment, excludes the possibility of influence – should not make us forget the common basis in sacrificial anthropology that underlies them both.[65] Dionysus's death has a much clearer sacrificial referent, since he is cut up, cooked, and eaten, in a perversion of the customary sacrificial rite (Detienne 1977). Christ's death is the result of a historical judicial process, but there are sacrificial elements in its theologization, by way of the identification with the Paschal Lamb, that cannot be brushed aside. This anthropological nearness explains why in what refers to the commemoration of the god's sacrifice there is a certain ambiguity on the Christian side when speaking about rituals surrounding the sacrifice of Dionysus (p. 355).

After death, both return to life. This clear resemblance allowed Christ and Dionysus to be fitted into the category, today well on the road to abandonment, of the "dying and rising god of vegetation" along with Osiris, Tammuz, Adonis, and Attis.[66] What can be said for certain is that in the cases of Christ and Dionysus the resurrection is, in narrative terms, an appendix to the central episode, the god's death: the Gospels dedicate much less space to the accounts of the Resurrection than to those of the Passion (as is also true of their commemoration during Holy Week), and in the same way, we find many fewer references to Dionysus's resurrection than to his death. However, the Christian elaboration of Christ's resurrection gives it much greater importance than Orphic poets and commentators gave to that of Dionysus: Christ's resurrection is essential for Christian faith, since it not only explains

---

65 Burkert's *Homo Necans* (1983) is already a classic work about the anthropological basis of sacrifice, including the divine one (pp. 76–78 on the Christian case).
66 This "Corn Spirit" or "Year Daimon" was theorized by Frazer in 1890 (1912^3) and enjoyed great popularity in the first half of the twentieth century, above all due to its enthusiastic reception by Jane Harrison (1903 = 1922^3). Nock (1964, 105–108) still admitted a certain similarity, although he underlined the differences of meaning to deny a possible influence on the first accounts of Christ's resurrection. The idea has been discredited for decades (Burkert 1979, 99–102, 105–111), since it unites, under the general pattern of a late allegorical explanation that identified the god with vegetation (e. g. Dionysus with the vine), several deities from different cultures that only in late antiquity came to converge, among other things due to Christian influence (Bremmer 2002, 52–54 *contra* Smith 1991 who denies any possible influence): Tammuz, for example, does not rise from the dead in the original Mesopotamian myth (Burkert 1979, 108–122).

his eternal existence and guarantees his divinity, but is also the prelude to that of man. In contrast, Dionysus's resurrection has scant theological function and seems to be simply a mythographic mechanism needed to reconcile the god's death with his undoubted actual presence in the Olympic pantheon and in the festivals and mysteries as a living god. It explains how he can continue to be present and in existence even after his death, since in Greece there is no god worthy of the name who is not alive: if he simply dies, he can be a hero and receive cult, but he does not cease to be a man.[67]

This essentially mythographic function accounts for the variety of versions of Dionysus' resurrection. Both the "Osirisized" version of the myth (*OF* 59), in which Rhea puts Dionysus back together, and the version that has him return to life on the basis of the heart saved by Athena (*OF* 325–327) are only documented beginning in the Hellenistic period.[68] It is even possible that some versions of the myth of Dionysus omitted this point as irrelevant, since it was not necessary to "narrate" his resurrection in order to know that he was alive. His resurrection is a mythographic rationalization to explain a fact characteristic of the pluriform and contradictory god, the fact that he can die and still live, can be simultaneously in Hades and on Olympus. Walter F. Otto vividly described how Dionysus unites death and life, like so many other contradictory principles, and argued with good reason that the transformation of his resurrection into a mythological episode was a late construct that divided into two phases what is really a single reality.[69] The religious function of this mythographic resurrection is scant, and the Orphic account of the soul's salvation could be imagined without it, utterly unlike the Pauline judgment, "If Christ has not risen, our faith is in vain" (*1 Cor.* 15:17). The difference in meaning between the death of Christ and that of Dionysus continues and increases in their resurrections.

Once there is a resurrection, the coincident detail of ascension into heaven after resurrection is easily explained by narrative necessity, since in both cases the divine Father has a heavenly dwelling. Justin and Origen are not

---

67 For this reason Celsus (*apud* Orig. *CC* 7.53) opposes Orpheus to Christ when he refers to *theioi andres* who die violently, while when he speaks of immortality he mentions, not Orpheus, but Dionysus, a god (*CC* 3.42). Heracles and Asclepius, intermediate figures between the divine and the human, appear in both quotations.
68 The first witness to the version with Athena is the poem of the third century BC that is the indirect source of Clement's account of the myth (p. 147f), since it derives the etymology of Pallas from the battering (*pallein*) of Dionysus' heart (*Protr.* 2.18.2).
69 Otto 1933, 175–187. Cole 1934, commenting on a funerary epigram in Bithynia, notes that contemplation of Dionysus is the link between the life and the death of the deceased.

Christianizing Orphism when they speak of "ascension" (p. 166), although there is no indication that the Orphic poems included a Dionysian scene resembling that in *Acts* 1:9–11. If there had been such a scene, Nonnus would not have omitted it when composing the *Dionysiaca*.

Finally, the greater importance of Christ's resurrection, the result of the different theologization of his death, leads to a different role after it. The Dionysus of the Orphic mysteries seems to act as a guide and intercessor for obtaining salvation, but he is not the one who grants it; Persephone is. In the scarce evidence we have, his eschatological role is generally limited to this intercessory function.[70] This intermediary role is undoubtedly also taken on by Christ, but in addition, as an integral part of the Trinity, his eschatological protagonism is far greater: for example, he holds a role of judge that Dionysus does not take on in spite of his frequent identification with Osiris. However, these differences must have seemed excessively subtle details compared to the fundamental correspondence that following the mysteries of one or the other god guaranteed life after death, for which reason the apologists preferred to tiptoe past the subject and draw a veil of silence over it.

Thus, the resemblances between the Orphic Dionysus and Christ are obvious on the narrative level, especially as a result of the shared episode of a god's death, rare in the Greek milieu. In addition, the similarities that we will see between Dionysian and Christian spiritual experience explain their similar roles as savior gods and the shared conception of them as sons of a divine Father.[71]

---

70   Johnston-McNiven 1996 describe this intercessory role of Dionysus befote Hades and Persephone while commenting on an Apulian krater in Toledo (Ohio), in connection with the mentions of Dionysus in the gold leaves and the Gurob papyrus. In other Bacchic mysteries that did not focus on the Zagreus myth, Dionysus could have had more importance in Afterlife hopes (cf. Nilsson 1935, Cole 1984), but not as a result of his death and resurrection.

71   A good parallel is the comparison between Cybele's mysteries and Christianity brilliantly undertaken by Fear 1996. There are similar parallels: resurrection; iconography of the Good Shepherd; tree and cross (Firm. Mat. *De err* 27.1, Arn. 5.17); Cybele as *theotokos* (Iul. *Hymn to Meter* 166b; *Contra Galileos* 262d; Aug. *CD* 2.26); the date of March 25 as celebration of Attis' resurrection and Christ's death; *taurobolium* and baptism; fasting. These parallels foster Christian reactive attacks, with all the ancient topoi of the critique of Cybele's cult (e. g. Seneca *apud* Aug. *CD* 6.10); at the same time, pagan resistance (e. g. Julian) adopts it as an anti-Christian alternative, aided by the antiquity and easy allegorization of Cybele's cult, which adopts some aspects of its rival (e. g. the *taurobolium*, a sacrifice, is transformed into a kind of baptism, and there is a new insistence on Attis' resurrection). These are three results very comparable to those produced by the similarity between the Orphic cult of Dionysus and Christianity.

However, the differences in interpretation and meaning are also very clear and result from several factors at least: the weight of biblical tradition in the interpretation of the figure of Christ (e.g., as Paschal Lamb), while Dionysus is imagined in conformity with the Greek tradition (e.g., with a secondary role with respect to Persephone in Hades); the fact that Jesus's death was a historical event with certain unchangeable characteristics (judicial process, death on the cross) that condition its interpretation, while Dionysus's death is a myth that, as such, permits greater flexibility in its details and its interpretation; the fact that, in addition, the theological elaboration of Christ's death and resurrection carried out by the Christians is far more complex than the consequences deduced from Dionysus's death and resurrection, among other things because there was no Orphic community to engage in this elaboration in dialectical confrontation with other communities (unlike the Christians in confrontation with Jews and Gnostics); and above all, finally, because Dionysus's death was interpreted far more from the perspective of sacrificial ritual than from that of theology.

Besides avoiding the projection of Christian details onto the myth of Dionysus, these differences should forewarn us against what Burkert (1999, 85) has considered the most significant factor in the unconscious Christianization of the myth of the Titans, due to the influence of the dogma of the sacrificed savior: making that myth the key to the edifice of Orphic theology. No religion can call itself Christian without referring to the death and resurrection of Christ as a fundamental redemptive episode. In contrast, there can be a great presence of Orphism where the death of Dionysus, and still more his resurrection, play a very secondary role (*Orphic Hymns*) or are even absent (*Derveni Papyrus*, at least in the preserved part). Let this warning serve as a reminder as we now turn to the anthropological consequences of the myth of the Titans.

2.2. Nature and destiny of man

Origen is the only Christian author who explicitly declares that the Greeks deduce theories about the soul from the myth of Dionysus (*CC* 4.17): he is probably referring to the impurity men inherit from their ancestors, the Titans. No other apologist makes the slightest allusion to this primordial stain: Gregory of Nazianzus does not mention it when in the *De anima* he attacks the theories of the soul contained in the *Rhapsodies*, and Augustine, when citing the *soma-sema* saying, explicitly denies that the pagans were familiar with the idea of the first man's fault. This silence can be explained by lack of knowledge of an interpretation always alluded to rarely and obscurely.[72] It is curious, however, that no ancient apologist noticed what many moderns have remarked: the similarity of the Titanic stain deduced from the Zagreus myth with the Christian doctrine of original sin, inherited from Adam and Eve.

The clear parallel of an ancestral fault expiated by all mankind, as descendants of the primeval sinners, is not free of differences, apart from the obvious disparity of the nature of each primordial sin. Following in Boulanger's footsteps, Ugo Bianchi identified an important distinction in meaning: the Christian idea of the original sin committed by the first human beings is not equivalent to the "antecedent sin" committed by the "ancestors" of human beings, the Titans.[73] Human beings are guilty due to moral solidarity with Adam and Eve, who are of the same nature as they are, while if they are born from the remains of the blasted Titans, they inherit "genetically" from them a physical impurity from which they need to be purified, not a moral responsibility that demands redemption. This subtle difference, however, does not hide the central parallelism of a construction by which men pay for the fault of another.

The origin and evolution of the two constructions is in fact very different: the fault inherited from the Titans' crime seems to be a theological elaboration arising from the traditional notion of the familial inheritance of ancestral fault (p. 19). The story of Adam and Eve, for its part, does not have this crucial interpretation in the Jewish milieu, but rather appears to be an account of the fall from a primordial state of happiness. In reality, the first chapters of *Genesis* are of marginal importance for Judaism and are practically ignored in the rest of the Old Testament, which is centered on the history of Israel beginning with Abraham in *Gn.* 12:1. Christians reinterpret the tale as the origin of the tendency to evil that lurks in all Adam and Eve's descendants. The Scriptural basis was a Pauline passage (*Rom.* 5:12ff) that contrasts Adam, the cause of perdition, with Christ, the agent of redemption. However, it will be four centuries later that, on the basis of this passage, the doctrine of original sin is explicitly formulated: Augustine stated that men are punished for their ancestors' guilt, which is shared by their descendants. It was probably his earlier allegiances to Manichaeanism and Neoplatonism that caused him to search in depth for the origin of evil until he came up with the theological construction of original sin.[74] After Paul and before

---

72 Cf. I n. 49 on the debate over the antiquity of this myth and its interpretation.
73 Boulanger 1925, 105–106, against Macchioro's direct derivation of Christian original sin from the Orphic myth, cf. p. 7; Bianchi 1966.
74 On the history of the doctrine of original sin in early Christianity, cf. Pagels 1989, Hauke 1993, Minois 2002. The attention paid to the apologists is scarce (cf. next note). A lengthy debate is still alive about the interpretation of Paul's passage.

Augustine, the apologists usually refer to the sin of Adam and Eve in quite general terms as the origin of the evil and corruption in which men have dwelt ever since.[75] If some of them knew the Zagreus myth, they decided to silence it: it was not scandalous enough to attack, and it may have seemed close to Christian doctrines, and yet not so equivalent to require an explanation, like other easier parallels. Ignorance, lack of interest and/or mistrust of Orphic similarities are the likeliest explanations for the apologetic silence on this myth.

However, there is little doubt that the Christian doctrine of an inherited guilt results from Greek influence on the interpretation of the biblical account, so in this case the genealogical relationship can explain the conceptual analogy. The primordial fault that leads to the soul's fall from its original divine position perhaps first arose in Greece with Orphism, but it would be too rash to take the myth of the Titans as the direct source of these ideas: the idea of ancestral fault was widespread in the ancient world, and there may have been other similar constructions.[76] It was not even necessary to know what this initial fault was in order to suppose its existence: the Gnostic systems presumed a fall of the soul, whose fault they did not always describe, and it was common to suppose an unknown and indeterminate fault. Celsus says, "Men are born bound to a body, whether because of the order of the universe, or in expiation of their faults (ποινὰς ἁμαρτίας ἀποτίνοντες), or because the soul is weighed down by passions until it purifies itself in certain periods" (*CC* 8.53). Like Empedocles (115 DK), he leaves it ambiguous whether he is referring to the primordial fault or to the faults of previous lives. Typically, Origen tiptoes around this subject in his response to Celsus: "Celsus is prudent in citing the theories of multiple authors about the cause of our birth without daring to affirm that any of them is false." Rather than coming directly from the myth of the Titans, Christian original sin seems rooted in the widespread idea of a primordial fault that caused the fall of man – or in Platonizing terms, the fall of the soul.

The soul's fall from its divine status as the consequence of an initial crime, whatever it was, had in Plato and, second in importance, Empedocles, representatives of a much higher caliber than any Orphic myth. Both were the great authorities to whom to refer on the subject of the fall of the soul: when pagan Middle Platonism elaborated and used a cento on the fall

---

75 E. g. Clem. Alex. *Protr.* 2.12.2: "that Eve by which error spread out." Theoph. *Autol.* 2.28.6: "this Eve who sinned at the beginning." The verbs used seem far from the implications of the Titanic myth.
76 Cf. Glotz 1904; Dodds 1951, 135–179; Bremmer 2002, 11–41; and Gagné's forthcoming monograph on ancestral fault.

of the soul, they were the star authors. Many of the texts included in this cento have been placed in relation with Orphism or considered to be the result of Orphic influence. However, the cento contains only one quotation from Orpheus, the *soma-sema* doctrine transmitted by Plato.[77] The scope of this expression goes beyond inherited guilt. It represents an entire dualistic vision of man, the introduction of which in Greece was due in great part to Orphism.

The *soma-sema* is simply a memorable slogan, but it reflects a true fact: Orphism is at the origin of the revaluation of the soul as the higher element of man and the consequent devaluation of the body and earthly life. This body/soul dualism makes it a direct precedent for the dimension of Christianity that considers this life to be a valley of tears and claims that complete happiness can be attained only after death.[78] Even if this dualism is not yet predominant in the biblical tradition or in the New Testament, in which the body-soul duality of Platonic origin has a very limited presence, the reception of Platonism beginning in the second century made it into a key component of Christian anthropology.[79] The Orphic *soma-sema* saying was taken up enthusiastically by ancient, medieval, and even modern Christian literature.[80] Two citations from Clement and Augustine shed light on the different possibilities of this anthropological dualism.

---

77 *Strom.* 3.3.16.3. Many of the texts from this cento on the fallen soul (cf. IV n. 146) quoted in *Stromata* III are also to be found in *OF* 439–469, where literary texts connected to Orphism are collected.
78 Bremmer 2002 presents the upgrading of the soul as a process beginning with Orphism and Pythagoreanism and continuing with Christianity, and even in later movements like Catharism. Cf. Dodds 1951, 139: "The new religious pattern made its fateful contribution: by crediting man with an occult self of divine origin, and thus setting the body and soul at odds, it introduced into European culture a new interpretation of human existence, the interpretation we call puritanical."
79 Platonic dualism only penetrates Judaism in Hellenized circles from the first century AD: cf. Bremmer 2002, 8f, 50f, 59f. The increasingly Platonic Christian theology must be differentiated from practice (e. g. *Acts of the Christian Martyrs*), where the opposition body/soul is conspicuously absent, and the resurrection of the same martyred body is crucial.
80 Cf. Courcelle 1965 on Neoplatonic, Jewish (Philo, Josephus) and Christian traditions of the body as prison, and Courcelle 1966 on the body as tomb. Cf. also De Vogel 1981. Even if criticized as a philo-Gnostic and Origenist image, it had great success in Christian literature. It was especially fruitful as an interpretative key for biblical passages like *Ps.* 5:10, "His throat is an open sepulcher," and *Mt.* 8:22, "Let the dead bury their dead." Even in 1963 Pope Paul VI had to declare formally, "The body is not the prison of the soul" (*apud* Courcelle 1965, 442). The expression also appears in late Christian epitaphs: cf. Bremmer 2002, 60 n. 27.

2.2. Nature and destiny of man

Clement's citation represents the intermediate position in a Christian reception of Platonism that seeks to avoid falling into the excesses of the Gnostics. His allusions to the *soma-sema* are part of a section of the *Stromata* (3.12.1–21.25.1) that aims to demonstrate that the Marcionites' negative vision of the world is rooted not in the Bible, but rather in misunderstanding the Greek philosophers, who nevertheless "did not consider it evil by nature, but rather with respect to the soul that has seen the good" (3.13.2). Clement considers correct a less radical interpretation of the devaluation of matter than the Gnostic one, taking it to be good in itself, but evil in its effects when it impedes the soul from reaching God. In contrast, Augustine's reference to the *soma-sema* (*Contra Iul. Pelag.* 4.15.78, 4.16.83) aims to refute the Pelagian opinions that denied man's original sin – opinions that, in their turn, arose in reaction to the demonization of matter by the Gnostics and the Manichaeans. Augustine also seeks to maintain an intermediate posture that devalues the world and the body as spaces where the soul finds opportunities to sin and separate itself from God, but that considers them to be divine works and therefore good. Once again, the Orphic image is used to confirm the Christian position, between Gnosis-Manichaeanism and Pelagianism.

Both texts make use of the image of the body as tomb of the soul in order to establish an intermediate position that devalues the body in comparison to the soul but does not consider it negative in itself. Does this interpretation by Clement and Augustine reflect the real sense of the Orphic expression? In principle, it would appear that it does. Jaap Mansfeld (1981, 290–293) points out that Gnostic pessimism, despite having Orphic and Platonic precedents, cannot be projected backward onto its Greek precedents. Cosmological monism encourages a devaluation of matter and, with it, of the body, similar to the Christian one, which does not consider the body entirely negative, but only inferior to the soul. That the body is a place of expiation (prison or tomb) for the soul implies that the life to come is superior to the earthly one, but not necessarily that the latter is essentially evil.[81] The fact that Augustine approves the *soma-sema* saying and Clement defends its "correct interpretation" seems to support this, but it is true that this does not cease to be an *interpretatio christiana* of Orphism. In the last analysis, Clement also recognizes that this idea is at the root of Gnostic pessimism, like other witnesses to Greek dualism, and in effect, the "deformation" denounced by

---

81 We could add that in traditional Greek poetry, from which Orphic poems take their formulas, the word σῆμα has a fairly positive connotation, since it grants the immortality of the hero (*Il.* 7.89, *Od.* 23.73, 110). The tomb does not have the negative connotations it took on later, even less so with reference to immortality.

Clement was all the easier given that in Orphism concepts and images were not fitted together in a solid doctrinal system, but rather spread practically autonomously. Let us recall that Augustine attributes the doctrine to those who "did not know original sin," revealing that the two elements could easily be separated. In the same way, it was easy for the *soma-sema* expression to become a symbol of the evil of matter, unconnected with cosmological monism. Plutarch's anecdote about the orpheotelestes whom King Leotychidas encourages to commit suicide in order to live happily in the Beyond is, despite its joking tone, symptomatic of this easy slippage into a negative consideration of the body. Many centuries later, the Cathars would once again use the *soma-sema* in a clearly Manichaean sense.[82]

In reality, anthropological dualism can lead both to a total pessimism that considers the body to be essentially evil and to a vision of the body as devalued in comparison with the soul that does not go so far as to demonize it. Christianity, once it adopted the fundamental Platonic body-soul distinction, chose the second option, in opposition to the Gnostics first and the Manichaeans later: biblical monism really mandated this choice, since the body does not cease to be a divine work and therefore good. The anthropological unitarianism of the biblical tradition, which does not distinguish body and soul, and the defense of the resurrection of the body also applied pressure in this direction. In contrast, the Gnostics and the Manichaeans, likewise heirs of the Platonic division but without the brake provided by the biblical tradition, turned to the first option, assisted by a cosmological dualism that provided them with a basis on which to consider all matter essentially evil. In sum, the Orphic image of the *soma-sema* has a destiny like that of its Christian counterpart of the *lacrimarum vallis* as a designation for earthly life. It entails a clear devaluation of the sensible world, and if weighty theological reasons do not sustain belief in the goodness of matter, it can easily lead to a total anthropological pessimism.

The dualism that Orphism shares with Hellenized Christianity brings with it a belief in the immortality of the soul that makes questions about its destiny after death inevitable. In this regard, reincarnation is one of the most famous innovations of Orphism and Pythagoreanism in Greek thought (Bremmer 2002). However, the Christian texts give little information on the subject of Orphic reincarnation. The fullest critiques, by Tertullian, Gregory of Nyssa and Augustine, do not mention Orpheus, but Plato, Empedocles and

---

82 Plut. *Apophth. Lacon.* 224d (*OF* 653). Bremmer 2002, 68f on Cathar recuperation of the Orphic slogan.

Pythagoras.[83] Only Clement of Alexandria seems to hint at the presence of metempsychosis in the Pythagorean circles from which come the Orphic fragments he quotes in the sections of the *Stromata* on symbolism and plagiarism, that is, while primarily discussing other subjects. Also, Gregory of Nazianzus seems to have taken Orphic poetry as an opponent, along with Empedocles and Pythagoras, in his attack on reincarnation in the poem *De anima* (p. 213). Gregory's text (App. 8) implies that the ideas of the soul entering the body from the air, the transmigration of souls (even in animals), and punishments beyond the grave coexisted in the *Rhapsodies*. As both texts show, reincarnation was an idea that could be combined with others and had varying functions in the Orphic tradition, at least in the late period. The *Rhapsodies* integrated, among other afterlife solutions, an extreme vision of the transmigration of souls. Nevertheless, other Orphic evidence alludes only very slightly to reincarnation, and in some cases it even appears to be entirely ignored.[84] Christian eagerness for the dialectical establishment of dogmatic truth was lacking in the Orphic milieu, and this is possibly the reason that the visions of the soul were maintained at a less systematized level, on which a variety of theories could coexist. We must recall that Orphism did not suffer dogmatic controversies leading to the acceptance or rejection of a theory, and could therefore remain ambiguous about its presence and its meaning. In effect, reincarnation can function as a process of progressive purification, as in Platonism and its epigone Origen, but also as a simple punishment, the cycle of which can be es-

---

83 Greg. Nys. *Dial. de an. et resur*. 88–101; Tert. *De an.* 28–31. Christian discussion of the transmigration of souls is very intense (Hoheisel 1984–1985, Scheffczyk 1985; Bremmer 2002, 60). While Justin briefly rejects it (*Dial.* 4, cf. Maritano 1992), Clement does not discuss the subject in his preserved works (cf. *Strom*. 7.32.8); yet Photius accuses him of defending reincarnation, perhaps taking him for a proto-Origenist (cf. Chadwick 1966, 48). Although Origen criticizes metensomatosis in animals (*CC* 1.20, 4.83, 5.29, 8.30), he defended the preexistence of souls before their entry into the body and a scheme of purification very similar to reincarnation, which he considers a "plausible" and "reasonable" doctrine (*Comm. in Joh.* 6.13–14: πιθανός; *CC*. 1.32: εὐλογότερον). The full formulation of his doctrine was in *De principiis*, only partially preserved (cf. Bianchi 1987, Chadwick 1966, 114–116, Solmsen 1972). After giving rise to heated polemics, Origenist doctrines were finally condemned in 553. In the neo-Platonic field there are also various positions: in Plato's footsteps, reincarnation is accepted, but some include animals in the cycle (Plot. *Enn.* 3.4.2), and others restrict it to rational beings (Porph. *apud* Stob. *Ecl.* 1.49.60, Iambl. *Myst.* 1.8, Sallust. *De dis* 20).
84 In the leaves, only the "painful circle of deep grief" in a Thurii leaf (*OF* 488) perhaps alludes to reincarnation, although other interpretations are possible (e.g. life as a wheel: Calame 2002; cf. Nock 1935). There is no place for reincarnation in the banquet of initiates described by Plato in *Resp.* 363c.

caped only through the purification provided by the *telete*, as the lamellae appear to imply. Reincarnation seems to have been an open option that Orphism could develop or pass over, and the scarce Christian critiques treat it as such.

In the *De anima* Gregory of Nazianzus takes aim at the torments of the Beyond not as such, but on account of the contradiction entailed by the physical torture of the incorporeal soul that is reincarnated in physical bodies. In combination with, or as an alternative to, reincarnation, the soul's happy destiny after death or its condemnation to torment is a fundamental preoccupation of Orphism and an area in which its affinity to Christianity is clear. The parallelism of a Beyond with rewards and punishments creates the opportunity to share images of both happiness and suffering beyond the grave. The apologists recognize that Christian eschatology is very similar in content to that of the Greek mysteries (and of Plato, p. 248). With their usual eagerness for boundary-setting, however, they insist on its different interpretation and practical effects. The way in which Origen responds as many as three times to Celsus's accusation (*CC* 2.5) that the Christians appeal to fear like the initiators of the Bacchic mysteries and predict the same torments as the mystagogues is revealing. Origen admits (*CC* 3.16) that they share the ancient tradition (παλαιὸς λόγος) of the Greeks and the Jews about "tribunals in the netherworld" and insists that the Christians are not inventing anything new in this regard. What he emphasizes is that the punishments of the Beyond that Christianity preaches have a meaning and consequences entirely different from those of the mysteries (*CC* 4.10). In *CC* 8.48, he insists:

> Celsus means that both we and the priests of the mysteries believe the same about eternal punishments, and would inquire which of the two are closer to the truth. I would say that those are right who are able to convince (διαθεῖναι) the people who hear what they say to live as though these things were real. Jews and Christians change the minds (διατίθενται) of their hearers with what they call the age to come, and that there are rewards in it for the just and punishment for sinners. Let Celsus, or whoever wishes, show who was so predisposed (διετέθησαν) by the eternal punishments announced by the initiators and mystagogues!

He appeals, then, not to the difference in content, but to the difference in meaning and practical consequences of one and the other eschatology. According to Origen, the rewards and punishments announced by Christianity succeed in changing the minds (*diatethenai*) of the faithful and aligning their lives to its moral doctrines, while those of the Greek mysteries do not have such an effect. We may now ask whether this difference in meaning and effects really existed.

On the Christian side, the debate already present in the New Testament between faith and works as conditions for salvation tilted toward works beginning at the end of the first century. As the immediate expectation of the Parousia faded, moralization (with many elements of Stoic origin) became the distinctive hallmark of Christianity, as can already be seen in the Pastoral Epistles. The custom of delaying baptism until the moment before death in order to enter purified into the Beyond did not undermine the moralizing essence of Christian salvation, since what the baptizand is purified from are all the previous sins that would lead to his condemnation were it not for baptism. Origen clearly idealizes reality when he says that the Christians live in accordance with moral principles, but it is indeed true that this is the goal toward which Christian eschatology is theoretically directed (practice is obviously a different question).

In the Orphic milieu the panorama is less clear, among other things due to the scarcity of sources. It is obvious that Platonic eschatology, of acknowledged Orphic roots, has a clear moral component inherited by pagans and Christians alike: both Celsus and Origen agree that the just will be rewarded and the evil punished, "and that it should never occur to anyone to abandon this thought" (*CC* 3.16, 8.49, 51). However, it is uncertain to what extent this moral component had any presence in early Orphic texts or cults. Neither the pre-Platonic texts that allude to Orphic eschatology nor the gold lamellae make reference to the requirement of specific conduct for salvation, apart from vague and customary references to justice, but rather to being initiated.[85] The theologization of morality that we find in Plato and in Christianity should not be extrapolated backward and projected onto ancient Orphism. However, whatever the ethical requirements of the early Orphic Afterlife may have been, it seems probable that the tendency to moralization perceptible in Greek ritual prescriptions (as we shall see) from Hellenistic times also affected eschatological speculation. The katabasis of the Bologna papyrus, with its list of sinners, suggests a conventionally moralized escha-

---

85 The Orphic leaves insist that the initiate must know the instructions and *symbola* in the Netherworld, and do not mention his virtues or faults. The requirement of purity (*katharos*) probably has a ritual meaning (though cf. p. 345). This emphasis on initiation and ritual purity is compatible with respect for poetic tradition. The traditional insistence on the benefits of justice, protected by the gods or personified as the goddess Dike, was probably taken up by Orphic poets: Dike already appears as πάρεδρος of Zeus "who sees all" in Orphic contexts from the fourth century BC (Ps. Demosth. 25.11, *OF* 32, *Orphic Hymn* 62: cf. Hes. *Op.* 232ff; Soph, *Oed. Col.* 1382); the εὔορκοι (Hes. *Op.* 285, Tyrt. fr. 12.30 West) paticipate in the Orphic banquet of the blessed (Plat. *Resp.* 363c).

tology in later Orphism.[86] The effect of these threats and warnings on the practical behavior of their hearers is hard to measure. The scarcity, not to say non-existence, of defined Orphic communities outside the moment of ritual undoubtedly led to the rite being more important than a conduct that could be controlled by neither the group nor the initiator afterward. Once again, the sociological difference between Orphism and Christianity is in direct correlation to their apparent ideological distance.

3. The ritual experience

3.1. Pagan and Christian *teletai*

Up to now we have been analyzing the theological concepts of Orphic literature in the light of the apologetic texts. However, it was not only stories about the gods (θεολογίαι) that were attributed to Orpheus, but also the patronage of the rites (τελεταί): man's relationship with the gods took form in the Orphic milieu in the *teletai*, both those that were actually celebrated and those that lived principally in the imaginations of those who spoke about them. As it was said in chapter I (p. 26ff), Orphism, as the mysteriosophy par excellence, had a share in both speculation (*mathein*) and experience (*pathein*). What can Christian evidence tell us about the second term? In principle, the apologists are not of great value for deepening our knowledge of the great experience of the mysteries, famously described by Walter Burkert (1987, 89–114). No matter how much they use the rhetoric of disclosure and profanation of the mysteries, Christian information on the Orphic *teletai* is almost always of literary origin and does not come from direct personal knowledge, and as a result, this material, valuable as it is for our knowledge of specific ritual elements, does not offer as much information on religious experience as it does on theological ideas and myths, which are easier to transmit in books and poems. In addition, the apologists are not interested, for obvious reasons, in giving any information that does not fit their aim of denigrating Greek mysteries. However, the Orphic cults lived in the intellectual tradition as much as or more than they did in actual practice, and their transmission took place through literature more than through cult. Furthermore, in chap-

---

86 On the Bologna papyrus, cf. pp. 39ff. The presence of *nomos* (or Nomos) in the gold leaf from Rome (*OF* 491, cf. pp. 70f) could also have a moral content absent from the earlier leaves. Bernabé/Jiménez 2008, 53f rightly warn against extrapolation of Platonic eschatology onto its Orphic model (*contra* Guthrie 1952, 177 and Harrison 1922³, 609).

ter II we saw that literary tradition, far from being mere erudition, was a major factor in creating true religious experience in the Imperial age. There are, therefore, some particular points on which the comments made by the apologists using literary sources can complement the light shed by the evidence arising directly from other, less-biased sources.

It is well known that Christians adopted the terminology of the mysteries in order to present and define their own religion (pp. 263ff). As we saw in chapter V, Clement of Alexandria and Gregory of Nazianzus present Christianity in the garb of the Bacchic and Eleusinian mysteries. Besides the rhetorical effectiveness that imposes symmetry ("abandon your mysteries and come to these"), their literary success makes clear that there was a great similarity in the experience of Christianity and the mysteries. As in the case of eschatological images, the polemic between Celsus and Origen sheds light on this resemblance, as well as their attempts to set differences (*CC* 3.59):

> Celsus says, "... Those who invite to the other mysteries (τὰς ἄλλας τελετὰς) proclaim this: 'Every one who has clean hands (χεῖρας καθαρός), and an intelligent tongue (φωνὴν συνετός)'; others again thus: 'He who is pure from all pollution (ἁγνός ἀπὸ παντὸς μύσους), and whose soul is conscious of no evil, and who has lived well and justly.' Such is the proclamation made by those who promise purification from sins. But let us hear what kind of persons these Christians invite. Every one, they say, who is a sinner, who does not understand (ἀσύνετος), who is a child, and, to put it simply, whoever is unfortunate, him will the kingdom of God receive ..." Now, in answer to such statements, we say that it is not the same thing to invite those who are sick in soul to be cured, and those who are in health to the knowledge and study of divine things. We, however, keeping both these things in view, at first invite all men to be healed, and exhort (προτρέπομεν) those who are sinners to come to the consideration of the doctrines which teach men not to sin, and those who do not understand to those which beget understanding, and those who are children to rise in their thoughts to manhood, and those who are simply unfortunate to good fortune, or – which is the more appropriate term to use – to blessedness. And when those who have been turned towards virtue have made progress, and have shown that they have been purified (κεκαθάρθαι) by the Word, and have led as far as they can a better life, only then do we invite them to participation in our mysteries (τὰς παρ ἡμῖν τελετὰς).

Celsus prefers the "other *teletai*," which demand physical and moral purity for initiation, to the Christian *telete*, which calls sinners. Origen responds that the Christians call the sinner so that he may first be converted and then enter into the deeper mysteries with a greater moral purity than is demanded by the pagan rites. Even if he stresses the differences in meaning, it does not occur to Origen to reject the molds of the *telete* into which Celsus fits the Christians; instead, he expands them, since both authors appear to be in agreement that this is the image that best defines the Christian experience. He puts forward three points in order to distinguish the pagan *telete* from the Christian one, whose accuracy we will examine in this order: gradual initiation, conversion, and moral purity.

Both Celsus and Origen accept the distinction between the initiated and the profane in pagan and Christian *teletai*. The consciousness of forming part of a chosen *élite* distinguished from the masses (οἱ πολλοί) and enjoying a privileged religious position is part of the essence of both Orphism and Christianity. This fundamental similarity is perceived by Clement and Theodoret when they identify the Orphic saying "many bear the thyrsus, but few are Bacchics" (πολλοὶ μὲν οἱ ναρθηκοφόροι, παῦροι δὲ βάκχοι) with the Gospel statement "many are called, but few are chosen" (πολλοὺς μὲν τοὺς κλητούς, ὀλίγους δὲ τοὺς ἐκλεκτούς).[87] Nevertheless, there may be greater complexity beyond the radical distinction between the profane and the initiated. Origen emphasizes the stepped arrangement and hierarchization of degrees of initiation, from the most superficial to the deepest. Both with reference to knowledge and theology and with reference to the practice of virtue, Christians recognize degrees of perfection.[88] The ranking of different degrees of initiation was also characteristic of Eleusis, the source of the popular terminology of initiatory ascent already used by Diotima in Plato's *Symposium*. In contrast, in Orphic poetry and in the itinerant *teletai* there seems to be no such complexity, and the sole distinction is between initiates and non-initiates, or those with knowledge and the ignorant: the βεβακχευμένος (*OF* 652) and the συνετός (*OF* 1) are distinguished from the μὴ βεβακχευμένος and the βέβηλος. This clear divergence is easily explained by the very different degree of social implantation and complexity.

As Origen implies, Christians consider passage from the status of profane to that of initiate a conversion. Clement's whole *Protrepticus* is an exhortation to conversion in the form of initiation into the mysteries of the Logos. Does this conversion that is so present in the Christian mystery reflect an element really present in the *teletai*, or is it specifically Christian? We enter here into a classic question for the study of the differences between

---

87 *Mt.* 22:14, *OF* 576. Clem. Alex. *Strom.* 1.19.92.3 ≈ 5.3.17.4; Thdt. *Affect.* 12.35.
88 Cf. p. 31. on Clement's trilogy from conversion to perfection. Cf. Lane Fox 1986, 336–340 on Christian perfectionists in the second to fourth centuries (already in *1 Cor* 7:7–10 about marriage).

ancient religion and Christianity. In 1933, A. D. Nock demonstrated in a celebrated book that Greek and Roman cults, unlike the Christian one, did not demand from their adepts a *conversion* that entailed the renunciation of other cults and complete dedication to one alone, but rather called for an *adhesion* compatible with the practice of other cults. The exclusivist monotheism of the biblical God is at the root of this fundamental change in religious mentality brought by Christianization. Nock's general thesis remains valid, since only a few vague references to religious conversion can be found in pagan milieus.[89] Conversion, like the literary genre of exhortation to it, the *Protrepticus*, has almost no precedents in the cultic sphere, but rather in that of philosophy: the philosophers (Aristotle, Cicero, Iamblichus) did indeed exhort their hearers to abandon ignorance and vice and turn toward the knowledge and virtue of the philosopher's life. Christianity takes up this tradition and easily adapts it to its religious frameworks.

However, given that Orphism unites elements of the mystery cults and of philosophy, it may be asked whether conversion might not have played a role in it, especially when the Jewish and Christian apologists offer the most glaring example, the conversion of Orpheus himself, who in the *Testament* abandons his earlier polytheism and proclaims biblical monotheism. Not only does the poem's text itself openly express conversion – "I proclaim the truth: let nothing of what once appeared in your heart deprive you of blessed eternity" – but all the apologists also introduce the text by emphasizing Orpheus's conversion: "he denies," "converting," "condemning his own dogmas," "he changed," "he intones a palinode" are phrases that underline the explicit renunciation of prior gods as a prerequisite for accepting the one God.[90]

The rhetorical emphasis on presenting Orpheus as a model of conversion could be enough to explain these references. The syncretistic tendency to equate the gods, and hence their cults, was a prevalent tendency in Or-

---

89 The numerous studies on conversion afterwards have generally started from the basis established by Nock 1933; cf. Herrero 2005b and Casadio 2009, with full bibliography, for the validity of Nock's model (cf. Price's position in n. 91 *infra*). Versnel 1990, 172 sees in Euripides' *Bacchai* some anticipations of later religiosity, among others a "dim reference to conversion" in line 944 (μεθέστηκας φρηνῶν: you changed your mind). Apuleius' *Metamorphoses* does not require from Lucius a formal renunciation of other cults in order to dedicate himself to Isis (it does, instead, require practical renunciations like sex). Only Christian influence in later paganism provokes some instances of exclusivism: Eunapius (*VS* 7.3.2–4) says that a devotee of Mithras cannot be hierophant at Eleusis.

90 *OF* 377–378, ll. 3–4; *OF* 368: ἀθετεῖ; *OF* 369: μετανοῶν; *OF* 373: τῶν ἑαυτοῦ δογμάτων κατεγνωκότα; *OF* 374: μετέθηκεν; *OF* 371: παλινῳδίαν ᾆσαι; *OF* 375: παλινῳδίαν ἀληθείας εἰσάγει.

phism and seems in principle incompatible with conversion in the Christian sense. Nevertheless, there is a precedent for the abandonment of one god for another in the myth of Orpheus that should be considered: in the *Bassarai*, Aeschylus dramatized how the Thracian abandoned the cult of Dionysus to honor the Sun-Apollo (*OF* 536), at the price of Dionysus's revenge. The neglect of a god's cult and his consequent revenge is a frequent episode in mythology. Granted, the neglect of Dionysus's cult is not due to Orpheus suddenly considering it false, but to his fascination with the cult of Apollo, which absorbs all his religious activity. It is not a matter of considering one cult truer than another, but rather of an individual believer relegating all other cults to second rank in favor of a single one. However, extreme adhesion may produce effects similar to conversion, even if there is no formal renunciation demanded by conversion. There is still another case of possible Orphic "conversion," vegetarianism, which entailed the refusal to participate in the sacrificial banquet with which the city honored its gods.[91] Figures close to Orphism like Empedocles and the Pythagoreans (or in literature, the chorus of Euripides's *Cretans*) proclaim as much. Vegetarianism appears to be a consequence of obsession with purity and horror at the shedding of blood (and/or belief in reincarnation); the renunciation of civic cult that it entails does not always arise from an explicit denial of community life, but it could certainly be perceived in this way. As in the case of Dionysus taking revenge against Orpheus, the city could react to vegetarianism with hostility because it perceived the effects of renunciation. Undoubtedly, some Orphic poems suggested changes in sacrificial practice.[92] However, this attitude did not come from religious conversion from one cult to another, but rather from the influence of philosophical ideas on the manner of ritual celebration. As a speculation about religion, therefore, Orphism did present, on a theoretical level, some of the elements of the conversion paradigm (renunciation and life-choice). The construction of Orphism as a movement essentially opposed to the city, albeit brilliantly defended by Marcel Detienne, has taken

---

91 Price 1999, 140f fully disagrees with Nock's paradigm, and uses the vegetarianism of "Orphics" as an example of religious conversion (also Apuleius': cf. n. 89), in order to show that the distinction between religion and philosophy is misleading. However, much closer to philosophical speculation than other Greek cults, Orphism is an exception in the Greek religious panorama.

92 E.g. Hieron. *Adv. Iov.* 2.14 and other testimonies to poems on vegetarianism collected in *OF* 630. Also, Clement's account (*Protr.* 2.17–18) shows an inversion of the usual sacrificial order, as Detienne 1977 detected. However, the ritual perversion of the impious sacrifice of the Titans is not a model to be followed in actual rites (cf. Herrero 2006).

this renunciation too far, since it presents "Orphics" as a unified group dedicated to religious conversion or political protest.[93] However, some "conversionist" tendencies may well have been present in Orphic poems, and detected by later Jewish and Christian apologists in the search for precedents for religious conversion.

In relation with this philosophical dimension of Orphism we arrive at the third question raised by the polemic between Celsus and Origen. A central element in pagan *teletai* is the purity of the initiates, who must be "free of all pollution": is this ritual or moral purity? This distinction is late and not universally applicable. The norms established by the *themis* (or its Roman equivalent the *fas*, divine law) encompassed both aspects. The clearest case is the crime that causes the primordial impurity in the Zagreus myth: the Titans' banquet is impious both from a ritual perspective, as a perversion of sacrifice, and from a moral one, and both aspects are united in this crime and its inheritors. In any case, it is clear that thanks to the influence of Platonic ethics, of the Stoic emphasis on moral philosophy, and of Eastern religions, the ethical element was gradually introduced into the religious milieu in such a way that external ritual purity came to imply internal moral purity as well.[94] Celsus in the aforementioned text shows that in the second century AD both had an equal footing. In the examples of pagan *teletai* he quotes, the terminology of ritual purity (*katharos, synetos, hagnos, mysos*) is smoothly given a moral meaning. The moralization of ritual precepts is a lengthy process but one without abrupt leaps, in which the formulas remain very much the same. In Orphic literature, at the moment in which ritual requirements become lifetime precepts (p. 19), their transformation into moral norms, upheld by a philosophical theory, is already underway. The process of moralizing the *teletai*, like what happens with regard to Orphic eschatological literature, must have reached its apogee only in the late period, but it had deep roots in ancient Orphism, which reflected on issues of ritual purity and tried to extend it through a whole lifetime in an *orphikos bios* that, even if it is doubtful that it existed in practice (except identified with the *pythagorikos bios*), did indeed exist at least as a concept that Plato (*Leg.* 782c) praised for its moral excellence.

Nevertheless, prescriptions of external purity continue to play an important role until the end of pagan antiquity, especially in milieus influenced

---

93 Detienne 1975 and 1977. Cf. Herrero 2008c.
94 Cumont 1949, 240f, Nock 1964, 17–23, and Gordon/Alvar 2008, 192ff on the morality of "Oriental" religions. On the notions of (im)purity, Parker 1983 (on pp. 321–327 he warns against taking the distich in Asclepius' temple at Epidaurus (cap. II n. 40) as a paradigm of the general situation).

by Neopythagoreanism, and they are a target of Christian mockery and attacks, which contrast them to the Christian search for internal purity.[95] What is curious, however, is that Christian asceticism coincides in a variety of practices with this same pagan ascesis that gives rise to apologetic mockery. Precisely due to the coincidence in practices, the Christians insist on the difference in motives. Whatever their deep psychological motivations, purity prescriptions can have three types of justification, of which we have found a variety of examples in the texts examined up to now. The first type is of a mythological order and etiologizes the ritual precept with a mythological story: for example, pomegranates should not be eaten because they carry Dionysus's blood. The second type is of a theoretical order and justifies the prescription with a philosophical theory: for example, vegetarianism is justified by the theory of reincarnation, or the taboo on eggs because the egg represents the *anima mundi*. The third type is of a practical order: abstinence from meat, sex, or alcohol is justified as an ascetic means for exercising oneself in virtue and having fewer occasions of sin.

Orphic literature clearly tends to justifications of the first type, since myths are its literary material and provide an efficacious etiology for ritual prescriptions, as we have seen.[96] However, the Neopythagoreans and Platonists who revived the Orphic tradition in the Imperial age tended, logically, to offer philosophical justifications of a theoretical order: in the footsteps of Empedocles, reincarnation and similar theories about the soul are repeatedly alluded to as justification for abstinence from meat (e.g. in young Plutarch's *De Esu Carnium* or Porphyry's *De Abstinentia*), and similarly, also from beans, eggs, hearts, and in extreme versions, sexual reproduction. In contrast, Christianity takes inspiration above all from Stoic ethics and frequently draws on a variety of medical theories for justifications of the third type for its ascetic practices. In this way, a series of behaviors coincide, even if their motives are different (in the apologists' orthodoxy). Clement says, "And if a just man refuses to impose on his soul the burden of eating meat, he has a praiseworthy reason, not that of Pythagoras and his disciples, who

---

95 E.g. Clem. Alex. *Strom.* 7.4.22.7. It is the same reproach that the Gospels make against Jewish strict following of the Torah. Clement follows Philo in allegorizing ritual passages of the Old Testament to express dogmatic notions: e.g. the eunuchs and the children of the prostitute of *Dt.* 23:1 are the atheists and the idolatrous (Clem. Alex. *Protr.* 2.25.1–2; Phil. *Mig.* 69, *Mut.* 205, *Conf.* 144).

96 Among the texts studied here, cf. the taboos on pomegranates (Clem. Alex. *Protr.* 19.3), eggs (Macr. *Somn. Scip.* 1.12.12), and beans (*Inscr. Smyrn.* 728 = *OF* 582 and probably Paus. 1.37.4). Also, the taboo on the heart could be easily justified by it being the only remnant of Dionysus' body (*Protr.* 18.1).

fantasize about the soul's imprisonment" (*Strom.* 7.32.8), and very shortly afterward, he gives the reason for Christian vegetarianism: "One of the wise will abstain from eating meat as an ascetic practice and in order to prevent his flesh from being greedy for sexual pleasures" (7.33.5).

Another, very similar passage in Origen (*CC* 8.30) has exactly the same reasoning, also directed not at refuting metempsychosis, but at differentiating the motives of a potential Christian asceticism from those of the Pythagoreans, and concludes, "To eat animal flesh is indifferent; to abstain is more reasonable."[97] Possibly not only the pagans, but also many Christian ascetic practitioners were not so clear on these differences. The psychological motivations for and physical manifestations of purity practices may offer a variety of points in common among Pythagoreanism, Christianity, and other religious movements, even Manichaeism, since there is great continuity in the ancient tradition of *enkrateia* (Bianchi 1985). However, the theoretical justification of these practices is distinct in each case, a difference that ultimately results in a difference in behavior as well, so that behavioral practices cannot simply be extrapolated from one movement to another: for example, the Christian emphasis on sexual purity for moral reasons is far greater than the scant emphasis, if any, that chastity could ever have had in Orphism (no poem mentions it, and only the chorus of the *Cretans*, a literary re-creation by Euripides, speaks of "separating oneself from generation": fr. 472 Kannicht), while vegetarianism and a variety of taboos on items of food and clothing had an importance in Orphism and Pythagoreanism that they never attained in Christian circles. In this case, the apologists were insisting on a real difference.

3.2. Ritual and belief

As both Celsus and Origen recognize, the pagan *teletai* and the Christian *telete* resemble one another and are comparable in many aspects. Of course, both authors stress above all the differences, as is to be expected from apologists of any side. Boundaries have to be traced more firmly precisely where continuity is more fluid. In this regard, the apologetic attitude resembles that of modern scholars, even if the latter act for other reasons. The logical concern to understand the Greek world without projecting our modern

---

97 This is the first Patristic quotation of Sextus' *Enchiridion*, a catalogue of moral precepts of Stoic coloration, very successful as a basic handbook of Christian morality (Chadwick 1959, 107–116). An appendix to the collection was called "Pythagorean precepts": the practices were the same or very similar, albeit with different justifications.

categories and interests has sometimes led to focusing on the differences between Greek religion and Christianity with such great emphasis that the final image is distorted. Let us focus on the point where the last texts on ritual prescription have led us: the supposed difference between a ritual-based approach to religion and a belief-based one.

As a reaction against nineteenth-century interpretations of Greek myths as if they had been dogmatic articles of faith, the twentieth century found a safe shield in the principle that in their attitude to the divine the Greeks did not care so much about belief as about ritual practice and festivals. The particular Greek notion of belief has been defined with great precision in the last years, and simplistic approaches have been abandoned.[98] However, that religious self-definition came for the Greeks more through participation in ritual than through sharing opinions seems well established. It was the Cambridge ritualist school that carried this principle the furthest, and in more or less nuanced forms, it has prevailed until today.[99] In her *Prolegomena*, Jane Harrison wrote a paragraph, in reference to the Eleusinian *symbola* cited by Clement, that despite its highly *démodé* tone and content, is still of unsurpassable expressivity:

> It is significant of the whole attitude of Greek religion that the confession is not a confession of dogma or even faith, but an avowal of ritual acts performed. This is the measure of the gulf between ancient and modern. The Greeks in their greater wisdom saw that uniformity in ritual was desirable and possible; they left a man practically free in the only sphere where freedom is of real importance, i. e. in the matter of thought. So long as you fasted, drank the *kykeon*, handled the *sacra*, no one asked what were your opinions or your sentiments in the performance of those acts; you were left to find in every sacrament the only thing you could find – what you brought. Our own creed is mainly a *Credo*, an utterance of dogma, formulated by the few for the many, but it has traces of the more ancient conception of *Confiteor*, the avowal of ritual acts performed. *Credo in unam sanctam catholicam et apostolicam ecclesiam* is immediately followed by *Confiteor unum baptismum* (sic), though the instinct of dogma surges up again in the final words *in remissionem peccatorum* (Harrison 1922, 156).

The ideas of ritual uniformity, Greek "sacraments," and the enthusiastic celebration of Greek "religious freedom" are characteristic of the time, but they do not affect the great fundamental intuition of the English scholar. The Greek *mystes* defines himself with his *symbola* not as a believer in a spe-

---

98 Veyne 1983, Pirenne 2009.
99 Price 1999, 3: "Practice, not belief, is the key, and to start from questions about faith or personal piety is to impose alien values on ancient Greece." This is also Burkert's approach (1985, 1987).

cific reality or myth, but rather as a participant in a ritual. "I have drunk the *kykeon*...," the Eleusinian initiate proclaims. The passwords that the initiate's soul repeats before the guardians in certain lamellae also coincide with this pattern of bearing witness to participation in ritual.

There is much truth in Harrison's paragraph. However, let us remember that it is based on the texts of Christian apologists, who obviously would be only too happy to support such a rigid boundary (or gulf) between Christianity and the mysteries. The criticisms levied by Clement, Arnobius, Origen, and Gregory at the myths, rituals, and *symbola* of the Greek mysteries are focused on rites and ignore or make fun of any possible doctrinal contents. The distinction between the two extremes of the *credo* and the *confiteor*, therefore, is largely based on ancient apologetic agendas, and should not entail denying the nuances and intermediate shadings present in both Christian and pagan milieus. For example, the ritual of baptism or the refusal to sacrifice in a pagan ritual can become the key to Christian self-definition in a variety of contexts. On the pagan side, if a purely ritual focus may have been true for some mystery cults, it is clearly false in the case of Orphism (and of many cults impregnated by it), where as we have said more than once, intellectual speculation is as important as ritual experience.

In effect, the Orphic initiate is not only *bebaccheumenos* or *bacchos*, but also *synetos*: the "knower" is not exactly the "believer," but he comes closer to self-definition through the defense of a truth. In the lamellae, the *mystes* has not only been initiated, but also instructed in what his true lineage is, so that in his self-definition as *bacchos* there are ritual elements and elements of knowledge. The opposition "falsehood/truth" in the lamellae of Olbia (*OF* 463) and its fellows (war/peace, death/life) suggest that these *orphikoi*, the only ones attested to have considered themselves as such, did not define themselves primarily with ritual *symbola*, but rather with conceptual oppositions that bring them close to the sphere of belief. Undoubtedly, there must have been a great variety of postures within the Orphic poetic and ritual tradition, as the Derveni commentator's criticisms of purely ritualistic forms of initiation and protests against the people's "lack of belief" (P. Derv. col. V) show. In general, voices from the philosophical camp, such as Plato, logically emphasize the doctrinal element at the expense of the ritual one: "The ancient *logoi* must be believed (πείθεσθαι)" (*Epist.* 7.335a). Plutarch, sensitive at once to the philosophical and the ritual side, maintains a perfect equilibrium between them: "You are impeded from believing it (πιστεύειν) by the doctrine (λόγος) of our fathers and the mystical symbols (σύμβολα) of the initiations of Dionysus" (*Cons. ad uxor.* 10).

The texts in chapter IV demonstrate that the Christians, who inherit the Greek tradition of philosophical critique of the blunt literalism of myths and superficial practice of rites, refuse nevertheless to accept any doctrinal content that might be arrived at through their interpretation. From the Christian perspective, the Greek mysteries are reduced, in Clement's words, to "murders and tombs" (*Protr.* 2.19.2). It is clear that there is a strong apologetic charge in this judgment, which leaves aside all the possible *legomena*, and therefore ignores the fundamental dimension of Orphism. Not only does it neglect to consider rituals of prayer that are as similar to the Christian ones as the *Orphic Hymns* (e. g. *OH* 55.28: "I invoke you with pious soul and sacred words"); it also leaves aside all the doctrinal interpretations that may have been attached to mystery rites and myths (e. g. theories about the soul).

However, even the Christian criticisms of pagan rituals, which put so much emphasis on the differences and thus set up some modern scholarly divisions, themselves reveal certain resemblances of Orphic rites to Christian ones. Let us end this section by examining a celebrated case on display in the apologists' texts, the parallels to the Christian sacraments.

3.3. Eating the god?

When Justin criticizes the demons for introducing wine into the mysteries of Dionysus (*Dial.* 69, *Apol.* 1.54), he acknowledges the strong resemblance in form and content to the Christian Eucharist. The same resemblance is revealed by the later apologists' silence about the consumption of wine in the Dionysian ritual. It is well known that Dionysus is identified with wine, and drinking it is a means to attain union with him, for example in the festival of the Anthesteria. When the rite is elaborated intellectually, the traditional allegory that equates Dionysus with wine suffices, in the same way as the one that equates Demeter with bread. In contrast, Christian theology debated the identification of Christ's body and blood with bread and wine for centuries before arriving at the concept of transubstantiation. Neither the Christian debate nor the solution can be imagined for the Bacchic consumption of wine. The Greeks seem to have been more concerned with performing the ritual than with explaining it in a way that went beyond allegory.[100]

---

100 For the Anthesteria, cf. Burkert 1983, 225. On the equation of Dionysus and wine, cf. Burkert 1987, 111; Henrichs 1982, 160; Obbink 1994, 70 ("There was a consumption, rather than sacramental, ritual"). Justin also accuses Mithras' ritual of shared bread and water of plagiarizing the Christian Eucharist (*Apol.* 1.66), but this is probably just a formal similarity, since there is no other evidence for Mith-

3.3. Eating the god?

The same combination of a certain basic identity and a very different representation applies to Dionysus's sacrifice in the Zagreus myth, for which the Christian sources are particularly interesting. Let us recall (p. 249) that both Clement (*Protr.* 18.1) and Arnobius (*Adv. Nat.* 5.19) avoid making express mention to the fact that the Titans ate Dionysus after sacrificing him. Instead, both authors describe in detail how the Titans killed and cooked the infant god, and then suddenly speed up the narration and precipitate Zeus's arrival, so that the eating is passed over in silence. Instead, Firmicus Maternus (*De err.* 6.3) delights in describing the banquet: "They cooked the boy's members in various ways and devoured them, thus feeding on a human cadaver, a banquet unheard of up to that day."

It is not by chance that in the first version the eaten body belongs to a god, while in Firmicus' euhemerist version it is a human corpse. Clement's and Arnobius's silence about a deed in principle so open to criticism as a god being eaten is intriguing. Perhaps they wanted to avoid discussing the awkward theme of theophagy, since Christians themselves were accused of cannibalism on account of the Eucharistic ritual. Porphyry condemns the Eucharist with the same energy with which, as a vegetarian, he attacks blood sacrifice.[101] We cannot rule out that they had some feeling of a certain deep identity between the theophagy of the pagan myth and the Eucharist. On the other hand, we know that Clement is following closely a pagan source, while Arnobius is probably following him. Perhaps they were – consciously or not – reproducing an omission of the Greek account on which their own accounts are based. In any case, it is clear that the eating of a god is the crux of the matter: since in Firmicus' tale Dionysus is a human child, he (and his Euhemeristic source) has no problem telling the details of the cannibalistic feast.

It is noteworthy that the Christians' behavior when telling this myth coincides with that of the pagan authors who recount it: Nonnus, Himerius, Proclus, Philodemus, Diodorus, Cornutus and Servius.[102] In each and every allusion to the episode, they omit mentioning at all that the Titans ate Dionysus. There are only two notorious exceptions, Plutarch and Olympiodorus,

---

    raic sacramentalism. On the evolution of Christian Eucharistic theology, cf. *TRE* s. v. "Abendmahl."

101 Porph. fr. 69 Harnack, *apud* Macarius of Magnesia *Monogenès* 3.15 (as Goulet 2003 has re-titled the work traditionally known as *Apocriticon*). Porphyry's attack, referring to Jn 6:53, and Macarius's response (3.23) are very illuminating for our subject.

102 Nonn. *Dion.* 6.204–210; Him. *Or.* 45.4; the various mentions by Proclus are collected in *OF* 311ff Bernabé; those by Philodemus, Diodorus, Cornutus and Servius are collected in *OF* 59 Bernabé; cf. also Pausanias' ambiguity: "dangers" (7.18.14); "sufferings" (8.37.5).

who do explicitly say that the Titans ate of the flesh of Dionysus. In fact, in these two texts it is imperative to mention that fact, in order to extract the myth's anthropological consequence – the double, Titanic and Dionysian nature of human beings, who originate in the ashes of the Titans who had eaten the dismembered Dionysus. Since both texts develop this interpretation, it was impossible to omit the eating, so at least Plutarch and Olympiodorus (or their source) mention it as cautiously as they can: the verb they use, to "taste of" (γεύομαι + genitive), describes the minimum possible act of ingestion. In contrast, when Plutarch speaks of human cannibalism in the same text, he has no problem saying "mutual eating" (ἀλληλοφαγίας).[103]

What these texts reveal is clear: the eating of a god, theophagy, was for the Greeks an unspeakable taboo, an *arreton*. As such, it was a matter with which to play in literature and in imaginary rituals, but without actually expressing it in explicit ways, in words or in actions. Especially in the ecstatic cult of Dionysus, in which the *bacchoi* attained union with the god, there were many possibilities for such playing. There are some ambiguous expressions in Euripides's *Bacchae*, perhaps even in its staging, and some iconographic representations of maenadism that play with the possible identification of Dionysus with the victim of the maenads' savage fury. However, this identification is not made explicit and, in any case, is restricted to the mythological level, because the *Bacchae* is more of a dramatic representation of a myth than a depiction of an actually existing ritual. Even if the myth has haunted the imagination of ancients and moderns as a real possibility for the expression of Dionysian ecstasy, the epigraphic traces of ritual maenadism are far from having even a hint of a Eucharistic atmosphere.[104]

---

103 Plut. *De esu carn.* 1.7, Olympiod. *In Plat. Phaed.* 1.3. Parallel cases are the accounts of the myth of Lycaon, where the sources do not say explicitly whether Zeus eats his son or not (Apoll. *Bibl.* 3.8.1; Nik. Damasc. *FGH* 90 F 38); and Tantalus' myth, where Demeter "tastes" (*Schol. Pind.* 1.40: ἀπογευσαμένης) Pelops (a necessary etiology of his ivory shoulder), in a softer version than that which Pindar refused to believe (*Ol.* 1.51f), i.e. that the gods ate human flesh. Such scruples are, of course, even greater if a god is not eater, but eaten. On these cannibalistic myths, cf. Burkert 1983, 89–212.

104 Henrichs 1978, 149–152; Burkert 1983 75–78, 141. Some ambiguous expressions in the *Bacchai* suggesting the identification of Pentheus with a sacrificial victim like the bull (*Ba.* 742–745, 1185), with which Dionysus is also identified (*Ba.* 920f) could seem to hint at a sacramental, supports the sacramental interpretation of maenadism (cf. chapter V n. 78). Perhaps artificial scenic effects, like the wig that Pentheus wore at the end of the play, contributed to his identification with Dionysus (cf. Kott 1974, 205–207).

The moment in which the Greeks come closest to an explicit formulation of theophagy is the myth of the Titans, which makes the god the victim of a perverse sacrifice. Nevertheless, here too it is impossible to go beyond the mythological level, because in order to postulate the sacramental ingestion of the god's flesh in animal form, it would be necessary to suppose that in the ritual actualization of the myth of the Titans (for which there is very little evidence), the sacrificed victim was identified with Dionysus. However, this identification, which would demonstrate the existence of ritual theophagy among the Greeks, appears only in three very late Christian witnesses (Firmicus, a scholiast on Clement, and Photius), whom we have already seen to be unreliable evidence, because they offer no more than a Christianizing re-creation of a reinvented paganism. Christians who did not consider Dionysus a god, and free of the Greek taboos, they went further than Euripides and any other Greek thinker and made the easy equation of the pagan god with the victim. These testimonies have misled many modern scholars, but they do not constitute evidence for Greek sacramental sacrifice in an actual (or imagined) rite.[105]

The Christians' projection of the Eucharist onto the maenadic-Titanic sacrifice that they construct, although distorting Greek religious reality, reveals nevertheless a certain basic anthropological identity between the Dionysiac sacrifice and the Christian Eucharist. The same affinity is the reason that Clement and Arnobius omit any mention of theophagy, a taboo for them as for pagan authors, and the basis for Porphyry's attacks upon the Eucharist as a bloody sacrifice. Both are based on the equation of the god with the victim.[106] Whatever deep anthropological roots this equation may have, or whether or not the Eucharist is a sublimation of blood sacrifice, are not our concern here. But the way in which each account of theophagy was elaborated in ritual and theory is revealing.

Christianity made theophagy explicit in ritual and theology, through the symbolism provided by the bread of the paschal meal, and elaborated the philosophico-theological concept of transubstantiation. In contrast, the theophagy of the myth of the Titans did not give rise to a sacramental ritual, since an animal sacrifice in which the killed victim was equated to the god was too explicit to serve as a symbolic substitute. For this reason, there is not a single piece of valid evidence for the existence of any such bloody

---

105 Firm. Mat. *De err.* 6.5, Schol. Clem. Alex. *Protr.* 12.119.1, Focio *s. v.* νεβρίζειν discussed on p. 269. On ritual reactualization of the Titanic myth, cf. *P. Gurob*, *PSI* 850 and *P. Argent.* 1313 discussed on p. 54f.
106 On the deep identity of blood sacrifice and the Eucharist (as a sublimation), cf. Dodd 1954, 339; Henrichs 1981, 229–231; Klauck 1982.

sacramental rite, not even for its explicit description in a fictitious setting. By contrast, equating gods with other type of food, like bread or wine, attained a higher degree of symbolization and was admitted as a rhetorical expression that could become on occasion a theological solution for a ritual puzzle.[107] The myth of the Titans served, instead, as the foundation for an anthropological theory of enormous consequences. Theophagy, in this case, did not create a ritual, but a doctrine.

Thus, thanks to the Christian texts about this celebrated myth, the relativity of the old opposition between belief and ritual in Orphism is demonstrated. Christian theology succeeded in giving full significance to a rite that is the center of ecclesial life. In contrast, the Orphic myth was the source of an anthropological theory that circulated in the literary tradition and not in ritual representation. Both preserve, or sublimate, the taboo on theophagy by different means, but if the Christian approach is based as much on belief (transubstantiation) as on rite (Eucharist), the Orphic approach starts from the imagination of a ritual (the sacrifice) recounted in a myth and ends up with a theory about the soul. The difference makes evident the disparate nature of two religious phenomena that nonetheless appeal to the same experience, the same almost instinctive equation of god and sacrificial victim. As so often, the opposition between the two is not so much that of belief vs. ritual or vice versa as it is that of an organized religion vs. a literary and ritual tradition.

4. Causes of the parallels

4.1. Typological resemblances

Some of the parallels between Orphism and Christianity probably have no other reason for being than the resemblance derived from a religious experience lived and transmitted in similar ways, without the need to postulate influence between the two. Both can be included in the general category of "religions of salvation," which, according to Max Weber's reasonable thesis, develop on the basis of similar social circumstances, the loss of political power by aristocracies. Jan Bremmer has successfully applied to Orphism an idea that is also valid for explaining aspects of early Christianity.[108] The

---

107 Cic. *ND* 3.42; Eur. *Ba.* 284; Tim. fr. 780.
108 Cf. Weber 1922, Bremmer 2002, 25; and Kippenberg 1991 for a reapplication of the Weberian thesis to Judaism, Christianity, and Shia Islam.

hope of salvation after death (in part as compensation for the loss of earthly privileges) and all that this idea brings with it, such as interest in eschatology, the experience of a liberating personal god, the obsession with purity, the distinction between the initiated and the profane, are shared by Orphism and Christianity. These parallels arise as natural developments of this fundamental identity, and it is therefore logical that they offer a basis for ideological coincidences, anthropological and ritual foundations that resemble one another, similar images, and mutual influences. Most of these have already been commented on as they have appeared in the texts (e.g. the parallel distinction called/chosen and *narthekophoroi/bacchoi*). Let it suffice to point out one new example here: beginning with St Paul, the image of the *agon* in which the Christian is to finish the contest crowned with the victory of salvation is very popular in Christianity, and it will become even more popular in martyrology. Some verses of the Orphic lamellae appear to point toward a similar conception of initiation as a victory in competition. It is clear that this is not a matter of influence, but rather of a common image in the Greek world that lends itself to use by religions of elitist salvation.[109]

Another factor that produces inevitable resemblances is that both Orphism and Christianity can also be classified under another general category, "the religions of the book," which start from the authority of divinely inspired texts, although it is necessary to insist that the authority of the canon of Judeo-Christian Scriptures is infinitely more rigid than the authority of the Orphic poems, an authority based on the weight of the traditional form and totally open to expansions, reworkings, and reinterpretations.[110] However, despite these differences, the textual dependence of both the Orphic and the Christian traditions leads not only to mutual assimilations, like the use of the term *hieros logos* for the Bible[111] or the comparison between Christian Scriptures and pagan "Scriptures" made by Celsus and Origen (*CC* 1.17), but also to coincident effects

---

109 Cf. 1 Cor. 9:25 and other passages studied by Pfitzner 1967, who shows how Paul adapts a Stoic topos. Clem. Alex. *Protr.* 1.2.3 also uses the image. On the other hand, an Orphic gold leaf (*OF* 488) says, "I stepped up to the crown with my swift feet." Ehrhardt 1957 suggests ascribing to Orpheus a quotation from "the theologian" in the scholia to Demosthenes that speaks about the "crowns for the competitors," but the relationship to the Pauline passages is not even indirect (cf. I n. 21.).

110 Cf. Henrichs 2003, 215 on the different religious function of Orphic writings and Christian scriptures (pp. 207 n.1 and 240 n. 118 for bibliography on ancient and modern *Buchreligionen*).

111 Henrichs 2003, 240–242, nn. 119–124 for several examples of Jewish (esp. Philo) and Christian usages of the terms ἱεροὶ λόγοι, ἱεραὶ γραφαί, ἱερὰ γράμματα and ἱεραὶ βίβλοι, which in pagan Greek and Egyptian contexts designate religious writings.

that arise almost inevitably from considering a text as an authority: allegorical interpretation and symbolism are necessary instruments for actualizing the text's meaning and preserving its authority, by giving it new senses without changing its words (in the case of the Bible) or by modifying and adapting it within the limits of previous tradition (in the case of Orphism). Christians and pagans in their mutual polemic reject allegory as a method of interpretation for their rivals' myths at the same time that they defend and claim it for the interpretation of their own. The resemblance of the reactions comes from a similar point of departure: dependence on a text.

Other parallels could be associated with this markedly textual character: predominance of doctrine over ritual and, within the ritual sphere, of *legomena* over *dromena*. It is especially interesting that both traditions make use of a very similar mechanism for arriving at abstract ideas, on the basis of metaphors offered by the literal sense of myth: e. g. creation as conceived as generation of matter, as transformation of matter, or *ex nihilo* are abstract notions constructed from the images of the Creator as father, as artisan, or as emitter of the creative word, respectively. Without a textually transmitted reflection, this type of evolution would be unthinkable.

It is in relation with these typological parallels that a very striking coincidence between Orphism and Christianity should be considered: the existence of a double level of understanding of the scheme of salvation, one of great intellectual and philosophical sophistication and another bordering on superstition that guarantees salvation mechanically. In fact, rather than of two levels, we should speak of two extreme poles between which the adepts of each religion move, since religion and magic are difficult, not to say impossible, to find in a "chemically pure" state. Like other apologists, Origen attacks the pagan *teletai* in the same terms in which Celsus attacks the Christian ones, and both sets of arguments are ultimately derived from the Platonic model of criticism of itinerant priests and charlatans who treated their initiations as a mere business matter, selling automatic salvation. In both Orphism and Christianity, this type of *goetes* coexisted with elevated interpretations containing large doses of speculation and mysticism. What is curious is that if the ideological coincidences of the high-end speculations on the divine and the nature of man arise from sharing both a hope of salvation and a textual transmission, the "low" end also results from the combination of these two factors: the fundamental instrument of the itinerant priests was the book, used almost as a magical spell, and the basic need of which they took advantage was the longing for salvation and purification. It is evident that exactly the same phenomenon was present in Christianity.[112] The venerable names of *Erlösungsreligionen* and *Buchreligionen* cover an infinitely wide range of ideas and practices, some of them not venerable at all.

Thus, none of these basic analogies demands a genealogical explanation entailing influence from one side on the other. However, within this general framework of appeal to similar religious needs by way of a textual medium that makes certain resemblances possible, even inevitable, the Orphic tradition and Christianity offer parallels that can only be explained by some form of contact. The following sections discuss the three ways in which that contact could have taken place.

4.2. Eastern waves

A first explanation of more specific parallels is a common origin in Middle Eastern mythology and speculation, which had a powerful influence on both the Bible and the beginnings of Greek poetry and philosophy: Canaanite, Egyptian, Mesopotamian, and Indo-Iranian elements are perceptible in both the Greek and biblical traditions.[113] Although they are incorporated and evolve differently in each case, they do not cease to maintain a certain parallel trajectory that facilitates their convergence under Christian influence. This is a very broad process moving in both directions between the Near East and Greece from the second millennium BC to the first millennium AD, within which I will limit myself here to describing the Orphic material.

It is in the cosmogonic material where the Christians draw most on these parallels. The idea of a god who is creator of the cosmos may have entered Orphic poetry through Eastern influence in archaic times (Burkert 2008), and more than a thousand years later the Christians, especially Lactantius, have no hesitation in assimilating this god to the Creator God of Genesis – a book heavily influenced by the same Eastern sources. Along with the influence of the Babylonian creation accounts, we must add the impact of Persian Mazde-

---

112 See e.g. the books used by charlatans in Plat. *Resp.* 364e, Eur. *Hipp.* 952–954, Dem. 18.259. Cf. Jiménez 2002, Henrichs 2003, 212–216. A very graphic example of the relation between books and dubious religious services is the etymology of Spanish *bribón* ("scoundrel") from βίβλον (cf. the English "bribe," originally the piece of bread given to a beggar).

113 Cf. West 1978 and 1997, Burkert 1992 and 2003 on the relationship between the Near East and Greece; Bernabé 1997 and 2008, and Burkert 2008 on the particular case of Orphism; Del Olmo 1998 for biblical correspondences with northern Semitic myths; Bottéro 1996 with Babylonian myths; also Albertz 1994.

ism on both milieus, the biblical and the Greek. The creation of the heaven, the stars, the earth, and the seas in *Genesis* (1:6–10), in this order, is identified by Lactantius (*Epitome* 3) with the Orphic creation of heaven, earth, stars, and sea (*OF* 247). However, more than in these elements, which are almost universal in creation stories and in which "influence" is difficult to prove, a common Middle Eastern origin can be exemplified in a much more concrete concept in which the coincidence cannot be due to chance: *pneuma*.

Pneuma in the sense of "spirit" – divine breath for the Jews, Holy Spirit for the Christians – appears in several late Orphic fragments cited by the apologists that are likely either forgeries or Orphic poems influenced by Judaism. The long version of the *Testament* says that God "guides the world with his spirit between the airs and the waters";[114] the *Smaller Krater*, a late Orphic poem influenced by Judaism, accompanies the creation of the cosmos with the whistling of the winds (*pneumasi*) mixed with voices (*OF* 414.2); Clement plays with the senses of neuma in his Christian adaptation of Orphic-Pythagorean imagery in *Protrepticus* 1.1–5; and last but not least, *OF* 853, cited by Didymus as a pagan intuition of the Trinity, makes God's impulse, "the wise force of the spirit," into the motor of all human accomplishment.

It is clear that Didymus manipulates the Orphic text in a Christianizing sense. Though it cannot be ruled out that he is citing a forgery like the *Testament*, it is probably a case of Jewish or Christian influence in a pagan Orphic poem (p. 199). However, in any case, the use of *pneuma* had precedents in ancient Orphism, enabling its easy Judeo-Christian adaptation or forgery. The evidence presents *pneuma* both in its primary meaning of "wind" in theogonic contexts and in the more abstract sense of "spirit" in more philosophical contexts. The first appearance of the concept in an Orphic context sets the pattern for its later development in Orphism. The Derveni commentator says that Orpheus calls the Moira *pneuma*, most likely on the basis of the presence of *pnoie* (breath, the poetic equivalent of what *pneuma* means in prose) in the Orphic theogony, in a verse similar to one in the later *Hymn to Zeus* (*OF* 31): Ζεὺς πνοιὴ πάντων Ζεὺς πάντων ἔπλετο μοῖρα.[115] The commentator appears

---

114 *OF* 378.27: πνεύματι δ' ἡνιοχεῖ. A secondary variant is πνεύματα (as object of ἡνιοχεῖ), but the instrumental dative is better attested (Riedweg 1993, 38). There may be a reference to Peripatetic cosmological theories (the next line, whose text is corrupt, seems to allude to heavenly phenomena), but one must not forget the reference to Gn 1:2 with the wind and the waters.

115 Janko 2001 and Bernabé (*OF* 14) accept the suggestion by Merkelbach 1967 and Claus 1981 of attributing that line to the Derveni theogony (against West 1983, 90 n. 36, and Betegh 2004, 126, who consider it a later Stoic addition), since the commentator says (col. XVIII.3) that Orpheus called (ὠνόμασεν) the Moira by

to be close to the ideas of Diogenes of Apollonia, who saw in air the principle of the world that governs men, and he finds this principle in the Orphic theogonic image of *pnoie*. Now, the verse that identifies Zeus with the "breath of all things" already goes beyond the physical image of breath and is a prelude to, and possible inspiration for, the Stoic idea of *pneuma* as the vital breath that runs through everything. This is no surprise, if we recall that, besides the aerocentric theories of Anaximenes and Diogenes, the Pythagorean cosmological theories already assigned *pneuma* a central role.[116]

In later Orphic evidence, *pneuma* appears both in its most literal sense and in more abstract senses. The *pneumata* appear together with Eros in a theogonic fragment of uncertain origin as the children of Time (*OF* 360). In the *Rhapsodies* the divine (θειώδης) *pneuma* plays an important role in catalyzing the formation of the primordial cosmic egg from the original chaos (*OF* 115, *OF* 117). The Christian apologetic novel (and its Jewish sources) known as the *Pseudoclementina* manifests great enthusiasm for this role of *pneuma* in the *Rhapsodies*. Of course, it is possible to see in this divine *pneuma* an element of the Stoic philosophy that impregnates the *Rhapsodies*, but it is clear that they are drawing on a much earlier theogonic image: the wind that fertilizes the egg is common to various Eastern cosmogonies.[117]

We find the same evolution from a theogonic image of wind to an abstract concept of creative impulse and divine breath in the Bible. Let us recall the beginning of *Genesis*: "The earth was without form, and void, and darkness covered the abyss, and the spirit (*pneuma* = *ruah*) of God moved upon the waters" (*Gn.* 1:2). The Hebrew *ruah* originally meant both "amorous desire" and "wind"[118] and was gradually elaborated as God's life-giving breath, which Christianity theologized as the Third Person of the Trinity. At a later stage, it would be easy for Jewish and Christian theologians to ap-

---

the name *pneuma*, which suggests that there was a line in the poem identifying both with Zeus.
116 Diog. Ap. fr. B5 D-K (cf. Betegh 2004, 306–323 for his relationship to the Derveni commentator). Cf. Aristot. *Phys.* 213b 22, *De Pythagoreis apud* Stob. *Ecl.* 1.18.1. Diodorus says (1.12.2), drawing on Hecataeus, that the first to identify Zeus and *pneuma* were the Egyptians. Other references in Gagné 2007.
117 E.g. the cosmogonies of Sanchuniaton and Moch (the latter also has an egg born from the wind), described by West 1997 in comparison with Orphic and Iranian cosmogonies (also West 1983, 199–204).
118 West 1978, 29. The parallel with *OF* 360, which makes the two senses two different entities by making Eros and the winds children of Cronus, is very clear and proves the Eastern roots of the image. Cf. Aristophanes' parodic cosmogony in *Birds*, with Eros being born from the cosmic egg "swift as the whirlwinds of the tempest" (697).

proximate it to the Stoic concept (Verbeke 1945), on the basis of the LXX translation of *ruaḥ* as *pneuma*, and for Didymus (or his source) also to approximate it to the Orphic theogonic image. It is clear that these approximations are not carried out only in the context of orthodoxy: Gnostic cosmogonies and speculations enthusiastically combine biblical and Greek ideas and images in which *pneuma* in its physical and philosophical senses plays a fundamental role.[119]

It seems clear that this parallel development of *pneuma* in the biblical and Greek traditions, which culminates in a final convergence, arises from a common origin in the Middle Eastern imagery that locates wind or air as a crucial agent in the cosmogonic process. In Greece this idea takes form both in the mythological cosmogonies – not only the Orphic one: the most explicit is that of Pherecydes, in which Time begets Fire, Wind (*pneuma*), and Water (fr. 60 Schibli) – and in the importance of *aer* as *arche* in Presocratic philosophy, which develops in philosophical prose what the poets continue to express in literary images. It is highly possible, in addition, that the central role of air in various Greek theories about the soul also originated in Eastern speculation, probably in a Persian and Indian milieu.[120] Some Orphic poems also contained the idea that the soul enters the body carried by the winds with the intake of breath, an idea probably tied to these ideas of Eastern origin.[121] And in the Bible too, on the other hand, the idea that air not only creates the cosmos but also gives life to man is perceptible, adapted to a unitary and not dualistic anthropology, in the word closest to the Greek "soul," *nephes*, a kind of vital breath that possibly comes from the same root as the verb "to breathe."[122] The second account of the Creation says, "And God shaped man from the clay of the earth and breathed into his nostrils the breath of life (*nephes* = πνοὴ ζωῆς in the translation of the LXX)" (*Gn.* 2:7).

Thus, in the three cited Orphic texts with Jewish / Christian sources (*Testament, Krater, OF* 853), the idea that *pneuma* is an agent that assists in

---

119 *Corpus Hermeticum* 3 N-F unites biblical and Stoic tradition; the Manichean *Kephalaia* (West 1978, 37) unite Iranian and Greek tradition.
120 West 1978 analyses the parallels between Pherecydes, Anaximenes and Heraclitus and Eastern cosmogonies in which air has a central role. On pp. 104ff he presents texts from Persia and the Indian Upanishads where the winds inspire life.
121 Aristotle, *De anima* 410b27 (*OF* 421). Gagné 2006 shows that Aristotle refers to the Orphic poem *Physika*, a theogony in which the Tritopatores were guardians of the winds that transported the soul and at the same time ancestors of mankind. Christian discussions of the virgin birth speak of this vivifying *pneuma* (ψυχοτρόφος, ζῳογόνος) with terms that are directly derived from the earlier Greek tradition (Orig. *CC* 1.37, Eus. *PE* 3.12, Aug. *CD* 21.5).
122 Bremmer 2002, 8 with bibliography. Cf. *Ex.* 23:12, 31:17, 2 *Sam.* 16:14.

creation and that moves and gives life to man has biblical roots, but it has close precedents in earlier Orphism that make assimilation or influence possible. It is easy to see where the circle begins and where it ends. The parallel between biblical ideas and Orphic texts, arising from a common Middle Eastern origin that facilitates their re-encounter in late antiquity, reveals a broader process: the various waves of Eastern influence in pre-classical times introduced into Greece theogonic and philosophical ideas that the Greeks, including the Orphic poets, developed within their own systems of thought. The same ideas also had an impact on the Bible, the starting point for Jewish and later Christian theology, with very different intellectual frameworks. The encounter between the biblical tradition and the Greek philosophical and literary tradition, from the translation of the LXX to the construction of Christian theology, was facilitated by the common origin of certain materials like the creative and life-giving *pneuma*, materials that had been inserted into and had evolved within both traditions in parallel ways. In reality, the Christianization of the Greek world was one more of the successive waves of Orientalism experienced by Greece throughout her history, and like the others, it cultivated ground already tilled by the earlier waves.

4.3. General Platonism

Practically all the elements that we find in Christianity in relation with anthropological dualism and with the soul as an entity separate from the body are the result of Greek influence, since Old Testament anthropology is unitary. Beginning in the Hellenistic age, in the so-called inter-testamentary period, ideas about the survival of the soul instead of the body appear in a Jewish milieu, for example in the *Book of Enoch*.[123] The Greek translation of the LXX already entails, inevitably, a certain Greek influence as it introduces into the biblical text terms loaded with four centuries of philosophical speculation like *psyche*.[124] Christianity inherits this reception of Greek dualism, the presence of which in the New Testament is still rather slight, but which increases beginning in the second century AD and reaches its culmination in the key authors for the definitive theological construction of Christianity, such as Origen, the Cappadocian Fathers, and Augustine.

---

123 1 *Enoch* 22 presents the just and unjust in different places in Sheol. However, traditional ideas of the Afterlife survived for a long time in Judaism in coexistence with the new. Cf. Bremmer 2002, 8f.

124 Cf. Bremmer 2002, 3 and 135 n. 23 on the Jewish/Christian reception of the Greek concept of *psyche*.

The reception of this anthropological dualism explains the coincidences between Orphism and Christianity in this field, like the soul's expiation of an inherited guilt (pp. 336ff). However, these coincidences are not the product of "Orphic influence," at least not directly. Orphism occupies a very marginal place in the wealth of Greek ideas that are gradually adapted to the biblical tradition in successive stages: Plato is the principal promulgator of dualistic anthropology and the immortality of the soul, and Platonism is the principal source of the diffusion of these ideas among ever-wider circles of society. Even the myths about the fate of the soul in dialogues like the *Republic*, the *Phaedrus*, the *Phaedo*, and the *Timaeus* are the starting points for new eschatological visions in an atmosphere of generalized Platonism that impregnates not only philosophy,[125] but also pagan and Judeo-Christian religion and a variety of intermediate camps like Gnosticism and, later, Manichaeism. Plato received and re-elaborated Orphic and Pythagorean ideas, but he became their inevitable point of reference: I have previously compared his work to Marx's *Capital* for contemporary Marxism, for which the earlier utopian socialists are very secondary and almost anecdotal references. In addition, besides Plato, other philosophers who may also have been inspired by Orphic ideas, like Empedocles and to a lesser extent Heraclitus and the Stoics, also had much greater standing than Orphic poetry as transmitters not only of ideas, but also of images with which to express them. It is a representative case that when St Paul in his discourse in the Areopagus appropriates the idea of a single lineage for god(s) and men, one of the most characteristic traits of the golden lamellae, he brings in a line from Aratus: "We are of His lineage."[126]

In fact, we have seen that in the majority of cases, Christian knowledge of Orphic literature comes not from direct contact with Orphic texts, but rather from the pagan philosophical literature that cites them. The ideological contacts are of the same sort, necessarily mediated by the philosophers who systematized and gave coherence to ideas that in earlier Orphism were more vague and dispersed. We might speak more properly of "indirect Orphic influence," if we consider Orphism to be at the root of the appearance of some of these ideas in Greece. However, I do not consider this to be useful, because in such an indirect influence, across six centuries of mediation, this word adds little. Searching at any cost for Orphic influence behind the ideo-

---

125 Chadwick 1966, 5–9 describes imperial philosophy as fundamentally Platonic in metaphysics and Stoic in ethics. Cf. Dillon 1988 on the general eclecticism of the time.
126 *Acts* 17:28 = Arat. *Phaen.* 5. Cf. *OF* 474. 5: *genos olbion euchomai einai*. Cf. Des Places 1964 about the *syggeneia* between men and gods from Homer to the Christian Fathers (without mention of Orphism).

logical parallels makes the label so general that it loses any useful meaning. For example, Guthrie (1952, 269) said that the Christian "idea of Purgatory had its origin in the Orphic notion of an intermediate stage between life on earth and the final bliss of the deified soul." Yet Purgatory as such was theorized in the twelfth century, although it is true that there are Patristic precedents for a process by which souls are purified before attaining definitive beatitude. However, if we want to spot its classical roots, the clear antecedent for this idea would be Plato, who develops the subject with all possible detail,[127] and perhaps Vergil in the literary sphere, not Orphism, in which it is not even certain that the cycle of reincarnation was conceived of as a progressive purification, and not merely an expiatory punishment. The problem with postulating Orphic influence in cases like this, in which the Orphic antecedent is very distant and highly mediated, is that it leads to projecting the Christian dogmatic framework onto Orphism and so to distorting the latter in the direction with which we are already familiar.

4.4. Mutual influence

We can indeed suppose a direct influence of Orphism on Christianity as the most probable explanation of some parallels, for which it is not necessary to postulate an intermediary. The clearest case is that of the images about the fate of the soul after death. Origen himself recognized (pp. 342–345) that the difference between Christian eschatology and that of the pagan *teletai* was one of meaning, not content. That the eschatological parallels are the result of Greek influence on the second generation of Christians can also be seen in the fact that in the New Testament concerns about the Beyond are almost entirely limited to two themes, the resurrection of the dead and the Last Judgment.[128] Both themes are ideas alien to the Greek world: the resurrection of the body is a constant motive for criticism of Christianity, and the collective judgment of the Second Coming is related to millenarian and apocalyptic ideas with Jewish roots, which are distinct from the individual judgment of each soul after death. It is only in the second century AD, coinciding with the spread of martyrdom and the reception of the Platonic sepa-

---

127 Solmsen 1972 shows that Origen is inspired by Plato for his theory of a progressive purification of the soul (probably through a transmigration cycle). On Purgatory, cf. Le Goff's 1981 classic study, and now Bremmer 2002, 64–69.
128 Luke is practically the only New Testament author who sometimes seems interested in the deceased's immediate destiny after death, before the final resurrection (e.g. *Lc.* 23:43). Cf. Bremmer 2002, 56f.

ration of body and soul, that the idea of an immediate voyage to the Beyond and all kinds of eschatological details of Greek origin appear in Christian literature. However, it must not be forgotten that the resurrection of the body, the Final Judgment, and other factors alien to Greek eschatology continue to condition the Christian image of the world beyond the grave and to lead it in directions different from those taken by Orphism.[129]

Research has progressed furthest in this area, for which Jewish and Christian eschatological literature offers wonderful material. In 1913, Albrecht Dieterich compared the recently discovered second-century-AD *Apocalypse of Peter* to the evidence for Greek (especially Orphic) eschatology and spotted multiple lines of continuity. Dieterich's underlying vision, typical of his time, that many Christians were converted Orphics, has been abandoned, and on the other hand, some central images of the *Apocalypse of Peter* (e.g. the tours of Hell) have been shown to stem from Jewish apocalyptic writings.[130] However, not a few of Dieterich's observations are still valid, and the probable Egyptian origin of this Christian work makes the transfer of images very plausible. For example, a particularly successful image of Orphic origin, constantly repeated from Plato to a variety of Christian passages, among them the *Apocalypse of Peter*, seems to have been the mud (βόρβορος) in which the condemned are portrayed as being mired.[131] Many other images of punishment also coincide with Greek precedents in this and other Christian writings, but their wide diffusion as elements of suffering or purification in a variety of contexts inside and outside Greece makes it difficult to know whether there is a direct connection. A convergence of universal motifs cannot be ruled out, as in the case of fire, which appears in the

---

129 E.g. the culmination of the love relationship with God in the Afterlife is alien to Greek eschatological tradition (cf. Bremmer 2002, 62 on the *Passio Perpetuae*). Orphic eschatological images more difficult to fit within orthodox Christianity were received in Gnostic literature (e.g. the ascent of the soul through obstacles on the way to the celestial Beyond).
130 Bremmer 2003, 1–7 tells the interesting story of the discussion of Dieterich's (and Usener and Norden's) idea: Himmelfarb (1983) accused Dieterich of neglecting, due to anti-Jewish bias, the fundamentally Jewish roots of the *Ap. Petri*. Bauckman 1998, 49–80 holds a more balanced position, according to which some specifically Greek roots are traceable within the general Jewish framework.
131 *Ap. Petri* 8.23; 9.24; Plat. *Phaed.* 69c; Aristoph. *Ra.* 145, Plot. *Enn.* I.6.6.5. Cf. Aubineau 1959 on this image; Bremmer 2003, 10–14 plausibly considers it the main proof of Orphic influence on the original Greek version (the Ethiopic version omits the mention of the mud). However, our knowledge that this torment was described in Orphic literature comes from intermediate sources like Plato and Aristophanes, so we cannot rule out that they were also mediators (like Vergil in the Latin tradition) of the transmission of Orphic images to Christian eschatological writings.

Apulian ceramics, although only indirectly in the texts, as an Orphic afterlife punishment.[132] However, fire as punishment can also be located in the *sheol* of the biblical tradition, and its importance as a purifying element is much greater in the Christian milieu, so it should not be automatically projected backward into Orphic eschatology.[133]

The images of the blessed also coincide, although it is sometimes difficult to go beyond a convergence of universal motifs. Light, for example, has a certain importance in Orphically colored descriptions of the Beyond, as a possible correlate of the initiatory experience, although in the Christian heaven *lux perpetua* is the overwhelmingly predominant element.[134] The case of the water drunk by the souls is clearer: the Egyptian origin of this image in the lamellae seems evident, due to the parallels, even verbal ones, with the *Book of the Dead*. Possibly the Christian *refrigerium*, in which the souls are imagined to refresh themselves in a similar way with the water of eternal life, originates in the Greek imaginary of Orphic roots. However, it may also originate in the same world of Egyptian eschatology that is at the root of the lamellae, or even in the universal conception (especially in the hot Mediterranean) of water as purification and rest.[135] Thus, the limited field of eschatological images, despite its anecdotal nature, reflects in miniature the spectrum of possibilities opened when discussing the root of the similarities between Christian and Orphic theology and experience: convergence of uni-

---

132 Although there are no references to fire as punishment in Orphic texts or in Plato, it does appear in the pseudo-Platonic dialogue *Axiochus* 371d (*OF* 430 IX), with motifs very similar to those on Apulian pottery. The cosmological function of fire in the Derveni Papyrus and the large Thurii leaf (*OF* 492) may have some relation to its eschatological role (Betegh 2004, 325–348).

133 Bremmer 2002, 63f. Clement (*Strom.* 5.8.45.4) alludes to fire just after the quotation of *OF* 438 on the fate of the soul. Gregory of Nazianzus in the poem *De Anima* (App. 8), criticizing the *Rhapsodies*, mentions punishment by fire (l. 46: cf. Herrero 2007b). Both texts may point to its presence in Orphic eschatology, although they could also be their authors' own projections of Christian imagery. Cf. Origen (*CC* 5.14–15) defending the purifying power of fire, contesting Celsus's mocking remarks about a cooking God.

134 Bremmer 2002, 60. For light in Orphic Afterlife imagery, cf. Pind. *Ol.* 2.63, fr. 129 S-M; in the death-like experience of the mysteries, Plut. fr. 178, 211 Sandbach; in the Christian Heaven, *Ap. Joh.* 22.5.

135 The Roman hypogeum of Viale Manzoni with Christian frescoes of the third century has some pagan imagery close to the Orphic leaves, and the *refrigerium* of the soul is specifically mentioned (p. 71). Cf. Chicoteau 1997, Bernabé-Jiménez 2008, 323ff. Cf. Merkelbach 1997 on the Egyptian roots of some elements of the gold leaves. Perhaps the same Egyptian origin can be posited for some eschatological Jewish and Christian images, without the need for an Orphic link.

versal motifs, common Eastern origin, indirect influence through the general Hellenistic tradition (especially Platonism), or direct influence.

It must be noted that the influence applies not so much to the ideological content as to the container, the image that represents it: the *Apocalypse of Peter* does not take from Orphism the condemnation of sinners in the Beyond, but the eternal mud as the image of torment. The iconography, like the texts, did not generally fuse Orpheus with Christ or David, but rather presented the latter with the traits of the former. The same constant applies in other areas in which direct transfer is also probable. It is impossible to know exactly whether these images were taken directly from Orphic literature or from intermediate sources, which nevertheless would not prevent a certain degree of consciousness of their Orphic origin. We have seen that Augustine appropriates the expression of the *soma-sema* (*Contra Iul. Pelag.* 4.78), Hippolytus the metaphor of the cosmic loom from the poem *Peplos* and from Pherecydes (*De Antichr.* 4), and Clement the image of Orphic-Pythagorean origin of the harmony of the cosmos caused by the divine song/instrument (*Protr.* 1.5). Let us recall another famous example: Gilles Quispel postulated, probably with good reason, an Orphic origin for the expressions of divine supremacy in the *Apocalypse of John*: "I am the Alpha and the Omega, the first and the last (ὁ πρῶτος καὶ ὁ ἔσχατος), the beginning and the end."[136] The *Apocalypse of John* does not take from Orphic literature the idea of God's eternity and supremacy over the world, which already appears in the Bible in expressions that proclaim God's eternity.[137] What might come from Orphism is the expression "beginning and end," which appears in a very similar formula (πρῶτος καὶ ὕστατος) in the first two lines of the different versions of the successful *Hymn to Zeus*.[138] As an image that expresses a shared theological monism, it is perfectly adapted to the biblical idea of

---

136 *Ap. Joh.* 22.13 (briefer formulations in 1.8, 21.6.) Quispel 1978, 17: "This is an echo of the old Orphic saying, for which there is no parallel in rabbinic literature ... the only passage in the New Testament where we can prove ... that the author was influenced ... by Orphic lore."
137 *Is.* 44:6: I am the first (*protos*) and the beyond (*meta tauta*); *Is.* 48:12: I am the first and for ever (*eis ton aionà*) *Hebr.* 13:8: Jesus Christ, yesterday, today and the same for ever (*eis tous aionas*).
138 *OF* 14, 31 and 243. Although it is also transmitted by other authors like Plato (*Leg.* 4.715e), the expression still keeps its Orphic hallmark (e.g. Apul. *Mund.* 37, and we may suppose that an apocalyptic text takes it rather from Orphic poems than from Plato. Josephus has similar expressions (*Ant. Iud.* 8.280, *Contra Apion.* 2.190), probably also due to direct or indirect Orphic influence.

God, as is demonstrated by its subsequent success in Christian iconography and literature.[139]

As might be logically expected, where there is the greatest possibility for direct influence is not in the sphere of the prose normally used by the apologists, but in that of Christian hexameter poetry, because it is there where Orphic poetic expressions can be most usefully and easily adapted. In the hexametric poem *De anima* by Gregory of Nazianzus, there are not only attacks (lines 22–52 in App. 8) that reflect the rival terminology (τιμή, ποινή, κύκλος, τίσις), but also some expressions in the description of his own thesis that could perfectly well have come from the Orphic poetry he is trying to supplant: χιτών (l. 115), νεκρόφορος (l. 116), πρωτόγονος (l. 128), μύστης (l. 67). Likewise, the section of *loci similes* in Bernabé's *Orphica* offers abundant parallels with Christian poetry and hymnody. Christian poets must have exploited the resources and formulas of pagan theological poetry, and the Orphic poems may have been a substantial source of inspiration for them, as for their contemporaries Nonnus and Claudian.[140] An examination of these poems is beyond my scope here, but it is coherent with the principle that inspires direct borrowings, both textual and iconographic: ideological resemblance in certain aspects favors the transfer of expressions and images that give shape to similar ideas.

Influence as an explanation of the resemblances between pagan religions and Christianity does not go only in one direction; rather, when the pagan evidence is late, it may well be a matter of reverse influence. The logical interest aroused by the first possibility in the nineteenth century caused the second to be neglected until the middle of the twentieth century, when scholars noticed that what they had taken to be very ancient patterns (e. g., Frazer's construct of the vegetable god who dies and returns to life) were in reality late convergences produced by the growing influence of Christianity.[141] This explanation can also be applied to some Orphic evidence, since it

---

139 The image of Alpha and Omega may be related to quasi-magical literature in which the alphabet was given magical properties: cf. Dornseiff 1925 on the mystical and magical uses of the alphabet. As a literary complement to the general presence of A and Ω in Christian symbology, cf. the *Pascual Hymn* (ll. 812–814) by Melito of Sardes.
140 E. g. when describing God in his poems, Gregory of Nazianzus uses epithets similar to the *Hymn to Zeus* of the *Rhapsodies* (*OF* 243): e. g. ἀπείριτος (*Carm. Arc.* 1.25; *OF* 243.2), οἶδμα θαλάσσης (*OF* 243.28; *PG* 37.770). Of course many of these expressions are also shared with other theological and oracular poetry described on p. 94. On Orphic traces in Nonnus and Claudian, cf. II n. 4.
141 Cf. n. 66.

is logical that if resemblance leads to the transfer of images to Christianity, the reverse process could also take place.

The ultra-sceptical theses of those who see in the myth of Dionysus and the Titans a result of the projection of the Christian idea of original sin can be rejected. The myth existed with its anthropological interpretation long before the Christians elaborated the dogma of original sin (p. 336). On the other hand, a possible Christianization of the myth of Dionysus is indeed observable in the passage of the rhetor Himerius that refers to it: "Zeus, observing, had seen it all and, after waking up Dionysus, as the tale says, he made the Titans disappear, according to the myths."[142] According to this version, Zeus decides to intervene at a certain moment, as if the Titans' attack and his son's suffering and return to life were part of a divine plan, in a clear projection of Christ's death and resurrection. The same influence of aspects of Christ on Dionysus, facilitated by the narrative resemblances in their lives (pp. 330ff), is visible in other evidence. The descent of Dionysus into Hades after his death is mentioned in a Rhodian inscription from the third century AD, apparently influenced by Christ's descent *ad inferos* (p. 49). However, the episode that seems to have had the greatest impact is the Nativity. Epiphanius describes a ritual in the temple of Core in Alexandria in which on 6 January a statue was carried, adorned with the sign of the cross, with the proclamation that "at this hour of this day Core, that is to say, the Virgin, gave birth to Aion." Core's role as mother of Dionysus appears to have suffered the influence of the Christian account of the Savior's virginal birth.[143] Epiphanius's text depicts a parallel case to that of a mosaic from Nea Paphos on Cyprus (325–350 A.D.) in which a child Dionysus on the lap of Hermes is represented amid personifications of Dionysian concepts clearly following the model of the adoration of the Magi (plate 5).[144]

Other late evidence reveals the Christianization of a paganism on the defensive that half-consciously adopted the forms of its rival in its own de-

---

142 *Or.* 45.4: ὁ γὰρ Ζεὺς ἐποπτεύων ἑώρα πάντα, καὶ τὸν Διονύσον ἐγείρας, ὡς λόγος, Τιτᾶνας ἐποίει παρὰ τῶν μύθων ἐλαύνεσθαι. There seems to be a contraposition between the *logos* and the *myths*. Perhaps the first was an interpretation derived from the mythic tale.

143 *Panar.* 51.22.10. Cf. Bowersock 1990, 22–28. It is not clear whether the words "that is, the Virigin" are said by the participants in the rite or are an assimilation by Epiphanius himself. In the first case, this title would be added to other obviously Christianizing elements like the date of the Christian Epiphany and the sign of the cross, since *parthenos* is not a traditional epithet of Core as mother of Dionysus, since that birth is due to rape by Zeus. Nonnus invokes her with this epithet in *Dion.* 6.155 to underline the violation of her virginity.

144 Cf. Daszewski 1985, Burkert 1987, 146 n. 22, Bowersock 1990, 49–53.

fense: when Celsus exalts Orpheus as *theios aner* and his works as the pagan response to the Christian Scriptures, the Christianization of Orphism by opposition can already be glimpsed.[145] Much more advanced is the case of the Egyptian ascetic Sarapion, who read only the Orphic poems, clearly imitating his neighbors, the monks of the desert, who read only the Bible, and when books acquire similar functions, it is logical to suppose that influence is also possible in both directions. The *Rhapsodies* codified the Orphic theogonies before Christianity, and in the *Orphic Hymns* no Christian influence is yet visible, but already in the catabasis of the *Bologna Papyrus* a certain Jewish and even Christian influence has been claimed in the punishment of abortion or infanticide: the Christian emphasis on moral themes forced the pagan opposition in its turn to take a more moralizing view of traditional rituals.[146] Nevertheless, in the same way that the general Platonizing atmosphere explains certain parallels between Orphism and Christianity without the need to resort to an indemonstrable direct influence, the parallel in this case as well can be explained more by the general tendency to the moralization of ancient ritual taboos than by Christian influence.

Without any doubt, however, where the Christianization by opposition of late Orphism had the greatest significance was in the final attempt to transform the poetic tradition, which had proceeded by the accumulation of images and myths, into a doctrinal system on Neoplatonic principles, in which the various ideas would be coherent with one another and stand in logical relation. Proclus, Damascius, and Olympiodorus fitted quotations from the *Rhapsodies* to their commentaries on Plato, making them agree with their own views. Syrianus appears to have been the most determined to carry out this task in two lost works, *On the Theology of Orpheus* and *Harmony of Orpheus, Pythagoras, and the Chaldean Oracles*. From the beginning of this study, I have insisted that Orphism never had this systematic character: it acquired it only just before its disappearance. The Orphic tradition is in this evolution a faithful mirror of the traditional paganism that, as much for the apologists as for their Neoplatonic rivals, it had come to represent.

---

145 Orig. *CC* 1.16–18, 7.53. One must note, however, that Celsus is forced to praise Orpheus due to polemical needs, but his natural tendency is to disdain the Bacchic mysteries and *teletai* (*CC* 2.55–56, 3.9, 4.10), and he prefers to cite Hesiod, Homer and other poets rather than Orpheus (*CC* 4.36, 6.42).

146 On the effect of Christian success on late paganism, cf. Bremmer 2002, 50–55. On Sarapion, p. 61. On the moralization of pagan religiosity, pp. 344ff. On the Bologna papyrus, cf. II. nn. 18–21.

Clement of Alexandria did not choose Orpheus's songs at random as the banner of Greek religion. From the classical age until the end of antiquity, Orphism brought together in traditional forms content that was varied and changing, Greek and foreign at the same time, trivial and profound, poetic and conceptual. All these diverse currents, nevertheless, had in common a particular religious vision of the world and of man, a stamp imposed by the Orphic seal. Anything that could be recounted in rites and poems of divine inspiration had a place in Orpheus' songs and so entered to form part of a wealth of ideas and images that soars over Greek spiritual history at a special level, parallel to the great creations of literature and philosophy, with which it maintains multiple contacts, but without ever fusing with them. For this reason, Orpheus's voice has been the object of interest, admiration, and rejection from the Presocratics to the apologists. The same is true today, even if the modern scholarly audience does not always hear the original music. Present-day distortions are added to the ancient ones, so that the permanent examination of inherited sources and concepts is indispensable in order to understand what Orphism meant in ancient Greece. Here is where authors like Clement and Lactantius turn out to be unexpectedly important sources for a tradition that they saw as a rival and at the same time as an ally when they presented the new religion to the Greeks. Ancient Christian literature has been too often abandoned to the theologians or the scholars of primitive Christianity and disdained as *munus alienum* by classicists, but it fully belongs in their sphere, and not only as a witness to Christian Hellenization. It also has a special value as a source and a beacon for getting to know the gods and poets of the Greeks. Not only did Athens enlighten Jerusalem. Cithaeron and Helicon may also receive light from Sion.

Plate 5: Mosaic from Nea Paphos, Cyprus (325–350 AD)

Appendices

The longest and most relevant texts have been collected here to facilitate consultation of the main sources. The English translations of the Apologists are drawn in large part from those of the Ante-Nicene Fathers collection, with several changes and adaptations.

1. Clement of Alexandria, *Protrepticus*, 1.1.1–1.5.4

   1.1. Amphion of Thebes and Arion of Methymna were both minstrels, and both were renowned in story. They are celebrated in song to this day in the chorus of the Greeks, the one for having allured the fishes, and the other for having surrounded Thebes with walls by the power of music. Another, a Thracian, a cunning master of his art (he also is the subject of a Hellenic myth), tamed the wild beasts by the mere might of song; and transplanted trees – oaks – by music. I might tell you also the story of another, a brother to these – the subject of a myth, and a minstrel – Eunomos the Locrian and the Pythic grasshopper. A solemn Hellenic assembly had met at Pytho, to celebrate the death of the Pythic serpent, when Eunomos sang the reptile's epitaph. Whether his ode was a hymn in praise of the serpent, or a dirge, I am not able to say. But there was a contest, and Eunomos was playing the lyre in the summer time: it was when the grasshoppers, warmed by the sun, were chirping beneath the leaves along the hills; but they were singing not to that dead dragon, but to God All-wise, – a lay unfettered by rule, better than the numbers of Eunomos. The Locrian breaks a string. The grasshopper sprang on the neck of the instrument, and sang on it as on a branch; and the minstrel, adapting his strain to the grasshopper's song, made up for the want of the missing string. The grasshopper then was attracted by the song of Eunomos, as the fable represents, according to which also a brazen statue of Eunomos with his lyre, and the Locrian's ally in the contest, was erected at Pytho. But of its own accord it flew to the lyre, and of its own accord sang, and was regarded by the Greeks as a musical performer.
   1.2. How, let me ask, have you believed vain myths and supposed animals to be charmed by music; while Truth's shining face alone, as would

seem, appears to you disguised, and is looked on with incredulous eyes? And so Cithæron, and Helicon, and the mountains of the Odrysi, and the initiatory rites of the Thracians, mysteries of deceit, are hallowed and celebrated in hymns. For me, I am pained at such calamities as form the subjects of tragedy, though but myths; but by you the records of miseries are turned into dramatic compositions. But the dramas and the Laenean poets, now completely drunk, crowned with ivy, completely senseless in their Bacchic rite, with the satyrs, and the frenzied thiasos and the rest of the chorus of demons, let us confine to Helicon and Cithæron, now antiquated, and let us bring from above, out of heaven, Truth, with Wisdom in all its brightness, and the sacred chorus of the prophets, down to the holy mount of God; and let Truth, darting her light to the most distant points, cast her rays all around on those who are wrapped in darkness, and deliver men from delusion, stretching out her very strong right hand, which is intelligence, for their salvation. And raising their eyes, and looking above, let them abandon Helicon and Cithæron, and take up their abode in Sion. "For out of Sion shall go forth the Law, and the Logos of the Lord from Jerusalem" (Is. 2:3) – the celestial Logos, the true athlete crowned in the theatre of the whole universe. What my Eunomos sings is not the melody of Terpander, nor that of Cepion, nor the Phrygian, nor Lydian, nor Dorian, but the immortal melody of the new harmony that bears God's name, the Levitic song, a song "of heartsease, free of gall, to make one forget all sorrows" (*Odyssey*, 4.221). A sweet and true charm of persuasion is mixed with this song.

1.3. To me, therefore, that Thracian Orpheus, that Theban, and that Methymnæan, – men, and yet unworthy of the name, – seem to have been deceivers, who, under the pretence of poetry corrupting human life, possessed by a spirit of artful sorcery for purposes of destruction, celebrating crimes in their orgies, and making human woes the materials of religious worship, were the first to entice men to idols; nay, to build up the stupidity of the nations with blocks of wood and stone, – that is, statues and images, – subjecting to the yoke of extremest bondage the truly noble freedom of those who lived as free citizens under heaven by their chants and enchantments. But not such is my song, which has come to loose, and that speedily, the bitter bondage of tyrannizing demons; and leading us back to the mild and loving yoke of piety, recalls to heaven those that had been cast prostrate to the earth. It alone has tamed men, the most intractable of animals; the frivolous among them answering to the fowls of the air, deceivers to reptiles, the irascible to lions, the voluptuous to swine, the rapacious to wolves. The silly are stocks and stones, and still more senseless than stones is a man who is steeped in ignorance. As our witness, let us adduce the voice of prophecy accordant with truth, and bewailing those who are crushed in ignorance and folly: "For God is able of these stones to raise up children to Abraham" (Mt. 3:9); and He, commiserating their great ignorance and hardness of heart who are petrified against the truth, has raised up a seed of piety, sensitive to virtue, of those stones – of the nations, that is, who trusted in stones. Again, therefore, some venomous and false hypocrites, who plotted against righteousness, He once called "a brood of vipers"(Mt. 3:7). But if one of those serpents even is willing to repent, and follows the Word, he becomes a man of God. Others he figuratively calls wolves, clothed in sheep-skins, meaning thereby monsters of rapacity in human form. And so all such most savage beasts, and all such blocks of stone, the celestial song has transformed into tractable men. "For even we ourselves were sometime foolish, disobedient, deceived, serving divers lusts and pleasures, living in malice and envy, hateful, hating one another." Thus speaks the apostolic Scripture: "But after that the kindness and love of God our saviour to man appeared, not by works of righteousness which we have done, but according to His mercy, He saved us" (Tit. 3:3–5). Behold the might of the new song! It has made men out of stones, men out of beasts. Those, moreover, that were as dead, not being partakers of the true life, have come to life again, simply by becoming listeners to this song.

1.5. It also composed the universe into melodious order, and tuned the discord of the elements to harmonious arrangement, so that the whole world might become harmony. It let loose the fluid ocean, and yet has prevented it from encroaching on the land. The earth, again, which had been in a state of commotion, it has established, and fixed the sea as its boundary. The violence of fire it has softened by the atmosphere, as the Dorian is blended with the Lydian strain; and the harsh cold of the air it has moderated by the embrace of fire, harmoniously arranging these the extreme tones of the universe. And this deathless strain, – the support of the whole and the harmony of all, – reaching from the centre to the circumference, and from the extremities to the central part, has harmonized this universal frame of things, not according to the Thracian music, which is like that invented by Jubal, but according to the paternal counsel of God, which fired the zeal of David. And He who is of David, and yet before him, the Logos of God, despising the lyre and harp, which are but lifeless instruments, harmonized by the Holy Spirit the cosmos and also, even more, the microcosmos, man, composed of body and soul, and makes melody to God on this instrument of many tones; and sings accordingly to this instrument – I mean man – :

"For you are my harp, and pipe, and temple." A harp for harmony; a pipe for breath; a temple by reason of the word; so that the first may sound, the second breathe, the third contain the Lord. A beautiful-breathing instrument of music the Lord made man, after His own image.

2. Eusebius, *Laudes Constantini*, 14.5.15

Thus, I say, did our common Saviour prove himself the benefactor and preserver of all, displaying his wisdom through the instrument of his human nature, just as a musician uses the lyre to evince his skill. The Grecian myth tells us that Orpheus had power to charm ferocious beasts, and tame their savage spirit, by striking the chords of his instrument with a master hand: and this story is celebrated by the Greeks, and generally believed, that an unconscious instrument could subdue the untamed brute, and draw the trees from their places, in obedience to its melodious power. But he who is the author of perfect harmony, the all-wise Word of God, desiring to apply every remedy to the manifold diseases of the souls of men, employed that human nature which is the workmanship of his own wisdom, as an instrument by the melodious strains of which he soothed, not indeed the brute creation, but savages endued with reason; healing each furious temper, each fierce and angry passion of the soul, both in civilized and barbarous nations, by the remedial power of his Divine doctrine. Like a physician of perfect skill, he met the diseases of their souls who sought for God in nature and in bodies, by a fitting and kindred remedy, and showed them God in human form.

3. Clement of Alexandria, *Protrepticus* 2.12.1–2-23.1

2.12.1) And what if I go over the mysteries? I will not divulge them in mockery, as they say Alcibiades did, but I will expose right well by the word of truth the sorcery hidden in them; and those so-called gods of yours, whose are the mystic rites, I shall display, as it were, on the stage of life, to the spectators of truth.

2) The *bacchoi* hold their orgies in honour of the frenzied Dionysus, celebrating their sacred frenzy by the eating of raw flesh, and go through the distribution of the parts of butchered victims, crowned with snakes, shrieking out the name of that Eva by whom error came into the World. The symbol of the Bacchic orgies is a consecrated serpent. Moreover,

according to the true interpretation of the Hebrew term, the name Hevia, aspirated, signifies a female serpent. Deo and Core have become the heroines of a mystic drama; and their wanderings, and seizure, and grief, Eleusis celebrates by torchlight processions.

2.13.1) I think that the etymology of orgies and mysteries ought to be traced, the former to the wrath (*orge*) of Demeter against Zeus, the latter to the nefarious wickedness (*mysos*) relating to Dionysus; but if Apollodorus says that from Myus of Attica, who was killed in hunting – 2) no matter, your mysteries do seem funeral honours. You may understand *mysteria* in another way, as *mytheria*, the letters of the two words being interchanged; for certainly myths of this sort hunt after the most barbarous of the Thracians, the most senseless of the Phrygians, and the most superstitious among the Greeks. 3) May he die, then, the man who was the author of this imposture among men, be he Dardanus, who taught the mysteries of the mother of the gods, or Eetion, who instituted the orgies and mysteries of the Samothracians, or that Phrygian Midas who, having learned the cunning imposture from the Odrysus, communicated it to his subjects. 4) For I will never be persuaded by that Cyprian Islander Cinyras, who dared to bring forth from night to the light of day the lewd rites of Aphrodité in his eagerness to deify a strumpet of his own country. 5) Others say that Melampus the son of Amythaon imported the festivals of Ceres from Egypt into Greece, celebrating her grief in song. These I would instance as the prime authors of evil, the parents of impious fables and of deadly superstition, who sowed in human life that seed of evil and ruin – the mysteries.

2.14.1) And now, for it is time, I will prove their rites to be full of imposture and quackery. And if you have been initiated, you will laugh all the more at these myths of yours which have been held in honour. I publish without reserve what has been involved in secrecy, not ashamed to tell what you are not ashamed to worship. 2) There is then the foam-born and Cyprus-born, the darling of Cinyras, – I mean Aphrodite, the lover of male genitals, because sprung from them, even from those of Uranus, that were cut off, – those lustful members, that, after being cut off, offered violence to the waves. Of members so lewd a worthy fruit – Aphrodite – is born. In the rituals of this marine pleasure, as a symbol of her birth a lump of salt and the phallus are handed to those who are initiated into the art of uncleanness. And those initiated bring a piece of money to her, as a courtesan's paramours do to her.

2.15.1) Then there are the mysteries of Deo, and Zeus's lustful unions with his mother, and the wrath of Deo (I know not what for the future I shall call her, mother or wife), on which account it is that she is called Brimo, as is said; also the entreaties of Zeus, and the drink of gall, the plucking out of the hearts of sacrifices, and unspeakable deeds. Such rites the Phrygians perform in honour of Attis and Cybele and the Corybantes. 2) And the story goes, that Zeus, having torn away testicles of a ram, brought them out and cast them at the breasts of Deo, paying thus a fraudulent penalty for his violent embrace, pretending to have cut out his own. 3) The symbols of initiation into these rites, when set before you in a vacant hour, I know will excite your laughter, although on account of the exposure by no means inclined to laugh: "I ate from the tympanon, I drank from the cymbal, I carried the sacred jars, I went into the nuptial chamber." Are not these tokens a disgrace? Are not the mysteries absurdity?

2.16.1) What if I add the rest? Demeter becomes a mother, Core is reared up to womanhood. And, in course of time, he who begot her, – this same Zeus – has intercourse with his own daughter Pherephatta, – after Deo, the mother, – forgetting his former abominable wickedness. Zeus is both the father and the seducer of Core, and shamefully courts her in the shape of a snake; 2) thus proving his true identity. The token of the Sabazian mysteries to the initiated is "the deity through the bosom," – the deity being this serpent crawling over the bosom of the initiated. Proof surely this of the unbridled lust of Zeus. And also Pherephatta has a child in the form of a bull, as an idolatrous poet says, –

"The bull, the snake's father, and the bull's father, the snake
On a hill the herdsman's hidden ox-goad," –

alluding, as I believe, under the name of the herdsman's ox-goad, to the thyrsos wielded by the *bacchoi*.

2.17.1) Do you wish me to go into the story of Pherephatta's gathering of flowers, her basket, and her seizure by Aidoneus, and the rent in the earth, and the swine of Eubouleus that were swallowed up with the two goddesses; for which reason those who go to the temples in the Thesmophoria thrust out swine? The women celebrate this myth variously in different cities in the festivals called Thesmophoria and Scirophoria, dramatizing in many forms the rape of Pherephatta.

2) The mysteries of Dionysus are wholly inhuman; for while still a child, and the Curetes danced around him clashing their weapons, and the Titans having come upon them by stealth, and having beguiled him with childish toys, these very Titans tore him limb from limb when but a child, as the poet of this ritual, the Thracian Orpheus, says: –

"Cone, and spinning-top, and limb-moving rattles,
And fair golden apples from the clear-toned Hesperides." (*OF* 306)

2.18.1) And the useless symbols of this mystic rite it will not be useless to exhibit for condemnation. These are dice, ball, hoop, apples, top, looking-glass, tuft of wool. And Athena, to resume our account, having abstracted the heart of Dionysus, was called Pallas, from the vibrating (*pallein*) of the heart; and the Titans who had torn him limb from limb, setting a caldron on a tripod, and throwing into it the members of Dionysus, first boiled them down, 2) and then fixing them on spits, "held them over Hephaistos." (*Il.* 2.426) But Zeus having appeared (since he was a god, perhaps he participated in the flavor, which your gods agree to "receive as their due share" [*Il.* 4.49]), strucks the Titans with his thunderbolt, and consigns the members of Dionysus to his son Apollo to be buried. And he – for he did not disobey his father – bore the dismembered corpse to Parnassus, and there deposited it.

2.19.1) If you wish to inspect the orgies of the Corybantes, then know that, having killed their third brother, they covered the head of the dead body with a purple cloth, crowned it, and carrying it over a bronze shield, buried it under the roots of Olympus. 2) These mysteries are, in short, murders and tombs. And the priests of these rites, who are called kings of the sacred rites (*Anaktotelestai*) by those who care to name them, give additional strangeness to the tragic occurrence, by forbidding celery with the roots from being placed on the table, for they think that celery grew from the Corybantic blood that flowed forth; 3) just as the women, in celebrating the Thesmophoria, abstain from eating the seeds of the pomegranate which have fallen on the ground, from the idea that pomegranates sprang from the drops of the blood of Dionysus. 4) Those Corybantes also they call Cabiric, by which they also denounce the Cabiric mystery. For these two identical fratricides, having abstracted the basket in which the phallus of Bacchus was deposited, took it to Etruria – dealers in honourable wares truly. They lived there as exiles, employing themselves in communicating the precious teaching of their superstition, and presenting phallic symbols and the basket for the Etruscans to worship. And some will have it, not improbably, that for this reason Dionysus was called Attis, because he was mutilated.

2.20.1) And what is surprising at the Etruscans, who were barbarians, being thus initiated into these foul indignities, when among the Athenians, and in the whole of Greece – I blush to say it – the shameful myth about Deo holds its ground? For Deo, wandering in quest of her daughter

Core, broke down with fatigue near Eleusis, a place in Attica, and sat down on a well overwhelmed with grief. This is even now prohibited to those who are initiated, lest they should appear to mimic the weeping goddess. 2) The indigenous inhabitants then occupied Eleusis: their names were Baubo, and Dysaules, and Triptolemus; and besides, Eumolpus and Eubouleus. Triptolemus was a herdsman, Eumolpus a shepherd, and Eubouleus a swineherd; from whom came the families of the Eumolpidae and that of the Kerykes – a lineage of hierophants – who flourished at Athens. 3) Well, then (for I shall not refrain from the recital), Baubo having received Deo hospitably, reaches to her the *kykeon*; and on her refusing it, not having any inclination to drink (for she was very sad), and Baubo having become annoyed, thinking herself slighted, uncovered her genitals, and exhibited them to the goddess. Deo is delighted at the sight, and takes a sip of the draught – pleased at the spectacle.

2.21.1) These are the secret mysteries of the Athenians! Orpheus records them too. I shall produce the very words of Orpheus, that you may have the mystagogue himself as witness for this piece of turpitude: –

> "Having thus spoken, she drew aside her garments, and showed all
> the inapropiate form of the body; there was the infant Iacchos,
> and with his own hand he kicked under Baubo's breasts.
> When the goddess noticed it, she rejoiced in her heart,
> and received the glancing cup in which was the *kykeon*." (*OF* 395)

2) And the following is the token of the Eleusinian mysteries: "I have fasted, I have drunk the *kykeon*; I have taken from the box; having done, I put it into the basket, and out of the basket into the chest." Fine sights truly, and becoming a goddess!

2.22.1) These are indeed mysteries worthy of the night, and flame, and the magnanimous or rather silly people of the Erechthidae, and the other Greeks besides, 2) "whom a fate they hope not for awaits after death." And in truth against these Heraclitus the Ephesian prophesies, as "the night-wanderers, the magi, *bacchoi, lenai, mystai*." These he threatens with what will follow death, and predicts for them fire. For they celebrate sacrilegiously what men regard as mysteries" (fr. 14 DK). 3) The mysteries are really a new custom and an (empty) supposition, an imposture of the serpent, which receives cult when men convert with bastard piety to profane mysteries and unholy rites.

4) What are these mystic chests? – for I must expose their sacred things, and divulge things not fit for speech. Are they not sesame cakes, and py-

ramidal cakes, and globular and flat cakes, embossed all over, and lumps of salt, and a snake the ritual instrument of Dionysus Bassareus? And besides these, are they not pomegranates, and branches, and rods, and ivy leaves? and besides, round cakes and poppy seeds? 5) And further, there are the unmentionable symbols of Themis, marjoram, a lamp, a sword, a woman's comb, which is a euphemism and mystic expression for the female sex. And be not drunk with wine, wherein is excess; but be filled with the Spirit.

3.22.6. O unblushing shamelessness! Once on a time night was silent, a veil for the pleasure of temperate men; but now for the initiated, the holy night is the tell-tale of the rites of licentiousness; and the glare of torches reveals vicious indulgences. Quench the flame, O Hierophant; reverence, O Torch-bearer, the torches. That light exposes Iacchus; let your mysteries be honoured, and command the orgies to be hidden in night and darkness. The fire dissembles not; it exposes and punishes what it is bidden.

4. Firmicus Maternus, *De errore profanarum religionum* 6.1–5

1. Thus, Most Holy emperors, have the elements been deified by the children of perdition. But there are still other superstitions whose secrets must be revealed, the mysteries and festivals of Liber, whose whole story in detail must be made known to your sacred intelligence, to make you aware that in these profane cults again it is the deaths of human beings that have been hallowed by worship.

2. Well then, Liber was the son of Jupiter – I mean the Jupiter who was king of Crete. In spite of being the progeny of an adulterous mother, Liber was reared under his father's eye with more zealous attention than was right and proper. Jupiter's wife, whose name was Juno, goaded by the fury of a stepmother's mentality, plotted in every sort of way to encompass the murder of the child. When the father was on the point of going abroad, he took steps, since he was aware of his wife's concealed indignation, to keep the angry woman from any treacherous behaviour, and entrusted his son to the protection of guards whom he deemed suitable. Then Juno had just the right opportunity for her designs, and she was all the more violently infuriated because the father at his departure had handed over the throne and scepter of the realm to the boy. First she corrupted the guards with bribes and gifts; then she stationed her minions, called Titans, in the inner apartments of the palace. With a rattle and a mirror of ingenious workmanship she so beguiled the fancy of the boy that he left his royal seat and let his childish desires lead him to the place of ambush.

3. There he was intercepted and killed, and to ensure that no trace of the murder might be found, the gang of minions chopped his members up into pieces and divided them among themselves. Next, piling one crime upon another, as they were egged on by mortal terror of their despot's cruelty, they cooked the boy's members in various ways and devoured them, thus feeding on a human cadaver, a banquet unheard of up to that day. The boy's sister Minerva (for she too was a party to the crime) saved his heart, which had fallen to her share; her double purpose was to have unambiguous evidence as she turned informer and likewise something to soften the brunt of her father's impetuous fury. When Jupiter returned, his daughter unfolded the tale of the crime.

4. Thereupon the father, infuriated by the gruesome and calamitous act of butchery and by the anguish of his bitter grief, put the Titans to various sorts of torture and killed them. In vengeance for his son he left untried no form of torment or punishment, but plunged madly though the whole gamut of penalties, thus avenging the murder of his so-called son, with a father's affection but a despot's display of power. Then, unable longer to bear the pangs of paternal grief, and seeing that no solaces could assuage the sorrow caused by his bereavement, he had a statue of the boy molded in plaster, and the artist placed the heart, whereby the crime had been revealed by the tattling sister, just in the spot where the contours of the breast were shaped. The next thing he did was to erect a temple in lieu of a tomb, and as priest he appointed the boy's paedagogus.

5. The latter's name was Silenus. Now the Cretans, wishing to allay the savage passion of their furious despot, established the anniversary of the death as a holyday, and arranged recurring sacred rites celebrated every two years, wherein they rehearse each and every thing that the boy did or suffered at his death. They tear a bull with their teeth, representing the cruel banquet with his regular commemoration; and amid the forest fastness they howl with dissonant outcries, feigning the insanity of madmen to create the belief that the crime was not done in treachery but in madness. In front of them is borne the basket in which the sister had secretly concealed the heart, and by the tootling of flutes and the din of cymbals they counterfeit the rattle which was used to beguile the boy. So, by the way of doing honor to a despot, a subservient rabble took a person who was unable to have any burial and made him into a god.

5. Athenagoras, *Plea for the Christians* 18.3–20.5

18.3. This then especially I beg you carefully to consider. The gods, as they affirm, were not from the beginning, but every one of them has come into existence just like ourselves. And in this opinion they all agree. Homer speaks of

"Oceanus, whence the gods have risen, and mother Tethys" (Il. 14.301);

and Orpheus, who, moreover, was the first to invent their names, and recounted their births, and narrated the exploits of each; whom they take for the truest theologian; and whom Homer himself follows in many things about the gods) – he, too, has fixed their first origin to be from water: –

"Oceanus, the origin of all" (Il. 14.246).

4. For, according to him, water was the beginning of all things, and from water mud was formed, and from both was produced an animal, a snake with the head of a lion growing to it, and between the two heads there was the face of a god, named Heracles and Cronos. 5. This Heracles generated an egg of enormous size, which, on becoming full, was, by the powerful friction of its generator, burst into two, the part at the top becoming Heaven, and the lower part becoming Earth. The goddess Earth, moreover, came forth with a double body; 6. and Heaven, by his union with Earth, begot females, Clotho, Lachesis, and Atropos; and males, the Hundred-Handed Cottys, Gyges, Briareus, and the Cyclopes Brontes, and Steropes, and Argos, whom also he bound and hurled down to Tartarus, having learned that he was to be ejected from his government by his children; whereupon Earth, being enraged, brought forth the Titans.

"The godlike Earth bore to Heaven
Sons who are by the name of Titans known,
Because they took vengeance (tisathen) on great starry Heaven"
(OF 83).

19.1. Such was the beginning of the existence both of their gods and of the universe. Let us then consider this: For each of those things to which divinity is ascribed is conceived of as having existed from the first. For, if they have come into being, having previously had no existence, as those say who treat of the gods, they do not exist. For, a thing is either uncreated and eternal, or created and perishable. ...

20.1. If the absurdity of their theology were confined to saying that the gods were created, and owed their constitution to water, since I have demonstrated that nothing is made which is not also liable to dissolution, I might proceed to the remaining charges. 2. But, on the one hand, they have described their bodily forms: speaking of Heracles, for instance, as a god in the shape of a snake coiled up; of others as hundred-handed; of the daughter of Zeus, whom he begot of his mother Rhea (or Demeter), as having two eyes in the natural place, and two in her forehead, and the face of an animal on the back part of her neck, and as having also horns, so that Rhea, frightened at her monster of a child, fled from her, and did not give her the breast (θηλή), whence mystically she is called Athela, but commonly Persephone and Core, though she is not the same as Athena, who is also called Core from her virginity –

3. And, on the other hand, they have described their admirable achievements, as they deem them: how Cronos, for instance, mutilated his father, and hurled him down from his chariot; and how he murdered his children, and swallowed the males of them; and how Zeus bound his father, and cast him down to Tartarus, as did Heaven also to his sons, and fought with the Titans for power; and how he persecuted his mother Rhea when she refused to wed him, and, she becoming a she-snake, and he himself being changed into a snake, bound her with what is called the Heraclean knot, and mated with her – of which the rod of Hermes is a symbol; and again, how he violated his daughter Persephone, in this case also assuming the form of a snake, and became the father of Dionysus. 4. In face of narrations like these, I must say at least this much: What that is becoming or useful is there in such story, that we must believe Cronos, Zeus, Core, and the rest, to be gods? Is it the descriptions of their bodies? What man of judgment and reflection will believe that a viper was begotten by a god? Thus Orpheus: –

"And Phanes begot another terrible offspring,
from his sacred womb: Echidna, frightful to see,
on whose head were hairs: its face was comely;
but the rest, from the neck downwards, bore the aspect
of a dread snake" (*OF* 81);

Or who will admit that Phanes himself, being a first-born god (for he it was that was produced from the egg), has the body or shape of a snake, or was swallowed by Zeus, so that Zeus might be infinite? 5. For if they differ in no respect from the vilest brutes (since it is evident that the Deity must differ from the things of earth and those that are derived from matter), they are not gods. How, then, I ask, can we approach them as suppliants, when their origin resembles that of cattle, and they themselves have the form of brutes, and are ugly to behold?

6. Origen, *Contra Celsum*. 1.16–18

1.16 *in fine*: And again, when making a list of ancient and learned men who have conferred benefits upon their contemporaries by their deeds, and upon posterity by their writings, Celsus excluded Moses from the number; while of Linus, to whom Celsus assigns a foremost place in his list, there exists neither laws nor discourses which produced a change for the better among any tribes; whereas a whole nation, dispersed throughout the entire world, obey the laws of Moses. Consider, then, whether it is not from open malevolence that he has expelled Moses from his catalogue of wise men, while asserting that Linus, and Musæus, and Orpheus, and Pherecydes, and the Persian Zoroaster, and Pythagoras, discussed these topics, and that their opinions were deposited in books, and have thus been preserved down to the present time. 17. And it is intentionally also that he has omitted to take notice of the myth, embellished chiefly by Orpheus, in which the gods are described as affected by human weaknesses and passions, while he attacks in the six books the Mosaic history because it is given a symbolical and allegorical signification. And here one might say to the writer of the "noblest and truest Discourse": "Why, good sir, do you make it a boast to have it recorded that the gods should engage in such adventures as are described by your learned poets and philosophers, and be guilty of abominable unions, and of engaging in wars against their own fathers, and of cutting off their secret parts, and should dare to commit and to suffer such enormities; while Moses, who gives no such accounts respecting God, nor even regarding the holy angels, and who relates deeds of far less atrocity regarding men (for in his writings no one ever ventured to commit such crimes as Cronos did against Uranus, or Zeus against his father, or that of the Father of men and gods, who had intercourse with his own daughter), …"

18. And challenging a comparison of book with book, I would say, "Come now, good sir, take down the poems of Linus, and of Musæus, and of Orpheus, and the writings of Pherecydes, and carefully compare these with the laws of Moses – histories with histories, and ethical dis-

courses with laws and commandments – and see which of the two are the better fitted to change the character of the hearer on the very spot, and which to harden him in his wickedness; and observe that your series of writers display little concern for those readers who are to peruse them at once unaided, but have composed their philosophy (as you term it) for those who are able to comprehend its metaphorical and allegorical signification; whereas Moses, like a distinguished orator who meditates some figure of rhetoric, and who carefully introduces in every part language of twofold meaning, has done this in his five books: neither affording, in the portion which relates to morals, any handle to his Jewish subjects for committing evil; nor yet giving to the few individuals who were endowed with greater wisdom, and who were capable of investigating his meaning, a treatise devoid of material for speculation. But of your learned poets the very writings would seem no longer to be preserved, although they would have been carefully treasured up if the readers had perceived any benefit in them, whereas the works of Moses have stirred up many, who were even aliens to the manners of the Jews, to the belief that, as these writings testify, the first who enacted these laws and delivered them to Moses, was the God who was the Creator of the world.

7. Lactantius, *Divinae Institutiones* 1.5.4–1.5.13

Orpheus, who is the most ancient of the poets, and coeval with the gods themselves – since it is reported that he sailed among the Argonauts together with the sons of Tyndarus and Hercules, – speaks of the true and great God as the first-born, because nothing was produced before him, but all things sprang from him. He also calls him Phanes because when as yet there was nothing he first appeared and came forth from the infinite. And since he was unable to conceive in his mind the origin and nature of this Being, he said that He was born from the boundless air: "The brilliant first-born son of the extended air;" for he had nothing greater to say. He affirms that he is is the father of all the gods, on whose account he framed the heaven, and provided for his children that they might have a habitation and place of abode in common: "He built for immortals an imperishable home." Thus, under the guidance of nature and reason, he understood that a power of principal greatness founded heaven and earth. And he could not say that Jupiter was the principle of all things since he was born from Saturn; nor could he say that Saturn himself was their principle, since it was reported that he was produced from Heaven; but he did not venture to set Heaven as the primeval god, because he saw that it was an element of the universe, and must itself have had an author. This reason led Orpheus to this first-born god, to whom he assigns and attributes the primacy.

Homer was able to give us no information relating to the truth, for he wrote of human rather than divine things. Hesiod was able, for he comprised in the work of one book the generation of the gods; but yet he gave us no hint of the truth, for he took his commencement not from God the Creator, but from chaos, which is a confused mass of rude and unarranged matter; whereas he ought first to have explained from what source, at what time, and in what manner, chaos itself had begun to exist or to have consistency. Without doubt, as all things were placed in order, arranged, and made by some artificer, so matter itself must of necessity have been formed by some being. Who, then, made it except God, to whose power all things are subject? But Hesiod shrinks from admitting this, for he dreads the unknown truth. He wished it to appear as if it was by the inspiration of the Muses that he poured forth that song on Helicon; but he had come after previous meditation and preparation.

Maro was the first of our poets to approach the truth, who thus speaks respecting the highest God, whom he calls Mind and Spirit ... Ovid also, in the beginning of his remarkable work, without any disguising of the name, admits that the universe was arranged by God, whom he calls the Framer of the world (*Met.* 1.57), the Artificer of all things (*Met.* 1.79). But if either Orpheus or these poets of ours had always maintained what they perceived under the guidance of nature, they would have comprehended the truth, and gained the same learning which we follow.

8. Gregory of Nazianzus, *Poemata Arcana* 7, *On the soul*: 22–52

I know of yet another account, which I will never accept,
for I could not believe in some common soul portioned between me and everyone else,
and drifting through the air. In that case, one who inhaled and
another who exhaled would be the same in all respects; thus everyone   25
who lives would be emptied into everyone else by breathing,
were the soul, in fact, of the nature of air, flowing from one person to another;
but if it resides somewhere, what held it, or what was already alive then

in my mother's womb, if, when I was outside, she drew me in?
And if you suppose a mother to have several children, 30
you honor her with all the more souls in process of destruction.
This myth, insipid trifling of books, is not for sensible people;
These people make the soul out to be passed along
from body to body, as befits its former lives, whether good or bad,
having either reward for virtue, or punishment for some wrongdoing; 35
and, as if they were sloppily changing a man's clothes,
struggling uselessly in putting them on and taking them off again.
They carry the wheel of the arch-sinner Ixion, making
a beast, a plant, a man, a bird, a snake, a dog, a fish,
and often each thing twice, since the cycle prescribes it. 40
How far then? I have never beheld the discouse of a wise beast,
nor a talking bush. Always a crow's good for cawing,
and always a fish is silent when swimming through the flowing sea.
Again, if there's a final retribution for the soul, as these themselves
say, this tenet of theirs is useless. If the soul is without flesh, 45
that were quite extraordinary. But if it is with flesh,
which among the multitude it had do you commit to the fire?
And what is most extraordinary, since you have bound me to many
bodies, and the bond has put me in acquaintance with many,
how has this alone escaped my mind, what skin it was that held me previously,
which one will do so next? How many have I died in? For it has not 50
grown rich with souls, as with money-bags, this bond of mine.
But this too results from aberration, that I should forget my former life.
But hear our account of the soul …

9. *Testament of Orpheus*: original version (*OF* 377)

I will speak to the lawful ones; shut the doors, profane,
all of you together. You, O Musaeus, child of the light-bearing Moon,
listen! for I am about to proclaim the truth. Let not the former
imaginings of your heart deprive you of the blessed life.
But look to the divine Logos, and adhere to it, 5
letting it guide your heart's deepest thoughts. And walk unwaveringly
upon the path, looking to the only king of the universe,
the immortal one. There is an ancient saying about Him: 7a

he is one, self-generated, and all things are made the progeny of one,
and among all things he circulates; but him no one among
mortals can see, although he sees all of them.   10
And he himself out of good things allows evil on mortals
as well as war, plague, and tearful sufferings.
There is no other one apart from the mighty God.
But I do not see him; for around him a cloud has settled,
for all mortals have in their eyes mortal pupils   15
too small, since they are implanted in flesh and bones;
too weak to see the sovereign through everything.
He indeed is firmly established hereafter over the vast heaven
on a golden throne; and earth stands under his feet,   20
and in his right hand to the extremities of the ocean
he stretches out on every side, the mountain base trembles before him,
and the rivers and the depths of the resplendent sea …

10. *Testament of Orpheus*: re-elaboration (*OF* 378)

I will speak to the lawful ones; shut the doors, profane,
since you flee the ordinances of the just, even though the divine sets them
for all of you together. You, O Musaeus, child of the light-bearing Moon,
listen! for I am about to proclaim the truth. Let not the former
imaginings of your heart deprive you of the blessed life.   5
But look to the divine Logos, and adhere to it,
letting it guide your heart's deepest thoughts. And walk unwaveringly
upon the path, looking to the only molder of the universe,
the immortal one. There is an ancient saying about Him:
he is the one, self-generated, and all has come into being as his offspring, 10
and among them he circulates; but him no one among
mortals can see in his soul, but with the mind.
And he himself out of good things does not enjoin evil on mortal
men. Even so, strife and hatred accompany them,
as well as war, plague, and tearful sufferings.   15
There is no other one, and you could easily see all things,
if you saw him. Yet, until that moment, at length here on earth,
my child, I will show you, when I see his

prints and the strong hand of the mighty God.
But I do not see him; for around him a cloud has been fixed   20
for me. But there are ten times more clouds for men;
for no one among mortals could see the ruler of men,
except a certain person, a unique figure, by descent an offshoot
of the Chaldaean race; for he expertly saw the movement of the stars
and of the sphere(s), which always rotates around its axle,   25
a perfect circle, all on their respective axes.
And with wind he created currents around both air and stream,
and he brings forth the flames of fire, lighting up the whole sphere …
He indeed is firmly established hereafter over the vast heaven
on a golden throne; and earth stands under his feet,   30
and in his right hand to the extremities of the ocean
he stretches out on every side, the mountain base trembles before him,
and it is not possible to endure his mighty force. But in every way
he himself is heavenly, and on earth brings all things to completion,
since he controls its beginning, its middle, and its end,   35
as a tradition of the ancients, as the one born in the undergrowth said,
having received the two-tablet law through the will of God.
But as it is not allowed to speak, I tremble throughout –
with reason, from the heights he rules over everything in order.
O child, be near to him in your thoughts,   40
and do not abandon this divine message, but keep it in your heart.

Bibliography

ABEL, E., *Orphica*, Leipzig-Prague, 1885.
ABINEAU, M., "Le thème du bourbier dans la littérature grecque profane et chrétienne", *Rev. Sc. Rel.* 47 (1959), 185–214.
AFONASIN, E., "A Christian Rethinking the Pythagorean Tradition: Clement of Alexandria and the Neopythagoreans", in *Abstracts of the XX World Congress of Philosophy*, Boston, 1998 (= http://www.bu.edu/wcp/Papers/Anci/AnciAfon.htm).
ALBERTZ, R., *A History of Israelite Religion in the Old Testament Period*, Westminster 1994.
ALBRILE, E., "… *in principiis lucem fuisse ac tenebras*. Creazione, caduta e rigenerazione spirituale in alcuni testi gnostici", *AION* 17 (1995) 109–155.
"L' Uovo della Fenice: aspetti di un sincretismo orfico-gnostico", *Le Muséon* 113 (2000) 55–85.
"Orfismo y gnosticismo", in Bernabé/Casadesús 2008, 1517–1516.
ALCOCK, S. E., CHERRY, J. F., ELSNER, J. (eds.), *Pausanias. Travel and Memory in Roman Greece*, Oxford, 2001.
ALDERINK, L. J., *Creation and Salvation in Ancient Orphism*, Chico, 1981.
ALFÖLDI, A., "Redeunt Saturnia regna VII: Frugifer-Triptolemos in ptolemäischen-römischen Herrscherkult", *Chiron* 9, 553–606.
ANDERSON, B., *Imagined Communities: Reflections on the Origin and Spread of Nationalism*, London 1983.
ANDERSON, G., *Sage, Saint and Sophist: Holy Men and Their Associates in the Early Roman Empire*. London: New York, 1994.
ATHANASSIADI, P., FREDE, M. (eds.), *Pagan Monotheism in Late Antiquity*, Oxford 1999.
ATHANASSIADI-FOWDEN, P., "A contribution to Mithraic theology. The emperor Julian's Hymn to King Helios", *JThS* 28 (1977) 360–371.
Julian and Hellenism. An Intellectual Biopgraphy, Oxford: 1981.
AULICH, J., *Orphische Weltanschauung der Antike und ihr Erbe bei den Dichtern Nietzsche, Hölderlin, Novalis und Rilke*, Frankfurt/Main 1994.
BARTELINK, G. J. M., "Die *Oracula Sibyllina* in den frühchristlichen griechischen Schriften von Justin bis Origenes (150–250 nach Chr.)" in J. Den

Boeft – A. Hilhorst (eds.), *Early Christian Poetry. A Collection of Essays*, Leiden, 1993, 23–33.

BARTON, S. C., HORSLEY, G. H. R., "A Hellenistic Cult Group and the New Testament Churches", *JAC* 24 (1981), 7–41.

BAUMGARTEN, R., *Heiliges Wort und Heilige Schrift bei den Griechen. Hieroi Logoi und verwandte Erscheinungen*, Tübingen 1998.

BEATRICE, P. F., "Soma chiton" in U. Bianchi (ed.), *La tradizione dell'enkrateia*, Roma 1985, 433–445.

"Diodore de Sicile chez les Apologistes", in B. Pouderon. J. Doré (eds.): *Les Apologistes chrétiens et la culture grecque*, Paris, 1998, 219–235.

BELAYCHE, N., "Hypsistos. Une voie de l'exaltation des dieux dans le polythéisme gréco-romain", *Archiv für Religionsgeschichte* 7 (2005), 34–55.

BEN LAZREG, N., 2002. "Roman and Early Christian burial complex at Leptiminus: first notice." *JRA* 15 (2002), 336–45

BERCHMAN, R. M., *Porphyry Against the Christians. Studies in. Platonism, Neoplatonism, and the Platonic Tradition*, Leiden/Boston, 2005.

BERNABÉ, A., "Una etimología platónica: σῶμα-σῆμα", *Philologus* 139 (1995) 204–237.

"Plutarco e l'orfismo" en I. Gallo (ed.): *Plutarco e la Religione, Atti del VI Convegno plutarcheo (Ravello, 29–31 maggio 1995)*, Napoli 1996a, 63–105.

"Elementos orientales en el orfismo", in: *Actas del Congreso Español de Antiguo Oriente Próximo, El Mediterráneo en la Antigüedad, Oriente y Occidente*, Madrid, Octubre de 1997. Internet (http://www.labherm.filol.csic.es/Es/Actas/Actas.html).

"Platone e l'Orfismo" in G. Sfameni Gasparro (ed.), *Destino e salvezza tra culti pagani e gnosi cristiana. Itinerari storico-religiose sull'orme di Ugo Bianchi*, Cosenza, 1998, 33–93.

"Tradiciones órficas en Diodoro", in M. Alganza Roldán, J. M. Camacho Rojo, P. P. Fuentes González, M. Villena Ponsoda (eds.), *ΕΠΙΕΚΕΙΑ. Studia Graeca in memoriam Jesús Lens Tuero*, Granada 2000, 37–53.

"La toile de Penélope: a-t-il existé un mythe orphique sur Dionysos et les Titans?", *RHR* 219 (2002a), 401–433.

"Referencias a textos órficos en Diodoro" in L. Torraca (ed.): *Scriti in onore di Italo Gallo*, Napoli, 2002b, 67–96.

"La théogonie orphique du Papyrus de Derveni", *Kernos* 15 (2002c), 91–129.

"Un 'resumen de historia del orfismo' en Strab. 7 fr. 18", *Actas del X Congreso de la Sociedad Española de Estudios Clásicos*, III, Madrid 2002d.

Hieros Logos. Poesía órfica sobre los dioses, el alma y el más allá, Madrid 2003a.

"Las *Ephesia Grammata*. Génesis de una fórmula mágica", *MHNH* 3 (2003b), 5–28.
Poetae Epici Graeci II: Orphicorum et Orphicis similium testimonia et fragmenta I–III, Munich–Leipzig, 2004–2006.
Textos órficos y filosofía presocrática, Madrid 2004b.
"The Derveni Theogony: Many questions and some answers", *HSCP* 103 (2007), 99–134
"Sur le rite décrit dans les colonnes II et VI du 'Papyrus de Derveni': que peut-on faire avec un oiseau?", *Etudes classiques*, 75.1–2 (2007b), 157–170.
"La teogonía órfica citada en las *Pseudoclementinas*", *Adamantius* 14 (2008), 79–99.

BERNABÉ, A., CASADESÚS, F., *Orfeo y la tradición órfica. un reencuentro*, Madrid 2008.

BERNABÉ, A., JIMÉNEZ SAN CRISTÓBAL, A., *Instructions for the Netherworld. The Orphic Gold Tablets*, Boston-Leyden 2008.

BETEGH, G., *The Derveni Papyrus: Cosmology, Theology and Interpretation*, Cambridge 2004.
"The Derveni Papyrus and Early Stoicism", *Rhizai* 4 (2007), 133–52.

BETTINI, M., "Un Dioniso di gesso: Firm. Mat. *De err. prof. rel.* 6, 1 sgg. (Orph. fr. 214 Kern)", *QUCC* 43 (1993) 103–108.

BETZ, H. D., "Fragments from a Catabasis Ritual in a Greek magical papyrus", *History of Religions* 19 (1980) 287–295.

BIANCHI, U., "Le problème des origines du gnosticisme", in *Colloque international sur les origines du gnosticisme* (= *Numen* 12), Messina, 1965, 236–237.
"Péché originel et péché antécedent", *RHR* 170 (1966), 117–126.
Le origini dello gnosticismo, Leiden, 1967
"L'orphisme a existé", in *Mélanges d'histoire des religions offerts à H.-C. Puech*, Paris 1974, 129–137.
(ed.), *La tradizione dell'enkrateia*, Roma 1985.
"Origen's treatment of the Soul and the Debate over Metemsomatosis", in L. Ries (ed.), *Origeniana Quarta*, Innsbruck, 1987, 270–81.

BICKEL, S., *La cosmogonie égyptienne avant le Nouvel Empire*, Göttingen 1994.

BIDEZ, J., CUMONT, F., *Les Mages hellenisés*. Paris, 1938.

BIEBUYCK, B, D. PRAET & I. VANDEN POEL, "Cults and Migrations. Nietzsche's Meditations on Orphism, Pythagoreanism and the Greek Mysteries" In: P. Bishop (ed.), *Nietzsche and Antiquity: His Reaction and Response to the Classical Tradition*. Woodbridge 2004, 151–169.

BLOCH, R., "Orpheus als Lehrer des Musaios, Moses als Lehrer des Orpheus", U. Dill/C. Walde (eds.) Antike Mythen: Medien, Transformationen und Konstruktionen, Berlin–New York, 2009, 469–486.

BOBICHON, P., *Justin Martyr. Dialogue avec Tryphon. edition critique, traduction, commentaire*, Fribourg 2003.

BONNECHÈRE, P., *Trophonios de Lebadée*, Leiden–Boston, 2003.

BOS, A. P., "Aristotle on the Etruscan Robbers: A Core Text of Aristotelian Dualism", *Journal of the History of Philosophy*, 41. 3 (2003) 289–306.

BOTTÉRO, J., *Initiation à l'Orient Ancien. De Sumer à la Bible*, Paris 1992.

BOTTINI, A., *Archeologia della salvezza. L'escatologia greca nelle testimonianze archeologiche*, Milano 1992.

BOULANGER, A., *Orphée: Rapports de l'Orphisme et le Christianisme*, Paris 1925.
"L'orphisme à Rome" *REL* 15 (1937), 121–135.

BOUSSET, W., *Kyrios Christos*, Göttingen 1913.

BOYANCÉ, P., *Le culte des Muses chez les philosophes grecs*, Paris 1936.

BOWERSOCK, G. W., *Hellenism in Late Antiquity*, Cambridge 1990.

BRÄNDL, M., *Der Agon bei Paulus: Herkunft und Profil paulinischer Agonmetaphorik*, Tübingen 2006.

BREMMER, J. N., *The Rise and Fall of the Afterlife*, London–New York, 2002.
"The Apocalypse of Peter: Greek or Jewish?", in J. Bremmer/I. Czaschez, *The Apocalypse of Peter*, Leuven 2003.
Greek Religion And Culture, The Bible And The Ancient Near East. Leiden–Boston.
"The Golden Bough: Orphic, Eleusinian, and Hellenistic-Jewish Sources of Virgil's Underworld in *Aeneid* VI", *Kernos* 22 (2009), 183–208.

BRISSON, L., "Orphée et l'Orphisme dans l'Empire romain, de Plutarque jusqu'à Jamblique", *Aufstieg und Niedergang der Römischen Welt*, II. 36.4, 1990, 2867–3931.
Orphée et l'Orphisme dans l'Antiquité gréco-romaine, London 1995.
"Le corps 'dionysiaque': l'anthropogonie décrite dans le *Commentaire sur le* Phédon *de Platon* (1, par. 3–6) attribué a Olympiodore est-elle orphique?", in: Goulet-Cazé, M. O.-Madec, G.-O'Brien, D. (eds.), Σοφίης Μαιήτορες *"chercheurs de sagesse": Hommage à Jean Pépin*, Paris 1992, 481–99.
Le sexe incertain: androgynie et hermaphrodisme dans l'Antiquité gréco-romaine, Paris 1997.
"Nascita di un mito filosofico: Giamblico (*VP* 146) su Aglaophamos", in Tortorelli Ghidini, M., A. Storchi Marino & A. Visconti (eds.), 2000: *Tra Orfeo e Pitagora. Origini e incontri di culture nell'antichità*. Atti dei Seminari Napoletani 1996–1998, Napoli 2000, 237–253.

"Sky, Sex and Sun. The Meanings of *aidoios/aidoion* in the Derveni Papyrus." *ZPE* 144 (2003), 19–29.

How Philosophers Saved Myths: Allegorical Interpretation and Classical Mythology, Chicago, 2004.

"El lugar, la función y la significación del orfismo en el neoplatonismo", in Bernabé/Casadesús 2008, 1491–1516.

"Zeus did not Commit Incest with his Mother. An Interpretation of Column XXVI of the Derveni Papyrus", *ZPE* 168 (2009) 27–39.

BROWN, P., *Society and the Holy in Late Antiquity*, Berkeley–Los Angeles, 1982.

BUELL, D. K., *Making Christians*, Princeton, 1999.

Why This New Race? Ethnic Reasoning in Early Christianity, New York, 2005.

BULTMANN, R., *Das Urchristentum im Rahmen der antiken Religionen*, Zürich 1949.

"Zur Geschichte der Lichtsymbolik im Altertum", *Philologus* 97 (1948), 1–36.

BURKERT, W., "Hellenistische Pseudopythagorica", *Philologus* 105 (1961), 16–43, 226–246.

"ΓΟΗΣ: Zum griechischen Schamanismus", *RhM* 105 (1962), 36–55.

Lore and Science in Ancient Pythagoreanism, Cambridge, Mass. 1972.

"Plotin, Plutarch und die platonisierende Interpretation von Heraklit und Empedokles", in: J. Mansfeld, L. M. de Rijk (eds): *Kephalaion. Studies in Greek Philosophy and its Continuation offered to Prof. C. J. de Vogel*, Assen 1975, 137–146.

"Orphism and Bacchic Mysteries: New Texts and Old Problems of Interpretation", *Colloquium of the Center for Hermeneutical Studies*, Berkeley, 1977.

Structure and History in Greek Mythology and Ritual, Berkeley, 1979.

"Craft versus Sect: The Problem of Orphics and Pythagoreans", in B. F. Meyer, E. P. Sanders (ed.), *Jewish and Christian Self-Definition* III, London 1982, 1–22.

Homo Necans: The Anthropology of Greek Sacrificial Ritual and Myth, Berkeley–Los Angeles–London, 1983.

Ancient Mystery Cults, Cambridge Mass.–London, 1987

The Orientalizing Revolution, Cambridge Mass., 1992.

"Bacchic Teletai in The Hellenistic Age" in J. Carpenter, C. Faraone (eds.), *Masks of Dionysus*, Ithaca–London, 1993, 259–275.

"Der geheime Reiz des Verborgenen: Antike Mysterienkulte", in H. G. Kippenberg, G. G. Stroumsa (eds.), *Secrecy and Concealment: Studies in the*

History of Mediterranean and Near Eastern Religions, Leiden–New York–Köln 1995, 79–101.

"The Logic of Cosmogony" in R. Buxton (ed.): *From Myth to Reason?* Oxford 1998.

Babylon, Memphis, Persepolis: Eastern Contexts or Greek Culture, Cambridge Mass. 2004.

"Kritiken, Rettungen und unterschwellige Lebendigkeit griechischer Mythen zur Zeit des frühen Christentums" in R. von Haehling (ed.), *Griechische Mythologie und frühes Christentum*, Darmstadt 2005, 173–194.

"El dios solitario. Orfeo fr. 12 Bernabé en contexto", in Bernabé–Casadesús 2008, 579–590.

BUSINE, A., *Paroles d'Apollon: Pratiques et traditions oraculaires dans l'Antiquite tardive (IIe–VIe siecle)*, Boston–Leiden 2005.

CAEROLS, J.J., "Sacrificuli ac uates ceperant hominum mentes (Liu. 25.1.8): religión, miedo y política en Roma·, G. Urso (ed.), *Terror et pavor. Violenza, intimidazione, clandestinità nel mondo antico*, Pisa 2006, 90–136.

CALAME, C., "La poésie attribuée à Orphée: qu'est-ce qui est orphique dans les *Orphica*?", *RHR* 219 (2002), 385–400.

CAMPENHAUSEN, H. FRHRR. VON, *Die Griechischen Kirchenväter*, Stuttgart 1967.

CARCOPINO, J., *La Basilique de Porta-Maggiore et l'influence du neopythagorisme à Rome*, Paris 1927.

CAROTTA, F.,"Orpheos Bakkikos: La Cruz desaparecida", *Isidorianum* 35, 2009, 179–217.

CASADESÚS, F., "El *Papiro de Derveni* y la técnica órfica de interpretación etimológica", Πρακτικὰ ια' Διέθνους Συνεδρίου Κλασικῶν Σπουδῶν, Athens 2001, 143–151.

"Orfismo y estoicismo", in Bernabé-Casadesús 2008, 1307–1338.

CASADIO, G., "Adversaria orphica et orientalia", *SMSR* 52 (1986), 291–322.

"Aspetti de la tradizione orfica all'alba del cristianesimo", in *La tradizione: Forme e modi*, Roma 1990, 185–204.

"Osiride in Grecia e Dioniso in Egitto", in I. Gallo (ed.): *Plutarco e la Religione, Atti del VI Convegno plutarcheo (Ravello, 29–31 maggio 1995)*, Napoli 1996, 201–227.

Antropologia gnostica e antropologia orfica nella notizia di Ippolito sui sethiani, Sangue e antropologia nella teologia, Roma 1989, 1295–1350 (= *Vie gnostiche all'immortalità*, Brescia 1997, 19–66).

"Ancient Mystic Religion, Emergence, New Paradigm from A.D. Nock to Ugo Bianchi", *Mediterraneo Antico: Economia Società Culture* 9.2 (2006) 485–534.

CASSIRER, E., *Philosophie der symbolischen Formen I–III*, Berlin 1923–1929.

CHADWICK, H., *Early Christian Thought and the Classical Tradition: Studies in Justin, Clement and Origen*, Oxford, 1966.
The Sentences of Sextus. A Contribution to the History of Early Christian Ethics, Cambridge, 1959.
CHICOTEAU, M., "The "Orphic" tablets depicted in a Roman Catacomb (c. 250 AD?)", *ZPE* 119 (1997) 81–83.
"Le 'Refrigerium' de l'hypogée du Viale Manzoni est-il méconnu?" *RBPh* 77.1 (1999), 205–208
CLASSEN, C.J., "The Creator in Greek Thought from Homer to Plato", *Class. & Med.* 23 (1962), 1–22.
CLAUS, D.B., *Toward the Soul. An Inquiry into the Meaning of ψυχή before Plato*, New Haven–London, 1981.
CLAUSS, M., *The Roman Cult Of Mithras: The God And His Mysteries*, New York 2001.
CLEMEN, C., *Der Einfluss der Mysterienreligionen auf das älteste Christentum*, Giessen 1913.
COLE, S., "Life and death: A New Epigram for Dionysus", *Epigraphica Anatolica* 4 (1984), 37–49.
COLLI, G., *La sapienza greca I: Dioniso, Apollo, Eleusi, Orfeo, Museo, Iperborei, Enigma*, Milano 1977.
COLLINS, D., "Nature, Cause, and Agency in Greek Magic", *TAPA* 133.1 (2003) 17–49.
CORNFORD, F.M., *Plato's Cosmology: The* Timaeus *of Plato Translated with a Running Commentary*, London, 1937.
COURCELLE, P., "Tradition platonicienne du corps-prison", *REL* 43 (1965), 406–443.
"Le corps-tombeau", *REA* 73 (1966) 101–122.
CRAHAY, R., "Eléments d'une mythopée gnostique dans la Grèce classique", in Bianchi 1967, 323–339.
CREUZER, G.F., *Symbolik und Mythologie der alten Völker*, Leipzig–Darmstadt 1810.
CSAPO, E., *Theories of Mythology*, Oxford 2005.
"Star Choruses: Eleusis, Orphism, and New Musical Imagery and Dance" in M. Revermann, P. Wilson (ed.), *Performance, Iconography, Reception: Studies in Honour of Oliver Taplin*. Oxford–New York 2008, 262–290.
CULLMAN, O., *Le problème littéraire et historique du roman pseudo-clémentin*, Paris 1930.
CUMONT, F., *Afterlife in Roman Paganism*, Yale 1922.
Les religions orientales dans le paganisme romain, Paris 1929³.
Lux Perpetua, Paris 1949.

CURTIUS, E.R., *European Literature and the Latin Middle Ages*, New York 1953.
DANIÉLOU, J., *Message évangelique et culture hellénistique aux IIe et IIIe siècles*, Paris–Tournais–New York–Roma 1961.
DASZEWSKI, W.A., *Dionysos der Erlöser: griechische Mythen im spätantiken Zypern*, Mainz 1985.
DELBRUECK, R., VOLLGRAFF, W., "An Orphic Bowl", *JHS* 54 (1934) 129–139.
DEMOEN, K., *Pagan and Biblical Exempla in Gregory Nazianzen. A Study in Rhetoric and Hermeneutics*, Turnhout 1996.
DETIENNE, M., "Les chemins de la déviance: Orphisme, Dionysisme, Pythagorisme" in *Orfismo in Magna Grecia. Atti del quattordicesimo Convegno di Studi sulla Magna Grecia*, (Taranto, 6–10 ottobre 1974) Napoli 1975, 49–79.
Dionysos mis à mort, Paris, 1977.
L'invention de la mythologie, Paris 1981.
DES PLACES, É., *Syngeneia. La parenté de l'homme avec Dieu d'Homère à la patristique*, Paris 1964.
DEVEREUX, G., *Baubo, la vulve mythique*, Paris 1983.
DICKIE, M.W., *Magic and Magicians in the Greco-Roman World*, London 2001.
DIETERICH, A., *Abraxas*, Leipzig 1891.
Nekyia. Beiträge zur Erklärung der neuentdeckten Petrusapokalypse, Leipzig–Berlin 1913².
DÍEZ DE VELASCO F., MOLINERO POLO, M.A., "Hellenoaegyptiaca I: Influences égyptiennes dans l'imaginaire grec de la mort: quelques exemples d'un emprunt supposé (Diodore I, 92, 1–4; I, 96, 4–8)", *Kernos* 7 (1994) 75–93.
DILLON, J.M., "'Orthodoxy' and 'eclecticism': Middle Platonists and Neo-Pythagoreans", in J.M. Dillon – A.A. Long (eds.): *The Question of "Eclecticism". Studies in Later Greek Philosophy*, Berkeley–Los Angeles–London 1988.
"Monotheism in the Gnostic Tradition" in Athanassiadi, P. – Frede, M., *Pagan Monotheism in Late Antiquity*, Oxford 1999, 69–79.
DILLON, J.M., HERSHBELL, J., *Iamblichus: On the Pythagorean Way of Life*, Atlanta 1991.
DODD C.H., *The Interpretation of the Fourth Gospel*, Cambridge 1953.
DODDS, E.R., *The Greeks and the Irrational*, Berkeley 1951.
Pagans and Christians in an Age of Anxiety, Cambridge 1965.
DÖLGER, F.J., "*Sacramentum infanticidii*: Die Schlachung eines Kindes und der Genuss seines Fleisches und Blutes als vermeitliches Einweihungsakt im ältesten Christentum", *Antike und Christentum* 4 (1934), 188–228.
DORNSEIFF, F., *Das Alphabet in Mystik und Magie*, Leipzig–Berlin 1922.

DROGE A. J., *Homer or Moses? Early Christian Interpretation on the History of Culture*, Tübingen 1989.

DUNAND, F., "Les associations dionysiaques au service du pouvoir lagide (III s^e av. J.-C.)" en *L'association Dionysiaque dans les societés anciennes. Actes de la Table ronde de l'École Française de Rome*, Roma 1986, 85–104.

EDMONDS, R. G., "Tearing apart the Zagreus Myth: A Few Disparaging Remarks on Orphism and Original Sin", *ClAnt* 18, 1999, 35–73.
Myths of the Underworld Journey: Plato, Aristophanes, and the "Orphic" Gold Tablets, Cambridge 2004.
"Recycling Laertes' Shroud: More on Orphism and Original Sin," 2008, (published online at the Center for Hellenic Studies: http://chs.harvard.edu/chs/redmonds).

EDSMAN, C. M., "Ein Orpheuszitat bei Platon als Stütze jüdisch-christlicher Zeitrechnung", *Mélanges Rudberg* (*Eranos* 1946) 488–499.

EDWARDS, M. J., „Atticizing Moses? Numenius, the Fathers and the Jews." *Vigiliae Christianae*, 44, (1990) 64–75.
"Xenophanes Christianus?', *GRBS* 32 (1991), 119–128.
"Gnostic Eros and Orphic Themes", *ZPE* 88 (1991) 25–40.
"Pagan and Christian Monotheism in the Age of Constantine", in Swain, S. / Edwards, M., *Approaching Late Antiquity: The Transformation from Early to Late Empire*, Oxford 2004.

EDWARDS, M. J., GOODMAN, M. / PRICE, S. (eds.), *Apologetics in the Roman Empire*, Oxford 1999.

EHRHARDT, A., "An unknown Orphic writing in the Demosthenes scholia and St. Paul", *Zeitschr. Neutest. Wiss.* 48 (1957), 101–110.

EISLER, R., *Orpheus the Fisher*. London, 1921.
Orphish-dionisische Mysteriengedanken in der christlichen Antike, Leipzig–Berlin 1925.

EIZENHOFER, L., "Die Siegelbildvorschläge des Clemens von Alexandrien", *JAC* 3 (1960), 51–69.

ELIADE, M., *Die Schöpfungsmythen: Aegypter, Sumerer, Hurriter, Hethiter, Kanaaniter und Israeliten*. Einsiedeln, 1964.

ELLINGER, P., *La légende nationale phocidienne. Artémis, les situations extrèmes*, Athens 1993, 147–195.

ELSNER, J., *Art and the Roman Viewer: The Transformation of Art from the Pagan World to Christianity*, Cambridge 1995.
Imperial Rome and Christian Triumph: The Art of the Roman Empire A.D. 100–450, Oxford 1998.
"Archaeologies and Agendas: Reflections on Late Ancient Jewish Art and Early Christian Art", *Journal of Roman Studies* 93 (2003), 114–128.

ESCHENBACH, A.C., *Epigenes de poesi Orphica, in priscas Orphicorum Carminum memorias liber commentarius*, 1702 (reed. M. Gesner, 1764).
EVANS, G.R., *Law and Theology in the Middle Ages*, London 2002.
FARAONE, CH., OBBINK, D., *Magika Hiera: Ancient Greek Magic and Religion*, Oxford 1991.
FARNELL, R., *Greek Hero Cults and Ideas of Immortality*, Oxford 1921.
FAUTH, W., *Helios Megistos*, Leiden–New York–Köln 1995.
FEAR, A.T., "Cybele and Christ" in E.N. Lane (ed.), *Cybele, Attis & Related Cults: Essays in Memory of M.J. Vermaseren*, Leiden, 1996, 37–50.
FESTUGIÈRE, A.J., "Les mystères de Dionysos", *R. Bi.* 4 (1935), 366–396 (= *Études de religion grecque et hellénistique*, Paris 1972, 13–63).
La révélation d'Hermes Trismégiste, 4 vols., Paris 1949–53.
FEULNER, R., *Clemens von Alexandrien*, Frankfurt am Main 2006.
FIEDROWICZ, M., *Apologie im frühen Christentum*, Paderborn 2001.
FITZGERALD, J.T., Olbricht, T.H., White, L.M. (eds.), *Early Christianity and Classical Culture: Comparative Studies in Honor of Abraham J. Malherbe*, Leiden–Boston 2003.
FÖGEN, M.T., *Die Enteignung der Wahrsager*, Frankfurt am Main, 1993.
FORBES, C., *Firmicus Maternus, The Error of the Pagan Religions*, New York 1970.
FOWDEN, G., "The Pagan Holy Man in Late Antique Society," *JHS* 102 (1982), 33–59.
The Egyptian Hermes: a Historical Approach Late Pagan Mind, Princeton 1986.
FOWLER, R.L., "Greek Magic, Greek Religion", *Ill. Class. Stud.* 20 (1995), 1–22.
FRASER, P.M., *Ptolemaic Alexandria* I–III, Oxford, 1972.
FRAZER, J.G., *The Golden Bough*, London 1912³.
FREDE, M., "Monotheism and Pagan Philosophy in Later Antiquity" in Athanassiadi, P.–Frede, M. (eds.), *Pagan Monotheism in Late Antiquity*, Oxford 1999, 41–67.
"Recherches sur le culte de Bacchus parmi les Grecs", *Histoire de l'Academie Royale des Inscriptions* 23 (1756), 242–270.
FRÉRET, N., "Recherches sur le culte de Bacchus parmi les Grecs", *Histoire de l'Academie Royale des Inscriptions* 23 (1756), 242–270.
FREUND, R., "The Ethics of Abortion in Hellenistic Judaism" *Helios* 10 (1983), 125–137.
FRIEDMAN, J.B., *Orpheus in the Middle Ages*, Cambridge Mass. 1970.
GAGNÉ, R., "Winds and Ancestors: The *Physika* of Orpheus", *HSCP* 103 (2007), 1–24.

"The Sins of the Fathers: C.A. Lobeck and K.O. Müller", *Kernos* 21 (2008), 109–124.

GAGNÉ, R., HERRERO, M., "Themis at Eleusis: Clement of Alexandria, *Protrepticus* 2.22.5", *CQ* 59.1 (2009), 270–274.

GAMBLE, H.Y., "Euhemerism and Christology in Origen, *Contra Celsum* III 22–43", *Vig. Christ.* 23 (1979), 12–29.

GEERLINGS, W., "Das Bild des Sängers Orpheus bei den griechischen Kirchenvaetern" in R. von Haehling (ed.), *Griechische Mythologie und früher Christentum*, Darmstadt 2005, 254–267.

GIGANTE, M., *L'ultima tunica*, Napoli 1973.

GIRARD, J., *Le Sentiment Religieux en Grèce*, 2nd ed., Grecé, Paris 1879².

GLOTZ, G., *La solidarité de la famille dans le droit criminel en Grèce*, Paris 1904.

GNILKA, C., *CHRÊSIS: Die Methode der Kirchenväter im Umgang mit der antiken Kultur II: Kultur und Conversion*, Basel 1993.

GODWIN, J., *Mystery Religions in the Ancient World*, New York 1981.

GOLDAMMER, K., "Christus Orpheus. Der μουσικὸς ἀνήρ als unerkanntes Motiv in der ravennatischen Mosaikikonographie", *Zeitschrift für Kirchengeschichte* 74 (1963), 217–243.

GORDON, R., ALVAR, J., *Romanising Oriental Gods: Myth, Salvation and Ethics, in the Cults of Cybele, Isis, and Mithras*, Boston–Leiden 2008.

GOULET, R., *Macarios de Magrésie: Le Monogénès*, Paris 2003.

GOVERS-HOPMAN, M., "Les jeux d'epithètes dans les *Hymnes Orphiques*", *Kernos* 14 (2001), 35–49.

GRAF, F., *Eleusis und die orphische Dichtung Athens in vorhellenistischer Zeit*, Berlin–New York 1974.
Magic in the Ancient World, Cambridge Mass. 1997.
"Orfeo, Eleusis y Atenas", in Bernabé/Casadesús 2008, 671–696.

GRAF F., JOHNSTON, S.I., *Ritual Texts for the Afterlife*, London 2007.
"Serious Singing: the Orphic Hymns as Religious Texts", *Kernos* 22 (2009), 169–182.

GRILLMEIER, A., "Der Gottessohn im Totenreich," *Zeitschrift für Katholische Theologie* 71 (1949), 1–53, 184–203.

GRUEN, E.S., *Heritage and Hellenism*, Berkeley–Los Angeles–London, 1993.

GRUPPE, O., *Griechische Mythologie und Religionsgeschichte*, München 1906.

GUTHRIE, W.K.C., *Orpheus and Greek Religion*, London 1952²

HABICHT, C., *Pausanias' Guide to Ancient Greece*, Berkeley 1985.

HALL, E., *Inventing the Barbarian*, Oxford, 1983.

HALL, J., *Ethnic Identity in Greek Antiquity*, Cambridge 1997.

HALTON, T., "Clement's Lyre: a Broken String, a New Song", *Second Century* 3 (1983), 177–199.
HARDIE, A., "Muses and Mysteries", in P. Murray – P. Wilson, *Music and the Muses*, Oxford 2004.
HARNACK A. VON, *Lehrbuch der Dogmengeschichte*, Freiburg, 1886–1894.
HARRISON, J., *Prolegomena to the Study of Greek Religion*, Cambridge 1903 (1922³).
Themis: A Study of the Social Origins of Greek Religion, Cambridge 1927.
HARTOG, F., *Le miroir d'Hérodote*, Paris 1980.
HAUKE, M.P., *Heilsverlust in Adam: Stationen griechischer Erbsündenlehre: Irenaeus, Origenes, Kappadozier*, Paderborn, 1993
HENGEL, M., *Judentum und Hellenismus*, Tübingen 1973.
HENRICHS, A., "Pagan Ritual and the Alleged Crimes of the Early Christians", in P. Granfield, J.A. Jungmann (eds.), *Kyriakon. Festschrift J. Quasten* I, Münster, 1970, 18–35
Die Phoinikika des Lollianos, Berkeley 1972.
"Greek Maenadism from Olympias to Messalina", *HSCP* 82 (1978), 149–152.
"Human Sacrifice in Greek Religion: Three Case Studies », in *Le Sacrifice dans l'Antiquité*, Entretiens Hardt 27, Vandœuvres–Genève 1981.
"Changing Dionysian Identities", in B.F. Meyer–E.P. Sanders (eds.): *Jewish and Christian Self-Definition* III, London 1982, 137–160.
"The Eumenides and Wineless Libations in the Derveni Papyrus", *Atti del XVII Congresso Internazionale di Papirologia*, Napoli 1984, II 255–268.
"*Hieroi Logoi* and *Hierai Bibloi*: The (Un)written Margins of the Sacred in Ancient Greece", *HSCP* 101 (2003), 207–266.
HERMANN, G., *Orphica*, Leipzig 1805.
HERNÁNDEZ DE LA FUENTE, D., "Elementos órficos en el canto VI de las *Dionisíacas*: el mito de Dioniso Zagreo en Nono de Panópolis", *Ilu. Revista de Ciencias de las Religiones* 7 (2002), 19–50.
HERRERO, M., "Técnicas de cristianización del léxico en el *Protréptico* de Clemente de Alejandría", *Interlingüística* 13 II (2002), 335–345.
"Derecho metafórico de familia: la ambigüedad del *nothos* desde la polis clásica a la apologética cristiana", *Actas del XI Congreso de la SEEC I*, Madrid 2005a, 637–646.
"La conversión como metáfora espacial: una propuesta de aproximación cognitiva al cambio cultural de la Antigüedad Tardía", *Ilu. Revista de Ciencias de las Religiones* 10 (2005b), 63–84.
"Le pluriel de dédain dans la reflexion religieuse des présocratiques", *Revue de Philosophie Ancienne* 24.2 (2005c), 55–74.

"Dionysos mi-cuit: l'étymologie de Mésatis et le festin inachevé des Titans", *Revue de l'histoire des religions* 223.4 (2006), 389–416.

"Las fuentes de Clem. Alex. *Protr.* 2.12–22: un tratado sobre los misterios y una teogonía órfica", *Emerita: Revista Española de Lingüística y Filología Clásica* 75.1 (2007a), 19–50.

"¿A quién dirige Gregorio de Nazianzo su crítica de la reencarnación (*De anima* 22–52)?", *Adamantius: Rivista del Gruppo Italiano di Ricerca su Origene e la tradizione alessandrina*, 13 (2007b), 231–247.

"Orphic Ideas of Immortality: Traditional Greek Images and a New Eschatological Thought", in M. Labahn/M. Lang (eds.) *Lebendige Hoffnung – ewiger Tod? Jenseitsvorstellungen im Hellenismus, Judentum und Christentum*, Leipzig 2007c, 247–273.

"Tradición órfica y tradición homérica", in A. Bernabé – F. Casadesús (eds.): *Orfeo y la tradición órfica: un reencuentro*, Madrid 2008a, 247–278.

"Orfismo en Roma" in A. Bernabé – F. Casadesús (eds.): *Orfeo y la tradición órfica: un reencuentro*, Madrid 2008b, 1383–1410.

"El orfismo, el *genos* y la *polis*" in A. Bernabé – F. Casadesús (eds.): *Orfeo y la tradición órfica: un reencuentro*, Madrid 2008c, 1603–1622.

"Orphic God(s): Theogonies and Hymns as Roads for Monotheism", in S. Mitchell/P. Van Nuffelen, *Pagan Monotheism in Late Antiquity*, Leuven 2009a, 77–99.

"Orphic Mediations Between Greek and Foreign Religion", in E. Cingano (ed.), *Ancient Literatures in the Mediterranean: Greece, Rome and the Near East*, Padova (2009b), 369–386.

HEUSSNER, A., *Die altchristlichen Orpheusdarstellungen*, Kassel 1893.

HOEK, A. VAN DER, *Clement of Alexandria and his Use of Philo in the Stromateis*, Leiden 1988.

"Techniques of Quotation in Clement of Alexandria", *Vig. Chr.* 50 (1996), 223–243.

"Etymologizing in a Christian Context: The Techniques of Clement and Origen", *Studia Philonica Annual* 16 (2004), 122–168.

"Apologetic and Protreptic Discourse in Clement of Alexandria", *L'apologétique chrétienne gréco-latine à l'époque prénicenienne*, Entr. Hardt 51, 2005, Vandoeuvres–Genève, 69–102

HOHEISEL, K., "Das frühe Christentum und die Seelenwanderung", *JAC* 27/29 (1984–85), 24–46.

HOLLADAY, C.R., "The Textual Tradition of Pseudo-Orpheus: Walter or Riedweg?" in *Geschichte-Tradition-Reflexion. Festschrift für Martin Hengel zum 70. Geburtstag, I: Judentum*, Tübingen 1996, 159–180.

HOLLMANN, A., "A Curse Tablet from the Circus at Antioch", *ZPE* 145 (2003), 67–82.
HOLZHAUSEN, J., "Gnostizismus, Gnosis, Gnostiker. Ein Beitrag zur antiken Terminologie", *JAC* 44 (2001), 58–74.
HONIGMAN, S., *The Septuagint and Homeric Scholarship in Alexandria*, Oxford 2003.
HORDERN, J., "Notes on the Orphic Papyrus from Gurôb (P. Gurôb 1; Pack² 2464)", *ZPE* 2000 (129) 131–140.
HUTTON, W., *Describing Greece. Landscape and Literature in the Periegesis of Pausanias*, Cambridge 2005.
IRWIN, E., "The song of Orpheus and the New Song of Christ", in J. Warden (ed.) *Orpheus: Metamorphoses of a Myth*, Toronto 1982, 51–62.
JACCOTTET, A.-F., *Choisir Dionysos. Les associations dionysiaques ou la face cache/e du dionysisme*, 2 vols, Zürich 2003.
JACOBS L., "Jewish Cosmology" in C. Blacker – M. Loewe (eds.), *Ancient Cosmologies*, London 1975, 66–68.
JÄGER, W., *The Theology of Early Greek Philosophers*, Cambridge Mass. 1947.
Early Christianity and Greek Paideia, Cambridge Mass. 1961.
JAKAB, A., *Ecclesia Alexandrina*, Bern 2001.
JANKO, R., "The Derveni Papyrus (Diagoras of Melos, *Apopyrgizontes logoi*?): A New Translation", *CPh* 96 (2001), 1–32.
JESNIK, J., *The Image of Orpheus in Roman Mosaic*, Oxford 1997.
JIMÉNEZ SAN CRISTÓBAL, A. I., "Los libros del ritual órfico", *EClás* 44 (2002), 109–23.
"Rasgos órficos en la epigrafía religiosa griega y romana", in Bernabé – Casadesús 2008, 1453–1490.
JOHNSON, A. P., *Ethnicity and Argument in Eusebius' Praeparatio Evangelica*, Oxford 2006.
JOHNSTON, S. I., MCNIVEN, T. J., "Dionysos and the Underworld in Toledo", *Museum Helveticum* 53 (1996), 25–36.
DE JONG, A., *Traditions of the Magi: Zoroastrianism in Greek and Latin Literature*, Leiden 1997.
JOURDAN, F., *Le Papyrus de Derveni*, Paris 2003.
"Dionysos dans le *Protréptique* de Clément d'Alexandrie. Initiations dionysiaques et mystères chrétiens", *RHR* 223.3 (2006), 265–282.
"Orphée, sorcier ou mage?", *RHR* 225.1 (2008a), 5–36.
"L'association poétique des citharèdes légendaires (Amphion, Arion et Orphée) chez Horace et Silius Italicus", *REA* 110 (2008b), 103–116.
"Le Logos et l'empereur, nouveaux Orphée. Postérité d'une image entrée dans la littérature avec Clément d'Alexandrie", *Vigiliae christianae*, 62.4 (2008c), 319–333.

Orphée et les chrétiens I: Orphée, du repoussoir au préfigurateur du Christ. Réécriture d'un mythe à des fins protreptiques chez Clément d'Alexandrie, Paris 2010.
Poème judeo-hellenistique attribué à Orphée, Paris 2010.
JUDEN, B., *Traditions orphiques et tendances mystiques dans le romantisme français (1800– 1855)*, Paris 1971.
KAHN, CH., *Pythagoras and the Pythagoreans: A Brief History*, Indianapolis 2001.
KERENYI, K., *Die Mysterien von Eleusis*, Zürich 1962.
KERN, O., "Die Herkunft des orphischen Hymnenbuchs" in *Genethliakon für C. Robert*, Berlin 1910, 89–101.
Orphicorum Fragmenta, Berlin 1922.
Die Religion der Griechen, 3 vols., Berlin 1938.
KING, K., *What is Gnosticism?*, Cambridge Mass. 2003.
KINGSLEY, P., *Ancient Philosophy, Mystery and Magic. Empedocles and Pythagorean Tradition*, Oxford 1995.
KIPPENBERG, H.G., *Die vorderasiatischen Erlösungsreligionen*, Frankfurt/Main 1991.
KIRK, G.S., *Myth: its Meaning and Function in Ancient and Other Cultures*, Berkeley–Cambridge 1970.
KLAUCK, H.-J., *Herrenmahl und hellenistischer Kult*, Munster 1982².
KLEINGÜNTHER, A., Πρῶτος εὑρετής, Leipzig 1933.
KOFSKY, A., *Eusebius of Caesarea against Paganism*, Leiden 2002.
KÖRTE, A., "Literarische Texte mit Ausschluss der christlichen", *Archiv für Papyrusforschung* 13 (1939), 103–150.
KOTANSKY, R., *Greek Magical Amulets: The Inscribed Gold, Silver, Copper and Bronze Lamellae I*, Köln 1994.
KOTT, J., *The Eating of the Gods. An Interpretation of Greek Tragedy*, New York 1973.
KOUREMENOS, T. PARASSOGLOU GM & TSANTSANOGLOU K. (EDS), *The Derveni Papyrus*. Firenze 2006.
LADA-RICHARDS, I., *Initiating Dionysus. Ritual and Theatre in Aristophanes' Frogs*, Oxford 1999.
LAGRANGE, M.-J., "Les mystères. L'orphisme", in *Introduction à l'étude du Nouveau Testament IV*, Paris 1937.
LAÍN ENTRALGO, P., *The Therapy of the Word in Classical Antiquity*, New Haven 1970.
LAKOFF, G., JOHNSON, M., *Metaphors We Live By*, Berkeley 1980.
LAKOFF, G., TURNER, M., *More than Cool Reason*, Berkeley 1989.
LAMBERTON, R., *Homer the Theologian*, Berkeley 1986.

Lampe, E., *A Patristic Greek Lexicon*, 1982⁶.
Lane Fox, R., *Pagans and Christians*, Harmondsworth 1986.
Lebedev, V., "Orpheus, Parmenides or Empedocles? The Aphrodite verses in the Naassene treatise of Hippolytus' *Elenchos*", *Philologus* 138 (1994), 24–31.
Le Boulluec, A., *Clement d'Alexandrie Stromate V, edition, traduction et commentaire*, 2 vols., Paris 1981.
La notion d'hérésie dans la litterature grecque IIe–IIIe siècles, Paris 1985.
Legge, F., *The Forerunners and Rivals of Christianity*, London 1915.
Le Goff, J., *La naissance du Purgatoire*, Paris 1981.
Lenger, M.T., *Corpus des Ordonnances des Ptolémées*, Bruxelles 1980².
Corpus des Ordonnances des Ptolémées. Bilan des additions et corrections. Compléments à la bibliographie, Bruxelles 1990.
Levaniouk, O., "The Toys of Dionysus", *HSCP* 103 (2007), 165–202.
Lieberg, G., *Poeta Creator. Studien zu einer Figur der antiken Dichtung*, Amsterdam 1982.
Liebeschuetz, W., "The Significance of the Speech of Praetextatus" en Athanassiadi, P. – Frede, M. (eds.), *Pagan Monotheism in Late Antiquity*, Oxford 1999, 185–205.
Lightfoot, J.L., *The Sibylline Oracles*, Oxford 2007.
Lilla, S.R.C., *Clement of Alexandria: A Study in Christian Platonism and Gnosticism*, Oxford, 1971.
Linforth, I.M., *The Arts of Orpheus*, Berkeley–Los Angeles 1941.
Lissarrague, F., "Danaé, métamorphoses d'un mythe", in S. Georgoudi, J.-P. Vernant (eds.), *Mythes grecs au figuré, de l'antiquité au baroque*, Paris 1996, 105–133.
Lizcano, S., "Orfismo en el *Corpus Philostrateum*", *Emerita* 71 (2004), 51–72.
Lloyd, G.E.R., *Polarity and Analogy*, Cambridge 1966.
Lloyd-Jones, H., *The Justice of Zeus*, Berkeley 1971.
Lloyd-Jones, H., Parsons, P., "Iterum de Catabasi Orphica", *Kyklos: Griechisches und Byzantinisches Rudolf Keydell zum neunzigsten Geburtstag*, Berlin–New York 1978, 88–100 (= *The Academic Papers of Sir Hugh Lloyd-Jones I*, Oxford 1990, 333–341).
Lobeck, C.A., *Aglaophamus sive de theologiae mysticae Graecorum causis libri tres*, Königsberg 1829.
Loisy, A., *Les mystères païens et le mystère chrétien*, Paris 1919.
Loucas, E. and I., "Un autel de Rhéa-Cybèle et la Grande Déese de Phlya", *Latomus* 45 (1986), 392–404.

Luck G., "Vergil and the Mystery Religions," *AJPh* 94, 1973, 147–166

Lugaresi, L., "Fuggiamo la consuetudine: pratiche sociali cristiane, rappresentazione e spettacoli in Clemente Alessandrino", *Adamantius* 9 (2003), 10–29.
Il teatro di Dio: il problema degli spettacoli nel cristianesimo antico (II–IV secolo). Supplementi Adamantius 1, Brescia, 2008.

Maass, E., *Orpheus: Untersuchungen zur griechischen, römischen, altchristlichen Jenseitdichtung und Religion*, München 1895.

Macchioro, V., *Orfismo e Paolinismo*, Montevarchi 1922.
From Orpheus to Paul: A History of Orphism, London 1930.

Majercik, R., *The Chaldean Oracles: Text, Translation and Commentary*, Leiden–New York 1989.

Malley, W.J., *Hellenism and Christianity: the Conflict between Hellenic and Christian Wisdom in the Contra Galilaeos of Julian the Apostate and the Contra Julianum of St. Cyril of Alexandria*, Roma 1978.

Mansfeld, J., "Bad World and Demiurge: A 'Gnostic' Motif from Parmenides and Empedocles to Lucretius and Philo" in R. van den Broek–M.J. Vermaseren (eds.), *Studies in Gnosticism and Hellenistic Religions presented to G. Quispel*, Leiden 1981, 261–314 = *Studies in Later Greek Philosophy and Gnosticism*, London 1989.
"Heraclitus, Empedocles, and Others in a Middle Platonist Cento in Philo of Alexandria", *Vigiliæ Christianæ* 39 (1985), 113–136 = *Studies in later Greek Philosophy and Gnosticism*, London 1989.
Heresiography in Context, Leiden–New York–Köln 1992.

Marcovich, M., "Orphic Fragment 226 Kern", *Rh. Mus.* 116 (1973), 359–60 (= *Studies in Greek Poetry*, Chicago 1991, 213–214).
"Phanes, Phicola and the Sethians", *JThS* 25 (1974), 447–451.
"Demeter, Baubo, Iacchus and a Redactor", *Vig.Christ.* 40 (1986), 294–301.
Heraclitus, Sankt Agustin 2001².

Maritano, M., "Giustino Martire di fronte al problema della metempsicosi", *Salesianum* 54 (1992), 231–281.

Markschies, Ch., "Odysseus und Orpheus – christlich gelesen" in R. Haehling, *Griechische Mythologie und frühes Christentum*, Darmstadt 2005, 227–253.

Martin D.B., *Inventing Superstition from the Hippocratics to the Christians*, Cambridge, Mass. 2004.

Martín, R., "La relación de Orfeo con la magia a través de los testimonios literarios", *MHNH* 3 (2003), 55–74.
La magia y el orfismo, Ph.D. thesis, Universidad Complutense, Madrid 2006

MARTÍNEZ MAZA, C., ALVAR, J., "Transferencias entre los misterios y el cristianismo: problemas y tendencias", *Antigüedad y cristianismo* 14 (1997) 47–59.
MARTÍNEZ NIETO, R. B., *La aurora del pensamiento griego. Las cosmogonías prefilosóficas griegas de Hesíodo, Alcmán, Ferecides, Epiménides, Museo y la Teogonía órfica antigua*, Madrid 2000.
MASTROCINQUE, A., "Orpheos Bakkhikos", *ZPE* 97 (1993), 16–32.
— *From Jewish Magic to Gnosticism*, München 2005.
— *Des mystères de Mithra aux mystères de Jésus*, Stuttgart 2009.
MAY, G., *Creatio ex Nihilo*, Edinburgh 1994.
MCGAHEY, R., *The Orphic Moment: Shaman to Poetic Thinker in Plato, Nietzsche and Mallarmé*, Albany 1994.
MEEREN, S. VAN DER, "Le *Protréptique* en philosophie: essaie de definition d'un genre", *Rev. Ét. Gr.* 115 (2002/2), 591–621.
MERKELBACH, R., *Roman und Mysterium in der Antike*, München–Berlin 1962.
— *Die Hirten des Dionysos*, Stuttgart 1988.
— "Die goldenen Totenpässe: ägyptisch, orphisch, bakchisch", *ZPE* 128 (1999), 1–13.
MERKELBACH, R., TOTTI, M., *Abrasax*, Köln 1990–1994 (4 vols).
METZGER, B., "Considerations of Methodology in the Study of Mystery Religions and Early Christianity", *HThR* 48 (1955), 1–20.
MINOIS, G., *Les Origines du mal: une histoire du péché originel*, Paris 2002.
MITCHELL, S., "The Cult of Theos Hypsistos between Pagans, Jews, and Christians" in Athanassiadi, P.–Frede, M. (eds.), *Pagan Monotheism in Late Antiquity*, Oxford 1999, 81–148.
MITCHELL, S., VAN NUFFELEN, P. (ed.), *Pagan Monotheism in Late Antiquity*, Leuven 2009.
MOLINA, M., *Orfeo y la mitología de la música*, PhD thesis, Madrid 1998.
MOLYVIATI-TOPTSIS, U., "Vergil's Elysium and the Orphic-Pythagorean Ideas of After-life", *Mnemosyne* 47.4 (1994), 33–46.
MOMIGLIANO, A., "Pagan and Christian Historiography in the IV Cent. A.D." in A. Momigliano (ed.): *The Conflict between Paganism and Christianity in the Fourth Century*, Oxford 1963, 17–38.
— *On Pagans, Jews and Christians*, Middletown Conn. 1987.
MONTSERRAT, M., *Los gnósticos*, 2 vols. Madrid 1983.
— "La notice d' Hyppolite sur les Séthiens. Étude de la partie systémathique", *Studia Patristica* 24 (1993), 390–398.
MORA, F., *Arnobio e i culti di mistero*, Roma 1994.
MORAND, A.-F., *Études sur les Hymnes orphiques*, Leiden–Boston–Köln 2001.

MORESCHINI, C., *Storia dell'ermetismo cristiano*, Brescia 2000.
MORESCHINI, C., Sykes, D. A., *St Gregory of Nazianzus: Poemata Arcana*, Oxford 1997.
MOST, G. W., "Presocratic Philosophy and Traditional Greek Epic", in A. Bierl, R. Lämmle, K. Wesselmann (ed.), *Literatur und Religion 2*. Berlin–New York: De Gruyte 2007, 271–302.
MOULINIER, L., *Orphée et l'orphisme à l'époque classique*, Paris 1955.
MURRAY, C., *Rebirth and Afterlife. A Study of Transmission of Some Pagan Imagery in Early Christian Funerary Art*, Oxford 1981.
MYLONAS, G. E., *Eleusis and the Eleusinian Mysteries*, Princeton 1961.
NAGY, G., "Eléments orphiques chez Homère", *Kernos* 14 (2001), 1–9.
NALDINI, M., "I miti di Orfeo e di Eracle nell' interpretazione patristica", *CCC* 14 (1993), 331–343.
NARDI, E., "Ce lo leggiamo, l'aborto?", *Iura* 21 (1970), 186–190.
"Codicillo", *Iura* 23 (1972), 135–136.
NIEHOFF, M. R., "Homeric Scholarship and Bible Exegesis in Ancient Alexandria: Evidence from Philo's 'Quarrelsome' Colleagues" *CQ* 57.1 (2007) 166–182.
NIETO IBÁÑEZ, J. M., "Dioniso, ¿Dios judío?", in J. G. Montes, M. Sánchez, R. J. Gallé (eds.), *Plutarco, Dioniso y el vino*, Madrid 1999, 327–336.
NILSSON, M. P., "Early Orphism and Kindred Religious Movements", *HThR* 28 (1935) 181–230.
The Dionysiac Mysteries of Hellenistic Times, Lund 1957.
NIMMO SMITH, J., *A Christian's Guide to Greek Culture: The Pseudo-Nonnus Commentaries on Sermons 4, 5, 39 and 43 by Gregory of Nazianzus*, Liverpool 2001.
NISBET, R. G. M., "Vergil's Fourth Eclogue: Easterner and Westerners", *BICS* 25, 1978, 59–78.
NOCK, A. D., *Conversion*, Oxford, 1933a.
"The Vocabulary of the New Testament", *JBL* 52 (1933b), 131–139 (= *Essays on Religion of the Ancient World I*, Oxford 1972, 341–347).
"Orphism or popular Philosophy?" *HThR* 28, 1935, 301–315.
"Hellenistic Mysteries and Christian Sacraments", *Mnemosyne* 5 (1952) 177–213 (= *Essays on Religion and the Ancient World*, Oxford 1972).
Early Gentile Christianity and its Hellenistic Background, New York 1928 (= reedited with additions in 1964).
NOLDEKE, TH., "Bar Choni über Homer, Hesiod und Orpheus", *ZDMG* 53 (1899), 501–507
NORDEN, E., *Agnostos Theos. Untersuchungen zur Formengeschichte religiöser Rede*, Leipzig–Berlin 1913.

P. Vergilius Maro Aeneis Buch VI, Darmstadt 1957[4].

OBBINK, D., "Dionysus Poured Out: Ancient and Modern Theories of Sacrifice and Cultural Formation", in T. Carpenter–C. Faraone (eds.), *Masks of Dionysus*, Ithaca–London 1993, 65–86.

"Cosmology as Initiation vs. the Critique of Orphic Mysteries", en A. Laks, G. W. Most (ed.), *Studies on the Derveni Papyrus*, Oxford 1997, 39–54.

OGILVIE, M., *The Library of Lactantius*, Oxford 1978.

O'HIGGINS, D. M., "Women's Cultic Joking and Mockery: Some Perspectives", en A. Lardinois, L. McClure, *Making Silence Speak: Women's Voices in Greek Literature and Society*, Princeton 2001, 137–160.

OLENDER, M., "Aspects de Baubo", *RHR* 102 (1985), 3–55.

OLMO LETE, G. DEL, *Mitos, leyendas y rituales de los semitas occidentales*, Madrid 1998.

OLMOS, R., "Appendix 2. Iconographical notes on the Orphic tablets", in Bernabé–Jiménez 2008, 273–315.

OPELT I., "Christianisierung heidnischer Etymologien", *Reallexikon für Antike und Christentum* 2, Stuttgart 1959, 70–85.

"Etymologie", *Reallexikon für Antike und Christentum* 6, Stuttgart 1966, 41–48.

"Fírmico Materno sobre las Bacanales (*De err.prof. rel.* 6.9)", *Helmantica* 19 (1968), 31–41.

OSBORN, E., *Clement of Alexandria*, Cambridge 2005.

OTTO, W. F., *Dionysos, Mythos und Kultus*, Frankfurt am Main 1933.

PAGELS, E., *Adam, Eve, and the Serpent*, New York 1988.

PAILLER, J.-M., *Bacchanalia. La répression de 186 av. J.-C. à Rome et en Italie*, Roma 1988.

PANYAGUA, E., "La figura de Orfeo en el arte griego y romano" *Helmantica* 18 (1967), 173–239.

PARKER, R., *Miasma*, Oxford 1983.

"Early Orphism" in A. Powell (ed.) *The Greek World*, London 1995, 483–510.

PATTON, K., Ray, B. (eds.), *A Magic Still Dwells: Comparative Religion in the Postmodern Age*, Los Angeles 2000.

PELLING, C. B. R., *Plutarch: Life of Antony*, Cambridge 1988.

PÉPIN, J., *Mythe et allégorie. Les origines grecs et les contestations judeo-chrétiennes*, Paris 1976.

"Christianisme et Mythologie. Jugements chrétiens sur les analogies entre paganisme et christianisme", *De la philosophie ancienne à la théologie patristique*, Paris 1986, VIII 18–44.

PERRONE, L., "Fra silenzio e parola: dall'apologia alla testimonianza del cristianesimo nel Contro Celso di Origene", in *L'apologétique chrétienne*

grécolatine à l'époque prénicénienne, Entretiens Hardt 51, Vandoeuvres–Genève 2005, 103–149.
PETERSEN, E., *ΕΙΣ ΘΕΟΣ. Epigraphische, formgeschichtliche und religionsgeschichtliche Untersuchungen*, Göttingen 1926.
PICARD, C., "L'épisode de Baubo dans les mystères d'Eleusis", *RHR* 95 (1927), 220–255.
PILHOFER, H., *PRESBYTERON KREITTON. Der Alterbeweis der jüdischen und christlichen Apologeten und seine Vorgeschichte*, Tübingen 1990.
PIRENNE-DELFORGE, V., *Retour à la source: Pausanias et la religion grecque*, Liège 2008.
— "Under Which Conditions Did the Greeks "Believe" in Their Myths? The Religious Criteria of Adherence", Dill, U.–Walde, Ch. (ed), *Ancient Myth: Media, Transformations and Sense-Constructions*, Berlin–New York 2009, 38–54.
PORTALUPI, F., "Sull'Interpretazione del mito di Orfeo in Frontone,". *Rivista di cultura classica e medioevale* 27 (1985) 125–34.
PÒRTULAS, J., "Orfeo en Bizancio", in M. Alganza Roldán–J. M. Camacho Rojo–P. P. Fuentes González–M. Villena Ponsoda (eds.), *ΕΠΙΕΙΚΕΙΑ. Studia Graeca in memoriam Jesús Lens Tuero*, Granada 2000, 399–405.
POUDERON, B., *D'Athènes à Alexandrie: études sur Athénagore et les origines de la philosophie chrétienne*, Québec 1998.
— "Hélène et Ulysse comme deux âmes en peine: une symbolique gnostique, platonicienne ou orphico-pythagoricienne?" *REG* 116 (2003), 132–151
— *Les apologistes chrétiens*, Paris 2005.
POUDERON, B., Doré, J. (eds.), *Les apologistes chrétiens et la culture grecque*, Paris 1998.
PREST, A., *Die Fragmente der griechischen Kultschriftsteller*, Berlin 1903.
PRICE, S., *Religions of the ancient Greeks*, Cambridge 1999.
PRINGENT, P., "Orphée dans l'iconographie chrétienne", *Revue d'histoire et de philosophie religieuses* 64 (1984), 205–221.
PROTT, J. VON ZIEHEN, L., *Leges Graecorum sacrae e titulis collectae. I. Fasti sacri*, Leipzig 1896.
QUANDT, G., *De Baccho ab Alexandri aetate in Asia Minore culto*, Halle 1913.
QUASTEN, J., *Musik und Gesang in den Kulten der heidnischen Antike und christlichen Frühzeit*, Münster 1930.
QUISPEL, G., "The Demiurge in the Apocryphon of John" en Wilson, R. McL. (ed.), *Nag Hammadi and Gnosis: Papers Read at the First International Congress of Coptology (Cairo, December 1976)*, Leiden 1978, 1–33.
RABINOWITZ, I., "The alleged Orphism of 11QPss 28:3–12", *ZATW* 76 (1964), 193–200.

RADICE, R., *La filosofia di Aristobulo e i suoi nessi con il "De mundo" atribuito a Aristotele: con due appendici contenenti i frammenti di Aristobulo, traduzione a fronte e presentazione delle varianti*, Milano 1995².

RAMELLI, I., *Allegoristi dell'età classica: Opere e frammenti*. Milan, 2007.

RAPISARDA E., *Clemente Fonte di Arnobio*, Torino 1939.

REINACH. S., "L'orphisme dans la IVᵉ Églogue de Vergile", *RHR* 42 (1900), 365–383.

"La mort d'Orphee" *RAr* 2 (1902), 242–79.

"Morale orphique et morale chrétienne", in *Cultes, mythes et religions* III, Paris 1905–1923, III 272–282 (= "Aoroi Biaiothanatoi", *Archiv für Religionswissenschaft* 9 (1900), 312–322).

REITZENSTEIN, R., *Poimandres*, Leipzig 1904.

Die hellenistische Mysterienreligionen 1927³.

RENAN, E., *Histoires des origines du christianisme: Les Apôtres*, Paris 1866.

RICCIARDELLI, G., *Inni Orfici*, Milano 2000.

RICHARDSON N. J., *The Homeric Hymn to Demeter*, Oxford 1976.

RIDINGS, D., *The Attic Moses*, Goteborg 1995.

RIEDWEG, C., *Mysterienterminologie bei Plato, Philo und Klemens von Alexandrien*, Berlin–New York 1987.

"Die Mysterien von Eleusis in rhetorisch geprägten Texten des 2./3. Jahrhunderts nach Christus", *Illinois Classical Studies* 13 (1988) 127–133.

Jüdisch-hellenistische Imitation eines orphischen Hieros Logos, München 1993.

Ps.-Justin (Markellos von Ancyra?) Ad Graecos de vera religione (bisher Cohortatio ad Graecos): Einleitung und Kommentar, Basel 1994.

"Iustinus Martyr II (pseudo-justinische Schriften)", *Reallexikon für Antike und Christentum* 19, Stuttgart 2001, 848–873.

"Poésie orphique et rituel initiatique. Éléments d' un *Discours Sacré* dans les lamelles d' or", *RHR* 219 (2002) 459–481.

Pythagoras: Werk, Leben und Nachwirkung, München 2004.

RIZZI, M., *Ideologia e retorica negli "exordia" apologetici. Il problema dell' 'altro'*, Milano 1993.

ROBERTSON, N., "Orphic Mysteries and Dionysiac Ritual", in M. B. Cosmopoulos (ed.), *The Greek Mysteries*, London 2003, 218–240.

ROBERTSON SMITH, W., *Lectures on the Religion of the Semites*, London 1894.

ROESSLI, J.-M., "Convergence et divergence dans l'interprétation du mythe d'Orphée", *RHR* 219 (2002), 503–513.

"Catalogues de sibylles, recueil(s) de *Libri Sibyllini* et corpus des *Oracula Sibyllina*. Remarques sur la formation et la constitution de quelques collections oraculaires dans les mondes gréco-romain, juif et chrétien", in E. Norelli (ed.), *Recueils normatifs et canons dans l'antiquité. Perspectives nouvelles sur la formation des canons juif et chrétien dans leur contexte culturel, Colloque de Genève, 11–12 Avril, 2002*, Lausanne 2004 47–68.

"Imágenes de Orfeo en el ámbito judío y Cristiano", in Bernabé–Casadesús 2008a, 179–226.

"¿Orfeo y el Orfismo en Qumrán?", in Bernabé–Casadesús, 2008b, 1015–1034.

"La cosmo-théogonie orphique du roman pseudo-clémentin", *Les Études Classiques* 76 (2008), 83–94.

ROHDE, E., "Die Religion der Griechen", *Kleine Schriften* II, Tübingen–Leipzig 1907, 320–339.

Psyche: Seelencult und Unsterblichkeitsglaube der Griechen, Tübingen 1907[4].

RÖHRICHT A., *De Clemente Alexandrino Arnobii in irridendo Gentilium Cultu Deorum Auctore*, Hamburg 1893.

ROIG LANZILLOTTA, L., "The Early Christians and Human Sacrifice", in J. Bremmer (ed.), *The Strange World of Human Sacrifice*, Leuven 2008, 81–102.

RUDHARDT, J., *Notions fondamentales de la pensée religieuse et actes constitutifs du culte dans la Grèce classique*, Paris 1958.

"Quelques réflexions sur les *Hymnes Orphiques*: avec texte et traduction des *Hymnes Orphiques* 1, 2, 9, 36 et 72", in P. Borgeaud (ed.), *Orphisme et Orphée*, Genève 1991, 263–288.

RUNIA, D. T., "Why Does Clement of Alexandria Call Philo The Pythagorean?," *Vigiliae Christianae* 49.1 (1995): 1–22.

"Plato's *Timaeus*, First Principle(s), and Creation in Philo and Early Christian Thought" in Reydams-Schils, G. J. (ed.), *Plato's Timaeus as Cultural Icon*, Notre Dame 2002.

RUSTEN, J., *Dionysius Schytobrachion*, Opladen 1982.

'Interim Notes on the Papyrus from Derveni', *HSCP* 89 (1985), 121–140.

SABBATUCCI, D., *Essai sur le mysticisme grec*, Paris 1965.

"Orfeo secondo Pausania", in Ph. Borgeaud (ed.), *Orphisme et Orphée, en l'honneur de Jean Rudhardt*, Genève 1991, 7–11.

SANDERS, J.A., "Psalm 151 in 11QPss" *ZATW* 75 (1963), 73–86 (with "Responsum", *ZATW* 76 (1964), 200).

SANTAMARÍA ÁLVAREZ, M.A., "Orfeo y el orfismo en los poetas helenísticos", in Bernabé–Casadesús 2008, 1339–1382.

SANZI, E., *Firmico Materno, L'errore delle religioni pagane*, Roma 2006.

SCARPI, P., *Le religioni dei misteri*, Firenze 2001.

SCHANZER, D., "Voices and Bodies: The Afterlife of the Unborn," *Numen* 56 (2009), 326–365
SCHEFFCZYK, L., *Die Reinkarnationslehre in der altchristlichen Literatur*, München 1985.
SCHEID, J., "Le thiase du Metropolitan Museum (*IGUR* I 160)" en *L'association dionysiaque dans les societés anciennes: Actes de la table ronde organisée par l'École française de Rome (Rome 24–25 mai 1984)*, Roma 1986, 275–290.
SCHIBLI, H. S., *Pherekydes of Syros*, Oxford 1990.
SCHIRONI, F., "L' Olimpo non è il cielo: esegesi antica nel Papiro di Derveni, in Aristarco e in Leagora di Siracusa", *ZPE* 136 (2001) 11–21.
SCHMIDT, H., "Dionys der Thraker", *Philologus* 7, 1852, 360–375.
SCHOLEM, G., *Über einige Grundbegriffe des Judentums*, Frankfurt am Main 1970.
SCHOLTEN, H., "Der Demeter- und Persephonemythos in der Auseinandersetzung christlicher Autoren" in R. von Haehling (ed.), *Griechische Mythologie und frühes Christentum*, Darmstadt 2005, 268–295.
SCHÜRER, E., *History of the Jewish People in the Age of Jesus Christ*, new edition revised by G. Vermes – F. Millar (eds.), Edinburgh 1973–1987.
SCHÜTZ, O., "Ein neuer orphischer Papyrustext", *Arch. für Papyrusf.* 13 (1939), 210–212.
SCOTT, J.M., "Dionysus in Philo of Alexandria. A study of *De vita contemplativa*" *Stud. Philon.* 20 (2008), 33–54.
SEAFORD, R., "Thunder, Lightning and Earthquake in the *Bacchae* and the Acts of the Apostles", in A.B. Lloyd (ed.), *What is a God? Studies in the Nature of Greek Divinity*, London 1997, 139–151.
SETAIOLI, A., "Nuove osservazioni sulla 'descrizione dell'oltretomba' nel papiro di Bologna", *SIFC* 42 (1970), 179– 224.
"L'imagine delle bilance e il giudizio dei morti", *SIFC* 44 (1972), 38–54.
"Ancora a proposito del papiro bolognese n. 4" *SIFC* 45 (1973), 124–133.
SEVERYNS, A., *Le cycle épique dans l'ecole d'Aristarque*, Paris–Liège 1928.
SFAMENI GASPARRO, G., *Misteri e culti mistici di Demetra*, Roma 1986.
Oracoli Profeti Sibille. Rivelazione e salvezza nel mondo antico, Roma 2002.
"Magie et magiciens: le débat entre chrétiens et paiens aux premiers siècles ap. J.C.", in *Res Orientales XIV, Magie et Magiciens, charmes et sortileges*, Brures–sur–Yvette 2002, 239–266.

SIDER, D., "Heraclitus in the Derveni Papyrus", in A. Laks–G.W. Most (eds.): *Studies in the Derveni Papyrus*, London 1997, 129–148.
SIEGERT, F., "Griechische Mythen im hellenistischen Judentum" in R. Haehling, *Griechische Mythologie und frühes Christentum*, Darmstadt (2005) 227-25.
SIMMONS, M., *Arnobius of Sicca. Religious Conflict and Competition in the Age of Diocletian*, Oxford 1995.
SKERIS, R.A., *XPΩMA ΘEOY: On the origin an theological interpretation of the musical imagery used by the ecclesiastical writers of the first three centuries, with special reference to the image of Orpheus*, Altötting 1976.
SMITH, M., "On the Wine God in Palestine", in S. Lieberman (ed.): *Salo W. Baron Jubilee Volume*, Jerusalen 1975, 815–829 (= S.J.D. Cohen (ed.) *Studies in the Cult of Yahweh* I, Leiden 1996, 227–237).
SMITH, M.S., "Psalm 151, David, Jesus and Orpheus", *ZATW* 92 (1980), 247–253.
SMITH, J.Z., "In Comparison a Magic Dwells" in *Imagining Religion: From Babylon to Jonestown*, Chicago 1982.
Drudgery Divine: On the Comparison of Early Christianities and the Religions of Late Antiquity, Chicago–London 1991.
SMITH, R.B.E., *Julian's Gods: Religion and Philosophy in the Thought and Action of Julian the Apostate*, London–New York 1995.
SNELL, B., "Papyrologische Bemerkungen", *Hermes-Einzelschr.* 5 (1937), 106–110.
SOKOLOWSKI, F., *Lois Sacrées de l'Asie Mineure*, Paris 1955.
Lois Sacrées des Cités Grecques, Supplément, Paris 1962.
Lois Sacrées des Cités Grecques, Paris 1969.
SOLMSEN, F., "Reincarnation in Ancient and Early Christian Thought", *Kleine Schriften* III, Hildesheim–Zürich–New York 1972, 465–494.
SORENSEN, J., *A Cognitive Theory of Magic*, Walnut Creek 2007.
SOURVINOU-INWOOD, C., "Festival and Mysteries, Aspects of the Eleusinian cult" en en M.B. Cosmopoulos (ed.), *The Greek Mysteries*, London 2003, 25–49.
SPEYER, W., *Die literarische Fälschung in heidnischen und christlichen Altertum*, München 1971.
„Porphyrios als religiöse Persönlichkeit und als religiöser Denker" in R. von Haehling (ed.), *Griechische Mythologie und frühes Christentum*, Darmstadt 2005, 68–84.
STEAD, CH., *Philosophy in Christian Antiquity*, Cambridge 1995.
STEMPLINGER, E., *Das Plagiat in der griechischen Literatur*, Berlin 1909.
STENEKER, H., *Peithous Demiurgia: observations sur la fonction du style dans le Protréptique de Clément d'Alexandrie*, Nijmegen 1967.

STEPHENS, S.A., *Seeing Double: Intercultural Poetics in Ptolemaic Alexandria*, Berkeley–Los Angeles 2003
STEPHENS, S.A., WINKLER, J.J., *Ancient Greek Novels: The Fragments*, Princeton 1995.
STERN. H., "The *Orpheus* in the Synagogue of Dura-Europos", *Journal of the Warburg Institute* 21 (1958), 1–6.
"Orphée dans l'art paléochrétien", *Cahiers Archéologiques* 23 (1974), 1–16.
STETTNER, W., *Die Seelenwanderung bei den Griechen und Römern*, Stuttgart 1934.
STOEHR-MONJOU, A., "Structure allégorique de *Romulea* 1: La comparaison Orphée-Felicianus chez Dracontius", *Vigiliae Christianae* 9.2 (2005), 187–203.
STRECKER, G., *Das Judenchristentum in der Pseudoklementinen*, Berlin 1981[2].
STROUMSA, G., *Barbarian Philosophy: The Religious Revolution of Early Christianity*, Tübingen 1999.
SUÁREZ DE LA TORRE, E., "Sibylles, mantique inspirée et collections oraculaires", *Kernos* 7 (1994), 179–205.
TABAGLIO, M., "La cristianizzazione del mito di Orfeo", in A.M. Babbi (ed.), *Le metarmofosi di Orfeo*, Verona 1999, 65–82.
TAKÁCS, S.A., "Politics and Religion in the Bacchanalian Affair of 186 B.C.E.", *HSCP* 100 (2000), 301–310.
TARDIEU, M., "La lettre à Hipparque et les réminiscences pythagoriciennes de Clément d'Alexandrie", *Vig. Christ.* 28 (1974), 241–247.
THESLEFF, H., *An Introduction to the Pythagorean Writings of the Hellenistic Period*, Åbo 1961.
THOM, J.C., *The Pythagorean Golden Verses*, Boston–Leiden, 1995
THRAEDE, M. "Erfinder II (geistesgeschichtlich)", *Reallexikon für Antike und Christentum* 5, Stuttgart 1962, 1191–1278.
TREU, M., "Die neue Orphische Unterweltsbeschreibung und Vergil", *Hermes* 82 (1954), 24–51.
TRISOGLIO, F., *San Gregorio di Nazianzo e il Christus patiens: il problema dell'autenticità gregoriana del dramma*, Firenze 1996.
TUELLER, M.A., *Literary Representations of the New God: Jesus and Dionysus*, BA thesis, Department of the Classics, Harvard University 1992.
TUILIER, A., *Grégoire de Nazianze, Christus Patiens*, SC, Paris 1969.
TULLIUS F., *Die Quellen des Arnobius im 4., 5. und 6. Buch seiner Schrift Adversus Nationes*, Berlin 1934 (diss.).
TURCAN, R. "L'oeuf orphique et les quatre élements (Martianus Capella *De nuptiis* II, 140)", *RHR* 160 (1961), 11–23.
Firmicus Maternus: De errore profanarum religionum, Paris 1982.

"Bacchoi ou Bacchants? De la dissidence des vivants à la ségregation des morts", in *L'association Dionysiaque dans les societés anciennes. Actes de la Table ronde de l'École Française de Rome*, Roma 1986, 227–246.

"L'elaboration des mysteres dionysiaques à l'époque hellénistique et romaine: de l'orgiasme à l'initiation" in A. Moreau (ed.) *L'initiation, Actes du Colloque International de Montpellier 11–14 avril, 1991*, Montpellier 1992, 215–233.

TURNER, E.G., "The Ptolemaic Royal Edict BGU VI 1211 is to be dated before 215–14 B.C." *Festschrift zum 100-jährigen Bestehen der Papyrussammlung der Österreichischen Nationalbibliothek Papyrus Erzherzog Rainer (P. Rainer Cent.)* Wien 1983, 148–152.

TURNER, J.D. *Sethian Gnosticism and the Platonic Tradition*, Québec 2001.

VAN BLADEL, K., *The Arabic Hermes: From Pagan Sage to Prophet of Science*, Oxford 2009.

VERBEKE, G., *L'évolution de la doctrine du pneuma du stoïcisme à S. Augustin*, Paris–Louvain 1945.

VERNANT J.-P., *Mythe et pensée chez les grecques*, Paris 1969.

VERSNEL, H., *Inconsistencies in Greek and Roman Religion I: Ter Unus*, Leiden 1990.

"The Poetics of Magical Charm", in Mirecki–Meyer (eds.) *Magic and Ritual in the Ancient World*, Leiden 1999, 105–156.

VEYNE, P., *Est-ce que les grecs ont-ils cru à leurs mythes?*, Paris 1983.

VICARI, P., "*Sparagmos*. Orpheus among the Christians", in J. Warden (ed.) *Orpheus: Metamorphoses of a Myth*, Toronto 1982, 63–83.

VIEILLEFON, L., *La figure d'Orphée dans l'antiquité tardive*, Paris 2003.

"Les mosaïques d'Orphée dans les maisons de l'antiquité tardive, fonctions décoratives et valeurs religieuses", *Mélanges de l'Ecole française de Rome* 116.2 (2005), 983–1000.

VOGEL, C.J. DE, "The *soma-sema* formula: its function in Plato and Plotinus compared to Christian writers", in H.J. Blumenthal–R.A. Markus (eds.), *Neoplatonism and early Christian thought. Essays in honour of A.H. Armstrong*, London 1981, 79–95.

WALKER, D.P., "Orpheus the Theologian and Renaissance Platonists", *Journal of the Warburg and Courtauld Institutes* 16 (1953), 100–120.

WALTER, N., *Der Thoraausleger Aristobulos. Untersuchungen zu seinen Fragmenten und zu epigraphischen Resten der jüdisch-hellenistischen Literatur*, Berlin 1964, 103–115.

WALZER, R., *Galen on Jews and Christians*, Oxford, 1949.

WEBER, M., *Wirtschaft und Gesellschaft*, Berlin 1922.

WEST, M.L., *Ancient Greek Philosophy and the Orient*, Oxford, 1971.

The Orphic Poems, Oxford, 1983

Ancient Greek Music, Oxford, 1992.

"Towards Monotheism", en Athanassiadi, P.–Frede, M. (eds.), *Pagan Monotheism in Late Antiquity*, Oxford 1999, 21–40.

WICK, P., "Jesus gegen Dionysos? Ein Beitrag zur Kontextualisierung des Johannesevangeliums", *Biblica* 85.2 (2004), 179–98.

WIDE, S., "ΑΟΡΟΙ ΒΙΑΙΟΘΑΝΑΤΟΙ", *Archiv für Religionswissenschaft*, 12 (1909), 224–233.

WIDENGREN, G., *Mani and Manichaeism*, London 1965.

WIESE, H., *Heraklit bei Klemens von Alexandrien*, Kiel 1963.

WILAMOWITZ-MÖLLENDORFF, U. VON, *Der Glaube der Hellenen*, Berlin 1931/2 (2 vols).

WILLERS, D., "Dionysos und Christus – ein archäologisches Zeugnis zur ‚Konfessionsangehörigkeit' des Nonnos," *MH* 49 (1992), 141–51.

WILLIAMS, M., *Rethinking Gnosticism: An Argument for Dismantling a Dubious Category*, Princeton 1996.

WILSON, S., *Saints and their Cults: Studies in Religious Sociology, Folklore and History*, Cambridge 1983.

WINIARCZYK, M., *Euhemeri Messenii Reliquiae*, Stuttgart–Leipzig 1991.

Euhemeros von Messene: Leben, Werk und Nachwirkung, München–Leipzig 2002.

WINKLER, J. J., "Lollianus and the Desperadoes", *JHS* 100 (1980), 239–260.

WLOSOK, A., *Laktanz und die Philosophische Gnosis*, Heidelberg 1960

ZEEGERS, N., *Les citations paiennes dans les apologistes grecs du II siècle*, Louvain 1972.

"Théophile d'Antiochie devant la culture grecque", in Pouderon, B., Doré, J. (eds.), *Les apologistes chrétiens et la culture grecque*, Paris 1998, 53–65.

ZELLER, L., "Zur Vorgeshichte des Christentums: Essener und Orphiker", *Zeit. Wiss. Theol.* 42 (1899), 195–269 (= *Kleine Schriften*, 1910, II, 120–184).

ZIEGLER, K., "Plagiat", *RE* XX.2 (1950), 1989–1991.

ZUCKER, F., "Euhemeros und seine Ἱερὰ ἀναγραφή bei den christlichen Schriftstellern", *Philologus* 64 (1905), 465–472.

ZUNTZ, G., "Once more: The so-called "Edict of Philopator on the Dionysiac Mysteries" (BGU 1211)", *Hermes* 91 (1963), 228–239 and *corrigendum* in p. 384.

"Aion Plutonios (Eine Gründungslegende von Alexandria)", *Hermes* 116 (1988), 291–303.

Index locorum

BIBLICAL PASSAGES

Gn. 1–3: 287, 292, 360
Gn. 1:8–31: 307
Gn 2:7: 364
Gn. 6:2: 280
Gn. 12:1: 336
Gn. 49:8–12: 165, 166
Ex. 15:25: 278
Ex. 20:21: 183
Ex. 23:12: 364
Ex. 31:17: 364
Deut. 32:9: 192
Deut. 32:39: 185
1 Sm. 16:23: 116, 286
2 Sm. 16.14: 364
Ps 5.10: 338
Ps 32:6: 197
Ps 33.3: 272
Ps 40.3: 272
Ps 47.3: 307
Ps 95.3–5: 277, 307
Ps 96.1: 272
Ps 98.1: 272
Ps 109:3: 274
Ps 148.2: 307
Is. 7:10–16: 165
Is. 9:1–11: 98
Is. 11.6: 122
Is 42.10: 272
Is. 44:6: 370
Is. 48:12: 370
Is 55.11: 198
Is 66.1: 184
Ez 18:23: 267

Am 4:13: 185, 192
Jer 10:12: 185
Jer 19:13: 192
Jer 4:23: 300
Dn 12:11: 114
Prov 8:9: 198
Wis 9:1: 197
Wis 14:15–16: 158, 234
Wis 12:3–7: 114
2 Mac 5–6: 114
2 Mac 7.28: 300, 301
*1 Enoch 22: 365
Is. 2. 3: 260, 290, 376
Mt 3:7: 377
Mt 3:9: 377
Mt 5:36–37: 198
Mt 8:8: 287
Mt 8:22: 338
Mt 22:14: 346
Lc 22:20: 272
Lc 23.43: 367
Jn 1:1–14: 274, 287, 304
Jn 2.1–11: 117
Jn 6:53: 355
Jn 15.1: 116
Act 1:9–11: 334
Act 5:30: 278
Act 5:39: 117
Act 12:7: 117
Act 16:25–26: 117
Act 13:29: 278
Act 17:16–34: 366
Act 17:28: 113, 244
Act . 26:14: 117

1 Cor 1:23: 331
1 Cor 2:9: 267
1 Cor 7:7–10: 346
1 Cor 8:6: 196
1 Cor 9:25: 359
1 Cor 10:20: 277
1 Cor 11:23–26: 270
1 Cor 15:17: 333
1 Cor 15:33: 244
2 Cor 12:2–4: 183
2 Cor 5:17: 272
Gal 6:15: 272
1 Thes 5:5: 256
Eph 4:22–24: 272
Tt 1:12: 244
1 Petr 2:24: 278
1 Petr 3:19: 49
Hebr 13:8: 370
1 Jn 2:7–8: 274
Ap. Joh. 5:9: 272
Ap. Joh. 1:8: 370
Ap. Joh. 14:10: 272
Ap. Joh. 21:6: 370
Ap. Joh. 22:5: 369
Ap. Joh. 22:13: 370
*Ap Petri 8.23: 368
*Ap Petri 9.24: 368

PAPYRI AND INSCRITPIONS
(see also OF)

P Argent 1313: 55f, 357
P Berol 44: 50, 95
P. Bonon. 4: cf. OF 717
BGU VI 1211: 52
P Cornell 55: 95
P Derveni col. VI:
– col. XIII: 319
– col. XIV: 319
– col. XVI: 327
– col. XX: 254
– col. XXII: 35
– col. XVIII: 292
P Gurob 1: cf. OF 578:
N H C II.1–32: 326
N H C VI.6.61: 102
N H C VI.6.63: 198
N H C VII.5: 102
PMG II: 59
PMG IV: 102
PMG V: 102
PMG VII: 59, 102, 288
PMG XIII: 102, 103, 288
PMG LXX: 60
PSI 850: 55, 357
PSI 1162: 58
PSI 1290: 58
P Vindob Gr 29456r°–29828r°: 10ig
IG III 74: 112
IG XII 787: 112
IG XII 5.227: 50
IG XIV 2241: 69
Sokolowski 1955, n. 20: 48
Sokolowski 1955, n. 48: 46
Sokolowski 1955, n. 84: 47
Sokolowski 1962, n.108: 48
Prott-Ziehen 1896, n. 46: 45
Prott-Ziehen 1896, n. 148: 48, 112
Quandt 1913, n. 177: 49
Quandt 1913, n. 204: 49
Corp Inscr Mon Rel Mithr 695: 72
Corp Inscr Mon Rel Mithr 475: 72
Inscr. Magn. 215(a), 35: 50
Inscr. Smyrn. 728: 47
SEG 1036a: 48
SEG 14.752: 47
SEG 16.478: 50
SEG 27.280: 50
SEG 34. 610: 50
TAM V 2, 1256: 48

Ancient Authors

Acta Martyrum
Mart. Pion. 19.163: 322

[Aelius Lampridius]
Alex. Sev. 29: 124

Aeschylus
Ag. 160: 326

Aëtius doxographus
Placita Philosophorum 1.6: 234

Alexander Aphrodisiensis
De fato 200. 22 Bruns: 301f

Alexis comicus
fr. 285 Kassel-Austin: 53f

Anthologia Palatina
9.524–525: 59

Apuleius
Apol. 27: 99
Apol. 56: 77
Met. 11.5: 318
Mund. 37: 370

Aratus
Phaen. 5: 244, 366

Aristides Quintilianus
De mus. 3.2: 38

Aristophanes
Ra. 31: 166
Ra. 145: 368
Ra. 1030–1036: 64,145, 226
Av. 690ff: 37, 107, 133, 239, 363

Aristoteles
Ath. 1: 28
De anima 410 b 27: 205, 364
EN 1154a.33: 274
Phys. 1.4.187a27: 301
Phys. 213b 22: 363
fr. 15 Rose: 26
fr. 59–61 Rose: 62, 216
*De mund. 401a 12: 311

Arnobius, *Adversus Nationes*
5.17: 334
5.19: 67, 153ff, 162, 249, 266f, 330,
    355
5.20: 155
5.24: 65
5.25: 50
5.32–45: 242

Arrianus
Alan. 1.11.2: 124

Artapanus
FGH 726F 3: 103, 111, 225, 233

Athanasius Alexandrinus
PG 26.1320: 144
Contra gent. 9: 234

Athenagoras Atheniensis,
Legatio pro Christianis
8:   305
17: 167, 229, 309, 314
18: 167f, 226f, 314, 384ff
19: 232, 384ff
20: 155, 169, 276, 384ff
22: 170, 242
24: 280

28: 103, 144, 225
29: 234
30: 234, 244
32: 169

Athenaeus
5.197c-203b: 52
24.632c: 124

Augustinus
Contra Faustum
– 13.2: 87, 103, 246, 280
– 23.1.15: 98, 103
Epistulae 234.1: 103
De Civitate Dei
– 2.26: 334
– 4.27: 234
– 6.10: 334
– 8.11–12: 280
– 10.9–10: 236
– 18.14: 95, 124, 140, 222, 246, 258
– 18.37: 95, 140, 280
– 21.5: 364
Confessiones
– 10.27: 274
– 12.27: 304, 315
Contra Iulianum Pelagianum
– 4.15.78: 90, 215, 249, 339
– 4.16.83: 90, 215, 339
In Iohannis Evangelium tractatus 7.6: 279

Callimachus
Epigr. 41: 164
Fr. 43.117 Pfeiffer: 24, 57

[Callisthenes]
1.42.6: 124

Callixenus
FGrH 627: 54

Cicero
Hortensius fr. 112 Grilli: 62, 90, 216
De natura deorum
– 1.41: 91
– 1.107: 32, 39, 62, 226
– 2.62: 234
– 3.39: 234
– 3.45: 234
– 3.56: 102
– 3.58: 62, 102
De legibus
– 2.19: 234
– 2.21.18: 237
– 2.37.4: 237

Clemens Alexandrinus
Protrepticus
1.1–1.5: 143, 375ff
1.1: 142, 291
1.2: 182, 253, 259, 260, 262, 272, 359
1.3: 141, 236, 238, 254259, 286f
1.4: 254259, 286f
1.5: 182, 212, 259, 286, 289, 292, 370
1.6: 182, 259, 272, 274, 287
1.7: 252, 259, 276, 278
2.11: 236, 238, 260
2.12–23: 147ff, 271, 378ff
2.12: 151, 236, 238, 261, 268, 271, 337
2.13: 47, 64, 145, 234, 256, 268
2.14: 234
2.15: 200
2.16: 155, 276
2.17: 48, 54, 55, 142, 228, 249, 261, 271, 330, 348

2.18: 149, 249, 333, 350, 355
2.19: 49, 146, 240, 243, 350, 354
2.21: 50, 142, 156
2.22: 142, 252, 164, 238, 257, 263, 268, 274, 276
2.24: 233, 234
2.25: 350
2.26: 234
2.27: 142
2.30: 234
2.36: 272
2.37: 244
2.40: 277
4.48: 53
4.49: 234
4.46–56: 239
4.58: 253
4.55: 277
5.58: 261
7.71: 254
7.73: 261
7.75: 261
7.74: 98, 186, 222, 279
8.77: 253, 261
8.79: 185, 192
8.81: 259
9.82: 261
9.87: 254
10.89–90: 253, 274
10.93: 252
10.104: 254
10.108: 253
10.110: 254
11.111: 260
11.115: 254
11.117: 254
12.118–120: 259, 260, 269, 271, 277, 357
12.120: 254, 259, 263
12.121: 253

12.123: 253
Paedagogus
1.1–3: 131
3.11.59: 120
3.18.84: 120
3.79: 198
Stromata
1.14.59: 95, 227
1.72.4: 109
1.79.2 : 233
1.19.91: 244
1.19.92.3: 216, 346
1.20.105.1: 233f
1.21.131: 32, 39, 62, 130, 140f, 203, 208, 223, 226, 229
1.22.150.1–4: 282
1.29.181: 290
2.20.106: 146
2.100.3: 109
3.1.1.1: 193
3.3. 12–25: 106, 339
3.3.15.3: 106
3.3.16.3–4: 90, 106, 215, 338
3.3.17.1–2: 90, 106, 107, 215, 249
4.13.90.2: 193
4.22.142.3: 48
5.1.9.4: 92
5.1.9.10: 279, 284
5.1.10.1: 282
5.1.14.40: 282
5.3.17.4: 216, 346
5.4.24.1: 206
5.4.28.4: 120
5.8.45.2–4: 60, 206, 242, 369
5.8.46.4: 206
5.8.48: 213
5.8.49.3: 207
5.12.70.3–6: 194, 331
5.12.78: 183, 185f
5.14.89–141: 190ff

5.14.116.1: *193, 204, 226, 229, 279*
5.14.122–124: *184ff, 187, 201, 324*
5.14.125: *187, 191, 195*
5.14.126–127: *185f, 187, 195*
5.14.128.3: *188ff, 312*
5.14.133: *185f*
6.2.5.3: *202, 226*
6.2.17: *203*
6.2.26.1: *65, 202, 226*
6.2.27: *203, 204*
7.4.22.7: *350*
7.32.8: *341, 350*
7.50–51: *198*
7.18.109
Excerpta ex Theodoto 32.1: *193*

[Clemens Romanus]
Homil. 6.2–13: *171f*
[Rufin. Recognit.] 10.17–19: *171f*
[Rufin. Recognit.] 10.30: *34f, 171f*

Cono
FGrHist 26 F 1.45.6: *124*
Corpus Hermeticum
CH 7.2: *101*
CH 13.7: *101*
fr. 3 Nock-Festugière: *364*
fr. 23 N-F: *102, 313*
fr. 66–67 N-F: *102*

Cyrillus Alexandrinus
Contra Iulianum
1.19: *225*
1.35: *141, 222, 226*
1.46: *196*
1.48: *103*
2.44a: *232*

Demosthenes
18.259: *29, 360*
*25. 11: *150, 343*

Didymus Alexandrinus
De Trinitate 2.27: *103, 199, 243f, 362f*

Dio Cassius
72.4: *58*

Dio Chrysostomus
Or. 33.2–4: *7*

Diodorus Siculus
1.11.2–3: *319*
1.12.2: *363*
1.23.2: *83, 144*
1.23.6: *74, 266*
1.94.1.2: *225*
1.96.2–4: *75, 145, 225f, 228*
3.58–59: *150*
3.62.6: *268*
3.65.5: *123*
3.65.6: *83, 144*
4.25.3: *74, 266*
4.43.1: *75, 228*
5.49.6: *75, 228*
5.64.4: *75, 228*
5.75.4: *75, 228*
5.77.3: *75, 145, 228*
6.1: *234*

Diogenes Apolloniates
fr. B5 D-K: *363*

Diogenes Laertius
1.5: *232*
8.17: *120*

Dionysius Halicarnassensis
Ant. Rom. 2.18–20: *255*
Ant. Rom. 2.19.1–2: *64f*

Empedocles
fr. 6 DK: 204
fr. 17 DK: 204
fr. 21 DK: 204
fr. 31 DK: 70
fr. 105 DK: 96
fr. 115 DK: 107, 337
fr. 117 DK: 107
fr. 118 DK: 106
fr. 126 DK: 70
fr. 141 DK: 96

Epiphanius Constantiensis
Panarion
51.22.10: 56, 194, 372
71: 136
1.182.13: 144f
Expositio fidei 10: 149f, 159, 243

Ephraim Syriensis
Carmina Nisibena, Hymn 36.5, 36.11: 141, 248

Euhemerus Messenius
fr. 36–37 Winiarczyk: 102

Eunapius
Vitae Sophistarum
7.3.2–4: 347
6.9.1: 102
6.15–17: 102
10.6–11: 102
11.10–12: 102

Euphronius lyricus
Priapeia, fr. 176–177 Powell: 52

Euripides
Alc. 357ff: 288
Alc. 967ff: 288

Androm. 170–177: 240
Ba. 45: 117
– 62ff: 46
– 105–110:
– 284: 358
– 325: 117
– 402: 20
– 447: 117
– 585: 117
– 742–745: 356
– 795: 117
– 918: 267f
– 920: 356
– 944: 347
– 1185: 356
– 1255: 117
Hippol. 952ff: 28, 360
Cret. fr. 472 Kannicht: 28, 271, 351
Melanipp. fr. 484 Kannicht: 37
Polyidos fr. 638 Kannicht: 106.
Adesp. fr. 912 Kannicht: 194, 331

Eusebius Caesariensis
Praeparatio Evengelica
1.6.4 : 227
1.10.40: 257
2.2.64: 131, 147, 159
3.1: 225
3.9–10: 190, 305
3.12: 222, 225, 364
3.9.14: 226
9.27: 111, 225, 233
10.4: 145, 227
10.8.1–16: 225
11.13.5: 282
11.19.1: 282
13.12.4–5: 184
13.13.55: 190
14.16.1: 233
Theophania 2.41: 221

De laudibus Constantini 14.5: 121,
125, 135, 139, 141, 221, 378,
Historia Ecclaesiastica 9.3–9.11: 236

Firmicus Maternus, Iulius
De errore profanarum religionum
1: 242
5: 192
6: 57, 67, 156, 234, 269, 271, 355ff
10–12:155
15: 156
16: 156
18: 155
22.3: 279
26: 155

Fronto, M. Cornelius
Epistulae 4.1: 125

Fulgentius
Mit. 3.9: 103

Galenus
Placit. Hippocr. et Plat. 3.4.15: 91
De usu part. 11.14: 301
De pulsuum differentiis 3.3: 308

Gregorius Nazianzenus
Orationes
4.115: 65, 142, 232, 261, 313
5.31: 150, 243, 264, 276
27.10: 146, 258
31.16: 243, 261
39.1: 264f
39.4–5: 142, 150, 243, 262, 264f, 276
Carmina Arcana 1.25 Sykes: 371
Carmina Arcana 7 (De anima): 133,
137, 213, 242, 335f, 341f, 371
Carm. quae spect. ad al. 1570: 95,
371

Gregorius Nyssenus
Dial. de an. et resurr. 88–101: 341

Harpocratio lexicographus
s. v. εὐοῖ σάβοι: 276

Hecataeus Abderita
FGH 264 F 25: 225

Heraclitus
fr. 14 DK: 235, 238, 268, 382
fr. 36 DK: 203–205
fr. 62–63 DK: 106f
fr. 129 DK: 204

Herodotus
1.132: 24
2: 144
2.53: 167, 226
2.81: 77, 161, 162
2.82: 51, 225
4.76–80: 30, 66

Hesiodus
Theog. 886–900: 176, 318
Op. 90: 206
Op. 285: 343
Op. 822: 206

Hesychius
s. v. Βαυβώ: 164
s. v. Ἠφέσια γράμματα: 60

Hieronymus
Epistula 41: 240
Epistula 117.6: 141
Chronicon s. a. 325–326: 134
Adversus Iovinianum 2.14: 146, 348

Himerius
Orationes 45.4: 331, 355, 372

Hippias Eleus
fr. 6 D-K: 226

Hippolytus
De Antichristo 4: 210f, 370
Refutatio omnium haeresium
– *1.3.1:* 107
– *5.8.39–40:* 262
– *5.8.43:* 96, 164
– *5.19.19–21:* 162
– *5.20.4:* 83, 95, 106, 107, 145f, 160ff
– *5.21.1:* 163
– *7.29.14–23:* 107
– *9.10.6:* 106f

Hippocrates
De morbo sacro 1.10: 47

Homerus
Ilias
1.1: 200
1.5: 305
1.399f: 157, 173
1.544: 173
1.580f: 191
2.426: 381
4.49: 381
4.61: 63
6.145ff: 20
7.89: 339
14.201: 175
14.246: 168
14.246a: 168, 385
14.302: 175, 385
15.134: 185
16.677: 149
17.53–56: 202

18.482–485: 178
20.213–241: 20
21.153–160: 20
21.194–7: 309
Odyssea
4.221: 376
5.340: 185
9.275: 193
9.372: 202
9.410f: 193
11.427: 202
23.73: 339
23.110: 339
24.3: 155
24.208f: 163
Hymn. Cer. 18: 318

Horatius Flaccus, Quintus
Ars poetica 391ff: 142, 216

Iamblichus
Vita Pythagorica
64: 288
146: 85
256: 120
267: 203
De mysteriis
1.2: 102
1.8: 341
7.5: 273
8.4: 314
Protrepticus 8: 216

Iohannes Malalas
Chronographia 2.4: 196ff
Chronographia 4.7: 306

Iosephus
Antiquitates Iudaicae 8.280: 370
Contra Apionem 2.14.145: 236

2.91–96: 240
2.190: 370

Irenaeus Lugdunensis
Adversus Haereses 2.14.1–2: 37, 107, 239, 240

Isocrates
Busiris 10.38: 24, 232

Iulianus
Hymn. Met. 166b: 334
Oratio 4.136a: 72, 85
Oratio 7.215–217: 85, 145
Oratio 11.136: 195
Epistulae 46: 80, 273
Epistulae 111: 80, 273
Epistulae 136: 80, 273
Contra Galileos 262d: 334

Iustinus Martyr et Ps.- Iustinus
Apologia
1.5: 277
1.21: 165, 234, 330
1.29: 234
1.43: 92
1.54: 123, 165ff, 249, 284, 330, 354
1.55: 123, 234
1.66: 354
2.7: 93
2.10.4–8: 232
Dialogus cum Tryphone
4: 341
8.1: 258
11.5: 256, 273
52: 165
54: 165
66: 165
69: 123, 165ff, 249, 284, 330, 354
70: 330f

*Cohortatio ad Graecos
    (Marcellus Ancyranus)
8.2: 292
9.3–4: 225
10.2: 144
14.2: 144, 225
15.1: 222, 227, 256f
15.2: 38, 196ff, 312
16.1: 98
17.1: 199, 201, 281f
17.2: 199ff, 226, 229
25.4: 281
36.4: 98
*De Monarchia
2.4: 143, 179f, 222

Lactantius
Divinae Institutiones
1.5.4: 140, 177, 280, 297, 300, 303, 313, 314, 323, 388
1.5.8: 177, 302, 388
1.5.13: 177, 280, 388
1.7: 324, 326
1.7.6: 143
1.7.11: 178
1.13.11: 98
1.15: 234
1.22.12: 142
1.22.15: 145
4.8.4: 177, 192
Epitome
3: 300, 361
23: 262

Liuius, Titus
1.16.4: 67
4.30.7: 68
25.1.6–8: 65, 68
25.1.12: 66
39.8–16: 65ff, 68, 235
40.29: 69

[Longinus]
De subl. 9.9: 302

Lucianus
Cataplus 5: 39
– 22: 262
De Saltatione 15: 145
– 79: 49, 74, 82f, 268
Adersus Indoctum 109: 44, 124

Lydus, Iohannes
De mensibus 4.53: 114

Macarius Magnes
Monogenes (Apocriticus) 3.15

Macrobius
Saturnales
1.17.42: 305
1.18: 114, 195
1.18.20: 319
1.18.22: 37, 162
7.6.18: 78
7.13.11: 120
Comentarii ad Somnium Scipionis
1.11.3: 216
1.12.12: 78, 350

Marinus
Vita Procli 26–38: 97, 326

Martianus Capella
De Nuptiis Philologiae et Mercurii
9.906–8: 142
9.923: 288

Maximus Tyrius
39.5: 318

Melitus Sardensis
Hymn. Pasch.: 274, 370

Menander comicus
Thais fr. 165 Kassel-Austin: 244

Menander rhetor
2.392.19: 142

Nonnus
Dionysiaca 6.155: 372
– 66.168ff: 48
– 6.204–210: 355

Olympiodorus
In Platonis Phaedonem 1.3: 356
7.10: 91

Oracula Sibyllina
3: 233
3.624: 98, 181.

Origenes
Contra Celsum
1.4: 240
1.14–16: 80
1.15: 282
1.16–18: 84, 95, 99, 173, 214, 240,
   252, 372, 386f
1.17: 100, 172, 242, 359
1.18: 313
1.20: 341
1.32: 213, 235, 341
1.37: 364
2.5: 240, 342
2.34: 236
2.49: 235
2.55: 84, 235, 237, 247, 372
3.9: 372
3.16: 84, 213, 235, 342f
3.22–43: 234, 248
3.23: 166, 172f, 214, 243, 248
3.36: 234
3.42: 333
3.59–61: 92, 264, 345

432 Index locorum

4.10: 84, 213, 235, 342, 372
4.11: 240
4.17: 166, 172, 231, 242, 248, 249, 286, 335
4.23: 235
4.33: 236
4.35: 173, 236
4.36: 372
4.41: 240
4.48: 65, 172f, 231, 243, 342
4.51: 231, 282, 302
4.83: 341
5.14: 235, 301, 369
5.29: 341
5.38: 282
5.45–46: 324
5.57: 282
6.22: 213, 309
6.25: 309
6.32: 114
6.42: 372
7.9–11: 235, 330
7.28: 213
7.50: 106
7.53: 44, 84, 124, 234, 247, 330, 333, 372
8.12: 318
8.30: 341, 351
8.48: 84, 213, 235, 277
8.49–51: 235, 343
8.53–54: 214, 337
8.58: 214
Comm. in Joh. 6.13–14: 341

Orphica
Hymni Orphici
2.1: 324
8.13: 194
10.3: 324
11.10: 324
16.9: 324
27.4: 324
34.13–23: 211f, 289, 300
36.1: 324
40.1: 324
42.2: 324
45.2: 324
50.1–2: 53, 324
52.1: 324
52.6: 48
52.9: 53
55.28: 353
56.1: 324
59.2: 324
62: 343
64: 71, 291
72.5: 71
83.2–4: 309
Fragmenta (ed. Bernabé)
1: 29, 171, 346
12: 22, 192, 327
14: 22, 175, 187, 192, 231, 278, 282, 305, 311, 322, 362, 370
16: 192, 302, 305, 309, 315
18: 302
22: 298
26: 24
31: 175, 187–190, 192, 230f, 244, 303, 311, 327, 362, 370
32: 343
34: 328
35: 328
36: 328
39: 328
44: 52ff
57: 95
58: 179, 328
59: 232, 328, 333, 355
60: 318, 319,
64: 37, 107

66: 37, 107
74: 170
75: 168
78–79: 299
81: 169, 386
83: 168, 385
89: 170
97: 306
114–117: 299, 363
124: 178
134: 48, 174, 177
139: 306
140–141: 176
149: 192
153: 177, 179
191: 174
200: 174
201: 173, 174, 175
215: 174
223: 202, 209
237: 178, 208
240: 175
243: 175, 187–190, 192, 243, 307, 311f, 315, 323, 327, 370, 371f
244: 173
247–248: 291, 361
282: 173
286–290: 211
303: 157
306: 149, 380
310: 55
311: 355
319: 157
325: 333
326: 333
327: 166, 333
330: 202, 209
334–336: 166
337–350: 39
348: 329

357: 206–208
360: 363
363: 178
364: 63
368–376: 179, 221, 347
377: 111, 180–186, 195f, 307, 311, 322, 347, 390f
378: 111, 180–186, 251, 292, 308, 311, 347, 362, 391f
384: 150
386: 200f
395: 149, 174, 176f, 382
398: 318, 324
406: 37
407: 37, 91, 206f, 210
414: 112, 196, 199, 292, 303, 362
417: 38, 63, 288
419: 63, 288
420: 288
421: 364
430: 368
437: 203–205, 209
438: 20, 206- 209
439–469: 338
444: 106
449–457: 106, 203
458: 194, 331
463: 15, 30, 353
467: 46
469: 69
474: 20, 29, 71, 366
476: 63
485–486: 1
488: 25, 48, 70, 341, 359, 369
491: 70f, 292, 344
492: 319, 369
493: 48
497: 83
502: 83
528: 68, 75

536: 319, 348
537: 319
538–545: 36, 195, 319
541: 37
543: 195, 243, 36, 54, 243, 312, 319, 323, 325
544: 305, 324
564: 28
567: 28, 351
570: 75
572: 160–164
576: 29, 216, 346
577: 68
578: 19, 27, 48, 54, 166
579: 152
581: 46
582: 47, 146, 350
583: 46
584: 68
585: 45, 72
589: 151
592: 150
593: 55
595: 76
602–624: 37
614–618: 38
619: 38, 197
620: 38, 112, 102, 196, 243, 289, 304, 306
621–624: 38, 58
623: 58
626: 64
630: 348
645–646: 47
648: 47
649: 42, 47
650: 47, 77
651: 47, 77
652: 20, 346
653–655: 28, 76, 235, 340

661: 48, 98, 182
662: 48, 177
669: 34
676: 174
678: 72, 319
679: 120, 123, 126, 247, 286
690: 193f, 195, 204, 209, 244, 323
691: 112, 191f, 195, 198, 209, 212, 230, 231, 243, 300, 323
695–704: 36
712: 60
717: 39–40, 63, 92
778: 102
784–791: 209
822: 144
830: 59, 60, 164
832: 59
833: 59
835: 162
844: 162
845: 182
846: 202, 209
848: 174, 176, 232, 313
853: 96, 199, 243f, 292, 362, 364
875–879: 140
1052: 124
1089: 120
* T 152 (Kern): 120
*33 (Kern): 210
* 55–56: 172
*352 (Kern): 96

Ouidius
Metamorphoses
1.57: 389
1.79: 389
10.11ff: 62
11.92: 47, 63

Pindarus
Ol.1.50ff: 232, 356
Ol.1.82–84: 1
Ol. 2.63: 369
Ol. 2.83–89: 235
fr. 129 Snell-Maehler: 369
fr. 137 SM: 106
fr. 169 SM: 290

Parmenides
fr. 13 DK: 302
292–299 DK: 301

Pausanias
1.5.1: 163
1.22.7: 43
1.31.4: 163
1.37.4: 42, 44, 146, 350
2.30.2: 43, 145,
3.13.2: 43
3.14.5: 43
3.20.5: 44, 124
4.1.7: 163
4.31.4: 276
5.26.3: 44, 124
6.20.18: 51
7.18.2: 45
7.18.14: 355
8.31.11: 43, 44
8.37.5–9: 43, 355
8.15.1: 42
8.31.11: 43
8.37.5: 32, 43, 162
9.27.2: 29, 42, 162, 163
9.3.5: 44
9.30.4: 44, 124
9.30.12: 29, 32, 36, 42, 162, 163
9.35.5: 43
10.7.2: 43
10.30.6: 45, 83
10.31.9–11: 45

Pherecydes Syrius
fr. 60 Schibli: 364

Philo Alexandrinus
De Aeternitate Mundi 15: 305
– 83: 312
De somnis 1.17: 102
1.25: 308
1.157: 312
De specialibus legibus. 1.280: 102
De Cherubim 94: 257
De Migratione Abrahami 69: 350
De Mutatione Nominum 205: 350
De confusione Linguarum 144: 350
De vita contemplativa: 109, 115

Philodemus
De Piet. 44. 16.1 Gomperz: 268
13 (P. Hercul. Vi 16 ff): 91

Philolaus
fr. 14 D.-K.: 106, 215f

Philostratus sophista
Vita Apolonii 4.14: 124
Heroicus 25.2: 176, 232, 313

Photius lexicographus
s. v. Nebrivzein: 269, 357

Plato
Apologia 41a: 226
Charm. 157°4
Cratilus 400c: 90
400e: 326
402b: 298
Euthyphro 5e: 24
Ion 534c: 292
Leges
715e: 184, 187, 231, 274, 281, 370

717d-e: 48
782c: 27, 349
808c: 274
909a: 235
933a: 235
Politicus 269e-273b: 303
Phaedo 69c: 216, 368
Phaedrus 264e: 308
Respublica
363c-d: 29, 50, 341, 343
364e: 235, 254, 360
595–607: 232
588b-589b: 106
Tim. 28c: 303, 313
51a: 305
91: 288
Epistulae 7.335a: 274
*Axiochus 371d: 368

Plotinus
Enneadae
1.6.6: 90, 368
2.9.6: 105
2.9.17: 105
3.4.2: 341
4.3.12: 90
5.8.4: 90

Plutarchus
Moralia
Apophthegmata laconia 224d: 76, 235, 340
Consolatio ad uxorem 10: 29, 76, 353
De animae procreatione e Timaeo 5: 301
De Iside et Osiride 9, 354d: 225
75, 364f: 76
De Pythiae Oraculis 404b: 292
Quaestiones Convivales 2.3.2: 78
– 4.671c-672b: 114
– 4.652: 120
– 8.9.2: 301
De facie in orbe lunae 938d: 168
De esu carnium 1.7, 996b: 76, 356
Septem sapientium convivium 163e: 226, 292
fr. 178 Sandbach: 369
fr. 211 Sandbach: 369
Vitae
Alexandri 2.7–9: 76, 152, 161, 268
– 14.5: 124
Antonii 24 - 75: 67
Caesaris 9.4: 68
Cleomenis 33–36: 52
Numae 22: 69
Themistoclis 1: 163

Polybius
12.24.5: 277

Porphyrius Tyrius
Ad Gaurum 2.2.9: 85
De abstinentia 2.19: 48
2.36: 85
165.3: 85
De statuis fr. 351–359 Smith: 85
Vita Pythagorae 42: 120
Quaestiones Homericae ad Odysseam pertinentes 24.208: 163
De antro nympharum 7, 14, 16: 85
10: 302
fr. 69 Harnack: 355

Proclus
Hymni 7.11: 166
In Platonis Timaeum
1.76.9: 102
1.303.27: 314
1.306: 179

1.433.31: 178
3.168.9: 85
3.227: 179
3.68: 179
Theologia Platonica 1.5: 85
1.28.5: 315

Psellus
Quaenam sunt Graecorum opiniones de daemonibus 3 (PG 122, c 878D 3–4): 151ff, 262, 271
Aurea Catena 164–167 Duffy: 294

Sallustius philosophus
De dis 20: 341

Scholia
Schol. Luc. Dial. Meretr. 2.1, 7.4, 52.9: 159
Schol. Plat. Gorg. 497c: 151
Schol. Clem. Protr. 12.119.1: 357
Schol. Pind. 1.40: 356

Semonides iambographus
fr. 7 West: 288

Seneca, Lucius Anneus
Medea 525ff: 62

Sextus Empiricus
Pyrrhonianae Institutiones 3.224: 47
Adversus Mathematicos 1.293: 226

Servius
Ad Aeneidem 6.741: 77
Ad Bucolicam 4.10: 63
Ad Georgicam 1.166: 77

Sozomenus Salaminius
Historia Ecclesiastica 7.40: 136

Statius
Silvae 2.2.60–61: 142
Thebais 5.1.23ff: 62

Stobaeus, Ioannes
Eclogae 1.18.1: 363
Eclogae 1.49.60: 341

Strabo
7, fr. 18: 68, 235, 254, 266
10.3.11: 75
10.3.16: 68, 75
10.3.18: 68

Suda
s. v. Ἑρμῆς: 196
s. v. Πλάτων: 282
s. v. Σαραπίων: 62

Suetonius
De grammatical et rhetorica 7: 57

Tacitus
Hist. 5.5.5: 114

Tatianus
Oratio ad Graecos 1.2: 140, 142, 145, 258
41.1–3: 130, 140, 141
42.5: 226
8.6: 170, 276
10.1: 170, 276
39: 233
27.1: 244

Tertullianus
Apologeticum 13.9: 234
– 21.7–9: 165, 234, 285, 329, 330
De anima 2.3: 103, 124, 280
15.4: 96

15.5–6: 103
28–31: 341
De Ieiunio 2.4.16.7: 240
Ad nationes 2.7: 262
De praescriptione haeresium 7.9: 295

Theo Smyrnaeus
Expositio Rerum Mathematicarum
104.20: 38, 59, 197
– 105.5: 102

Theodoretus Cyrensis
Graecarum Affectionum Curatio
1.21–22: 143, 145, 150f, 261
1.114: 145
2.30–32: 222
2.47: 140
2.95: 145
2.112: 233
3.4: 233
3.29: 140
3.58: 324f
5.13: 90, 215
6.26: 282
11.33: 213, 257
12.35: 216, 346
Epistulae 118.5: 257, 273

Theophilus Antiochenus
Ad Autolycum 2.3: 222
2.28.6: 337
2.30: 140,
2.38: 281
3.2: 143, 179
3.7: 233
3.8: 234

Theophrastus
Charact. 16.11: 235

Theosophorum Graecorum Fragmenta
Theosophia Tubingensis. 55–56: 180, 222
– 169: 324

Tyrtaeus
fr. 12.30 West: 343

Tzetzes Iohannes
Exegesis in Homeri Iliadem 26.5: 200

Valerius Maximus
1.3.3: 114

Vergilius
Bucolica.
4.22–26: 70
6.30: 62
Georgica
4.453ff: 62
Aeneis
6.428: 39
7.385–405: 67
7.580: 67

Xenophanes
Fr. 23 DK: 196, 317

GENERAL INDEX

Alexandria: 56f, 61, 98, 111f, 131f, 144, 159, 170f, 190, 195, 199, 201f, 207, 217, 225f, 229, 233; cf. also Egypt.
Allegory: 34f, 60f, 78, 85f, 91, 142f, 167, 169, 171, 173ff, 197, 202–208f, 226, 229–232, 243, 249, 279, 293, 319, 326f, 332, 334, 350, 354, 359f.
Apologetics: vi, 3f, 9–14, 87–89, 127–138, 199–212, 217f, 219–224, 293–295.
Arreton: cf. taboo.
Asia Minor: 36f, 46–51, 113, 120, 126, 137f, 177, 217, 248
Bacchoi: 29, 72, 216, 268, 356, 378ff.
Baubo: 50, 59, 149–154, 164, 176f, 224, 240, 382.
Catabasis: 8, 22f, 32, 38–40, 45, 48f, 60–63, 71, 92, 202, 248, 296, 343, 373
Celsus: 80, 84f, 99f, 124, 131, 134, 173, 213f, 219f, 232–237, 240–252, 264, 273, 277, 282–287, 324, 327, 330, 333, 337, 342–346, 349–351, 359f, 372.
Conversion: 89, 132–137, 143, 147, 181f, 219–222, 245, 251–260, 264, 272, 346–349,
Creation: 24f, 35, 175, 178, 191, 193, 195–198, 289–292, 299–316, 323f, 360–364,
Chronologies: 95, 98, 119f, 132, 137, 140f, 167, 178, 200f, 204, 223, 226f, 233, 244, 247, 273, 279, 281, 283, 294.
Descensus ad inferos: cf. catabasis.

David: 98, 115f, 119–122, 245, 260, 286, 370, 377
Demeter: 33f, 41–44, 47, 50f, 59f, 82, 144, 147–153, 157, 160, 169–171, 177, 200, 228, 231, 242f, 299, 318, 324f, 329, 333, 354, 356
Deo: cf. Demeter.
Derveni papyrus: 16, 21–25, 30, 33, 35, 76, 91, 101, 170, 175, 178, 187, 192, 230f, 238, 254, 268, 281, 292, 296, 298f, 302, 305, 307, 311, 318f, 324, 327f, 335, 353, 362, 369
Dionysus: 6f, 10–16, 20–24, 33, 36f, 41–59, 62, 66–76, 78, 82, 102, 114–118, 123f, 144–168, 169–171, 177, 194f, 202, 213f, 224, 231, 233f, 240, 248f, 259f, 266–271, 276, 284f, 299, 319, 328–335, 348, 350, 353–357, 371f.
Egypt: 51–62, 74f, 83, 100–103, 107, 110f, 113, 118, 130, 136, 144f, 192, 194, 198, 206, 217, 222, 225–229, 281–283, 299, 303, 305, 368f, 373.
Eleusis: 16f, 33, 42–45, 54, 56, 68, 75f, 81f, 95, 132f, 147–152, 160–164, 170f, 228, 262–267, 271, 329, 345–347, 352f.
Empedocles: 24f, 30, 70, 76, 90, 96, 106f, 160–164, 187, 203f, 210, 213, 218, 231, 242, 337, 340f, 348, 350, 356.
Ephesia grammata: 60, 206f. Cf. also magic.

Eschatology: 21–28, 36–39, 44f, 63f, 76, 80, 122, 187f, 213, 248, 334, 342–345, 366–369.

Etymologies: 45, 76, 140, 152, 191, 268, 276–278, 290, 297, 333, 360.

Eucharist: 6, 8, 240, 269–271, 310, 332, 354–358; cf. also sacramentalism.

Euhemerism: 57, 136, 149, 156–159, 171, 178, 224, 231–235, 239, 249, 278, 330, 355.

Gnostic/ Gnosticism: 12f, 26, 38, 58f, 61, 71, 88, 100–108, 113, 118, 131–135, 160–162, 192–194, 215, 220, 239, 256, 273, 282, 301, 307, 309f, 324, 335–340, 363, 366, 368.

Goes/goeteia: 235–237, 254, 290, 360; cf. also magic.

Gold leaves/tablets: 1, 15–17, 20, 22, 24–31, 39, 51, 58, 69–71, 334, 341, 343f, 369

Greece (geog.): 41–46, 217f

Helios: cf. Sun.

Henotheism: 21, 36, 54, 72, 130, 167, 179, 191, 312, 317–320, 323.

Heraclitus: 89f, 106, 203–205, 209f, 231, 235, 237f, 268, 282, 364

Hermeticism: 12, 26f, 61, 79, 100–104, 111, 113, 135, 196–198, 225, 233f, 314, 364,

Hieronymus and Hellanicus, (Theogony): 33, 57, 91, 130, 168–172, 175, 229, 232, 276, 298, 306.

Hieroi logoi: 42–45, 53–57, 61, 77, 93, 181, 359

Iconography: 73, 80, 107, 116–126, 139, 141, 143, 245, 260, 271, 186, 330, 356, 370f.

Initiators: 19, 28, 85, 90, 235–237, 342–346, 360

Isis: 27, 51, 130, 144, 150, 329, 347

Judaism: 3f, 12f, 40, 88, 92f, 98, 104f, 108–116, 191, 205, 220f, 272, 301, 321, 336f, 358, 362, 365.

Linus: 94f, 99, 124, 160, 205, 222, 252, 387.

Magic: 52, 58f, 61, 70, 77, 81f, 88f, 207, 225, 237, 253f, 259, 266, 286, 290, 306, 360

Manichaeism: 102–105, 137, 215, 217, 237, 336, 339f, 351, 364, 366

Maenadism: 37, 46, 50, 67, 81f, 147, 158, 177, 266–271, 276f, 356f.

Mithraism: 12, 27, 72, 75, 123, 125f, 165, 213, 309, 319, 347, 354.

Moses: 59, 100, 103, 110f, 140f, 145, 165, 178, 183f, 224–227, 231, 233, 236, 279, 281f, 308, 311.

Monotheism: 97f, 112, 122, 129, 143, 179, 190, 192, 195f, 200, 221–223, 231, 239, 243, 248, 253, 264, 283, 296, 316–324, 328, 347.

Moralization: 48, 92, 112, 238, 343, 349, 373.

Musaeus: 29, 43, 93–96, 99, 103, 111, 124, 141, 160, 179, 184, 201, 205, 222–226, 233, 251f, 256

Music: 38, 63, 93f, 116, 120–123, 131, 140–142, 211f, 259f, 265f, 277, 288–293, 309.

Nomos: 71, 259, 274, 277, 290–292, 309, 344.

Pythagoras / (neo-)pythagoreanism: 16f, 25–32, 35–39, 47, 51, 60–64, 68–71, 77f, 81, 85, 90–99, 106, 109, 115, 120, 122, 124, 129, 132, 137, 141, 146, 202–215, 223–231, 242, 244, 257, 259, 282, 288–293, 306–308, 314, 338, 340f, 348–351, 363, 366, 370, 373.

Plato / (neo-)platonism: 4, 15f, 29–35, 46, 51, 61, 63, 74, 78–81, 84–109, 124, 129–139, 151, 173, 175, 178f, 183, 187f, 194, 204, 210, 213–217, 221, 225, 227f, 230–232, 235–238, 244f, 248, 250f, 254, 257f, 264f, 273–275, 278, 280–282, 288, 292–315, 320f, 326f, 329, 336–344, 346, 349f, 353, 365–373.

Oaths: 37f, 58f, 196–198, 243, 289, 304f.

Omophagy: 8, 28, 46, 158, 265, 269, 270f; cf. also maenadism.

Oracles (Chaldean): 97, 184, 192, 326, 373.

Oracles (Sibylline): 49, 87, 97f, 103, 111, 178, 181f, 192, 199f, 233, 279.

Orgia: 14, 43, 63, 82, 149.

Original sin / primordial fault: 14, 19, 23, 215f, 250, 336f, 339, 371.

Orpheus / David / Christ: 115f, 118–125, 139–144, 246–251, 254, 259f, 272–275, 286–293.

Orphic life: 14, 17, 19, 27, 349. Cf. also vegetarianism.

"Orphics": 5, 12–30, 78f, 86, 327, 348, 368.

Osiris: 51, 57, 144, 150, 217, 329, 332–334.

Panorphism / "Orpheoscepticism": 4–8, 14–18, 21, 23, 51, 70, 78, 142, 153, 271f, 328, 371f,

Phlya: 29, 32, 36, 42f, 79, 83, 160–164.

Paganism: 12–14, 78–88, 127–138, 251–255, 265–275.

Pelagianism: 137, 215f, 249f, 339, 380.

Persephone / Core: 14, 21, 23, 37f, 43, 45, 53f, 56, 59f, 64, 68, 71, 169–171, 216, 261, 268, 285, 319, 325, 329, 331, 334f, 372.

Phanes / Protogonos: 72, 123, 169, 172, 174–178, 192, 242, 297–299, 314, 319, 313, 318f

Plagiarism: 103, 117, 123, 129, 132, 160, 165–167, 192, 194, 201–205, 209f, 229, 241, 248f, 279–284, 306, 329f, 341, 354.

Pneuma: 107, 124, 172, 199, 244, 259, 284, 292, 302, 312, 362–365.

Priority: cf. chronologies.

Ptolemies: 29, 46, 52–57, 61, 57, 61, 67, 84, 110, 194, 202.

Rhapsodies: 23, 26, 32f, 35, 38f, 43f, 47f, 51, 53, 57, 63, 72, 83, 91, 133, 136f, 157, 162, 165, 166, 168f, 170–172, 175f, 178f, 187–190, 202, 211, 213f, 230, 242f, 249, 291, 297f, 302f, 307, 309, 311–316, 326, 335, 341, 363, 369, 371, 373.

Rhea: cf. Demeter.

Reincarnation: 14, 20, 25, 33, 35, 93, 133f, 137, 205, 208f, 213f, 242, 288, 328, 340–342, 348, 350f, 367.

Renaissance: 104, 108, 179, 247, 293f.

Resurrection: 6, 49, 84, 117, 130, 165f, 217f, 230, 234, 237, 244, 248f, 284, 301, 324, 330, 332–335, 338, 340, 367, 372.

Rome: 62–73, 76, 92, 110, 126.

Rites: 27–30, 41–86, 144–166, 223, 224f, 228, 235f, 257f, 261–272, 344–358; cf. also teletai.

Sacramentalism: 6, 8, 270f, 284, 310, 352, 354–358; cf. also eucharist.

Sarapion: 62, 102, 373.

Sethians: 104, 106f, 133, 160–164, 239.

Sonship: 95, 165, 248f, 256, 285, 330f.

Soma-sema: 20, 69, 90, 107, 215f, 250, 335, 338ff, 370.

Sun: 36f, 72, 85, 125, 195f, 213, 231, 241, 305, 319f, 323f, 348,

Soul: 1, 14–16, 19–25, 31, 33, 38f, 48, 60, 63, 69–71, 76–78, 83, 89f, 90, 94, 96, 100f, 104, 106f, 115f, 121f, 129, 133, 141, 175, 203–210, 213–217, 231, 247, 249–251, 257, 259, 288–293, 296, 307, 313, 331, 333, 335, 337–342, 350, 353f, 364–369.

Sibyl: 49, 87, 97f, 103, 111, 144, 178, 181f, 192, 199f, 233, 279.

Stoicism: 31, 33, 35, 63, 91f, 168, 170, 172, 180, 187, 192, 202, 204f, 208–210, 229f, 232, 242, 244, 258, 275, 291, 301, 306–131, 320, 343, 349–351, 359, 362–364, 366.

Symbola/synthemata: 54, 76, 146, 149–152, 164, 224, 242, 262, 343, 352f

Syncretism: 4, 8, 13, 36, 61, 72f, 85, 88, 112–126, 189f, 192, 195f, 198, 217, 219, 245, 247f, 250, 253, 278, 286f, 193, 217–224, 347.

Ritual taboo: 14, 42, 44, 47f, 80, 82, 93, 146, 223, 270, 325, 331, 350f, 356ff

Telete: 14–19, 27–29, 38, 44, 46, 52–27, 74f, 84f, 92, 114, 116, 142, 146, 149, 213, 236, 243, 263f, 270, 278, 342, 354–351, 360, 367, 372.

Theogonies: 15f, 21–24, 32–35, 47, 49, 57, 60–63, 107, 167–179, 214, 229, 257, 276, 296–298, 302, 305, 307, 314, 318f, 323, 325. Cf. also Derveni, Hieronymus and Hellanicus, Rhapsodies.

Testament of Orpheus: cf. index locorum, OF 377–378.

Titans: 6f, 14, 17, 19, 23–25, 33, 42–49, 55–58, 67, 74–76, 78, 80, 82, 98, 104, 148, 156–158, 162, 168f, 214, 228, 243, 249, 262, 268f, 328, 331, 335–337, 348f, 355–358, 371f, 380f, 383–386.

Vegetarianism: 14, 25, 27f, 137, 146, 348–351, 355. Cf. also Orphic life.

Zeus: 6, 14, 21–24, 35–37, 44, 53f, 57, 70–72, 75, 80, 90, 125, 149, 151–157, 162, 165–179, 187–195, 197f, 207f, 214, 226, 231f, 240, 242, 244, 249, 278, 281, 191, 298f, 302, 305, 307, 311–315, 318f, 322–327, 329–331, 343, 355f, 362f, 370–372, 37–381, 385–387.

www.ingramcontent.com/pod-product-compliance
Lightning Source LLC
Chambersburg PA
CBHW050847160426
43194CB00011B/2065